■ THE RESOURCE FOR THE INDEPENDENT TRAVELER

"The guides are aimed not only at young budget travelers but at the indepedent traveler; a sort of streetwise cookbook for traveling alone."

—The New York Times

"Unbeatable; good sight-seeing advice; up-to-date info on restaurants, hotels, and inns; a commitment to money-saving travel; and a wry style that brightens nearly every page."

—The Washington Post

"Lighthearted and sophisticated, informative and fun to read. [Let's Go] helps the novice traveler navigate like a knowledgeable old hand."

—Atlanta Journal-Constitution

"A world-wise traveling companion—always ready with friendly advice and helpful hints, all sprinkled with a bit of wit."

—The Philadelphia Inquirer

■ THE BEST TRAVEL BARGAINS IN YOUR PRICE RANGE

"All the dirt, dirt cheap."

—People

"Anything you need to know about budget traveling is detailed in this book."

—The Chicago Sun-Times

"Let's Go follows the creed that you don't have to toss your life's savings to the wind to travel—unless you want to."

—The Salt Lake Tribune

■ REAL ADVICE FOR REAL EXPERIENCES

"The writers seem to have experienced every rooster-packed bus and lunar-surfaced mattress about which they write."

—The New York Times

"A guide should tell you what to expect from a destination. Here Let's Go shines."

—The Chicago Tribune

"[Let's Go's] devoted updaters really walk the walk (and thumb the ride, and trek the trail). Learn how to fish, haggle, find work—anywhere."

—Food & Wine

LET'S GO PUBLICATIONS

TRAVEL GUIDES

Alaska 1st edition **NEW TITLE**
Australia 2004
Austria & Switzerland 2004
Brazil 1st edition **NEW TITLE**
Britain & Ireland 2004
California 2004
Central America 8th edition
Chile 1st edition
China 4th edition
Costa Rica 1st edition
Eastern Europe 2004
Egypt 2nd edition
Europe 2004
France 2004
Germany 2004
Greece 2004
Hawaii 2004
India & Nepal 8th edition
Ireland 2004
Israel 4th edition
Italy 2004
Japan 1st edition **NEW TITLE**
Mexico 20th edition
Middle East 4th edition
New Zealand 6th edition
Pacific Northwest 1st edition **NEW TITLE**
Peru, Ecuador & Bolivia 3rd edition
Puerto Rico 1st edition **NEW TITLE**
South Africa 5th edition
Southeast Asia 8th edition
Southwest USA 3rd edition
Spain & Portugal 2004
Thailand 1st edition
Turkey 5th edition
USA 2004
Western Europe 2004

CITY GUIDES

Amsterdam 3rd edition
Barcelona 3rd edition
Boston 4th edition
London 2004
New York City 2004
Paris 2004
Rome 12th edition
San Francisco 4th edition
Washington, D.C. 13th edition

MAP GUIDES

Amsterdam
Berlin
Boston
Chicago
Dublin
Florence
Hong Kong
London
Los Angeles
Madrid
New Orleans
New York City
Paris
Prague
Rome
San Francisco
Seattle
Sydney
Venice
Washington, D.C.

COMING SOON:

Road Trip USA

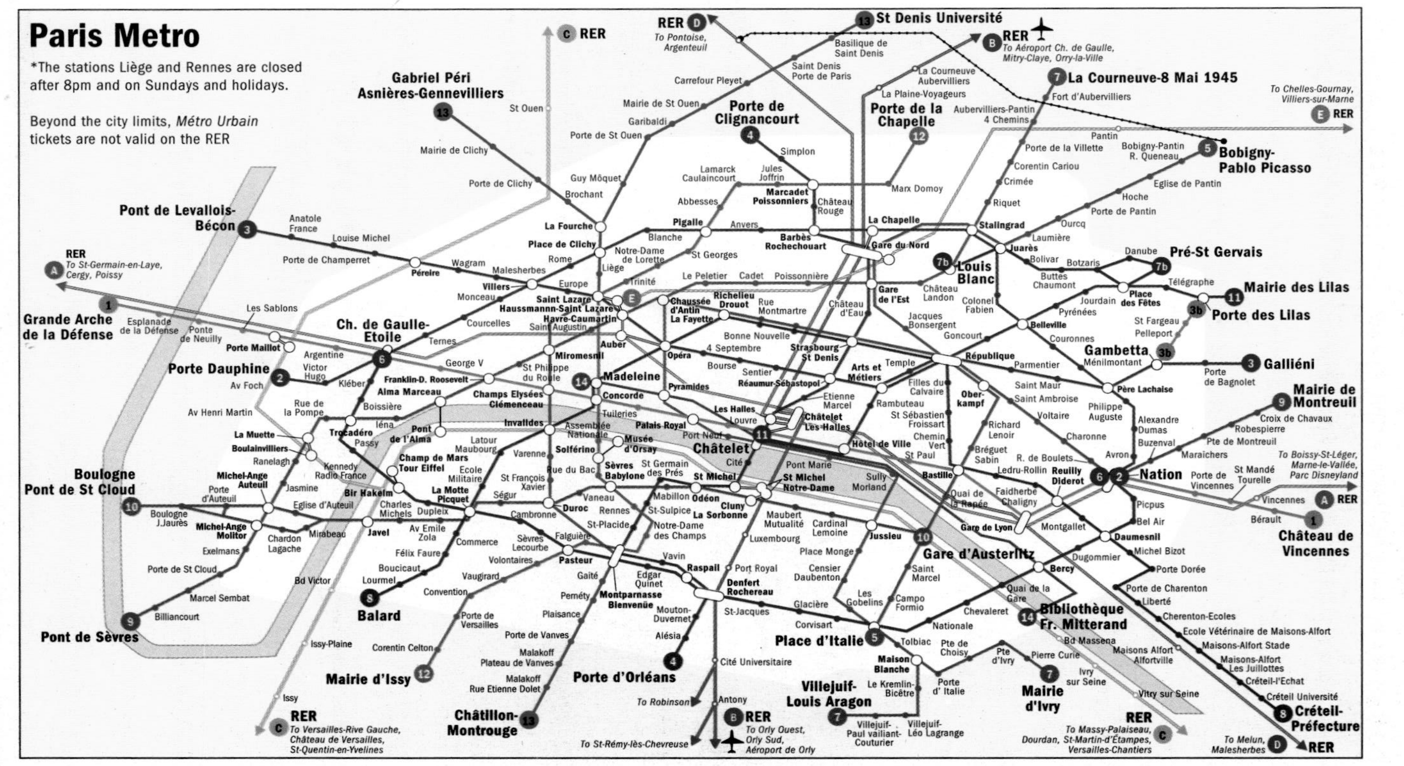

Paris Metro
*The stations Liège and Rennes are closed after 8pm and on Sundays and holidays.
Beyond the city limits, Métro Urbain tickets are not valid on the RER
RER A To St-Germain-en-Laye, Cergy, Poissy
1 Grande Arche de la Défense
Esplanade de la Défense
Pont de Neuilly
Les Sablons
Porte Maillot
Argentine
Ch. de Gaulle-Etoile
Pont de Levallois-Bécon
Anatole France
Louise Michel
Porte de Champerret
Pereire
Wagram
Malesherbes
Villiers
Monceau
Courcelles
Ternes
Gabriel Péri Asnières-Gennevilliers
Mairie de Clichy
Porte de Clichy
St Ouen
C RER
Guy Môquet
Brochant
La Fourche
Place de Clichy
Rome
Europe
Liège
Porte de St Ouen
Garibaldi
Mairie de St Ouen
Carrefour Pleyet
Saint Denis Porte de Paris
Basilique de Saint Denis
St Denis Université
RER D To Pontoise, Argenteuil
RER B To Aéroport Ch. de Gaulle, Mitry-Claye, Orry-la-Ville
La Courneuve Aubervilliers
La Plaine-Voyageurs
La Courneuve-8 Mai 1945
Fort d'Aubervilliers
Aubervilliers-Pantin 4 Chemins
Porte de Clignancourt
Simplon
Porte de la Chapelle
Marx Domoy
Lamarck Caulaincourt
Jules Joffrin
Marcadet Poissonniers
Château Rouge
Abbesses
Pigalle
Anvers
Barbès Rochechouart
La Chapelle
Gare du Nord
Blanche
Notre-Dame de Lorette
St Georges
Trinité
Le Peletier
Cadet
Poissonnière
Saint Lazare
Haussmann-Saint Lazare
Havre-Caumartin
Saint Augustin
Chaussée d'Antin La Fayette
Richelieu Drouot
Rue Montmartre
Château d'Eau
Gare de l'Est
Château Landon
Colonel Fabien
Louis Blanc
Stalingrad
Jaurès
Riquet
Crimée
Corentin Cariou
Porte de la Villette
Pantin
Bobigny-Pantin R. Queneau
Bobigny-Pablo Picasso
Eglise de Pantin
Hoche
Porte de Pantin
Ourcq
Laumière
Bolivar
Botzaris
Buttes Chaumont
Danube
Pré-St Gervais
Place des Fêtes
Télégraphe
Mairie des Lilas
Porte des Lilas
St Fargeau
Pelleport
Gambetta
Ménilmontant
Gallieni
Porte de Bagnolet
Jourdain
Pyrénées
Belleville
Couronnes
Goncourt
Jacques Bonsergent
République
Parmentier
Saint Maur
Saint Ambroise
Père Lachaise
Philippe Auguste
Alexandre Dumas
Buzenval
Avron
Maraîchers
Pte de Montreuil
Robespierre
Croix de Chavaux
Mairie de Montreuil
To Chelles-Gournay, Villiers-sur-Marne
E RER
To Boissy-St-Léger, Marne-le-Vallée, Parc Disneyland
Nation
Porte de Vincennes
St Mandé Tourelle
Vincennes
A RER
Bérault
Château de Vincennes
Picpus
Bel Air
Daumesnil
Michel Bizot
Porte Dorée
Porte de Charenton
Liberté
Charenton-Ecoles
Ecole Vétérinaire de Maisons-Alfort
Maisons-Alfort Stade
Maisons-Alfort Les Juillottes
Créteil-l'Echat
Créteil Université
Créteil-Préfecture
To Melun, Malesherbes
D RER
RER C To Massy-Palaiseau, Dourdan, St-Martin-d'Étampes, Versailles-Chantiers
Vitry sur Seine
Ivry sur Seine
Maisons Alfort Alfortville
Bd Massena
Pierre Curie
Mairie d'Ivry
Pte d'Ivry
Pte de Choisy
Porte d' Italie
Tolbiac
Maison Blanche
Le Kremlin-Bicêtre
Villejuif-Léo Lagrange
Villejuif-Paul vaillant-Couturier
Villejuif-Louis Aragon
Place d'Italie
Nationale
Chevaleret
Bibliothèque Fr. Mitterand
Quai de la Gare
Bercy
Dugommier
Montgallet
Reuilly Diderot
R. de Boulets
Faidherbe Chaligny
Gare de Lyon
Quai de la Rapée
Gare d'Austerlitz
Saint Marcel
Campo Formio
Les Gobelins
Jussieu
Cardinal Lemoine
Place Monge
Censier Daubenton
Sully Morland
Bastille
Ledru-Rollin
Bréguet Sabin
Richard Lenoir
Oberkampf
Voltaire
Charonne
Chemin Vert
St Paul
St Sébastien Froissart
Filles du Calvaire
Rambuteau
Temple
Arts et Métiers
Strasbourg St Denis
Bonne Nouvelle
Hôtel de Ville
Pont Marie
Châtelet Les Halles
Châtelet
Les Halles
Etienne Marcel
Réaumur-Sébastopol
Sentier
Bourse
4 Septembre
Opéra
Pyramides
Auber
Madeleine
Concorde
Tuileries
Palais Royal
Louvre
Pont Neuf
Cité
St Michel Notre-Dame
St Michel
Odéon
Cluny La Sorbonne
Maubert Mutualité
Luxembourg
Port Royal
Denfert Rochereau
St-Jacques
Glacière
Corvisart
Cité Universitaire
Antony
RER B To Orly Ouest, Orly Sud, Aéroport de Orly
To Robinson
To St-Rémy-lès-Chevreuse
Porte d'Orléans
Alésia
Mouton-Duvernet
Raspail
Edgar Quinet
Vavin
Montparnasse Bienvenüe
Gaîté
Pernéty
Plaisance
Porte de Vanves
Malakoff Plateau de Vanves
Malakoff Rue Etienne Dolet
Châtillon-Montrouge
Pasteur
Falguière
Notre-Dame des Champs
St-Placide
Rennes
St-Sulpice
Mabillon
St Germain des Prés
Sèvres Babylone
Rue du Bac
Vaneau
Duroc
Musée d'Orsay
Solférino
Assemblée Nationale
Invalides
Varenne
St François Xavier
Ségur
Cambronne
Sèvres Lecourbe
Volontaires
Vaugirard
Convention
Porte de Versailles
Corentin Celton
Mairie d'Issy
Commerce
La Motte Picquet
Ecole Militaire
Latour Maubourg
Champs Elysées Clémenceau
Miromesnil
St Philippe du Roule
Franklin-D. Roosevelt
George V
Alma Marceau
Pont de l'Alma
Champ de Mars Tour Eiffel
Bir Hakeim
Dupleix
Av Emile Zola
Félix Faure
Boucicaut
Lourmel
Balard
Javel
Charles Michels
Kennedy Radio France
Passy
Iéna
Trocadéro
Boissière
Kléber
Victor Hugo
Porte Dauphine
Av Foch
Rue de la Pompe
Av Henri Martin
La Muette
Boulainvilliers
Ranelagh
Jasmine
Eglise d'Auteuil
Michel-Ange Auteuil
Porte d'Auteuil
Michel-Ange Molitor
Mirabeau
Chardon Lagache
Exelmans
Boulogne Pont de St Cloud
Boulogne J.Jaurès
Porte de St Cloud
Marcel Sembat
Billiancourt
Pont de Sèvres
Bd Victor
Issy-Plaine
Issy
RER C To Versailles-Rive Gauche, Château de Versailles, St-Quentin-en-Yvelines

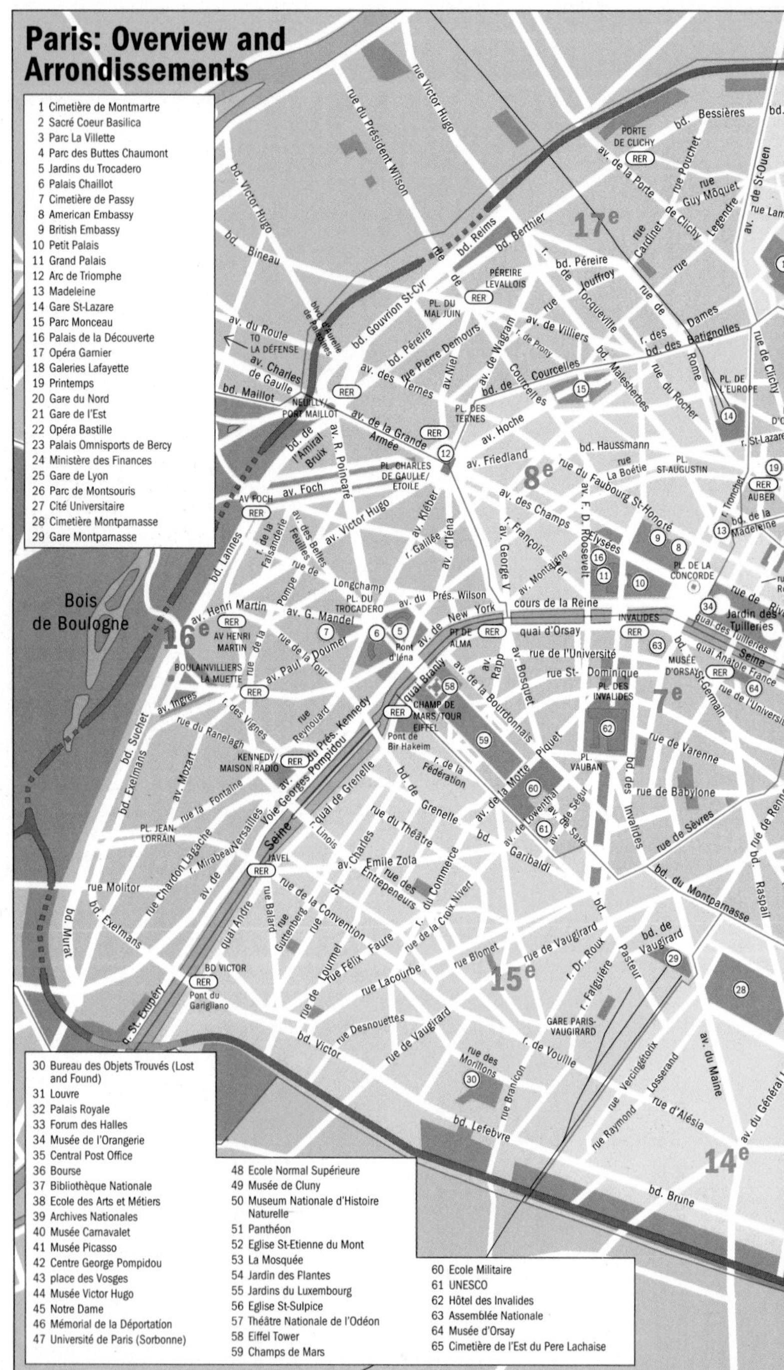

Paris: Overview and Arrondissements
1 Cimetière de Montmartre
2 Sacré Coeur Basilica
3 Parc La Villette
4 Parc des Buttes Chaumont
5 Jardins du Trocadero
6 Palais Chaillot
7 Cimetière de Passy
8 American Embassy
9 British Embassy
10 Petit Palais
11 Grand Palais
12 Arc de Triomphe
13 Madeleine
14 Gare St-Lazare
15 Parc Monceau
16 Palais de la Découverte
17 Opéra Garnier
18 Galeries Lafayette
19 Printemps
20 Gare du Nord
21 Gare de l'Est
22 Opéra Bastille
23 Palais Omnisports de Bercy
24 Ministère des Finances
25 Gare de Lyon
26 Parc de Montsouris
27 Cité Universitaire
28 Cimetière Montparnasse
29 Gare Montparnasse
30 Bureau des Objets Trouvés (Lost and Found)
31 Louvre
32 Palais Royale
33 Forum des Halles
34 Musée de l'Orangerie
35 Central Post Office
36 Bourse
37 Bibliothèque Nationale
38 Ecole des Arts et Métiers
39 Archives Nationales
40 Musée Carnavalet
41 Musée Picasso
42 Centre George Pompidou
43 place des Vosges
44 Musée Victor Hugo
45 Notre Dame
46 Mémorial de la Déportation
47 Université de Paris (Sorbonne)
48 Ecole Normal Supérieure
49 Musée de Cluny
50 Museum Nationale d'Histoire Naturelle
51 Panthéon
52 Eglise St-Etienne du Mont
53 La Mosquée
54 Jardin des Plantes
55 Jardins du Luxembourg
56 Eglise St-Sulpice
57 Théâtre Nationale de l'Odéon
58 Eiffel Tower
59 Champs de Mars
60 Ecole Militaire
61 UNESCO
62 Hôtel des Invalides
63 Assemblée Nationale
64 Musée d'Orsay
65 Cimetière de l'Est du Pere Lachaise
17e
8e
16e
7e
15e
14e
Bois de Boulogne
Seine
TO LA DÉFENSE
PORTE DE CLICHY
PÉREIRE LEVALLOIS
PL. DU MAL JUIN
NEUILLY/PORT MAILLOT
PL. DES TERNES
PL. CHARLES DE GAULLE/ETOILE
AV FOCH
PL. DU TROCADERO
AV HENRI MARTIN
BOULAINVILLIERS LA MUETTE
KENNEDY/MAISON RADIO
CHAMP DE MARS/TOUR EIFFEL
PT DE ALMA
Pont d'Iéna
Pont de Bir Hakeim
INVALIDES
PL. DES INVALIDES
PL. VAUBAN
MUSÉE D'ORSAY
PL. DE LA CONCORDE
Jardin des Tuilleries
PL. ST-AUGUSTIN
PL. DE L'EUROPE
AUBER
JAVEL
PL. JEAN-LORRAIN
BD VICTOR
Pont du Garigliano
GARE PARIS-VAUGIRARD
RER
bd. Bessières
av. de la Porte de Clichy
rue Pouchet
rue Guy Môquet
av. de St-Ouen
rue Lamarck
rue Cardinet
rue Legendre
bd. Berthier
bd. Reims
bd. Péreire
rue Jouffroy
rue de Tocqueville
rue des Dames
bd. des Batignolles
rue de Rome
rue du Rocher
rue de Clichy
rue Victor Hugo
rue du Président Wilson
bd. Victor Hugo
bd. Bineau
bd. Gouvion St-Cyr
av. du Roule
av. Charles de Gaulle
bd. Maillot
av. des Ternes
rue Pierre Demours
av. Niel
av. de Wagram
av. de Villiers
rue de Prony
rue de Courcelles
bd. de Courcelles
bd. Malesherbes
av. Hoche
av. de la Grande Armée
bd. de l'Amiral Bruix
av. R. Poincaré
av. Friedland
bd. Haussmann
rue La Boétie
rue du Faubourg St-Honoré
r. St-Lazare
r. Tronchet
bd. de la Madeleine
av. Foch
av. Victor Hugo
av. Kléber
r. Galilée
av. d'Iéna
av. des Champs Elysées
r. François 1er
av. George V
av. F. D. Roosevelt
av. Montaigne
rue de la Faisanderie
av. des Belles Feuilles
rue de Longchamp
rue de la Pompe
av. Henri Martin
av. G. Mandel
av. du Prés. Wilson
av. de New York
cours de la Reine
rue de Rivoli
quai des Tuilleries
quai Anatole France
quai d'Orsay
rue de l'Université
rue St-Dominique
bd. St-Germain
rue de la Tour
av. Paul Doumer
av. Ingres
r. des Vignes
rue du Ranelagh
rue Reynouard
av. du Prés. Kennedy
quai Branly
av. Rapp
av. Bosquet
av. de la Bourdonnais
rue de Varenne
rue de Babylone
bd. des Invalides
av. de la Motte Piquet
av. de Ségur
av. de Saxe
av. de Lowenthal
rue de Sèvres
rue de Rennes
bd. du Montparnasse
bd. Raspail
bd. Suchet
bd. Exelmans
av. Mozart
rue la Fontaine
av. de Versailles
Voie Georges Pompidou
quai de Grenelle
r. de la Fédération
bd. de Grenelle
rue du Théâtre
bd. Garibaldi
r. Linois
rue Mirabeau
rue Chardon Lagache
rue Molitor
bd. Murat
av. de Versailles
quai André Citroën
rue Balard
rue St. Charles
av. Emile Zola
rue des Entrepeneurs
rue du Commerce
rue de la Croix Nivert
rue de la Convention
rue Guttenberg
rue Félix Faure
rue de Lourmel
rue Lacourbe
rue Blomet
rue de Vaugirard
r. Dr. Roux
r. Falguière
bd. Pasteur
bd. de Vaugirard
av. du Maine
rue Desnouettes
bd. Victor
r. de Vouille
rue des Morillons
rue Brancion
rue Vercingétorix
rue Raymond Losserand
rue d'Alésia
av. du Général Leclerc
bd. Lefebvre
bd. Brune
r. St. Exupéry

N
LG
bd. Ney
bd. Macdonald
Canal de l'Ourcq
18e
Championnet
bd. Ornano
rue de la Chapelle
rue Ordener
rue Duhesme
Poissonniers
cadet
r. l'Evangile
rue de l'Ourcq
av. Corentin Cariou
rue Archereau
bd. Sérurier
av. Jean Lolive
rue Riquet
rue Custine
rue de Clignancourt
bd. Barbès
rue des
rue Marx Dormoy
rue d'Aubervilliers
rue de Flandre
rue de Crimée
Bassin de la Villette
av. Jean Jaurès
bd. Indochine
19e
bd. de Rochechouart
bd. de la Chapelle
PL. DE STALINGRAD
r. Armand Carel
rue Manin
r. David d'Angiers
bd. d'Algérie
PL. PIGALLE
av. Trudaine
RER
av. Secrétan
9e
rue Poissonnière
rue La Fayette
Canal St-Martin
PL. DU COLONEL FABIEN
bd. de la Villette
de Châteaudun
r. Paradis
rue du Fg. Poissonnière
r. d'Hauteville
r. de Fg. St-Denis
bd. de Strasbourg
bd. de Magenta
10e
bd. Mortier
bd. Montmartre
bd. Poissonnière
r. Château d'Eau
rue du Faubourg du Temple
rue des Pyrénées
PL. GAMBETTA
2e
St-Denis
bvd. St-Martin
av. Parmentier
rue St-Maur
bd. de Belleville
av. Gambetta
rue Montmartre
rue Réaumur
PL. DE LA RÉPUBLIQUE
rue Oberkampf
av. de la République
bd. de Sébastopol
rue St-Martin
rue de Turbigo
3e
1er
r. Etienne Marcel
rue du Louvre
rue Beaubourg
rue du Temple
bd. Beaumarchais
11e
av. Gambetta
20e
rue St-Honoré
r. des Halles
rue des Archives
rue Vieille du Temple
bd. Ménilmontant
rue de Rivoli
Louvre
Pont Neuf
rue du Chemin Vert
bd. Voltaire
rue de la Roquette
bd. R. Lenoir
av. Philippe Auguste
bd. de Charonne
rue de Rivoli
rue St-Antoine
quai St-Michel
r. de Seine
St-Germain
ST-MICHEL
Ile de la Cité
4e
Ile St-Louis
bd. Henri IV
rue de Charonne
rue du Faubourg St-Antoine
rue de Lyon
rue Rollin
quai de la Tournelle
PL. MAUBERT
Pont de Sully
rue de Montreuil
NATION
bd. Davout
6e
r. des Écoles
LUXEMBOURG
bd. St-Michel
rue Monge
5e
quai St-Bernard
av. Ledru
bd. Diderot
Cours de Vincennes
PL. DE LA NATION
bd. Picpus
PL. DE LA CONTRE-SCARPE
Pont d'Austerlitz
Seine
av. Daumesnil
12e
rue de Picpus
av. du Dr. Arnold Netter
rue d'Ulm
rue Mouffetard
r. G. St-Hilaire
rue Buffon
rue Censier
rue Guy Lussac
r. C. Bernard
PORT ROYAL
GARE D'AUSTERLITZ
Pont de Bercy
bd. de Bercy
PL. FÉLIX ÉBOUÉ
av. Daumesnil
M. Bizot
bd. Soult
bd. St-Marcel
bd. de Port Royal
rue St-Jacques
av. des Gobelins
bd. de l'Hôpital
rue de Bercy
quai de Bercy
rue de Charenton
av. du Gén
bd. Poniatowski
bd. Arago
Pont de Tolbiac
Parc Zoologique
bd. St-Jacques
PL. D'ALESIA
bd. de la Gare
rue Jeanne d'Arc
rue du Chevaleret
bd. A. Blanqui
av. de Choisy
rue de Tolbiac
rue National
Pont National
Bois de Vincennes
13e
d'Alésia
rue de Tolbiac
av. d'Italie
av. d'Ivry
rue Regnault
BD. MASSÉNA
bd. de Masséna
rue de Paris
bd. Kellerman
CITÉ UNIVERSITAIRE
0
1 mile
0
1 km

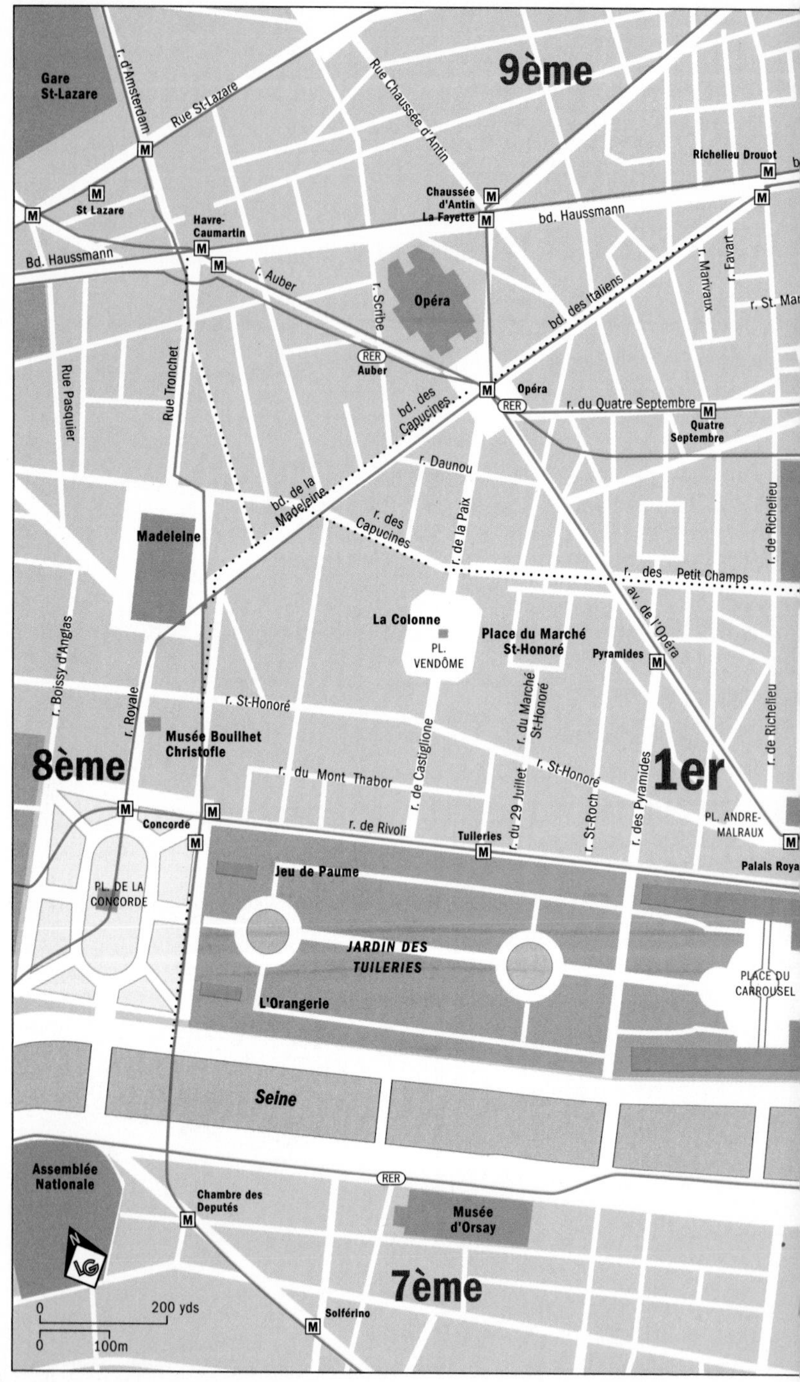
9ème
8ème
1er
7ème
Gare St-Lazare
r. d'Amsterdam
Rue St-Lazare
Rue Chaussée d'Antin
St Lazare
Havre-Caumartin
Chaussée d'Antin La Fayette
Richelieu Drouot
bd. Haussmann
Bd. Haussmann
r. Auber
r. Scribe
Opéra
bd. des Italiens
r. Marivaux
r. Favart
r. St. Mar
Auber
Rue Pasquier
Rue Tronchet
bd. des Capucines
Opéra
r. du Quatre Septembre
Quatre Septembre
r. Daunou
bd. de la Madeleine
r. des Capucines
r. de la Paix
r. de Richelieu
Madeleine
r. des Petit Champs
av. de l'Opéra
La Colonne
PL. VENDÔME
Place du Marché St-Honoré
Pyramides
r. Boissy d'Anglas
r. Royale
r. St-Honoré
Musée Boulhet Christofle
r. de Castiglione
r. du Marché St-Honoré
r. du Mont Thabor
r. St-Honoré
r. du 29 Juillet
r. St-Roch
r. des Pyramides
PL. ANDRE-MALRAUX
Concorde
r. de Rivoli
Tuileries
Palais Roya
Jeu de Paume
PL. DE LA CONCORDE
JARDIN DES TUILERIES
PLACE DU CARROUSEL
L'Orangerie
Seine
Assemblée Nationale
RER
Chambre des Deputés
Musée d'Orsay
Solférino
0
200 yds
0
100m

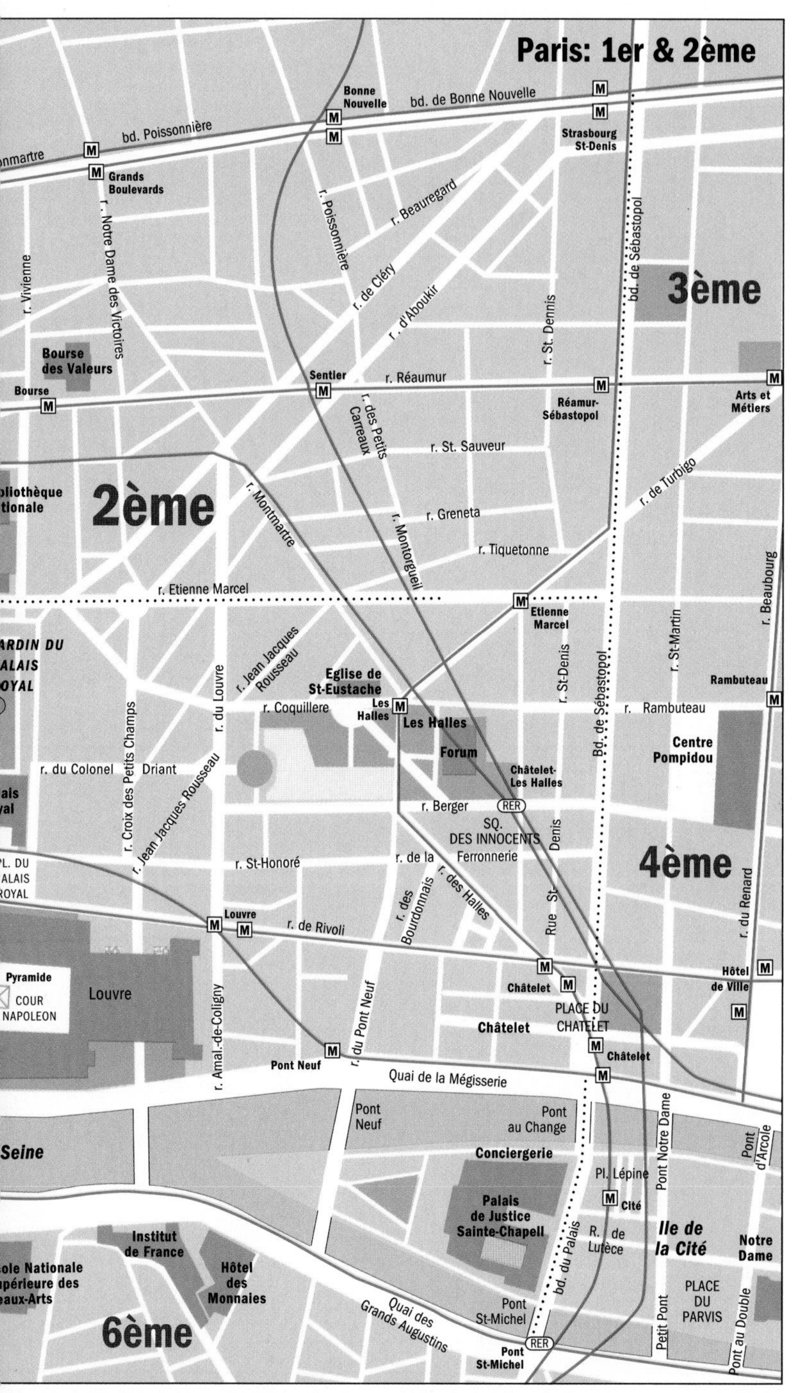
Paris: 1er & 2ème
bd. de Bonne Nouvelle
Bonne Nouvelle
bd. Poissonnière
Strasbourg St-Denis
Grands Boulevards
r. Notre Dame des Victoires
r. Vivienne
r. Poissonnière
r. Beauregard
r. de Cléry
r. d'Aboukir
bd. de Sébastopol
3ème
r. St. Dennis
Bourse des Valeurs
Bourse
Sentier
r. Réaumur
Réaumur-Sébastopol
Arts et Métiers
r. des Petits Carreaux
r. St. Sauveur
r. de Turbigo
2ème
r. Montmartre
r. Greneta
r. Montorgueil
r. Tiquetonne
r. Etienne Marcel
Etienne Marcel
r. Beaubourg
r. St-Martin
r. St-Denis
r. Jean Jacques Rousseau
Eglise de St-Eustache
r. du Louvre
Rambuteau
r. Rambuteau
r. Coquillere
Les Halles
Forum
Centre Pompidou
r. Croix des Petits Champs
r. du Colonel Driant
Châtelet-Les Halles
r. Berger
RER
SQ. DES INNOCENTS
Bd. de Sébastopol
r. de la Ferronnerie
r. St-Honoré
4ème
r. des Bourdonnais
r. des Halles
Rue St Denis
r. du Renard
Louvre
r. de Rivoli
Pyramide
COUR NAPOLEON
Châtelet
Hôtel de Ville
r. Amal.-de-Coligny
r. du Pont Neuf
PLACE DU CHATELET
Pont Neuf
Quai de la Mégisserie
Pont Neuf
Pont au Change
Seine
Conciergerie
Pont Notre Dame
Pont d'Arcole
Pl. Lépine
Cité
Palais de Justice Sainte-Chapell
R. de Lutèce
Ile de la Cité
Notre Dame
Institut de France
Hôtel des Monnaies
bd. du Palais
PLACE DU PARVIS
Quai des Grands Augustins
Pont St-Michel
Petit Pont
Pont au Double
6ème

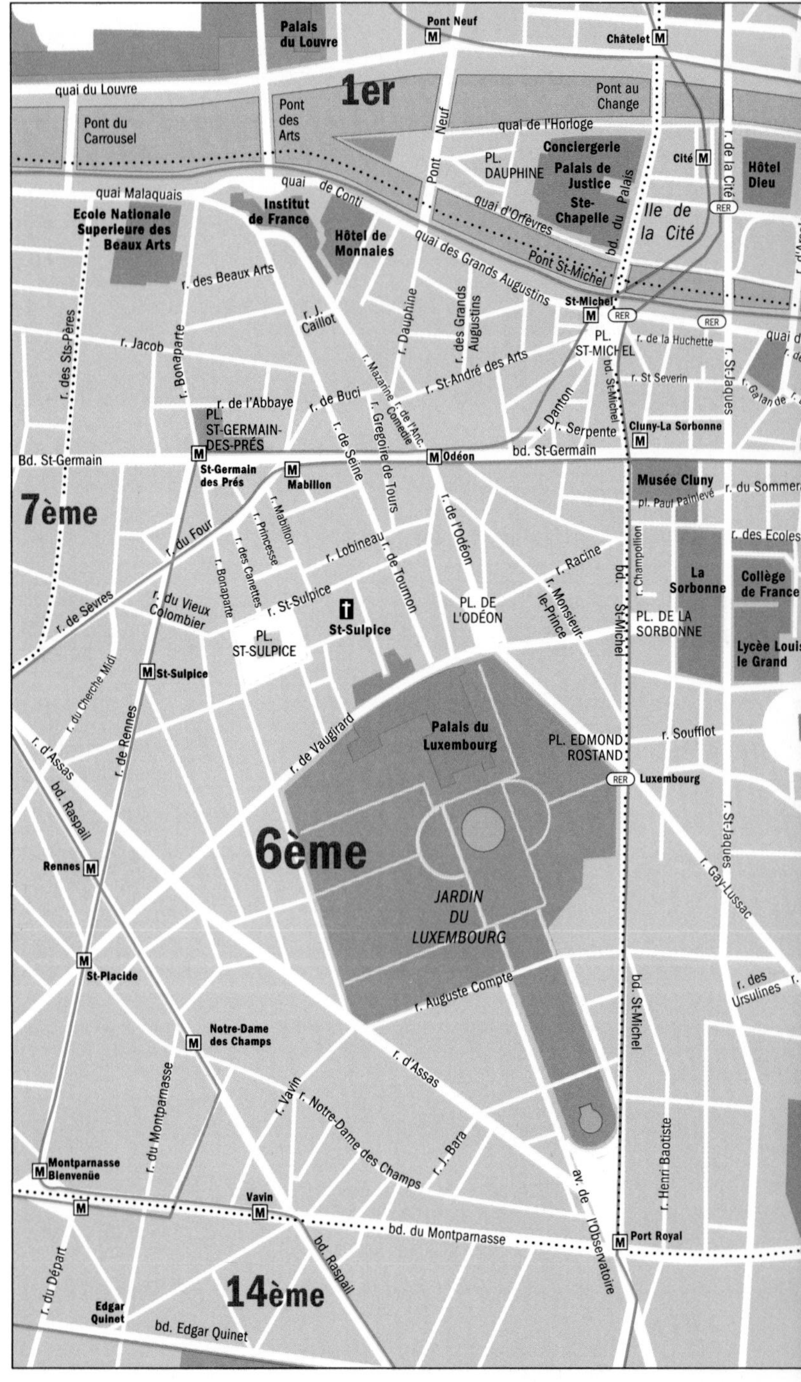

Palais du Louvre
Pont Neuf
Châtelet
1er
quai du Louvre
Pont du Carrousel
Pont des Arts
Pont au Change
quai de l'Horloge
Conciergerie
PL. DAUPHINE
Palais de Justice
Ste-Chapelle
Cité
Hôtel Dieu
r. de la Cité
quai Malaquais
quai de Conti
Institut de France
Ecole Nationale Superieure des Beaux Arts
Hôtel de Monnaies
quai d'Orfèvres
bd. du Palais
Ile de la Cité
quai des Grands Augustins
Pont St-Michel
r. des Beaux Arts
r. J. Caillot
r. Dauphine
r. des Grands Augustins
St-Michel
RER
r. des Sts-Pères
r. Jacob
r. Bonaparte
PL. ST-MICHEL
r. de la Huchette
r. St-Jaques
r. St-André des Arts
r. Mazarine
r. de l'Anc. Comédie
bd. St-Michel
r. St Severin
r. Galande
r. de l'Abbaye
r. de Buci
r. Danton
r. Serpente
PL. ST-GERMAIN-DES-PRÉS
r. de Seine
r. Grégoire de Tours
Cluny-La Sorbonne
Bd. St-Germain
Odéon
bd. St-Germain
St-Germain des Prés
Mabillon
Musée Cluny
pl. Paul Painlevé
r. du Sommerard
7ème
r. Mabillon
r. Princesse
r. de l'Odéon
r. des Ecoles
r. du Four
r. des Canettes
r. Lobineau
r. de Tournon
r. Champollion
La Sorbonne
Collège de France
r. Racine
r. de Sèvres
r. du Vieux Colombier
r. St-Sulpice
PL. DE L'ODÉON
r. Monsieur-le-Prince
PL. DE LA SORBONNE
PL. ST-SULPICE
St-Sulpice
Lycée Louis le Grand
St-Sulpice
r. du Cherche Midi
r. de Rennes
r. de Vaugirard
Palais du Luxembourg
PL. EDMOND ROSTAND
r. Soufflot
r. d'Assas
Luxembourg
bd. Raspail
Rennes
6ème
r. Gay-Lussac
JARDIN DU LUXEMBOURG
St-Placide
r. Auguste Compte
r. des Ursulines
Notre-Dame des Champs
r. d'Assas
r. du Montparnasse
r. Vavin
r. Notre-Dame des Champs
r. J. Bara
r. Henri Baotiste
Montparnasse Bienvenüe
av. de l'Observatoire
Vavin
bd. du Montparnasse
Port Royal
bd. Raspail
r. du Départ
14ème
Edgar Quinet
bd. Edgar Quinet

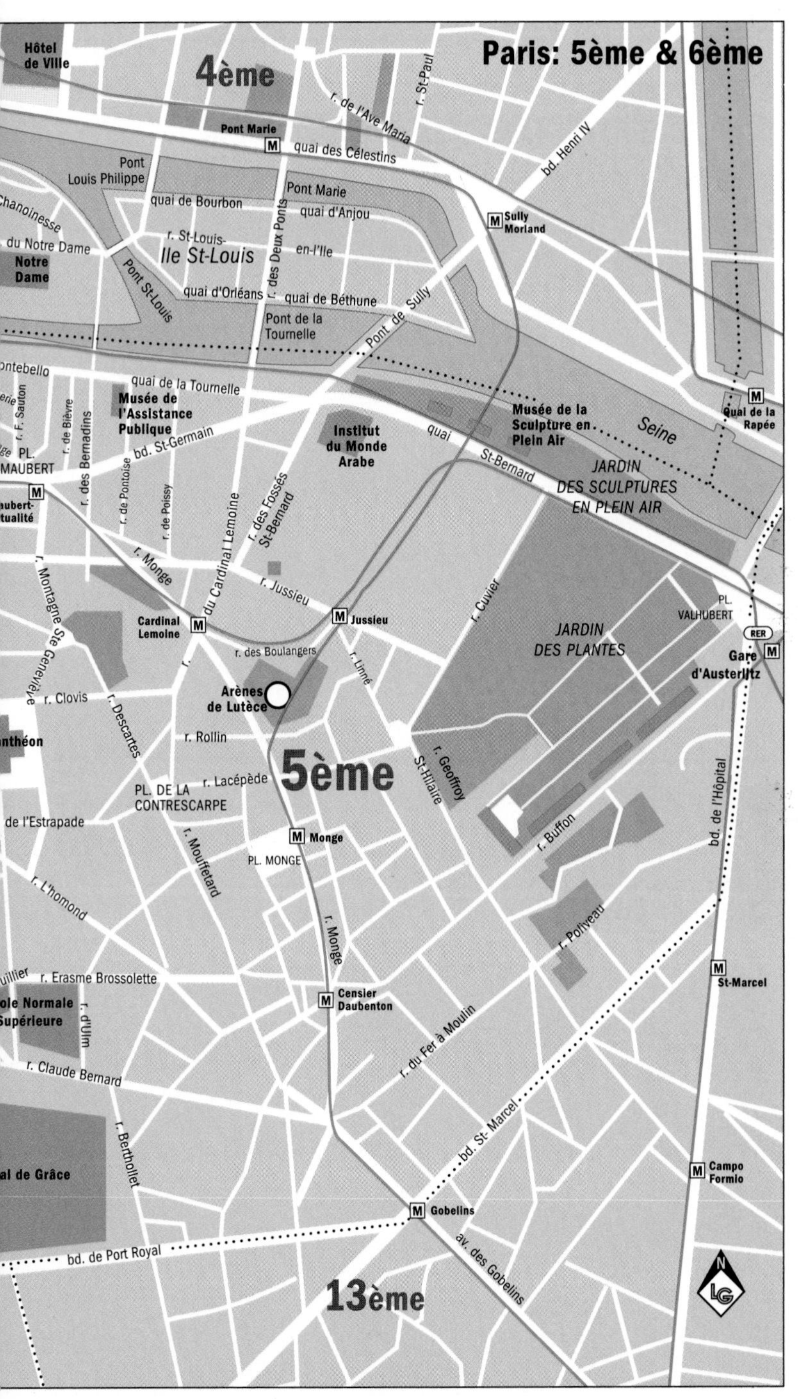

Paris: 5ème & 6ème
4ème
5ème
13ème
Hôtel de Ville
Pont Marie
quai des Célestins
r. de l'Ave Maria
r. St-Paul
bd. Henri IV
Sully Morland
Pont Louis Philippe
quai de Bourbon
quai d'Anjou
r. St-Louis-en-l'Ile
Ile St-Louis
r. des Deux Ponts
Notre Dame
Pont St-Louis
quai d'Orléans
quai de Béthune
Pont de Sully
Pont de la Tournelle
quai de la Tournelle
Musée de l'Assistance Publique
bd. St-Germain
PL. MAUBERT
r. F. Sauton
r. de Bièvre
r. des Bernadins
r. de Pontoise
r. de Poissy
Institut du Monde Arabe
quai St-Bernard
Musée de la Sculpture en Plein Air
Seine
JARDIN DES SCULPTURES EN PLEIN AIR
Quai de la Rapée
r. du Cardinal Lemoine
r. des Fossés St-Bernard
r. Monge
r. Jussieu
Jussieu
Cardinal Lemoine
r. Cuvier
JARDIN DES PLANTES
PL. VALHUBERT
RER
Gare d'Austerlitz
r. Montagne Ste Geneviève
r. des Boulangers
r. Linné
Arènes de Lutèce
r. Clovis
r. Descartes
r. Rollin
r. Lacépède
PL. DE LA CONTRESCARPE
r. Geoffroy St-Hilaire
r. Buffon
bd. de l'Hôpital
de l'Estrapade
Monge
PL. MONGE
r. Mouffetard
r. L'homond
r. Poliveau
r. Erasme Brossolette
r. d'Ulm
Censier Daubenton
St-Marcel
r. Claude Bernard
r. du Fer à Moulin
bd. St-Marcel
r. Berthollet
Campo Formio
Gobelins
bd. de Port Royal
av. des Gobelins
N
LG

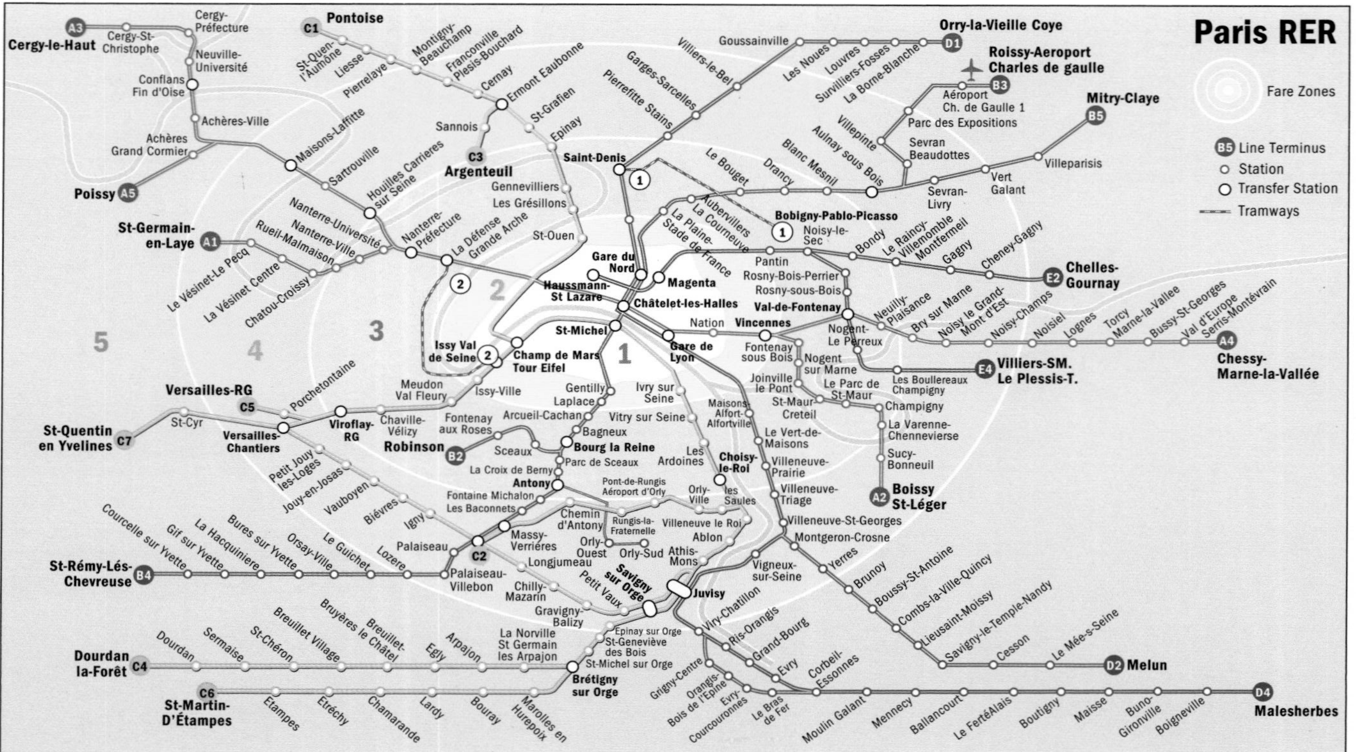

Paris RER
Fare Zones
B5 Line Terminus
Station
Transfer Station
Tramways
1
2
3
4
5
A3 Cergy-le-Haut
Cergy-St-Christophe
Cergy-Préfecture
Neuville-Université
Conflans Fin d'Oise
Achères-Ville
Achères Grand Cormier
Poissy A5
Maisons-Laffitte
Sartrouville
Houilles Carrieres sur Seine
Nanterre-Université
Nanterre-Ville
Rueil-Malmaison
Chatou-Croissy
Le Vésinet Centre
Le Vésinet-Le Pecq
St-Germain-en-Laye A1
Nanterre-Préfecture
La Défense Grande Arche
C1 Pontoise
St-Ouen-l'Aumône
Liesse
Pierrelaye
Montigny-Beauchamp
Franconville Plessis-Bouchard
Cernay
Ermont Eaubonne
Sannois
C3 Argenteuil
St-Grafien
Epinay
Gennevilliers
Les Grésillons
St-Ouen
Saint-Denis
Pierrefitte Stains
Garges-Sarcelles
Villiers-le-Bel
Goussainville
Les Noues
Louvres
Survilliers-Fosses
La Borne-Blanche
Orry-la-Vieille Coye D1
Roissy-Aeroport Charles de gaulle
Aéroport Ch. de Gaulle 1 B3
Parc des Expositions
Sevran Beaudottes
Villepinte
Mitry-Claye B5
Villeparisis
Vert Galant
Sevran-Livry
Aulnay sous Bois
Blanc Mesnil
Drancy
Le Bouget
Aubervilliers La Courneuve
La Plaine-Stade de France
Bobigny-Pablo-Picasso
Noisy-le-Sec
Bondy
Le Raincy-Villemomble Montfermeil
Gagny
Cheney-Gagny
E2 Chelles-Gournay
Pantin
Rosny-Bois-Perrier
Rosny-sous-Bois
Val-de-Fontenay
Neuilly-Plaisance
Bry sur Marne
Noisy le Grand-Mont d'Est
Noisy-Champs
Noisiel
Lognes
Torcy
Marne-la-Vallee
Bussy-St-Georges
Val d'Europe
Serris-Montévrain
A4 Chessy-Marne-la-Vallée
Nogent-Le Perreux
Les Boullereaux Champigny
E4 Villiers-SM. Le Plessis-T.
Gare du Nord
Magenta
Haussmann-St Lazare
Châtelet-les-Halles
St-Michel
Nation
Vincennes
Gare de Lyon
Fontenay sous Bois
Nogent sur Marne
Joinville le Pont
Le Parc de St-Maur
St-Maur Creteil
Champigny
La Varenne-Chennevierse
Sucy-Bonneuil
A2 Boissy St-Léger
Issy Val de Seine
Champ de Mars Tour Eifel
Issy-Ville
Meudon Val Fleury
Chaville-Vélizy
Viroflay-RG
Porchetontaine
Versailles-RG C5
St-Quentin en Yvelines C7
St-Cyr
Versailles-Chantiers
Petit Jouy les-Loges
Jouy-en-Josas
Vauboyen
Biévres
Igny
Gentilly
Laplace
Arcueil-Cachan
Fontenay aux Roses
Robinson B2
Sceaux
Bagneux
Bourg la Reine
Parc de Sceaux
La Croix de Berny
Antony
Fontaine Michalon
Les Baconnets
Massy-Verrières
C2
Palaiseau
Palaiseau-Villebon
Lozere
Le Guichet
Orsay-Ville
Bures sur Yvette
La Hacquiniere
Gif sur Yvette
Courcelle sur Yvette
St-Rémy-Lés-Chevreuse B4
Ivry sur Seine
Vitry sur Seine
Les Ardoines
Choisy-le-Roi
Maisons-Alfort-Alfortville
Le Vert-de-Maisons
Villeneuve-Prairie
Villeneuve-Triage
Villeneuve-St-Georges
Montgeron-Crosne
Yerres
Brunoy
Boussy-St-Antoine
Combs-la-Ville-Quincy
Lieusaint-Moissy
Savigny-le-Temple-Nandy
Cesson
Le Mée-s-Seine
D2 Melun
Pont-de-Rungis Aéroport d'Orly
Orly-Ville
les Saules
Chemin d'Antony
Rungis-la-Fraternelle
Orly-Ouest
Orly-Sud
Villeneuve le Roi
Ablon
Athis-Mons
Longjumeau
Chilly-Mazarin
Gravigny-Balizy
Petit Vaux
Savigny sur Orge
Juvisy
Vigneux-sur-Seine
Viry-Chatillon
Ris-Orangis
Grand-Bourg
Evry
Corbeil-Essonnes
Grigny-Centre
Orangis-Bois de l'Epine
Evry-Courcouronnes
Le Bras de Fer
Moulin Galant
Mennecy
Ballancourt
Le FertéAlais
Boutigny
Maisse
Buno-Gironville
Boigneville
D4 Malesherbes
Epinay sur Orge
St-Geneviève des Bois
St-Michel sur Orge
Brétigny sur Orge
La Norville St Germain les Arpajon
Arpajon
Egly
Breuillet-Bruyères le Châtel
Breuillet Village
St-Chéron
Sermaise
Dourdan
Dourdan la-Forêt C4
C6 St-Martin-D'Étampes
Etampes
Etréchy
Chamarande
Lardy
Bouray
Marolles en Hurepoix

PARIS 2004

ABIGAIL K. JOSEPH EDITOR
MEGAN MORAN-GATES ASSOCIATE EDITOR

RESEARCHER-WRITERS
WILLIAM LEE ADAMS
NEASA COLL
BRENDAN MCGEEVER

AMELIA AOS SHOWALTER MAP EDITOR
ARIEL FOX MANAGING EDITOR

MACMILLAN

HELPING LET'S GO If you want to share your discoveries, suggestions, or corrections, please drop us a line. We read every piece of correspondence, whether a postcard, a 10-page email, or a coconut. **Address mail to:**

Let's Go: Paris
67 Mount Auburn Street
Cambridge, MA 02138
USA

Visit Let's Go at **http://www.letsgo.com,** or send email to:

feedback@letsgo.com
Subject: "Let's Go: Paris"

In addition to the invaluable travel advice our readers share with us, many are kind enough to offer their services as researchers or editors. Unfortunately, our charter enables us to employ only currently enrolled Harvard students.

Published in Great Britain 2004 by Macmillan, an imprint of Pan Macmillan Ltd.
20 New Wharf Road, London N1 9RR
Basingstoke and Oxford
Associated companies throughout the world
www.panmacmillan.com

Published in the United States of America by St. Martin's Press.

ISBN: 1 4050 3328 2
First edition
10 9 8 7 6 5 4 3 2 1

Let's Go: Paris is written by Let's Go Publications, 67 Mount Auburn Street, Cambridge, MA 02138, USA.

ADVERTISING DISCLAIMER All advertisements appearing in Let's Go publications are sold by an independent agency not affiliated with the editorial production of the guides. Advertisers are never given preferential treatment, and the guides are researched, written, and published independent of advertising. Advertisements do not imply endorsement of products or services by Let's Go, and Let's Go does not vouch for the accuracy of information provided in advertisements.

If you are interested in purchasing advertising space in a Let's Go publication, contact: Let's Go Advertising Sales, 67 Mount Auburn St., Cambridge, MA 02138, USA.

HOW TO USE THIS BOOK

PRICES & RANKINGS. In each *arrondissement,* we rank establishments by value (from best to worst); our favorites get the Let's Go thumbs-up (☒). Each listing falls within a price range (❶-❺); see p. xii for a price range breakdown.

ORGANIZATION. The coverage in this book, like the city of Paris, is divided into 20 *arrondissements.* The **Discover Paris** chapter is organized roughly as the city is laid out; the **Sights, Museums, Food & Drink, Nightlife, Accomodations,** and **Shopping** chapters are organized numerically (fromfirst *arrondissement* to twentieth).

INSIDE SCOOP. Throughout this book, you'll find sidebars in black boxes and longer articles—built-in reading material for the airplane, waiting in line, or whiling away the afternoon in a café. You can read researchers' tales **From the Road,** get **The Local Story** from Parisians, learn what's been going on **In Recent News,** dive into the **Insider's City** with mini-walking tours, hear about some of the city's **Local Legends,** decipher items you'll see **On the Menu,** discover **Hidden Deals** and the best ways to blow your budget on **Big Splurges,** and get **No Work All Play** with Paris's coolest festivals. Don't miss the book's **Articles:** a history of postwar Parisian intellectuals from a leading French literature scholar (p. 178), plus discussions of 18th-century garden design (p. 284) and 19th-century urban planning (p. 102).

WHEN TO USE IT

1-2 MONTHS BEFORE YOU GO. Our book is filled with practical information to help you before you go. **Planning Your Trip** (p. 303) has advice on passports, plane tickets, insurance, and more. The **Accommodations** (p. 251) section can help you with booking a room from home.

2 WEEKS BEFORE YOU GO. Start thinking about your ideal trip. **Discover Paris** (p. 1) lists the city's top 25 sights, along with suggested itineraries, walking tours, Let's Go Picks (the best and quirkiest that Paris has to offer), Top 10 lists, and the dirt on each of Paris's neighborhoods. Read up on Parisian history and culture in the **Life & Times** chapter (p. 39).

ON THE ROAD. Once in Paris (see p. 23) will be your best friend once you've arrived, with all the practical information you'll need. You'll do a lot of flipping through the listings in **Sights, Museums, Food & Drink, Nightlife, Entertainment,** and **Shopping.** When you feel like striking out, turn to **Daytripping** for one-day and weekend trips away from Paris into historic towns in the Île de France. The **Service Directory** contains a list of local services. The **Phrasebook** has a list of useful French phrases and words to help you navigate most every situation in French. Should you decide that you want to do something more than see the sights, turn to **Alternatives to Tourism** for information on volunteering, studying, and working in Paris. Finally, just remember to put down this guide once in a while and go exploring on your own; you'll be glad you did.

A NOTE TO OUR READERS The information for this book was gathered by *Let's Go* researchers from May through August of 2003. Each listing is based on one researcher's opinion, formed during his or her visit at a particular time. Those traveling at other times may have different experiences since prices, dates, hours, and conditions are always subject to change. You are urged to check the facts presented in this book beforehand to avoid inconvenience and surprises.

Paris

Auberge Internationale des Jeunes

Hostel in the city centre of Paris

Bastille Area

- Rooms for 2, 3, 4 persons only
- Very clean
- English speaking staff
- Breakfast included
- Free luggage storage
- Free showers
- Free safe for your valuables
- Internet access
- Credit cards & travellers cheques accepted
- Access to all sights
- NO CURFEW

The best value downtown

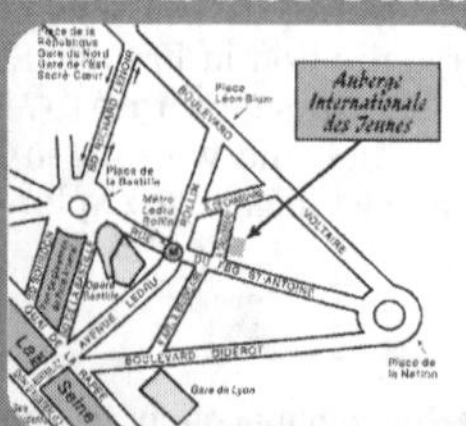

13 € from November to February

14 € from March to October

An ideal location for young people,
a lively and safe area with many cafes and pubs.
Laundromats, boulangeries and supermakets nearby.
International atmosphere.
Bookings are possible by fax or email.

10, rue trousseau . 75011 Paris
Tel (+33) 01 47 00 62 00
Fax (+33) 01 47 00 33 16
Metro Ledru-Rollin, line 8
Email aij@aijparis.com
http//www.aijparis.com

Contents

bold denotes a map

RESEARCHER-WRITERS

William Lee Adams *Île de la Cité, 3ème, 4ème, 9ème, 12ème, 13ème, 17 ème, 20ème*

Having survived the heat of *Let's Go: Southeast Asia 2003*, William took his Georgia sass to Paris, where he cruised his way through the Marais and never gave up in his quest for that perfect leather bag. Through it all, this psychology major sent back hilarious, insightful, and impeccably formatted copy enhanced with tales of his exploits in the bars and boutiques of the City of Love.

Neasa Coll *Île St-Louis, 5ème, 6ème, 7ème, 8ème, 15ème, 16ème*

This social anthropology major from Calgary went to Paris as a pilgrim to the shrine of *couture*, but came back forswearing materialism for contemporary art and socialist theater. Nonetheless, she managed to hunt down the best shopping in the city, conquer the cafés of the Latin Quarter, write brilliant features (even at the very last minute)—and look uniquely fabulous the whole time.

Brendan McGeever *1er, 2ème, 10ème, 11ème, 14ème, 18ème, 19ème*

After getting his MBA from Harvard, this Indianapolis native took a Parisian sojourn before returning to NYC. Aided by his girlfriend Yvonne and beautiful language skills developed as a French and marketing major at the University of Pennsylvania, he served as surrogate dad to his fellow RWs, made far too many calls to FedEx, ate a lot of ice cream, and infused his copy with signature humor and energy.

CONTRIBUTING WRITERS

Verena Andermatt Conley teaches Romance Languages and Literatures at Harvard University. Her publications include *Hélène Cixous: Writing the Feminine* (1981; 1991); *Rethinking Technologies*, ed. (1993; 1997); *Ecopolitics: the Environment in Poststructuralist Thought* (1997); and *The War Against the Beavers* (2003), a personal account about life in Minnesota's North Woods. A book on postwar Parisian intellectuals is forthcoming.

Charlotte Houghteling was the editor of *Let's Go: Middle East 2003*, *Egypt 2003*, and *Israel 2003.* She is currently completing her M.Phil. at Cambridge on the consumer society of Revolutionary Paris.

Sara Houghteling was a Researcher-Writer for *Let's Go: France 1999* and has taught at the American School in Paris. She is now a graduate student in creative writing at the University of Michigan.

Maryanthe Malliaris was a Researcher-Writer for *Let's Go: Greece 2000*. She has also served as a Production Manager and Managing Editor of New Media for the *Let's Go* series. She now lives in Paris and studies at the Sorbonne.

Meredith Martin is a Ph.D. candidate in the Department of the History of Art and Architecture at Harvard university. She is currently researching a dissertation on garden architecture and social formation in 18th-century France, with a focus on aristocratic women and their pleasure diaries.

ABOUT LET'S GO

GUIDES FOR THE INDEPENDENT TRAVELER

Budget travel is more than a vacation. At *Let's Go,* we see every trip as the chance of a lifetime. If your dream is to grab a knapsack and a machete and forge through the jungles of Brazil, we can take you there. Or, if you'd rather enjoy the Riviera sun at a beachside cafe, we'll set you a table. If you know what you're doing, you can have any experience you want—whether it's camping among lions or sampling Tuscan desserts—without maxing out your credit card. We'll show you just how far your coins can go, and prove that the greatest limitation on your adventure is not your wallet, but your imagination. That said, we understand that you may want the occasional indulgence after a week of hostels and kebab stands, so we've added "Big Splurges" to let you know which establishments are worth those extra euros, as well as price ranges to help you quickly determine whether an accommodation or restaurant will break the bank. While we may have diversified, our emphasis will always be on finding the best values for your budget, giving you all the info you need to spend six days in London or six months in Tasmania.

BEYOND THE TOURIST EXPERIENCE

We write for travelers who know there's more to a vacation than riding double-deckers with tourists. Our researchers give you the heads-up on both world-renowned and lesser-known attractions, on the best local eats and the hottest nightclub beats. In our travels, we talk to everybody; we provide a snapshot of real life in the places you visit with our sidebars on topics like regional cuisine, local festivals, and hot political issues. We've opened our pages to respected writers and scholars to show you their take on a given destination, and turned to lifelong residents to learn the little things that make their city worth calling home. And we've even given you Alternatives to Tourism—ideas for how to give back to local communities through responsible travel and volunteering.

OVER FORTY YEARS OF WISDOM

When we started, way back in 1960, Let's Go consisted of a small group of well-traveled friends who compiled their budget travel tips into a 20-page packet for students on charter flights to Europe. Since then, we've expanded to suit all kinds of travelers, now publishing guides to six continents, including our newest guides: *Let's Go: Japan* and *Let's Go: Brazil.* Our guides are still annually researched and written entirely by students on shoe-string budgets, adventurous travelers who know that train strikes, stolen luggage, food poisoning, and marriage proposals are all part of a day's work. Even as you read this, work on next year's editions is well underway. Whether you're reading one of our new titles, like *Let's Go: Puerto Rico* or *Let's Go Adventure Guide: Alaska,* or our original best-seller, *Let's Go: Europe,* you'll find the same spirit of adventure that has made *Let's Go* the guide of choice for travelers the world over since 1960.

GETTING IN TOUCH

The best discoveries are often those you make yourself; on the road, when you find something worth sharing, please drop us a line. We're Let's Go Publications, 67 Mt. Auburn St., Cambridge, MA 02138, USA (feedback@letsgo.com).

For more info, visit our website: www.letsgo.com.

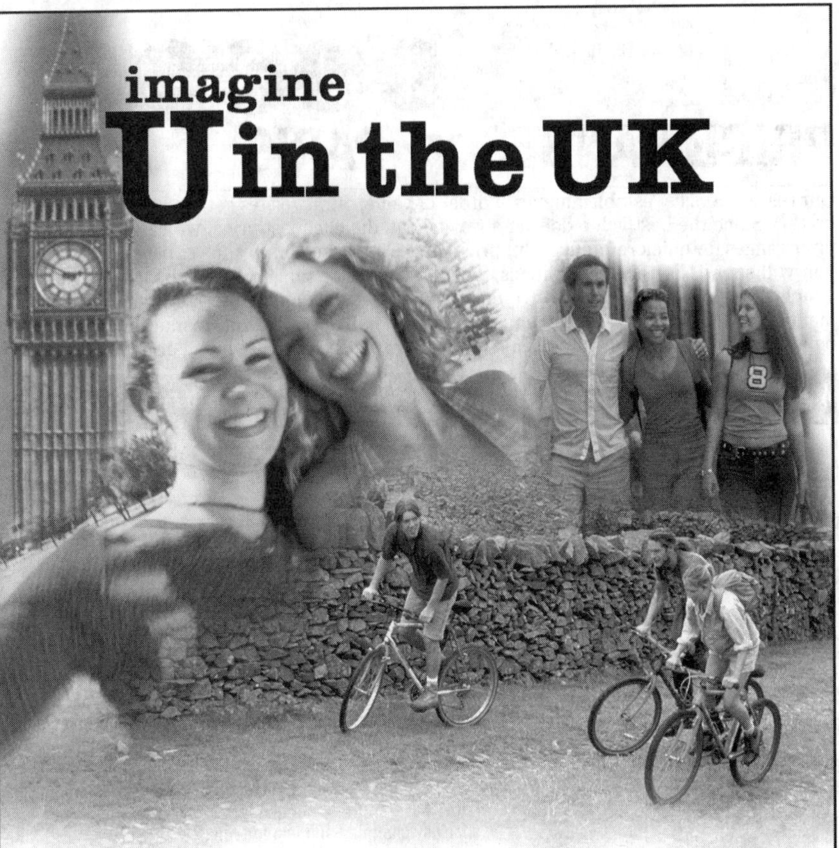

1 2 3 4 5

PRICE RANGES >> PARIS

Our researchers list establishments in order of value; our favorites get the Let's Go thumbs-up (☒). Since the best value doesn't always mean the cheapest price, we have a system of price ranges for quick reference. Our price ranges are based on a rough expectation of what you will spend. For **accommodations,** we base our price range off the cheapest price for which a single traveler can stay for one night. For **restaurants** and other dining establishments, we estimate the average amount that you will spend in that restaurant. The table below tells you what you will typically find in Paris at the corresponding price range.

ACCOMMODATIONS	RANGE	WHAT YOU'RE LIKELY TO FIND
❶	under €30	Mostly hostels; expect a basic dorm-style room and hall bathrooms. There may be lockout and/or curfew. Breakfast is often included.
❷	€31-50	Small hotels, usually in less central areas. Expect basic but clean and comfortable rooms and hall bathrooms.
❸	€51-75	Small hotels in more central areas, and with more amenities or better decor. Most rooms have shower and/or toilets, TV, and phone.
❹	€76-95	Nicer hotels in convenient areas, often with unique decor and atmostphere. Rooms should have shower and toilet, as well as TV and phone.
❺	above €96	Upscale hotels. If you're paying this much, your room should have all the amenities you want, and should be especially charming and comfortable.

FOOD	RANGE	WHAT YOU'RE LIKELY TO FIND
❶	under €10	Mostly take-out food, like sandwiches or falafel. Also some cafés and crêperies.
❷	€11-15	Small restaurants, cafés, and brasseries; you'll usually get a basic 1 or 2 course sit-down meal.
❸	€16-25	Nicer restaurants, usually featuring lunch or dinner *menus*; expect at least 2 courses (*plat* and *entrée* or dessert) and good service.
❹	€26-35	Restaurants with great atmosphere, great service, and great food. You'll usually get a *menu* with 2 or 3 courses, wine, and coffee.
❺	above €36	Classy, dressy restaurants with amazing food and flawless service; you'll most likely have one of those meals that you'll remember for a lifetime.

ACKNOWLEDGMENTS

Abigail thanks: My researchers, for doing beautiful work despite apartment and computer disasters, illness, many sketchy men, and my insanity; Yvonne Pollack, Verena Conley, and Meredith Martin for their contributions; Ariel, for keeping me (and my index!) calm and on track; Amelia, for being on top of everything and lovely to work with; Megan, for being amazingly helpful and competent; Scrobins, for saving all of our lives basically every day, dealing with my anxiety and the Gothic doubling of the food chart, and being so unfailingly sweet about it; all of the city guide editors (and the racoon) for being the most wonderful set of freaks I'll ever work with (Stef and her apartment for the, uh, study breaks); my Dane St. boys for building a delightful domicile with me; shame and performativity; Bravo, HBO, TBS, Dedo, the Enormous, and the Colo for providing the summer's entertainment; my family, especially my mom, for the occasional dinner and listening to endless complaints; friends (and Friendsters) both here and far away (Naomi, EB, Kara, I love you freaks); and Mike (Dr. Chicken) and Allie for numerous lunches, dinners, drinks, spectacles of various kinds, and for being the people I couldn't live without.

Megan thanks: Abigail for making it all come together and having fun along the way. Scrobins for the unrelenting support, cookies, and laughs. The rest of the pod, for the absurd discussions, constant distractions, and tomfoolery. Special thanks to Chez Renard for good times and a rent-free summer. Mom, Dad, Taylor, Adri, and Rob: thanks for your love and friendship.

Amelia thanks: Many thanks to Abigail for making everything run so smoothly, to Mapland for a lovely summer, to Mike, Christine and Elizabeth for great meals and company, to Amanda for being my favorite utensil, to my extended blocking group for keeping more or less in touch, and to my family for taking my calls, wherever I happened to be walking.

Editor Abigail K. Joseph
Associate Editor Megan Moran-Gates
Managing Editor Ariel Fox
Map Editor Amelia Aos Showalter
Typesetter Ankur Ghosh
Photographer Luke Marion

INSIDE

Discover Paris

City of light, city of love, unsightly city, invisible city—Paris somehow manages to do it all. From alleys that shelter the world's best bistros to broad avenues flaunting the highest of *haute couture*, from the centuries-old stone of Notre Dame's gargoyles to the futuristic motions of the Parc de la Villette, from the masterpieces of the Louvre to the installations of avant-garde galleries, from the relics of the first millennium to the celebrations of the third, Paris presents itself as both a harbor of tradition and a hotbed of impulse. You can't conquer Paris, old or new, in one week or in thirty years—you can get acquainted in a day, though, and in a week, you may find you're old friends.

Paris has been a center of commerce, culture, and conflict for centuries. Great novels have been written, great ideas born, great loves lost and found here; students have protested, artists have starved, kings have been beheaded—and in the midst of it all, this city became the Western world's symbolic capital of romance, revolution, heroism, and hedonism. No wonder that it's the world's most heavily touristed city—or that intellectuals in the later 20th century, in inimitable French style, started to question whether "Paris" has become nothing more than a conglomeration of illusions in the imagination of the tourist. You might find yourself wondering the same thing, as you sit in some perfect sidewalk café with a view of the Eiffel Tower, sipping an espresso or savoring a croissant, surrounded by beautiful people in brooding black: can this place exist? But it does.

Facts & Figures

Population:
metropolitan area
11,330,700

city proper
2,110,400

Surface Area:
roughly 64 sq. km

Length Of The Seine Within Paris:
13km

Length of the Tunnels Running Under Paris:
300km

Total Number of Steps on the Eiffel Tower:
1792

Priciest Cup of Coffee:
US$12

Estimated "Romantic Encounters" Per Day:
4,959,476

Estimated Pounds Of Lingerie Purchased Per Day:
238

Revolutions To Date:
4

Revolutions To Come?
C'est la vie.

And when you shake yourself out of that romantic swoon, you just might find yourself face to face with postmodernity, whether it takes the form of daring new architecture, fashion, and music, multiethnic and multilingual (not to mention multi-culinary!) communities, or intellectual activity and progressive politics taking on the complex, exciting, difficult realities of the city. Paris seems, incredibly, to live up to its mythical reputation while simultaneously defying it; to be everything that everyone expects and at the same time a constant surprise; at once a living monument to the past and a city full of the life of the present.

ORIENTATION

Flowing from east to west, the **Seine River** crosses the heart of the city of Paris. The two islands **Île de la Cité** and neighboring **Île St-Louis** sit at the geographical center of the city, while the Seine splits Paris into two large expanses—the **Rive Gauche** (Left Bank) to the south of the river and the **Rive Droite** (Right Bank) to the north. Modern Paris is divided into **20 arrondissements** (districts) that spiral clockwise outward from the Louvre. Each *arrondissement* is referred to by its number (e.g. the 3rd, 12th). The French equivalent of the English numerical indicator "th" (as in 18th) is "*ème.*" The proper way to pronounce the name of an *arrondissement* in French is to add "iemme" to the French word for its number; for example, the 16*ème* is *seizième* (SEZ-yem). The exception to this is the 1st, for which the abbreviation is 1*er* (*premier*, PREM-yay).

NEIGHBORHOODS

The neighborhoods below are divided into the Rive Gauche and Rive Droite, listed within each region by number. In most other chapters of this guide, neighborhoods are listed in numerical order from 1*er* to 20*ème*.

SEINE ISLANDS

ÎLE DE LA CITÉ & ÎLE ST-LOUIS

NEIGHBORHOOD QUICKFIND: ***Sights,*** *p. 67;* ***Food & Drink,*** *p. 169;* ***Shopping,*** *p. 235;* ***Accommodations,*** *p. 254.*

It's appropriate that all distance points in France are measured from *kilomètre zéro*, a circular sundial in front of Notre Dame on Île de la Cité. After all, if any place can be called the heart of Paris, it is this slip in the river. Île de la Cité sits in the very center of the city and at the center of the Île de France, the geographical region surrounding Paris. It was the first part of the city to be settled (by the Gauls; see **Life & Times,** p. 39), and the first spot to be named "Paris." From the 6th century, when Clovis crowned himself king of the Franks, until Charles V abandoned it in favor of the Louvre in the 14th century, the island was the seat of the monarchy. Construction of the **Notre Dame** cathedral began here in 1163, and the presence of the cathedral along with other historically significant buildings (including **Ste-Chapelle** and **La Conciergerie**) ensured that the island would remain a center of Parisian religious, political, and cultural life—and, now, a major center of touristic interest.

Île St-Louis had less illustrious beginnings. Originally two small islands—the Île aux Vâches (Cow Island) and the Île de Notre Dame—the Île St-Louis was considered suitable for duels, cows, and little else throughout the Middle Ages. In 1267, the area was renamed for **Louis IX** after he departed for the Crusades. The two islands merged in the 17th century under the direction of architect Louis Le Vau, and Île St-Louis became residential as a result of a contractual arrangement between Henri IV and the bridge entrepreneur Christophe Marie, after whom the **Pont Marie** is named. The island's *hôtels particuliers* attracted an elite citizenry including Voltaire, Mme. de Châtelet, Daumier, Ingres, Baudelaire, Balzac, Courbet, George Sand, Delacroix and Cézanne. In the 1930s, inhabitants declared the island an independent republic.

Île St-Louis still retains a certain remoteness from the rest of Paris. Older residents say "Je vais à Paris" ("I'm going to Paris") when leaving by one of the four bridges linking Île St-Louis and the mainland. All in all, the island looks remarkably similar to its 17th-century self, retaining an incredible sense of history as well as a unique calm. While tourists might clog the streets on weekends, the island is nonetheless a haven of boutiques, specialty food shops, and art galleries that can provide for a pleasant wander.

DON'T MISS: **Ste-Chapelle** (p. 70); **Berthillon** ice cream (p. 170).

RIVE GAUCHE (LEFT BANK)

The *"gauche"* in Rive Gauche once signified a secondary, lower-class lifestyle, the kind flaunted by the perennially impoverished students who stayed there. Today, the Left Bank's timeless appeal is ensured by its inexpensive cafés and bars, great shopping and sightseeing, and literary caché both past and present.

FIFTH & SIXTH ARRONDISSEMENTS: LATIN QUARTER

NEIGHBORHOOD QUICKFIND: ***Sights,*** *p. 86;* ***Museums,*** *p. 148;* ***Food & Drink,*** *p. 177;* ***Nightlife,*** *p. 211;* ***Shopping,*** *p. 239;* ***Accommodations,*** *p. 259.*

The 6*ème* and the western half of the 5*ème* make up the *Quartier Latin* (Latin Quarter), which takes its name from the language used in the 5*ème*'s prestigious *lycées* and universities prior to 1798. The 5*ème* has been right in the intellectual thick of things since the founding of the **Sorbonne** in 1263, and its hot-blooded student population has played a major role in uprisings from the French Revolution to the revolution of May 1968 (see **Life & Times,** p. 49). The cafés of the now-legendary **boulevard St-Germain** in the 6*ème* are the former stomping grounds of Hemingway, Sartre, Picasso, Camus, Baudelaire, and just about anyone else who was in Paris during the first half of the 20th century.

Some naysayers argue that this *quartier* has lost its rebellious vigor since the 60s: the new, concrete sidewalk slabs that replaced the loose cobblestones used as missiles in the protests are proof enough. Yet while areas like **boulevard St-Michel** (the boundary between the 5*ème* and 6*ème*), with their chain stores and hoards of camera-toting tourists, are notable victims of commodification, the smaller byways of the student quarter still hold fast to their progressive, edgy, and multiethnic tone. Dusty bookstores, art-house cinemas, smoky jazz clubs, and international food abounds. Pl. de la Contrescarpe and **rue Mouffetard,** both in the *5ème*, are quintessential Latin Quarter; the Mouff' has one of the liveliest street markets in Paris.

Despite its high-class fashion and shameless materialism, the *6ème* is home to two of Paris's most vibrant cultural staples: literary cafés and art galleries. In addition to classic St-Germain cafés, there is a vibrant literary life around **Carrefour de l'Odéon.** The area's prestigious galleries (see p. 159) display exciting contemporary work.

DON'T MISS: **Institut du Monde Arabe** (p. 90); **Jardin des Plantes** (p. 89).

SEVENTH ARRONDISSEMENT

NEIGHBORHOOD QUICKFIND: ***Sights,*** *p. 96;* ***Museums,*** *p. 149;* ***Food & Drink,*** *p. 183;* ***Nightlife,*** *p. 213;* ***Shopping,*** *p. 242;* ***Accommodations,*** *p. 262.*

The *7ème* became Paris's most elegant residential district in the 18th century, and the 1889 completion of the **Eiffel Tower** at the river's edge, though it was met with mixed feelings, ensured that the area would remain in the spotlight. The World Fairs that followed helped to cement the landmark in Parisian history. Many of the neighborhood's stunning residences have been maintained as foreign embassies, while the **National Assembly** and the **Invalides** add much historical merit and French character to this section of the Left Bank. Keep your eye out for the tip of the Eiffel Tower, sometimes visible beyond the rooftops of the area. In the grass of the **Champ de Mars** or the fashionable sidestreets surrounding **rue de Sèvres,** the *7ème* offers both some of the most touristy and most intimate sights in Paris. Predictably, the area is not cheap when it comes to food and accommodations.

DON'T MISS: **Musée Rodin** (p. 140).

THIRTEENTH ARRONDISSEMENT

NEIGHBORHOOD QUICKFIND: ***Sights,*** *p. 111;* ***Food & Drink,*** *p. 190;* ***Nightlife,*** *p. 216;* ***Accommodations,*** *p. 268.*

Until the 20th century, the *13ème* was one of Paris's poorest neighborhoods, with conditions so bad in the 19th century that Victor Hugo used parts of the neighborhood as a setting for *Les Misérables.* Traversed by the **Bièvre,** a stagnant stream clogged with industrial refuse, the *13ème* was also the city's worst-smelling district.

Happily, the 20th century has seen many changes to the *13ème*, olfactory and otherwise. In 1910, the Bièvre was filled in. Environmentalists eventually won a campaign to close the neighborhood's tanneries and paper factories. If city planners have their way, the influx of construction that began with Mitterand's ultra-modern **Bibliothèque de France** in 1996 will continue with **ZAC (Zone d'Aménagement Concerté),** a project which will make the quai banks of the *13ème* into the largest cultural center in Paris. Next to come are a new university, numerous blocks of office space, a cinema complex, and a film education center. The area is also home to several immigrant communities residing in a thriving **Chinatown.**

DON'T MISS: The music, the drinks, and the view at **Batofar** (p. 216); the bargain gourmet food in the charming **Butte-aux-Cailles** (p. 190).

LET'S NOT GO: Be careful near the sleazy nightlife at av. du Maine's northern end.

FOURTEENTH ARRONDISSEMENT: MONTPARNASSE

NEIGHBORHOOD QUICKFIND: ***Sights,*** *p. 113;* ***Museums,*** *p. 152;* ***Food & Drink,*** *p. 191;* ***Nightlife,*** *p. 216;* ***Accommodations,*** *p. 269.*

Montparnasse (Mount Parnassus), one of the areas of Paris most imbued with the mythology of the bohemian past, was named after the Greek gods by the students who gathered here to recite poetry in the 18th century. The first of many generations of immigrants to settle in the 14*ème* were Bretons who came to the neighborhood in the 19th century (Breton *crêperies*, handicraft shops, and cultural associations still line busy **rue du Montparnasse**). But the area's heyday was the interwar period, when it became a haven for artists, writers, and political exiles, including Man Ray, Modigliani, Henry Miller, and Lenin. The avant-garde set up studios in Montparnasse and talked, drank, and danced all night in cafés like **Le Select** and **Le Dôme.**

The area where the chic 6*ème* meets the commercial 14*ème* just south of the Latin Quarter (near the ever-fashionable **boulevard du Montparnasse**) never lost its sense of style. While gentrification has forced struggling artists out of those now upscale quartiers, the 14*ème's* affordability and well-entrenched café culture still attract young artists and students, who debate at the **Cité Universitaire.** Restaurants (of both the cheap and Lost-Generation chic varieties), a few remaining galleries, and cafés make the 14*ème* well worth a visit.

DON'T MISS. Cimetière du Montparnasse (p. 113); **L'Entrepot** (p. 216).

FIFTEENTH ARRONDISSEMENT

NEIGHBORHOOD QUICKFIND: ***Sights,*** *p. 114;* ***Museums,*** *p. 152;* ***Food & Drink,*** *p. 192;* ***Accommodations,*** *p. 270.*

Unlike its neighbors to the east, the Latin Quarter and Montparnasse, the 15*ème* never gained a reputation as being either upstart or overly literary. Instead, it drew a working middle-class population. Today, the 15*ème* is the city's most populous *arrondissement*, and still middling in incomes and politics. The expansive **Parc André Citroën** (p. 114) attracts families on weekends. Aside from that, the 15*ème* doesn't have sights to speak of, and you'll find the atmosphere crowded, busy, and very industrial around Gare Montparnasse. Hotels scramble for guests in the summer, and budget travelers can benefit from low room rates. Don't overlook the lively establishments in the western segment of the neighborhood, particularly along the border with the seventh. Locals have their favorites among the grocers on r. du Commerce, the cafés at the corner of r. de la Convention and r. de Vaugirard, and the specialty shops along av. Emile Zola.

DON'T MISS: The view from the **Tour Maine-Montparnasse** (p. 115).

Ritz Hotel

Notre Dame

Jardin du Luxembourg

RIVE GAUCHE (LEFT BANK)

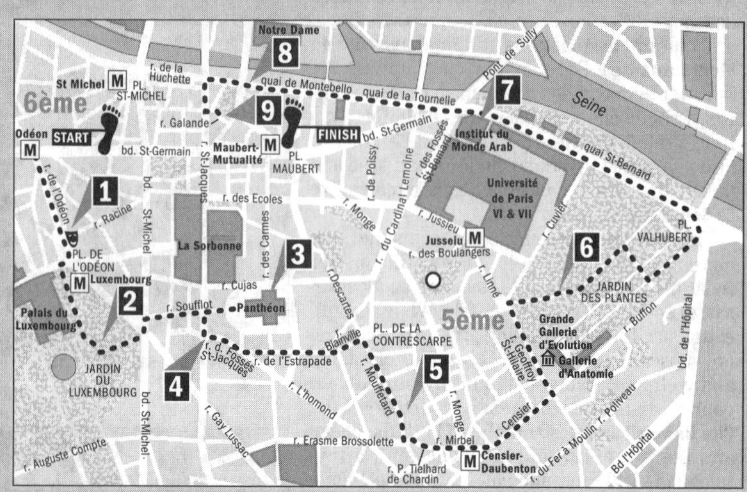

START: M: Odéon

FINISH: M: St-Michel

DISTANCE: 6.1km (3¾ mi.)

DURATION: 3-4hr.

WHEN TO GO: Start in the afternoon

1 THÉÂTRE DE L'ODÉON. When you get off the métro, take a look at the impressive facade of the Odéon, Paris's oldest and largest theater. (See p. 93.)

2 JARDIN DU LUXEMBOURG. Architectural excesses, beautiful lawns, miniature sailboats, and plenty of shady spots make this garden a favorite. (See p. 91.)

3 PANTHÉON. The inscription reads: "To great men from a grateful fatherland." The Panthéon indeed houses some great men (and women): its crypt contains the remains of Emile Zola, Marie Curie, Victor Hugo, and others. And the fatherland must have been grateful to have put them up in a building as beautiful as this one. (See p. 87.)

4 AU PORT SALUT. The traditional three-course lunch at this boisterous former cabaret is pure gastronomic joy. (163bis, r. St-Jacques; see p. 177.)

5 RUE MOUFFETARD. The Mouff' has held onto its charm since the 2nd century. Hemingway and Paul Verlaine both came to stay. Have some of (arguably) the best ice cream in Paris at **Octave,** no. 138. (See p. 88.)

6 JARDIN DES PLANTES. The Jardin's rare plants and exquisite *roserie* draw visitors. The **Galerie d'Anatomie** is the unlikely star of the garden's many museums. (See p. 89.)

7 INSTITUT DU MONDE ARABE. This modern building has excellent exhibits, striking architecture , and a great (free!) view of the city. (See p. 90.)

8 SHAKESPEARE & CO. Stroll along the Seine until you reach Shakespeare & Co. No visit to the Latin Quarter would be complete without a stop in at this famed bookstore. (37, r. de la Boucherie; see p. 90.)

9 LE CAVEAU DE LA HUCHETTE. This club serves refreshing *digestifs* upstairs and great jazz downstairs. (5, r. de la Huchette; see p. 220.)

RIVE DROITE (RIGHT BANK)

The *Rive Gauche* has long been considered the more fashionable side of the Seine. The first four *arrondissements* comprise what has historically been central Paris and contain the oldest streets in the city, along with many of its most famous sights and best (if not cheapest) restaurants, nightlife, and shopping.

Quai St-Michel

FIRST ARRONDISSEMENT

NEIGHBORHOOD QUICKFIND: ***Sights,*** *p. 73;* ***Museums,*** *p. 146;* ***Food & Drink,*** *p. 171;* ***Nightlife,*** *p. 206;* ***Shopping,*** *p. 235;* ***Accommodations,*** *p. 254.*

Paris's royal past is conspicuous in much of the 1*er*. Its prized possession, the **Louvre**, is the former home of French royalty. Louis XIV, who seemed to take his garden fetish with him wherever he went (see **Daytripping**, p. 284), made sure the greenery here was well-tended, evidenced in the **Tuileries.**

Today, the bedchambers and dining rooms of innumerable rulers house the world's finest art, and the Sun King's prized gardens are more a playground for sunbathers and children with sailboats than debauched kings. Royalty still dominates here, though: Chanel and the Ritz Hotel hold court. The Ritz stands in the regal **place Vendôme,** while less ritzy souvenir shops crowd **rue du Rivoli** and **Les Halles.** Elegant boutiques line the **rue St-Honoré,** the street that passes the Comédie Française, where actors still pay tribute to Molière, the company's founder. Farther west, smoky jazz clubs pulse on **rue des Lombards** while restaurants on **rue Jean-Jacques Rousseau** serve up France's most divine culinary finery.

Opéra

DON'T MISS: The **Palais-Royal** (p. 74).

LET'S NOT GO: Although above ground the 1*er* is one of the safest areas in Paris, the area's métro stops (Châtelet and Les Halles) are best avoided at night.

SECOND ARRONDISSEMENT

NEIGHBORHOOD QUICKFIND: ***Sights,*** *p. 77;* ***Food & Drink,*** *p. 172;* ***Nightlife,*** *p. 206;* ***Shopping,*** *p. 235;* ***Accommodations,*** *p. 255.*

The 2*ème* has a long history of trade and commerce, from the lovely 19th-century **passageways** (the world's first indoor shopping malls) to the ancient **Bourse** where stocks and bonds were traded. The oldest and most enduring trade of the area, prostitution, has thrived on **rue St-Denis**

Arc de Triomphe

Top Ten Places to Kiss

You are, after all, in the "City of Love," or so they say ...embrace that romanticization, and each other. *Vive l'amour!*

1. On **Pont Neuf** or in the garden just to the left (p. 71). One of the city's most popular make-out spots.

2. The garden of the **Musée Rodin,** preferably near "Le Baiser" (p. 140).

3. The stairs of **Montmartre,** particularly between nos. 30 and 32, r. des Trois Frères (p. 119).

4. The exquisite rose garden in the **Bois de Boulogne** (p. 125).

5. The 9th-floor terrace of **Samaritaine** (p. 247), where the view of the city will rival your view of each other.

6. Trocadéro esplanade, under the **Eiffel Tower**–or on the top of the tower (p. 116).

7. **Place des Vosges,** especially on a sunny afternoon (p. 85).

8. Strolling along the lovely **Canal St-Martin** (p. 108).

9. At the top of the ferris wheel at the **Jardin des Tuileries**–just be careful not to fall out! (p. 73).

10. At any **café** after 11pm–that's where Parisians seem to do it most.

From cinema: outside the **Théâtre du Châtelet** in pl. du Châtelet *(Diva)*; on the métro at **Bir-Hakeim** *(Last Tango in Paris)*.

since the Middle Ages. Many cheap little restaurants and hotels populate this mostly working-class area and make it an excellent place to stay; **rue Montorgeuil** is full of great bakeries and food shops. The area known as **Etienne-Marcel** bursts with fabulous and fabulously cheap clothing—come here to get outfitted for wild nights of clubbing. For those either tired of chasing skirts or up for a laugh, the Opéra Comique, now known as the **Théâtre Musicale,** can be found between bd. des Italiens and r. de Richelieu.

DON'T MISS: Galleries and Passages (p. 77).

LET'S NOT GO: (At least not with the kids, anyway.) R. St-Denis is a seedy center of prostitution and pornography.

THIRD & FOURTH ARRONDISSEMENTS: MARAIS

NEIGHBORHOOD QUICKFIND: ***Sights,*** *p. 79;* ***Museums,*** *p. 146;* ***Food & Drink,*** *p. 174;* ***Nightlife,*** *p. 207;* ***Shopping,*** *p. 237;* ***Accommodations,*** *p. 257.*

Drained by monks in the 13th century, the Marais ("swamp") was land-filled to provide building space for the Right Bank. With Henri IV's construction of the glorious **place des Vosges** at the beginning of the 17th century, the area became the city's center of fashionable living. Leading architects and sculptors of the period designed elegant **hôtels particuliers** with large courtyards. Under Louis XV, the center of Parisian life moved to the *faubourgs* (then considered suburbs) St-Honoré and St-Germain, and construction in the Marais ceased. During the Revolution, the former haunts of the sovereign gave way to slumlords and their tenements; at the same time, the majority of *hôtels* fell into ruin or disrepair. The Jewish population, which had been a presence in the Marais since the 12th century, grew with influxes of immigrants from Russia and North Africa—and, tragically, was effectively depleted during the Holocaust. Fortunately, in the 1960s the Marais was declared an historic neighborhood. A 30-year period of gentrification and renovation has allowed the Marais to regain its pre-Revolutionary glory.

Once-palatial mansions have become exquisite museums, and the tiny twisting streets have been adopted by hip bars, avant-garde galleries, and some of the city's most unique boutiques. **Rue des Rosiers,** in the heart of the *4ème*, is still the focal point of the city's Jewish population. Superb kosher delicatessens neighbor Middle Eastern and Eastern European restaurants, and on Sundays, when much of the city is closed, the Marais remains lively. The Marais is also unquestionably the center of gay Paris, with its hub around the intersection of **rue Ste-Croix de la Brettonerie** and **rue Vieille-du-Temple.** This corner is a microcosm of the entire district: an accessible, fun, and friendly mix of old and new, queer and straight, cheap and chic, classic and cruisy, hip and historic. No pilgrim to Paris should miss it.

DON'T MISS: Place des Vosges (p. 85).

EIGHTH ARRONDISSEMENT

NEIGHBORHOOD QUICKFIND: ***Sights,*** *p. 100;* ***Museums,*** *p. 150;* ***Food & Drink,*** *p. 184;* ***Nightlife,*** *p. 213;* ***Shopping,*** *p. 243;* ***Accommodations,*** *p. 263.*

Once home to both *nouveau riche* wannabes and true blue bloods, the *8ème* didn't really take off until the turn of the 19th century, after the aristocrats had been chased out by the Revolution and Napoleon had given deserving officers and *haute bourgeoisie* titles and prestige of their own. The *8ème* became a hub of social and commercial activity under Napoleon's nephew, Louis Napoleon, who, with Haussman, finished construction of the **place de l'Etoile.**

Lined with expansive mansions, expensive shops and restaurants, and grandiose monuments, the *8ème's* broad boulevards are filled with Parisians out for the latest in fashion and tourists who may feel schlumpy next to all of the showy elegance. Stylistic contrasts are especially jarring on the **Champs-Elysées,** which is long past its heyday but still retains some of the glamour that comes with being one of the world's most famous streets.

A stroll along **avenue Montaigne, rue du Faubourg St-Honoré,** or around the **Madeleine** will give a taste of what life in Paris is like for those with money to burn. Obscenely upscale *haute couture* boutiques mix with McDonald's and Monoprix along the Champs, and the US Embassy stands opposite one of Paris's most expensive hotels. Don't expect inexpensive eateries and hidden deals in this neighborhood—instead, visit the *8ème's grands boulevards* to gawk, and if you dare, blow a day's budget on unforgettably fine dining.

DON'T MISS: Parc Monceau (p. 105); **Musée Jacquemart-André** (p. 150).

NINTH ARRONDISSEMENT

NEIGHBORHOOD QUICKFIND: ***Sights,*** *p. 105;* ***Food & Drink,*** *p. 186;* ***Museums,*** *p. 151;* ***Nightlife,*** *p. 214;* ***Accommodations,*** *p. 264.*

The *9ème* was a major benefactor of Haussmannization, which gave its southern half the *grands boulevards* and the air of glamour that extends south into the *8ème.* The *9ème* caught everyone's attention beginning in the late 19th century, when the magnificent **Opéra Garnier** was finished and the glitzy auction house **Drout** opened its doors. Today, the *9ème* is a veritable diagram of Paris's cultural extremes. The lower *9ème* proudly displays the highest of highs: the high art of the Opéra Garnier, the high-falutin' panoramic cinemas, and the high-class *couture* of the swanky department stores **Galeries Lafayette** and **Au Printemps.** The upper *9ème,* near the northern border with the *18ème,* however, offers a striking contrast: the infamously low-brow porn shops, X-rated cinemas, and the culture of prostitution and drugs that dominate the neon-lighted area known as **Pigalle.** Separating these two oddly located sectors is the *9ème's* geographical center: a sleepy, residential neighborhood that holds these two extravagant extremes of materialism at bay. There are plenty of hotels, but many to the north are used for the local flesh trade. Nicer but not-so-cheap hotels are available near the respectable and central bd. des Italiens and bd. Montmartre.

DON'T MISS: Opéra Garnier (p. 105); **Galeries Lafayette** (p. 247).

LET'S NOT GO: Place Pigalle and M: Barbès-Rochechoart are notorious for prostitution and drugs, both of which become apparent at an astonishingly early hour. Tourists (especially young women) should avoid Pigalle, especially after dark.

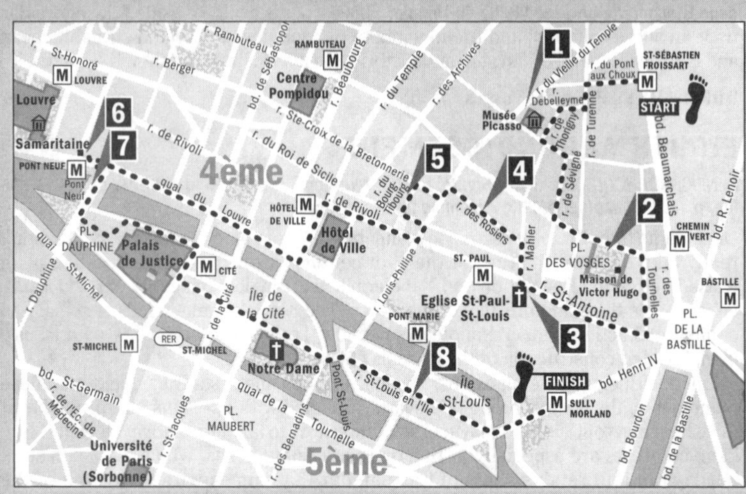

START: M: St-Sébastien Froissart

FINISH: M: Sully Morland

DISTANCE: 5.2km (3¼ mi.)

DURATION: 3-4hr.

WHEN TO GO: Start in the late morning

1 MUSÉE PICASSO. This museum traces Picasso's life and work chronologically, all the way from Paris to the Riviera, from blue to pink, from first mistress to last. (5, r. de Thorigny; see p. 142.)

2 PLACE DES VOSGES. The exquisite manicured grass of Paris's oldest public square has been tread by the likes of Molière and Victor Hugo (no. 6 is a museum of his life and work), not to mention a good number of royals. An arcade runs around all four of its sides and houses restaurants, art galleries, and shops. (See p. 85.)

3 EGLISE ST-PAUL-ST-LOUIS. This Jesuit cathedral dominates r. St-Antoine and offers the weary traveler a break from the heat and car exhaust on the *rue.* The church's Baroque interior houses Eugène Delacroix's dramatic *Christ in the Garden of Olives* (1826). (See p. 84).

4 RUE DES ROSIERS. This quintessential Marais street is filled with bakeries, off-beat boutiques, and kosher restaurants. For lunch, enjoy a delicious falafel sandwich at the perpetually crowded **L'As du Falafel.**, no. 34. (See p. 81.)

5 MARIAGE FRÈRES. This classic and classy *salon de thé* has 500 varieties of tea to choose from. (30, r. du Bourg-Tibourg; see p. 198.)

6 SAMARITAINE. Eleven floors of shopping for him, her, and home are topped off with an unbeatable panoramic view of the city. Markers name every dot on the horizon, making this Art Deco department store worth a visit, even if shopping isn't on the agenda. (67, r. de Rivoli; see p. 77.)

7 PONT NEUF. By way of the very long, very straight, rue de Rivoli and the scenic quai du Louvre, make your way to the Pont Neuf, Paris's oldest bridge (c. 1607). Its gargoyles have seen peddlers and pickpockets, and a whole lot of bubble wrap (see p. 71).

8 RUE ST-LOUIS-EN-ÎLE. Wander down the charming 17th-century-esque main street of the Île St-Louis, popping into a chic boutique or two and stopping for a scoop of **Berthillon** ice cream (no. 34) or gelato at **Amarino** (no. 47). (See p. 72.)

TENTH ARRONDISSEMENT

NEIGHBORHOOD QUICKFIND: ***Sights,*** *p. 107;* ***Museums,*** *p. 151;* ***Food & Drink,*** *p. 187;* ***Accommodations,*** *p. 265.*

The **place de la République** was once a hotbed of Revolutionary fervor, but Haussmann put an end to that with a some clever urban planning (see **Sights,** p. 102). Since then, the 10*ème* has quieted down. In general, the area is one of striking juxtapositions—regal statues scrawled with graffiti and peaceful, sunny squares next to packed boulevards full of seedy wares. Though the 10*ème* is not known for drawing tourists, it should not be written off completely. Good, cheap restaurants abound, and the area near **Canal St-Marin** makes for very pleasant wandering.

DON'T MISS: Canal St-Martin (p. 108).

LET'S NOT GO: The 10*ème* is far from sights and certain areas may be unsafe at night; take care around the bd. St-Martin and parts of r. de Faubourg St-Denis no matter the time of day. Use caution west of pl. de la République along r. du Château d'Eau.

ELEVENTH ARRONDISSEMENT

NEIGHBORHOOD QUICKFIND: ***Sights,*** *p. 108;* ***Food & Drink,*** *p. 188;* ***Nightlife,*** *p. 214;* ***Accommodations,*** *p. 266.*

The 11*ème* is most famous for hosting the Revolutionary kick-off at the **Bastille** prison on July 14, 1789 (see **Life & Times,** p. 43). The French still storm this area—nightly, in fact—in search of the latest cocktail, culinary delight or up-and-coming artist. The 1989 opening of the glassy **Opéra Bastille** on the bicentennial of the Revolution breathed new life into the 11*ème*. In the early 1990s, the neighborhood near the Opéra Bastille was touted as the next Montmartre, the next Montparnasse, and the next Latin Quarter: the city's latest Bohemia. Today, with its numerous bars along **rue de Lappe,** impressive international dining options on **rue de la Roquette,** and off-beat cafés and avant garde galleries, the Bastille area appears to have lived up to these expectations. Crowds also surge north of the Bastille to **rue Oberkampf** and **rue Ménilmontant,** where lively bars and nightclubs provide the perfect end to an all-night bar crawl. Five métro lines converge at M: République and three at M: Bastille, making the 11*ème* a transport hub and mammoth center of action, the hangout of the young and fun. Budget accommodations line these streets and are likely to have space.

Best Spots for Late Night...

Can't sleep? Neither can we. Check out the following for all of your 4am needs.

Anglo fun: party with the late-night anglo crowd at **Mustang Café** in the 14*ème* until 5am (see p. 217).

Cheap food & coffee: hang out with the cab drivers at **Taxi Club** in the 1*er*, open until 6am (see p. 171).

Cigarettes: most tabacs close around 6pm, but the one at **10, r. Washington** in the 8*ème* is open till 2:30am. Look for the long line of desperate smokers.

Dinner: Babylone Bis in the 2*ème* is open till 8am and serves food and fun all night (see p. 173).

Flowers: romantic emergency at dawn? **Elyfleur** in the 17*ème* is open 24hr. (82, av. de Wagram, ☎01 46 66 87 19).

Music: at **Aux Trois Mailletz** in the 5*ème* you can enjoy smoky jazz till dawn with the Latin Quarter's coolest (see p. 220).

Museum: For that midnight museum fix, the **Musée de l'Érotisme** in the 18*ème*is open until 2am (see p. 156).

Packing tape & stamps: Need to mail a letter at 5am? No worries. **Poste du Louvre** in the 1*er* is open 24 hours a day (see p. 344).

Posh, Pricey Cocktails: drink with the it-boys and girls of St-Germain until 6am at **Café Mabillon** in the 6*ème* (see p. 212).

Top Ten Métro Stations

1. **Abbesses** in the 18*ème*—climb the never-ending spiral stairs to see all of the funky paintings.

2. **Cluny-La Sorbonne** in the 5*ème*: try to decipher the signature of the Sorbonne's luminaries on the tiles.

3. **Arts et Métiers** in the 3*ème* is covered entirely in copper, designed by the nearby Musée des Arts et Métiers. You'll feel like you're inside a submarine.

4. **Montparnasse-Bienvenüe** in the 14*ème:* witness the *trottoir roulant rapide* (fast-rolling pavement), a revolution in urban travel. But be careful not to fall!

5. **Louvre** in the 1*er* is filled with replicas of artwork from the museum.

6. **St-Germain des Prés** in the 6*ème* has poetry, cartoons, and quotations projected onto its curved walls.

7. **Palais Royal's** entrance in the 1*er* is appropriately bejeweled.

8. **Cité & St-Michel** in the 5*ème* let you fulfill that spaceship fantasy in the uber-modern elevators that count down and take off.

9. **Porte Dauphine** in the 16*ème* has one of the best of the Hector Guimard's brilliant Art Nouveau entrances.

10. **Line 14:** Any stop on this new, super-swank line will seduce you with its speed, glass doors, and multilingual instructions.

DON'T MISS: The young, up-and-coming nightlife scene on **rue de Lappe** (p. 214).

TWELFTH ARRONDISSEMENT

NEIGHBORHOOD QUICKFIND: ***Sights,*** *p. 110;* ***Museums,*** *p. 152;* ***Food & Drink,*** *p. 189;* ***Nightlife,*** *p. 215;* ***Shopping,*** *p. 243;* ***Accommodations,*** *p. 267.*

The 12*ème's* **place de la Nation** was the setting for Louis XIV's wedding in 1160. The neighborhood was the site of much revolutionary fervor during the revolutions of 1830 and 1848. In the mid-1900s, the neighborhood calmed down, only to raise its shackles later on—in response to the building of the controversial **Opéra Bastille** in 1989. Today, the 12*ème* borrows youthful momentum from the neighboring 4*ème* and 11*ème.* Its northwestern fringes are decidedly funky (the **Viaduc des Arts, rue de la Roquette,** and **rue du Faubourg St-Antoine** are lined with galleries and stores), and its core is working class, with a large immigrant population. The streets around the Bois de Vincennes offer some of the city's most pleasant places to stay, but are removed from the city center.

DON'T MISS: If only to see what all the fuss is about, the **Opéra Bastille** (p. 110).

LET'S NOT GO: The area is generally safe, but be careful around Gare de Lyon, which attracts some sketchy characters.

SIXTEENTH ARRONDISSEMENT

NEIGHBORHOOD QUICKFIND: ***Sights,*** *p. 116;* ***Museums,*** *p. 153;* ***Food & Drink,*** *p. 193;* ***Nightlife,*** *p. 217;* ***Accommodations,*** *p. 272.*

When Notre Dame was under construction, this now elegant suburb was little more than a couple of tiny villages in the woods, and so it remained for several centuries, as kings and nobles chased deer and boar through its forests. With the advent of Haussmann, however (see **Sights,** p. 102), the area was transformed. The wealthy villages of **Auteuil, Passy,** and **Chaillot** banded together and joined the city, forming what is now the 16*ème.*

Today, the well-kept streets of this elegant *quartier* provide peaceful release from the mobbed sidewalks of the neighboring 8*ème.* Home to impressive Art Nouveau and Art Deco architecture in addition to Paris' best view of the famous Eiffel Tower, the 16*ème* also hosts an impressive density of **museums** of all types and specializations. Showcasing everything from cutting-edge contemporary art to second-century Asian statuary, this *arrondissement* has countless museums of every shape, size, and style are sure to satisfy any appetite. Aside from museums, most property in the area tends to be that of rich landlords; you'll see more mansions, townhouses, and apartment buildings than businesses or restaurants in the sixteenth.

DON'T MISS: site creation contemporaine (p. 153).

SEVENTEENTH ARRONDISSEMENT

NEIGHBORHOOD QUICKFIND: ***Sights,*** *p. 118;* ***Museums,*** *p. 156;* ***Food & Drink,*** *p. 194;* ***Nightlife,*** *p. 217;* ***Accommodations,*** *p. 273.*

While barricades were erected, nobles beheaded, and novels written in the heart of the city, **Les Batignolles** of the *17ème* was little more than farmers' fields until the mid-19th century. By the end of the 19th century, however, the area became a center for the **Impressionists** (see **Life & Times,** p. 61) who came for the cheap rent and stayed for the views. Today, hugging the northwestern edge of the city and sandwiched in between the aristocratic *8ème* and *16ème arrondissements* and the more tawdry *18ème* and Pigalle, the *17ème* is a working-class residential neighborhood bespeckled with restaurants both cheap and gourmet. Some of its hotels cater to prostitutes, others to visiting businesspeople. The **Village Batignolles** offers a nice change of pace from central Paris, and is a great place for a stroll (during daylight). Hip bars like **L'Endroit** (see **Nightlife,** p. 217) cater to stylish young crowds, while the **Musée Jean-Jacques Henner** (see **Museums,** p. 156) affords the discerning art enthusiast a stimulating afternoon.

DON'T MISS: Nightlife on wheels at the roller-disco **La Main Jaune** (see p. 217).

LET'S NOT GO: Be careful where the *17ème* borders the *18ème* near pl. de Clichy.

EIGHTEENTH ARRONDISSEMENT: MONTMARTRE

NEIGHBORHOOD QUICKFIND: ***Sights,*** *p. 119;* ***Museums,*** *p. 156;* ***Food & Drink,*** *p. 195;* ***Nightlife,*** *p. 218;* ***Shopping,*** *p. 245;* ***Accommodations,*** *p. 273.*

Like Montparnasse and the Latin Quarter, Montmartre (one of the few neighborhoods Haussmann left intact when he redesigned the city and its environs) still glows with the lustre of its artsy-bohemian past. Named "Mount of the Martyr" for St-Denis, who was beheaded here by the Romans in AD 260, the hill was for centuries a rural village covered with vineyards, wheat fields, windmills, and gypsum mines. In the late 19th and early 20th centuries, the area became a center of the city's rebellious artistic energies. During the Belle Epoque, its picturesque beauty and low rents attracted bohemians like painter HenriToulouse-Lautrec and composer Erik Satie as well as performers and impresarios like Aristide Bruant. Toulouse-Lautrec, in particular, immortalized Montmartre with his paintings of life in disreputable nightspots like the **Bal du Moulin Rouge.** Filled with cabarets like "Le Chat Noir," satirical journals, and proto-Dada artist groups like *Les Incohérents* and *Les Hydropathes*, the whole *butte* became the Parisian center of free love, fun, and *fumisme:* the satiric jabbing of social and political norms. A generation later, just before WWI smashed its spotlights and destroyed its crops, the *butte* welcomed eccentric innovators like Picasso, Modigliani, Utrillo, and Apollinaire into its artistic circle and its cabarets.

Nowadays, Montmartre is a mix of nostalgic history, pseudo-artistic schmaltz (pl. du Tertre), upscale bohemia (above r. des Abbesses) and sleaze (along bd. de Clichy). The rather strenuous climb up to the **Basilique du Sacré-Coeur** is worth it for the beauty of the church itself and the dramatic panoramas of the city in front of it. The northwestern part of the *butte* retains some village charm, with breezy streets speckled with interesting shops and cafés; cinephiles have been flocking recently to this area where the hit film *Amélie* was set. At dusk, gas lamps trace the stairways up the hillside to the basilica. Hotel rates rise as you climb the hill to Sacré-Coeur. Downhill and south at seedy pl. Pigalle, hotels tend to rent by the hour.

DON'T MISS: Picasso's favorite: the **Lapin Agile** (p. 120).

LET'S NOT GO: At night, avoid **M: Anvers, M: Pigalle,** and **M: Barbès-Rochechouart;** use M: Abbesses instead. Always be careful in areas near the northern *9ème.*

NINETEENTH ARRONDISSEMENT

NEIGHBORHOOD QUICKFIND: ***Sights,*** *p. 123;* ***Food & Drink,*** *p. 197;* ***Accommodations,*** *p. 274.*

The 19*ème* never got the patronage of the bohemian artists that made its neighbor, Montmartre, so famous. Many of its buildings were constructed without attention to building codes and were later replaced by housing projects.

Like Paris's other peripheral *arrondissements,* the 19*ème* is a predominantly working-class quarter, far from most central sights. However, the *arrondissement* does boast a number of charming streets and two of Paris' finest parks, the Romantic **Parc des Buttes-Chaumont** and the ultra-modern **Parc de la Villette.** The 19*ème* is also home to a large Asian community, and full of wonderful, inexpensive eateries.

LET'S NOT GO: Be careful at night particularly in the emptier northwestern corner of the *arrondissement* as well as along r. David d'Angiers, bd. Indochine, and av. Corentin Cariou, r. de Belleville, and by the "Portes" into the area.

TWENTIETH ARRONDISSEMENT

NEIGHBORHOOD QUICKFIND: ***Sights,*** *p. 123;* ***Museums,*** *p. 157;* ***Food & Drink,*** *p. 197;* ***Nightlife,*** *p. 218;* ***Accommodations,*** *p. 275.*

As Haussmannization expelled many of Paris's workers from the central city in the mid 19th century, thousands migrated east to **Belleville** (the northern part of the 20*ème*), **Ménilmontant** (the southern), and **Charonne** (the southeastern). By the late Second Republic, the 20*ème* had come to be known as a "red" *arrondissement,* characterized as both proletarian and radical. Some of the heaviest fighting during the suppression of the Commune took place in these streets, where the *communards* made desperate last stands on their home turf. Caught between the Versaillais troops to the west and the Prussian lines outside the city walls, the Commune fortified the Parc des Buttes-Chaumont and the **Cimetière du Père Lachaise** but soon ran out of ammunition. On May 28, 1871, the *communards* abandoned their last barricade and surrendered (see **Life & Times,** p. 45). The 20*ème* remained the fairly isolated home of those workers who survived the retributive massacres following the government's takeover.

Today, the *arrondissement* has a similar feel, with busy residential areas and markets that cater not to visitors but to locals. The area is also the home to sizable Greek, North African, Russian, and Asian communities.

DON'T MISS: **Père Lachaise Cemetery (p. 123).**

BANLIEUE

The *banlieue* are the suburbs of Paris. They have recently gained international attention in the film *La Haine* as sites of poverty and racism, although they in fact range in socioeconomic status from extremely wealthy to extremely depressed. The nearest, *proche-banlieue,* are accessible by the métro and bus lines from the city. These include the Vallé de Chevreuse towns to the south; St-Cloud, Neuilly, and Boulogne to the west past the Bois de Boulogne (see **Sights,** p. 125); St-Mandé and Vincennes to the east past the Bois de Vincennes (see **Sights,** p. 128); and to the north, the towns of housing projects known as *zones* or *cités,* Pantin, Aubervilliers, and La Courneuve, which have recently experienced high levels of crime and drug traffic. Apparently, the Paris *Commune* of 1871 (see **Life & Times,** p. 45) was not completely in vain, since the *banlieue rouges* (red suburbs)—Montreuil, Bagnolet, Bobigny, and Kremlin-Bicêtre—flourish with communist governments. The *grandes banlieue* (Versailles, Chantilly, and St-Germain-en-Laye), farther afield and boasting some awesome sights (see **Daytripping,** p. 279), can be reached by RER or commuter train. The *banlieue* have also become sites of some of Paris's more exciting cultural productions. Every summer brings the annual *Banlieue Jazz* and *Banlieue Blues* festivals to the greater Paris area; throughout the year, artists communes take advantage of government-controlled rents in the *banlieue rouges.* A radical artistic spirit continues to thrive at Parisian theater collectives, in particular at **La Cartoucherie** (see p. 225)—perhaps the most vibrant current incarnation of that storied Parisian Bohemia. In the poorer suburbs, disaffection has in some cases been articulated as artistic expression; young people of Arab and North African descent in particular have been mixing their varied musical and cultural traditions to produce exciting, incendiary fusion music of all types.

TOP 25 SIGHTS

25. Passages of the 2ème arrondissement. Shopping, old school. Here you can behold glorious stained glass and well-tiled boutiques (see p. 77).

24. Île St-Louis. Filled with bistros, gourmet shops, and purveyors of Paris's prized Berthillon ice-cream, this island looks just as it did in the 17th century (see p. 170).

23. Institut du Monde Arabe. This modern left-bank beauty hosts art from the Near and Middle East, film festivals, and a luxe rooftop terrace. The nearby **Mosquée de Paris** has soothing fountains and lush cloisters (see p. 90).

22. La Défense. Where Paris does business and where you wander among corporate towers or lounge beneath the giant arch. An alternate universe (see p. 131).

21. Panthéon. This big dome in the Latin Quarter contains the world's favorite physics experiment, **Foucault's Pendulum** (see p. 87).

20. Centre Pompidou. Plumbing on the outside, contemporary art on the inside, and a squiggly fountain. Not your average museum (see p. 139).

19. Parc André Citroën. Perfect for a sunny summer picnic. Vast expanses of grass that you can actually sit on–none too common in this city of well-manicured greenery. Splash in the fountain or take a hot-air balloon ride (see p. 114).

18. Catacombs. Because, like Jacques Cousteau, we like to dive low. And see tunnels and tunnels of subterranean skulls (see p. 113).

17. Les Puces de St-Ouen. The largest flea market in France. Clothing, antiques, housewares, car parts, and the kitchen sink (see p. 248).

16. Montmartre. A former artists' quarter and now perhaps a tourist trap. The holy whiteness of **Basilique Sacré-Coeur** and heavenly view are your reason for scaling the heights of Montmartre's well-café-ed hill (see p. 119).

15. Rue Mouffetard. One of the Latin Quarter's treasures–this lively street combines creative boutiques, friendly bars, a fresh produce market, and ample space for strolling (see p. 88).

14. Arc de Triomphe. Don't try to fight the traffic in the *Etoile*–go underground to arrive at the tomb of the unknown soldier, an "eternal" flame, and a great view from the roof. It's the big, yellow arch in the middle of all those speeding cars (see p. 100).

13. Musée Rodin. Parisians don't hesitate to call this the best museum in Paris. The sculptures are breathtaking, and the gardens exquisite (see p. 140).

12. The Champs-Elysées. No trip to Paris would be complete without a walk down this flashy avenue (see p. 100).

11. Père Lachaise Cemetery. Practically a city in its own right, immense Père Lachaise is riddled with famous dead folk, including Jim Morrison, Oscar Wilde, and Edith Piaf. Your mausoleum should look so good (see p. 123).

10. Opéra Garnier. The Phantom of the Opera allegedly swept through the basement of this decadent red-and-gilt opera hall. Venture into the boxes and imagine the 19th-century Parisians who went to see and be seen (see p. 105).

Let's Go Picks

Forget Notre Dame for a minute or two–these unsung heroes of Paris deserve a mention, and a visit.

Best stained glass: Ste-Chapelle's (p. 70) three large walls made of 1136 panes of stained glass will blow you away.

Best fake cliffs: It's funny because it's true. It's a bit of a trek out to the 19*ème's* **Parc au Buttes-Chaumont** (p. 123), but it's worth it for an overdose of Romanticism.

Best place to unleash your inner child: Parc de la Villette (p. 143). Go wild.

Best place to meditate: The quiet Japanese garden at **UNESCO** (p. 97).

Most secure shoes: On the top floor of **Le Bon Marché,** *haute chaussures* have glass cases and their own security guards (p. 246).

Best place to mourn your poverty: Avenue Montaigne in the 8*ème,* with the best clothes in Paris that you'll never afford.

Best pot: Take your pick among the funky ceramic vases in the stellar **Musée Picasso** (p. 142).

Best place to feel like (and maybe see) a movie star: Super-swanky **buddha-bar** (p. 184).

Best place to witness the spirit of '68 in action: socially conscious, artistically innovative theater at **La Cartoucherie (p. 225)**.

9. The Eiffel Tower. No matter how many desk-sized reproductions you may have seen, nothing can prepare you for the sheer height and grace of this iron lady. A romp on the **Champ de Mars,** the lawn stretching from her feet, is good for your sense of proportion (see p. 96).

8. Musée d'Orsay. An architectural beauty, this former train station now shelters the masterpieces of Impressionism and more (see p. 138).

7. Jardin du Luxembourg. Pitch *boules,* see the *grand guignol,* and sail a toy boat in the most popular of Paris's formal gardens (see p. 91).

6. The Marais. Never before have so many lovely bars, bistros, cafés, boutiques, and boys come together in one neighborhood (see p. 79).

5. Place des Vosges. Surrounded by an arcade of red-brick 17th-century townhouses, Paris's oldest public square is one of the city's loveliest spots to spend an afternoon reading in the sun. (see p. 85).

4. St-Germain-des-Prés. This charming, historic area boasts exciting galleries, upscale boutiques, and legendary cafés perfect for smoking, sipping, people-watching, and communing with the ghost of Sartre.

3. Musée du Louvre. Once a palace of kings, and now the home of *Mona Lisa, Victory of Samothrace, Venus de Milo,* and legions of appreciators. Come at night to see the glass pyramid aglow (see p. 135).

2. Notre Dame Cathedral. The famous home of the hunchback and so many gargoyles, so much history and such beautiful stained glass. The view of the illuminated buttresses at night truly deserves to be called "awe-inspiring" (see p. 67).

1. The Seine. At night by boat or for a daytime stroll with wine and baguette in tow; strolling across the bridges or reading on the *quais*; staring across the water in a fit of romantic agony or elation; glistening in the sun or misting in the rain–in any of its (or your) moods, this river is glorious. This is center of Paris's (and France's) history and mythology, and the city, or any visit to it, is unimaginable without it.

PARIS IN ONE WEEK (OR LESS)

THREE DAYS

DAY 1: CENTRAL SIGHTS

Begin on the **Île de la Cité** with **Notre Dame** (p. 67), then move inland over the **Pont Neuf** to the **Louvre** (p. 135). If you're up for it, the **Marais** (p. 79) is a good afternoon option—with some low-key sights and plenty of cafés for cooling your heels.

The *3ème's* **Musée Picasso** (p. 142) and **Musée Carnavalet** (p. 146) are both fascinating places to spend your time in the area.

DAY 2: THE TOWER, ORSAY, & RODIN

Step out of the métro and behold **The Eiffel Tower** (p. 96), a masterpiece or a monstrosity, depending on whom you ask—and then scale her if you dare. Bop along the Seine to the **Musée d'Orsay** (p. 138) and if you can stomach any more art, lounge in the delicious gardens of the **Musée Rodin** (p. 140) for the remains of the day. Sample some of Paris's Champs-Elysées **nightlife** (p. 213) when the sun goes down.

DAY 3: THE LATIN QUARTER

The Left Bank is full of romantic students and fancy-pants intellectuals. Visit the **Sorbonne** (p. 86) to catch them where they live, or stroll the **Mouff'** (rue Mouffetard; p. 88) to view the places they shop. The **Musée de Cluny** (p. 142) has classy medieval art. The **Jardin des Plantes** (p. 89) holds gorgeous vegetation. The **Mosquée de Paris** (p. 90) has a lovely facade and an even lovelier tea room; its sister, the **Institut du Monde Arabe du Paris** (p. 90) exhibits art from the Arab world. Enjoy the jazz at central **Au Duc des Lombards** (p. 219) on your last night out.

FIVE DAYS

Take **Three Days,** and add two more, because you just can't get enough.

DAY 4: MONTMARTRE

Though Montmartre is one of the most heavily touristed areas in Paris, the neighborhood still has loads of charm from when it was all vineyards and windmills (try **rue St-Vincent**). If Picasso, Modigliani, and Apollinaire thought it was up to snuff, you probably will, too. If you're here in October, don't miss the **Fête du Vendages,** when the vineyards are opened to all for dancing and, *bien sûr*, much drinking of wine.

DAY 5: OPÉRA & SHOPPING

Because no trip to Paris would be complete without a little self-indulgence on the **Champs-Elysées** (p. 100). Begin at the **Arc de Triomphe** (p. 100) and end at **place de la Concorde** (p. 103). Follow this up with some Empire pomp at the grand old Paris **Opéra Garnier** (p. 105), and perhaps purchase yourself some tickets for later that evening. And if you haven't spent enough money, there's always the *grands magasins* (department stores) next door: **Galeries Lafayette** and **Au Printemps** (p. 246).

Best place to pretend to be an artist: The *atelier* at **Musée Zadkine** (p. 148).

Best bridge by night: The ornate **Pont Alexandre III** (p. 98) connects the Esplanade des Invalides to the Grand and Petit Palais. Built for the 1900 Exposition Universelle, this bridge is a sight to behold when the Seine floodlights go on.

Best place to speak English and be proud of it: The **House of Live** (p. 213) in the *8ème*. You'll feel right at home.

Best place to learn about sex: The **Musée de l'Erotisme** (p. 156)–and it's open until 2am!

Most Exaggerated Breasts: Madonna's enormous bosom at the **Musée Grevin** (Wax Museum; p. 151).

Best place to show some Canadian pride: the friendly **Moosehead** bar and restaurant (p. 212). Oh Canada!

Best place for a makeover: the cosmetics wonderland **Sephora** on the Champs-Elysées (p. 243).

Best borrowed glamour: the couture gowns for rent at **La Femme Ecarlarté** (p. 242).

Best place to speak drunken French: the back of a taxi–after the driver knows where you're going (p. 28).

Best place for drunken "intellectual" conversation: the Latin Quarter classic **Le Bar Dix** (p. 212). Have some sangria with your Sartre, *cheri*.

Easiest, cheapest way to get drunk: "Un pression, s'il vous plaît." Rinse, repeat.

SEVEN DAYS

Five Days came and went. You're still in the City of Light. Whatcha doin'?

DAY 6: MUSEUMS IN THE 16ÈME & BOIS DE BOULOGNE

Begin at M: Iéna and visit the **Palais de Tokyo** (p. 116), the **Musée d'Art Moderne** (p. 153), the **Musée de Mode et Costume** (Museum of Fashion and Clothing; p. 155), and the **Musée National des Arts Asiatiques** (p. 154) in one fell swoop. Then rest your newly-cultured self at the **Bois de Boulogne** (p. 125).

DAY 7: VERSAILLES

Go out with a bang. Hop on a train early in the morning and head out on Paris's most Baroque daytrip to see the **Hall of Mirrors,** Marie-Antoinette's **Hameau,** and some intensely landscaped **gardens** packed with fountains and statuary (p. 279).

FESTIVALS & NATIONAL HOLIDAYS

For information on festivals, the Office de Tourisme (see p. 345) has a home page (www.paris-touristoffice.com) and a pricey info line (☎08 36 68 31 12). You can also get a listing of festivals before you leave home by writing the French Government Tourist Office. *Let's Go* lists its favorite **Festivals** below. This isn't all of them, just the ones that promise to keep you fat, happy, or drunk (or all three). Be sure to check listings in *Time Out* and *Pariscope* (€0.40 at any newsstand) a week or more ahead of time for updates and details on all events.

SPRING

Foire du Trône, late Mar.-late May (☎01 46 27 52 29; www.foiredutrone.com). M: Porte Dorée. On Reuilly Lawn, Bois de Vincennes, 12*ème*. A European fun fair replete with carnival rides (€1.50-3), *barbe à papa* (cotton candy), and a freak show. Open M, Tu, and Th 1:30-11pm; W and Su 11am-11pm; F 1:30pm-1am; Sa 11am-11pm.

Ateliers d'Artistes-Portes Ouverts, May-June. Call tourist office or check *Pariscope* for details. For selected days during the year, each *quartier*'s resident artists open their workshops to the public for show-and-tell, though the majority of expositions are in the 13*ème*.

SUMMER

Festivals du Parc Floral de Paris, May-Sept. (☎01 55 94 20 20; www.parcfloraldeparis.com). Three separate festivals held at the Kiosque Géand de la Vallée des Fleurs (Route de la Pyramide, Bois de Vincennes). *Théâtre pour Enfants* offers kids a different show every W at 2:30pm. The *Festival à Fleur de Jazz* offers jazz concerts Sa at 3pm. And the *Festival Classique au Vert* offers classical concerts Su at 4:30pm. All shows free with €1.50 park entrance. Schedules at the tourist office and in *Pariscope.*

Grandes Eaux Musicales de Versailles, early Apr.-early Oct. (☎01 30 83 78 88). Outdoor concerts of period music and fountain displays every Sa and Su at Parc du Château de Versailles, RER C7. A magical event that displays Versailles's gardens in all their excess and glory. Tickets €5.50, reduced €3. For reservations through **FNAC,** call ☎08 92 70 18 92.

Gay Pride, last Sa in June (☎08 36 68 11 31; www.gaypride.fr). See **Paris Pride,** p. 82. For additional information on dates and events, call the **Centre Gai et Lesbien** (☎01 43 57 21 47), **Le Duplex** bar (☎01 42 72 80 86), or **Les Mots à la Bouche** bookstore (☎01 42 78 88 30; www.motsbouche.com). Or check Marais bars and cafés for posters.

Course des Serveuses & Garçons de Café, mid-June (☎01 42 96 60 75). If you thought service was slow by necessity, let this race change your mind. Over 500 tuxedoed waiters and waitresses sprint through the streets on an 8km course carrying a full bottle and glass on a tray. Starts and finishes at Hôtel-de-Ville, 4*ème*. If you're in town, you don't want to miss this.

Festival Chopin, mid-June-mid-July (☎01 45 00 22 19; www.frederic-chopin.com). Route de la Reine Marguerite. From M: Porte Maillot, take bus #244 to Pré Catelan, stop #12. Concerts and recitals held at the Orangerie du Parc de Bagatelle in the Bois de Boulogne. Not all Chopin, but all piano, arranged each year around a different aspect of the master's *oeuvre.* Prices vary (usually €16-31).

Jazz à la Villette, late June to early July (☎01 40 03 75 75 or 01 44 84 44 84; www.la-villette.com). M: Porte de Pantin. At Parc de la Villette. A week-long celebration of jazz from big bands to new international talents, as well as seminars, films, and sculptural exhibits. Past performers have included Herbie Hancock, Ravi Coltrane, Taj Mahal, and B.B. King. Marching bands parade every day and an enormous picnic closes the festival. Some concerts are free. Others €16, reduced price €13, ages under 18 €7.

Fête des Tuileries, late June to late Aug. (☎01 46 27 52 29). M: Tuileries. A large fair held on the terrace of the Jardin des Tuileries. Huge ferris wheel with views of nighttime Paris offers proof positive that the carnival ethos is the same the world over. Open M-Th 11am-midnight, F-Sa 11am-1am. Free entrance; ferris wheel €5, under 10 €3.

Fête de la Musique, June 21 (☎01 40 03 94 70). See **Night Musique,** p. 220. Also called "Faîtes de la Musique" ("Make Music"), this summer solstice celebration gives everyone the chance to make as much racket as possible, as Paris's usual noise laws don't apply for the duration of the festival.

Feux de la St-Jean Baptiste (Fête Nationale du Québec), June 24 (☎01 45 08 55 61 or 01 45 08 55 25). Magnificent fireworks at 11pm in the Jardin de Tino Rossi at quai St-Bernard, 5*ème,* honoring the Feast of St. John the Baptist. Sacré-Coeur offers a spectacular bird's-eye view. The festival also includes an elaborate display at the Canal de l'Ourcq in the Parc de la Villette. In addition, Québec's National Holiday is celebrated by Paris's Québecois community with dancing, *drapeaux fleurs-de-lys,* and music at various spots throughout Paris, including: the Délégation Générale du Québec, 66, r. Pergolèse, 16*ème* (☎01 40 67 85 00); the Association Paris-Québec, 5, r. de la Boule Rouge, 9*ème*; and the Centre Culturel Québecois, 5, r. de Constantine, 7*ème* (M: Invalides).

Fête du Cinéma, late June (www.feteducinema.com). In 2004, this Parisian institution will celebrate its 20th anniversary, showing films in about 5000 cinemas throughout France. Purchase 1 ticket at regular movie price (€6.10-7.75) and receive a passport for unlimited showings (of participating films) for €1.50 each. Arrive early for popular favorites, and expect long lines. Full listings of movies and events for this 3-day festival can be found online, at theatres, or in métro advertisements. Don't miss this

Louvre

Shopping

Montmartre

opportunity to join the millions of movie-goers who relish the blockbusters, the indie flicks, the imports, and the ever-enduring classics that make Parisian cinema one of the most diverse—and enjoyable—in the world.

Paris, Quartier d'Eté, mid-July to mid-Aug. (☎01 44 94 98 00; www.quartierdete.com). This city-wide, multifaceted festival features dance, music from around the world, a giant parade, promenade concerts, and jazz. Locations vary, but many events are usually held in the Jardin des Tuileries, Jardin du Luxembourg, and Parc de la Villette. This festival is one of Paris's largest and includes both world-class (i.e. international ballet companies and top-ten rock bands) and local artists, musicians, and performers. Prices vary, but much is free. Pick up a brochure at the tourist office.

Bastille Day (Fête Nationale), July 14. France's independence day. Festivities begin the night before, with traditional street dances at the tip of Île St-Louis. The *Bals Pompiers* (Firemen's Balls) take place inside every Parisian fire station the night of the 13th, with DJs, bands, and cheap alcohol (entrance €5). These balls are the best of Paris's Bastille Day celebrations. The fire stations on r. Blanche, bd. du Port-Royal, r. des Vieux-Colombiers, and the Gay Ball near quai de la Tournelle in the 5*ème* are probably your best bets. For information on the *Bals,* call the **Sapeurs Pompiers** (☎01 47 54 68 18) or visit them at 1, pl. Jules Renard in the 17*ème.* There is dancing at pl. de la Bastille with a concert, but be careful as young kids sometimes throw fireworks into the crowd. July 14 begins with the army parading down the Champs-Elysées at 10:30am (be prepared to get in place by 8 or 9am) and ends with fireworks at 10:30-11pm. The fireworks can be seen from any bridge on the Seine or from the Champs de Mars. Be aware that for the parade and fireworks the métro stations along the Champs and at the Trocadéro are closed. Groups also gather in the 19*ème* and 20*ème* (especially in the Parc de Belleville) where the hilly topography allows a long-distance view to the Trocadéro. Unfortunately, the entire city also becomes a nightmarish combat zone with firecrackers underfoot; avoid the métro and deserted areas if possible. *Vive la France!*

Tour de France, enters Paris 4th Su in July (☎01 41 33 15 00; www.letour.fr). See **Tour de Force,** p. 229. The Tour de France, the world's premier long-distance bicycling event, ends in Paris and thousands turn out at the finish line to see who will win the *chemise d'or.* Expect huge crowds at pl. de la Concorde as well as along the av. des Champs-Elysées.

Le Festival de Cinema en Plein Air, late July-late Aug. (www.cinema.arbo.com). M: Porte de Pantin. At the Parc de la Villette. Families, couples, and large groups lounge on the grass and enjoy some of the greatest movies ever made. A limited number of lounge chairs are provided, so many people bring their own picnic blankets. Films start around 10pm, but arrive early to get a good spot on the grass.

FALL

Fête de l'Humanité, 2nd weekend of Sept. (☎01 49 22 72 72 or 01 49 22 73 86). At the Parc de la Courneuve. Take the métro to Porte de la Villette and then bus #177 or one of the special buses. The annual fair of the French Communist Party. Charles Mingus, Marcel Marceau, the Bolshoi Ballet, and radical theater troupes have appeared. 3-day pass €8.

Festival d'Automne, mid-Sept. to late Dec. (☎01 53 45 17 17; www.festival-automne.com). Notoriously highbrow and *avant* drama, ballet, cinema, and music arranged around a different theme each year. Many events held at the Théâtre du Châtelet, 1*er;* the Théâtre de la Ville, 4*ème;* and the Cité de la Musique, 19*ème.* Ticket prices vary according to venue.

Journées du Patrimoine, 3rd weekend of Sept. (☎01 40 15 37 37). The few days each year when certain ministries, monuments, and palaces are opened to the public. The Hôtel-de-Ville should be on your list, as well as the Palais de l'Elysée and the Matignon, the palace of the Prime Minister. Offerings vary from year to year; check with the tourist office 2-3 days in advance. Free.

Fête des Vendanges à Montmartre, first weekend in Oct. R. des Saules, 18*ème* (☎01 46 06 00 32). M: Lamarck-Caulaincourt. A celebration of the harvest from Montmartre's vineyards. Folk songs, parades, and the picking and stomping of grapes. Much wine is consumed.

WINTER

Christmas (Noël), Dec. 24-25. At midnight on Christmas eve, Notre Dame becomes what it only claims to be the rest of the year: the cathedral of the city of Paris. Midnight mass is celebrated with pomp and incense. Get there early to get a seat. Christmas Eve is more important than Christmas Day in France. Families gather to exchange gifts and eat Christmas food, including *bûche de Noël* (Christmas Yule Log), a rich chocolate cake. During the season leading up to Dec. 24, the city illuminates the major *boulevards,* including the Champs-Elysées, in holiday lights and decorations. A huge *crèche* (nativity scene) is displayed on pl. Hôtel-de-Ville. Restaurants offer Christmas specialties and special *menus.*

New Year's Eve & Day, Dec. 31-Jan. 1. Young punks and tons of tourists throng the Champs-Elysées to set off fireworks, while restaurants host pricey evenings of *foie gras* and champagne galore. On New Year's Day, there is a parade with floats and dolled-up dames from pl. Pigalle to pl. Jules-Joffrin.

NATIONAL HOLIDAYS

When a holiday falls on a Tuesday or Thursday, the French often take Monday or Friday off, a practice known as *faire le pont* (to make a bridge). Banks and public offices close at noon on the nearest working day before a public holiday.

DATE	FESTIVAL	
January 1	Le Jour de l'An	New Year's Day
April 1	Le Lundi de Pâques	Easter Monday
May 1	La Fête du Travail	Labor Day
May 8	L'Anniversaire de la Libération	Anniversary of the Liberation of Europe
May 9	L'Ascension	Ascension Day
May 20	Le Lundi de Pentecôte	Whit Monday
July 14	La Fête Nationale	Bastille Day
August 15	L'Assomption	Feast of the Assumption
November 1	La Toussaint	All Saints' Day
November 11	L'Armistice 1918	Armistice Day
December 25	Le Noël	Christmas

PIPER

INSIDE

Once in Paris

GETTING IN TO PARIS

TO & FROM THE AIRPORTS

ROISSY-CHARLES DE GAULLE (ROISSY-CDG)

Most transatlantic flights land at **Aéroport Roissy-CDG,** 23km northeast of Paris. For info, call the 24hr. English-speaking information center (☎01 48 62 22 80) or look it up on the web at **www.parisairports.com.** The two cheapest and fastest ways to get into the city from Roissy-CDG are by RER or bus.

RER. The RER train from Roissy-CDG to Paris leaves from the Roissy train station, which is in Terminal 2. To get there from Terminal 1, take the free shuttle bus called the Navette (every 10min.). From there, the RER B (one of the Parisian commuter rail lines) will transport you to central Paris. To transfer to the métro, get off at Gare du Nord, Châtelet-Les-Halles, or St-Michel, all of which are RER and métro stops. To go to Roissy-CDG from Paris, you will need a ticket covering five zones. Take the RER B to "Roissy," which is the end of the line. Get on the free shuttle bus if you need to get to Terminal 1 (30-35min.; RER every 15min. 5am-12:30am; €7.70, children €5.30).

BUS. Taking a shuttle bus the whole distance from the airport to Paris is somewhat simpler than the RER, and takes about the same time. The **Roissybus** (☎01 49 25 61 87) leaves from 9, r. Scribe near M: Opéra, and stops at terminals 1, 2, and T9. From de Gaulle, the bus leaves from terminals 1, 2, and T9 and stops at 9, r. Scribe. Tickets can be bought on the bus. (45min. To airport every 15min. 5:45-11pm; from airport every 15min. 6am-11pm; €8).

The **Daily Air France Buses** (recorded info available in English ☎08 92 35 08 20) run to two areas of the city. Tickets can be purchased on the bus itself. **Line 2** runs to and from the Arc de Triomphe (M: Charles de Gaulle-Etoile) at 1, av. Carnot (35min.; every 15min. 5:45am-11pm; one-way €10, round-trip €17, children one-way €5; 15% group discount), and to and from the pl. de la Porte de Maillot/Palais des Congrès (M: Porte de Maillot) on bd. Gouvion St-Cyr, opposite the Hôtel Méridien (same schedule and prices). **Line 4** runs to and from r. du Commandant Mouchette opposite the Méridien Hotel (M: Montparnasse-Bienvenüe; to airport every 30min. 7am-9:30pm; one-way €11.50, round-trip €19.55, children one-way €5.75; 15% group discount); and to and from Gare de Lyon, at 20bis, bd. Diderot (same schedule and prices). The shuttle stops are at or between terminals 2A-F and at terminal 1 on the departures level of the airport.

DOOR-TO-DOOR SERVICE. While the RER B and buses are the cheapest means of transportation, it can be a somewhat harrowing experience to navigate the train and métro stations if you are loaded down with heavy baggage. As taxis are exorbitantly expensive (€40-50 to the center of Paris), **shuttle vans** are the best option for door-to-door service. Several companies run shuttles to and from both airports. See the **Service Directory,** p. 346, for services and phone numbers.

For the motion-impaired, **Airhop** (☎01 41 29 01 29; reserve 48hr. in advance) and **GIHP** (☎01 41 83 15 15) offer transport to and from the airport.

ORLY

Aéroport d'Orly (☎01 49 75 15 15 for info in English; 6am-11:45pm), 18km south of the city, is used by charters and many continental flights.

RER. From Orly Sud gate G or gate I, platform 1, or Orly Ouest level G, gate F, take the **Orly-Rail** shuttle bus (every 15min. 6am-11pm; €5.15, children €3.55) to the **Pont de Rungis/Aéroport d'Orly** train stop, where you can board the **RER C2** for a number of destinations in Paris. (Call RATP ☎08 36 68 41 14 for info in English. 35min., every 15min. 6am-11pm, €5.15.) The **Jetbus** (every 15min. 6am-10pm, €4.58), provides a quick connection between Orly Sud, gate H, platform 2, or Orly Ouest level 0, gate C and M: Villejuif-Louis Aragon on line 7 of the métro.

BUS. Another option is the RATP **Orlybus** (☎08 36 68 77 14), which runs to and from métro and RER stop Denfert-Rochereau, 14*ème* to Orly's south terminal. (30min.; every 10-15min. 6am-11:30am from Orly to Denfert-Rochereau, 5:35am-11pm from Denfert-Rochereau to Orly; €5.60.) You can also board the Orlybus at Dareau-St-Jacques, Glacière-Tolbiac, and Porte de Gentilly. **Air France Buses** run between Orly and **Gare Montparnasse,** near the Hôtel Méridien, 6*ème* (M: Montparnasse-Bienvenüe), and the Invalides Air France agency, pl. des Invalides (30min.; every 15 min. 6am-11pm; one-way €7.50, round-trip €12.75). Air France shuttles stop at Orly Ouest and then Orly Sud, at the departures levels.

ORLYVAL. RATP also runs **Orlyval** (☎01 69 93 53 00), a combination of métro, RER, and VAL rail shuttle, and probably your fastest option. The VAL shuttle goes from Antony (a stop on the RER line B) to Orly Ouest and Sud. You can either get a ticket just for the VAL (€7), or combination VAL-RER tickets that include the VAL ticket and the RER ticket (€8.75 and up). Buy tickets at any RATP booth in the city, or from the Orlyval agencies at Orly Ouest, Orly Sud, and Antony. **To Orly:** Be careful when taking the RER B from Paris to Orly, because it splits into 2 lines right before the Antony stop. Get on the train that says "St-Rémy-Les-Chevreuse" or just look for the track that has a lit-up sign saying "Antony-Orly." (35min. from Châtelet; every 10min. M-Sa 6am-10:30pm, Su and holidays 7am-11pm.) **From Orly:** Trains arrive at

Orly Ouest 2min. after reaching Orly Sud. (32min. to Châtelet, every 10min. M-Sa 6am-10:30pm, Su 7am-11pm.)

DOOR-TO-DOOR SERVICE. See **Service Directory,** p. 346, for information **shuttle van service. Taxis** from Orly to town cost around €25. Allow about 30min., though traffic can make the trip much, much longer.

BEAUVAIS

Ryanair, Easyjet, and other intercontinental airlines often fly into and depart from **Aeroport Beauvais.** Buses take you from the airport to M: Porte Maillot. Tickets can be purchased at 1, blvd. Pershing, 17*ème* (☎01 58 05 08 45). Consult www.aeroportbeauvais.com for bus schedules and other information.

ESSENTIAL INFORMATION

EMERGENCY & CRISIS NUMBERS

Police:
☎17.

Ambulance:
☎15. Also has info on nearby medical care.

Fire (pompiers):
☎18.

English language crisis line:
☎01 46 21 46 46 (3-11pm).

Emergency (mobile phone):
☎112.

TRAIN STATIONS

GENERAL INFORMATION

Each of Paris's six train stations is a veritable community of its own, with resident street people and police, cafés, *tabacs*, banks, and shops. Locate the ticket counters *(guichets)*, the platforms *(quais)*, and the tracks *(voies)*, and you will be ready to roll. Each terminal has two divisions: the *banlieue* (suburb) and the *grandes lignes* (big important trains). Some cities can be accessed by both regular trains and **trains à grande vitesse (TGV;** high speed trains). TGVs are more expensive, much faster, and require reservations that cost a small fee. For **train information** or to make reservations, contact SNCF (☎08 92 35 35 35, €0.34 per min.; www.sncf.fr). A telephone with direct access to the stations is to the right of the Champs-Elysées tourist office (see **Service Directory,** p. 345). Yellow **ticket machines** *(billetteries)* at every train station sell tickets. You'll need to have a MasterCard, Visa, or American Express card and know your PIN (MC and V only at ticket booths). **SNCF** offers discounted round-trip tickets for travelers in France, which go under the name **Tarifs Découvertes**—you should rarely have to pay full price.

TIPS ON RIDING THE RAILS

Don't forget to **validate** *(composter)* your ticket at the orange machines on the platform before boarding the train. If you fail to do so, the *contrôleur* will severely reprimand you in fast-paced French, and could slap you with a heavy fine. Remember that Gare du Nord and Gare d'Austerlitz can become unsafe at night, when drugs and prostitution are more common. Also, it is not advisable to buy tickets in the stations except at official counters. The SNCF doesn't have any outfits in refrigerator boxes, no matter what you're told.

BUS STATIONS

International buses arrive in Paris at **Gare Routière Internationale du Paris-Gallieni** (M: Gallieni), just outside Paris at 28, av. du Général de Gaulle, Bagnolet 93170. **Eurolines** (☎01 49 72 57 80, €0.34 per min.; www.eurolines.fr) sells tickets to most destinations in France and neighboring countries.

GETTING AROUND PARIS

BY PUBLIC TRANSPORTATION

The **RATP (Régie Autonome des Transports Parisiens)** coordinates a network of subways, buses, and commuter trains in and around Paris. For info, contact **La Maison de la RATP,** right across the street from M: Gare de Lyon (190, r. de Bercy); the **Bureau de Tourisme RATP,** pl. de la Madeleine, *8ème* (☎01 40 06 71 45; M: Madeleine; open daily 8:30am-6pm) or the **RATP helpline** (☎ 08 92 68 41 14; in English, daily 6am-9pm, €0.34 per min). The RATP also has a helpful **English website** for visitors (http://www.ratp.fr/ParisVisite/Eng/index.htm) with extensive information on fares, routes, passes, and services for disabled visitors. For wheelchair or seeing-impaired métro services, see **Travelers With Disabilities,** p. 324.

FARES. Individual tickets for the RATP cost €1.30 each, or can be bought in a *carnet* of 10 for €9.60. Say, "Un ticket, s'il vous plaît" (AHN ti-KAY...), or "Un carnet..." (AHN CAR-nay...), to the person behind the window. Each métro ride takes one ticket, and the bus takes at least one, sometimes more, depending on connections you make and the time of day. For directions on using the tickets, see **Métro,** below.

PASSES. If you're staying in Paris for several days or weeks, a **Carte Orange** can be very economical. Bring an ID photo (taken by machines in most major stations for €3.81) to the ticket counter and ask for a weekly *carte orange hebdomadaire* (€13.75) or the equally swank monthly *carte orange mensuelle* (€46.05). These cards have specific start and end dates (the weekly pass runs M-Su, and the monthly starts at the beginning of the month). Prices quoted here are for passes in Zones 1 and 2 (the métro and RER in Paris and suburbs), and work on all métro, bus, and RER modes of transport. If you intend to travel to the suburbs, you'll need to buy RER passes for more zones (they go up to 5). If you're only in town for a day or two, a cheap option is the **Carte Mobilis** (€5 for a one-day pass in Zones 1 and 2; available in métro stations; ☎01 53 90 20 20), which provides unlimited métro, bus, and RER transportation within Paris. Always write the number of your *carte* on your coupon.

Paris Visite tickets are valid for unlimited travel on bus, métro, and RER, as well as discounts on sightseeing trips, bicycle rentals, and shopping at stores like Galeries Lafayette. These passes can be purchased at the airport or at métro and RER stations. The passes are available for one day (€8.35), two days (€12.95), three days (€18.25), or five days (€22.85), but the discounts you receive do not necessarily outweigh the extra cost.

MÉTRO

In general, the Métro system is easy to navigate (pick up a colorful map at any station or use the handy one in the center of this book), and trains run swiftly and frequently. Métro stations, in themselves a distinctive part of the Paris landscape, are marked with an "M" or with the "Métropolitain" lettering designed by Art Nouveau legend Hector Guimard. See **Discover,** p. 12, for our favorite métro stations.

GETTING AROUND. The first trains start running around 5:30am, and the last ones leave the end-of-the-line stations (the *portes de Paris*) for the center of the city at about 12:15am. For the exact departure times of the last trains, check the poster in the center of each station marked *Principes de Tarification* (fare guidelines), the white sign with the platform's number and direction, or the monitors above the platform. Transport maps are posted on platforms and near turnstiles; all have a *plan du quartier* (map of the neighborhood). Connections to other lines are indicated by orange *correspondance* signs, exits by blue *sortie* signs. Transfers are free if made within a station, but it is not always possible to reverse direction on the same line without exiting the station.

USING TICKETS. To pass through the turnstiles, insert the ticket into the small slot in the metal divider just to your right as you approach the turnstile. It disappears for a moment, then pops out about a foot farther along, and a little green or white circle lights up, reminding you to retrieve the ticket. If the turnstile makes a whining sound and a little red circle lights up, your ticket is not valid; take it back and try another. When you have the right light, push through the gate and retrieve your ticket. **Hold onto your ticket** until you exit the métro, and pass the point marked **Limite de Validité des Billets;** a uniformed RATP *contrôleur* (inspector) may request to see it on any train. If caught without one, you must pay a hefty fine. Also, any *correspondances* (transfers) to the RER require you to put your validated (and uncrumpled) ticket into a turnstile. Otherwise you might need to buy a new ticket in order to exit.

LATE AT NIGHT. Do not count on buying a métro ticket home late at night. Some ticket windows close as early as 10pm, and many close before the last train is due to arrive. **Always have one ticket more than you need,** although large stations have ticket machines that accept coins. Avoid the most **dangerous stations** (Barbès-Rochechouart, Pigalle, Anvers, Châtelet-Les-Halles, Gare du Nord, Gare de l'Est). Although most of these neighborhoods are safe above ground, the stations are frequented by criminals looking to prey on tourists. When in doubt, take a taxi.

RER

The RER (Réseau Express Régional) is the RATP's suburban train system, which passes through central Paris. Introduced in 1969, the RER travels much faster than the métro. There are five RER lines, marked A-E, with different branches designated by a number, such as the C5 line to Versailles-Rive Gauche. The newest line, the E, is called the Eole (Est-Ouest Liaison Express), and links Gare Magenta to Gare St-Lazare. The principal stops within the city, which link the RER to the métro system, are **Gare du Nord, Nation, Charles de Gaulle-Etoile, Gare de Lyon,** and **Châtelet-Les-Halles** on the Right Bank and **St-Michel** and **Denfert-Rochereau** on the Left Bank. The electric signboards next to each track list all the possible stops for trains running on that track. Be sure that the little square next to your destination is lit up. To get to the suburbs, you'll need to buy special tickets (one-way €4.25-7.60). You'll need your ticket to exit RER stations. Insert your ticket just as you did to enter, and pass through. Like the métro, the RER runs from about 5:15am to midnight.

BUS

Although slower and often costlier than the métro, bus rides can be cheap sightseeing tours and helpful introductions to the city's layout.

TICKETS. Bus tickets are the same as those used in the métro, and can be purchased either in métro stations or on the bus from the driver. Enter the bus through the front door and punch your ticket by pushing it into the machine by the driver's seat. If you have a *carte orange* or other transport pass flash it at the driver. Inspectors may ask to see your ticket, so hold onto it until you get off. Should you ever wish to leave the earthly paradise that is the RATP autobus, just press the red button and the *arrêt demandé* sign will magically light up.

ROUTES. The RATP's *Grand Plan de Paris* includes a map of the bus lines for day, evening, and nighttime (free at métro stations). The free bus map *Autobus Paris-Plan du Réseau* is available at tourist offices and at métro information booths. Buses with **three-digit numbers** travel to and from the suburbs, while buses with **two-digit numbers** travel exclusively within Paris.

NIGHT BUSES. Most buses run daily 6:30am-8:30pm, although those marked **Autobus du nuit** continue until 1am. Still others, ominously named **Noctambus,** run all night. Night buses (starting at €2.30; price dependent upon how far you go) start their runs to the portes of the city from the "Châtelet" stop and leave daily every hour on the half hour from 1:30 to 5:30am. Buses departing from the suburbs to

Châtelet run every hour on the hour 1-6am. Noctambuses I through M, R, and S have routes along the Left Bank en route to the southern suburbs. Those marked A through H, P, T, or V have routes on the Right Bank going north. Look for bus stops marked with a bug-eyed moon sign. Ask at a major métro station or at Gare de l'Est for more information on Noctambuses.

TOUR BUSES. Balabus (call the RATP ☎08 36 68 41 14 for info in English) stops at virtually every major sight in Paris (Bastille, St-Michel, Louvre, Musée d'Orsay, Concorde, Champs-Elysées, Charles de Gaulle-Etoile; whole loop takes 1¼hr.). The fare is the same as any standard bus (3 tickets, since it covers more than the 2-zone region), and the loop starts at the Grande Arche de La Défense or Gare de Lyon.

BY TAXI

For taxi companies, see **Service Directory,** p. 345. If you have a complaint, or have left personal belongings behind, contact the taxi company, or write to **Service des Taxis de la Préfecture de Police,** 36, r. des Morillons, 75015 (☎01 55 76 20 00; M: Convention). Ask for a receipt; if you want to file a complaint, record and include the driver's license number.

RATES. Tarif A, the basic rate, is in effect in Paris 7am-7pm (€0.60 per km). **Tarif B** is in effect Monday-Saturday 7pm-7am, all day Sunday, and during the day from the airports and immediate suburbs (€1 per km). **Tarif C,** the highest, is in effect from the airports 7pm-7am (€1.20 per km). In addition, there is a *prix en charge* (base fee) of €2, and a minimum charge of €5. You should wait for taxis at the nearest **taxi stand;** oftentimes, taxis will not stop if you attempt to flag them down on the street. Lines at taxi stands can get long in the late afternoon during the week and on weekend nights. Should you call a taxi rather than hail one at a taxi stand, the base fee will increase according to how far away you are and how long it takes the driver to get there. For all cabs, stationary time (at traffic lights and in traffic jams) costs €24.30 per hour. Additional charges (€0.90) are added for luggage over 5kg. Taxis take three passengers; there is a €2.45 charge for a fourth. For **tipping,** see p. 36. Some take credit cards (AmEx/MC/V).

BY CAR

Irwin Shaw wrote, "One driver out of every twelve in Paris has killed a man. On foot, the Parisian is as courteous as the citizen of any other city. But mounted, he is merciless." The infamous rotary at the Arc de Triomphe is a perfect example of this: police are stationed on the Champs-Elysées side to keep unwitting tourists from walking directly across eight lanes of traffic to the Arc. As a rule, the fastest and biggest car wins. **Priorité à droite** gives the right of way to the car approaching from the right, regardless of the size of the streets, and Parisian drivers make it an affair of honor to take this right even in the face of grave danger. Technically, drivers are not allowed to honk their horns within city limits unless they are about to hit a pedestrian, but this rule is often broken. The legal way to show discontent is to flash your headlights. If you don't have a map of Paris marked with one-way streets, the city will be impossible to navigate. Parking is expensive and hard to find.

FINDING YOUR WHEELS. Expect to pay at least US$180 per week, plus 20.6% tax, for a teensy car; you'll probably have to purchase **insurance** as well (see below). Automatic transmission is often unavailable on cheaper cars. Reserve well before leaving for France and pay in advance if at all possible; it's always significantly less expensive to reserve a car from home than from France. Always check if prices quoted include tax, unlimited mileage, and collision insurance; some credit card companies will cover this automatically. Ask about discounts and check the terms of insurance, particularly the size of the deductible. Non-Europeans should check with their national motoring organization (like AAA) for international coverage. Airlines sometimes offer special fly-and-drive packages, with up to a week of free or discounted rental. The minimum rental age in France is 21; those under 25 will often have to pay a surcharge. At most agencies, all that's needed to rent is a valid driver's license and proof that you've had it for a year; bring your passport just in case. For agencies, see the **Service Directory,** p. 342.

INTL. DRIVING PERMIT (IDP). Those with an EU-issued driving license are entitled to drive in France with no further ado. While others may be legally able to drive in France on the strength of their national licenses for a few months, it's safest to get an International Driving Permit (IDP), a translation of your regular license into 10 languages, including French. The IDP, valid for one year, must be issued in your own country before you depart. You must be 18 years old to receive the IDP. The IDP is in addition to, not a replacement for, your home license, and is not valid without it. An application for an IDP usually includes one or two photos, a current local license, and an additional form of ID, and requires a fee. To apply, contact the local branch of your home country's Automobile Association.

CAR INSURANCE. EU residents driving their own cars do not need extra insurance coverage in France. For those renting, paying with a gold credit card usually covers standard insurance. If your home car insurance covers you for liability, make sure you get a **green card,** or **International Insurance Certificate** to prove it. If you have an accident abroad, it will show up on your domestic records if you report it to your insurance company. Also, be prepared to pay US$8-10 per day for rental car insurance. Leasing should include insurance and the green card in the price. Some travel agents offer the card; it may also be available at border crossings.

BY TWO-WHEELER

BICYCLES. During the 1995 métro strike, bike stores came to the rescue of carless Parisians, and the community of cyclists dreaming of an autoless Paris became more vocal. Nonetheless, if you have never ridden a bike in heavy traffic, don't use central Paris as a testing ground. The Bois de Boulogne and the Bois de Vincennes, on the city's periphery, should be more your speed. Bicycles can be transported on all RER lines anytime except rush hour (M-F 6:30-9am and 4:30-7pm) and on métro line 1 Sunday before 4:30pm. Ask for a helmet and inquire about insurance. For bike rental listings, see the **Service Directory,** p. 341.

Métro

Rue Mouffetard

Rue du Temple

SCOOTERS. *"Les Scooters"* (motorized two-wheelers, also called *motos* or *mobylettes*) are ubiquitous in Paris. Everyone seems to own one, and just as many seem to have been injured on one. If you want to sacrifice safety for the speed and style that only a scooter can provide, you can rent one; no special license is required, though a helmet most definitely is. See **Service Directory,** p. 341.

CONSULAR SERVICES IN PARIS

Call before visiting any of these embassies, since different services have different hours. Visa services tend to be available only in the morning. In a dire situation, your country's embassy or consulate should be able to provide legal advice, and may be able to advance you some money in a serious emergency. Dual citizens of France cannot call on the consular services of their second nationality for assistance.

Australia, Australian Embassy and Consulate, 4, r. Jean Rey, 15*ème* (☎01 40 59 33 00; after-hours emergency 01 40 59 33 01; fax 01 40 50 33 10; www.austgov.fr). M: Bir-Hakeim. Open M-F 9:15am-noon and 2-4:30pm.

Canada, Canadian Embassy and Consulate, 35, av. Montaigne, 8*ème* (☎01 44 43 29 02; www.amb-canada.fr). M: Franklin Roosevelt. Open 9am–noon and 2-5pm.

Ireland, Embassy of Ireland, 12, ave. Foch, 16*ème* (☎01 44 17 67 00; emergency 01 44 17 67 67; fax 01 44 17 67 60; www.irlande-tourisme.fr). Open M-F 9:30am-1pm and 2:30-5:30pm.

New Zealand, New Zealand Embassy and Consulate, 7ter, r. Leonardo de Vinci, 16*ème* (☎01 45 01 43 43; fax 45 01 43 44; www.nzembassy.com/france). Open July-Aug. M-Th 9am-1pm and 2-5:30pm, F 9am-2pm; Sept.-June M-Th 9am-1pm and 2-5:30pm, F 9am-1pm and 2-4pm.

South Africa, South African Embassy, 59, quai d'Orsay, 7*ème*; mailing address 59, quai d'Orsay, 75343 Paris Cedex 07 (☎01 53 59 23 23; emergency 86 09 67 06 93; www.afriquesud.net). Open M-F 8:30am-5:45pm; visa services 9am-noon.

United Kingdom, British Embassy, Consulate Section, 18bis, r. d'Anjou, 8*ème* (☎01 44 51 31 00 (including emergency); fax 44 51 31 27; www.amb-grandebretagne.fr). Open M and W-F 9:30am-12:30pm and 2:30-5pm, Tu 9:30am-4:30pm.

United States, Consulate General, 2, r. St-Florentin, 1*er*. Mailing address 2, r. St-Florentin, 75382 Paris Cedex 08 (☎01 43 12 22 22; fax 01 42 61 61 40; www.amb-usa.fr). M: Concorde. Open M-F 9am-12:30pm and 1-6pm, notarial services Tu-F 9am-noon. Don't wait in the long line; go to the right and tell the guard that you are there for American services.

KEEPING IN TOUCH

BY MAIL

SENDING MAIL FROM PARIS

Post offices are marked on most Paris maps by their abstract flying-letter insignia; on the streets, look for the yellow and blue PTT signs. In general, post offices in Paris are open Monday to Friday 8am-7pm (they stop changing money at 6pm) and on Saturday 8am-noon, though the **Poste du Louvre,** 52, r. du Louvre, 1*er* (☎01 40 28 20 40; M: Louvre), is open 24hr. even on holidays, and takes MasterCard and Visa. Buy stamps at *tabacs* or from vending machines inside post offices.

Air mail between Paris and North America takes five to ten days and is fairly dependable. To airmail a 20g (about 1 oz.) letter or postcard from France to the US or Canada costs €0.90; a 200g package costs €5.20. It is vital to distinguish your airmail from surface mail by labeling it clearly **par avion.** If you plan on sending multiple letters or postcards to international destinations, the best deal by far is to purchase a packet of **enveloppes internationales;** these pre-posted, priority mail envelopes reach most destinations in a few days. To airmail a package to a destination outside France, you must complete one of the small green customs slips provided at the post office.

In France there are two grades of express mail: letters sent *prioritaire* cost the same as regular airmail letters and arrive within four or five days to North America, although anything heavier than a letter will cost more than regular airmail. **Chronopost** arrive in one to three days at a soaring cost of €35.84 for a letter. Chronopost is available until 6pm in most post offices, until 8pm at major branches; call ☎ 08 25 80 18 01. You must go to a window for *prioritaire* or chronopost. The idiot-proof machines in the lobbies of most post offices hold your hand through the process, weighing your package/letter and printing out a sticker with the right amount of postage. The **aerogramme,** a sheet of fold-up, pre-paid airmail paper, requires no envelope and costs more (€0.76 to the US or Canada). Registered mail is called *avec recommandation;* the cost starts at €4.33 and depends upon where the mail is going. To be notified of a registered letter's receipt, ask for an *avis de récéption* and pay an additional €1.22.

RECEIVING MAIL IN PARIS

There are several ways to arrange pickup of letters sent to you while you are abroad. If you do not have a mailing address in Paris, you can receive mail through the **Poste Restante** system, handled by the 24hr. Louvre post office (see above). Address *Poste Restante* letters to: LAST NAME, First Name; Poste Restante: Recette Principale; 750xx (where xx is the arrondissement you want to send to, e.g. 75006 for the 6*ème*, 75016 for the 16*ème*) PARIS; FRANCE; mark the envelope "hold." When picking up your mail, bring a form of photo ID, preferably a passport. There is a €0.46 charge per letter to pick up. If the clerks insist that there is nothing for you, have them check under your first name as well. Note that post offices will not accept courier service deliveries (e.g., Federal Express) for Poste Restante, nor will they accept anything that requires a signature for delivery. Also, there is a 15-day hold limit.

American Express: AmEx's travel offices throughout the world offer a free Client Letter Service (mail held up to 30 days and forwarding upon request) for cardholders who contact them in advance. Address the letter to the recipient at the Paris American Express Office (11, r. Scribe, 75009 Paris). Some offices will offer these services to non-cardholders (especially AmEx Travelers Cheque holders), but call ahead.

BY PHONE

CALLING WITHIN FRANCE

Almost all French pay phones accept only microchip phonecards called **Télécartes;** you'll be hard-pressed to find a coin-operated payphone (though some bars and restaurants do have them, around €0.40 per call). Cards come in two denominations: €7.50 for 50 *unités*, and €15 for 120 *unités*. Value of the units varies; land line calls are 1 unit per minute. **FranceTelecom** cards charge you four units for every call, even if no one answers. *Télécartes* are available at post offices, métro stations, and *tabacs*. Don't buy cards from street vendors, who sometimes recycle used cards. Emergency and collect calls require neither coins nor *Télécartes*.

Phone numbers in Paris and the Île-de-France require **01** in front, in the northwest of France **02,** in the northeast **03,** in the southeast and Corsica **04,** and in the southwest **05.** Emergency calls and numbers beginning with **0 800** are free. Most numbers beginning with **08** are expensive.

To call abroad from France, dial **00** followed by the appropriate **country code,** the local area/city code (dropping any leading zeros), then the phone number. France's country code is **33;** the United States and Canada's is **1;** Australia's is **61;** Ireland's is **353;** New Zealand's is **64;** South Africa's is **27;** and the UK's is **44.**

the hidden deal

Rent-A-Phone

Whether you're in Paris for one week or one year, having a cell phone can make life a lot easier. When an emergency strikes you'll call for help, and when you meet that hottie at the bar, he or she will be able to contact you for another rendez-vous. Purchasing a cell phone for a short-term stay, however, may not bode well with your wallet. The solution? **Call'Phone,** a free cell phone rental service that provides a sleek telephone, a battery, a leather carrying case, and a charger in exchange for 5 minutes of daily cell phone use. Incoming calls are free, and outgoing calls within France are €0.70 a minute. Phones can be ordered before you arrive in France via the company's website, **www.callphone.com,** and picked up at any Parisian airport, or delivered (free of charge) to your hotel. Call'Phone will send itemized call-by-call billing statements to both postal and e-mail addresses and deduct the fees from your credit card. Considering that overpriced calling cards add up fast, renting a phone for a short-term stay is both economical and fashionable—who wants to be the only person in Paris without a mobile?

See **Service Directory** (p. 342) for more information.

Directory information: ☎12. English rarely spoken.

International information: 00 33 12 + country code (Australia 61; Ireland 353; New Zealand 64; UK 44; US and Canada 1).

International Operator: ☎00 33 11.

PHONE CARDS. Let's Go has recently partnered with ekit.com to provide a calling card that offers a number of services, including email and voice messaging. Before purchasing any calling card, always be sure to compare rates with other cards, and to make sure it serves your needs (a local phonecard is generally better for local calls, for instance). For more information, visit www.letsgo.ekit.com.

CELL PHONES. Cell phones are an increasingly popular option for travelers calling within Europe. Virtually all areas of Europe receive excellent coverage, and the widespread use of the **Global System for Mobiles (GSM)** allows one phone to function in multiple countries. A small chip called a **Subscriber Identity Module Card** (**SIM** or **"smart card"**) can be purchased from carriers in each European country to provide a local number for any GSM phone. However, some companies lock their phones to prevent switches to competitor carriers, so inquire about using the phone in other countries before buying it. Phones in Europe generally cost around US$100, and instead of requiring a service contract, they often run on prepaid minutes that are easily purchased at a variety of locations. Frequently, incoming calls are free. For more info about GSM phones, try: www.vodafone.com, www.orange.co.uk, www.roadpost.com, www.cellularabroad.com, www.t-mobile.com, or www.planetomni.com. Another option is to rent a ceullar phone; see the box **Rent-A-Phone,** at left, for information.

GETTING MONEY FROM HOME

If you run out of money while traveling, the easiest and cheapest solution is to have someone back home make a deposit to your credit card or cash (ATM) card. Failing that, consider one of the following options:

WIRING MONEY. Travelers from the US, Canada, and the UK can wire money abroad through Western Union's international money transfer services. **Western Union** has many locations worldwide, including many French post offices. To find one, visit www.westernunion.com, or call in the US ☎800-325-6000, in Canada ☎800-

235-0000, in the UK ☎0800 83 38 33, in Australia ☎800 501 500, in New Zealand ☎800 27 0000, in South Africa ☎0860 10003, and in France 08 25 00 98 98. The rates for sending cash are generally US$10-11 cheaper than with a credit card, and the money is usually available at the place you're sending it to within an hour.

US STATE DEPARTMENT (US CITIZENS ONLY). In dire emergencies only, the US State Department will forward money within hours to the nearest consular office, which will then disburse it according to instructions for a US$15 fee. Contact the Overseas Citizens Services division of the US State Department (☎202-647-5225; nights, Su, and holidays 647-4000; http://travel.state.gov).

SAFETY & SECURITY

EXPLORING. To avoid unwanted attention, try to blend in as much as possible. Avoid clothing and accessories that will make you look like a stereotypical "tourist." Familiarize yourself with your surroundings before setting out, and carry yourself with confidence. Check maps in shops and restaurants rather than on the street. If you are traveling alone, be sure someone at home knows your itinerary, and never admit that you're by yourself. When walking at night, stick to busy, well-lit streets and avoid dark alleyways. If you feel uncomfortable, leave as quickly and directly as you can, but don't allow fear of the unknown to turn you into a hermit.

CON ARTISTS & PICKPOCKETS. In Paris, as in other large cities, **con artists** often work in groups, and children are among the most effective. Beware of certain classics: sob stories that require money, rolls of bills "found" on the street, mustard spilled (or saliva spit) onto your shoulder to distract you while they snatch your bag. **Never let your passport and your bags out of your sight.** Beware of **pickpockets** in city crowds, especially on public transportation. Also, be alert in public telephone booths: If you must say your calling card number, do so very quietly; if you punch it in, make sure no one can look over your shoulder.

DRUGS & ALCOHOL. A meek "I didn't know it was illegal" will not suffice. Possession of **drugs** in France can end your vacation abruptly; convicted offenders can expect a jail sentence and fines. Never bring any illegal drugs across a border. Trains from Amsterdam, especially, are often met by guard dogs ready to sniff out drugs. It is vital that **prescription drugs,** particularly insulin, syringes, or narcotics, be accompanied by the prescriptions themselves and a statement from a doctor and left in original, labeled containers. In France, police may stop and search anyone on the street—no reason is required. Also, a positive result of the gentlemanly drinking age (16) is that public drunkenness is virtually unseen, even in younger crowds.

MEDICAL CARE. France's socialized medical system provides care that is widely available and of high quality, but it may seem unfamiliar and intimidating to a foreigner, especially one who does not speak French fluently (though many medical professionals speak English). A visit to a doctor will cost around €20, though your insurance may reimburse you. **Pharmacies** are everywhere; look for the green cross. Almost every drug (including allergy medications and fever reducers) requires a prescription. The shelves of pharmacies display only skin care products and other ephemera; for non-prescription medications you'll have to ask the pharmacist. See **Service Directory** for medical services (p. 342) and pharmacies (p. 345).

PROTECTING YOUR VALUABLES. There are a few steps you can take to minimize the financial risk associated with traveling. First, bring as little with you as possible. Second, buy a few combination padlocks to secure your belongings either in your pack or in a hostel or train station locker. Third, carry as little cash as possible. Keep your traveler's checks and ATM/credit cards in a money belt—not a "fanny pack"—along with your passport and ID cards. Fourth, keep a small cash reserve separate from your primary stash—around US$50 sewn into or stored in the depths of your pack, along with your traveler's check numbers and important photocopies.

SELF-DEFENSE. There is no sure-fire way to avoid all the threatening situations you might encounter while traveling, but a good self-defense course will give you concrete ways to react to unwanted advances. **Impact, Prepare, and Model Mugging** can refer you to local self-defense courses in the US (☎800-345-5425). Visit the website at www.impactsafety.org for a list of nearby chapters. Workshops (2-3hr.) start at US$50; full courses (20hr.) run US$350-500.

TERRORISM. Terrorism has not been as serious a problem in France as in other European countries. In the post-September 11 world, however, it is of increased concern in France as in most of the world. Due to its troubled colonialist history, France has always been an enemy of unstable Algeria. France contains cells of Al Qaeda and other terrorist groups; several September 11 hijackers lived in neighboring Germany. Several cities have recently experienced unrest, though because of immigrant conditions rather than terrorism. Several synagogues have been firebombed, though by domestic anti-Semites rather than Al Qaeda. The French government has heightened security at public places, with various side effects: for example, certain train stations no longer permit luggage storage.

If you are concerned about terrorism, avoid areas with lots of people—popular restaurants and shops, public transportation, famous sights. That said, it will be very hard to enjoy your vacation without being around other people. See the box on **travel advisories** below for more info.

PARIS ETIQUETTE, ABRIDGED

In Paris they simply stared when I spoke to them in French; I never did succeed in making those idiots understand their language.

-Mark Twain

ANTI-AMERICANISM. The notoriously rocky relationship between the French and Americans became news again during the spring of 2003, when Prime Minister Chirac and most of the French people vehemently opposed President Bush and the war with Iraq. The hyper-patriotic American boycott of French exports like cheese and wine did nothing to warm the hearts of the French towards the Yanks, and potential tourists may feel anxious about venturing into this apparently unfriendly environment. For the most part, though, Parisians are not overtly hostile towards individuals Americans. You may find yourself engaged, willingly or unwillingly, in passionate political debates in which Americans leaders and policies will be summarily dismissed. Stay calm, and enjoy these arguments (lectures?) for what they are: a rather delightful, if somewhat exasperating, part of the Parisian experience.

ARGUING. Avoid doing this with Parisians. Do not assume you can talk your way into something. When the concierge sitting in front of a rack of keys tells you there are no vacancies, or when the maître d' insists that he cannot seat you in a restaurant full of empty tables, move on.

AUGUST. Be aware that Parisians clear out of their beloved city for nearly the entire month of August while they take their *grands vacances*: many establishments, including hotels, shut down, and Anglophones flood the city's sights.

BLENDING IN. Trying to blend in as much as possible is always a good idea when traveling, and in Paris it will take you far. The French tend to dress more conservatively than people in other countries; they also live up to their reputation for being particularly stylish, so don't worry about being overdressed. Leave the shorts, t-shirts, and sneakers at home, and bring along (or purchase in Paris!) some well-fitting black pants, cute shoes, and sunglasses, and you'll be well on your way to looking like a Parisian.

CHURCHES. Cutoff, tight, short, bare-shouldered, sloppy, or dirty are words that should never be used in describing what you are wearing into a church. Do not walk into the middle of a mass or other service unless you plan to give an impromptu homily. Do not take flash photographs, and do not walk directly in front of the altar.

DRIVING. The French have a not-undeserved reputation for aggressive, dangerous driving. Still, while they will zoom past slow cars or space cadets, they will in all likelihood not hit you. Parisians jaywalk for sport.

ETAGES (FLOORS). In France, they call the ground floor the *rez-de-chaussée* and start numbering with the first floor above the ground floor *(premier étage)*. The button labeled "R" and not "1" is typically the ground floor. This system can cause unpleasant surprises, as when your "fourth-floor hotel room" is in reality above the tree line.

GIFTS. If you are invited to someone's house for lunch or dinner, it is expected that you won't arrive at their door empty-handed. Wine is a common and perfectly adequate thank-you gift, as is food or flowers. A word to the wise: unless you will be attending to a wake, don't bring a bouquet of chrysanthemums—mums are they're flowers of mourning.

GREETINGS & SALUTATIONS. Although the Parisian concept of customer service leaves much to be desired, there is no end to the pleasantries that one encounters when entering or exiting a business, hotel, or restaurant. Always, always say *"Bonjour, Madame/Monsieur"* when entering an establishment, and *"Au revoir"* when leaving. If you bump into someone on the street or while awaiting/pushing your way into a subway, bus, train, or the like, always say *"Pardon"* to excuse yourself. The proper way to answer the telephone is *"âllo,"* but if you use this on the street as a personal greeting, you'll immediately blow your cover as a tourist.

ESSENTIAL INFORMATION

TRAVEL ADVISORIES

The following offices provide travel information by telephone, by fax, or via the web:

Australian Department of Foreign Affairs and Trade: ☎1300 55 5135; faxback service 02 6261 1299; www.dfat.gov.au.

Canadian Department of Foreign Affairs & International Trade (DFAIT): In Canada and the US call ☎800-267-6788, elsewhere call 613-944-6788; www.dfait-maeci.gc.ca. Call for their free booklet, *Bon Voyage...But.*

New Zealand Ministry of Foreign Affairs: ☎04 494 8500; fax 494 8506; www.mft.govt.nz/trav.html.

United Kingdom Foreign and Commonwealth Office: ☎020 7008 0232; fax 7008 0155; www.fco.gov.uk.

US Department of State: ☎202-647-5225, faxback service 647-3000; http://travel.state.gov. For *A Safe Trip Abroad,* call ☎512-1800.

HOURS. Most restaurants open at noon for lunch and then close for the afternoon before reopening for dinner, while some bistros and most cafés will remain open throughout the afternoon. Small businesses, as well as banks and the post office close for "lunch," which, clocking in at a hefty three hours, must include a sizable nap (typically noon-3pm).

LANGUAGE. Even if your French is near-perfect, waiters and salespeople who detect the slightest accent will often immediately respond in English. This can be frustrating—especially if you came to Paris to practice your French, and also if the Parisian in question speaks poor English. If your language skills are good, continue to speak in French. More often than not, they will both respect and appreciate your fortitude, and speak to you, in turn, in French.

POCKET CHANGE. Cashiers and tellers will constantly ask you *"Avez-vous de la monnaie?"* ("Do you have the change?") as they would rather not break your €20 note for a pack of gum. If you don't have it, smile ever-so-sweetly and say *"Non, désolée."* A nasty look is the worst you could get in return.

POLITESSE. Parisians are polite, especially to older people. In Paris, the difference between getting good and bad service is the difference between a little meek *politesse* and careless rudeness. Tone and facial expressions can work wonders. Maintain composure at all times and act like you mean business; speak softly and politely (*do* employ the standard *"monsieur/madame"* and *"s'il vous plaît"*) to Parisians in official positions, especially if they are older than you.

PUBLIC RESTROOMS. The streetside public restrooms *(pissoirs)* in Paris are worth the €0.30 they require. For this paltry sum, you are guaranteed a clean restroom, as these magic machines are self-cleaning after each use. Toilets in train stations, major métro stops, and public gardens are tended to by *gardiens* and generally cost €0.40. However, cleanliness should not be expected in your average café, as they tend to have squat toilets. Most cafés reserve restrooms for their clients only.

SERVICE. There is no assumption in Paris that "the customer is always right," and complaining to managers about poor service is rarely worth your while. Your best bet is to take your business elsewhere. When engaged in any official process (e.g., opening a bank account, purchasing insurance, etc.), don't fret if you get shuffled from one desk to another or from one phone number to the next. Hold your ground, patiently explain your situation as many times as necessary, and you will prevail. The pace of life in Paris is noticeably slower than in the United States, and this applies to service; that waiter smoking at the bar *will* serve you eventually, so just sit back, relax, and get used to those 3 hour lunches. And those smoking waiters.

SMOKING. A very large number of Parisians smoke cigarettes, and do not appreciate anti-tobacco evangelism. Although some restrictions have been placed on smoking in public areas (such as métro platforms) and eating establishments are technically required to have a clearly marked non-smoking section, these laws are not strictly enforced. Tourists who smoke will find this atmosphere liberating; those who do not may find themselves constantly coughing in smoky restaurants, bars, and cafés—or might find themselves taking up the habit, seduced by the romance of it all (damn you, health hazards!). Cigarettes can be purchased only in *tabacs*.

SNOBBERY. Paris is the hottest tourist destination in Europe. Naturally, Parisians become progressively more and more annoyed as the tourists flood in during the summer months, with July and August being the height of the tourist season. Most Parisians are not blatantly rude to tourists, but don't take it personally if you catch your waiter snickering about you in French to his co-workers.

SUNDAY. Paris appears to shut down entirely on Sundays (excepting the Marais). Minimarkets, supermarkets, shops, and restaurants will generally be closed, though some services may be available in the morning. Do as *Parisiens* do, and head for open-air markets to pack a picnic. Many establishments and most museums are closed Mondays, and other hours vary: calling ahead is always a good idea.

TIPPING. Service is almost always included in meal prices in restaurants and cafés, and in drink prices at bars; look for the phrase *service compris* on the menu or just ask. If service is not included, tip 15-20%. Even when service is included, it is polite to leave a *pourboire* at a café, bistro, restaurant, or bar—€0.50 to 5% (a larger tip may be considered insulting). Do tip your hairdresser well; do not tip taxis more than 15% of the metered charge.

MEDIA

TELEVISION & RADIO

For most of the post-war period, French **television** was in the hands of a state-run monopoly, but in the mid-80s, several public stations were privatized, including **TF1**, now the most popular station in France. The public channel **ARTE** appeals to the stubbornly intellectual. Cable TV is also available; the pay channel **Canal Plus** shows recent films and live sporting events. TV guides are the most popular publications in France, with **Télé 7 jours** leading the pack. Second banana is **Télérama,** which provides commentary not only on TV but also on culture in general. French **radio** went commercial in 1984, although the success of large conglomerates means few stations remain independent. National stations include **Fun Radio** for teens; **RTL2,** a pop rock station; **Skyrock,** a noisy and provocative rock station; and **Nostalgie,** an adult-oriented station with quiz shows and easy-listening music. Public stations include **France-Inter,** a quality general interest station, and **France Info,** an all-news station.

NEWSPAPERS & OTHER PUBLICATIONS

NEWSPAPERS. The French are bombarded with many different views from many newspapers (and the various political factions that they represent). On the left are **Libération** (€1.20), a socialist newspaper that offers comprehensive news coverage of world events, and **L'Humanite** (€1.20), produced by the communist party. More to the middle (though sometimes with a socialist streak) is the widely read **Le Monde** (€1.20) which offers especially thorough political coverage. To the right are **Le Figaro** (€1) and **La Tribune,** the latter of which is like France's version of the *Wall Street Journal,* providing international financial coverage. For something lighter, try **Le Canard Enchaine** (€1.20)—a weekly satirical newspaper published on Wednesdays (just make sure you read *Figaro* first to get all the jokes).

MAGAZINES. Magazines offer more in-depth coverage of news and culture. **Le Nouvel Observateur** (€3) proffers an inquisitive take on French culture and society; the cultural magazine **Nova** (€7) has a special summer guide to Parisian cultural events; **Express** (€2.30) is a weekly publication similar to *Time* magazine, with coverage of national and international news; **Marianne** (€2.50) resembles a French *Vanity Fair,* filled with gossip and world news; **Tetu** (€5) has the latest in queer politics, fashion and events; and **Technik Art** (€6) is a monthly communique for the Parisian dandy. For the best selection of English language magazines, as well as copies of the Sunday edition of the *New York Times* (after noon on Mondays) try **W.H. Smith** (see **Shopping,** p. 236). Of course, if you are after cultural listings and reviews, you need only venture as far as the nearest *tabac,* as all carry the vital publications.

GOINGS-ON. Pariscope (€0.40) and **Officiel des Spectacles** (€0.35), both published Wednesdays, have the most comprehensive listings of movies, plays, exhibits, festivals, clubs, and bars. *Pariscope* may well be worth the extra €0.05; it has an English-language section called **Time Out Paris** and an easy-to-use (free) online counterpart at **www.pariscope.fr.** Also free is the tourist office monthly **Where: Paris,** which highlights exhibits, concerts, walking tours, and events, and the Mairie de Paris's monthly **Paris le Journal,** which has articles about what's going on around the city. For other listings, check **Figaroscope,** a Wednesday supplement to **Le Figaro,** which lists happenings about Paris, **Free Voice,** a monthly English-language newspaper published by the American Church, and the bi-weekly **France-USA Contacts (FUSAC)** both of which provide job and housing listings, as well as general information for English speakers and are available for free from English-speaking bookstores, restaurants, and travel agencies throughout Paris (see **Alternatives to Tourism,** p. 336).

INSIDE

Life & Times

HISTORY

ANCIENT PARIS

ROMAN BEGINNINGS. The area that would become Paris was first settled by the Gallic Parisii clan around 300 BC, who lived peacefully on the Île de la Cité until conquest by **Julius Caesar's** troops in 52 BC initiated 300 years of Roman rule. The Romans, who named the new colony **Lutetia Parisiorum** (Latin for "the Midwater-Dwelling of the Parisii"), expanded the city, building new roads (including r. St-Jacques), public baths (now the **Musée de Cluny,** p. 142), and gladiatorial arenas (**Arènes de Lutèce,** p. 90). By AD 360, the Romans had shortened the name of the now-resplendent outpost to "Paris."

CHRISTIANITY & CHARLEMAGNE. Despite Roman prosperity, the advance of **Christianity** and barbarians, as well as the declining strength of Rome's trade and military power, threatened the Roman-pagan rule. By the time Rome finally fell in AD 476, Gaul had suffered assaults by Germanic tribes such as the Vandals, Visigoths, and Franks, as well as Attila and his marauding Huns, who tried to take the city in 450 and were supposedly stopped by the prayers of **St. Genevieve,** who became the patron saint of Paris. It was the **Franks** who eventually dominated Gaul and bequeathed it their name. In 476, **King Clovis** of the Franks defeated the Gallo-Romans and took control of Paris, founding France's first royal house, naming Paris the capital, and converting the entire city to Christianity. The

c. 300 BC
The Parisii settle on Île de la Cité

52 BC
Conquest by Julius Caesar and the beginning of Roman Rule

AD 260
St-Denis is beheaded by the Romans for attempting to Christianize Paris

476
Fall of the Roman Empire; King Clovis comes to power

800
Charlemagne is named Holy Roman Emperor

987
Hugh Capet elected to the throne

1163
Construction of Notre Dame Cathedral begins

1170
Chanson de Roland (Song of Roland); Marie de France, *Lais*

1215
University of Paris is founded

1348-49
The Black Death ravages Paris

1337-1453
The Hundred Years' War: England vs. France

1430
Joan of Arc is burned at the stake for heresy after leading the French troops to victory

Merovingian Dynasty (481-751) enjoyed almost 300 years of rule before **Pepin the Short's** son, **Charlemagne,** took power in 768 and established the **Carolingian Dynasty** (751-987). On Christmas Day, 800, Charlemagne had himself crowned Holy Roman Emperor by **Pope Leo III.** Charlemagne expanded his territorial claims and, despite his own illiteracy, renewed interest in the art and literature of the ancients, initiating the **Carolingian Renaissance.** Despite Charlemagne's conquest of most of the Western world, Paris suffered when Charlemagne moved his capital to Aix-la-Chapelle (Aachen, in northwestern Germany). When invading **Normans** and **Saracens** menaced Europe in the 9th and 10th centuries, Charlemagne's empire fell and France crumbled into fragments.

MIDDLE AGES TO THE RENAISSANCE

MEDIEVAL PARIS. As the first millennium approached, France was a disparate collection of independent kingdoms with their own languages and traditions. These kingdoms were organized in the **feudal system,** which bonded peasant-worker vassals to their lords.

Paris returned to prominence with the 987 election of the Count of Paris, **Hugh Capet,** to the throne. Under the rule of the **Capetian Dynasty** (987-1328), Paris flourished as a center of trade, education, and power. Capet's descendants attempted to unite the various kingdoms into one centralized country. In 1163, construction began on **Notre Dame** (see **Sights,** p. 67), which would take over 170 years to complete. The Capetians' most famous king, **Philippe-Auguste** (1179-1223), expanded Paris's territory, refortified its walls, and paved the city's streets. With the establishment of the University of Paris in 1215 and the **Sorbonne** in 1253 (see **Sights,** p. 86), Paris was reorganized into two parts: the commercial Rive Droite (Right Bank) and the academic Rive Gauche (Left Bank). Both trade and papal power transferred to France in the 14th century when Pope Clement V moved to Avignon in 1309.

PLAGUE & WAR. Like most of France's cities, 14th-century Paris suffered the ravages of both the **Black Death** (1348-49) and the **Hundred Years' War** (1337-1453), in which the Burgundians allied with the English against the French and Paris was trapped in the middle. When **Charles IV,** the last of the Capetian dynasty, died in 1328, Edward III of England claimed his right to the throne. Were it not for the mythic **Joan of Arc,** who allied with the Valois king **Charles VII** against Henry V of England, Paris might have become an English colony. Joan, a peasant girl from Orléans who heard angelic voices telling her to save France, led the Valois troops to a string of victories before she was captured by the English and burned at the stake in Rouen for heresy. Charles VII reclaimed Paris in 1437 and drove the English back to Calais. The Valois Dynasty took over where the Capetians left off and moved toward securing a unified France.

THE RENAISSANCE. The influence of the **Italian Renaissance** sparked interest in literature, art, and architecture in 16th-century Paris. In 1527, **François I** commissioned Pierre Lescot to rebuild the **Louvre** (see **Museums,** p. 135) in the open style of the Renaissance, and moved the royal residence there. During the reign of François's successor, **Henri II,** mansions were added to the **place Royale** (now called pl. des Vosges; see **Sights,** p. 85), a masterpiece of French Renaissance architecture. However, when Henri II died in the square's Palais des Tournelles in 1563 after a jousting accident, his wife, **Catherine de Médicis,** ordered it destroyed and began work on the **Tuileries Palace,** the **Pont Neuf,** and the **Jardin des Tuileries** (see **Sights,** p. 73).

RELIGIOUS BLOODSHED. Religious conflict between **Huguenots** (French protestants) and **Catholics** initiated the **Wars of Religion** (1562-1598). After the death of her husband, Henri II, Catherine de Médicis effectively became France's ruler. A fervent Catholic, she was ruthless in the wars against the French Protestants from the southwestern kingdom of Navarre. **Henri de Navarre** agreed to marry Catherine de Médicis's daughter, **Marguerite de Valois** (Queen Margot), in an effort to bring peace to the two warring kingdoms. But the wedding was a trap: when the leading Protestants in France had assembled in Paris for the royal union in 1572, Catherine signaled the start of the **St. Bartholomew's Day Massacre.** A wild Parisian mob slaughtered some 2000 Huguenots. Henri's life and throne were saved only by a not-exactly-voluntary conversion to Catholicism. In 1589, Henri de Navarre acceded to the throne as **Henri IV de Bourbon,** ensuring peace, uniting France, and establishing the last of France's royal houses, the **Bourbons.** Upon his ascension to the throne at St-Denis (see **Sights,** p. 132), Henri IV waved off the magnitude of his conversion with the remark, *"Paris vaut bien une messe"* ("Paris is well worth a mass."). His heart still lay with the Huguenots, though: in 1598, he issued the **Edict of Nantes,** which granted tolerance for French Protestants and quelled religious wars for almost a century.

SEVENTEENTH CENTURY

LOUIS XIII & RICHELIEU. The French monarchy reached its height of power and opulence in the 17th century. First of the Bourbon line, Henri IV succumbed to an assassin's dagger in 1610 and was succeeded by **Louis XIII.** Louis's capable and ruthless minister, **Cardinal Richelieu,** consolidated political power in the hands of the monarch and created the centralized, bureaucratic administration characteristic of France to this day. He expanded Paris and built the **Palais du Luxembourg** (see **Sights,** p. 92) for the Queen mother, **Marie de Médicis,** and the Palais Cardinal (today the **Palais-Royal;** see **Sights,** p. 74) for himself. Richelieu manipulated the nobility and taunted the bourgeoisie with promises of social advancement, tightening the monarchy's hold over the state.

1461
François Villon, *Le Testament*

1527
François I sets up royal residence in the Louvre

1532
François Rabelais, *Gargantua*

c. 1558
Marguerite de Navarre, *Héptameron*

1562-98
The Wars of Religion: Huguenots vs. Catholics

1572
St. Bartholomew's Day Massacre

1580
Michel de Montaigne, *Essais*

1598
Henri VI de Bourbon issues the Edict of Nantes, proclaiming religious tolerance

1610
Beginning of the reign of Louis XIII and Cardinal Richelieu

1642
Five-year old Louis XIV comes to the throne

1637
René Descartes, *Discours de la Méthode (Discourse on Method)*

1648
The Académie Française is founded under the direction of Charles le Brun

1658
Blaise Pascale, *Pensées*

1661
Louis XIV, the Sun King, moves the court to his new chateaux at Versailles

1664
Molière, *Tartuffe*

1667
Jean Racine, *Phèdre*

1701-13
War of Spanish Succession

1715
Louis XIV dies and is succeeded by Louis XV

1752
Denis Diderot and Jean D'Alembert, *Encyclopédie*

1756
François Boucher, *Madame de Pompadour*

1758
Voltaire, *Candide*

1774
Louis XVI and Marie Antoinette take the throne

1766
Jean-Jacques Rousseau, *Confessions*

1778
France allies with the United States in the American Revolution

SUN KING SHINES. Richelieu and Louis died within months of each other in 1642 and were replaced by **Louis XIV** and **Cardinal Mazarin.** Since Louis was only five years old at the time, the cardinal took charge, but by 1661 the 24-year-old monarch had decided he was ready to rule alone. Not one known for modesty, Louis adopted the title **Sun King** and took the motto *"L'état, c'est moi"* ("I am the state"). He brought a distinctly personal touch to national affairs, moving the government to his new 14,000 room palace, the outrageously extravagant **Château de Versailles** (see **Daytripping,** p. 279). Louis transformed Versailles into a magnificent showcase for regal opulence and noble privilege (see **Garden Party,** p. 284). The King himself was on display: favored subjects could observe him and his queen rise in the morning, groom, and dine. Louis XIV strove to put down any form of dissent, operating on the principle of *"un roi, une loi, une foi"* ("one king, one law, one faith"). Louis reigned for 72 years, revoking the Edict of Nantes in 1685 at the behest of his mistress, and initiating the ruinous **War of the Spanish Succession** (1701-1713). Louis brought the nobility with him to Versailles to keep a close eye on them and avoid any unpleasant uprisings. The nobles vegetated at court, and most didn't bother to notice their complete loss of political power. From Versailles, Louis XIV commissioned the landscape architect **André Le Nôtre** to build a tree-lined boulevard called the Grand Cours, today known as the **Champs-Elysées** (see **Sights,** p. 101). The Sun King also built the **place Vendôme** (see **Sights,** p. 73) and his daughter, the Duchesse de Bourbon, commissioned the **Palais Bourbon,** which today houses the **Assemblée Nationale** (see **Sights,** p. 99). Louis finally died in 1715 and was succeeded by the two-year-old **Louis XV.** The light that had once emanated from the French throne could no longer eclipse domestic problems. The lavish expenditures of the Sun King left France in debt, and after his death, the weakened nobility's resentment toward the monarchy began to brew.

THE FRENCH REVOLUTION

REVOLUTION BUILDS. When **Louis XVI** succeeded to the throne in 1774, the country was in desperate financial straits. Peasants blamed the soon-to-be-*ancien régime* for their mounting debts, while aristocrats detested the king for his gestures toward reform. In 1789, in an attempt to resolve this no-win situation, Louis XVI called a meeting of the **Estates General,** an assembly of delegates from the three classes of society: aristocrats, clergy, and the bourgeois-dominated **Third Estate.** This anachronistic body had not met since 1614, and after weeks of legal wrangling, the Third Estate broke away and declared itself the National Assembly. Locked out of its chamber, the delegation moved to the tennis courts at Versailles where the **Oath of the Tennis Court,** a promise to draft a new constitution, was sworn on June 20, 1789. The King did not dismiss the Assembly; instead he sent in troops to intimidate it and received the immortal riposte "the assembled nation cannot receive orders." As rumors multiplied, the initiative passed to the Parisian mob, known as the *sans-culottes* (those without breeches), who were angered by high bread prices and the disarray of the government.

STORMING OF THE BASTILLE. When they stormed the old fortress of the Bastille (see **Sights,** p. 108) on July 14th, peasants across France burned the records of their debts. July 14th *(le quatorze juillet)* is now the Fête Nationale (see **Festivals,** p. 20). The Assembly joined in the Revolution in August with the abolishment of feudal law and the Declaration of the Rights of Man, which embodied the principles *liberté, égalité,* and *fraternité.*

REIGN OF TERROR. When the petrified king, now under virtual house arrest, tried to flee the country in 1791, he was arrested and imprisoned; meanwhile, Austria and Prussia mobilized in order to stamp out the democratic disease. In 1793, as the revolutionary armies miraculously defeated the invaders, the radical **Jacobin** faction, led by **Maximilien Robespierre** and his **Committee of Public Safety,** took over the Convention and began a period of suppression and mass execution known as the **Reign of Terror.** In January, the Jacobins guillotined the King and his cake-savoring Queen, **Marie-Antoinette,** abolishing the monarchy. The ironically named **place de la Concorde** (Harmony Square) was the site of more than 1300 beheadings (see **Sights,** p. 103). With a **Republic** declared, the *ancien régime* was history. The Revolution had taken a radical turn. The Church refused to be subjugated to the National Assembly and was replaced by the oxymoronical **Cult of Reason.** Their 10-day weeks did not catch on, but their metric system is now the standard. As counter-revolutionary paranoia set in, power lay with **Robespierre** and his McCarthyesque Committee of Public Safety. The least suspicion of royalist sympathy led to the block; Dr. Guillotine himself did not escape the vengeance of his invention. Robespierre ordered the execution of his rivals before his own denunciation and death in 1794. The **Terror** was over and power was entrusted to a five-man **Directory.**

NAPOLEON & EMPIRE

RISE OF NAPOLEON... Meanwhile, war continued as a young Corsican general swept through northern Italy and into Austria. Fearful of his rising popularity, the Directory jumped at **Napoleon Bonaparte's** idea of invading Egypt to threaten Britain's colonies in India. Although successful on land, the destruction of his fleet at the Battle of the Nile left his disease-ridden army marooned in Cairo. Napoleon responded by hurrying back to France to save his career. Riding a wave of public support, he deposed the Directory, declared himself First Consul of a triumvirate, Consul for Life in 1802, and ultimately **Emperor** in 1804. Portions of his **Napoleonic**

1784
Caron de Beaumarchais, *Le Mariage de Figaro*

1789
The French Revolution begins with the Oath of the Tennis Court and the storming of the Bastille

1793-4
Thousands are beheaded during the Reign of Terror

1793
Jean-Paul Marat, publisher of the revolutionary newspaper *L'Ami du peuple,* is assassinated in his bathtub by Charlotte Corday

1793
Jacques-Louis David, *Marat assassiné (The Death of Marat)*

1795
Marquis de Sade, *La Philosophie dans le boudoir (Philosophy in the Bedroom)*

1802
Madame de Staël, *Delphine*

1803-1815
Napoleonic Wars extend the French empire

1804
Napoleon Bonaparte declares himself emperor

1805
Construction of the Arc de Triomphe begins

1812
Napoleon's troops occupy, freeze in, and withdraw from Moscow

1814
Jean-Auguste-Dominique Ingres, *La Grande Odalisque*

1815
Napoleon is defeated at the Battle of Waterloo and exiled to St. Helena by the British

1829-48
Honoré de Balzac, *La Comedie humaine (The Human Comedy)*

1830
Charles X's army invades Algeria; the July Revolution leads to a constitutional monarchy under Louis-Philippe

1830
Eugene Delacroix, *La Liberté guidant la peuple (Liberty Leading the People)*

1831
Victor Hugo, *Notre Dame de Paris (The Hunchback of Notre Dame)*

1832
George Sand, *Valentine*

Code still exist today, although it structured an autocratic approach to life, re-establishing slavery and requiring wives to show obedience to their husbands.

Paris benefited from Napoleon's conquests and international booty. His interest in the ancient Egyptian and Roman worlds brought countless sculptures from Alexandria and Italy into Paris, including the Louvre's *Dying Gladiator* and *Discus Thrower* (see **Louvre** p. 135). He ordered the constructions of the two triumphal Roman arches, the **Arc de Triomphe** (see **Sights,** p. 100) and the **Arc du Carrousel** (see **Louvre,** p. 135) topping the latter with a gladiatorial sculpture stolen from St. Mark's Cathedral in Venice. Napoleon's many new bridges, like the **Pont d'Austerlitz,** the **Pont Iéna,** and the **Pont des Arts** (see **Sights,** p. 96) spanned the Seine in style. He ordered the construction of a neo-Greco-Roman style temple, the **Madeleine** (see **Sights,** p. 104), and he finished the Cour Carrée of the Louvre, originally ordered by Louis XIV. The monument that perhaps best exemplifies Napoleon's Empire style is the **Château de Malmaison.** Meanwhile, when Josephine failed to produce an heir, she and Napoleon amicably annulled their marriage. The Emperor got re-married to **Marie Louise d'Autriche** and his armies pushed east to Moscow.

...AND HIS DOWNFALL. In 1812, after occupying a deserted Moscow, Napoleon was forced to withdraw at the onset of winter. The freezing cold decimated the French ranks, and of the 700,000 men he had led out to Russia, barely 200,000 returned. Having lost the support of a war-weary nation, Napoleon abdicated in 1814. In return, he was given the Mediterranean island of **Elba,** and the monarchy was reinstated under **Louis XVIII,** brother of his headless predecessor. Napoleon left Elba and landed near Cannes on March 26th, 1815. He marched north as the king fled to England. The adventure of the ensuing **Hundred Days' War** ended on the field of **Waterloo** in Flanders, Belgium, where the **Duke of Wellington** triumphed. The ex-Emperor threw himself on the mercy of the English, who banished him to remote **St. Helena** in the south Atlantic, where he died in 1821. Napoleon is still popularly regarded as a hero in France; thousands still pay their respects at his tomb at **Les Invalides** (see **Sights,** p. 98). The **Restoration** of the monarchy saw Louis XVIII at the helm, as the **Bourbon** dynasty went on and on.

RESTORATION & MORE REVOLUTION

THE JULY REVOLUTION. Although initially forced to recognize the achievements of the Revolution, the reinstated monarchy soon returned to its despotic ways. When **Charles X** restricted the press and limited the electorate to the landed classes, the people had had enough. Remembering the fate of his brother, Charles abdicated quickly following the **July Revolution** of 1830, and a constitutional monarchy was created under **Louis-Philippe,** Duke of Orléans, whose more modest bourgeois lifestyle garnered him the name **"the Citizen King."** In a symbolic gesture, he kept his flag tricolor and his monarchy constitutional. The middle classes prospered, but the industrialization of France created a class of urban poor receptive to the new ideas of **socialism.**

FEBRUARY REVOLUTION. When the king and his bourgeois government refused to reform, the people were well practiced: there followed the **February Revolution** of 1848 and the declaration of the **Second Republic** and France's first universal male suffrage. The late Emperor's nephew, **Louis Napoleon,** was elected president. The constitution barred him from seeking a second term, though he ignored it and seized power in a coup in 1851. Following a referendum in 1852, he declared himself **Emperor Napoleon III** to popular acclaim. Napoleon III's reign saw the industrialization of Paris and the rise of the urban population, pollution, and poverty that Balzac and Hugo's novels describe (see p. 53). Still, during his reign, France's prestige was restored: her factories hummed and **Baron Georges Haussmann** rebuilt Paris, replacing the medieval street plan (too conducive to street demonstrations) with *grand boulevards* along which an army could be deployed (see p. 60).

FRANCO-PRUSSIAN WAR. Despite Napoleon III's reconstruction of Paris, his downfall came in July 1870 with France's defeat in the **Franco-Prussian War.** The confident French did not notice the storm clouds gathering across the Rhine, where **Bismarck** had almost completed the unification of Germany. After tricking the French into declaring war, the Iron Chancellor's troops swiftly overran the country. The Emperor was captured and as German armies advanced, the **Third Republic** was declared. Paris held out for four months, with the residents so desperate for food that they slaughtered and devoured most of the animals in the zoo (see **Sights,** p. 89).

PARIS COMMUNE. When the government admitted defeat, placing a conservative regime led by Adolphe Thiers in power, the Parisian mob revolted again; in 1871 they declared the Paris Commune. For four months, a committee of leftists, the *communards,* assumed power and rejected the Thiers government, throwing up barricades and declaring the city a free Commune. When French troops were sent in to recapture the city, the *communards* burned the Hôtel-de-Ville, the Palais-Royal, and Catherine de Médicis's Tuileries Palace before retreating to their last stand, Père Lachaise cemetery (see **Sights,** p. 123). The crushing of the Commune was quick and bloody. Many estimate that over 20,000 Parisians died, slaughtered by their compatriots in about a week. The last of the *communards* were shot against Père Lachaise's Mur des Fédérés on May 21, 1871. The defeat broke both the power of Paris over the provinces and that of the Parisian proletariat over the city.

1848
The February Revolution and the declaration of the Second Republic; Baron Georges Haussmann begins redesigning Paris

1848
French conquest of Vietnam begins

1852
Louis Napoleon declares himself emperor

1856
Gustave Flaubert, *Madame Bovary*

1857
Charles Baudelaire, *Les Fleurs du mal (The Flowers of Evil)*

1861
Construction begins on the Opéra Garnier

1863
Edouard Manet, *Dejeuner sur l'Herbe (Lunch on the Grass)*

1870
France is defeated in the Franco-Prussian War

1871
The Paris Commune

1874
The Impressionists have their first exhibition

1875
Georges Bizet, *Carmen*

1876
Stephane Mallarmé, *L'Apres-midi d'un faune*

1880
Emile Zola, *Nana*

1883
Guy de Maupassant, *Une Vie*

1889
Eiffel Tower is constructed for the Universal Exposition

1890-1914
Belle Epoque

1894
A Jewish army captain is falsely accused of treason in the Dreyfus Affair

1904
The French unite with the British in the Entente Cordiale

1905-6
Henri Matisse, *Le Bonheur de Vivre (Joy of Life)*

1907
Pablo Picasso, *Les Demoiselles d'Avignon*

1913
Igor Stravinsky's *The Rite of Spring* has its riotous debut

1913-27
Marcel Proust, *A la recherce du temps perdu*

1914
Beginning of World War I

1917
Marcel Duchamp, *La Fontaine*

1918
WWI ends with victory for France and its allies and the signing of the Treaty of Versailles

BELLE EPOQUE

ART & INDUSTRIALIZATION. After over 80 years of revolutions, violence, and political instability, it is easy to understand why the period of peace, prosperity, and culture that followed between roughly 1890 and 1914 is called the **Belle Epoque** (Beautiful Period). The colors of the **Impressionists** (see p. 61), the novels of **Marcel Proust** (see p. 57), and the **World Expositions** of 1889 and 1900, which gave Paris the **Eiffel Tower** (see **Sights,** p. 96), the **Pont Alexandre III,** the **Grand** and **Petit Palais** (see **Sights,** p. 103), and the first **métro** line, all reflected the optimism and energy of the Belle Epoque. At the same time, industrialization introduced many new social problems to the Third Republic. While the government's reforms laid the foundation for the contemporary social welfare state, social tensions continued to grow.

DREYFUS AFFAIR. The Third Republic was further undermined by the **Dreyfus affair.** Alfred Dreyfus was a Jewish army captain convicted and exiled in 1894 on trumped-up charges of treason. When the army refused to consider the case even after proof of Dreyfus's innocence was uncovered, France became polarized between the *Dreyfusards*, who argued for his release, and the reactionary right-wing *anti-Dreyfusards*, to whom Dreyfus was an unpatriotic traitor, regardless of the evidence. These ethnic tensions foreshadowed the conflicts that France would later confront in its colonial territories.

WORLD WAR I

TENSIONS BUILD. After centuries of mutual dislike, the **Entente Cordiale** brought the British and the French into cooperation in 1904. Together with czarist Russia, this **Triple Entente** faced the **Triple Alliance** of Germany, Italy, and the Austro-Hungarian Empire. Tensions exploded in 1914, when a Serbian nationalist assassinated the heir to the Austrian throne, **Archduke Franz-Ferdinand,** in Sarajevo. Germany did not encourage Austria to exercise restraint, so they marched on Serbia. Russia responded, and suddenly virtually all of Europe was at war.

HELL IN THE TRENCHES. After advancing within 50km of Paris, the German offensive stalled at the **Battle of the Marne.** Four years of agonizing trench warfare ensued. Germany's unrestricted submarine warfare on ships entering European waters provoked the **United States** to enter on the side of the Triple Entente. American troops tipped the balance of power in favor of the British and the French (Russia had withdrawn in 1917 in the midst of its own violent revolution), and on November 11, 1918, fighting ended, but not before an entire generation of European men and boys was lost to the trenches.

TREATY OF VERSAILLES. The Germans were forced to sign the humiliating **Treaty of Versailles** in the Hall of Mirrors, where Prussian King Wilhelm I had been crowned Kaiser of the German Reich in 1870 at the end of Germany's victory in the Franco-Prussian War. The treaty contained a clause ascribing the blame for the war to Germany. The foundations for the great resentment that would aid Hitler's rise to power were laid in the Sun King's château.

ROARING 20s & 30s DEPRESSION

EXPAT FUN. Parisians danced in the streets with British, Canadian, and American soldiers at the end of WWI. The party continued into the **Roaring 20s,** when artists like **Cocteau, Picasso, Chagall,** and **Man Ray;** performers like **Josephine Baker,** who, like other black Americans, found greater tolerance in France than at home; and expatriates like **Gertrude Stein, Ernest Hemingway, Ezra Pound,** and **F. Scott Fitzgerald** (see p. 57) flooded Paris's cafés and salons.

RISE OF FASCISM. The party ended with the **Great Depression** in the 1930s, and was exacerbated by the violent right-wing **fascist demonstrations,** in which thousands of Parisians marched on pl. de la Concorde and stormed the Assemblée Nationale. To combat the Fascists, Socialists and Communists united together under **Léon Blum's** left-wing **Front Populaire,** seeking better wages, unionization, and vacation benefits. The Popular Front split over Blum's decision not to aid the Spanish Republicans against the Fascist General Franco in the Spanish Civil War. Tensions between left and right made France ill-equipped to deal with the dangers of Hitler's rapid rise to power and his impending mobilization on the opposite shores of the Rhine.

WORLD WAR II

NAZI OCCUPATION. After invading Austria, Czechoslovakia, Poland, Norway, and Denmark, Adolf Hitler's armies swept through the Ardennes in Luxembourg and blitzkrieged across Belgium and the Netherlands before entering Paris on June 13, 1940. Curators at the Louvre, sensing the inevitable **Nazi Occupation,** removed many works of art, including the *Mona Lisa,* and placed them in hiding. Photographs of Nazi footsoldiers and SS troops goosestepping through the Arc de Triomphe are as chilling as the images of shocked Parisians lined up along the Champs-Elysées watching the spectacle of Nazi power. The French signed a truce with the Germans ceding the northern third of the country to the Nazis and designating the lower two-thirds to a collaborating government set up in Vichy. The puppet **Vichy** government under **Maréchal Pétain** cooperated with Nazi policy, including the **deportation** of over 120,000 French and foreign Jews to **Nazi concentration camps** between 1942 and 1944.

1920S
The heyday of American expatriate culture in Paris

1920
Colette, *Cheri*

1924
André Gide, *Les Faux-Monnayers (The Counterfeiters);* André Breton, *The Surrealist Manifesto*

1938
Jean-Paul Sartre, *La Nausée (Nausea)*

1940-44
Nazi occupation of Paris

1942-44
Deportation and murder of thousands of French Jews

1942
Albert Camus, *L'Etranger (The Stranger)*

1944
Liberation of Paris and declaration of the Fourth Republic under Charles de Gaulle

1946
French women win the right to vote

1949
Simone de Beauvoir, *Le Deuxieme Sexe (The Second Sex)*

1953
Samuel Beckett, *En Attendant Godot (Waiting for Godot)*

DEPORTATION OF THE JEWS. Soldiers broke down doors on the streets surrounding the rue des Rosiers in the largely Jewish neighborhood of the Marais in the 4th *arrondissement* and hauled Jewish families to the Vélodrome d'Hiver, an indoor winter cycling stadium. Here, Jews awaited transportation to concentration camps like **Drancy,** in the northeast industrial suburb of Paris near St-Denis, or to camps in Poland and Germany (the **Mémorial de la Déportation** on the Île de la Cité honors those who perished in the Holocaust; see **Sights,** p. 71). France was plagued by many profiteering and anti-Semitic **collaborators** *(collabos)* who aided the **Gestapo.** Recently, the French government and the Roman Catholic Church in France have acknowledged some responsibility for the deportations and for their moral apathy, but the issue remains a controversial one.

CULTURE DURING THE OCCUPATION. Paris's theaters, cinemas, music-halls, and cafés continued to operate for the Nazi soldiers and officers who flocked to Paris for rest and relaxation. Many restaurants and entertainers who continued to serve and sing for Nazi clients, including the **Moulin Rouge, Maxim's, Yves Montand, Maurice Chevalier,** and **Edith Piaf,** were criticized at the end of the war. Women who took German lovers had their heads shaved after the war and were forced to walk in the streets amid spitting and jeering.

RESISTANCE. Today, France prefers to commemorate the brave men and women of the **Résistance,** who fought in secret against the Nazis throughout occupation. In Paris, the Résistance fighters (or *maquis*) set up headquarters below the boulevards, in the **sewers** (see **Museums,** p. 149) and **catacombs** (see **Sights,** p. 113). In London, **Général Charles de Gaulle** established the **Forces Françaises Libres** (Free French Forces), declared his **Comité National Français** the government-in-exile, and broadcast inspirational messages to his countrymen on the BBC (the first of which is now engraved above the **Tomb of the Unknown Soldier** under the Arc de Triomphe).

LIBERATION & POSTWAR RECOVERY. On June 6, 1944, British, American, and Canadian troops launched the D-Day invasion on the Normandy coast. On August 25th, after four years of occupation, Paris was free. Again, Parisian civilians and Résistance fighters danced and drank with the American, Canadian, and British soldiers. De Gaulle evaded sniper fire to attend mass at Notre Dame and give thanks for the **Liberation of Paris.** His procession down the Champs-Elysées was met with the cheers of thousands of elated Parisians. After the war, as monuments to French bravery were established in the Musée de l'Armée and the Musée de l'Ordre de la Libération (see **Museums,** p. 141), and as thousands of French Jewish survivors began to arrive at the main Repatriation Center in the **Gare d'Orsay** (see **Museums,** p. 138), there was a move to initiate change and avoid returning to the stagnation of the pre-war years. De

Gaulle promised new elections once deportees and exiled citizens had been repatriated, and France drafted a new constitution. In 1946, French women finally gained the right to vote.

POSTCOLONIAL PARIS: THE 50s & 60s

FOURTH REPUBLIC. The **Fourth Republic** was proclaimed in 1944. Charles de Gaulle quit in 1946, unable to adapt to democratic politics. The Fourth lacked a strong replacement for de Gaulle, and 14 years saw 25 governments. Despite these problems, the Fourth Republic presided over an economically resurgent France.

COLONIAL INDEPENDENCE. The end of the war also signaled great change in France's residual 19th-century **colonial empire.** France's defeat in 1954 at the Vietnamese liberation of **Dien Bien Phu** inspired the colonized peoples of France's other protectorates and colonies, which all gained their **independence** in rapid succession: Morocco and Tunisia in 1956, Mali, Senegal, and the Ivory Coast in 1960. But in Algeria, France drew the line when Algerian nationalists, backed by the resistance efforts of the **FLN (Front Libération National),** moved for independence. With a population of over one million French *colons*, or **pied-noirs** (literally "black feet" in French), who were either born in or had immigrated to Algeria, France was reluctant to give up a colony that it had come to regard as an extension of the French *hexagone*.

ALGERIAN WAR. Fighting in Algeria lasted from 1954 to 1962. The Fourth Republic came to an end in the midst of this chaos overseas. De Gaulle was called out of retirement to deal with the crisis and voted into power by the National Assembly in 1958. Later that year, with a new **constitution** in hand, the nation declared itself the **Fifth Republic.** This did nothing to resolve the Algerian conflict. Terrorist attacks in Paris by desperate members of the FLN were met by curfews for African immigrants. At a peaceful demonstration against such restrictions in 1961, police opened fire on the largely North African crowd, killing hundreds. Amid the violence in Paris and the war in Algeria, a 1962 referendum granted Algeria independence. One hundred years of French colonial rule in Algeria came to an end, and the French colonial empire crumbled in its wake.

The repercussions of colonial exploitation continue to haunt Paris, where racial tensions today complicate relations between middle-class French, Arab North Africans, Black West Africans, and Caribbeans, many of whom are second- and third-generation citizens.

REVOLUTION OF 1968. De Gaulle's foreign policy was a success, but his conservatism brought growing domestic problems. In **May 1968,** what started as a student protest against the university system rapidly grew into a full-scale revolt, as workers striked in support of social

1954
Vietnam is liberated from French colonial rule at Dien Bien Phu

1957
Roland Barthes, *Mythologies*; Jean Genet, *La Balcon (The Balcony)*

1958
The Fourth Republic ends and de Gaulle is voted back into power

1954-1962
The Algerian War

1961
Police kill hundreds of peaceful protestors in Paris

1960
Eugène Ionesco, *Rhinoceros*

1967

Jacques Derrida, *De La Grammatologie (Of Grammatology)*

1968

Student-led revolution of May 1968

1975

Hélène Cixous, *La Rire de la Méduse (The Laugh of the Medusa)*

1976

Michel Foucault, *Histoire de la sexualité (The History of Sexuality, Volume I)*

1977

Jacques Lacan, *Écrits*

1981

Beginning of Socialist François Mitterrand's presidency

1983

Medhi Charef, *Le thé au harem d'Archie Ahmed (Tea in the Harem)*

1984

Marguerite Duras, *L'Amant (The Lover)*

1986

Marc Augé, *Un Ethnologue dans le métro (In the Métro)*

reform. Frustrated by racism, sexism, capitalism, an outdated curriculum, and the threat of a reduction in the number of students allowed to matriculate, students seized the **Sorbonne.** Barricades were erected in the **Latin Quarter,** and an all-out student revolt began. Students dislodged cobblestones to hurl at riot police, and their slogan, *"Sous les pierres, la plage"* ("Under the pavement, the beach"), symbolized the freedom of shifting sand that lay beneath the rock-hard bureaucracy of French institutions. The situation escalated over the next several weeks. Police used tear gas and clubs to storm the barricades, while students fought back by throwing Molotov cocktails and lighting cars on fire. When 10 million state workers went on **strike** in support of the students, the government deployed tank and commando units.

The Parisian university system was almost immediately decentralized, with various campuses scattered throughout the city and the nation so that student power could never again come together so explosively. The National Assembly was dissolved and things looked to be heading for revolution yet again. Only when elections returned the Gaullists to power were future crises averted. However, the aging General had lost his magic touch, and he resigned following a referendum in 1969.

80s & 90s

POMPIDOU & D'ESTAING. Four parties have dominated French politics since de Gaulle. On the (moderate) right are two parties formed when de Gaulle's old allies split in 1974: the Union pour la Démocratie Française (UDF), led by **Valéry Giscard d'Estaing,** and the Rassemblement pour la République (RPR), led by **Jacques Chirac.** On the left is the Parti Socialiste (PS), in power through the 1980s under **François Mitterrand,** and the Parti Communiste Français (PCF), which holds few seats and little power. After de Gaulle's exit, many feared the Fifth Republic's collapse. It has endured, but with change. De Gaulle's Prime Minister, **Georges Pompidou,** won the presidency, held a *laissez-faire* position toward business and a less assertive foreign policy than de Gaulle. In 1974, Pompidou died suddenly, and his successor was conservative **Valéry Giscard d'Estaing.** D'Estaing's term saw the construction of the **Centre Pompidou** (see **Museums,** p. 139), an arts center incorporating gallery and performance spaces. D'Estaing carried on de Gaulle's legacy by concentrating on economic development and strengthening French presence in international affairs.

MITTERRAND & COHABITATION. In 1981, Socialist **François Mitterrand** took over the presidency, and the Socialists gained a majority in the Assemblée Nationale. Within weeks they had raised the minimum wage and added a fifth week to the French worker's annual vacation. The political collapse of the Left during Mitterrand's presidency forced him to compromise with the right. Mitterrand began his term with widespread nationalization, but the international climate could not support a socialist economy. In the wake of the 1983 recession, the Socialists met with serious losses in the **1986 parliamentary elections.** The right gained control of parliament, and Mitterrand had to appoint the conservative **Jacques Chirac** as Prime Minister.

Meanwhile, in an unprecedented power-sharing relationship known as "cohabitation," Mitterrand withdrew to control foreign affairs, allowing Chirac to assume domestic power. Chirac privatized many industries, but a large-scale transport strike and widespread terrorism hurt the right, allowing Mitterrand to win a second term in 1988. He proceeded to run a series of unpopular Socialist governments, one led briefly by **Edith Cresson,** France's first female Prime Minister.

GRANDS PROJETS. Mitterrand's **Grands Projets** (see p. 51) transformed the architectural landscape of Paris with grand millennial style. Seeking immortality in stone, steel, concrete, Mitterrand was responsible for the **Musée d'Orsay** (see **Museums,** p. 138), **Parc de la Villette** (see **Museums,** p. 143) the **Institut du Monde Arabe** (see **Museums,** p. 148), the **Louvre Pyramid** (see **Museums,** p. 135), the **Opéra Bastille** (see **Sights,** p. 110), the **Grande Arche de la Défense** (see **Sights,** p. 131), and the new **Bibliothèque de France** (see **Sights,** p. 112). Although expensive and at times as controversial as the Eiffel Tower was in 1889, Mitterrand's vision for a 21st-century Paris has produced some of the city's most breathtaking new architecture. Mitterrand's other great legacy was his Socialist project to decentralize financial and political power from Paris to local governments outside the Île de France. But the people were more concerned with scandals involving Mitterrand's ministers than his grandiose plans. In the mid-90s, Mitterrand revealed two startling facts—that he had worked with the Vichy government in WWII before joining the Résistance and that he had been seriously ill with cancer since the beginning of his presidency.

CHIRAC TAKES OVER. In 1995, Mitterrand chose not to run again because of his failing health, and Chirac was elected president. With unemployment at 12.2% at the time of the election, Chirac faced a difficult year. The crisis ended in a prolonged **Winter Strike** by students, bus drivers, subway operators, electricians, and postmen, who protested against budget and benefit cuts proposed by Chirac and his unpopular Prime Minister, **Alain Juppé.** For weeks, Paris was paralyzed. Stores kept reduced hours, mail delivery came to a halt, and occasional blackouts and traffic jams plagued the city. Despite hardships, many Parisians were glad to see the spirit of 1968 still alive and to rediscover their neighbors, local cafés, and corner markets while grounded in their neighborhoods by the transport strikes. 1996 proved to be a tough year as well. The nation mourned the loss of François Mitterrand, who died in early January, and later that year, Chirac was denounced around the globe for conducting underground **nuclear weapons tests** in the South Pacific.

1986
In the parliamentary elections, the Socialists suffer major losses and the far-right wins 10% of the vote

1991
The Maastricht treaty and the formation of the European Union

1993
The Law Pasqua gives police greater freedom to interrogate immigrants

1995
Jacques Chirac elected president; Paris paralyzed by the Winter Strike

1996
Mitterrand dies; Chirac criticized for nuclear weapons tests

1999
Border controls abolished for the entire EU; the PACS extends benefits to homosexual couples

2002
The Euro replaces the franc as France's official currency; far-right nationalist Jean-Marie Le Pen wins a shocking number of votes in the presidential election

2003
France comes into conflict with the United States over the war in Iraq

2003
Etienne Balibar, *Nous, citoyens d'Europe? Les frontières, l'Etat, le peuple (We, Citizens of Europe? Borders, the State, the People)*

The ascendancy of the right was short-lived; in 1997, Chirac dissolved the parliament, but elections reinstated a Socialist government. Chirac was forced to accept his one-time presidential rival, majority leader **Lionel Jospin,** as Prime Minister.

EUROPEAN UNION. One of the most important challenges in the 80s and 90s was the question of European integration. Despite France's support of the creation of the **European Economic Community (EEC)** in 1957, the idea of a unified Europe has met with considerable resistance. Since the inception of the 1991 **Maastricht Treaty,** which significantly strengthened economic integration by expanding the 13-nation EEC to the **European Union (EU),** the French have manifested fear of a loss of French national character and autonomy. Hoping that a united Europe would strengthen cooperation between France and Germany, Mitterrand led the campaign for a "Oui" vote in France's 1992 referendum on the treaty. This position lost him prestige; the referendum scraped past with a 51% approval rating. The **Schengen Agreement** of 1995 created a six-nation zone without border controls. 1999 saw the extension of this zone to the entire EU (barring the UK, Ireland, and Denmark), as well as the birth of the European single currency, the **euro** (see **Planning Your Trip,** p. 307), which in 2002 superceded the French franc as France's official currency.

PARIS TODAY

2002 ELECTION. In the political arena, it looked as though the left was firmly in place to lead France well into the 21st century. The 2002 presidential election was slated to be a lackluster showdown between **Chirac** and his unglamorous prime minister, **Lionel Jospin.** But things got interesting when far-right nationalist **Jean-Marie Le Pen** unexpectedly edged out Jospin in the April preliminaries. Shocked out of their previous apathy, citizens took to the streets in protest, condemning the politics of Le Pen, who has publicly blamed France's immigrants for a wide variety of social problems in France. Before the elections, one million people, 200,000 of them in Paris, took part in a country-wide May Day demonstration. Hoisting signs that said *"Honte de mon pays"* ("Ashamed of my country"), protesters demanded that citizens vote for Chirac, whom they identified as the lesser of two evils. Chirac won with 82% of the vote. Parliamentary elections one month later dramatically marked the end of cohabitation between President and Prime Minister. With a landslide victory for the center-right and the appointment of conservative **Jean Pierre Raffarin** as Prime Minister, Chirac faces few barriers in fulfilling his pledges for tax cuts, institutional reform, and a crackdown on crime.

Le Pen's unexpected victory in the 2002 preliminary elections is only the most visible sign of the constant national debate on immigration policy. France has passed a record amount of legislative changes in its immigration policy, issuing forth seven reforms in the last 25 years. Anti-immigration sentiment increased substantially in 1993, when then Interior Minister Charles Pasqua proposed "zero-immigration" and initiated the **Law Pasqua,** allowing police greater freedom to interrogate immigrants. Jospin's 1998 law on immigration mitigated the effects of the Law Pasqua by allowing foreign scientists and scholars more relaxed conditions of entry.

ANTI-SEMITISM. In related news, anti-Semitic violence has been on the rise. In March and April of 2002, France experienced an alarming wave of anti-Semitic violence. Jewish schools, synagogues, and cemeteries became targets of terrorists. In response, thousands of French police were called in to protect Jewish neighborhoods throughout France. The violence has reflected not only escalating conflict in the Mideast, but also the growing tension over demographic changes in France and across Europe.

GAY RIGHTS. In 1999, France became the first traditionally Catholic country in the world to legally recognize homosexual unions. The **Pacte Civil de Solidarité,** known by its acronym **PACS,** was designed to extend to homosexual and unmarried heterosexual couples greater welfare, tax and inheritance rights. While PACS is now such a common term that it is used as both a noun *(pacser)* and an adjective *(pacsé)*, it is has faced a number of detractors. For many, PACS is strictly a legal term; gay marriage is still an unwelcome concept to many conservative French. Gay activists are currently struggling to attain the same rights to adoption and reproductive technologies that heterosexual married couples enjoy.

IRAQ & AMERICA. In the spring of 2003, the everpresent cultural conflict between France and America entered the political sphere when Chirac firmly refused to ally himself with President George W. Bush in the war against Saddam Hussein in **Iraq.** In a frenzy of patriotism, many Americans boycotted French products and, absurdly, tried to change the names of items like "French fries" and "French toast" to "Freedom fries" and "Freedom toast" (this book hereby swears to refrain from making any "Freedom" jokes), while thousands demonstrated in the streets of Paris against Bush's aggressive foreign policies. Bush and Chirac appeared to make up at the June 2003 G8 **Evian summit** (which met with its own share of protests), but how relations—both political and cultural—between the two countries will look in the coming years is just one of the questions currently facing Paris and its people.

LITERATURE & PHILOSOPHY

MEDIEVAL CHANSONS & FABLIAUX. Medieval France produced an extraordinary number of literary texts, starting at the beginning of the 12th century with popular **chansons de gestes,** stories written in verse that recount tales of 8th-century crusades and conquests. The most famous of these, the **Chanson de Roland** (1170), dramatizes the heroism of Roland, one of Charlemagne's soldiers, killed in battle in the Pyrenées in 778. While *chansons de geste* entertained 12th-century masses, the aristocracy enjoyed more refined literature extolling knightly honor and courtly love, such as the *Lais* (narrative songs) of **Marie de France,** the romances of **Chrétien de Troyes,** and Béroul's adaptation of the Irish legend of **Tristan et Iseult.**

During the 13th century, popular satirical stories called **fabliaux** celebrated all that was bawdy and scatological with tales of cuckolded husbands, saucy wives, and shrewd peasants. The 14th and 15th centuries produced the proto-feminist writings of **Christine de Pisan** and the ballads of **François Villon,** along with comic theater like the *Farce de Maître Pathelin.*

RENAISSANCE INNOVATION. The Renaissance in France produced literary texts challenging medieval notions of courtly love and Christian thought. Inspired by Boccaccio's *Decameron* and the Italian Renaissance, Marguerite de Navarre's *Héptaméron* employed pilgrim stories to explore innovative Humanistic ideas. **Calvin's**

Villon en Ville

Paris's first major poet was the great, the bawdy, the mysterious **François Villon** (1431-?), who wrote a number of *ballades* from the point of view of aging prostitutes, as well as a will in verse, *Le Grand Testament*. Excess was never enough for Monsieur Villon, who thieved, whored, drank himself silly, and spent too much time in prison. He narrowly escaped the gallows in 1463. Leaving Paris soon after this incident (even if he liked death, he did not like to die), Villon disappeared, although one poem remains in which he describes his close encounter with the gallows. Behold one of the earliest mentions of the city of Paris in poetry:

Quatraine
Je suis François, dont il me poise,
Né de Paris emprès Pontoise,
Et de la corde d'une toise
Saura mon col que mon cul poise.

Quatrain
I'm François, that's what they
accuse me of,
Born in Paris near Pontoise,
And by the noose of a gallows,
My neck shall be no more
than what my ass can pull.

humanist treaties criticized the Church and opened the road to the Reformation in France. With Jacques Cartier's founding of Nouvelle France (Québec) in 1534, French writers began to expand their perspectives on themselves and the world. **Rabelais's** fantastical *Gargantua and Pantagruel* imaginatively explored the world from giants' points of view, and **Montaigne's** *Essais* pushed the boundaries of individual intellectual thought. While the poetry of **Ronsard** and **Du Bellay,** the memoirs of **Marguerite de Valois,** and the works of **Louise Labé** contributed to the Renaissance's spirit of optimism and change, they also expressed anxiety over the atrocities of the 16th-century Wars of Religion.

RATIONALISM & THE ACADÉMIE. The founding of the **Académie Française** in 1635 assembled 40 men to regulate and codify French literature and language. The Académie has since acted as the church of French letters (see **Sights,** p. 92), though 17th-century French literature was not all as strict as the Académie. French philosophers reacted to the mushy musings of humanists with **Rationalism,** a school of thought championing logic and order. Map-lover **René Descartes** placed his trust in his own good sense, and set out to understand the world. In his 1637 *Discourse on Method*, Descartes proved his own existence with the catchy deduction, "I think, therefore I am." The equally diverse genius **Blaise Pascal** misspent his youth inventing the mechanical calculator and the science of probabilities. He later became a devotee of Jansenism, a Catholic reform movement that railed against the worldliness of the Jesuit-dominated Church. Retiring from public life, he expounded the virtues of solitude in his best-known work, *Pensées* (1658). **Jean-Baptiste Molière,** the era's comic relief, satirized the social pretensions of his age. Molière founded the great **Comédie Française,** the world's oldest national theater company, which still produces the definitive versions of French classics at its theater in Paris (see **Entertainment,** p. 224).

ENGLIGHTENMENT. The Enlightenment in France was informed by advances in the sciences and aimed at the promotion of reason in an often backward world. The Bible of the Enlightenment philosophers was **Denis Diderot** and **Jean D'Alembert's** *Encylopédie* (1752-1780), a record of the entire body of human knowledge with entries by the **philosophes** themselves. This staggeringly modest corpus included entries by such luminaries as **Jean-Jacques Rousseau** and **Voltaire,** who illuminated the century with his insistence on liberty and tolerance. Voltaire is best known for his satire *Candide* (1758), a refutation of the claim that "all is for the best in the best of all possible worlds." Satire was also the pet medium of playwright **Beaumarchais,** whose incendiary comic masterpieces *Le Barbier de Seville* (1775) and *Le Mariage de Figaro* (1784) were banned by Louis XVI. Voltaire was tame when compared to **Jean-Jacques Rousseau** who, something of a misfit, advocated a complete overhaul of society instead of happily satirizing it away. In his *Confessions* (1766-1769) and in novels like *Emile* (1762) and *Julie, ou La Nouvelle Héloïse* (1761), Rousseau argues that leaving society behind is better than living in a corrupt world.

REVOLUTIONARY PORN. The traumas of the period of the **French Revolution** are perhaps best represented in literature by the works of the **Marquis de Sade.** In libertine novels like *Philosophy in the Bedroom* (1795) and *Justine* (1791), de Sade attacked hypocrisy and repression and dealt with a mad world through the violently excessive representation of the sexual practice which was named for him.

ROMANTICISM. The 19th century saw an emotional reaction against Enlightenment rationality. Though anticipated in some ways by Rousseau, the expressive ideals of **Romanticism** first came to prominence in Britain and Germany rather than analytically minded France. One of the initial steps into the Romantic era in France came with the publication of **François-René de Chateaubriand's** novel *Attala* (1801), inspired by the time he spent waiting out the excesses of the revolution with native Americans around Niagara Falls. Goethe and the German Romantics were greatly admired by the stylish **Mme. de Staël,** whose *Delphine* (1802) and *Corinne* (1807) reflect upon the injustices of being a talented woman in a chauvinist world.

19TH CENTURY NOVELS. It was during this time that the novel became the pre-eminent literary medium, with such great writers as **Stendhal** and **Balzac,** but it was **Victor Hugo** who dominated the Romantic age. While his novels *The Hunchback of Notre Dame* (1831), and *Les Misérables* (1862) have achieved near-mythical status, he was also a prolific playwright and poet. An early blow for feminism was struck by **Aurore Dupin.** After leaving her husband and her childhood home of La Châtre in 1831, she took the pen-name **Georges Sand** and started a successful career as a novelist, condemning the social conventions which bound women into unhappy marriages in books such as *Valentine*

Rebel Without A Cause

The life of **Arthur Rimbaud** puts most modern teen idols to shame. During the Franco-Prussian War of 1870, the 16-year-old Rimbaud ran away from home to start a revolution, but was foiled when he was arrested at the train station for traveling without a ticket. Undeterred, a year later he ran away again to defend the Paris Commune, abandoning that cause just days before its suppression. The disillusioned Rimbaud set out to change the world through poetry. By abandoning traditional forms, trusting to his visions, and torturing himself to achieve new experiences, he aimed to "derange all the senses." The confident 17-year-old sent some verses to Paul Verlaine, who was so impressed that he invited Rimbaud to stay with him. Rimbaud seduced the older man, who abandoned his wife and child; after two years they separated acrimoniously, with Verlaine shooting Rimbaud in the wrist.

In 1875, at 21, Rimbaud abandoned poetry and set off to explore the world. Traveling to Indonesia and Egypt, he settled down to a career running guns into Ethiopia. Cancer forced his return to France in 1891, and he died that year in Marseille. During his absence, Verlaine, believing him dead, published the works of "the late Arthur Rimbaud," and today he is recognized as one of France's great poets.

We'll Always Have Paris

After WWI, a "lost generation" of writers found their way to Paris from Ireland, England, and America—**James Joyce, Ernest Hemingway, Ford Maddox Ford, Ezra Pound, Gertrude Stein,** and **F. Scott Fitzgerald** among them. These expatriates sought a freedom in Paris they could not find at home; as Gertrude Stein liked to say, "America is my country, but Paris is my hometown."

To read about Paris through smiling Irish—or otherwise Anglo—eyes, check the following list, all expatriate classics: Henry James's ***The Ambassadors*** and ***The American,*** Ernest Hemingway's ***A Moveable Feast,*** James Baldwin's ***Giovanni's Room,*** Henry Miller's ***Tropic of Cancer,*** Djuna Barnes's ***Nightwood***, Anaïs Nin's ***Journals,*** Gertrude Stein's ***Autobiography of Alice B. Toklas,*** W. Somerset Maugham's ***The Moon and Sixpence,*** and George Orwell's ***Down and Out in Paris and London.*** Art Buchwald's memoirs, ***I'll Always Have Paris*** and ***Leaving Home*** recount stories of post-WWII Paris after Liberation. A singularly elegant expatriate yarn or two can be found in Edmund White and Hubert Sorin's ***Our Paris: Sketches from Memory***. *New Yorker* correspondent Adam Gopnik's funny, moving ***Paris to the Moon*** is the latest entry in the expat genre.

(1832). Sand was as famous for her scandalous lifestyle as for her prose, with a string of high-profile relationships, including a 10-year dalliance with **Frédéric Chopin** (see p. 63). Normandy also provided the setting for **Gustave Flaubert's** novel *Madame Bovary* (1856), in which the author developed his characters' psychology through detailed descriptions of their experiences. Prosecuted for immorality in 1857, Flaubert was narrowly acquitted. Six months later, **Charles Baudelaire** was not so lucky; the same tribunal fined him 50 francs. The poet gained a reputation for obscenity, despite the fact that the condemned work, *The Flowers of Evil*, is now recognized as the most influential piece of French poetry of the 19th century.

SOCIALISM & SCIENCE. Baudelaire participated in the 1848 revolution, and his radical political views closely resembled those of the anarcho-socialist innovator **Pierre-Joseph Proudhon.** Born into poverty, Proudhon's sharp mind won him a scholarship to college at Besançon and then Paris where, in 1840, he published the leaflet *What is Property?* His inflammatory reply was that "property is theft." Put on trial in 1842, he only escaped punishment because the jury refused to condemn ideas it could not understand. A pivotal figure in the history of socialism, Proudhon inspired the *syndicaliste* trade-union movement of the 1890s. A more optimistic philosophy was provided by the **Positivism** of **Auguste Comte.** Comte anticipated that science would give way to a fully rational explanation of nature. Science certainly demonstrated a great deal of progress at the time; **Louis Pasteur** showed that disease and fermentation were both caused by microorganisms; famous for his **pasteurization** process, he also solved the problem of transporting beer long distances without spoilage (see **Sights,** p. 115).

NATURALISM & SYMBOLISM. Like its artistic counterpart Impressionism, literary **Symbolism** reacted against stale conventions and used new techniques to capture instants of perception. Led by **Stéphane Mallarmé** and **Paul Verlaine,** the movement was instrumental in the creation of modern poetry as we understand it today, particularly through the work of the precocious **Arthur Rimbaud.** In 1880, a loose grouping of novelists proclaimed the birth of **Naturalism,** a development of Realism that attempted to use a scientific, analytic approach to dissect and reconstruct reality. In practice, there is little to unite the works of such writers as **Emile Zola** and **Guy de Maupassant.** Zola, who went to school with Cézanne, defended the maligned Impressionists during his early days as a journalist, but his life work was *Les Rougon-Macquart*, a 20-novel series which uses the life of the title family to examine every aspect of French life during the Second Empire.

BELLE EPOQUE. Works that confronted the **Dreyfus Affair's** anti-Semitism, like Zola's *J'accuse*, laid the foundation for a whole new literature in France that would explore issues of individual identity—including sexuality, gender, and ethnicity—in 20th-century France. The decadence and social snobbery of the turn of the century was captured by **Marcel Proust** in the seven volumes of *Remembrance of Things Past* (1913-1927). Revolutionary in technique, this autobiographical portrait of Belle Epoque upper-class society inspires a fanaticism which puts Star Wars to shame. Like most serious French authors of the time, Proust was published in the influential *Nouvelle Revue Française*. Founded in 1909, this journal rose to prominence under the guidance of **André Gide,** who won the Nobel Prize in 1947 for morally provocative novels such as *The Counterfeiters* (1924). Throughout his career, Gide was engaged in a rivalry with Catholic revivalist **Paul Claudel.** Claudel struggled unsuccessfully to persuade Gide that divine grace would eventually overcome greed and lust, the basic theme behind plays such as *The Satin Slipper* (1924).

QUEER MODERNISM. Like Proust, Gide and novelist/playwright **Colette** wrote frankly about homosexuality. Proust's portraits of Belle Epoque Parisians in *Sodom and Gomorrah*, Gide's homoerotic novels like *l'Immoraliste*, and Colette's sensual descriptions of opium dens in the 1920s and cabarets in the 1930s in *Le pur et l'impur* and *La Vagabonde* inspired later feminist and homoerotic writing. Authors that continued to explore these new themes include **Jean Genet** in *Querelle* (1947), **Monique Wittig** in *Les Guerillères* (1967), and **Hervé Guibert** in *Fou de Vincent (Crazy about Vincent)*. That particular sexual freedom that seems to characterize the City of Romance, at least in the artistic imagination, was also represented by American and British expatriate writers like **Gertrude Stein** (whose home, shared with Alice B. Toklas, was a gathering place for the expat avant-garde), **Djuna Barnes, F. Scott Fitzgerald**, and **Henry Miller** (see **We'll Always Have Paris,** at right).

DADAISM & SURREALISM. As in art, film, dance, and music, 20th-century French literature moved toward abstraction. Inspired by the nonsensical art movement called Dadaism, the theatrical collaborations of choreographer Serge Diaghilev, set-designer Pablo Picasso, composer Erik Satie, and writer **Jean Cocteau** during WWI laid the foundation for even further abstraction following the war. In France, Dadaism took a literary bent under the influence of Romanian-born **Tristan Tzara,** whose poems of nonsensically scrambled words attacked the structure of language. Tzara's colleagues **André Breton** and **Louis Aragon** soon became dissatisfied with the anarchy of Dada, and set about developing a more organized protest which burst out in 1924 with the publication of Breton's first *Surrealist Manifesto*, in which he expounded its guiding principle: the artistic supremacy of the subconscious. What was not created consciously was difficult to understand consciously—most Surrealist poetry defies analysis. Surrealism exercised a great influence on later absurdist French theater, such as **Eugène Ionesco's** *Rhinocéros*, expatriate **Samuel Beckett's** *Waiting for Godot*, and **Sartre's** *Huis Clos (No Exit)*. Meanwhile, the rising threat of Nazi Germany spurred a call to arms by writers, led by the indomitable **André Malraux.** Active in the Chinese and Spanish civil wars, Malraux drew inspiration from the former for his masterpiece, *The Human Condition* (1933). Another adventurer, **Antoine de St-Exupéry,** used his experiences as an early aviation pioneer to create classics such as *The Little Prince* (1943).

EXISTENTIALISM. The period following the war was intellectually dominated by **Jean-Paul Sartre,** the Grand High Master of **Existentialism.** This philosphy held that life, in itself, was meaningless; only by choosing and then committing oneself to a cause could existence take on a purpose. Sartre committed his own ideas to the stage, dominating French theater in the 1940s and 1950s.

FEMINISM. Existentialist and seminal feminist, Sartre's companion **Simone de Beauvoir** made waves with *The Second Sex* (1949), an essay attacking the myth of femininity. Its famous statement, "One is not born, but becomes a woman" inspired a new generation of feminists in the 50s-70s. With their exploration of gender identity, writers like **Marguerite Duras** *(L'Amant)*, **Nathalie Sarraute** *(Tropismes)*, **Marie Cardinal** *(Les Mots Pour le Dire)*, **Christine Rochefort** *(Les Stances à Sophie)*, **Hélène Cixous** *(Le Rire de la Méduse)*, **Luce Irigaray** *(Ce Sexe Qui n'en est Pas Un)*, and **Marguerite Yourcenar** *(Le Coup de Grace)* sparked feminist movements worldwide. **French Feminism** came into conflict with the American version; the American feminists of were most interested in practical action, while French writes like Cixous, Irigaray, and **Julia Kristeva,** influenced by the psychoanalytic thought of **Jacques Lacan,** were interested in analyzing the ways in which language is gendered and "phallocentric." The founding of the publishing house *Des Femmes* in the 70s ensured that French women writers would continue to have a means of expressing themselves in print.

CAMUS & ABSURDIST THEATER. Though **Albert Camus** is often classed with Sartre, he could hardly be more different. Born into poverty in Algeria, Camus edited the Résistance newspaper *Combat.* Camus's existentialism was marked by a sense of decency; commitment was not enough if it was unfair to others. He achieved fame with his debut novel *The Outsider* (1942), which tells the story of a dispassionate social misfit condemned to death for an unrepentant murder. Camus's play *Caligula* (1945) was an early example of **Anti-Théâtre,** whose adherents laid bare the strangeness of life and the inadequacies of language. In the 50s, existentialists met at Montparnasse cafés to discuss the absurd world around them. In Irish emigré **Samuel Beckett's** *Waiting for Godot* (1953), two men wait and wait, without knowing why or for whom. *Rhinocéros* (1960), by Romanian immigrant **Eugène Ionesco,** portrays the protagonist's perplexity as everyone else turns into a horned African mammal.

POSTCOLONIAL VOICES. In the 20th century, many voices emerged from France's former colonies and protectorates in the **Antilles** (Martinique and Guadeloupe), the **Caribbean** (Haiti), **North America** (Québec), **North Africa** (Algeria, Tunisia, and Morocco, known as the **Maghreb**), and **West Africa** (Senegal, Mali, Côte d'Ivoire, Congo, and Cameroon). Although written in French, these works speak out against France's colonial exploitation, from the 16th-18th century conquest of the Antilles and Caribbean and the 19th-century occupation of North and West Africa to 1960s decolonization and independence (see p. 49). Beginning in 1920s Paris with the foundation of the **Négritude** movement by intellectuals **Aimé Césaire** (Martinique) and **Léopold Sédar Senghor** (Senegal), Francophone literature began to flourish. Césaire's *Cahiers d'un retour au pays natale* and Senghor's *Anthologie de la poésie nègre et malgache* attempted to define a shared history and identity among black Francophones. Their work and the subsequent founding of the press **Présence Africaine** inspired generations of Francophone intellectuals on both sides of the Atlantic, the most celebrated of whom is Antilles writer **Frantz Fanon** *(Les damnées de la terre)*.

MAGHRÉBIN LITERATURE. While France relinquished its protectorates Morocco and Tunisia with relatively little resistance in the 1950s, its refusal to part with Algeria, where over one million French *pied-noirs* resided, erupted into the Algerian War in the 1960s (see p. 49). As a result, much Maghrébin writing is marked by a search for cultural identity, a conflict between colonial and postcolonial history and subjectivity. Some of the most prolific of these writers are **Assia Djébar** *(Les femmes d'Alger dans leur appartement)* from Algeria; **Driss Charibi** *(La civilisation...ma mère!)* from Morocco; and **Albert Memmi** *(La statue de sel)* from Tunisia. North African immigration to France in the 70s, 80s, and 90s has had a profound impact on French language, culture, and politics. Many second- and third-generation Maghrébin writers in France, such as **Mehdi Charef** *(Le thé au harem d'Archi Ahmed)*, have written about *beur* (slang for an Arab in France) culture, racism, and the difficulties of assimilation.

EXPERIMENTAL NOVELS. Experimentation with narrative and perspective in the 50s and 60s led to the **nouveau roman** (the new novel), which abandoned conventional narrative techniques and created new ones, such as *sous conversation* (what people think while in conversation). Among its best known exponents are Sarraute, Duras, and **Alain Robbe-Grillet** *(Projet pour une révolution à New York)*.

POSTMODERN -ISMS. From the 70s to the present day, criticism, **theory**, and philosophy have exerted a great influence over literary, political, and intellectual life in France. **Postmodernism** rejects the possibility of stable meaning and identity, instead seeking to analyze the fragmented and constructed nature of society and the individual. In *The Postmodern Condition: A Report on Knowledge* (1979), **Jean François Lyotard** turned a routine report commissioned by the Canadian government into a postmodernist manifesto, arguing that Modernist thought was too stable and thus constraining. Among the most influential French theorists of the late 20th century are structuralist **Ferdinand de Saussure,** historical "archaeologist" **Michel Foucault** *(Discipline and Punish, The History of Sexuality)*, psychoanalysts **Jacques Lacan** and **Hélène Cixous,** and cultural critic **Jean Baudrillard,** all of whose works have had a profound influence on the practices of feminist and queer theory. Theory and literary criticism, both in France and in the United States, was transformed by **deconstruction,** a practice founded by **Jacques Derrida,** whereby a text's inherent oppositions are examined through careful analysis of language and form. Foucault and Lacan, among others, gave legendary weekly seminars open to the public, suggesting that even the most esoteric theoretical musings are of interest to a large number of Parisians. To many, these thinkers and their various modes of critical inquiry represent the most important intellectual developments of the post-war world. For more on postwar French intellectuals and writers, see **Parisian Intellectuals Abuzz,** p. 178.

FINE ARTS & ARCHITECTURE

ROMAN STONES. Paris's first achievements in architecture were the baths, arenas, and roads created by the Romans, which include the partially reconstructed Arènes de Lutèce and the baths preserved in the **Musée de Cluny** (see **Museums**, p. 142).

GOTHIC CATHEDRALS. Most **Medieval art** aimed to instruct the average 12th- and 13th-century churchgoer on religious themes: as most commoners were illiterate, stained glass and intricate stone facades, like those at **Chartres** (see **Daytripping,** p. 289), **Ste-Chapelle,** and **Notre Dame** (see **Sights,** p. 67), served as large reproductions of the Bible. These churches are stunning examples of **Gothic** architecture, characterized by flying buttresses that allowed for ceilings which soared 15m into the air and enormous stained-glass windows. Monastic industry brought the art of illumination to its height, as monks added ornate illustrations to manuscripts. The **Cluny** and the **Chantilly** museums (see **Daytripping,** p. 295) display manuscripts, including the illuminated **Très Riches Heures du Duc de Berry.**

THE RENAISSANCE. Inspired by the painting, sculpture, and architecture of the Italian Renaissance, 16th-century France imported its styles from Italy. François I had viewed such re-born art during his Italian campaigns, and when he inherited France in 1515, he decided the time had come to put France, artistically, on the map. The king implored friends in Italy to send him works by **Titian** and **Bronzino.** He also imported the artists themselves to create **Fontainebleau** (see **Daytripping**, p. 287), the most perfect example of French Renaissance architecture. **Leonardo da Vinci** appeared soon after with the **Mona Lisa** smilingly in tow as a gift to the French monarch at the Louvre (see **Museums,** p. 135).

BAROQUE EXCESS. In the 17th century under Louis XIV, the delightfully excessive Baroque style swept up from Italy to France. The architecture of **Versailles** (see **Daytripping,** p. 279) benefited from this Italian infusion. The palace, first built over a period of three years (1631-1634), was extravagantly reimagined by Louis XIV during the second half of the century, inspired by the château of **Vaux-le-Vicomte** (see **Daytripping,** p. 293), the 1657 accomplishment of the architect-artist-landscaper triumvirate **Louis Le Vau, Charles Le Brun,** and **André Le Nôtre** (see **Garden Party,** p. 284But the Baroque period had room for realism, even as it indulged a monarch's penchant for gilt and high-heels—the brothers **Le Nain** (who worked together on all their canvases) and **Georges de La Tour** (1593-1652) produced representations of everyday life.

ACADÉMIE ROYALE. Baroque exuberance was subdued by the more serious and classical works of **Nicolas Poussin** (1594-1665). Poussin believed that reason should be the guiding principle of art; he was fortunate enough to enjoy the support of the French **Académie Royale.** Under director **Charles Le Brun** (1619-1690), the traditionalist Academy, founded in 1648, became the sole arbiter of taste in matters artistic, holding annual **salons,** the "official" art exhibitions held in vacant halls of the Louvre, and setting strict, conservative guidelines for artistic technique and subject matter.

ROCOCO. The early 18th century brought on the playful **Rococo** style. Its asymmetric curves and profusion of ornamentation are more successful when kept in the closet, in **Louis XV** interior design, than in architecture. **Antoine Watteau** (1684-1721) captured the secret *rendez-vous* of the aristocracy and **François Boucher** (1703-1770) painted landscapes and scenes from courtly life.

NEOCLASSICISM & REVOLUTIONARY ART. After the Revolution wreacked havoc on symbolic strongholds of the aristocracy like Versailles and Notre Dame, Napoleon I's reign saw the emergence of **Neoclassicism**, exemplified architecturally by the **Eglise de la Madeleine** (see **Sights,** p. 104), a giant imitation of a Greco-Roman temple, and the imposing **Arc de Triomphe** (see **Sights,** p. 100), both begun in 1806. The influence of painter **Jacques-Louis David** (1748-1825) spanned the period from Revolution to Empire; his *Death of Marat* (1793) was a rallying point for Revolutionaries and is considered by some critics to mark the onset of "modernity;" later, he created giant canvases on Classical themes and facilitated the emergence of **Empire style** in fine and decorative art and fashion, which exploited the Greek and Roman iconography so admired by Napoleon. The French Revolution had inspired painters to create heroic depictions of scenes from their own time. Following David, and encouraged by the deep pockets of Napoleon, painters created large, dramatic pictures, often of the emperor as Romantic hero and god, all rolled into one *petit* package. But after Napoleon's fall, few artists painted nationalistic *tableaux*. One exception was **Théodore Géricault** (1791-1824), whose *Raft of the Medusa* (1819) can be seen in the Louvre (see **Museums,** p. 135).

ROMANTICISM AND ORIENTALISM. 19th-century France was ready to settle into respectable, bourgeois ways after the troubling years of France's shift from Republic to Empire. The paintings of **Eugène Delacroix** (1798-1863) were a shock to salons of the 1820s and 1830s. The *Massacre at Chios* (1824) and *The Death of Sardanapalus* (1827) both display an extraordinary sense of color and a penchant for melodrama. Delacroix went on to do a series of "Moroccan" paintings; he shared this Orientalist territory with **Jean-Auguste-Dominique Ingres** (1780-1867), among others. Ingres's most famous representation of the sexual and racial otherness that so fascinated the Romantic imagination is the nearly liquid reclining nude, *La grande odalisque*. Another influential Romantic, **Paul Delaroche** (1797-1859) created charged narratives on large canvases (*The Young Martyr*, 1855).

CLASSICISM & HAUSSMANNIZATION. Aside from a romantically inspired **Gothic revival** led by the so-called "great restorer" **Viollet-le-Duc,** Neoclassicism reigned in nineteenth century architecture, supported by the dominant Ecole de Beaux-arts's strictly classical curriculum. The ultimate expression of 19th-century classicism is **Charles Garnier's** Paris **Opéra** house, built 1862-1875 (see **Sights,** p. 105). Although traces of the past abound, today's city is essentially the Paris remade under the direction of **Baron Georges Haussmann.** From 1852 to 1870, Haussmann transformed Paris from an medieval city to a modern metropolis. Commissioned by Napoleon III to modernize the city, Haussmann tore long, straight boulevards through the tangled clutter and narrow alleys of old Paris, creating a unified network of **grands boulevards.** For more information on Haussmann, see **Haussmania,** p. 102).

REALISM. The late 19th and early 20th century saw the reinvention of painting in France: first, a shift of subject matter to everyday life, and then a radical change in technique. **Impressionism** found its beginnings in the mid-19th century with **Théodore Rousseau** (1812-1867) and **Jean-François Millet** (1814-1875) who were leaders of the **Ecole de Barbizon,** a group of artists who painted nature for its own sake. Landscape painting capturing a "slice of life" paved the way for **Realism.** The Realists were led by **Gustave Courbet** (1819-1877), who focused on everyday subjects but portrayed them larger-than-life on tremendous canvases.

MANET'S MODERNITY. Edouard Manet (1832-1883) facilitated the transition from the Realism of Courbet to what we now consider **Impressionism;** in the 1860s, he began to shift the focus of his work to color and texture. Manet's *Déjeuner sur l'herbe* was refused by the Salon of 1863 due to its naughty Naked Lunch theme (two suited men and a naked woman are shown picnicking in the forest, in a formation taken from Raimondi's *Judgement of Paris*) and revolutionary technique; it was later shown proudly at the Salon des Refusés, along with 7000 other rejected salon works. In the equally scandalous *Olympia* (1862), appropriating the form of Titian's *Venus of Urbino,* Manet boldly reimagined the classically idealized female nude. He depicted a distinctly contemporary Parisian prostitute, wearing only a shoe and staring unapologetically at the viewer, a figure whose fleshly modernity, inserted into the grand Western tradition, disconcerted viewers and earned accusations of pornography and inspired numerous caricatures—and, later, iconic status. Both works can be seen at Paris's fantastic Musée d'Orsay. (see **Museums,** p. 138).

IMPRESSIONISM & POST-IMPRESSIONISM. By the late 1860s Manet's new aesthetic had set the stage for **Claude Monet** (1840-1926), **Camille Pissarro** (1830-1903), and **Pierre-Auguste Renoir** (1841-1919), who began to further explore new techniques. They strove to attain a sense of immediacy; colors were used to capture visual impressions as they appeared to the eye, and light became subject matter. In 1874, these revo-

Painting Paris

Impressionists and Post-Impressionists found inspiration in the landmarks, streets, and inhabitants of their rapidly changing city.

PONT NEUF. Monet and Renoir both painted Paris's oldest bridge looking from the southeast corner in 1872. Renoir's painting captures the bustle of carriages on a sun-drenched day, while Monet's depicts a crowd of gray and purple umbrellas on a misty, dreary one. Pissarro's 1901 view, more colorful and energetic, includes the newly-erected Samaritaine department store.

JARDIN DU LUXEMBOURG. Van Gogh's *Terrace of the Luxembourg Gardens* (1886) experiments with the bright colors of the grove of trees west of pl. Edmond Rostrand. William Singer Sargent's more restrained *Luxembourg Gardens at Twilight* (1879) evokes the calm of the main fountain in the setting sun.

GRANDS BOULEVARDS. Pissarro's *Boulevard Montmartre* (1897) and Van Gogh's *Boulevard de Clichy* (1887) both took advantage of the open spaces created by the new *grands boulevards* to present more distant, abstract views of street life. Gustave Caillebotte's *Street in Paris: Rainy Day* (1877) represents the bourgeois body in the modern city.

GARE ST-LAZARE. For Manet, Monet, and Caillebotte, this seemingly mundane location represented all that was modern and industrial.

lutionary artists had their first group exhibition, and a critic snidely labeled the group "Impressionists." The artists themselves found the label accurate, and their Impressionists' show became an annual event for the next seven years. In the late 1880s, the members of the group inspired **Edgar Degas** (1834-1917), **Gustave Caillebotte** (1848-1894), **Berthe Morisot** (1841-1895), **Henri Fantin-Latour** (1836-1904), and Monet's *Water Lilies* in the early 1900s.

The **Post-Impressionists,** also called **Neo-Impressionists,** were loners. **Paul Cézanne** (1839-1906) painted landscapes using an early Cubist technique in isolation at Aix-en-Provence; **Paul Gauguin** (1848-1903) took up residence in Tahiti where he painted in sensuous color; **Vincent van Gogh** (1853-1890) projected his tortured emotions onto the countryside at Arles (see **Daytripping,** p. 298). **Georges Seurat** (1859-1891) revealed his **Pointillist** technique at the Salon des Indépendants of 1884. Sculptor **Auguste Rodin** (1840-1917) focused on energetic, muscular shaping of bronze (see **Museums,** p. 140).

BOHEMIA & ART NOUVEAU. As the 19th century drew to a close, Bohemia had moved its center to the cabarets and cafés of Montmartre, a refuge from the chaos of the modern city below. **Henri de Toulouse-Lautrec** (1864-1901) captured the spirit of the Belle Epoque in vibrant silkscreen posters that covered Paris, as well as in his paintings of brothels, circuses, and can-can cabarets. The curves of **Art Nouveau** transformed architecture, furniture, lamps, jewelry, fashion, and even the entrances to the Paris **Métropolitain**. The Universal Exhibitions of 1889 and 1900 led to the construction of the **Grand** and **Petit Palais** and the **Eiffel Tower,** which, a century after its controversial construction, remains the best loved landmark in France. Meanwhile, **Charles Frederick Worth** opened the first house of *haute couture*, turning fashion into a sort of commodified art form; for more on Parisian fashion, see **Shopping,** p. 233.

CUBISM & FAUVISM. **Pablo Picasso,** one of the most prolific artists of the 20th century, first arrived in Paris from Spain in 1900 and made a reputation for himself with collectors like writer **Gertrude Stein. Cubism** was a radical movement developed by Picasso and his friend **Georges Braques** (1882-1963) emphasizing an object's form by showing all its sides at once. The word "Cubism" was coined by **Henri Matisse** (1869-1964) as he described one of Braque's landscapes. Matisse, who was engaged in a lifelong contest of rivalry and inspiration with Picasso, moved to squeezing paint from the tube directly onto canvas. This aggressive style earned the name **Fauvism** (from *fauves*, wild animals) and characterizes Matisse's mature works, like *The Dance* (1931-32; see **Museums,** p. 135).

DADAISM & SURREALISM. **Marcel Duchamp** (1887-1968) put Cubism in motion with his *Nude Descending a Staircase* (1912). **Marc Chagall** (1887-1985) moved to Paris from Russia and found himself in La Ruche or "The Beehive" (an artists' colony on the outskirts of Montmartre; see **Sights,** p. 115) with artists like **Fernand Léger** (1881-1955) and **Jacques Lipchitz** (1891-1973). The disillusionment that pervaded Europe after WWI was Duchamp's dropcloth, as he led the **Dada** movement in Paris. The production of "non-art" was for Dadaists a rejection of artistic conventions and traditions. This movement culminated in the exhibition of Duchamp's *La Fontaine* (*The Fountain*, 1917), a urinal that Duchamp turned upside-down.

Surrealism's goal was a union of dream and fantasy with the everyday, rational world in "an absolute reality, a surreality," according to poet and leader of the movement, **André Breton.** The bowler-hatted men of **René Magritte** (1898-1967), the dreamscapes of **Joan Miró** (1893-1983), the patterns of **Max Ernst** (1891-1976), and **Salvador Dalí's** (1904-1989) melting time-pieces arose from time spent in Paris.

1930S PHOTOGRAPHY & ARCHITECTURE. During the 30s, photographers like **Georges Brassaï** (1889-1984), **André Kertész** (1894-1985), and **Henri Cartier-Bresson** began using small cameras to record the streets and *quartiers* of Paris in black and white. Meanwhile, architects began to incorporate new building materials in their designs. A Swiss citizen who lived and built in Paris, Charles-Edouard Jeanneret, known as **Le Corbusier,** was the architectural pioneer in reinforced **concrete.** A prominent member of the legendary **International School,** Le Corbusier dominated his field from the 1930s until his death in 1965, and is famous for such buildings as the Villas La Roche and Jeanneret, which are today all preserved by the **Fondation Le Corbusier** (see **Museums,** p. 155).

NAZI DESTRUCTION & THEFT. The arrival of WWII forced many artists working in Paris to move across the continent or the ocean, and, as the Nazis advanced, the Louvre's treasures were sent to the basements of Paris. On May 27, 1943, hundreds of "degenerate" paintings by Picasso, Ernst, Klee, Léger, and Miró were destroyed in a bonfire in the garden of the Jeu de Paume. Tens of thousands of masterpieces belonging to Jewish collectors were appropriated by the Germans, and only recently have serious inquiries into stolen art been made .

GRANDS PROJETS. The 80s and 90s produced some of Paris's most controversial architectural masterpieces. Inspired by President Giscard d'Estaing's daring **Centre Pompidou** in the late 70s, President Mitterrand initiated his famous 15-billion-franc *Grands Projets* program to provide a series of modern monuments at the dawn of the 21st century (see p. 50). New projects such as the **ZAC (Zone d'Aménagement Concerté)**—which plans to build a new university, sports complex, public garden, and métro in the 13*ème*—continue to transform the city.

CONTEMPORARY ART. Later 20th-century—and early 21st-century—experiments in photography, installation art, video, and sculpture can be seen in the collections and temporary exhibitions of the **Centre Pompidou** and the **Fondation Cartier pour l'Art Contemporain** (see **Museums,** p. 139), as well as in the numerous galleries throughout the city, which are evidence of the continuing vibrancy and creativity of the Parisian art scene (see **Museums,** p. 146).

MUSIC

EARLY MUSIC TO THE REVOLUTION. The early years of music in Paris date back to the Gregorian chant of 12th-century monks in Notre Dame. Other early highlights include the ballads of medieval troubadours, the Renaissance masses of **Josquin des Prez** (c. 1440-1521) and the Versailles court opera of **Jean-Baptise Lully** (1632-87).

During the reign of **Robespierre,** the people rallied to the strains of **revolutionary music,** such as **Rouget de Lisle's** *War Song of the Army of the Rhine.* Composed in 1792, it was taken up with gusto by volunteers from Marseille; as *La Marseillaise*, it became the national anthem in 1795.

GRAND & COMIC OPERA. With the rise of the middle class in the early part of the 19th century came the spectacle of **grand opera,** as well as the simpler **opéra comique.** These styles later merged and culminated in the Romantic **lyric opera,** a mix of soaring arias, exotic flavor, and tragedy (usually death); examples include **Gounod's** *Faust* (1859), **St-Saëns's** *Samson et Dalila* (1877), **Bizet's** *Carmen* (1875), and **Berlioz's** *Les Troyens* (1856-58).

ROMANTICISM TO THE BEGINNINGS OF MODERNISM.. Paris served as musical center for foreign composers during the Romantic period. The half French, half Polish **Frédéric Chopin** (1810-1849) started composing at the age of seven, and his mature works went on to transcend the Romantic style. Chopin mixed with the Hungarian **Franz Liszt,** the Austrian **Félix Mendelssohn,** and the French **Hector Berlioz.**

Music at the turn of the 20th century began a new period of intense, often abstract invention. **Impressionist Claude Débussy** (1862-1918) used tone color and nontraditional scales in his instrumental works *Prélude à l'après-midi d'un faune* (1894) and *La Mer* (1905), as well as his opera *Pelléas et Mélisande* (1902). **Ravel's** use of Spanish rhythm betrayed his Basque origins. When a listener screamed "but he is mad!" at the 1928 premiere of his *Boléro*, the composer retorted, "Aha! She has understood." The music of **Igor Stravinsky,** whose ballet *The Rite of Spring* caused a riot at its 1913 premiere at the Théâtre des Champs-Elysées (see **Sights,** p. 101), was violently dissonant and rhythmic, and began the **Modernist** movement.

KLEIN & NEOSERIALISM. Already famous for his monochromatic *Blue* paintings, in 1960 **Yves Klein** presented *The Monotone Symphony:* three naked models painted a wall blue with their bodies, while the artist conducted an orchestra on one note for 20 minutes. Composer **Pierre Boulez** (born 1925) was an adept of the **Neo-serialist** school, which uses the 12-tone system developed in the 1920s by Austrian Arnold Schoënberg. Always innovative, Boulez's work includes aleatory music and partial compositions, but his greatest influence on modern music has been as director of the **IRCAM** institute in the Centre Pompidou (see **Museums,** p. 139).

JAZZ & CHANSONS. France recognized the artistic integrity of jazz sooner than the United States. In the 1930s, French musicians copied the swing they heard on early Louis Armstrong sides, but the 1934 Club Hot pair of violinist **Stéphane Grapelli** and stylish Belgian-Romany guitarist **Django Reinhardt** were already innovators. After WWII, American musicians streamed into Paris. A jazz festival in 1949 brought the young **Miles Davis** across the pond for a dreamy April in Paris. Pianist **Bud Powell,** drummer **Kenny Clarke,** and others found the respect, dignity, and gigs accorded them reason enough to stay. **Duke Ellington** and others played clubs like the Left Bank hot spot, **Le Caveau de la Huchette** (see **Nightlife,** p. 218), and jazz classics helped the city's rain-slicked streets take on a saxophonic gloss.

the Parisian public has been happiest with the songs of crooner **Charles Aznavour** and the unforgettable **Edith Piaf. Jacques Brel's** and **Juliette Grecco's** popular *chansons* charmed smoky cabarets in the 1960s. Divas like Piaf, the Egyptian-born **Dalida,** and the Québecoise **Fabienne Thibeault** have made way for such new *chanteuses* as **Patricia Kaas, Isabelle Boulay,** and the seductive **Mylène Farmer.**

WORLD MUSIC. A vibrant music scene also emerged from the immigrant communities of the *banlieue* in the 80s and 90s, combining rap, hip hop, and the sounds of African, Arab and French traditions. Some claim that the artistic output of the *banlieue*, including this music and its often caustic lyrics exploring the tensions of racism and ethnic identities, is the where the most important and exciting possibilities for the present and future of French culture lie.

FILM

FRENCH CINEMA. Not long after he and his brother Louis presented the world's first paid screening in a Paris café in 1895, **Auguste Lumière** remarked, "The cinema is a medium without a future." In defiance of this statement, the French strive to reveal the broadest possibilities of film. The French government subsidizes the film industry, and American studios, which dominate the French market, think this policy unfair. But Paris wins in the end, retaining a vibrant film culture.

BEGINNINGS & SURREALISM. The trick cinema of magician-turned-filmmaker **Georges Méliès** astounded audiences with "disappearing" objects, but gave way by 1908 to an emphasis on narrative. At 14 minutes in length, Méliès's *Journey to the Moon* (1902) was the first motion picture to realize the story-telling possibilities of the medium. Paris was the Hollywood of the early days of cinema, dominating production worldwide. New movements in art engaged film and yielded the slapstick *Entr'acte* (1924) by **René Clair,** starring that grand-Dada of impertinence, **Marcel Duchamp,** and **Luis Buñuel's** *Un Chien Andalou* (1928), a marvel of jarring associations featuring the work of Salvador Dalí. The Dane **Carl Dreyer's** *Passion of Joan of Arc* (1928) exhibits a notable passion for close-ups.

THE 20S AND 30S. Although WWI allowed Hollywood to wrest celluloid dominance from a shattered Europe, in the 1920s and 1930s French cinema was the most critically acclaimed in the world under such great directors as **Jean Renoir,** son of the Impressionist painter. *La Grande Illusion*, which he directed in 1937, is a powerful anti-war statement, set in the prisoner of war camps of WWI. His *Les Règles du Jeu* (1939) reveals the erosion of the French bourgeoisie and his country's malaise at the doorstep of war. The 1930s brought sound, crowned by **Jean Vigo's** *Zero for Conduct* (1933), prefiguring the growth of **Poetic Realism** under **Marcel Carné** and writer **Jacques Prévert** (*Daybreak*, 1939). Censorship during the Occupation led to a move from political films to nostalgia and escapist cinema. Carné and Prévert's epic *Children of Paradise* (1943-5) finds in 1840s Paris the indomitable spirit of the French.

NEW WAVE AUTEURS. **Jean Cocteau** carried the poetic into fantasy with *Beauty and the Beast* (1946) and *Orphée* (1950). The Surrealist *Beauty and the Beast* featured an early use of special effects. A group of young intellectuals gathered by critic **André Bazin** took issue with "cinema of quality." Encouraged by government subsidies, they swapped pen for the camera in 1959. **François Truffaut's** *The 400 Blows* and **Jean-Luc Godard's** *A Bout du Souffle (Breathless)* were joined the same year by **Alain Resnais's** *Hiroshima, Mon Amour* (written by Marguerite Duras) and announced the French New Wave *(Nouvelle Vague)*. Aznavour starred in Truffaut's *Shoot the Piano Player* (1960). Three years earlier, a star was born when **Jean Vadim** sent the incomparable **Brigitte Bardot** shimmying naked across the stage in *And God Created Woman*. For more on the New Wave, see **Parisian Intellectuals Abuzz,** p. 178. Other directors of the New Wave are **Jean Rouch** (*Chronicle of a Summer*, 1961), **Louis Malle** (*The Lovers;* 1958), **Eric Rohmer** (*My Night with Maud;* 1969), **Agnès Varda** (*Cléo from 5 to 7;* 1961), and **Chris Marker** (*La Jetée;* 1962). These directors are unified by their interest in categories of fiction and documentary, the fragmentation of linear time, the thrill of youth, speed, cars, and noise, and Hitchcock and Lang's American films. The filmmaker as *auteur* (author) remains a concept crucial to French film, as does the term *"Art et Essai"* to describe what Anglophones call "Art Cinema." Godard emerged as the New Wave oracle of the 60s. His collaborations with actors **Jean-Paul Belmondo** and **Anna Karina,** including *Vivre Sa Vie* (1962) and *Pierrot le Fou* (1965), inspired a generation of filmmakers.

NEW CLASSICS. The world impact of French cinema in the 60s brought wider recognition of French film stars in the 70s and 80s, such as stunning **Catherine Deneuve** *(Belle de jour, Les Parapluies de Cherbourg)* and (*Danton, 1492, Camille Claudel*), as well as, more recently, **Juliette Binoche** *(Blue)* and **Julie Delpy** (*Europa, Europa*). **Jean-Jacques Beineix's** *Betty Blue* (1985), **Claude Berri's** *Jean de Florette* (1986) and sequel *Manon des Sources* (1986), **Louis Malle's** heart-wrenching WWII drama *Au Revoir les Enfants* (1987), **Marc Caro** and **Jean-Pierre Jeunet's** dystopic *Delicatessen* (1991), and Polish **Krzysztof Kieslowski's** three colors trilogy, *Blue* (1993), *White* (1994), and *Red* (1994), have all become classics of 20th-century French cinema. Several recent French films explore the issue of sexual identity, including Belgian **Alain Berliner's** transgender tragicomedy *Ma vie en rose* (1997). The art cinema now prospers under **Marcel Hanoun** (*Bruit d'Amour et de Guerre*; 1997) and **Jacques Doillon** (*Ponette;* 1997). A group of incendiary young directors like **Gaspar Noe** (*Irreversible*; 2003), **Catherine Breillat** (*Romance*; 1999) and **Claire Denis** *(Trouble Every Day*; 2002) have stirred controversy in their attempts to blur the boundaries between pornography and art while exploring some pretty heavy themes, and proving that the French tradition of embracing content and technique far too provocative for Hollywood is alive and well. In 2001, **Jean-Pierre Feunet's** international hit *Le Fabuleux Destin d'Amélie Poulain (Amélie)* was the highest grossing film of the decade in France.

INSIDE

Sights

SEINE ISLANDS

ÎLE DE LA CITÉ

NEIGHBORHOOD QUICKFIND: ***Discover,*** *p. 2;* ***Food & Drink,*** *p. 169;* ***Accommodations,*** *p. 254.*

see map p. 380-381

NOTRE DAME

M: Cité. ☎ 01 53 40 60 87; crypt 01 43 29 83 51. ***Cathedral*** *open daily 8am-6:45pm.* ***Towers*** *open Jan.-Mar. and Oct.-Dec. 10am-5:30pm; Apr.-June and Sept. 9:30am-7:30pm; July-Aug. 9am-7:30pm.* ***Admission*** *€6.10, ages 18-25 €4.10.* ***Tours*** *begin at the booth to the right as you enter. In English W-Th noon, Sa 2:30pm; in French M-F noon, Sa 2:30pm. Free.* ***Confession*** *can be heard in English. Roman Catholic* ***Mass*** *M-F 8, 9am, noon, 6:15pm; Sa 8, 8:45, 10, 11:30am, 12:45, 6:30pm;* ***Vespers*** *sung 5:30pm in* *the choir.* ***Treasury*** *open M-Sa 9:30-12:30pm and 1:30-5:30pm, Su 1:30-5:30pm; last ticket at 5pm. €2.50, students and ages 12-17 €2, 6-12 €1, under 6 free.* ***High Mass*** *with Gregorian chant is celebrated Su 10am, with music at 11:30am, 12:45, 6:30pm. Before Vespers, one of the cathedral organists gives a free recital starting at 4:30pm.* ***Crypt*** *open daily 10am-5:30pm; last ticket sold 30min. before closing. €3.90, over 60 €2.80, under 27 €2.20, under 13 free.*

Once the site of a Roman temple to Jupiter, the ground upon which Notre Dame stands housed three churches before Maurice de Sully began construction of the Catholic cathedral in 1163. De Sully, the bishop of Paris under King Philip II, was concerned with preventing the kind of poor interior design that made Notre Dame's predecessor unbearably dark and cramped. He aimed to create an edifice filled with air and light, in a style that would later be dubbed **Gothic** (see **Life & Times,** p. 59). He died before his plan was completed; it was up to later centuries to rework the cathedral into the composite masterpiece, finished in 1361, that stands today. Royals used Notre Dame for marriage ceremonies, most notably that of **Henri of Navarre** to Marguerite de Valois (see **Life & Times**, p. 41). Royal burials were performed at the St-Denis cathedral, coronations took place at Reims (with the exception of **Henri VI's**, performed at Notre Dame in 1431), and relics went to Ste-Chapelle (See p. 70). But from the beginning, Notre Dame had a particular hold on the public's attention.

In addition to its royal functions, the cathedral was also the setting for notable events like **Joan of Arc's** trial for heresy in 1455. During the Revolution, secularists renamed the cathedral Le Temple de la Raison (The Temple of Reason) and covered its Gothic arches with plaster facades of virtuous Neoclassical design. The church was reconsecrated after the Revolution, and was the site of **Napoleon's** papal coronation in 1804, but the building fell into disrepair and was used to shelter livestock before **Victor Hugo's** 1831 novel *Notre-Dame de Paris (The Hunchback of Notre Dame)* revived the cathedral's popularity and inspired Napoleon III and Haussmann to invest time and money in its restoration. Modifications by **Eugène Viollet-le-Duc** (including a new spire, gargoyles, and a statue of himself admiring his own work) reinvigorated the cathedral in the public consciousness: Notre Dame once again became a valued symbol of civic unity. Indeed, in 1870 and again in 1940 thousands of Parisians attended masses to pray for deliverance from the invading Germans. On August 26, 1944, **Charles de Gaulle** braved Nazi sniper fire to come here and give thanks for the imminent liberation of Paris. All of these upheavals (not to mention the hordes of tourists who invade its sacred portals every day, and the equally sacrilegious 1996 Disney movie of Hugo's novel) seem to have left the cathedral unmarked. In the words of poet e.e. cummings, "The Cathedral of Notre Dame does not budge an inch for all the idiocies of this world."

EXTERIOR

Notre Dame is still in the throes of a massive cleaning project, as it has been for several years, but at least now its newly glittering **West Facade** has been set free from scaffolding. Such restorative efforts are in line with tradition: work on the exterior started in the 12th century and continued into the 17th, when artists were still adding Baroque statues. The oldest work is found above the **Porte de Ste-Anne** (right), mostly dating from 1165-1175. The **Porte de la Vierge** (left), relating the life of the Virgin Mary, dates from the 13th century. The central **Porte du Jugement** (Door of Judgement) was almost entirely redone in the 19th century; the figure of Christ dates from 1885. Revolutionaries wreaked havoc on the facade during the ecstasies of the 1790s when, not content with decapitating Louis XVI, they attacked the statues of the Kings of Judah above the doors, which they interpreted as his ancestors. The heads were found in the basement of the Banque Française du Commerce in 1977 and were installed in the Musée de Cluny (see **Museums,** p. 142).

TOWERS

The two towers—home to the cathedral's most famous fictional resident, Quasimodo the Hunchback—stare with gray solemnity across the square below. Streaked with black soot, the twin towers of Notre Dame were an imposing shadow on the

Paris skyline for years. No more. After two years of sandblasting, the blackened exterior has been brightened, once again revealing the rosary windows and rows of saints and gargoyles that line the cathedral. There's usually a line to make the 422-step climb (look for the mass of people to the left of the cathedral entrance), but it's well worth it. The claustrophobia-inducing staircase emerges onto a spectacular perch, where rows of gargoyles survey the heart of the city, particularly the Left Bank's Latin Quarter and the Marais on the Right Bank. In the South Tower, a tiny door opens onto the 13-ton bell that even Quasimodo couldn't ring: it requires the force of eight people to move. For a striking view of the cathedral, cross Pont St-Louis (behind the cathedral) to Île St-Louis and turn right on quai d'Orléans. At night, the cathedral's buttresses are lit, and the sight is truly awe-inspiring. The Pont de Sully, at the far side of Île St-Louis, also affords an impressive view of the cathedral.

Notre Dame

INTERIOR

The fact that the cathedral can seat over 10,000 people is not the only thing at which to marvel upon entering. From the inside, the cathedral seems to be constructed of soaring, weightless walls. This effect is achieved by the spidery **flying buttresses** that support the vaults of the ceiling from outside, allowing light to fill the cathedral through delicate stained glass windows. Walk down the **nave** (the long, open part of the church) to arrive at the **transept** and an unforgettable view of the **rose windows.** The North window (to the left) is still almost entirely 13th-century glass, and the south and west windows are equally enchanting, though they contain more modern glass. At the center of the 21m north window is the Virgin, depicted as the descendent of the Old Testament kings and judges who surround her. The base of the south window shows Matthew, Mark, Luke, and John on the shoulders of Old Testament prophets, and in the central window Christ is surrounded by the 12 apostles. The cathedral's **treasury,** south of the choir, contains an assortment of glittering robes, sacramental cutlery, and other gilded artifacts from the cathedral's past. The famous Crown of Thorns, supposedly worn by Christ, is "not ordinarily exposed" and is only presented on Fridays during Lent, from 5 to 6pm.

Pont Neuf Garden

Far below the cathedral towers, beneath the pavement of the square in front of the cathedral, the **Crypte Archéologique,** pl. du Parvis du Notre Dame, houses artifacts that were unearthed in the construction of a parking garage. The crypt

Quai d'Anjou

is a virtual tour of the history of Île de la Cité; it houses architectural fragments from various eras throughout Paris's history—from Roman Lutèce up through the 19th-century sewers—as well as temporary art exhibitions.

ELSEWHERE ON THE ÎLE DE LA CITÉ

PALAIS DE LA CITÉ

4, bd. du Palais. M: Cité.

The Palais de la Cité houses the infamous **Conciergerie,** a Revolutionary prison, and **Ste-Chapelle,** the private chapel of St-Louis. Both are remnants from St-Louis's 13th-century palace. Most of the modern Palais is occupied by the **Palais de Justice,** which was built after the great fire of 1776 and is now home to the district courts of Paris.

PALAIS DE JUSTICE

*Within Palais de la Cité, 4, bd. du Palais; use the entrance for Ste-Chapelle. M: Cité. ☎01 44 32 51 51. **Courtrooms** open M-F 9am-noon and 1:30-6pm. Free.*

A wide set of stone steps at the main entrance of the Palais de Justice leads to three doorways: you have your choice of entering through one marked Liberty, Equality, or Fraternity, words that once signified revolution and now serve as the bedrock of French tradition. All trials are open to the public, and even if your French is not up to legalese, the theatrical sobriety of the interior makes a quick visit worthwhile. Choose a door and make your way through the green gates that stand beyond "Equality." Climb the stairs to the second floor and go immediately left (look for signs for "Cour d'Appel"), where guards will let you into a viewing gallery.

STE-CHAPELLE

*4, bd. du Palais. M: Cité. Within Palais de la Cité. ☎01 53 73 78 51, www.monum.fr. **Open** daily Apr.-Sept. 9:30am-6pm. Last admission 30min. before closing. **Admission** €6.10, seniors and ages 18-25 €4.10, under 18 free. Twin ticket with Conciergerie €9, seniors and ages 18-25 €6, under 18 free. Occasional candlelit, classical music **concerts** (€16-30), held in the Upper Chapel mid-March-Oct. Check with FNAC (www.fnac.fr) or inquire at the booth to the left of the ticket-taker for details.*

Ste-Chapelle remains the foremost example of flamboyant Gothic architecture and a tribute to the craft of medieval stained glass. The chapel was constructed in 1241 to house the most precious of King Louis IX's possessions: the Crown of Thorns from Christ's Passion. Bought along with a section of the Cross by the Emperor of Constantinople in 1239 for the ungodly sum of 135,000 pounds, the crown required an equally princely home. Although the crown itself—minus a few thorns that St-Louis gave away in exchange for political favors—has been moved to Notre Dame, Ste-Chapelle is still a wonder to explore. In the comparatively simple Lower Chapel a few "treasures," platter-sized portraits of saints, remain beneath the blue vaulted ceiling dotted with golden fleur-de-lis, though a gift shop takes away some of the effect. But the real star of the building is the Upper Chapel. On sunny days, light pours through its walls of stained glass, illuminating frescoes of saints and martyrs and creating one of the most breathtaking sights in Paris. Read from bottom to top, left to right, the 1136 windows narrate the Bible from Genesis to the Apocalypse.

CONCIERGERIE

*1, quai de l'Horloge, entrance on bd. du Palais, to the right of Palais de Justice. M: Cité. ☎01 53 73 78 50, www.monum.fr. **Open** daily Apr.-Sept. 9:30am-6:30pm; Oct.-Mar. 10am-5pm. Last ticket 30min. before closing. **Admission** €6.10, students €4.10. Includes **tour** in French, 11am and 3pm. For English tours, call in advance.*

The effect of walking into this dark, historically rich monument to the Revolution is a far cry from that of entering its illuminated neighbor, the Ste-Chapelle. Built by Philip the Fair in the 14th century, the Conciergerie is a good example of secular medieval architecture. The name Conciergerie refers to the administrative officer of the Crown who acted as the king's steward, the *Concierge* (Keeper). When Charles

V moved the seat of royal power from Île de la Cité to the Hôtel St-Pol and then to the Louvre, he left this one man in charge of the Parliament, Chancery, and Audit Office on the island. Later, this edifice became a royal prison and was taken over by the Revolutionary Tribunal after 1793. The northern facade, blackened by auto exhaust, is an appropriately gloomy introduction to a building in which 2780 people were sentenced to death between 1792 and 1794. Among its famous prisoners were the 21 Girondins, Napoleon III, and Robespierre. At the farthest corner on the right, a stepped parapet marks the oldest tower, the **Tour Bonbec,** which once housed torture chambers. The modern entrance lies between the **Tour d'Argent,** stronghold of the royal treasury, and the **Tour de César,** used by the Revolutionary Tribunal.

Past the entrance hall, stairs lead to rows of cells complete with replicas of prisoners and prison conditions. Plaques explain how, in a bit of opportunism on the part of the Revolutionary leaders, the rich and famous could buy themselves private cells with cots and tables for writing while the poor slept on straw in pestilential cells. Marie-Antoinette was imprisoned in the Conciergerie for five weeks and the model of her room is one of the most crowded spots on the touring circuit. To escape the crowds, follow the corridor named for "Monsieur de Paris," the executioner during the Revolution; you'll be tracing the final footsteps of Marie-Antoinette as she awaited decapitation on October 16, 1793. Other exhibits tell the story of the Revolutionary factions. In 1914, the Conciergerie ceased to be used as a prison. As visitors can see today, occasional concerts and wine tastings in the Salle des Gens d'Armes have, happily, replaced torture and beheadings.

MÉMORIAL DE LA DÉPORTATION

M: Cité. At the very tip of the island on pl. de l'Île de France, a 5min. walk from the back of the cathedral, and down a narrow flight of steps. ***Open*** *daily Apr.-Sept. 10am-noon and 1-7pm; Oct.-Mar. 10am-noon and 1–5pm. Free.*

This haunting memorial commemorates the 200,000 French victims of Nazi concentration camps. Inside, the focal point is a tunnel lined with 200,000 quartz pebbles, reflecting the Jewish custom of placing stones on the graves of the deceased. To the sides are empty cells and wall carvings of concentration camp names and humanitarian quotations. Near the exit is the simplest and most arresting of these, the injunction, "*Pardonne. N'Oublie Pas*" ("Forgive. Do Not Forget"). The park in which the memorial is located is perfect for a breather after a visit to the tunnel, and is filled with a bevy of sunbathers on nice days.

HÔTEL DIEU

1, pl. du Paris, to the side of Notre Dame. ☎ 01 42 34 82 34. Open daily, 7am-8pm. Free.

A hospital today, the Hôtel Dieu was built in the Middle Ages to confine the sick rather than to cure them. It had guards posted to keep the patients from getting out and infecting the city. More recently, Pasteur did much of his pioneering research inside (see **Life & Times,** p. 56). In 1871, the hospital's proximity to Notre Dame saved the cathedral—*communards* were dissuaded from burning the church for fear that the flames would engulf their hospitalized comrades. The hospital's serene gardens, found within the inner courtyard, regularly feature sculpture exhibitions.

PONT NEUF

Leave Île de la Cité by Paris's oldest bridge, the Pont Neuf (New Bridge), behind pl. Dauphine. Completed in 1607, the bridge was innovative because its sides were not lined by houses. Before the construction of the Champs-Elysées, the bridge was Paris's most popular thoroughfare, attracting peddlers, performers, and thieves. More recently, Bulgarian artist Christo wrapped the bridge in 44,000 sq. m of nylon. You can see the comic gargoyle faces carved into the supports from a Bâteau-Mouche (see **Service Directory,** p. 346), or from the park at the base of the bridge, Square du Vert-Galant. Visiting around sunset is one of the most romantic experiences in Paris: just ask the innumerable couples getting acquainted on its sides.

ÎLE ST-LOUIS

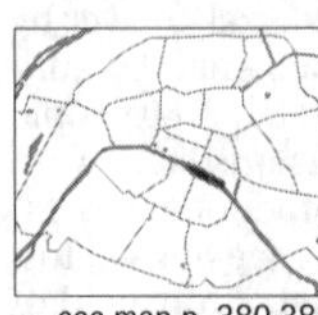

see map p. 380-381

*NEIGHBORHOOD QUICKFIND: **Discover,** p. 2; **Food & Drink,** p. 170; **Shopping,**p. 235.*

QUAI DE BOURBON

Visible immediately to the left after crossing the Pont St-Louis, the quai de Bourbon wraps around the northwest edge of the island.

Sculptor **Camille Claudel** lived and worked at **no. 19** from 1899 until 1913, when her brother, the poet Paul Claudel, had her incarcerated in an asylum. Because she was the protegé and lover of sculptor Auguste Rodin, Claudel's most striking work is displayed in the Musée Rodin (see **Museums,** p. 140). At the intersection of the quai and r. des Deux Ponts sits the café **Au Franc-Pinot,** whose wrought-iron and grilled facade is almost as old as the island itself. The grapes that decorate the ironwork gave the café its name; the *pinot* is a grape from Burgundy. Closed in 1716 after authorities found a basement stash of anti-government tracts, the café-cabaret reemerged as a treasonous address during the Revolution. Cécile Renault, daughter of the proprietor, mounted an unsuccessful attempt on Robespierre's life in 1794. She was guillotined the following year. Today the Pinot houses a mediocre jazz club (live music most nights of the week) and serves lunch and dinner in its vaulted basement.

QUAI D'ANJOU

The quai wraps around the northeast edge of the island to the left after the Pont Marie.

Some of the island's most beautiful old *hôtels* line quai d'Anjou, between Pont Marie and Pont de Sully. **No. 37** was home to John Dos Passos; **No. 29** housed the Three Mountains Press, which was edited by Ezra Pound and published works by Hemingway and Ford Maddox Ford; and **No. 9** was the address of Honoré Daumier, realist painter and caricaturist, from 1846 to 1863, during which time he painted, among other works, *La Blanchisseuse* (*The Washer Woman*), now hanging in the Louvre. The **Hôtel Lambert,** at **no. 2,** was designed by Le Vau in 1640 for Lambert le Riche and was home to Voltaire and Mme. de Châtelet, his mathematician mistress.

RUE ST-LOUIS-EN-L'ÎLE

This street bisects the island lengthwise.

The main thoroughfare of Île St-Louis, r. St-Louis-en-L'Île is home to an enticing collection of shops such as clothing boutiques, gourmet food stores, galleries, and ice cream shops, including the famous Berthillon *glacerie* (see **Shopping,** p. 235 and **Food & Drink,** p. 170).

EGLISE ST-LOUIS-EN-L'ÎLE

*19bis, r. St-Louis-en-l'Île. ☎01 46 34 11 60. **Open** Tu-Su 9am-noon and 3-7pm. Check with FNAC (www.fnac.com) or call the church for concert details; ticket prices vary, around €20 general admission and €15 for students.*

Built by Le Vau in 1726 and much vandalized during the Revolution, this church has more to offer than initially meets the eye. Beyond the building's sooty, humdrum facade, you'll find an ostentatious Rococo interior lit by more windows than appear to exist from the outside. Gilded carvings and paintings are well-labelled in all of the chapels. Legendary for its acoustics, the church hosts concerts (usually classical) throughout the year.

QUAI DE BÉTHUNE

The quai is on the southeast side of the island.

Marie Curie lived at **no. 36,** quai de Béthune, until she died of radiation-induced cancer in 1934. French President **Georges Pompidou** died just a few doors down at **no. 24.**

FIRST ARRONDISSEMENT

NEIGHBORHOOD QUICKFIND: *Discover,* p. 7; *Museums,* p. 146; *Food & Drink,* p. 171; *Nightlife,* p. 206; *Shopping,* p. 235; *Accommodations,* p. 254.

see map p. 374-375

EAST OF THE LOUVRE

Jardin des Tuileries

JARDIN DES TUILERIES

M: Tuileries. ☎01 40 20 90 43. ***Open*** *daily Apr.-Sept. 7am-9pm; Oct.-Mar. 7:30am-7:30pm. English* ***tours*** *from the Arc de Triomphe du Carrousel. Free.* ***Amusement park*** *open late June to mid-Aug. Rides €2-15.*

Sweeping down from the Louvre to the pl. de la Concorde, the Jardin des Tuileries celebrates the victory of geometry over nature. Missing the public promenades of her native Italy, Catherine de Médicis had the gardens built in 1564. In 1649, André Le Nôtre (gardener for Louis XIV and designer of the gardens at Versailles) imposed his preference for straight lines and sculpted trees upon the landscape of the Tuileries. The elevated terrace by the Seine offers remarkable views, including ones of the **Arc de Triomphe du Carrousel** and the glass pyramid of the Louvre's Cour Napoleon. Sculptures by Rodin and others stand amid the garden's cafés and courts. In the summer, the r. de Rivoli terrace becomes an amusement park with children's rides, food stands, and a huge ferris wheel.

Chanel

JEU DE PAUME & L'ORANGERIE

Flanking the pathway at the Concorde end of the Tuileries are the holdings of the **Galerie National du Jeu de Paume** and the **Musée de l'Orangerie** (see **Museums,** p. 146).

PLACE VENDÔME

Stately pl. Vendôme, three blocks north along r. de Castiglione from the Tuileries, was begun in 1687 by Louis XIV. Designed by Jules Hardouin-Mansart, the square was intended to house embassies, but bankers built lavish private homes for themselves here instead. Today, the smell of money is still in the air: bankers, perfumers, and jewelers (including Cartier, at no. 7), line the square.

In the center of pl. Vendôme, Napoleon stands atop a large column dressed as Caesar. In 1805, Napoleon erected the work, modeled after Trajan's Column in Rome and fashioned out of the

Place Vendôme

from the road

Non Means No

"Excuse me, mademoiselle, but may I take some photographs of your feet?" It might be 11am on a Sunday, but that's not too early for a girl walking down a Parisian street to be harassed simply because she exists. Constantly besieged by lewd comments, suggestive gestures, and even late-night grabbing, Paris taught me not only to be thick-skinned, but how to tell a dangerous situation from a merely irritating one—and, of course, how to talk back, in French.

There was the elderly man, wine bottle in hand, who shouted "vive l'amour!" while I searched for a friend, and the scruffy kids who bothered me even when I wore headphones. There was the petrifying evening when, although I was with two friends, a slimy young guy grabbed me by the arm and jeered "oh la la" as he leaned towards his car.

If you're a girl traveling alone in Paris, you might start to wish that you were invisible. Usually, a solid "laissez-moi tranquille" or a "non!" ends the unwanted attention. Learn to keep certain phrases on the tip of your tongue, and avoid being alone after dark. Take care, wear sunglasses, and stand tall. Enjoy the city for all of its pleasures, and try to let the unpleasant encounters become no more than part of the backdrop.

—Neasa Coll

bronze from 1250 cannons he captured at the Battle of Austerlitz. After Napoleon's exile, the Royalist government arrested the sculptor and forced him, on penalty of death, to get rid of the statue. For all his pains, the return of Napoleon from Elba soon brought the original statue back to its perch. Over the next 60 years it would be replaced by the white flag of the monarchy, a renewed Napoleon in military garb, and a classical Napoleon modeled after the original. During the Commune, a group led by uppity artist Gustave Courbet toppled the entire column, planning to replace it with a monument to the "Federation of Nations and the Universal Republic." The original column was recreated with new bronze reliefs, at Courbet's expense. (The painter was subsequently jailed and sent to Switzerland, where he died a few years later; see **Life & Times,** p. 61.)

PALAIS-ROYAL & SURROUNDINGS

PALAIS-ROYAL

Palace closed to the public. Fountain open June-Aug. daily 7am-11pm; Sept. 7am-9:30pm; Oct.-Mar. 7am-8:30pm; Apr.-May 7am-10:15pm. Free.

One block north of the Louvre along r. St-Honoré lies the once regal and racy Palais-Royal. It was constructed between 1628 and 1642 by Jacques Lemercier as Cardinal Richelieu's Palais Cardinal. After the Cardinal's death in 1642, Queen Anne d'Autriche moved in, preferring the Cardinal's palace to the Louvre. She brought with her a young Louis XIV. Louis was the first king to inhabit the palace, but he fled during the Fronde uprising. In 1781, a broke Duc d'Orléans rented out the elegant buildings that enclose the palace's formal garden, turning the complex into an 18th-century shopping mall with boutiques, restaurants, theaters, wax museums, and gambling joints—its covered arcades were a favorite for prostitutes. On July 12, 1789, 26-year-old Camille Desmoulins leapt onto a café table here and urged his fellow citizens to arm themselves, shouting, "I would rather die than submit to servitude." The crowd filed out and was soon skirmishing with cavalry in the Jardin des Tuileries (the Revolutions of 1830 and 1848 began with similar scuffles). In the 19th century, Haussmann's boulevards re-gentrified the area and aristocrats moved back in.

Visitors are free to enjoy the palace from the outside, and in summer, the fountain in the palace garden becomes a mecca for those in need of a foot bath. On the sides of the garden are futuristic metal sculptures by Arnaldo Pomodoro that attract almost as much attention as the palace. In the central courtyard, the **Colonnes de Buren**—a set of black and white striped pillars—are as controversial today as they were when artist Daniel Buren installed them in 1986.

COMÉDIE FRANÇAISE

Located on the southwestern corner of the Palais-Royal (as you're facing the Louvre), the Comédie Française is home to France's leading dramatic troupe (see **Entertainment,** p. 224). Built in 1790 by architect Victor Louis, the theater was the first permanent home for the Comédie Française troupe, created by Louis XIV in 1680. The entrance displays busts of famous actors by equally famous sculptors, including Mirabeau by Rodin, Talma by David d'Angers, and Voltaire by Houdon. Molière, the company's founder, took ill here on stage while playing the role of the Imaginary Invalid. The chair onto which he collapsed is still on display. At the corner of r. Molière and r. Richelieu, Visconti's **Fontaine de Molière** is only a few steps from where Molière died at no. 40.

LES HALLES & SURROUNDINGS

EGLISE DE ST-EUSTACHE

M: Les Halles. Above r. Rambuteau. ☎01 42 36 31 05. ***Open*** *M-F 9am-7:30pm, Su 9:15am-7:30pm. High* ***mass*** *with choir and organ Su 11am and 6pm. Free organ recital Su 5:30-6pm. Hours and masses vary in August; call in advance.*

There is a reason why Richelieu, Molière, and Mme. de Pompadour were all baptized in the Eglise de St-Eustache, and it's probably the same reason why Louis XIV received communion in its sanctuary, and why Mozart chose to have his mother's funeral here. This church is a magnificent blend of history, beauty, and harmony. Eustache (Eustatius) was a Roman general who adopted Christianity upon seeing the sign of a cross between the antlers of a deer. As punishment for converting, the Romans locked him and his family into a brass bull that was placed over a fire until it became white-hot. Construction of the church in his honor began in 1532 and dragged on for over a century. In 1754, the unfinished facade was demolished and replaced with the Romanesque one that stands today—incongruous with the rest of the Gothic building but appropriate for its Roman namesake. The chapels contain paintings by Rubens, as well as the British artist Raymond Mason's bizarre relief *Departure of the Fruits and Vegetables from the Heart of Paris*, commemorating the closing of the market at Les Halles in February 1969. In the summertime, organ concerts commemorate St-Eustache's premieres of Berlioz's *Te Deum* and Liszt's *Messiah* in 1886. Outside the church, Henri de Miller's 1986 sculpture *The Listener* depicts a huge stone human head and hand. Perhaps the glory days of St-Eustache will soon return, as parts of the church are under renovation.

LES HALLES

M: Les Halles.

The métro station Les Halles exits directly into the underground mall. To see the gardens above, use one of the four "Portes" and ride the escalators up towards daylight. Emile Zola called Les Halles *"le ventre de Paris"* ("the belly of Paris"). A sprawling food market since 1135, Les Halles received a much-needed facelift in the 1850s with the construction of large iron-and-glass pavilions to shelter the vendors' stalls. Designed by Victor Baltard, the pavilions resembled the one that still stands over the small market at the Carreau du Temple in the *3ème*. In 1970, authorities moved the old market to a suburb near Orly. Politicians and city planners debated next how to fill *"le trou des Halles"* ("the hole of Les Halles"), 106 open acres that presented Paris with the largest urban redesign opportunity since Haussmannization. Most of

Samaritaine

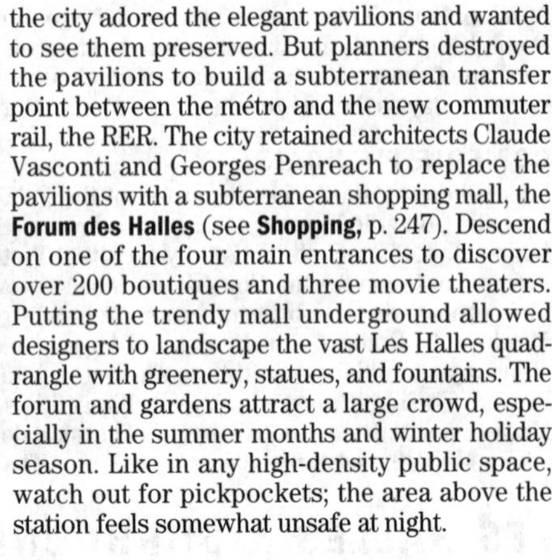

the city adored the elegant pavilions and wanted to see them preserved. But planners destroyed the pavilions to build a subterranean transfer point between the métro and the new commuter rail, the RER. The city retained architects Claude Vasconti and Georges Penreach to replace the pavilions with a subterranean shopping mall, the **Forum des Halles** (see **Shopping,** p. 247). Descend on one of the four main entrances to discover over 200 boutiques and three movie theaters. Putting the trendy mall underground allowed designers to landscape the vast Les Halles quadrangle with greenery, statues, and fountains. The forum and gardens attract a large crowd, especially in the summer months and winter holiday season. Like in any high-density public space, watch out for pickpockets; the area above the station feels somewhat unsafe at night.

Going for a Swim

BOURSE DU COMMERCE

M: Louvre-Rivoli. ☎01 55 65 55 65; www.ccip.fr. ***Open*** *M-F 8:30am-5:30pm.* ***Tours*** *available in French and English. Free; call in advance.*

Between r. du Louvre and the Forum des Halles, the round Bourse du Commerce brokers commodities trading. The beautiful interior makes it worth taking a tour for more than just the business-minded. Inside, the recently restored iron-and-glass cupola forms a tremendous skylight, and the room is surrounded by frescoes. In the Middle Ages, a convent of repentant sinners occupied the site. Catherine de Médicis threw them out in 1572, when a horoscope convinced her that she should abandon construction of the Tuileries and build her palace here instead. Most of the palace was demolished in 1763, leaving only the observation tower of her personal astrologer, as a memorial to her superstition. Louis XV later replaced the structure with a grain market. In 1889, it was transformed into the commodities market that it is today.

FONTAINE DES INNOCENTS

From M: Châtelet, take r. de la Ferronnerie to pl. Joachim du Bellay.

Built in 1548 and designed by Pierre Lescot, the Fontaine des Innocents is the last trace of the Eglise and Cimetière des Sts-Innocents, which once bordered Les Halles. Until its demolition in the 1780s, the edges of the cemetery were crowded by merchants selling produce amid the smell of rotting corpses. The cemetery closed during the Enlightenment's hygienic reforms, and the corpses moved to the catacombs (see p. 113). The fountain is now a hangout for alterna-teens and the overflow crowd from McDonald's.

Les Halles

EGLISE ST-GERMAIN L'AUXERROIS

2, pl. du Louvre. M: Louvre. ☎ 01 42 60 13 96. ***Open*** *daily 9am-12:45pm, 2:30-6pm.* ***Vespers*** *Su 6:30pm.* ***Mass*** *with organ Su 10am.*

Tucked directly behind the Louvre along r. de l'Amiral de Coligny is the Gothic Eglise St-Germain l'Auxerrois. On August 24, 1572, the church's bell sounded the signal for the St. Bartholomew's Day Massacre. Thousands of Huguenots were rounded up by the troops of the Duc de Guise and slaughtered in the streets, while King Charles IX shot at the survivors from the palace window. Visitors are allowed inside to view the violet stained glass windows or listen to Sunday evening vespers.

SAMARITAINE

Starting at 67, r. de Rivoli.

Samaritaine, one of the oldest department stores in Paris, spans a total of three blocks. Founded in 1869, it helped to usher in the age of conspicuous consumption. The building began as a delicate iron and steel construction in 1906 and was revamped in Art Deco style in 1928. The roof, accessible by a quick elevator ride, has one of the best free views of the city. For more information, see **Shopping,** p. 247.

Passages

Bateau-Mouche

Marché Montorgueil

SECOND ARRONDISSEMENT

NEIGHBORHOOD QUICKFIND: ***Discover,*** *p. 7;* ***Food & Drink,*** *p. 172;* ***Nightlife,*** *p. 206;* ***Accommodations,*** *p. 255;* ***Shopping,*** *p. 235.*

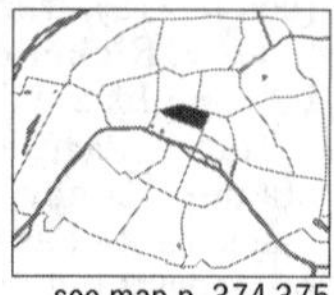
see map p. 374-375

TO THE WEST

GALLERIES & PASSAGES

Behold the world's first shopping malls. In the early 19th century, speculators built **passageways** designed to attract window shoppers ("window lickers," in French), using sheets of glass held in place by lightweight iron rods. This startling new design allowed the daylight in, and gas lighting and electric heating ensured customers (of every sort) would be flocking here at all hours of the day and night. Today, these lovely passages and galleries (the posher version) house a delightful mix of upscale clothing boutiques, cafés, food shops, and gift shops (look for the several that sell antique postcards). Follow our **Insider's City** tour (p. 78) for the best of the *passages*.

the insider's CITY

SHOPPING A L'ANCIENNE

Easy to miss, these mid-block early 19th-century passages are the world's first indoor malls. Afternoon, when the shops are open, is the best time to tour the galleries.

1 Passage du Grand Cerf, 10, r. Dussoubs to 145, r. St-Denis. The most beautiful of the passages; exquisite iron-work and great boutiques, too.

2 Passage de Panoramas, 10, r. St-Marc to 11, bd. Montmartre. The stores at nos. 8 and 47 have been open since the 1830s. A bevy of stamp collector's shops as well.

3 Passage Jouffry, across bd. Montmartre from Panoramas. Bookstores, toy shops, and a phenomenal pastry and candy store–Le Valentin at no. 32.

4 Galerie Vivienne, 4, r. des Petits Champs to 6, r. Vivienne. The grande dame of the *passages*, with marble mosaics and the boutique of bad-boy designer Jean-Paul Gaultier.

BIBLIOTHÈQUE NATIONALE: SITE RICHELIEU

58, r. de Richelieu. M: Bourse. Just north of the Galeries Vivienne and Colbert, across r. Vivienne. Info line ☎ 01 53 79 59 59; galleries 01 47 03 81 10; cabinet 01 47 03 83 30; www.bnf.fr. ***Library*** *open M-Sa 9am-7pm. Books available only to researchers who prove they need access to the collection with a letter of introduction from their university, research advisor, or editor.* ***Tours*** *of the former reading room (through a window), La Salle Labrouste, first Tu of the month 2:30pm in English and French; €6.83; ☎ 01 53 79 86 87.* ***Galleries*** *open Sa 10am-7pm, Su noon-7pm, only when there are exhibits.* ***Admission*** *€5, students €4.* ***Cabinet des Médailles*** *open M-F 1-6pm, Sa 1-5pm. Free.*

With a 12 million volume collection that includes Gutenberg Bibles and first editions dating back to the 15th century, the Bibliothèque Nationale is possibly the largest library in Continental Europe. Since 1642, every book published in France has been required to enter the national archives here, which evolved out of the Bibliothèque du Roi, the royal book depository. To accommodate the ever-increasing volume of books, the government purchased annexes near the library. At one point, books considered a little too titillating for public consumption descended into a room named "Hell," to which only the most qualified scholars were granted access. In the late 1980s, the French government eschewed annexes as a short-term solution and resolved to build the mammoth **Bibliothèque de France** in the 13*ème* (see p. 112), where the collections from the 2*ème's* Richelieu branch were relocated between 1996 and 1998.

Today, Richelieu still holds collections of stamps, money, photography, medals, and maps, as well as original manuscripts written on everything from papyrus to parchment. Scholars must pass through a strict screening process to gain access to the main reading room of the library; be prepared with a letter of introduction from your university, research advisor, or editor that clearly states the nature of your research.

For the viewing of the general public, the **Galerie Mazarin** and **Galerie Mansart** host excellent temporary exhibits of books, prints, and lithographs taken from the collection. Upstairs, the **Cabinet des Médailles** displays coins, medallions, and *objets d'art* confiscated from the French Revolution. Across from the library's main entrance is the **place Louvois.** This *place's* sculpted fountain personifies the four great rivers of France—the Seine, the Saône, the Loire, and the Garonne—as heroic women.

BOURSE DES VALEURS & GALERIE JUNK BOND

r. Notre-Dame des Victoires. M: Bourse. ☎01 49 27 55 55. Open to the public for ***tours*** *Sept.-July M-F 9am-4pm; call to reserve.* ***Admission*** *€8, students €5.*

The Bourse des Valeurs, Paris's stock exchange, had a rather frivolous beginning. Founded in 1724, it soon became a treasure chest for the Bourbon kings, who enjoyed issuing worthless bonds to finance their taste for palaces and warfare. The Jacobins closed the exchange during the Revolution to fend off war profiteers. It was reopened under Napoleon, who loved all things Neoclassical and relocated it to its current somber building, complete with requisite Corinthian columns. Computers have made the edifice all but redundant—a fact perhaps missed by the **Galerie Junk Bond,** an artists' squat across from the Bourse. Junk Bond began in 1999 as a colorful, if belated, protest, with a paint-splattered facade pointedly contrasting its stately neighbor—only to be shut down the following summer. Both buildings now have a sleepy, abandoned feel. The Bourse houses a museum of itself which explains its history and ambiguous present function.

THÉÂTRE MUSICAL POPULAIRE (OPÉRA COMIQUE)

M: Richelieu-Drouot. To the west of the Bourse, between r. Favart and r. Marivaux. For performance information, see ***Music, Opera, and Dance,*** *p. 227.* ***Tickets*** *€7-50. For* ***tours,*** *reserve in advance; ☎01 42 44 45 40. €19.*

Laughs and sobs have resonated at the Opéra Comique for two centuries. Originally built as the Comédie Italienne, it burned down twice in the 1840s and was rebuilt for good in 1898. It was here that Bizet's Carmen first hitched up her skirts, cast a sweltering glance at the audience, and seduced Don José. Under new management, the opera has changed its name and expanded to embrace all kinds of musical theater, including Broadway musicals and operettas.

TO THE EAST

RUE SAINT-DENIS

M: Strasbourg-St-Denis.

In the mid-1970s, Paris's prostitutes demonstrated in churches, monuments, and public squares, demanding unionization. They marched down r. St-Denis, the central artery of the city's prostitution district, to picket for equal rights and protection under the law. Their campaign was successful and prostitution is now legal in France. Officially, sex workers are still not allowed to work the streets, and only the prostitutes themselves can use the money they earn on the job. This creates a problem, since even if a woman uses her earnings to support her family, her husband can be prosecuted as a procurer. Despite its legalization, prostitution is far less common in France than it is in the Netherlands. You might think otherwise along r. St-Denis, an enclave of debauchery, sex shops, and sketchy clubs in the otherwise G-rated *2ème*.

THIRD ARRONDISSEMENT

NEIGHBORHOOD QUICKFIND: ***Discover,*** *p. 8;* ***Museums,*** *p. 79;* ***Food & Drink,*** *p. 174;* ***Nightlife,*** *p. 207;* ***Shopping,*** *p. 237;* ***Accommodations,*** *p. 257.*

see map p. 376-377

CONSERVATOIRE NATIONAL DES ARTS & MÉTIERS

On the corner of r. St-Martin and r. Réaumur. M: Arts et Métiers or Réaumur-Sébastopol. ***Museum:*** *60, r. Réaumur. ☎01 53 01 82 00; www.arts-et-metiers.net.* ***Open*** *Su, Tu-W, F-Sa 10am-6pm, Th 10am-9:30pm.* ***Admission*** *€6.50, students and seniors €4.50, under 18 free.*

Formerly the Abbey St-Martin-des-Champs, this flamboyant Gothic structure became the National Conservatory of Art and Mechanics in 1794, with the goal of perfecting French industry. Its collection of over 80,000 various scientific and mechanical objects and nearly 15,000 detailed scientific drawings is now gathered into the collections of the informative **Musée des Arts et Métiers.** The conservatory's developing design ideas don't stop within its walls; the Arts et Métiers métro station that serves this area is entirely covered in copper tiling in homage to the museum and the conservatory.

RUE VIEILLE-DU-TEMPLE

M: Hôtel-de-Ville or St-Paul. ***Hôtel de Rohan:*** *☎ 01 40 27 63 94 for info on guided tours.*

This street is lined with many stately residences, including the 18th-century **Hôtel de la Tour du Pin** (no. 75) and the more famous **Hôtel de Rohan** (no. 87). Built between 1705 and 1708 for Armand-Gaston de Rohan, Bishop of Strasbourg and alleged love-child of Louis XIV, the *hôtel* has housed many of his descendants. Frequent temporary exhibits allow access to the interior *Cabinet des Singes* and its original decorations. The Hôtel de Rohan, now a part of the National Archives, also boasts an impressive courtyard and fragrant rose garden. Equally engaging are the numerous art galleries that have taken root on the street (see **Museums,** p. 157, for further gallery listings in this area). At the corner of r. des Francs-Bourgeois and r. Vieille-du-Temple are the Gothic turrets of the **Hôtel Hérouët,** which were built in 1528 for Louis XII's treasurer, Hérouët.

ARCHIVES NATIONALES

60, r. des Francs-Bourgeois. M: Rambuteau. ☎ 01 40 27 60 96. ***Open*** *M-F 10am-12:30pm and 2-5:30pm, Sa-Su 2-5:30pm.*

Located in the 18th-century building that once housed the plush Hôtel de Soubise, the **Musée de l'Histoire de France** (see **Museums,** p. 147) is today home to the most famous documents in the National Archives. The Treaty of Westphalia, the Edict of Nantes, the Declaration of the Rights of Man, Marie-Antoinette's last letter, Louis XVI's diary, letters between Benjamin Franklin and George Washington, and Napoleon's will are all preserved here. Louis XVI's entry for July 14, 1789, the day the Bastille was stormed, reads simply "*Rien*" ("Nothing"): out at Versailles, far from the uprising in Paris, it had been a bad day for hunting. Not all of the documents are on display; only those featured in the museum's current exhibit are available for viewing. Call for upcoming events.

MÉMORIAL DU MARTYR JUIF INCONNU

37, r. de Turenne. Near M: St-Paul. ☎ 01 42 77 44 72; fax 01 48 87 12 50. ***Exposition*** *open M-Th 10am-1pm and 2-5:30pm, F 10am-1pm and 2-5pm.* ***Archives*** *open M-W 11am-5:30pm, Th 11am-8pm.*

The Memorial to the Unknown Jewish Martyr was created in 1956 by a committee that included Charles de Gaulle, Winston Churchill, and David Ben-Gurion; it commemorates European Jews who died at the hands of the Nazis and their French collaborators. Usually located in the *4ème*, the memorial is under renovation in 2003, due to the construction of an accompanying museum on the site; the address above is a temporary one.

OTHER SIGHTS

The **Eglise St-Denys du St-Sacrement** is at 68bis, r. de Turenne (M: Chemin Vert or St-Sébastien-Froissart), and houses a dark, well-hidden fresco by celebrated painter Eugène Delacroix. Farther east at 51, r. de Montmorency (M: Etienne-Marcel), is **L'Auberge Nicolas Flamel,** the oldest remaining house in all of Paris, built in 1407. The inscription on the building's facade, "Here, one eats and drinks," still holds true: the ground floor of the home remains a working bistro, though history has lent some weight to its prices.

FOURTH ARRONDISSEMENT

NEIGHBORHOOD QUICKFIND: ***Discover,*** *p. 8;* ***Museums,*** *p. 147;* ***Food & Drink,*** *p. 175;* ***Nightlife,*** *p. 209;* ***Shopping,*** *p. 237;* ***Accommodations,*** *p. 258.*

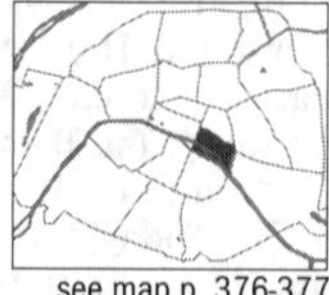

see map p. 376-377

TO THE NORTH: BEAUBOURG

CENTRE POMPIDOU

M: Rambuteau or Hôtel-de-Ville.

One of the most visible examples of renovation in the *4ème* is the Centre Pompidou, the ultramodern exhibition, performance, and research space considered alternately an innovation and an eyesore (see **Museums,** p. 139). Dominating Beaubourg, a former slum *quartier* whose high rate of tuberculosis earned it classification as an *îlot insalubre* (unhealthy block) in the 1930s, the Pompidou shocked Parisians when it opened in 1977, and continues to be the subject of aesthetic debate today. Its architects, Richard Rogers, Gianfranco Franchini, and Renzo Piano, designed an unconventional building whose color-coded electrical tubes (yellow), water pipes (green), and ventilation ducts (blue) line its exterior. Initially designed to accommodate 5000 visitors a day, the center and its **Musée National d'Art Moderne** attract more like 20,000. In fact, more people visit the Pompidou every year than visit the Louvre. The cobblestone square out front gathers artists, musicians, rebels, and passersby. As in all crowded spaces, hold on to belongings and be careful at night.

RUE DES ROSIERS

4 blocks east of Beaubourg, parallel to r. des Francs-Bourgeois. M: St-Paul.

At the heart of the Jewish community of the Marais, the r. des Rosiers is packed with kosher shops, butchers, bakeries, and falafel counters. Until the 13th century, Paris's Jewish community was concentrated in front of Notre Dame. When Philippe-Auguste expelled the Jewish population from the city limits, many families moved to the Marais, just outside the walls. Since then, this quarter has been Paris's Jewish center, taking in the influx of Russian Jews in the 19th century and new waves of North African Sephardim fleeing Algeria in the 1960s. During WWII, many who had fled to France to escape the pogroms of

Hôtel-de-Ville

Centre Pompidou

Musée Picasso

Paris Pride

A short walk through the winding streets of the Marais reveals that Paris's gay community has come out of the closet, nailed the door shut, and painted it pink. Parisian queers celebrate this fact the last weekend of June with the annual **Gay Pride Festival:** boisterous parties, film screenings, demonstrations, art exhibits, concerts, and a lively parade on Saturday afternoon.

The parade begins at place d'Italie and treks northward toward place de la République. Traffic stops. Madonna blasts. The boys get down right on the *rue*. The theme of the parade changes annually. Various groups within the homosexual community march behind their own banners and ride on elaborate and sometimes ostentatious floats. Among groups showing solidarity in 2003 were the "Retired Homos" (who glided by on a float decked with lawn chairs) and the "Aqua Homos" (who chose to play volleyball and wear speedos on their float), and a solitary "Midget Homo" who proudly marched behind the "Asian Homos." Beyond listening to loud music and basking in the spectacle of fabulously dressed drag queens, festival-goers (if lucky) can catch condoms and lubricant thrown from the floats.

Gay Pride Paris, last weekend in June (☎08 36 68 11 31; www.gaypride.fr).

Eastern Europe were murdered by the Nazis. Assisted by French police, Nazi soldiers stormed the Marais and hauled Jewish families to the Vélodrome d'Hiver, an indoor cycling stadium. Here, French Jews awaited deportation to work camps like Drancy, in a northeastern suburb of Paris, or to camps farther east in Poland and Germany. **The Mémorial de la Déportation** on the Île de la Cité commemorates these victims (see p. 71). Today, the Jewish community thrives in the Marais, with two synagogues at 25, r. des Rosiers and 10, r. Pavée, designed by Art Nouveau architect Hector Guimard. The mix of Mediterranean and Eastern European Jewish cultures gives the area a unique flavor, with kugel and falafel served side by side. The gay community also thrives here, though the beautiful androgynous types for which the Marais is famous are more apparent on r. Vielle du Temple and r. Ste-Croix de la Bretonnerie.

RUE VIEILLE-DU-TEMPLE & RUE STE-CROIX DE LA BRETTONERIE

M: St-Paul or Hôtel-de-Ville. One block north of r. de Rivoli, runs the parallel r. du Roi de Sicile (which becomes r. de la Verrerie); r. Vieille-du-Temple meets it and then, 1 block north, r. Ste-Croix de la Brettonerie.

Winter, spring, summer, fall—the intersection of rue Vieille-du-Temple and rue Ste-Croix de la Brettonerie is always hot. The epicenter of Paris's thriving gay community, these streets boast beautiful boys in tight pants and droves of super-stylish men out to cruise and be cruised. Although many establishments fly the rainbow flag, gay and straight go together: chic women wander through trendy boutiques while intellectuals of all orientations sip merlot at **La Belle Hortense,** a bookish oasis in this on-the-move and in-the-scene enclave (see **Food & Drink,** p. 210). Day or night, café or bar, come play where the boys are—that is, if you can stand the heat.

HÔTEL-DE-VILLE & SURROUNDINGS

HÔTEL-DE-VILLE

*29, r. de Rivoli. M: Hôtel-de-Ville. ☎01 42 76 43 43. **Open** M-F 9am-6:30pm when there is an exhibit, until 6pm otherwise. **Tours** given by individual lecturers available for groups with advance reservations; the Hôtel provides a list of lecturers, their dates, and phone numbers; some lecturers offer English tours.*

Paris's grandiose city hall dominates pl. Hôtel-de-Ville, a large square with fountains and Belle Epoque lampposts. The present structure is the second reincarnation of an original edifice built during medieval times. That building served as a meeting hall for water merchants who controlled traffic on the Seine. In 1533, King François I appointed Boccador to expand and reconstruct the structure into a City Hall worthy of Parisians. The result was an impressive building in the Renaissance style of the Loire Châteaux. The building was witness to municipal executions on the *place*. In 1610, Henri IV's assassin was quartered alive here by four horses bolting in opposite directions.

On May 24, 1871, the *communards* (see **Life & Times,** p. 45) doused the building with petrol and set it afire. Lasting a full eight days, the blaze spared nothing but the frame. The Third Republic built a virtually identical structure on the ruins, with a few significant changes. The Republicans integrated statues of their own heroes into the facade: historian Michelet flanks the right side of the building while author Eugène Sue surveys the r. de Rivoli. They also installed brilliant crystal chandeliers, gilded every interior surface, and created a Hall of Mirrors in emulation of Versailles. When Manet, Monet, Renoir, and Cézanne offered their services, they were all turned down in favor of ponderous, didactic artists whose work decorates the Salon des Lettres, the Salon des Arts, the Salon des Sciences, and the Salon Laurens. The Information Office holds exhibits on Paris in the lobby.

Originally called pl. de Grève, the pl. Hôtel-de-Ville made a vital contribution to the French language. Poised on a marshy embankment *(grève)* of the Seine, the medieval square served as a meeting ground for angry workers, giving France the useful phrase *en grève* (on strike). Strikers still gather here amid riot police. Less frequently, the square hosts concerts, TV broadcasts, and light shows against the Hôtel-de-Ville; during the 1998 World Cup and the Euro 2000, fans watched the French victory on huge screens erected on the square.

TOUR ST-JACQUES

39-41, r. de Rivoli. M: Hôtel-de-Ville. Two blocks west of the Hôtel-de-Ville.

The Tour St-Jacques stands in its own park. This flamboyant Gothic tower is the only remnant of the 16th-century Eglise St-Jacques-la-Boucherie. The 52m tower's meteorological station and the statue of Pascal at its base commemorate Pascal's experiments on the weight of air, performed here in 1648. The tower marks Haussmann's *grande croisée* of r. de Rivoli and the bd. Sébastopol, the intersection of his east-west and north-south axes for the city (see p. 102 for more on Haussmann).

SOUTH OF RUE ST-ANTOINE & RUE DE RIVOLI

EGLISE ST-GERVAIS-ST-PROTAIS

R. François-Miron. M: Hôtel-de-Ville. Gregorian chant at matins (Tu-Sa 7:30am), vespers (Tu-Sa 6pm, Su 6:30pm), and high mass (Su 11am).

St-Gervais-St-Protais was named after Gervase and Protase, two Romans martyred under Nero. The classical facade, flamboyant Gothic vaulting, stained glass, and Baroque wooden Christ by Préault are part of a working monastery.

HÔTEL DE BEAUVAIS

68, r. François-Miron. M: Hôtel-de-Ville.

The Hôtel de Beauvais was built in 1655 for Pierre de Beauvais and his wife Catherine Bellier. Bellier, Anne d'Autriche's chambermaid, had an adolescent tryst with the Queen's son, 15-year-old Louis XIV. Later, from the balcony of the *hôtel*, Anne d'Autriche and Cardinal Mazarin watched the entry of Louis XIV and his bride, Marie-Thérèse, into Paris. A century later, as a guest of the Bavarian ambassador, Mozart played his first piano recital here. Restored in 1967, the half-timbered 14th-century **Maison à l'Enseigne du Faucheur** and **Maison à l'Enseigne du Mouton** give a little taste of medieval Paris.

Place des Vosges

Vosges Arcades

Mosquée de Paris

HÔTEL DE SENS

1, r. du Figuier. M: Pont Marie. ***Courtyard*** *open to the public.* ***Library*** *open Tu-F 1:30-8:30pm, Sa 10am-8:30pm; closed July 1-16.*

One of the city's few surviving examples of medieval residential architecture, the Hôtel de Sens was built in 1474 for Tristan de Salazar, the Archbishop of Sens. Its military features reflect the violence of the day; the turrets were designed to survey the streets outside; the square tower served as a dungeon. An enormous Gothic arch entrance—complete with chutes for pouring boiling water on invaders—make the mansion all the more intimidating. The former residence of Queen Margot, Henri IV's first wife, the Hôtel de Sens has witnessed some of Paris's most daring romantic escapades. In 1606, the 55-year-old queen drove up to the door of her home, in front of which her two current lovers were arguing. One opened the lady's carriage door, and the other shot him dead. Unfazed, the queen demanded the execution of the other, which she watched from a window the next day. The *hôtel* now houses the **Bibliothèque Forney** and a quite beautiful courtyard.

LA MAISON EUROPÉENNE DE LA PHOTOGRAPHIE

5-7, r. de Fourcy. M: St-Paul. ☎01 44 78 75 00; www.mep-fr.org. ***Open*** *W-Su 11am-8pm.* ***Admission*** *€5, students and seniors €2.50, under 8 free, W 5-8pm free. Wheelchair accessible.*

Rotating galleries, an in-depth library, and a *vidéothèque* with almost 600 films by photographers are housed in the Hôtel Hénault de Cantobre. La Maison hosts both temporary exhibits featuring international contemporary photography and works from its permanent collection.

EGLISE ST-PAUL-ST-LOUIS

99, r. St-Antoine. M: St-Paul. ☎01 49 24 11 43. ***Open*** *M-Sa 8am-9pm, Su 9am-8:30pm. Free* ***tours*** *at 3pm, every 2nd Su of the month.* ***Mass*** *M 7pm; Tu, W and F 9am and 7pm; Th 9am, 7, 10pm; Sa 9am and 6pm; Su 9:30, 11:15am, 7pm.*

Dating from 1627 (when Louis XIII placed its first stone), the Eglise St-Paul dominates r. St-Antoine. Its large dome—a trademark of Jesuit architecture—is visible from afar, but hidden by ornamentation on the facade. Paintings inside the dome depict four French kings: Clovis, Charlemagne, Robert the Pious, and St-Louis. The embalmed hearts of Louis XIII and Louis XIV were kept in vermeil boxes carried by silver angels before they were destroyed during the Revolution. The church's Baroque interior is graced with three 17th-century paintings of the life of St-Louis and Eugène Delacroix's dramatic *Christ in the Garden of Olives* (1826). The holy-water vessels were gifts from Victor Hugo.

17, RUE BEAUTREILLIS

Jim Morrison died (allegedly of a heart attack) here in his bathtub on the third floor. Don't look for any commemorative plaques: today the building houses a massage parlor. In memoriam, visit his grave at the Cimetière Père Lachaise (see p. 123).

PLACE DES VOSGES & SURROUNDINGS

PLACE DES VOSGES

M: Chemin Vert or St-Paul.

At the end of r. des Francs-Bourgeois sits the magnificent pl. des Vosges, Paris's oldest public square. The *place* is one of the most charming spaces for a picnic or afternoon siesta. The central park, lined with manicured trees centered around four fountains, is surrounded by 17th-century Renaissance townhouses. Kings built several mansions on this site, including the Palais de Tournelles, which Catherine de Médicis ordered destroyed after her husband Henri II died there in a jousting tournament in 1563. Henri IV later ordered the construction of a new public square.

Each of the 36 buildings lining the square has arcades on the street level, two stories of pink brick, and a slate-covered roof. The largest townhouse, forming the square's main entrance, was the king's pavilion; opposite is the smaller pavilion of the queen. Originally intended for merchants, the pl. Royale attracted the wealthy, including Mme. de Sevigné and Cardinal Richelieu. In the 18th century, Molière, Racine, and Voltaire filled the grand parlors with their *bon mots*, and Mozart played a concert here at the age of seven. Even when the city's nobility moved across the river to the Faubourg St-Germain, pl. Royale remained among the most elegant spots in Paris. During the Revolution, however, the 1639 Louis XIII statue in the center of the park was destroyed (the statue there now is a copy), and the park was renamed pl. des Vosges in 1800 after the first department in France to pay its taxes. Follow the arcades around the edge of pl. des Vosges for an elegant promenade, window shopping, and a glimpse of plaques that mark the homes of famous residents. **Théophile Gautier** and **Alphonse Daudet** lived at no. 8. **Victor Hugo** lived at no. 6, which is now a museum of his life and work (see **Museums,** p. 147). The corner door at the right of the south face of the *place* (near no. 5) leads into the garden of the Hôtel de Sully.

HÔTEL DE SULLY

62, r. St-Antoine. M: St-Paul. Info on the Centre ☎01 44 61 20 00. ***Open*** *M-Th 9am-12:45pm and 2-6pm, F 9am-12:45pm and 2-5pm.*

Built in 1624, the Hôtel de Sully, was acquired by the Duc de Sully, minister to Henri IV. Often cuckolded by his young wife, Sully would say when giving her money, "*Voici tant pour la maison, tant pour vous, et tant pour vos amants*" ("Here's some for the house, some for you, and some for your lovers"). The inner courtyard offers fatigued tourists benches and a formal garden. On the side of the *Hôtel* along St-Antoine is the **Centre d'Information des Monuments Nationaux,** which distributes free maps and brochures on monuments and museums.

HÔTEL DE LAMOIGNON

22, r. Malher. M: St-Paul. Exhibition: ☎01 44 59 29 60. ***Open*** *Tu-Sa 10am-6pm, Su noon-7pm.* ***Admission*** *€4, students and seniors €2.* ***Bibliothèque*** *open M-Sa 9:30am-6pm, Su noon-7pm.*

Built in 1584 for Henri II's daughter, Diane de France, the Hôtel de Lamoignon is one of the finest *hôtels particuliers* in the Marais. The facade's Colossal style was copied later in the Louvre. Lamoignon and the adjacent buildings now house the **Bibliothèque Historique de la Ville de Paris,** a non-circulating library of Parisian history with 800,000 volumes. An exhibition hall next door hosts rotating exhibits.

FIFTH ARRONDISSEMENT

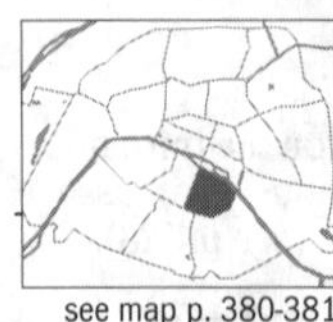

see map p. 380-381

NEIGHBORHOOD QUICKFIND: ***Museums,*** *p. 148;* ***Food & Drink,*** *p. 177;* ***Nightlife,*** *p. 211;* ***Shopping,*** *p. 239;* ***Accommodations,*** *p. 259.*

TO THE WEST: LATIN QUARTER

PLACE ST-MICHEL

M: St-Michel.

The busiest spot in the Latin Quarter, pl. St-Michel holds much political history: the Paris Commune began here in 1871, as did the 1968 student uprising. The majestic 1860 fountain (one of the *5ème's* great meeting places) features bronze dragons, an angelic St-Michel slaying a dragon, and a WWII memorial commemorating the citizens who fell defending their *quartier* during the August 1944 Liberation of Paris.

For those with more of a bent for books than battles, the *place* is still eager to please. Several branches of Gibert Jeune dot the beginning of bd. St-Michel, welcoming visitors to a *quartier* rich in literary history. There are scores of antiquarian booksellers and university presses here, ready to indulge even the most arcane of literary appetites (see **Shopping,** p. 239). For the more gastronomically inclined, the surrounding streets offer a panoply of delights; ice cream shops and crêpe stands line **rue St-Séverin,** while Greek *gyro* (say it with us now, "YEE-row") counters compete for customers on the bustling corridors and bazaar-like alleyways of **rue de la Huchette**. Be sure to **watch your belongings** here, as pickpockets frequent the area.

Lest you're roaming through the *5ème* with your face buried in a book (or a plate of food), the area around pl. St-Michel has some awe-inspiring sights that should not go unnoticed. The nearby **Eglise St-Julien-le-Pauvre** (a right off bd. St-Michel and another right onto r. St-Julien le Pauvre), which dates back to 1170, is one of the oldest churches in Paris. Across bd. St-Jacques is another architectural behemoth, the huge, bizarre, and wonderful **Eglise St-Séverin.** Spiraling columns and sweepingly modern stained glass ornament the interior of the Gothic complex. At the intersection of bd. St-Germain and bd. St-Michel, the **Musée de Cluny's** extraordinary collection of medieval art, tapestries, and illuminated manuscripts has something to suit just about everyone (see **Museums,** p. 142). A major tourist and student thoroughfare, **boulevard St-Michel** (or "*boul' Mich*"") doesn't offer too much charm or flavor—for that, visitors have only to travel a bit farther afield, as many of the traditional bistros of the quarter still hold their ground on nearby streets like **rue Soufflot** and **rue des Fossés St-Jacques**.

LA SORBONNE

45-7, r. des Ecoles. M: Cluny-La Sorbonne or RER: Luxembourg. Walk away from the Seine on bd. St-Michel and turn left on r. des Ecoles to see the main building.

Founded in 1253 by Robert de Sorbon as a dormitory for 16 poor theology students, the Sorbonne is one of Europe's oldest universities. Soon after its founding, it became the administrative base for the University of Paris and the site of France's first printing house, opened in 1469. As it grew in power and size, the Sorbonne often contradicted the authority of the French throne, even siding with England during the Hundred Years' War. But today, the university is safely in the folds of governmental administration, officially known as *Paris IV*, the fourth of the University of Paris's 13 campuses. Its main building, **Ste-Ursule de la Sorbonne,** which is closed to the public, was commissioned in 1642 by Cardinal Richelieu, and is located on r. des Ecoles. Security has been drastically tightened following September 11, but visitors can still stroll through the **Chapelle de la Sorbonne** (entrance off of the pl. de la Sorbonne), an impressive space which houses temporary exhibitions on the arts and letters. Nearby **place de la Sorbonne,** off bd. St-Michel, boasts a flavorful assortment of cafés, bookstores, and—during term-time—students.

COLLÈGE DE FRANCE

11, pl. Marcelin-Berthelot. M: Maubert-Mutualité. From the métro, walk against traffic on bd. St-Germain, turn left on r. Thenard; the entrance to the Collège is at the end of the road, across r. des Ecoles and up the steps. Courses run Sept.-May. Info ☎ 01 44 27 12 11; www.college-de-france.fr. Closed Aug.

Created by François I in 1530 to contest the university's authority, the Collège de France stands behind the Sorbonne with the humanist motto "Doce Omnia" ("Teaches Everything") emblazoned in mosaics on the interior courtyard. The outstanding courses at the Collège, given by such luminaries as Henri Bergson, Pierre Boulez, Paul Valéry, and Milan Kundera, are free and open to all. You'll find lecture schedules posted around the courtyard upon entrance.

PANTHÉON

pl. du Panthéon. M: Cardinal Lemoine. From the métro, walk down r. Cardinal Lemoine and turn right on r. Clovis; walk around to the front of the building to enter. ☎ 01 44 32 18 00. ***Open*** *daily summer 10am-6pm; winter 10am-6pm; last admission 5:15pm.* ***Admission*** *€7, students €4.50, under 18 free. Free entrance first Su of every month Oct.-Mar.* ***Guided tours*** *in French leave from inside the main door daily at 2:30 and 4pm.*

The Panthéon is one of the most beautiful buildings in all of Paris. Visible all the way from the Luxembourg gardens to St-Germain to the Ecole Normale Supérieure, it is an extravagant landmark in a city known for its extravagance. Unreal airiness and geometric grandeur are its architectural claims to fame. But the architecture itself can't take all the credit for the building's renown; its crypt is the final resting place of some of France's most distinguished citizens. The remains of scientists Marie and Pierre Curie, politician Jean Jaurès, Louis Braille, and writers Voltaire, Jean-Jacques Rousseau, Emile Zola, and Victor Hugo are all here. At Hugo's burial in 1885, two million mourners and Chopin's *Marche Funèbre* followed the coffin to its resting place. Fans of *Le Petit Prince* may want to pay homage at the memorial to Antoine de St-Exupéry in the main rotunda. The most recent addition, in November 2002, was Alexandre Dumas.

The inscription in stone across the front of the Panthéon dedicates the building "To great men from a grateful fatherland," but originally, the Panthéon was simply one man's dedication to his wife. In 507, King Clovis converted to Christianity and had a basilica designed to accommodate his tomb and that of his wife, Clotilde. In 512, the basilica became the resting place of **Ste-Geneviève,** who was believed to have protected Paris from the attacking Huns with her prayers. Her tomb immediately became a pilgrimage site, and so many people came to visit the patron saint of Paris that a set of worshippers dedicated themselves to the preservation of her relics and remains, calling themselves *Génovéfains*.

Louis XV was also feeling pretty grateful after surviving a grave illness in 1744, a miracle he ascribed to the powers of Ste-Geneviève. He vowed to build a prestigious monument to the saint and entrusted the design of the new basilica to the architect Jacques-Germain Soufflot in 1755. Louis laid the first stone himself in 1764 and after Soufflot's death, the Neoclassical basilica was continued by architect Jean-Baptiste Rondelet and completed in 1790. The walls of the basilica got an enviable redesign in 1874 when the director of the Musée des Beaux-Arts commissioned some of the finest artists of the time to depict the saint's story.

The Revolution converted the church into a mausoleum of heroes on April 4, 1791, in an attempt to find a place for proletariat poet Mirabeau's body. The poet was interred, only to have his ashes expelled the next year when his correspondence with King Louis XVI was revealed to the public. In 1806, Napoleon reserved the crypt for the interment of those who had given "great service to the State."

The Panthéon's other main attraction is like a fifth-grade experiment taken to new extremes: **Foucault's Pendulum.** The plane of oscillation of the pendulum stays fixed as the Earth rotates around it. The pendulum's rotation is confirmation of the rotation of the Earth for nonbelievers, who included Louis Napoleon III and a large crowd in 1851.

Panthéon

Rue Mouffetard

Sorbonne

EGLISE ST-ETIENNE DU MONT

pl. de l'Abbé Basset, just east of the Panthéon. M: Cardinal Lemoine. Follow directions to the Panthéon; the church is to the right. **Prayers** *sung M-F 4:30-6:30pm.*

While everyone's dying to get in, not all of France's legends are buried in the Panthéon. Pascal and Racine are buried next door in the Eglise St-Etienne du Mont, whose facade takes a lot of artistic license, blending Gothic windows, ancient belfry, and Renaissance dome. Inside, the star of the sanctuary is the outrageous **rood-screen** (the central balcony where priests delivered sermons) made of wildly ornate marble fretwork and flanked on both sides by spiral staircases. On the right side of the nave, check out a Herculean Samson holding up the wood-carved pulpit.

ECOLE NORMALE SUPÉRIEURE

45, r. d'Ulm. Closed to the public.

France's premier university, the Ecole Normale Supérieure is located southeast of the Sorbonne and is part of the *Grands Ecoles*, a consortium of France's best schools. Normale Sup' (as its students, the *normaliens*, call their alma mater) accepts only the most gifted students in its programs in literature, philosophy, and the natural sciences. Its list of prestigious graduates includes Jean-Paul Sarte, Michel Foucault, and Louis Pasteur.

TO THE EAST: PLACE DE LA CONTRESCARPE

RUE MOUFFETARD

M: Cardinal Lemoine, Place Monge, or Censier Daubenton.

South of pl. de la Contrescarpe, **rue Mouffetard** is home to one of the liveliest street markets in Paris (see **Food & Drink,** p. 202), and is generally crowded with a friendly mix of Parisians and visitors. Along with **rue Monge,** the Mouff' is the center, at least in spirit, of the Latin Quarter's tourist and student social life. This most storied of Latin Quarter streets went through various incarnations before ending up as the snaking alley of charming boutiques and restaurants that you see today. It began as a Roman road, and then was the main thoroughfare of a wealthy villa from the 2nd century until the 13th century; some current buildings date back to the 12th century. Poet Paul Verlaine died at no. 39, r. Descartes in 1844. Hemingway lived down the Mouff' at no. 74, r. du Cardinal Lemoine. Perfectly picturesque for an afternoon stroll or

Quartier Latin people-watching is the winding stretch up r. Mouffetard past pl. de la Contrescarpe, and onto **rue Descartes** and **rue de la Montagne Ste-Geneviève.** After working up an appetite, you may want to grab lunch at one of the many reasonably-priced restaurants (see **Food & Drink,** p. 177) and finish off the day with a visit to one of the nearby sights.

JARDIN DES PLANTES

M: Gare d'Austerlitz, Jussieu, or Censier-Daubenton. ☎01 40 79 37 94. ***Jardin des Plantes, Ecole de Botanique, Jardin Alpin,*** *and* ***Roserie*** *open daily summer 7:30am-8pm; winter 7:30am-5:30pm. Free.* ***Grandes Serres,*** *57, r. Cuvier. Open M and W-Su 1-5pm, Apr.-Oct. Sa-Su until 6pm. €2.30, students €1.50.* ***Menagerie Zoo,*** *3, quai St-Bernard and 57, r. Cuvier. Open daily Oct.-Mar. 10am-5:30pm, Apr.-Sept. until 6pm. Last ticket 30min. before closing. €4.60, students €3.05. For admission information to the* ***Musée d'Histoire Naturelle,*** *see* ***Museums,*** *p. 148.*

In the eastern corner of the *5ème* is the Jardin des Plantes 45,000 sq. m of carefully tended flowers and lush greenery. Created in 1635 by Louis XIII's doctor, the gardens originally grew medicinal plants to promote His Majesty's health. Now they're better suited to sunbathers and families than those seeking cures (though joggers still puff by). The gardens are also a sanctuary for the natural sciences, surrounded on both sides by a score of museums, research institutions, and scientific libraries.

If you want to stick to greenery, start in the center, where the charming, rustic **Jardin Alpin** contains more than 2000 different kinds of plants from mountain ranges including the Alps, the Pyrenees, and the Himalayas. The **Ecole de Botanique** is a landscaped botanical garden tended by students, horticulturists, and amateur botanists. The **Roserie** is filled with roses from all over the world (in full bloom in mid-June). On the southern base, the two botanical boxes of the **Grandes Serres** (Big Greenhouses) span two climates: the *serre mexicaine* has desert-dwelling flora, and the *serre tropicale* simulates a humid rain forest with banana plants, orchids, and (yikes!) a few carnivorous plants.

The gardens also include the tremendous **Musée d'Histoire Naturelle** (see **Museums,** p. 148) and the **Ménagerie Zoo.** Although no match for the Parc Zoologique in the Bois de Vincennes (see p. 128), the zoo is home to 240 mammals, 500 birds, and 130 reptiles. During the siege of Paris in 1871, officials raided the zoo for meat, and elephants were served to starving Parisians.

the insider's CITY

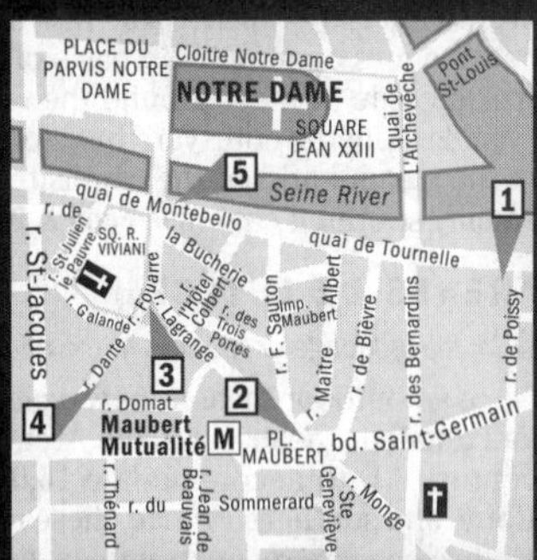

LATIN LOVING

If Paris is for lovers, then its Latin Quarter is for lovers of literature. The 5ème reminds us that the city's literary spirit is still alive and kicking.

1 45, quai de la Tournelle. In 1919, John Dos Passos began writing *Three Soldiers* in a rented apartment here.

2 Pl. Maubert. In 1546, Etienne Dolet was burned here for heresy, with his own library used to fuel the blaze.

3 R. de Fouarre. In the Middle Ages, people sat here on *fouarres* (bales of hay) to listen to lectures at a makeshift open-air college.

4 Librairie Gourmande, 4, r. Dante (☎01 43 54 37 27). There's no better combination: books, food, and wine.

5 Quai de Montebello. Paris's serious booksellers are clustered here. Come to browse or to view a most literary sight: the spired home of Victor Hugo's hunchback.

MOSQUÉE DE PARIS

Behind the Jardin des Plantes at pl. du Puits de l'Ermite. M: Censier Daubenton. From the métro, walk down r. Daubenton; mosque at the end of the street, on the left. ☎ *01 48 35 78 17.* ***Open*** *daily 10am-noon and 2-5:30pm, June-Aug. closes at 6:30pm. Guided* ***tour*** *€3, students €2.* ***Hammam*** *open for men Tu 2-9pm and Su 10am-9pm; women M, W-Th, Sa 10am-9pm and F 2-9pm; €15. 10min. massage €10, 30min. massage €30, bikini wax €11. MC/V.*

The Institut Musulman houses the beautiful Persian gardens, elaborate minaret, and shady porticoes of the Mosquée de Paris, a mosque constructed in 1920 by French architects to honor the role played by the countries of North Africa in WWI. The cedar doors open onto an oasis of blue and white where Muslims from around the world come to meet around the fountains and pray in the carpeted prayer rooms (visible from the courtyard but closed to the public). Frenzied tourists can also relax in the steam baths at the exquisite *hammam* (Turkish bath) or sip mint tea at the equally soothing café (see **Food & Drink,** p. 180).

ARÈNES DE LUTÈCE

M: Place Monge or Jussieu. At the intersection of r. de Navarre and r. des Arènes.

Once an outdoor theater, now a glorified sand-pit (used for pick-up games of soccer and amateur theatricals), the Arènes de Lutèce were built by the Romans in the 1st century AD to accommodate 15,000 spectators. Similar to oval amphitheaters in Rome and southern France, these ruins were unearthed in 1869 and restored in 1910; all the seats are reconstructions. Look for free music festivals and other events happening at the Arènes throughout the summer.

ALONG THE SEINE

SHAKESPEARE & CO. BOOKSTORE

37, r. de la Bucherie. M: St-Michel. ***Open*** *daily noon-midnight.*

A legend among Parisian Anglophones, this shop seeks to reproduce the atmosphere of Sylvia Beach's establishment of the same name at 8, r. Dupuytren (later at 12, r. de l'Odéon), which was a gathering place for expatriates in the 20s, as described memorably by Hemingway in *A Moveable Feast.* Beach famously published James Joyce's *Ulysses* in 1922 after it had been deemed too obscene to print in England and America. The original shop closed in 1941, and George Whitman, alleged grandson of the poet Walt Whitman, opened his rag-tag bookstore, which has itself become a cultish landmark, in 1951. Frequented by Allen Ginsberg and Lawrence Ferlinghetti, Shakespeare (as it is known among its followers) hosts poetry readings, Sunday evening tea parties, a literary festival, and other funky events. No real traces of the Lost Generation, other than in spirit and memory—but plenty of lost boys and girls who call its burlap couches home. For more, see **Shopping,** p. 240.

INSTITUT DU MONDE ARABE

1, r. des Fossés St-Bernard. ☎ *01 40 51 38 38. M: Jussieu. Walk down r. Jussieu away from the Jardin des Plantes and make your first right onto r. des Fossés St-Bernard.* ***Museum*** *open Tu-Su 10am-6pm. €4, reduced rate €3, under 12 free.* ***Library*** *open Tu-Sa 1-8pm, July-Aug. Tu-Sa 1-6pm. Free.*

The Institut du Monde Arabe (IMA) is housed in one of the city's most striking buildings. Facing the Seine, the IMA was built to look like a ship to represent those on which Algerian, Moroccan, and Tunisian immigrants sailed to France. The southern face is comprised of 240 Arabesque portals that open and close, powered by light-sensitive cells that determine how much light is needed to illuminate the interior of the building without damaging the art. Inside, the IMA houses permanent and rotating exhibitions on Maghrébin, Near Eastern, and Middle Eastern Arab cultures as well as a library, research facilities, lecture series, film festivals, and a rooftop terrace; you don't have to eat in the Institut's restaurant to see the gorgeous views of the Seine, Montmartre, and Île de la Cité. For more on the IMA, see **Museums,** p. 148.

JARDIN DES SCULPTURES EN PLEIN AIR

M: Jussieu or Gare d'Austerlitz. From either station, head toward the Seine; the garden stretches along quai St-Bernard.

The Jardin boasts a collection of modern sculpture, including works by Zadkine and Brancusi, on a long stretch of green along the Seine. It's a nice place to read and relax by the river, although in recent years the beauty of many of the embankments has been marred by graffiti.

SIXTH ARRONDISSEMENT

NEIGHBORHOOD QUICKFIND: ***Discover,*** *p. 3;* ***Museums,*** *p. 148;* ***Food & Drink,*** *p. 181;* ***Nightlife,*** *p. 212;* ***Shopping,*** *p. 239;* ***Accommodations,*** *p. 91.*

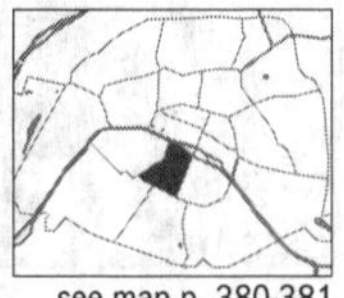

see map p. 380-381

The sleek and stylish *6ème* gives Sorbonne students a run for their intellectual money. The *5ème's* better-kempt older brother, the *6ème* is home to two of Paris's still-vibrant cultural staples: literary cafés and art galleries. The cafés line **boulevard St-Germain-des-Prés** (see **Food & Drink,** p. 181) and are the former stomping grounds of Hemingway, Sartre, Picasso, Camus, Baudelaire, and just about anyone else who was in Paris during the first half of the 20th century. The galleries (see **Museums,** p. 157) display some of the city's (and the world's) most exciting contemporary work, while the **Ecole Nationale Supérieure des Beaux-Arts** (see p. 95) provides a glimpse of future Picassos, even before they hit the galleries. Fashion-as-art also thrives in the *6ème,* with couture boutiques next to unique independent designers. Look, but you probably won't buy—a peek at the price tags, and you'll feel faint (see **Shopping,** p. 239). It's the perfect neighborhood to spend a day admiring beautiful things and reconsidering your own materialism.

JARDIN DU LUXEMBOURG & ODÉON

JARDIN DU LUXEMBOURG

M: Odéon or RER: Luxembourg. ***Open*** *daily dawn-dusk. The wrought-iron gates of the main entrance are on bd. St-Michel. Guided* ***tours*** *in French Apr.-Oct. first W of every month at 9:30am; depart from pl. André Honorat behind the observatory—but it's more pleasant to wander.*

"There is nothing more charming, which invites one more enticingly to idleness, reverie, and young love, than a soft spring morning or a beautiful summer dusk at the Jardin du Luxembourg," wrote Léon Daudet in an absolute fit of sentimentality in 1928. Parisians from all over the flock to these formal gardens to sunbathe, write, stroll, read, and gaze at the rose gardens, central pool, and, of course, at each other. A residential area in Roman Paris, the site of a medieval monastery, and later the home of naughty 17th-century French royalty, the gardens were liberated during the Revolution and are now free to all. Children can sail toy boats in the fountain, ride ponies, and see the *grand guignol* (a puppet show; see **Entertainment,** p. 230) while their parents and granddads pitch *boules.* Saunter through the park's sandy paths, passing sculptures of France's queens, poets, and heroes; challenge the local cadre of aged chessmasters to a game under the shady chestnut trees; sit by the Renaissance facade of the **Palais du Luxembourg;** or have an ice cream at the Buvette des Marionettes. One of the loveliest spots in the Jardin is just east of the Palais, at the **Fontaine des Médicis,** a viney Romantic grotto complete with a murky fish pond and wild, baroque fountain sculptures. A mammoth task-force of gardeners tends this most beloved of Parisian gardens; each spring they plant or transplant 350,000 flowers and move the 150 palm and orange trees out of winter storage. Like in most public parks in Paris, you'll notice "Pelouse Interdit" signs forbidding you from sitting on the grass; use the benches provided or find the grass in the park where lounging is permitted and join the crowds of Parisians picnicking, tanning, and making out.

St-Germain-des-Prés

Palais du Luxembourg

St-Sulpice

PALAIS DU LUXEMBOURG

*About half a dozen **tours** are conducted each summer May-Sept. Places must be reserved the M prior to each tour. Schedule is available from the reception (just ask the guards) or telephone for more information. ☎01 44 54 19 49 to reserve space on the tours; www.monum.fr.*

The Palais du Luxembourg, located within the park and now serving as the home of the French Senate, was built in 1615 at Marie de Médicis's request. Homesick for her native Tuscany, she tried to recreate its architecture and gardens in central Paris. Her builders finished the Italianate palace in a mere five years and Marie moved in 1625. But a feud with the powerful Cardinal Richelieu made her time there brief. Wielding great power, Richelieu banished the Queen Mother in 1630 to Cologne, where she died penniless. The palace went on to house a number of France's most elite nobility, and in later years, became a prison for those nobles awaiting the guillotine and then for Revolutionary Jacobin perpetrators.

The Luxembourg again took center stage during the First and Second Empires. Imprisoned in the palace during the Revolution with her Republican husband, Beauharnais, the future Empress Josephine returned five years later to take up official residence with her second husband, the new Consul Napoleon Bonaparte. During WWII, the palace was occupied by the Nazis, who made it the headquarters of the *Luftwaffe*. In 1879, the palace first served its current function as the meeting place for the Sénat, the upper house of the French Parliament. The president of the senate lives in Petit Luxembourg, originally a conciliatory gift from Marie de Médicis to her nemesis Richelieu.

MUSÉE DU LUXEMBOURG

19, r. de Vaugirard. ☎01 42 34 25 95. M: Odéon or RER: Luxembourg. From the métro, walk through the Carrefour de l'Odéon and down r. de Conde; turn right on r. Vaugirard; the museum entrance is on the left.

Run by the Ministère de la Culture et la Communication, the Musée du Luxembourg is housed in the historic Palais du Luxembourg and offers rotating art exhibitions featuring everything from classical to contemporary artists. **Renovations** are currently making the museum wheelchair-accessible; call for date of reopening.

PALAIS DE L'INSTITUT DE FRANCE

Pl. de l'Institut. M: Pont Neuf. From the métro, walk west on quai du Louvre and cross the Seine on the Pont des Arts. 1 block to the east of the ENSB-A on quai Malaquai. Check Pariscope or L'Officiel des Spectacles for listings of frequent seminars, lectures, and openings.

The Palais de l'Institut de France broods over the Seine beneath its famous black- and gold-topped dome, added to the building in 1663. Designed by Le Vau to lodge a college established in Cardinal Mazarin's will, it has served as a school (1688-1793), a prison (1793-1805), and is now home to the **Académie Française,** which devotes itself entirely to the patronage of the arts, letters, and sciences. The glorious building has housed this branch of the Institut de France since 1806 and is also home to the Bibliothèque Mazarine, founded in 1643. Although the building is not open to the public, peek inside the courtyard to the right (if the doors are open) and get a glimpse of Mazarine's enormous funeral sculpture. The grounds are frequently opened for historical seminars, conferences, and guides; check *Pariscope* for listings.

Musée d'Orsay

THÉÂTRE DE L'ODÉON

M: Odéon. From the métro, walk down r. de l'Odéon to the pl. de l'Odéon.

The Théâtre de l'Odéon is Paris's oldest and largest theater (see **Entertainment,** p. 224). Completed in 1782, it was bought by Louis XVI and Marie-Antoinette for the Comédie Française, a celebrated theater troupe founded by Molière in the 17th century which did not have a theater of its own. Beaumarchais's *Marriage of Figaro*, nearly banned by Louis XVI for its attacks on the nobility, premiered here in 1784 before delighted aristocrats. In 1789, the actor Talma staged a performance of Voltaire's *Brutus* in which he imitated the pose of the hero in Jacques-Louis David's painting. As the Revolution approached, the Comédie Française splintered over the issue of political loyalties. Republican members followed Talma to the Right Bank, settling into the company's current location near the Louvre. Those actors who remained behind were jailed under the Terror and the theater was closed. It later earned the name *théâtre maudit* (cursed theater) after two fires and a chain of failures left it nearly bankrupt. Its present Greco-Roman incarnation dates from an 1818 renovation overseen by David (for more on David, see **Life & Times,** p. 60). The Odéon's fortunes changed after WWII, when it became a venue for experimental theater. On May 17, 1968, student protesters seized the building and destroyed much of its interior before police quelled the rebellion (see **Life & Times,** p. 49).

Eiffel Tower

EGLISE ST-SULPICE

M: St-Sulpice or Mabillon. From the Mabillon métro, walk down r. du Four and make a left onto r. Mabillon. R. Mabillon intersects r. St-Sulpice at the entrance to the

Musée Rodin

kids IN THE CITY

For All the Little People Out There

A world of parks awaits all those touring Paris too cool for Disneyland and too young for Beaujolais and Chanel. The Jardin du Luxembourg (see p. 91) offers ponies, mini sail boats, and enough cotton candy to make a dentist see dollar signs. Explore Parc Monceau (see p. 105), among whose architectural *folies* half of France's ruling elite was wheeled as babies; the Parc des Buttes-Chaumont (see p. 123), whose cliffs and waterfalls will impress pre-teens, and whose *guignols* and explorable creeks are the favorites of many a muddy local child; the expansive Parc de la Villette (see p. 123), whose Cité des Science et de l'Industrie is fun and (gasp!) educational, and whose other gardens are the best in the city for romping about; and the Jardin d'Acclimatation (see p. 126), which has pony rides, mini-golf, a zoo, bumper cars, and carousels. Almost all of the parks also feature *guignols*, traditional French puppet shows which delight both kids and adults. For more on these, see **Entertainment,** p. 230).

church. 2 blocks west of the theater. ☎ *01 46 33 21 78 or 01 42 34 59 60.* **Open** *daily 7:30am-7:30pm. Guided* **tour** *in French daily 3pm.*

The balconied, soot-darkened facade of the Eglise St-Sulpice dominates the large square of the same name, home to children, street vendors, and a lovely fountain. The building was designed by Servadoni in 1733, but remains unfinished despite the efforts of architects over the years to complete it. While the outside may not be all that aesthetically pleasing, the same cannot be said for the church's magnificent interior. In the first chapel on the right are a set of fierce, gestural Delacroix frescoes (*Jacob Wrestling with the Angel* and *Heliodorus Driven from the Temple*). A *Virgin and Child* by Jean-Baptiste Pigalle and an enormous organ are in a rear chapel. In the transept, an inlaid copper band runs along the floor from north to south, connecting a plaque in the south to an obelisk in the north. A ray of sunshine passes through a hole in the upper window of the south transept during the winter solstice, striking marked points on the obelisk at mid-day. A beam of sunlight falls on the copper plaque during the summer solstice and behind the communion table during the spring and autumn equinoxes.

ST-GERMAIN-DES-PRÉS

Known as *le village de Saint-Germain-des-Prés*, the crowded area around **boulevard St-Germain** between St-Sulpice and the Seine is packed with cafés, restaurants, galleries, cinemas, and expensive boutiques.

BOULEVARD ST-GERMAIN

M: St-Germain-des-Prés.

Most famous as the ex-literati hangout of Existentialists (who frequented the Café de Flore) and Surrealists like André Breton (who preferred Deux Magots), the boulevard St-Germain is stuck somewhere between a nostalgia for its intellectual café-culture past and an unabashed delight with all things fashionable and cutting edge. It is home to scores of cafés, both new and old, where expensive cups of coffee can be sipped while watching stylish Parisians. The Boulevard and its many side-streets around r. de Rennes have become a serious shopping area (see **Shopping,** p. 239), filled with designer boutiques from Louis Vuitton to Armani. Together, the appeal of the enduring *vie intellectuelle* and of (somewhat less enduring) fashion trends combine to make the Boulevard one of Paris's busiest and most enticing areas.

EGLISE ST-GERMAIN-DES-PRÉS

3, pl. St-Germain-des-Prés. M: St-Germain-des-Prés. From the métro, walk into pl. St-Germain-des-Prés to enter the church from the front. ☎01 55 42 81 33. **Open** *daily 8am-8pm. Info office open M 2:30-6:45pm, Tu-Sa 10:30am-noon and 2:30-6:45pm. Mass in Spanish Su 5pm.*

The Eglise St-Germain-des-Prés is the oldest standing church in Paris, and it shows: the only decorations on the church's exterior are the pink and white hollyhocks growing to the side. King Childebert I commissioned a church on this site to hold relics he had looted from the Holy Land. Completed in AD 558, it was consecrated by St-Germain, Bishop of Paris, on the very day of King Childebert's death—the king had to be buried inside the church's walls.

The rest of the church's history reads like an architectural Book of Job. Sacked by the Normans and rebuilt three times, the present-day church dates from the 11th century. On June 30, 1789, the Revolution seized the church in a dress rehearsal for the storming of the Bastille. The church then did a brief stint as a saltpeter mill and in 1794, the 15 tons of gunpowder that had been stored in the abbey exploded. The ensuing fire devastated the church's artwork and treasures, including much of its monastic library. Baron Haussmann destroyed the last remains of the deteriorating abbey walls and gates when he extended r. de Rennes to the front of the church and created pl. St-Germain-des-Prés.

Completely redone in the 19th century, the magnificent interior is painted in shades of maroon, deep green, and gold with enough regal grandeur to counteract the building's modest exterior; especially striking are the royal blue and gold-starred ceiling, frescoes (by a pupil of Ingres) depicting the life of Jesus, and decorative mosaics along the archways. In the second chapel—on the right after the apse—a stone marks the interred heart of 17th-century philosopher René Descartes, who died of pneumonia at the frigid court of Queen Christina of Sweden, as well as an altar dedicated to the victims of the September 1793 massacre, in which 186 Parisians were slaughtered in the courtyard. Free maps, with information in English on St-Germain's history, are available at the entrance to the church. The info window has a schedule of the Eglise's frequent concerts (see **Entertainment,** p. 228). As in most churches built for an age without microphones, the acoustics are amazing.

ECOLE NATIONALE SUPÉRIEURE DES BEAUX-ARTS

14, r. Bonaparte, at quai Malaquais. From M: St-Germain-des-Prés. walk down r. Bonaparte. ☎01 47 03 50 00; application info 01 47 03 50 65; www.ensba.fr. **Tours** *on M afternoons by reservation; contact ☎01 47 03 52 15 or marie-paule.delnatte@ensba.fr.* **Exhibition Hall** *(☎01 47 03 50 74) admission €4, students €2. Open Tu-Su 1-7pm. Open days each year allow the opportunity to peruse the studios and teaching areas of the school. Call for schedule and info.*

France's most acclaimed art school, the Ecole Nationale Supérieure des Beaux-Arts was founded by Napoleon in 1811 and soon became the stronghold of French academic painting and sculpture. The current building, the Palais des Etudes, was finished in 1838 and is a mix of architectural styles. Though the public is not normally permitted to tour the building itself, you may be able to prowl around its gated courtyard. The best shot at a glimpse of the lifeblood of the Ecole des Beaux-Arts, however, is to go to the **Exhibition Hall** at no. 13, quai Malaquais, where you can get a look at the cutting-edge painting, photography, and installation work of an exciting new generation of Parisian *artistes*.

ODÉON

Cour du Commerce St-André, branching off bd. St-Germain to the North, is one of the most picturesque walking areas in the *6ème*, with cobblestone streets, centuries-old cafés (including **Le Procope;** see **Food & Drink,** p. 182), and outdoor seating in the summer months. Beyond the arch stands the **Relais Odéon,** a Belle Epoque bistro whose stylishly painted exterior, decked with floral mosaics and a hanging sign, is a fine example of Art Nouveau (see **Life & Times,** p. 62), as is the doorway of no. 7, r. Mazarine, several blocks north. Farther down this passageway, on the top floor of the building on the left, is the site where a Revolutionary-era clandestine press published Marat's *L'Ami du Peuple.* Marat was assassinated by Charlotte Corday in the bathtub of his home, which once stood at the spot where the courtyard meets r. de l'Ancienne Comédie.

Just to the south of bd. St-Germain-des-Prés, the **Carrefour d'Odéon,** a favorite Parisian hangout, is a delightfully boisterous square, filled with bistros, cafés, outdoor seating and cinemas. The **Comptoir du Relais** still holds court here, while newcomer cafés strut their flashy selves across the street. The cafés here are a little quieter than their counterparts on the bd. St-Germain, but that might be because their denizens are thinking and scribbling—there is a nascent wave of literary life swelling up here, and an incursion by the occasional laptop bears witness to it.

PONT DES ARTS

The footbridge across from the Institut, appropriately called the Pont des Arts, is celebrated by poets and artists for its delicate ironwork, beautiful views of the Seine, and its spiritual locus at the heart of France's prestigious Academy of Arts and Letters. Built as a toll bridge in 1803, it was the first bridge to be made of iron. On the day it opened, 65,000 Parisians paid to walk across it; today, it is less crowded, absolutely free, and perfect for a picnic dinner, for viewing the sunset, and for a little romancing.

SEVENTH ARRONDISSEMENT

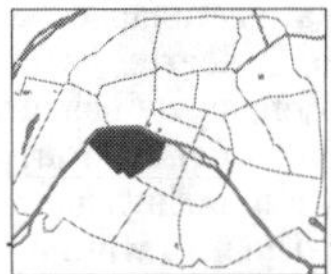

see map pp. 382-383

NEIGHBORHOOD QUICKFIND: ***Discover,*** *p. 4;* ***Museums,*** *p. 149;* ***Food & Drink,*** *p. 183;* ***Nightlife,*** *p. 213;* ***Shopping,*** *p. 242;* ***Accommodations,*** *p. 262.*

TO THE WEST

EIFFEL TOWER

M: Bir-Hakeim or Trocadéro. ☎01 44 11 23 23; www.tour-eiffel.fr. ***Open*** *daily mid-June through Aug. 9am-midnight; Sept.-Dec. 9:30am-11pm (stairs 9:30am-6pm); Jan. through mid-June 9:30am-11pm (stairs 9:30am-6:30pm).* ***Elevator*** *to 1st fl. €3.70, under 12 € 2.10; 2nd fl. €7/€3.80; 3rd fl. €10.20/ €5.30.* ***Stairs*** *to 1st and 2nd fl. €3. Under 3 free. Last access to top 30min. before closing.*

Gustave Eiffel, who also engineered the Statue of Liberty, wrote of the tower he planned: "France is the only country in the world with a 300m flagpole." Designed in 1889 as the tallest structure in the world, the Eiffel Tower was conceived as a monument to engineering that would surpass the Egyptian pyramids both in size and notoriety. But before construction had even begun, shocks of dismay reverberated through the city. Critics dubbed it a "metal asparagus" and the Parisian Tower of Babel. After the building's completion, writer Guy de Maupassant ate lunch every day at its ground-floor restaurant—the only place in Paris, he claimed, from which he couldn't see the offensive thing.

Nevertheless, when it was inaugurated in March 1889 as the centerpiece of the Universal Exposition, the tower earned the love of Paris; nearly 2 million people ascended it during the event. Numbers dwindled during the following decades. As the 20-year property lease approached expiration, Eiffel faced the imminent destruction of his masterpiece. The structure survived due to its importance as a communications tower, a function Eiffel had helped cultivate in the 1890s. The radiotelegraphic center atop the tower worked during WWI to intercept enemy messages, including the one that led to the arrest and execution of Mata Hari, the Danish dancer accused of being a German spy.

With the 1937 World Exposition, the Eiffel Tower again became a showpiece. Eiffel himself walked humbly before it, remarking: "I ought to be jealous of that tower. She is more famous than I am." Luckily, the gold bust of Eiffel at the base of the tower is unmissable. Since the Expo, Parisians and tourists alike have reclaimed the monument in over 150 million visits. An icon of Paris represented on everything from postcards to neckties and umbrellas, Eiffel's wonder still takes the heat from some who see it as Maupassant did: an "excruciating nightmare" overrun with tourists and their trinkets. Don't believe the anti-hype, though. The tower may not be beautiful, but it is a wonder of design and engineering. The top floor, with its unparalleled view, is especially deserving of a visit. And despite the 7000 tons of metal and 2.5 million rivets, which hold together its 12,000 parts, the tower appears light and elegant, especially at night, when it sparkles every hour on the hour.

The cheapest way to ascend the tower is by walking up the first two floors. The **Cinémax** on the first floor is a good excuse to catch your breath and to see films about the tower. But you might as well pay to go all the way up if you're going to go at all; captioned aerial photographs (in English) help you locate landmarks. On a clear day it is possible to see Chartres Cathedral, 88km away.

NEAR THE TOWER

CHAMPS DE MARS

The Champs de Mars (Field of Mars) is a tree-lined expanse that stretches from the Ecole Militaire to the Eiffel Tower. The field is close to the *7ème's* military monuments and museums, and its history suggests a number of reasons why it should celebrate the Roman god of war. The name comes from the days of Napoleon's Empire, when the field was used as a drill ground for the adjacent Ecole Militaire. In 1780, Charles Montgolfier launched the first hydrogen balloon from this site. During the Revolution, the park witnessed civilian massacres and political demonstrations. Today, the god of war would be ashamed to see his park turned into a series of daisy-strewn lawns filled with tourists and hordes of children, where playgrounds, basketball court, and a carousel all encourage fun and games. Perhaps most disturbing for Mars would be the new glass monument to international peace that was erected at the end of the Champs in 2000. Named the *Mur pour la Paix* (Wall for Peace), this structure consists of two large glass walls covered from top to bottom with the word "peace" written in 32 languages. Directly facing the Ecole Militaire, this monument stands in quiet defiance of the formidable façade of the Ecole.

ECOLE MILITAIRE

1, pl. Joffre. M: Ecole Militaire. ☎01 44 42 41 96. Tours available; call ahead for schedule.

In 1751, Louis XV founded the Ecole Militaire at the urging of his mistress, Mme. de Pompadour, who hoped to make officers of "poor gentlemen." In 1784, 5-year-old **Napoleon Bonaparte** enrolled. A few weeks later, he presented administrators with a comprehensive plan for the school's reorganization. By the time he graduated three years later, he was a lieutenant in the artillery. Teachers foretold he would "go far in favorable circumstances." Louis XVI made the building into a barracks for the Swiss Guard, but it was converted back into a military school in 1848. Today, French and foreign officers attend the School of Advanced War Studies.

UNESCO

7, pl. de Fontenoy. M: Ségur. ☎01 45 68 10 60; cinema ☎01 45 68 00 68; www.unesco.org. Bookshop and exhibitions open M-F 9:30am-12:45pm and 2:15pm-5:45pm. Tours M-F 3pm. Free. Pick up a map of the building at the information desk to your left, beyond the elevators after you enter.

The Ecole Militaire's architectural and spiritual antithesis, UNESCO (United Nations Educational, Scientific, and Cultural Organization) occupies the Y-shaped building across the road. Established in 1958 to foster science and culture throughout the world, the agency built this major international monument in Paris. It represents 188 nations and is the creation of three different architects: the American **Breurer,** the Italian **Nervi,** and the Frenchman **Zehrfuss.** Don't be deterred by the institutional exterior: the organization welcomes visitors, and the exhibitions as well as

Ghosts of Paris Past

The *7ème's* quai Voltaire, generally known for its lovely views of Seine bridges, boasts an artistic heritage more distinguished than any other block in the city. At no. 27, Voltaire himself spent his last days. No. 19 housed the cultural powerhouses: Baudelaire from 1856 to 1858 while he wrote *Les Fleurs du Mal (Flowers of Evil)*, Richard Wagner as he composed *Die Meistersinger* between 1861 and 1862, and Oscar Wilde while he was in exile. Eugène Delacroix lived at no. 13 from 1829 to 1836, followed by the landscape painter Jean-Baptiste-Camille Corot. At no. 11, Jean-Auguste-Dominique Ingres died in 1867. The famous Russian ballet dancer Rudolf Nureyev lived at no. 23 from 1981 until his death in 1993.

For more on Parisian literature and fine arts, see **Life & Times**, p. 53.

the permanent pieces are worth the trouble of navigating the entrance. Visitors are encouraged to join the 3pm tour, and the bookshop, just inside on your right, sells everything from United Nations publications to educational computer games, as well as folk music and literature. Temporary exhibitions often have unique pieces of art and craft for sale, while bulletin boards around the elevators list upcoming events and opportunities for language classes, music and dance classes, and even apartments for rent.

In the outer courtyard a huge sculpture by **Henri Moore** called *Figure in Repose* is joined by a mobile by the American artist **James Calder** and a walking man by Swiss sculptor **Alberto Giacometti.** The large framework globe by Danish artist **Erik Reitzel** is eyecatching amongst the hedges. Two murals by **Joán Miró** and **Josep Llorens Artigas,** *The Wall of the Sun* and *The Wall of the Moon*, reside in the Miró Halles. Inside the foyer of Room I is a painting by **Picasso** entitled *The Fall of Icarus*, and next door in the Salle des Actes is a tapestry by architect **Le Corbusier.** Behind Ségur Hall sit a lovely Japanese garden and meditation area, complete with goldfish and turtles to relax the frenzied traveller. By the garden are a set of metal sculptures by **Vassilakis Takis** and an angel from the facade of a Nagasaki church destroyed by the atomic bomb during WWII.

AMERICAN CHURCH IN PARIS

65, quai d'Orsay, at the corner of quai d'Orsay and r. A. Moissan. M: Invalides. ☎ *01 40 62 05 00; www.acparis.org.*

The first American church founded on foreign soil, this brick and stone Gothic church surrounds a charming courtyard. Besides being a good place to find almost every kind of information for visitors (such as apartment listings, language courses, jobs, and *FUSAC* magazine), the church hosts concerts, usually classical chamber or solo music, Sept.-May on Sundays at 6pm.

TO THE EAST

INVALIDES

127, r. de Grenelle. M: Invalides.

The gold-leaf dome of the Hôtel des Invalides shines at the center of the *7ème*. The green, tree-lined **Esplanade des Invalides** runs from the *hôtel* to the **Pont Alexandre III,** an ornate bridge with gilded lampposts from which you can catch a great view of the Invalides and the Seine. The **Musée de l'Armée, Musée des Plans-Reliefs,** and **Musée de l'Ordre de la Libération** are housed within the Invalides museum complex (see

Museums, p. 141), as is **Napoleon's tomb,** in the **Eglise St-Louis.** Enter from either pl. des Invalides or pl. Vauban and av. de Tourville. To the left of the Tourville entrance, the **Jardin de l'Intendant** offers benches among impeccably groomed trees for those who've had their fill of guns and emperors. Lined with foreign cannons, the ditch used to be a moat and still makes it impossible to leave by any but the two official entrances. Be aware that certain areas are blocked to tourists in order to respect the privacy of the war veterans who still live in the hospital.

ASSEMBLÉE NATIONALE

33, quai d'Orsay. M: Assemblée Nationale. ☎01 40 63 61 21; www.assemblee-nat.fr.

The Palais Bourbon's original occupants probably would not recognize their former home. Built in 1722 for the Duchesse de Bourbon, daughter of Louis XIV, the palace is now the home of the French parliament. Guided visits are available, but check website for details. Be prepared to present your passport or national identity card for entrance.

PALAIS DE LA LÉGION D'HONNEUR

At the corner of r. de Lille and r. de Bellechasse. M: Solférino. From the métro, walk up r. Solférino, turn right onto r. de Lille; the short r. de la Légion d'Honneur will be on your left. ☎01 40 62 84 25.

Once the elegant **Hôtel de Salm,** the Palais de la Légion d'Honneur was built in 1786 by architect Pierre Rousseau for the Prince de Salm-Kyrburgh. The mansion came into the hands of Napoleon in 1804. It was burned down during the Commune of 1871, but the members of the Légion rebuilt it soon after, using the original plans. Now it houses the **Musée National de la Légion d'Honneur** (see **Museums,** p. 150). Both the Palais and the museum are **closed for renovations** until early 2004.

LA PAGODE

57bis, r. de Babylone. M: St-François-Xavier. ☎01 45 55 48 48. Movie tickets €7.30; over 60, under 21, students, and M and W €5.80. The café is open daily between show times; coffee €2.50. MC/V.

A Japanese pagoda built in 1895 by the Bon Marché department store magnate M. Morin as a gift to his wife, La Pagode endures as an artifact of the Orientalist craze that swept France in the 19th century. When Mme. Morin left her husband just prior to WWI, the building became the scene of Sino-Japanese soirées, despite the tension between the two countries. In 1931, La Pagode opened its doors to the public, becoming a cinema and swank café where the likes of silent screen star Gloria Swanson were known to raise a glass. The theater closed during the Nazi occupation, despite the Axis allegiance. Although it reopened in 1945, it closed again in 1998 due to a lack of funding, despite having been declared an historic monument by the Ministry of Culture in 1982. It was reopened under private ownership in November 2000. The two-screen cinema continues to show smaller, independent films. See also listing in **Entertainment,** p. 227.

HÔTEL MATIGNON

57, r. Varenne. M: Varenne.

Once owned by Talleyrand, Hôtel Matignon is now the official residence of the prime minister. The Hôtel does not permit visitors. Nearby, at 53, r. Varenne, a plaque commemorates American novelist Edith Wharton, one of the first of the early 20th century expatriates. She lived at this address from 1910-1920.

EGLISE ST-THOMAS D'AQUIN

On r. de Gribeauval, off r. du Bac. M: Rue du Bac. ☎ 01 49 24 11 43. Open M-F 8:45am-7pm, Sa 8:45am-noon and 2:30-7pm, Su and daily during the summer 8:45am-noon and 4-7pm.

The 17th-century Eglise St-Thomas d'Aquin was originally dedicated to St-Dominique but was reconsecrated by revolutionaries as the Temple of Peace. While the church facade is an unassuming continuation of the city block, the interior is fantastically decorated with murals on the walls and ceiling, particularly behind the altar. The church holds occasional organ concerts., and information about group pilgrimages within Europe can be found on the bulletin boards inside the main entrance.

EGLISE ST-FRANÇOIS-XAVIER

12, pl. du Président Mithouard, on bd. des Invalides. M: St-François-Xavier. Open M and Tu-Th 7:45am-noon and 2:30-7:45pm, W and F 7:45am-12:45pm and 2:30-7:45pm, Sa 8:45am-12:30pm and 2:30-7:45pm, Su 8:45am-12:45pm and 3-7:45pm.

Within its blue and red stained-glass windows, this beautiful church offers sanctuary from the endless noise and chaos of city streets. Built between 1861 and 1874, its grand size provides much room for reflection, and candles may be lit for an offering.

EIGHTH ARRONDISSEMENT

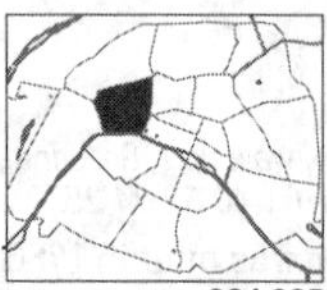

see map pp. 384-385

NEIGHBORHOOD QUICKFIND: ***Discover,*** *p. 9;* ***Museums,*** *p. 150;* ***Food & Drink,*** *p. 184;* ***Nightlife,*** *p. 213;* ***Shopping,*** *p. 243;* ***Accommodations,*** *p. 263.*

ALONG THE CHAMPS-ELYSÉES

ARC DE TRIOMPHE

M: Charles de Gaulle-Etoile. ☎01 44 09 89 84. ***Open*** *daily Apr.-Sept. 10am-11pm; Oct.-Mar. 10am-10:30pm. Last entry 30min. before closing.* ***Admission*** *€7, ages 18-25 €4.50, under 17 free. Expect lines even on weekdays, although you can escape the crowds if you go before noon. You will kill yourself trying to dodge the 10 "lane" merry-go-round of cars (and face a hefty fine), so use the pedestrian underpass on the right side of the Champs-Elysées facing the Arc. Buy your ticket in the pedestrian underpasses before going up to the ground level. AmEx/MC/V for charges over €14.*

It's hard to believe that the Arc de Triomphe, looming gloriously above the Champs-Elysées at pl. Charles de Gaulle-Etoile, was first designed as a huge, bejeweled elephant. The world's largest triumphal arch crowns a flattened hill between the Louvre and Pont de Neuilly—an ideal vantage point that, in 1758, excited the imagination of the architect Ribart, whose ambition it was to erect an animal of monumental proportions. Fortunately for France, construction of this international symbol of her military prowess was not actually undertaken until 1806, when Napoleon envisioned a monument somewhat more appropriate for welcoming troops home. Unfortunately for Napoleon, however, he was exiled before the monument was completed. Louis XVIII ordered the completion of the Arc in 1823 and dedicated it to the war in Spain and its commander, the Duc d'Angoulême. Designed in the end by Chalgrin, the Arc de Triomphe was consecrated in 1836; the names of Napoleon's generals and battles are engraved inside.

Since Napoleon, the arch has been a magnet for various triumphant armies. The victorious Prussians marched through in 1871, inspiring the mortified Parisians to purify the ground with fire. On July 14, 1919, however, the Arc provided the backdrop for an Allied celebration parade headed by Maréchal Foch. His memory is now honored by the boulevard that bears his name and stretches out from the Arc into the 16*ème*. French sanctification of the Arc was frustrated once more during WWII; Frenchmen were reduced to tears as the Nazis goose-stepped through their beloved arch. After the torturous years of German occupation, a sympathetic Allied army made sure a French general would be the first to drive under the famous edifice.

The **Tomb of the Unknown Soldier** has lain under the Arc since November 11, 1920. Its marker bears the inscription, "Here lies a French soldier who died for his country, 1914-1918" and represents the 1,500,000 Frenchmen who died during WWI. Inside the Arc, visitors can climb 205 steps up a winding staircase to the *entresol* between the Arc's two supports, and 29 farther to the museum. There is an elevator for the less ambitious; the lines for it are always long. Forty-six steps beyond the museum, the **terrasse** observation deck, at the top of the Arc, provides a brilliant view of the Champs-Elysées, the tree-lined av. Foch, and the "Axe Historique"—from the Arc de Triomphe du Carrousel and the Louvre Pyramid (see p. 73) at one end to the Grande Arche de la Défense (see p. 131) at the other.

AVENUE DES CHAMPS-ELYSÉES

M: Charles de Gaulle-Etoile. The Champs runs from the pl. Charles de Gaulle-Etoile southeast to the pl. de la Concorde.

The avenue des Champs-Elysées is the most famous of the 12 symmetrical avenues radiating from the huge rotary of pl. Charles de Gaulle-Etoile. The Champs is lined with chain stores ranging from the most celebrated (and guarded) clothing boutiques to the low-budget Monoprix. Expensive cafés stand in contrast to fast-food outlets, and most restaurants along the Champs cater to the abundant tourists with English menus and service. Although it has been a fashionable avenue since Marie de Médicis ploughed its first incarnation, the Cours-la-Reine, through fields and marshland in 1616, it remained unkempt until the early 19th century, when the city built sidewalks and installed gas lighting. From that point on, the Champs flourished, and where elegant houses, restaurants, and less subdued bars and panoramas sprung up, the *beau monde* was guaranteed to see and be seen. The infamous Bal Mabille opened in 1840 at no. 51. At no. 25, visitors have the rare chance of seeing a true *hôtel particulier* from the Second Empire—here the Marquise de Paiva, adventuress, famous courtesan, and spy, entertained the luminaries of the era. In recent years, the Champs has become thoroughly commercialized, and its glamor has faded. But Jacques Chirac has made a concerted effort to resurrect the avenue, widening the sidewalks, planting more trees, and building underground parking lots. Today, the avenue is an intriguing mixture of old and new, inviting tourists to tramp through enormous superstores and dance till dawn in glitzy nightclubs, while managing to preserve pockets of greenery along with remnants of timeless glamor. Crowds walk the avenue day and night, but do take care when hailing taxis in the mad post-clubbing rush. The tree-lined streets merge with park space just past av. Franklin D. Roosevelt, one of the six avenues that radiate from the Rond Point des Champs-Elysées. Av. Montaigne, lined with Paris's finest houses of *haute couture*, runs southwest. For help conquering the Champs-Elysées along with the rest of Paris, visit the enormous **tourist office** at no. 127 (see **Service Directory,** p. 345).

FOUQUET'S

99, av. des Champs-Elysées (☎01 47 23 70 60). M: George V.

Today, you can watch others cling desperately to the Champs's glorious past at Fouquet's, a famous and outrageously expensive café-restaurant where French film stars (supposedly) hang out. Open since 1899, the red-awninged eatery still hosts the French answer to the Oscars, the annual César awards (see **Food & Drink,** p. 185).

THÉÂTRE DES CHAMPS-ELYSÉES

*15, av. Montaigne. M: Alma-Marceau. ☎01 49 52 50 50. For **tours,** call ☎01 44 54 19 30; €3.80.*

Built by the Perret brothers in 1912 with bas-reliefs by Bourdelle, the Théâtre des Champs-Elysées is best known for staging the controversial premiere of Stravinsky's *Le Sacre du Printemps*. Vaslav Nijinsky's choreography had the dancers dressed in feathers and rags, hopping about pigeon-toed to evoke primitivism, and a riot ensued. The three *salles* still host operatic, orchestral, and dance performances (see **Entertainment,** p. 230, for full listing).

PALAIS DE L'ELYSÉE

M: Champs-Elysées-Clemenceau.

The guards pacing around the house at the corner of av. de Marigny and r. du Faubourg St-Honoré are protecting the Palais de l'Elysée. Built in 1718, the Palais was later home to Louis XV's mistress Madame de Pompadour; after her divorce from

How Paris Cleaned Up Its Act

Like a clock, twelve straight boulevards radiate outwards from the pl. Charles de Gaulle. A view through the arc at the foot of the Louvre aligns with the Obelisk in the pl. de la Concorde, the Arc de Triomphe, and the modern arch at La Défense. Café-lined streets and wide tree-lined boulevards seem as organic to Paris as the murky snaking of the Seine. Yet none of this is an accident. And, despite our modern notions that Paris is a city to which pleasure—be it amorous, gastronomic, artistic, or commercial—comes naturally, the city's charm is as calculated as the strategic application of paint to a courtesan's lips, and the city wasn't always so beautiful.

Social commentator Maxime Du Camp observed in the mid-19th century: "Paris, as we find it in the period following the Revolution of 1848, was uninhabitable. Its population…was suffocating in the narrow, tangled, putrid alleyways in which it was forcibly confined." Sewers were not used until 1848, and waste and trash rotted in the Seine. Streets followed a maddening 12th-century design; in some *quartiers*, winding thoroughfares were no wider than 3.5m. Toadstool-like rocks lined the streets allowing pedestrians to jump to safety as carriages sped by. In the hands of the Seine prefect, Baron Georges-Eugène Haussmann, bureaucrat and social architect under Emperor Louis Napoleon, the city's medieval layout was demolished and replaced with a new urban vision guided by the second emperor's technological, sanitary, and political agenda.

Haussmann replaced the tangle of medieval streets with his sewers, trains, and *grand boulevards*. The prefect's vision bisected Paris along two central, perpendicular axes: the r. de Rivoli and the bd. de Sébastopol (which extended across the Seine to the bd. St-Michel). Haussmann, proclaiming the necessity of unifying Paris and promoting trade among the different *arrondissements*, saw the old streets as antiquated impediments to modern commercial and political progress. His wide boulevards swept through whole neighborhoods of cramped row houses and little passageways; incidentally, he displaced 350,000 of Paris' poorest residents.

The widespread rage at Haussmann's plans reinforced the emperor's desire to use the city's layout to reinforce his authority. The old, narrow streets has been ideal for civilian insurrection in preceding revolutions; rebels built barricades across street entrances and blocked off whole areas of the city from the government's military. Haussmann believed that creating *grands boulevards* and carefully mapping the city could bring to an end the use of barricades, and more importantly, prevent future uprisings. However, he was gravely mistaken. During the 1871 revolt of the Paris Commune, which saw the deposition of Louis Napoleon and the rise of the Third Republic, the *grands boulevards* proved ideal for the construction of higher and stronger barricades.

Despite the underlying political agenda of Haussmannization, many of the prefect's changes were for the better. Haussmann transformed the open-air dump and grave (for the offal of local butchers and the bodies of prisoners) at Montfauçon with the whimsical waterfalls, cliffs, and grottoes of the Parc des Buttes-Chaumont. Paris became eminently navigable, and to this day a glance down one of Paris's many grands boulevards will offer the *flâneur* (lit. "wanderer") an unexpected lesson in the layout of the city. Stroll down the bd. Haussmann, the street bearing its architect's name. En route to the ornate Opéra Garnier, one glimpses the Church of the Madeleine and the Gare St-Lazare; Haussmann's layout silently links these monuments to religion, art, and industry. The facades of the *grands magasins* (department stores) Printemps and Galeries Lafayette, respectively resemble a temple and a theater, again suggesting something of the religious and the panoptic in the art of strolling and shopping along Paris's grand streets.

It is hard to imagine the city of Paris as a sewer-less, alley-ridden metropolis; but it is perhaps all the more beautiful today if we do so.

***Charlotte Houghteling** has worked on Let's Go's* Middle East, Egypt, *and* Israel *titles. She wrote her senior thesis on the development of department stores during the Second Empire and is completing her M.Phil. at Cambridge on the consumer society of Revolutionary Paris.*

***Sara Houghteling** was a Researcher-Writer for* Let's Go: France 1999 *and has taught at the American School in Paris. She is now a graduate student in creative writing at the University of Michigan.*

Napoleon, Josephine Bonaparte lived here. Napoleon III was also once a resident. Since 1870, it has served as state residence of the president of France, currently Jacques Chirac. Entrance requires personal invitation.

GRAND & PETIT PALAIS

M: Champs-Elysées-Clemenceau.

At the foot of the Champs-Elysées, the Grand and Petit Palais face one another on av. Winston Churchill. Built for the 1900 World's Fair, they were widely received as a dazzling combination of "banking and dreaming," exemplifying the ornate art nouveau architecture. While the Petit Palais houses an eclectic mix of artwork, its big brother has been turned into a space for temporary exhibitions on architecture, painting, sculpture, and French history. The Grand Palais also houses the **Palais de la Découverte,** a science museum/playground for children (see **Museums,** p. 150). The Palais is most beautiful at night, when its statues are backlit and the glass dome glows greenly from within.

AROUND PLACE DE LA CONCORDE

PLACE DE LA CONCORDE

M: Concorde.

Paris's largest and most infamous public square forms the eastern terminus of the Champs-Elysées. If you are standing between the Champs-Elysées and the Tuileries Gardens, the *place* affords a fine view of the gold-domed Invalides, the columns of the Assemblée Nationale (across the river to your right) and the Madeleine (to your left). Constructed between 1757 and 1777 to provide a home for a monument to Louis XV, it soon became a billboard of public grievance and accusation against the King. It is not hard to imagine why this vast area was to become pl. de la Révolution, the site of the guillotine that severed 1343 heads from their blue-blooded bodies. On Sunday, January 21, 1793, Louis XVI was beheaded by guillotine on a site near where the Brest statue now stands. The celebrated heads of Marie-Antoinette, Charlotte Corday (Marat's assassin), Lavoisier, Danton, Robespierre, and others rolled into baskets here and were held up to the cheering crowds who packed the pavement. After the Reign of Terror, the square was optimistically renamed **place de la Concorde** (Square of Harmony), though the noise pollution of the cars zooming through this intersection today hardly makes for a harmonious visit.

Much favored by film crews for its views of Paris's monuments, this square has been featured in many films, such as the dream sequence in Gene Kelly and Stanley Donen's *An American in Paris.* On Bastille Day, a military parade led by the President of the Republic marches through pl. de la Concorde (usually around 10am) and down the Champs-Elysées to the Arc de Triomphe (see **Discover,** p. 20). In the evening, an impressive fireworks display lights up the sky over pl. de la Concorde. At the end of July, the Tour de France finalists pull into the home stretch on the Champs-Elysées and the pl. de la Concorde.

In the center of the *place* is the monumental **Obélisque de Luxor.** Recalling a little scuffle called the Revolution, ignited by the pompous statue of his predecessor, King Louis-Philippe opted for a more apolitical monument when he chose this, a gift from the Viceroy of Egypt to Charles X in 1829. Getting the obelisk to Paris was no simple task—it had to travel by sea, with a special boat built to transport it up the Seine. Erected in 1836, Paris's oldest monument dates back to the 13th century BC and recalls Ramses II's deeds. At night, the obelisk, fountains, and lamps are illuminated, creating a romantic glow, somewhat eclipsed by the hordes of cars rushing by here.

Flanking the Champs-Elysées at pl. de la Concorde stand Guillaume Coustou's **Cheveaux de Marly.** Also known as *Africans Mastering the Numidian Horses*, the original sculptures are now in the Louvre to protect them from the effects of city pollution. Perfect replicas graciously hold their places on the Concorde. Eight large statues representing France's major cities also grace the *place.*

MADELEINE

pl. de la Madeleine. M: Madeleine. ☎01 44 51 69 00. ***Open*** *daily 7:30am-7pm. Regular organ and chamber concerts; contact the church for a schedule and Virgin or FNAC for tickets.*

Mirrored by the Assemblée Nationale across the Seine, the Madeleine—formally called Eglise Ste-Marie-Madeleine (Mary Magdalene Church)—was built to look like a Greek temple. Construction, overseen by Louis XV, began in 1764 and was halted during the Revolution, when the Cult of Reason proposed transforming the building into a bank, a theater, or a courthouse. Characteristically, Napoleon decreed that it should become a temple to the greatness of his army, while Louis XVIII shouted, "It shall be a church!" Completed in 1842, the structure stands alone amongst a medley of Parisian churches, distinguished by four ceiling domes, 52 exterior Corinthian columns, and a curious altarpiece adorned by an immense sculpture of the ascension of Mary Magdalene, the church's namesake. A colorful flower market thrives alongside the church facing the Assemblée Nationale. **Marcel Proust** spent most of his childhood nearby at no. 9, bd. Malesherbes, which might explain his penchant for his aunt Léonie's *madeleines* with tea. You, too, can enjoy a few *madeleines* or pick up some chocolate *macarons* at the world-famous **Fauchon,** 24-30, pl. de la Madeleine, behind the church (see **Food & Drink,** p. 201). Today, expensive clothing and food shops line the surrounding square, which is the terminus of the new métro line 14.

OTHER SIGHTS

Directly north of pl. de la Concorde, like two sentries guarding the gate to the Madeleine, stand the **Hôtel de Crillon** (on the left) and the **Hôtel de la Marine** (on the right). Architect Jacques-Ange Gabriel built the impressive colonnaded facades between 1757 and 1770. On February 6, 1778, the Treaty of Friendship and Trade was signed here by Louis XVI and American statesmen including Benjamin Franklin, making France the first European nation to recognize the independence of the United States of America. Chateaubriand lived in the Hôtel de Crillon between 1805 and 1807. Today, it is one of the most expensive, elegant hotels in Paris. The Hôtel de la Marine is the headquarters for the French national marines. World-renowned **Maxim's** restaurant, 3, r. Royale, won't even allow you a peek into what was once Richelieu's home, but is more than happy for you to visit the shop next door.

TO THE NORTH

CHAPELLE EXPIATOIRE

29, r. Pasquier, inside pl. Louis XVI, just below bd. Haussmann. M: Madeleine. ☎01 44 32 18 00. ***Open*** *Th-Sa 1-5pm. €2.50, under 18 free.*

Pl. Louis XVI is comprised of the immense Chapelle Expiatoire, its monuments to Marie-Antoinette and Louis XVI, and a lovely, quiet park. During the Revolution, when burial sites were in high demand, lime-filled trenches were dug here. Although Louis XVIII had his brother's and sister-in-law's remains removed to St-Denis in 1815, the Revolution's Most Wanted still lie here. Marat's assassin, Charlotte Corday, and Louis XVI's cousin, Philippe-Egalité (who voted for the king's death only to be beheaded himself), are buried on either side of the staircase. Statues of the expiatory King and Queen, with their crowns at their feet, stand inside the Chapelle, on either side of a tomb-shaped altar (is anyone missing the symbolism here?). Their final letters are engraved in French on the base of the sculptures.

GARE ST-LAZARE

M: St-Lazare.

The Gare St-Lazare's platforms and iron-vaulted canopy are a bit grubby, but not to be missed by train riders and fans of Monet's painting *La Gare St-Lazare* (at the Musée d'Orsay; see p. 138) and Zola's novel about the station and its trains, *La Bête Humaine.* The Gare attracts some sketchy characters; take care, especially at night.

PARC MONCEAU

M: Monceau or Courcelles. ***Open*** *daily Apr.-Oct. 7am-10pm; Nov.-Mar. 7am-8pm. Gates close 15min. before closing.*

The Parc Monceau, an expansive urban oasis guarded by gold-tipped, wrought-iron gates, borders the elegant bd. de Courcelles. It's packed at lunchtime when young and old converge on the park to eat, play, unwind, or read in the shade. Also popular with joggers, the park was designed by painter Carmontelle for the Duc d'Orléans; it was completed by Haussmann in 1862. The park boasts the largest tree in the capital: an oriental platane, 7m thick and two centuries old. An array of architectural *follies*—a pyramid, a covered bridge, an East Asian pagoda, Dutch windmills, and Roman ruins—make this formal garden and kids' romping ground (complete with roller rink) a Kodak commercial waiting to happen. The well-stocked park *chalet* (open daily 10am-7pm; sandwiches €3-4, crêpes €2-4) is great for a quick bite to eat.

CATHÉDRALE ALEXANDRE-NEVSKI

12, r. Daru. M: Ternes. ☎01 42 27 37 34. ***Open*** *Tu, F, Su 3-5pm.* ***Services*** *in French and Russian, Su 10am, Sa 6-8pm, other times posted on church calendar.*

Built in 1860, the onion-domed Eglise Russe, also known as Cathédrale Alexandre-Nevski, is a Russian Orthodox church. The golden domes are spectacular from both outside and in. They were intricately painted by artists from St. Petersburg in gold, deep reds, blues, and greens, and were recently restored to their former splendor. Today, the cathedral is the center of Russian culture in Paris, and Russian restaurants can be found in the surrounding streets. Be sure to dress appropriately; no shorts or uncovered shoulders are allowed in the cathedral.

NINTH ARRONDISSEMENT

NEIGHBORHOOD QUICKFIND: ***Discover,*** *p. 9;* ***Museums,*** *p. 151;* ***Food & Drink,*** *p. 186;* ***Nightlife,*** *p. 214;* ***Accommodations,*** *p. 264.*

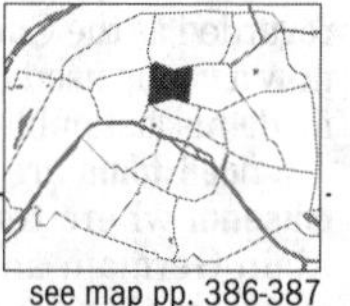
see map pp. 386-387

OPÉRA & SURROUNDINGS

The area around the southernmost border of the *9ème* is known simply as *l'Opéra* after the area's distinguishing landmark, the **Opéra Garnier.** *L'Opéra* and the Haussmann-designed *grands boulevards* which surround it are, without a doubt, the *9ème's* most prosperous and touristed area and contain all the spill-over glamor from its more celebrated western neighbor, the ritzy *8ème.* Those who aren't thrilled at the thought of seeing a world-class performance of a Massenet opera in the Garnier's stunning Second Empire hall can walk down the road to the **Olympia** (see **Entertainment,** p. 229), which remains today one of the leading concert venues for American, European, and Brazilian pop, jazz, and rock performances. Just to the north of the Opéra is the most trafficked area in the *9ème:* the city's enormous department stores, **Galeries Lafayette** and **Au Printemps** (see **Shopping,** p. 246), which offer some of the best large-scale shopping in Paris—especially in July, when the ubiquitous summer sale season begins.

OPÉRA GARNIER

M: Opéra. General info and reservations ☎08 36 69 78 68, tour info 01 40 01 22 63; www.opera-de-paris.fr. ***Concert hall and museum*** *open Sept. to mid-July daily 10am-5pm, last entry 4:30pm; mid-July to Aug. 10am-6pm, last entry 5:30pm. Concert hall closed during rehearsals; call ahead.* ***Admission*** *€6; ages 10-16, students, and over 60 €3.* ***English tours*** *daily at noon and 2pm. €10; students, ages 10-16, and over 60 €8; under 10 €4. See also* ***Entertainment,*** *p. 229.*

The stunning exterior of the Opéra Garnier—with its newly restored multi-colored marble facade, sculpted golden goddesses, and ornate columns and friezes—is one of the most impressive sights in Paris. Designed by Charles Garnier under Napoleon

III in the showily eclectic style of the Second Empire, the Opéra is perhaps most famous as the home of the Phantom of the Opera. But today, towering high above the grands boulevards of the Haussmaniacally geometric lower *9ème*, the Opéra Garnier remains one of the city's most extravagant architectural wonders. Having recently undergone massive renovations (work on the Grand Foyer will continue until April 2004), on bright days its brilliant exterior shimmers like gold. It's no wonder that Oscar Wilde once swore he saw an angel floating on the sidewalk while he was sitting next door to the Opéra at the Café de la Paix.

With its amalgam of vastly different styles and materials, its odd flourishes, and its emphatic rejection of any single formal tradition, the building epitomizes both the Second Empire's ostentatiousness and its rootlessness. Asked whether his building was in the style of Louis XIV, Louis XV, or Louis XVI, Garnier responded that his creation belonged only to Napoleon III, who financed the project. Garnier's plans outshone hundreds of others in an 1861 competition to design the building, including the entry of the "Pope of Architects," Viollet-le-Duc, who restored Notre Dame. Garnier was just 35 and virtually unknown at the time, and the commission made him famous. After 15 years of construction, the Opéra opened its doors in 1875.

No less impressive than the view from the outside, the Opéra's interior is decorated with Gobelin tapestries, gilded mosaics, and an eight-ton chandelier that fell on the audience in 1896. The incident, along with spooky lake underneath the building, provided the inspiration for *Le Fantôme de l'Opera (The Phantom of the Opera)*, which began life as a 1910 novel by Gaston Leroux and went through several film incarnations before bursting into song in 1986 with Andrew Lloyd Webber's megamusical (be sure to pay a visit to the Phantom's box, Number 5). The Opéra's red and gold auditorium has 1900 red velvet seats and a brilliant, whimsical ceiling painted by Marc Chagall in 1964. This five-tiered auditorium was designed as a stage not only for operas but for 19th-century bourgeois social life: balconies were constructed so audience members could watch the show and one another.

Since 1989, most operas have been performed at the **Opéra de la Bastille,** generally regarded as the Garnier's heinously ugly stepsister (see p. 110). The Opéra Garnier is now a venue used mainly for ballet. In 1992, shortly before his death, Rudolf Nureyev made his last public appearance here, his home since his defection from the USSR.

Guided tours are available in several languages. The Opéra houses a **library** and **museum** where temporary exhibits on theatrical personages, such as director Alain Germain and dancer Vaslav Nijinsky, are held throughout the year. The museum also displays a permanent collection, which includes sculptures by Degas and scale models of famous opera scenes. Paul Baudry's portrait of Charles Garnier himself hangs by the entrance to the museum.

CAFÉ DE LA PAIX

12, bd. des Capucines.

Located next to the Opéra Garnier, the Café de la Paix is the quintessential 19th-century café. Like the Opéra, it was designed by Charles Garnier and sports frescoes, mirrored walls, and Neoclassical ceilings with winking "epicurean cherubs." Oscar Wilde frequented the café; today it caters to the after-theater crowd and anyone else who doesn't mind paying €4.58 for coffee (see **Food & Drink,** p. 186).

NORTH OF OPÉRA

The upper *9ème*, with its infamous red-light district, is a destination for those in search of cheap and not-so-cheap thrills, and the less carnivorous will probably choose to stay near its southern border. The middle *9ème*, with a high density of synagogues and temples, is home to a substantial Jewish population; there are a handful of kosher food stores along the main drag, which is comprised of **rue Notre Dame de Lorette** and **rue du Faubourg Montmartre.** This noisy street is also filled with discount shops, pizza parlors, and car exhaust.

EGLISE NOTRE DAME DE LORETTE

M: Notre Dame de Lorette. Exit the métro and the church will be in front of you on pl. Kossuth. Mass Tu, W, F and Sa, 8am, 12:15, 6:45pm; Th 8am and 6:45pm; Su 9:30am and 6:30pm.

Built in 1836 to "the glory of the Virgin Mary," Eglise Notre Dame de Lorette is an example of Neoclassical architecture. Frescoes inside its elevated chapel depict the four evangelists contemplating Mary and the four prophets hailing her. The statue at the middle of the nave portrays Mary gazing at the baby Jesus. The serenity of these works is a far cry from the noise of **Rue Notre Dame de Lorette.** Far less saintly than its namesake, this street was the debauched hangout of Emile Zola's *Nana* (whose name is now slang for chick or babe) and a thoroughfare of serious ill repute in the late 1960s. *Lorette* came to be a term used to refer to the quarter's young prostitutes. Nowadays, for the most part the only business being transacted on the Lorette is at the street's Jewish markets and cheap pizza joints.

PIGALLE

M: Pigalle. Let's Go *does not recommend that travelers (in particular young women) walk alone in the Pigalle area at night.*

The home of famous cabarets-*cum*-nightclubs (Folies Bergère, Moulin Rouge, Folies Pigalle) and well-endowed newcomers with names like "Le Coq Hardy" and "Dirty Dick," this mawkish, dirty, neon neighborhood is raunchy enough to make even Jacques Chirac blush. Stretching along the trash-covered bd. de Clichy from pl. Pigalle to pl. Blanche, Pigalle earned its infamous reputation as the extravagant un-chastity belt of Paris during WWII, when American servicemen stationed in Paris nicknamed it "Pig-alley." Like its southern neighbor, **rue St-Denis,** sex shops, brothels, porn stores, and lace, leather, and latex boutiques fill up almost every block of Pigalle's back alleys. At "night," a time which seems to start well before dark in Pigalle, prostitutes, pimps, and drug dealers begin prowling the streets and subway stations in the area; as a result, the entire district swarms with police. Though it is supposedly undergoing a slow gentrification, Pigalle shows no signs of shedding its sleazy reputation any time soon. Even the RATP makes regular announcements in neighborhood métro stops warning visitors against pick-pockets. The areas to the north of bd. Clichy and south of pl. Blanche are comparatively calm, but visitors should exercise caution at all times.

EGLISE DE LA STE-TRINITÉ

M: Trinité. M-Sa 11am-8pm, Su 10:30am-8pm. Mass M-S noon and 7pm, Su noon.

Built at the end of the 19th century in Italian Renaissance style, this church has beautiful, painted vaults and is surrounded by an ornately fountained park replete with tree-shaded benches, a playground, and ping-pong tables.

TENTH ARRONDISSEMENT

NEIGHBORHOOD QUICKFIND: ***Discover,*** *p. 11;* ***Food & Drink,*** *p. 187;* ***Museums,*** *p. 151;* ***Accommodations,*** *p. 265.*

see map p. 388

PORTES ST-DENIS & ST-MARTIN

M: Strasbourg-St-Denis. When you exit the métro you will see the portes to either side of you (look between the trees).

At the end of r. Faubourg St-Denis, the grand **Porte St-Denis** looms triumphantly. Built in 1672 to celebrate the victories of Louis XIV in Flanders and the Rhineland, the gate imitates the Arch of Titus in Rome. Once the site of a medieval entrance to the city, the present arch now serves as a rotary for traffic and a gathering place for pigeons and loiterers alike. In the words of André Breton, *"c'est très belle et très inutile"* ("it's very beautiful and very useless."). On July 28, 1830, revolutionaries scrambled to the top and rained cobblestones on the monarchist troops below (see **Life & Times,** p. 45). The 1674 **Porte St-Martin** at the end of r. du Faubourg St-Martin is a smaller copy, with a herculean Louis XIV on the facade, wearing nothing but a wig and a smile.

THÉÂTRES DE LA RENAISSANCE & DE ST-MARTIN

M: Strasbourg-St-Denis or République.

The stretch from Porte St-Martin to pl. de la République along r. René Boulanger and bd. St-Martin served as a lively theater district in the 19th century but is now quite shabby, with loiterers and sex shops. If you want to see vestiges of the glory days, go to where bd. St-Martin and r. René Boulanger meet, and check out the still-working theaters, whose sculpted facades are now their only draw for tourists.

PLACE DE LA RÉPUBLIQUE

M: République.

Though Haussmann created it to divide and conquer the revolutionary *arrondissements* that border it, the pl. de la République serves as a bustling meeting point for the vastly different *3ème*, *10ème*, and *11ème arrondissements*. It also serves as the disorienting junction of av. de la République and bds. Magenta, Voltaire, Temple, Turbigo, and St-Martin. At the center of the *place*, Morice's sculpture of La République glorifies France's many revolutionary struggles, and the host of chain restaurants lining it feed the diverse crowds. The area buzzes with people during the day, but it can be dangerous at night.

CANAL ST-MARTIN

M: République or Goncourt will take you to the most beautiful end of the canal.

The most pleasant area of the *10ème* is unquestionably the tree-lined Canal St-Martin. Measuring 4.5km, the canal has several locks, which can be observed on one of the Canauxrama trips (see **Service Directory,** p. 346). It was built in 1825 as a shortcut for river traffic on the Seine, and it also served as a defense against the upstart eastern *arrondissements*. This residential area is being rediscovered by Parisians and tourists alike, who stroll the tree-lined canal to check out new upscale shops and restaurants and the Sunday antique market that takes place along the quai de Valmy.

HÔPITAL ST-LOUIS

M: Colonel Fabien or Goncourt. From métro Fabien walk down r. de la Grange-aux-Belles; from Goncourt take av. Parmentier north. Pedestrian entrances to the Carré are on r. de la Grange-aux-Belles, r. Bichat, and av. Claude Vellefaux. ***Open*** *to pedestrians daily 5:30am-9:45pm.*

Built in 1607 by Henri IV as a sanctuary (read: prison) for plague victims, the Hôpital St-Louis was across a marsh and downwind of the rotting Buttes-Chaumont (see p. 123). Its distance from any water source suggests that it was intended more to protect the city from contamination than to help the unfortunates. Today, the hospital boasts the lovely **Carré St-Louis,** a flowered courtyard in the middle of the original hospital buildings; the newer buildings of the hospital complex still serve the sick.

ELEVENTH ARRONDISSEMENT

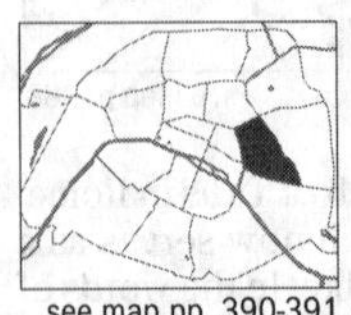

see map pp. 390-391

NEIGHBORHOOD QUICKFIND: ***Discover,*** *p. 11;* ***Food & Drink,*** *p. 188;* ***Nightlife,*** *p. 214;* ***Accommodations,*** *p. 266.*

BASTILLE PRISON

M: Bastille.

The Bastille Prison is the most visited sight in Paris that is actually nonexistent. A Parisian mob stormed this symbol of the monarchy's tyranny on July 14, 1789, sparking the French Revolution. Two days later, the National Assembly ordered the prison to be demolished. Today, the July Column (see below), at one corner of the pl. de la Bastille, commemorates the site where the prison once stood.

The prison was originally commissioned by Charles V to safeguard the eastern entrance to Paris. Strapped for cash, Charles "recruited" a press-gang of passing civilians to lay the stones for the fortress. The Bastille towers rose 100 ft. above Paris by the end of the 14th century. Under Henri IV they became the royal treasury; Louis XIII made them a state prison. Internment here, generally reserved for heretics and political dissidents, was the king's business and, as a result, often arbitrary. But it was hardly the hellhole that the Revolutionaries who tore it down imagined it to be—Bastille's titled inmates were allowed to furnish their suites, have fresh linen, bring their own servants, and receive guests: the Cardinal de Rohan held a dinner party for 20 in his cell. Notable prisoners included Mirabeau, Voltaire, and the Marquis de Sade (for more on these dandies, see **Life & Times,** p. 54).

Having sacked the Invalides for weapons, Revolutionary militants stormed the Bastille for munitions. Supposedly an impenetrable fortress, the prison had actually been attacked during other periods of civil unrest. Surrounded by an armed rabble, too short on food to entertain a siege, and unsure of the loyalty of the Swiss mercenaries who defended the prison, the Bastille's governor surrendered. His head was severed with a pocket knife and paraded through the streets on a pike. Despite the gruesome details, the storming of the Bastille has come to symbolize the triumph of liberty over despotism. Its first anniversary was the cause for great celebration in Revolutionary Paris. Since the late 19th century, July 14 has been the official state holiday of the French Republic and is usually a time of glorious firework displays and consumption of copious amounts of alcohol (see **Discover,** p. 20).

JULY COLUMN

M: Bastille. In the center of pl. de la Bastille.

Yes, the column topped by the conspicuous gold cupid doing an arabesque at the center of pl. de la Bastille is in fact a statue of Liberty. In 1831, King Louis-Philippe laid the cornerstone for the July Column to commemorate Republicans who died in the revolutions of 1789 and 1830. Emblazoned names commemorate the 504 martyrs of 1830 buried inside, along with, strangely enough, two mummified Egyptian pharaohs. The column isn't open to the public.

in recent news

Modern Mariannes

The face of **Marianne,** a symbol of the French Republic and "Liberté, Egalité, Fraternité" since the Revolution, has, in recent years, been modeled on legendary Gallic beauties like Brigitte Bardot and Catherine Deneuve.

In 2003, however, the face of Marianne changed drastically: Thirteen women, more than half of them of North African or African descent, were selected to represent the ideals of France. On Bastille Day, enormous color photographs of the women, all wearing the Phyrigian bonnet, were hung on the Neoclassical facade of the Assemblée Nationale.

"Mariannes of Today" is a project of a movement called Ni Putes Ni Soumises (Neither Whores nor Doormats), whose goal is to address the problems faced by women in the impoverished immigrant communities of the suburbs. Trapped in a fiercely traditional culture that forces them into one of those two roles, many girls have been victims of assault, gang rape, and even murder. The exhibit, following a mass protest last March, demands recognition of the gender-based violence and discrimination that, they claim, have worsened in these largely Muslim communities in recent years—and a place for the women who have endured it in the citizenry and iconography of the French Republic.

RUE DE LA ROQUETTE

M: Bastille-Voltaire.

Quieter than its neighbor, jumping r. de Lappe, the winding r. de la Roquette does have some hidden gems. This 17th-century byway was home to poet Paul Verlaine, who lived at no. 17, and is now lined with off-beat cafés, bars, creative boutiques, an avant-garde church, and countless restaurants, serving everything from Italian to Thai food. The charming **square de la Roquette** is an ideal endpoint to a stroll along this up-and-coming street.

TWELFTH ARRONDISSEMENT

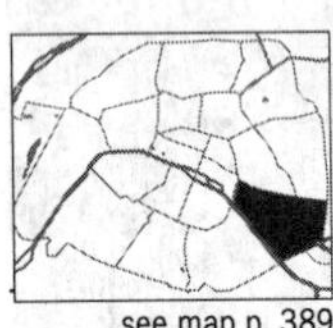

see map p. 389

NEIGHBORHOOD QUICKFIND: ***Discover,*** *p. 12;* ***Museums,*** *p. 152;* ***Food & Drink,*** *p. 189;* ***Nightlife,*** *p. 215;* ***Shopping,*** *p. 243;* ***Accommodations,*** *p. 267.*

AROUND PLACE DE LA BASTILLE

OPÉRA BASTILLE

130, r. de Lyon. Look for the words "Billeterie" on the building. M: Bastille. ☎01 40 01 19 70; www.opera-de-paris.fr. 1hr. ***tour*** *almost every day, usually at 1 or 5pm; call ahead (tours in French, but groups of ten or more can arrange for English).* ***Admission*** *€10, over 60 €8, students and under 26 €5. For concert info, see* ***Entertainment,*** *p. 229.*

Once known as the "Red Belt" around Paris because of its residents' participation in both the 1830 and 1848 Revolutions, the 12*ème* was also a hotbed of Parisian Resistance during WWII. But the only rebellions staged these days are over the Opéra Bastille, one of Mitterrand's *Grands Projets.* Presiding over the **place de la Bastille** and designed by Carlos Ott, a Canadian mall architect, the Opéra opened in 1989 (on the eve of Bastille Day) to protests over its unattractive and questionable design (nets still surround parts of the building to catch falling tiles). The "People's Opera" has been described as a huge toilet because of its resemblance to the coin-operated *pissoirs* in the streets of Paris. Also, many complain that the acoustics of the hall are defective. The Opéra has not struck a completely sour note, though, as it has helped renew local interest in the arts. The guided tour (expensive but interesting and extremely impressive) offers a behind-the-scenes view of the largest theater in the world. The immense auditorium, which seats 2703, comprises only 5% of the building's surface area. The rest of the Opéra houses exact replicas of the stage (for rehearsal purposes) and the workshops for both the Bastille and Garnier operas. The building employs almost one thousand people, from techies to actors to administrators to wig- and shoe-makers. The 2003-2004 season includes performances of the operas *Tosca* and *La Traviata* as well as the ballets *Don Quichotte* and *Giselle.* On Bastille Day, all performances are free, though the queues are long; your best bet is to join the line very early in the morning and bring a book.

VIADUC DES ARTS & PROMENADE PLANTÉE

9-129, av. Daumesnil. M: Bastille. The viaduc extends from r. de Lyon to r. de Charenton. Entrances to the Promenade are at Ledru Rollin, Hector Malot, and bd. Diderot. ***Open*** *M-F 8am, Sa-Su 9am; closing hours vary, around 5:30pm in winter and 9:30pm in summer.*

The *ateliers* in the **Viaduc des Arts** house artisans who make everything from *haute couture* fabric to hand-painted porcelain to space-age furniture. Restorators of all types fill the arches of the old railway viaduct, and they can make your oil painting, 12th-century book, grandmother's linen, or childhood dollhouse as good as new. Interspersed among the stores are gallery spaces that are rented by new artists each month (see **Museums,** p. 160). High above the avenue, on the "roof" of the viaduct, runs the lovely, rose-filled **Promenade Plantée,** Paris's skinniest park.

ELSEWHERE IN THE TWELFTH

BERCY QUARTER

M: Bercy.

East of the **Gare de Lyon,** the Bercy quarter has seen rapid construction, beginning with Mitterrand's **Ministère des Finances** building, a hulking modern monolith to match the Bibliothèque across the river. Sit in one of the many new cafés and brasseries along the **rue de Bercy** and ogle the mammoth grass-and-glass **Palais Omnisports** concert and sports complex. Each of its sloping sides is covered in green grass which local youth and the occasional tourist (unsuccessfully) try to scale. The **Parc de Bercy** stops just short of being calming, thanks to its uneasy man-made details, like the perfectly calibrated hills. A far lovelier (and far less weird) site is the **Yitzhak Rabin Garden,** with its rose arbors, grape vines, and playground dedicated to the Nobel Prize-winning Prime Minister of Israel.

To top off this bizarre 21st-century construct, **Frank Gehry** added one of his ultramodern, psychedelic, turreted buildings at **no. 51, rue de Bercy,** to be dedicated to the history of cinema. On the eastern side of the park is what used to be Paris's wine depot; the rows of old wine storage buildings have now been converted into a pretty if somewhat unsettling Club Med (M: Cour St-Emilion). The club cafés lining Cour St-Emilion are cute in a rather contrived way; one even has hammocks outside instead of chairs.

THIRTEENTH ARRONDISSEMENT

NEIGHBORHOOD QUICKFIND: ***Discover,*** *p. 4;* ***Food & Drink,*** *p. 190;* ***Nightlife,*** *p. 216;* ***Accommodations,*** *p. 268.*

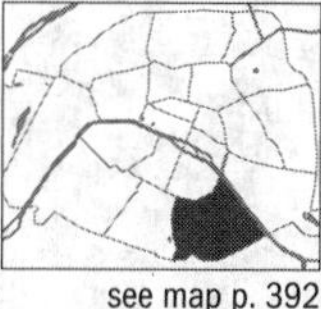

see map p. 392

MANUFACTURE DES GOBELINS

42, av. des Gobelins. ☎01 44 61 21 69. M: Gobelins. 1½hr. ***tours*** *in French Tu-Th 2:15 and 2:30pm; arrive 30min. in advance. Call in advance for group tours in English.* ***Admission*** *€8, ages 7-25 €6, under 7 free.*

The Manufacture des Gobelins, a tapestry workshop over 300 years old, is all that is left of the 13*ème's* manufacturing past. Established in 1662 by Henri IV for his imported Flemish tapestry artists, the Gobelins produced the priceless 17th-century tapestries now displayed in the Musée de Cluny (see **Museums,** p. 142). Still an adjunct of the state, the factory receives commissions from French ministries and foreign embassies. The tours are great if you have an interest in the intricacies of weaving: you can actually see the artists at work on each step of the process. Tours are also the only way inside the Gobelins.

QUARTIER DE LA BUTTE-AUX-CAILLES

M: Corvisart. From the métro, exit onto bd. Blanqui, and turn onto r. Barrault, which will meet r. de la Butte-aux-Cailles.

The Butte-aux-Cailles (Quail Knoll) district is like a mini-village in the heart of the big city, with **rue de la Butte-aux-Cailles** and **rue des Cinq Diamants** sharing duties as the village's main drags. However, this little hamlet isn't exactly a tranquil one: the area was one of the first to fight during the Revolution of 1848, and, 120 years later, its citizens were up in arms again, hosting the unofficial headquarters of the *soixante-huitards*, the student and intellectual activists behind the 1968 riots in Paris. Today, the fight continues in the Butte's cooperative bar, **La Folie en Tête** (see **Nightlife,** p. 216), as well as the neighborhoods intellectual hang-out, **Le Temps des Cerises** (see **Food & Drink,** p. 191). The nascent gentrification of the entire *arrondissement* has attracted trend-setters, artists, and intellectuals to this area, but this process is—luckily for long-time residents—still slow-moving.

the insider's CITY

CHINATOWN'S BEST

While the edges of the 13ème pursue a trendy rebirth, Chinatown manages to preserve its traditions. The area is rich with gems that make it worth a visit:

1 Dong Nam A. You'll be amazed by this store's selection of exotic produce.

2 L'Empire des Thés (☎01 45 85 66 33). A delightful tea shop—eat in on sesame eclairs, or take home a pot of one of 220 Chinese teas.

3 Hoa Ly (☎01 45 83 96 63). Beautiful Mandarin dresses *(cheongsams)*, jackets and blouses, in colors for any wedding except a white one.

4 Ka Sun Sas (☎01 56 61 98 89). You may just find a priceless Ming Vase here.

5 Lycée Gabriel Fauré. Brilliant orange and blue tilings and swirling statues decorate this neighborhood school.

EGLISE STE-ANNE DE LA BUTTE-AUX-CAILLES

188, r. de Tolbiac. ☎01 45 89 34 73. M: Tolbiac. ***Open*** *Sa-Th 9am-7:30pm, F 7:30am-7:30pm. Mass M 7pm, Tu and Th 9am and 7pm, W 9am and noon, F 7:30am and noon, Sa 9am.*

This Byzantine church owes its completion to the Lombard family who, in 1898, donated funds from their chocolate store on av. de Choisy to finish it. The front of the church is nicknamed *la façade chocolat* in their honor.

CHINATOWN

M: Porte d'Ivry, Porte de Choisy, Tolbiac, or Maison Blanche are all near Chinatown.

Paris's Chinatown lies in the area bounded by r. de Tolbiac, bd. Massena, av. de Choisy, and av. d'Ivry. It is home to large Chinese, Vietnamese, and Cambodian communities, and to a host of Asian restaurants, shops, and markets like **Tang Frères** (see **Food & Drink,** p. 201). Window-shopping along av. de Choisy and av. d'Ivry provides a glimpse of the neighborhood's rich offerings: beautiful embroidered shoes and dresses, elegant chopstick sets, ceramic Buddha statuettes, exotic (and often delicious) fruits and vegetables. See **Insider's City** (p. 112) for more on Chinatown's sights.

BIBLIOTHÈQUE NATIONALE DE FRANCE: SITE FRANÇOIS MITTERRAND

Quai F. Mauriac. ☎01 53 79 59 79; www.bnf.fr. M: Quai de la Gare or Bibliothèque François Mitterrand. Open Su noon-7pm, Tu-Sa 10am-8pm; closed 1st-3rd Su of Sept. and the 2nd half of Aug. Open to those over the age of 16. Admission €3. Annual membership €30. MC/V.

Opened in 1996, the Bibliothèque de France is the last and most expensive of Mitterrand's *grand projets*. In fact, the library was unable to realize its full design because work had to be hurried to have the building complete before Mitterrand's death (so he could have the building named after him). Replacing the old Bibliothèque Nationale in the *2ème* (still open to scholars), the new library is open to the public (except the research rooms, entrance to which requires special permission). The L-shaped towers of Dominique Perrault's controversial design are meant to look like open books from above. Inside, the modern building features grand reading rooms and multiple galleries displaying exhibits on photography and the history of sound, among other things. On sunny days, visitors bask in pleasant views of the Seine along the multitude of stairs surrounding the building.

FOURTEENTH ARRONDISSEMENT

NEIGHBORHOOD QUICKFIND: **Discover,** p. 4; **Museums,** p. 152; **Food & Drink,** p. 191; **Nightlife:** p. 216; **Accommodations,** p. 269.

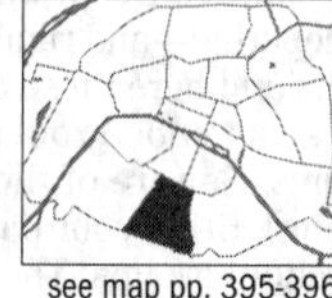

see map pp. 395-396

BOULEVARD DE MONTPARNASSE

M: Montparnasse-Bienvenüe or Vavin.

In the early 20th century, Montparnasse became a center for avant-garde artists such as Modigliani, Utrillo, Chagall, and Montmartre transplant Léger. Political exiles like Lenin and Trotsky talked strategy over cognac in the cafés, including **Le Dôme, Le Sélect,** and **La Coupole,** along bd. Montparnasse. After WWI, Montparnasse attracted American expatriates and artistic rebels like Calder, Hemingway, and Henry Miller. The Spanish Civil War and WWII, however, ended this bohemian golden age. Montparnasse has since seen heavy commercialization; chain restaurants and tourists now crowd the boulevard. The street still has its draws, however, even for those unimpressed by its illustrious past: the classic restaurants still hold their own (the best is the pricey **La Coupole**) and provide a classically "Parisian" place to sip a café express, read Apollinaire, and sigh longingly.

CIMETIÈRE DU MONTPARNASSE

3, bd. Edgar Quinet. M: Edgar Quinet. With your back to Café Odessa, walk to your left down bd. Quinet until you hit sq. Delambre. ☎ 01 44 10 86 50. ***Open*** *mid-Mar. to Oct. M-F 8am-6pm, Sa 8:30am-6pm, Su and holidays 9am-6pm; Nov.-Mar. M-F 8am-5:30pm, Sa 8:30am-5:30pm, Su and holidays 9am-5:30pm. A few guided* ***tours*** *in French July-Dec., call ☎ 01 40 71 75 60 for times. Free.*

In the shadow of the modern Tour Montparnasse (see p. 115) hides the beautiful Cimetière du Montparnasse, opened in 1824 as the burial grounds for some of the most famous (and fashionable) residents of the city. Enter the cemetery off bd. Edgar Quinet (the main entrance is just east of M: Edgar Quinet), grab a free *Index des Célébrités* (available to the left of the entrance), and take the following route. Go right on the av. du Boulevard, pausing to ponder the shared *tombeau* of existentialists Jean-Paul Sartre and Simone de Beauvoir in the 20th *division* at right. Durkheim is a bit farther ahead in the 5th *division*. Rounding the corner on av. de l'Ouest, you'll pass by the homes of Charles Baudelaire, Eugène Ionesco, Man Ray, and Robert Desnos. Farther east, composer Camille St-Saëns lies not far from shagadelic 70s pop singer Serge Gainsbourg, whose graffitied grave resembles Jim Morrison's across town at Père Lachaise (see p. 123). Also resting in peace here are Samuel Beckett, Guy de Maupassant, and sculptors Constantin Brancusi and Frédéric Bartholdi (who did the Statue of Liberty). Finally, visit the graves of wrongly accused Jewish colonel Alfred Dreyfus (see **Life & Times**, p. 46), just across r. Emile Richard, and author Marguerite Duras, located in the 21st division on your way out. Cimetière Montparnasse is still an active cemetery, so be sure to be respectful of those who are visiting their departed loved ones.

CATACOMBS

1, pl. Denfert-Rochereau. M: Denfert-Rochereau. From the métro, take exit pl. Denfert-Rochereau, cross av. du Général Leclerc. The entrance is the dark green structure straight ahead. ☎ 01 43 22 47 63; www.paris-france.org/musees. ***Open*** *Tu 10am-4pm, W-Su 10am-4pm. €5, seniors €3.30, ages 14-26 €2.50, under 14 free.* ***Tour*** *lasts 45min.*

At the intersection of six avenues, a lion sculpted by Bartholdi commemorating La Défense Nationale de 1870-1871 dominates pl. Denfert-Rochereau. Most visitors observe Bartholdi's Leo from their place in the line to visit the Catacombs, a series of tunnels 20m below ground and 1.7km in length. They were originally excavated to provide stone for building the city. By the 1770s, much of the Left Bank was in danger of caving in and digging promptly stopped. The former quarry was then used as a mass grave to relieve the stench emanating from Paris's overcrowded cemeteries.

The entrance warns "Stop! Beyond Here Is the Empire of Death." In 1793, a Parisian got lost and became a permanent resident, so stick to the tour. During WWII, the Empire of Death was full of life when the Resistance set up headquarters among the departed—and rumor has it that a group of young Parisians, called cataphiles, prowl around here these days in a radical kind of urban exploration. The catacombs are like an underground city, with street names on walls lined with femurs and craniums. Beware of the low ceilings and bring a sweater (and a flashlight if you have one). Bring your patience, too, as you'll likely be waiting in line with the numerous school groups. The catacombs are not recommended for the faint of heart or leg; there are 85 steep steps to climb on the way out.

CITÉ UNIVERSITAIRE

*Main entrance 21, bd. Jourdain. M: Porte d'Orléans. From the métro, take the pl. du 25 Août 1944 exit and walk down bd. Jourdain past intersection with r. Henri Barboux. RER: Cité Universitaire. Bus 88: Porte d'Arceuil. With your back to r. E.D. de la Meurthe, walk down bd. Jourdain. Guided **tours** starting at the Maison Internationale. For information about staying at the Cité Universitaire, call the Administration office ☎01 44 16 64 48; www.ciup.fr. Free. Lunch or dinner €2.50 with valid student ID.*

On bd. Jourdain, upwards of 6000 students from 122 countries study, argue, and drink themselves silly at the **Cité Universitaire.** If you make the trek to this idyllic 40-hectare campus, you'll find it was well worth it. At the main entrance is the central **Maison Internationale,** whose fancy topiary mazes and high *mansarde* roofs dominate the complex. The building's old marble halls house the information center and cafeteria for the university, where visitors with a valid student ID can grab a quick bite on the fly while getting the dirt on Parisian college life from students in line. Though the houses are closed to the public, the grounds are free for exploration. The oldest and most happening place to be is the **Maison Deutsch de la Meurthe.** Le Corbusier's **Pavilion Suisse** (1932) and **Maison du Brésil** (1959) are architectural wonders; the former reflects the architect's dream of a vertical city. Its roof garden housed anti-aircraft guns during WWII. While the **Maison des Etats-Unis** houses Americans in prison-like squalor, the **Maison Suédoise** and **Maison Japonaise** offer delightful accommodations. Just across bd. Jourdain, you'll find various corduroy-clad intellectuals discussing Heidegger and young drama students running lines by the duck pond of **Parc Montsouris.**

FIFTEENTH ARRONDISSEMENT

see map p. 393

*NEIGHBORHOOD QUICKFIND: **Discover,** p. 5; **Museums,** p. 152; **Food & Drink,** p. 192; **Accommodations,** p. 270.*

The 15*ème* has few tourist sites—you'll probably only explore here if your stay extends beyond a week. Its varied neighborhoods, generally calm and safe at night, are similar to those of smaller French cities like Nantes or Rouen.

LE PARC ANDRÉ CITROËN

*2, r. de la Montagne de la Fage. ☎01 44 26 20 00; www.volenballon.com. M: Javel-André Citroën or Balard. **Open** M-F 7:30am-9:30pm, Sa-Su 9am-9:30pm. **Tours** of the park in English; June-Sept. Sa 10:30am; €5.80; call ☎01 40 71 75 60 for more info. **Balloon rides** €12, ages 12-17 €10, ages 3-11 €6, under 3 free.*

The futuristic Parc André Citroën was created by landscapers Alain Provost and Gilles Clément in the 1970s. Rides in the hot-air balloon that launches from the central garden offer spectacular aerial views of the park and all of the city of Paris. Located alongside the Seine, the six gardens contain a variety of fountains, huge glass greenhouses, and a wild garden whose plant life changes from one year to the next. In the summer months, the grassy expanses of the park are crowded with sunbathers and picnickers of all ages.

TOUR MAINE-MONTPARNASSE

33, av. du Maine. M: Montparnasse-Bienvenüe. ☎01 45 38 52 56; Ciel ☎01 40 64 77 64. ***Tower*** *open May-Sept. daily 9:30am-11:30pm; Oct.-Apr. M-F 9:30am-10:30pm.* ***Ciel*** *open daily 8am-2pm.* ***Admission*** *€8, students and seniors €6.80, under 14 €5.50, disabled €5.20.*

The modern Maine-Montparnasse Tower dominates the *quartier's* northeast corner. Standing 59 stories tall and completed in 1973, the controversial building looks jarringly out of place amid Montparnasse's otherwise sedate 19th-century architecture. Shortly after it was erected, the city forbade the construction of skyscrapers, designating the outer reaches of the La Défense district (see p. 131) as the sole home for future *gratte-ciels*. For an open-air, all-encompassing view of Paris that rivals that from the Eiffel Tower—and lacks the walls of tourists—bypass the 52 floors of office space and ride the elevator to the 56th floor, then climb three flights to the rooftop. You'll be amazed at the view from 207m, and historical photographs and maps (inside on the 56 floor) help you locate landmarks. On your way down, stop on the 56th floor for a meal at the **Ciel**, or, if the prices make you queasy, try the café instead (*plats* €5-9.50).

PLACE DU 18 JUIN 1940

At the intersection of r. de l'Arrivé and bd. Montparnasse. M: Montparnasse-Bienvenüe.

This traffic-heavy square commemorates two important events of World War II. On June 18, 1940, General de Gaulle broadcast his first BBC radio address from London, urging France to resist the Nazi occupiers. And it was here that General Leclerc, then the leader of the French forces, accepted the surrender of General von Choltitz, the Nazi commander of the Paris occupation, on August 25, 1944.

INSTITUT PASTEUR

25, r. du Docteur Roux. M: Pasteur. Turn right on bd. Pasteur; r. du Docteur Roux is the first right. ☎01 45 68 82 83; www.pasteur.fr. Before entering the museum, you must obtain a name tag from the small office across from the Institute. ***Open*** *Sept.-July M-F 2-5:30pm.* ***Admission*** *€3, students €1.50. Guided* ***tours*** *in English easily arranged, just ask at the reception.*

Founded by the French scientist Louis Pasteur in 1887, the Institut Pasteur is now a center for biochemical research, development, and treatment. It was here that Pasteur, a champion of 19th-century germ theory, developed pasteurization, his technique for purifying milk products and beer. The institute, now primarily dedicated to research laboratories, has turned Pasteur's somber but magnificent home into a museum. Inside, the very instruments with which the scientist discovered a vaccine for anthrax and the cure for rabies will wow even the least scientifically-minded visitors. The grand portraits of Pasteur and his family, including several painted by a teenage Louis, offer a closer look a his life, as do the magnificently preserved rooms. It was also here in 1983 that Dr. Luc Montaigner (in conjunction with Robert Gallo) first isolated HIV, the virus that causes AIDS. Pasteur's tomb, an awe-inspiring, marble and mosaic construction dedicated to faith, hope, charity, and science, is also open to visitors as part of the short museum tour.

LA RUCHE

52, r. de Dantzig - on the passage de Dantzig. M: Convention. Follow r. de la Convention toward pl. Charles Vallin; r. de Dantzig will be on the right.

Built as a wine pavilion by Gustave Eiffel for the 1900 exhibition, the building known as "the Beehive" eventually became a home to industrious artists after it was bought and renovated by Alfred Boucher, himself a struggling sculptor. Chagall, Soutine, Modigliani, and Léger are some of the more famous residents who vied for a "cell" here, and whose work is preserved in the gardens of la Ruche, along with that of other residents, past and present. Today, the Fondation La Ruche offers grants, studios, and housing to young artists. **It is not open to visitors,** but modern art buffs may still find it interesting.

SIXTEENTH ARRONDISSEMENT

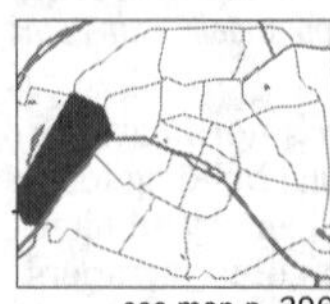

see map p. 396

NEIGHBORHOOD QUICKFIND: ***Discover,*** *p. 12;* ***Museums,*** *p. 153;* ***Food & Drink,*** *p. 193;* ***Nightlife,*** *p. 217;* ***Accommodations,*** *p. 272.*

TROCADÉRO & SURROUNDINGS

PLACE D'IÉNA

M: Iéna.

The pl. d'Iéna positions you next to the rotunda of the **Conseil Economique** and in front of a sweep of popular museums, including the round, Palladian facade of the **Panthéon Bouddhique (Musée Guimet),** which houses an outstanding collection of Asian art. It is a 5min. walk west to the Trocadéro, and 5min. east to the museums of the **Palais de Tokyo** (see **Museums,** p. 153).

PALAIS DE TOKYO

11, av. du Président Wilson. M: Iéna.

Built for the 1937 World Expo, the Palais is home to the **Musée d'Art Moderne de la Ville de Paris** (see **Museums,** p. 153), which has a world-class collection of 20th-century art. The west wing of the Palais houses the warehouse-like **site creation contemporaine** (see **Museums,** p. 153) which shows thought-provoking exhibits of today's hottest (and most controversial) contemporary art. The building's austere, Neoclassical portico and Trocadéro-esque courtyard also contain a cheerful café, La Terrasse du Musée (see **Food & Drink,** p. 193).

PALAIS GALLIERA

Across from the Palais de Tokyo. M: Iéna.

The Palais Galliera was built for the Duchess of Galliera by Louis Ginain as a repository for her collection of Italian Baroque art, although her collection was eventually sent to Genoa instead. The Italianate structure, completed in 1892, houses the more unorthodox **Musée de la Mode et du Costume** (see **Museums,** p. 155). The Palais's gardens are currently under renovation, but the museum is open for business.

PLACE DU TROCADÉRO

M: Trocadéro.

In the 1820s, the Duc d'Angoulême built a memorial to his victory at Trocadéro—hence the present name. Jacques Carlu's more modern design for the 1937 World Exposition (which beat out Le Corbusier's) for the **Palais de Chaillot** features two white stone wings cradling an Art Deco courtyard that extends from the *place* over spectacular cannon-shaped fountains. Enigmatic gold inscriptions by Paul Valéry claim, among other things, that "the hand of the artist is equal and rival to thoughts of the artist, and each is nothing without the other." Surveyed by Henri Bouchard's 7.5m bronze *Apollo* and eight other figures, the terrace attracts tourists, vendors, skateboarders, and in-line skaters, and offers panoramic views of the Eiffel Tower and Champs de Mars. Be aware of pickpocketers and traffic as you gaze upward.

PALAIS DE CHAILLOT

17, pl. de Trocadéro.

The Palais de Chaillot houses the **Musée de l'Homme** and the **Musée de la Marine** (see **Museums,** p. 155), the **Théâtre National de Chaillot** (see **Entertainment,** p. 225), and the **Cinémathèque Française** (see **Entertainment,** p. 227). It is actually the last of a series of buildings on this site. Catherine de Médicis had a château here, transformed into a convent by Queen Henrietta of England. Napoleon razed the convent and planned a palace for his son, but rotten luck at Waterloo brought construction to a halt.

JARDINS DU TROCADÉRO

Below the palace, the Jardins du Trocadéro extend their impressive swaths of green to the Seine. The Gardens offer a stunning picnic spot, a ride on a two-storied **carousel** (€2) in the pl. de Varsovie, and, at night, an incredible view of the Eiffel Tower. The unlit parts of the garden are best avoided after dark.

CIMETIÈRE DE PASSY

2, r. du Commandant-Schloesing. M: Trocadéro. ☎01 47 27 51 42. From the métro, walk toward the right-hand wing of the Palais de Chaillot, turn right on av. Paul Doumer, and veer right onto r. du Commandant-Schloesing. ***Open*** *Mar.16-Nov. 5 M-F 8am-6pm, Sa 8:30am-6pm, Su 9am-6pm; Nov. 6-Mar.15 M-F 8am-5:30pm, Sa 8:30am-5:30pm, Su 9am-5:30pm.*

Less tourist-infested and more peaceful than the Palais Chaillot, the Passy Cemetery offers an alternative (if somewhat obscured) view of the Eiffel Tower. This hilly grotto, hanging high over the Trocadéro hustle-bustle since 1850, is the perfect place to wander, listen to the sounds of street performers below, and gaze out at the rooftops. Art fiends can pay homage to painter Edouard Manet and composers Claude Débussy and Gabriel Fauré. The enormous wall holding the cemetery up on the Trocadéro side was designed in the same Neoclassical style as the Palais Chaillot.

PASSY & AUTEUIL

Located southwest of Trocadéro, **Passy** and **Auteuil** were once famous for their restorative waters (which attracted such visitors as Molière, Racine, and Proust) and later for their avant-garde architecture. Now, this famous pair of ex-hamlets is best known as the site where *Last Tango in Paris* was filmed, and as a pricey shopping district. The glitziest in glamour-wear is around the intersection of **rue Passy, rue Mozart,** and **avenue Paul Doumer,** near M: La Muette. The narrow, winding streets named after famous composers, writers, and artists (Guy de Maupassant, Nicolas Poussin, and Donizetti are a few) recall 18th-century *salon* culture. **No. 59, rue d'Auteuil** was the site of Mme. Helvetius's house, where the so-called "Notre Dame d'Auteuil" hosted her notorious *salons*, frequented by the *Rive Droite's* well-read and best-dressed.

RUE LA FONTAINE

M: Michel-Ange Auteuil, Jasmin, or Eglise d'Auteuil, or RER: Kennedy. R. La Fontaine extends from the intersection at M: Michel-Ange Auteuil to the Maison de Radio-France, where it turns into r. Rayounard.

Its name comes from the spring which brought the residents of Auteuil their water, but now this celebrated street is Paris's free-flowing fountain of Belle Epoque architecture, much of it designed by Art Nouveau master Hector Guimard. **Castel Béranger** (1898), at no. 14, launched Guimard's career, and has turquoise iron flourishes, carbuncular seahorses, and columns bulging with floral sea-growth. No. 17 (1911) continued it, and now houses **Café Antoine,** complete with painted glass ceiling and Art Nouveau tiles. Off r. La Fontaine is **rue Agar,** which was micro-managed by Guimard through-and-through, down to the viney street signs. The building at no. 60 (1911), which now houses the **Ministère de l'Education Nationale,** is also his, and features a fence made of gnarled iron "branches." Proust enthusiasts will want to pause at no. 96—it's where the writer was born on July 10, 1871.

PLACE D'AUTEUIL

M: Eglise d'Auteuil.

This pleasantly jumbled, asymmetrical intersection features several shady, tree-lined cafés and the rather eclectic **Eglise Notre Dame d'Auteuil,** a Romanesque-Byzantine amalgam of a church.

Place de la Concorde

La Madeleine

Place de la République

RUE BENJAMIN FRANKLIN

M: Passy.

This street commemorates the statesman's one-time residence in Passy. Franklin lived at 66, r. Raynouard from 1777 to 1785 while negotiating a treaty between the new US and the old Louis XVI. The present building was built long after his stay, but it was on this site that Franklin experimented with his electrifying lightning rod.

STATUE OF LIBERTY

M: Passy or Mirabeau. Walk down av. du Président Kennedy (from Mirabeau, toward the Tour Eiffel; from Passy, away from it), until the Pont de Grenelle. Access to the Allée des Cygnes from the Pont Bir-Hakeim.

On a man-made islet in the middle of the Seine, the **Allée des Cygnes,** stands a very miniature version of the very grand Lady Liberty of New York fame. This version of the monument, by French sculptor Frédéric Bartholdi, was donated by a group of American expatriates in 1885 and was moved to this spot for the 1889 World Exposition. The shady, sandy island is good for wandering.

JARDIN DE RANELAGH

M: La Muette. From the métro, head away from the Eiffel Tower down Chaussée de la Muette to av. Ranelagh.

The lovely Jardin de Ranelagh has playgrounds, a carousel, and puppets and is the perfect place for a romantic picnic after a day of architectural sight-seeing or marathon museum visits.

SEVENTEENTH ARRONDISSEMENT

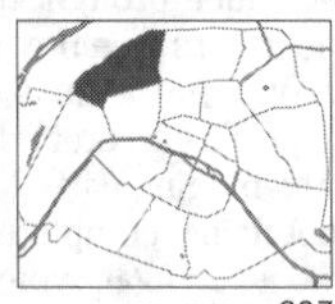
see map p. 397

NEIGHBORHOOD QUICKFIND: ***Discover,*** *p. 13;* ***Museums,*** *p. 156;* ***Food & Drink,*** *p. 194;* ***Nightlife,*** *p. 217;* ***Accommodations,*** *p. 273.*

VILLAGE BATIGNOLLES

In the eastern half of the 17*ème*, **rue des Batignolles** is considered the center of the Village Batignolles, a quiet, old-fashioned village of shops and residences starting at Boulevard des Batignolles to the south and extending up to **place du Dr. Félix Lobligeois.** Just north of the *place*, the craggy waterfalls and duck-ponds of the Romantic park, **square des Batignolles,** recall its more famous neighbor to the south, the English-style Parc Monceau (see p. 105); it was from the park's western end that Monet painted the train tracks running from the southern Gare St-Lazare. To the west, restaurants and cafés line **rue des Dames,** while shops stand on **rue de Lévis** (M: Villiers). On the other side of r. des Batignolles, at **rue Lemercier** between r. Clairaut and r. des Moines (M: Brochant), is a daily covered market filled with meat, cheese, flowers, produce, and old women who have shopped here since WWII. **La Cité des Fleurs,** 59-61, r. de la Jonquière (at the intersection with r. des Epinettes), is a row of exquisite private homes and gardens that look like they were lifted out of a Balzac novel. Designed in 1847, this prototypical condominium required each owner to plant at least three trees in the gardens.

CIMETIÈRE DES BATIGNOLLES

8, r. St-Just. M: Port-de-Clichy. From the métro, walk north along av. Port-de-Clichy and turn right onto av. du Cimetière des Batignolles. ☎01 46 27 03 18. ***Open*** *Mar. 16 to early Nov. M-F 8am-6pm; early Nov. to Mar. 15 M-F 8am-5:30pm, Sa 8:30am-5:30pm, Su 9am-5:30pm. Last entrance 15min. before closing. Free.*

The Cimetière des Batignolles, sandwiched between a noisy *lycée* and the car horns of the Périphérique, is surprisingly serene given its surroundings. André Breton, Paul Verlaine, and Benjamin Peret are buried here.

EIGHTEENTH ARRONDISSEMENT

NEIGHBORHOOD QUICKFIND: ***Discover,*** *p. 13;* ***Museums,*** *p. 156;* ***Food & Drink,*** *p. 195;* ***Nightlife,*** *p. 218;* ***Shopping,*** *p. 245;* ***Accommodations,*** *p. 273.*

see map pp. 386-387

MOUNTING MONTMARTRE

Funicular runs cars up and down the hill every 2min. Open 6am-12:30am. €1.30 or métro ticket.

One does not merely visit Montmartre; one climbs it. The standard approach is from the south, via M: Anvers or M: Abbesses, although other directions provide interesting, less crowded climbs. From M: Anvers, the walk up r. Steinkerque to the ornate switchbacked stairway is short but sometimes overcrowded with tourists and associated commerce. The longer climb from M: Abbesses, also the safest at night, passes by more worthwhile cafés and shops; follow r. de la Vieuville to r. Drevet, turning right on r. Gabrielle and left up the stairs to r. du Cardinal Dubois. For an easier ascent, take the glass-covered **funiculaire** from the base of r. Tardieu (from M: Anvers, walk up r. Steinkerque and take a left on r. Tardieu). Something like a ski lift, it is operated by the RATP and you can ride it with a normal métro ticket.

Every Sunday at 2:30pm from May 1 to October 15, the city organizes historic 2hr. walking tours in French of Montmartre, which allow a unique view into some of the less-touristed spots of the *butte* (meet at the exit of the funicular station; €6).

BASILIQUE DU SACRÉ-COEUR

35, r. du Chevalier de la Barre. M: Anvers, Abbesses, or Château-Rouge. ☎01 53 41 89 00. ***Open*** *daily 7am-10:30pm. Wheelchair-accessible through back.* ***Admission*** *free.* ***Dome and crypt*** *open daily 9am-6:45pm. €5.*

The Basilica of the Sacred Heart floats above Paris like an exotic headdress. In 1873, the Assemblée Nationale selected the birthplace of the *Commune* (see **Life & Times,** p. 45) as the location for Sacré-Coeur, "in witness of repentance and as a symbol of hope," although politician Eugène Spuller called it "a monument to civil war." The Catholic establishment hoped that the Sacré-Coeur would "expiate the sins" of France after the bloody civil war in which thousands of *communards* were massacred by government troops. After a massive fund-raising effort, the basilica was completed in 1914 and consecrated in 1919. Its hybrid style of onion domes, arches,

the local story

Un Vrai Artiste

Pl. du Tertre was, in its day, a true artists' haven. Like most of Montmartre, though, it has since degenerated into a big, square-shaped tourist trap. Street artists crowd the place, hoping to peddle their wares to tourists. But artists like ***Steven Petrovic*** *prove that the artistic spirit is still alive and well in Montmartre. Petrovic comes to the square every day, sets up his easel, and gets to work.*

LG: How long have you been drawing portraits here?
SP: Oh, for about 20 years.

LG: Twenty years, wow! How many do you draw a day?
SP: It's hard because the problem isn't how many portraits but how good a portrait; it's better to draw two or three in a day than 50.

LG: So who asks for a portrait most often? Children, women, men...
SP: It could be someone elderly or it could be a child. It's sentimental. It depends on the person's intelligence. And the people who are attracted to my work, I draw them with pleasure because to do a good job there has to already be communication with the people.

and white color set it apart from the smoky grunge of most Parisian buildings. Most striking inside the basilica are the many **mosaics,** especially the depiction of Christ on the ceiling and the mural of the Passion at the back of the altar. The narrow climb up to the top of the dome offers the highest vantage point in all of Paris and a view that stretches as far as 50km on clear days. Farther down, the **crypt** contains a relic of what many believe to be a piece of the sacred heart of Christ. While the views up the grassy slopes to the Basilica are among the most beautiful in the city, the streets beneath the winding pedestrian pathways leading up to the famed Basilica are hideously over-touristed; to circumvent the onslaught, walk up r. des Trois Frères instead of those streets. Likewise, try to avoid the sacrilegiously commodified streets surrounding Sacré-Coeur.

LAPIN AGILE

22, r. des Saules. M: Lamarck-Caulaincourt. Walk uphill from the métro, turn left on r. Caulaincourt, and right on r. des Saules. ☎01 46 06 85 87; www.au-lapin-agile.com. Call to reserve. ***Entrance*** *and 1 drink €24 (Su-F except holidays, students under 26 €17).* ***Shows*** *start daily at 9pm and go until 2am. Knock on the door if you arrive after 9pm.*

Still going strong among quaint shuttered houses is the Lapin Agile cabaret. Frequented by Verlaine, Renoir, Modigliani, and Max Jacob, the establishment was first known as the "Cabaret des Assassins" until André Gill decorated its facade with a painting of a *lapin* (rabbit) balancing a hat on its head and a bottle on its paw. The cabaret immediately gained renown as the "Lapin à Gill," (Gill's rabbit). By the time Picasso began to frequent the establishment, walking over from his first studio at no. 49, r. Gabrielle, the name had contracted to "Lapin Agile." Today, you can sip a delicious *cerises maison* (€7) while taking in a delightful mix of French *chanson* and comedy (see **Entertainment,** p. 225).

BATEAU-LAVOIR

11bis, pl. Emile Godeau. M: Abbesses. Facing the church, head right up r. des Abbesses, and turn right (uphill) on r. Ravignan; follow the steps to pl. Emile Godeau. Closed to the public.

Given its strange name by sardonic residents Max Jacob and André Salmon, who thought the building's winding corridors resembled the interior of a ship *(bateau)*, the Bateau-Lavoir has been home to several artists' *ateliers* since the turn of the century. Still serving as studio space for 25 contemporary painters and sculptors, the building's undisputed heyday was in the first quarter of the 20th century, when great artists like Picasso, Juan Gris, Modigliani, Apollinaire, and Jacob (among others) stayed here. In his apartment here in 1907, Picasso finished his cubist manifesto, the remarkable *Demoiselles d'Avignon.* Alas, the original building burned down in 1970, so all that distinguishes this building from its neighbors is a plaque in French describing the site's history.

LES VIGNES

r. des Saules. M: Lamarck-Caulaincourt. Follow directions to the Lapin Agile. On the corner of r. des Saules and r. St-Vincent. Closed to the general public, except during the Fête des Vendages.

In the 16th century, Montmartre was known for its vineyards and revitalizing wines; so much so, that a 17th-century saying promises that *"c'est du vin de Montmartre qui on boit pinte et pisse quarte"* ("With Montmartre wine, you drink a pint and piss out a quart"). Now this lone surviving vineyard, perched on the hilly slope across from the Lapin Agile, is one of the few remaining vineyards in all of Paris. More than a wine-grower, the *vignes* of Montmartre is a tradition: every October, the vineyard hosts the **Fête des Vendages,** a boisterous festival of wine-drinking, dancing, and folklore, when the wine produced on the grounds is sold to the public (see **Discover,** p. 20). The area around the vineyard, on the northern slope of the *butte*, is one of the loveliest in Montmartre. Still unspoiled by tourism, the streets around r. St-Vincent have maintained their rural village charm with old stone walkways and farm houses.

PLACE DU TERTRE

M: Abbesses. With your back to the church in pl. des Abbesses, walk up r. de la Vieuville, turn left on r. Drevet, left again on r. Gabrielle, and go right uphill on r. du Calvaire.

One of the most heinously over-touristed spots in the 18*ème*, pl. du Tertre teems with amateur artists, hordes of pushy portrait painters, and has-been cafés. But the *place* was once the haunt of artists and intellectuals, and the cheapness of the area has not destroyed its celebrated vista of the *butte*.

DOWNHILL

RUES ABBESSES, LEPIC & D'ORSEL

These days tasty restaurants, trendy cafés, and *boulangeries* crowd this corner of Montmartre around r. des Abbesses and r. Lepic. Fans of the international hit film *Amélie* (2002) have been

LG: Have you studied art?
SP: Yes. I went to the School of Beaux-Arts in Yugoslavia, in Belgrade. For five years you learn not only how to draw and paint, but you learn the job, like in the Renaissance Period. Because what people don't realize is that drawing and painting is a job, like philosophy, like music, like mathematics.

LG: So it takes five years?
SP: Minimum. And your whole life.

LG: Do you like your job?
SP: Oh, of course.

LG: And do you ever get annoyed with the tourists and all that?
SP: With stupid people, one is always annoyed. But, no, you have to love humanity in order to continue to exist.

LG: Have you ever drawn a portrait of someone famous?
SP: No, because it has nothing to do with fame. Of course there are famous actresses and famous actors or politicians who pass by, but who cares? There are people who are very simple but who have a goodness, something in their face that is just as good as all the celebrities and all the riches of the world. I'm not interested in drawing famous people. Because one doesn't try to become famous by drawing famous people. One becomes famous by doing real things.

Montmartre

Sacré-Coeur

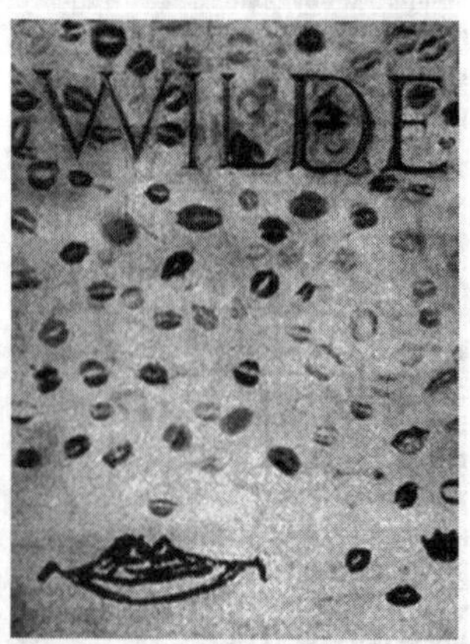

Père Lachaise

making pilgrimages to this home of the (either charmingly or frighteningly) adorable title character, and cafés and shops have accordingly thematized themselves. Longtime residents have, predictably, been complaining about the "Amélie Poulainization" of their neighborhood, but to little avail. Tall iron gates hide the beautiful gardens of several 18th-century townhouses. Walking down r. Lepic will carry you past the **Moulin Radet,** one of the last remaining windmills on Montmartre. Farther down is the site of the **Moulin de la Galette,** depicted in a painting by Auguste Renoir during one of the frequent dances held there (*Bal au Moulin de la Galette*, 1876, now in the Musée d'Orsay). Even farther down is one of Vincent van Gogh's former homes at 54, r. Lepic. Attractive boutiques cluster along r. d'Orsel near Abbesses.

CIMETIÈRE MONTMARTRE

20, av. Rachel. M: Place de Clichy or Blanche. ☎01 53 42 36 30. Follow r. Caulaincourt parallel to r. Lepic downhill to get to the cemetery. Open M-F 8am-6pm, Sa 8:30am-6pm, Su 9am-6pm; winter closes 5:30pm.

Though less star-studded than the legendary Père Lachaise (see p. 123), Cimetière Montmartre is beautifully landscaped and more secluded than its famous neighbor. Writers Alexandre Dumas and Stendhal, painter Edgar Degas, physicists André Ampère and Léon Foucault, composer Hector Berlioz, filmmaker François Truffaut, and dancer Vaslav Nijinksy are buried here, among others. The cemetery was also the site of countless mass graves after the siege of the Commune in 1871. Emile Zola was interred here until his corpse joined those of other famous artists in the Panthéon in 1908.

BAL DU MOULIN ROUGE

82, bd. de Clichy. M: Blanche. Directly across from the métro. ☎01 53 09 82 82; www.moulin-rouge.com. Shows 7, 9, 11pm.

Along the bd. de Clichy and bd. de Rochechouart, you'll find many of the cabarets and nightclubs that were the definitive hangouts of the Belle Epoque, including the infamous cabaret Bal du Moulin Rouge, immortalized by the paintings of Toulouse-Lautrec, the music of Offenbach, and, most recently, Baz Luhrmann's Hollywood blockbuster. At the turn of the century, Paris's bourgeoisie came to the Moulin Rouge to play at being bohemian. After WWI, Parisian bohemians relocated to the Left Bank and the area around pl. Pigalle became a world-renowned seedy red-light district (see p. 107). Today, the crowd consists of tourists out for an s, and skin. The revues are still risqué, but the price of expensive—a show and dinner cost €130. You can be ket for a spot at the bar for €63, which includes two you'll have somewhere to sit.

au Rouge, Marcadet-Poissonniers.

tracks, the 18*ème* becomes an immigrant ghetto in the filled with crumbling buildings, the quarter takes its ie medieval vineyard that once stood here. During the e (see **Life & Times,** p. 49), the presence of the Algerian N) kept the area relatively segregated. Today, the area heap housing in the city, but ambitious plans may soon unt clothing shops line bd. Barbès, and you'll find Afri- s around r. Doudeauville and r. des Poissonniers. **Tati,** a od for rummaging, is at no. 13, pl. de la République (see ickpocketers are ready and waiting to prey on unsus- unfamiliar with the area should avoid it at night.

ARRONDISSEMENT

NEIGHBORHOOD QUICKFIND: ***Discover,*** *p. 14;* ***Food & Drink,*** *p. 197;* ***Accommodations,*** *p. 274.*

see map p. 398

PARC DE LA VILLETTE

The best sight in the 19*ème* is the Parc de la Villette. See p. 143.

PARC DES BUTTES-CHAUMONT

M: Buttes-Chaumont and Botzaris are both situated right along the park. ***Open*** *daily 7am-11pm; gates close 15min. early.*

In the south of the 19*ème*, Parc des Buttes-Chaumont is a mix of man-made topography and transplanted vegetation, all of it created on a whim of nostalgia; Napoleon III commissioned it in 1860 out of a longing for London's Hyde Park, where he spent much of his time in exile. Before he placed the order, the *quartier* had been, since the 13th century, host to a *gibbet* (an iron cage filled with the rotting corpses of criminals), a dumping-ground for dead horses, a breeding-ground for worms, and a gypsum quarry (the source of "plaster of Paris"). Making a park out of the existing mess took four years and 1000 workers. Designer Adolphe Alphand had all of the soil replaced and the quarried remains built up with new rock to create enormous fake cliffs surrounding a lake. Today's visitors walk the winding paths surrounded by lush greenery and dynamic hills, and enjoy a great view of the *quartier* from the cave-filled cliffs topped with a Roman temple. Watch out for the ominously-named *Pont des Suicides* (Suicide Bridge).

TWENTIETH ARRONDISSEMENT

NEIGHBORHOOD QUICKFIND: ***Discover,*** *p. 14;* ***Museums,*** *p. 157;* ***Food & Drink,*** *p. 197;* ***Nightlife,*** *p. 218;* ***Accommodations,*** *p. 275.*

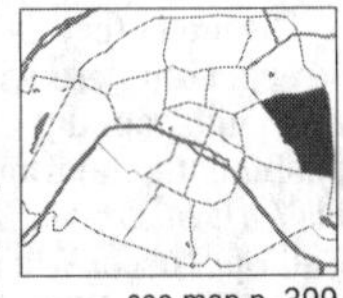

see map p. 399

PÈRE LACHAISE CEMETERY

16, r. du Repos. M: Père Lachaise. ☎01 55 25 82 10. ***Open*** *Mar.-Oct. M-F 8am-6pm, Sa 8:30am-6pm, Su and holidays 9am-6pm; Nov.-Feb. M-F 8am-5:30pm, Sa 8:30am-5:30pm, Su and holidays 9am-5:30pm. Last entrance 15min. before closing. Free. Free* ***maps*** *supposedly available at guard booths by main entrances, but they're usually out; it is worth the €2 to buy a detailed map from a nearby tabac*

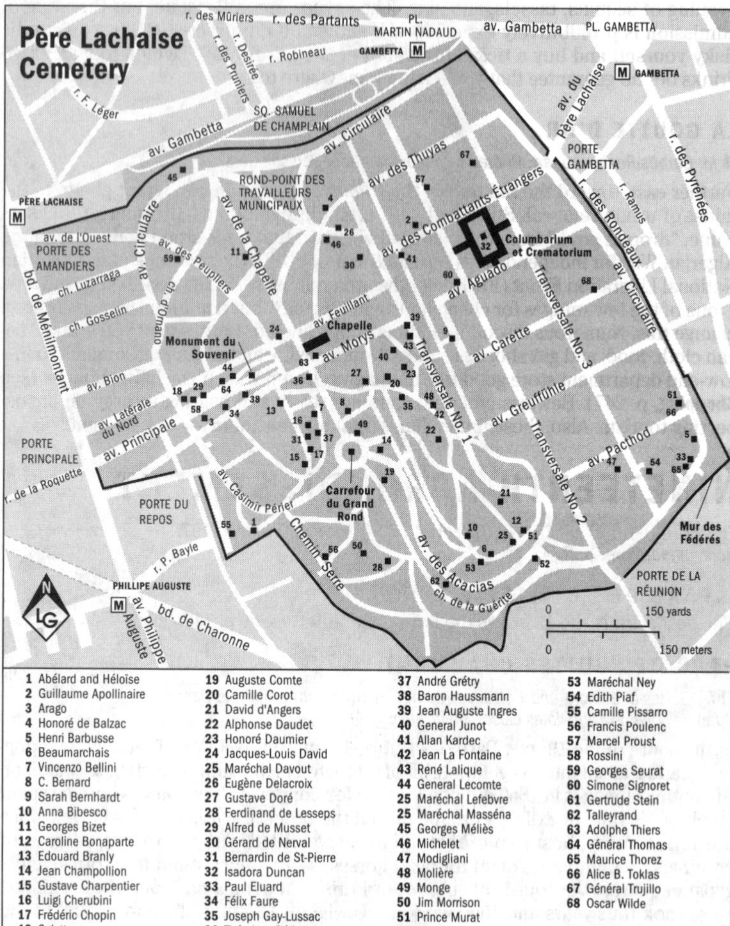

before entering. 2hr. ***guided tour*** *in English June-Sept. Sa 3pm; in French Sa 2:30pm, occasionally Tu 2:30pm and Su at 3pm as well as numerous "theme" tours. €6, students €4. Tours meet at the bd. de Ménilmontant entrance; call ☎ 01 40 71 75 60 for info.*

With its winding paths and elaborate sarcophagi, Cimetière du Père Lachaise has become the final resting place of French and foreign giants. Balzac, Colette, Jacques Louis David, Delacroix, La Fontaine, Haussmann, Molière, and Proust are buried here, as are Chopin, Jim Morrison, Gertrude Stein, and Oscar Wilde. With so many tourists, however, they're hardly resting in peace.

The cemetery is a bustling 19th-century neighborhood-of-the-dead laid out in streets complete with sarcophagi that resemble little houses. Many of the tombs in this landscaped grove strive to remind visitors of the dead's many worldly accomplishments: the tomb of French Romantic painter **Géricault** wears a reproduction of his *Raft of the Medusa* (the original is in the Louvre); on **Chopin's** tomb sits his muse Calliope. **Oscar Wilde's** grave is marked by a larger-than-life striking Egyptian figure. Shortly after Wilde's burial, there was a scandal over the generous proportions of the Egyptian's Nile jewels. The director of the cemetery, exhausted by all the fuss, took matters into his own hands: he allegedly removed the offending parties with a small hammer, condemning them to eternal life as a paperweight. Though the jewels are gone, dozens of lipstick marks from adoring fans cover the tomb today. **Haussmann,** the man of the boulevards, wanted to destroy the cemetery as part of his urban-renewal project, but obviously relented; he now occupies a mausoleum in Père Lachaise. Remembered by plaques here are dancer **Isadora Duncan,** author **Richard Wright,** opera diva **Maria Callas,** and artist **Max Ernst.** The most visited grave is that of **Jim Morrison,** the former lead singer of The Doors. His graffiti-covered bust was removed from the tomb, leaving his fans to fill the rest of the cemetery with their messages. In summer, dozens of people bring flowers, joints, beer, poetry, and Doors paraphernalia to his tomb each day; the sandbox in front of the stone is now the sanctioned site for the creative expression of such pensive mourners. A guard polices the spot at all times.

Over one million people are buried in the cemetery. Curiously, there are only 100,000 tombs. The discrepancy is due to the old practice of burying the poor in mass graves. Corpses are removed from these unmarked plots at regular intervals to make room for new generations of the dead. Even with such purges, however, the 44 hectares of Père Lachaise are filled to bursting, so the government makes room by digging up any grave that has not been visited in a certain number of years. To avoid this fate, some solitary (and rich) souls who sense they are about to kick the bucket resort to hiring a professional "mourner."

Perhaps the most moving sites in Père Lachaise are those that mark collective deaths. The **Mur des Fédérés** (Wall of the Federals) has become a site of pilgrimage for left-wing sympathizers. In May 1871, a group of *communards* murdered the Archbishop of Paris, who had been taken hostage at the beginning of the Commune. They dragged his mutilated corpse to their stronghold in Père Lachaise and tossed it in a ditch. Four days later, the victorious *Versaillais* found the body. In retaliation, they lined up 147 Fédérés against the eastern wall of the cemetery, shot them, and buried them on the spot. Since 1871, the Mur des Fédérés has been a rallying point for the French Left, which recalls the massacre's anniversary every Pentecost. Near the wall, a number of moving monuments commemorate the Resistance fighters of WWII as well as Nazi concentration camp victims.

PARC DE BELLEVILLE

27, r. Piat, in front of La Maison de l'Air. M: Pyrénées.

Built in the side of a hill, this well-landscaped park is a series of terraces connected by stairs and footpaths. At its highest points, the park offers spectacular views of Parisian landmarks, including Sacre Coeur, Centre Pompidou, and the Eiffel Tower. Fountains, flowers, and families dot the park's serene landscape, the only noise coming from the playground located at the entrance.

PERIMETER SIGHTS

BOIS DE BOULOGNE

M: Porte Maillot, Sablons, Pont de Neuilly, Porte Dauphine, or Porte d'Auteuil. Open 24hr.

The Bois de Boulogne is an 846-hectare (over 2,000 acre) green canopy at the western edge of Paris and a popular place for walks, jogs, boating, and picnics. In a past life, it was the vast Forêt de Rouvray, a royal hunting ground where deer and wild boar ran with wolves and bears. In 1852 the Bois had become "a desert used for dueling and suicides," and was given to the city of Paris by Napoleon III. Acting on imperial instructions, Baron Haussmann dug lakes, created waterfalls and cut winding paths through thickly wooded areas. By the turn of the century, the park was square enough that aristocratic families rode there to spend a Sunday afternoon "in the country." In harder times, the pleasure park also served a decidedly utilitarian purpose—its trees were felled for firewood during the Revolution; it was occupied by a "ragged army" of citizens scrounging for edible plants during the starvation of the Prussian siege in 1870; it was a site for the execution of political undesirables ("men with intelligent faces") by the Communards in 1871; and during WWII people grew vegetable gardens to supplement meager rations. In 1991, a flood of newly liberated Eastern Europeans camped in the park. And more recently, the Bois by night has been a bazaar of sex and drugs, complete with transvestite prostitutes and violent crime. Police are stepping up patrols, but the boulevards around the periphery of the Bois continue to be lined with fleshly wares at night and so are best avoided then. Take care if wandering the park alone, and try to stay on main paths and roads.

STADIUMS

The Bois de Boulogne contains several stadiums, the most famous of which are the **Hippodromes de Longchamp** and **d'Auteuil,** a flat racecourse and a steeplechase, respectively. The June Grand Prix at Longchamp was one of the premier annual events of the Belle Epoque. Today, these stadiums host events ranging from music festivals to sports. Also within the *bois*, the **Parc des Princes** hosts football (soccer) matches, and the **Stade Roland Garros** is home of the **French Open** tennis tournament.

LAKES

M: Porte Dauphine. Boathouses open late Feb. to early Nov. daily 10am-7pm, weather permitting. Rentals €7 per hr., €.65 deposit.

There are two artificial lakes stretching down the eastern edge of the Bois. The manicured islands of the **Lac Inférieur** can be reached only by rowboat. Visitors can also stroll under a cascading waterfall between the two lakes, a refreshing break from sweltering summer temperatures.

JARDIN D'ACCLIMATATION

M: Sablons. Cross the street, pass Monoprix, and walk three blocks. ☎01 40 67 90 82. Open daily 10am-7pm; ticket office closes 5:45pm. €2.30, under 3 free. No dogs allowed.

The Jardin d'Acclimatation offers a small zoo, some sports (mini-golf, riding, bowling), and carnival rides. Sneakily mixed in are educational museums that parents will adore (see below), picnic areas, and outdoor jazz concerts. Pick up a map from the ticket counter as you enter.

MUSÉE EN HERBE

Directly on your left at the Entrée Sablons. ☎01 40 67 97 66. Open daily 10am-6pm. €3. Call to make reservations for special studio sessions.

The Musée en Herbe is a European art-history museum designed for children ages 4-11. Temporary exhibits range from farm animals to artists like Manet, Chagall, and Picasso. The museum also offers studio workshops on sculpture, pottery, papier mâché, painting and collage for children two and older. A participatory theater company for children stages plays and puppet shows.

PRÉ CATELAN

From M: Porte Maillot (exit av. de Neuilly), take bus #244 to Bagatuel-Pré-Catelan. Open daily 8:30am-7:30pm.

The Pré Catelan could be named after Théophile Catelan, master of the hunt under Louis XIV, but legend has it that this neatly manicured meadow was named after a murdered delivery boy, Arnault Catelan, who rode from Provence to Paris to deliver gifts to Philippe le Bel from Beatrice de Savoie, and who hired a group of men to protect him on his journey. The men robbed and murdered him at night, believing that Arnault carried gold, though he only had rare perfumes from the South of France. Authorities later captured the marauders, who, doused in a rare Provençale scent, were easily identifiable. Inside the Pré Catelan, the **Jardin de Shakespeare** is a popular open-air theatre. *(☎01 46 47 73 20. Open daily for wandering 2-4pm.)*

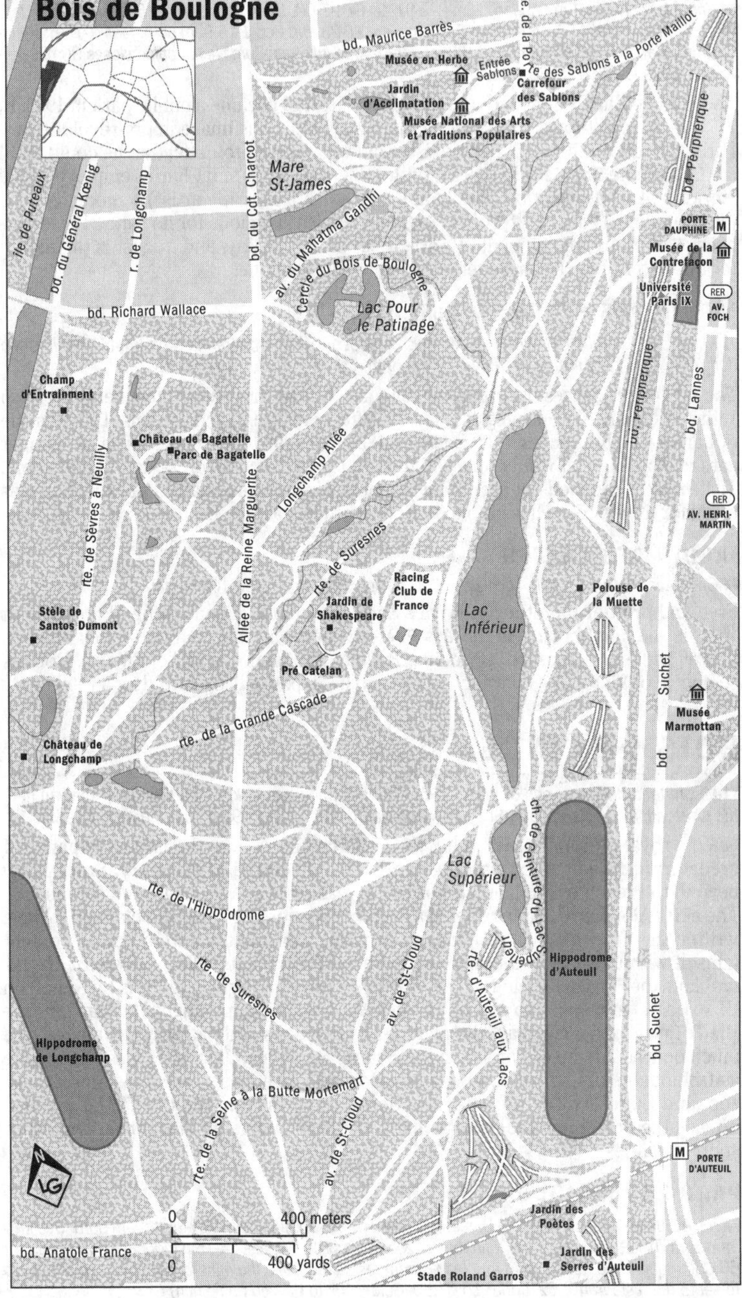
Bois de Boulogne
bd. Maurice Barrès
Musée en Herbe
Entrée Sablons
rte. de la Porte des Sablons à la Porte Maillot
Jardin d'Acclimatation
Carrefour des Sablons
Musée National des Arts et Traditions Populaires
bd. Périphérique
Mare St-James
PORTE DAUPHINE
Musée de la Contrefaçon
Université Paris IX
AV. FOCH
av. du Mahatma Gandhi
Cercle du Bois de Boulogne
Lac Pour le Patinage
bd. du Cdt. Charcot
r. de Longchamp
bd. du Général Kœnig
île de Puteaux
bd. Richard Wallace
Champ d'Entraînment
Château de Bagatelle
Parc de Bagatelle
Longchamp Allée
bd. Lannes
AV. HENRI-MARTIN
rte. de Sèvres à Neuilly
Allée de la Reine Marguerite
rte. de Suresnes
Racing Club de France
Jardin de Shakespeare
Lac Inférieur
Pelouse de la Muette
Stèle de Santos Dumont
Pré Catelan
bd. Suchet
Musée Marmottan
rte. de la Grande Cascade
Château de Longchamp
ch. de Ceinture du Lac Supérieur
Lac Supérieur
rte. de l'Hippodrome
av. de St-Cloud
rte. d'Auteuil aux Lacs
Hippodrome d'Auteuil
rte. de Suresnes
Hippodrome de Longchamp
rte. de la Seine à la Butte Mortemart
PORTE D'AUTEUIL
0
400 meters
400 yards
Jardin des Poètes
bd. Anatole France
Jardin des Serres d'Auteuil
Stade Roland Garros

PARC DE BAGATELLE

Same bus stop as Pré Catelan, above. ☎01 40 67 97 00. Open daily Jan. 1-15 9am-4:30pm; Jan. 16-Feb. 15 and Oct. 16-Nov. 30 9am-5:30pm; Feb. 16-28 and Oct. 1-15 9am-6pm; Mar. 1-15 8:30am-6:30pm; Mar. 16-Apr. 30 and Sept. 8:30am-7pm; June-July 9am-8pm. Ticket office closes 30min. earlier. €1.50, ages 6-10 €0.75.

The Parc de Bagatelle was once a private estate and became a public park in 1905. In 1777, in an impetuous act that could not have helped his image in pre-revolutionary Paris, the future Charles X bet his sister-in-law, Marie-Antoinette, that he could build the **Château de Bagatelle** in three months. She was game, and Charles employed 1000 workers of all descriptions (including a Scottish landscape artist) to complete the job (see **Garden Party,** p. 284). The **Bagatelle Garden** is famous for its June 21 **rose exhibition.** Tulips are magnificent in April, irises bloom in May, and August is the month for the water lilies the gardener added in tribute to Monet.

JARDIN DES SERRES D'AUTEUIL

M: Porte d'Auteuil or Michel-Ange Molitor. Enter at 1, av. Gordon-Bennett, off bd. d'Auteuil. Open daily May-Aug. 10am-6pm; Sept.-Apr. 10am-5pm. €0.75; reduced fare €0.35.

The Jardin des Serres d'Auteuil (Greenhouse Garden) represents the merging of two 19th century loves: iron and glass (see the **Eiffel Tower,** p. 96) and gardens. This was one of Paris's first hothouses, built between 1895 and 1898 to allow the green of summer gardens to bloom all winter long and today it is still in action, or, rather, in full bloom. Tickets were rationed out according to a person's moral standards; an exception was made for drunkards, whose "condition" the garden was supposed to cure.

JARDIN DES POÈTES

Open Apr. 16-Oct. 15 daily 9am-8pm; Oct. 16-Apr. 15 W and Sa-Su 10am-7pm.

Free and prettier than the Jardin des Serres d'Auteuil, if something of a make-out spot, is the neighboring **Jardin des Poètes.** Poems are marked on stones on each flower bed: scan Ronsard, Corneille, Racine, Baudelaire, and Apollinaire. Rodin's sculpture of Victor Hugo is also to be found here, partially obscured by a thicket.

BOIS DE VINCENNES

*M: Château de Vincennes or Porte Dorée. To best enjoy the park, rent a **bike** from the van near the Château, in the Esplanade St-Louis, **open** Sa-Su and holidays 9am-7pm; about €4 per hr.*

Once a royal hunting forest, the Bois de Vincennes is now the largest expanse of greenery in Paris, encompassing nearly 1000 hectares of greenery. Since it lay beyond the reach of Parisian authorities, it was once a favorite ground for dueling. The elder Alexandre Dumas dueled a literary collaborator here who claimed to have written the *Tour de Nesle.* Dumas's pistol misfired and the author had to content himself with using the experience as the basis for a scene in *The Corsican Brothers.* Like the Bois de Boulogne, the Vincennes forest was given to Paris by Napoleon III, to be transformed into an English-style garden. Not surprisingly, Haussmann (see **Life & Times,** p. 60) oversaw the planning of the lakes and pathways. Annexed to a much poorer section of Paris than the Bois de Boulogne, Vincennes was never quite as fashionable or as formal. Today, the Bois de Vincennes's bikepaths, horsetrails, zoo, and Buddhist Temple offer wonderful escapes from the city. The park also houses the **Vélodrome Jacques Anquetil,** the **Hippodrome de Vincennes,** and other sports facilities.

PARC ZOOLOGIQUE DE PARIS

*53, av. de St-Maurice. M: Porte Dorée. ☎01 44 75 20 10. **Open** daily May-Sept. 9am-6pm; Oct.-May 9am-5pm. Ticket office closes 30min. before zoo. **Admission** €8; ages 4-16, students 16-27, and over 60 €5; under 4 free. Kiddie train tour leaves from restaurant (take the right fork after you enter the zoo to get to the restaurant); €2, under 10 €1.50. Guidebook to the zoo (in French) €5.*

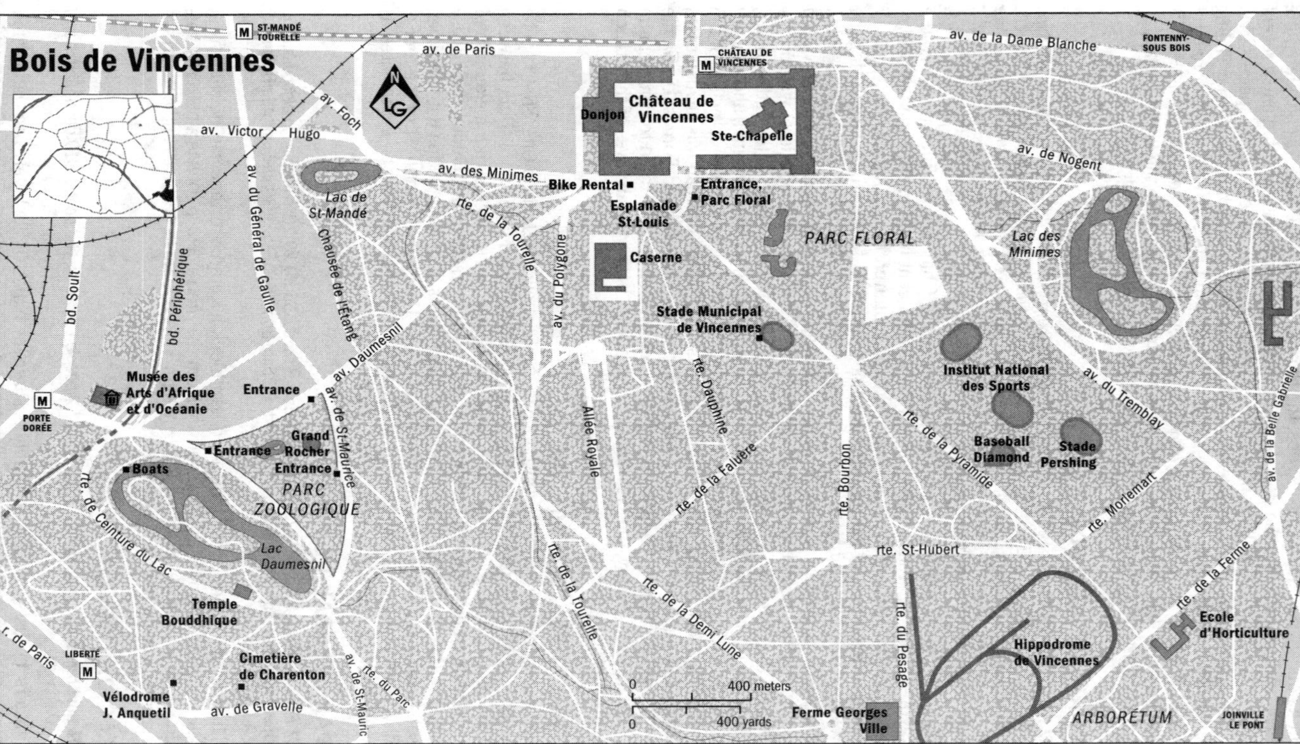

Bois de Vincennes
ST-MANDÉ TOURELLE
av. de Paris
CHÂTEAU DE VINCENNES
av. de la Dame Blanche
FONTENNY-SOUS BOIS
av. Foch
av. Victor Hugo
Château de Vincennes
Donjon
Ste-Chapelle
av. de Nogent
av. des Minimes
Bike Rental
Entrance, Parc Floral
Esplanade St-Louis
Lac de St-Mandé
rte. de la Tourelle
PARC FLORAL
Lac des Minimes
bd. Soult
bd. Périphérique
av. du Général de Gaulle
Chaussée de l'Étang
av. du Polygone
Caserne
Stade Municipal de Vincennes
av. Daumesnil
Musée des Arts d'Afrique et d'Océanie
PORTE DORÉE
Entrance
av. de St-Maurice
rte. Dauphine
Allée Royale
Institut National des Sports
av. du Tremblay
av. de la Belle Gabrielle
Grand Rocher
Entrance
Entrance
Boats
PARC ZOOLOGIQUE
rte. de la Pyramide
Baseball Diamond
Stade Pershing
rte. de la Faluère
rte. Bourbon
rte. Mortemart
rte. de Ceinture du Lac
Lac Daumesnil
rte. St-Hubert
rte. de la Tourelle
rte. de la Demi Lune
rte. de la Ferme
Temple Bouddhique
rte. du Pesage
Ecole d'Horticulture
Hippodrome de Vincennes
r. de Paris
LIBERTÉ
Cimetière de Charenton
av. de St-Mauric
rte. du Parc
0
400 meters
0
400 yards
Vélodrome J. Anquetil
av. de Gravelle
Ferme Georges Ville
ARBORÉTUM
JOINVILLE LE PONT

In a country not known for its zoos, the Parc Zoologique de Paris is considered the best of the bunch. It is the Bois de Vincennes's most popular attraction and a recent effort has been made to improve the environments in which its 135 species live. Don't miss the impressive collection of Japanese macaques who pass the day sliding down rocks, swinging from trees, and chewing on hats thrown into their habitat (don't feed the animals!). The *phoques* (the French word for *seal*—pronounced just as you think it is) are fed daily at 4pm. The park is also home to the **Grand Rocher,** an observatory, which offers a breathtaking view of the surrounding *bois.*

CHÂTEAU DE VINCENNES

M: Château de Vincennes. On the northern edge of the park. ☎01 48 08 31 20. ***Open*** *Apr.-Sept. daily 10am-noon and 1:15-6pm; Oct.-Mar. 10am-noon and 1:15-5pm.* ***Tour*** *of the Ste-Chapelle (45min.) 10:15, 11:45am, 1:30, 4:15pm, summer also 5:15pm. €4, 18-25 €2.50, under 18 free.* ***Tour*** *of Ste-Chapelle, ramparts, and moat (1¼hr.) 11am, 2:15, 3, 3:45pm, in summer also 4:30pm. €5.50, ages 18-26 €3.50, under 18 free.*

Called "the Versailles of the Middle Ages," the Château de Vincennes was the favored court of French kings as early as the 13th century, and although the Louvre was royalty's principal home, every French monarch from Charles V to Henri IV spent at least part of his time at Vincennes. Henri III took refuge here during the Wars of Religion, and Mazarin and the court found the château's defenses useful in the wake of the Fronde. In the 18th century, Vincennes became a country-club prison for well-known enemies of the state like Mirabeau. When Diderot was imprisoned in the château, Rousseau walked through the forest to visit. In the 19th century, the complex resumed its military functions, serving as fortress, arsenal, and artillery park. In 1917, the infamous spy Mata Hari, convicted of espionage on behalf of the Germans, faced a firing squad within its walls. In 1940, the château was headquarters for General Maurice Gamelin, Commander of the French Land Forces. De Gaulle criticized Gamelin for holing up in Vincennes, without even a radio to connect him with the front. Today, the 17th-century apartments house the archives of the French armed forces.

STE-CHAPELLE & DONJON

Not to be confused with the (also lovely) Ste-Chapelle on Île de la Cité, Ste-Chapelle is looking better than ever these days after restoration of its exterior. Built between 1336 and 1370, the 52m high *donjon* (big square tower) is a striking example of medieval architecture. It has been closed for restoration (and hidden under very unattractive scaffolding) since 1995, however, and still no completion date has been set. Guided tours are the only way to get inside the church, but most of the tour is devoted to historical background, and much of their beauty can be appreciated as well from the outside as from inside the ramparts.

PARC FLORAL DE PARIS

Esplanade du Château. M: Château de Vincennes. ☎01 55 94 20 20; www.parcfloraldeparis.com. ***Open*** *daily Mar.-Apr. 9:30am-6pm; Apr.-Sept. 9:30am-8pm; Oct.-Feb. 9:30am-5pm.* ***Admission*** *€1, ages 6-17 and over 60 €0.50, under 6 free.*

The Parc Floral de Paris's ultra-modern block-lettered entrance can be seen from the château entrance that faces away from the métro. The park has a butterfly garden, miniature golf, and assorted games for kids, and hosts festivals and concerts in summer. Check the park's web site for details.

LAC DAUMESNIL

Boat rental *Mar.-Nov. daily 9:30am-7pm. 1-2 people €9 per hr., 3-4 people €10 per hr.; additional €10 deposit.*

Joggers, cyclists, and people-watchers share the banks of the lovely Lac Daumesnil, and rowboats share its waters. The mysterious caves near the lake—topped off by a small temple—are not to be missed.

FERME GEORGES VILLE (FERME DE PARIS)

☎01 43 28 47 63. ***Open*** *Su, Tu-Sa and holidays summer 1:30-7pm; winter 1:30-6pm.* ***Admission*** *€3.50, ages 6-12 €2.00, under 6 free.*

Visitors to the farm enjoy the company of real live chickens, cows, goats, and more. This is a great place to bring the kids, and all other petting-zoo enthusiasts.

LA DÉFENSE

M/RER: La Défense, or the #73 bus. The RER is faster, but the métro is a bit cheaper. If you take the RER, buy the RER ticket before going through the turnstile. A normal métro ticket may get you into the RER station in Paris, but won't get you out without a fine at La Défense. Consider either coming or going by the Esplanade de la Défense métro stop so you can savor the architecture and outdoor sculpture near the arch. ***Grande Arche*** *open daily 10am-8pm; ticket office closes 7:30pm, roof closes 8:30pm.* ***Admission*** *€7.50; under 18, students, and seniors €5.50. Beyond the small lawn, the* ***Info Défense*** *booth offers free maps, guides, and a free permanent exhibit on the architectural history and future of La Défense. ☎01 47 74 84 24. Open M-F 9:30am-5:30pm.* ***French petit train tours*** *Apr.-Oct. daily every hr. 10am-5pm (6pm in Aug.), lasting 35min., from under the Grande Arche; €5, under 16 €3.*

Just outside Paris's most exclusive suburbs lies a gleaming, teeming space crammed with eye-popping contemporary architecture, enormous office buildings, and one very geometric arch. Great efforts have been made since La Défense's initial development in 1958, especially by Mitterrand and his *Grands Projets* program, to inject social spaces, monuments, and art into La Défense's commercial landscape. Shops, galleries, gardens, and sculptures by **Miró, Calder,** and **César** cluster around the **Grande Arche de la Défense,** a 35-story building in the shape of a white hollow cube.

After the construction of the Tour Montparnasse in 1973 (see p. 115), Parisian authorities restricted further construction of *gratte-ciels* (skyscrapers) within the 20 *arrondissements* for fear that new highrises would alter the Paris skyline. As a result, new building projects moved to La Défense. To maintain the symmetry of the **Axe Historique** (the line that stretches from the Arc de Triomphe du Carrousel in front of the Louvre, up the Champs-Elysées to the Arc de Triomphe, and then up the av. de la Grande Armée to La Défense), I.M. Pei suggested a plan for a monument to anchor the Défense end of the axis (you'll see that the Arche is at a slight angle from the Axe—the RER station below required the variance). Danish architect Otto von Spreckelsen's Grande Arche was chosen for the La Défense monument, and Pei was asked to design the eastern terminus in the courtyard of the Louvre. Spreckelsen backed out of the project, disheartened by red tape and by his own design, which he deemed a "monument without a soul." British engineer Peter Rice finished the work and designed the canvas tent "clouds" suspended to soften the arch's austere angles.

The Arche was inaugurated on the French Republic's bicentennial, July 14, 1989. It took 300,000 tons of steel, 2800 marble and glass facade pieces, 2.6 billion francs and the efforts of 2000 workmen (two of whom died in construction accidents) to complete this 87,000 sq. m office building. The roof of this unconventional office building covers one hectare—Notre Dame could nestle in its hollow core. The arch's walls are covered with white marble and mirrors, so that it gleams in sunlight (bring your shades or you'll be squinting all morning long). The outdoor glass elevators make for a unique ride. The view from the top of the Arche, however, is less than spectacular given the number of tall buildings between it and the far-off city center. You're much better off with the views you get from the Eiffel Tower, the Basilica of Sacré-Coeur and the café at the top of the Centre Pompidou.

OTHER SIGHTS

Other Défense buildings include the **Bull Tower,** the tent-like **Palais Défense,** a space-age **IMAX dome,** and the **CNIT building,** a center for congresses, exhibitions, and conferences that, at 37 years old, is La Défense's oldest building. Underneath the Arche is the **Sources d'Europe** European information center, which houses a quiet café and holds exhibits on such topics as the European Union. (Open M-F 10am-6pm. Free.)

The Arche is surrounded by eight gardens (maps available at Info Défense). The huge **Quatre Temps** shopping center, one of the largest shopping malls in Europe, contains cafés, supermarkets, a cinema, and 30 restaurants. But visitors expecting to find a fashionable shopping mecca will probably be disappointed by the stores themselves—serious shoppers are better off staying in Paris proper. *(Enter from the Grande Arche métro, or from behind the Miró sculpture. Shops open M-Sa 10am-8pm. Supermarkets open M-F 9am-10pm, Sa 8:30am-10pm. Cinema and restaurants open until 11pm.)*

SAINT-DENIS

North of the 18*ème* and accessible by métro (see below), the town of St-Denis is most noted for its stunning 12th-century basilica, an architectural marvel—especially in comparison to the rather grubby modern buildings that stand beside it—with a long and storied past that is closely linked to the history of the French monarchy. The town itself has little else to offer in the way of tourist destinations, and if you're looking for a bite to eat, you'll find plenty of fast-food outlets and cheap eats, but not much in the way of fine dining. Its most recent claim to fame was as the venue for the 1998 World Cup, which necessitated the construction of a new 75,000-seat stadium, which today plays host to rock concerts in addition to sporting events. An open-air market is held three times a week (Tu, F, Su) in the square by the Hôtel-de-Ville (on the way from the métro stop to the basilica).

PRACTICAL INFORMATION

The most direct route to St-Denis is by métro (M: St-Denis-Basilique, line 13); visitors headed to the Stade should take the RER (RER: Stade de France, line B, or RER: St-Denis, line D). The **tourist office,** 1, r. de la République, has English-speaking guides, information on the basilica and the town of St-Denis, maps, suggested walks, restaurant guides, and a ticket outlet for sporting events or concerts in the Stade de France. From the métro, turn left down r. Jean Jaurès, following the signs to the tourist office, and turn right on r. de la République. (☎01 55 87 08 70; fax 01 48 20 24 11; www.ville-saint-denis.fr. Open M-Sa 9:30am-1pm and 2-6pm, Su and bank holidays 10am-1pm and 2-4pm.)

SIGHTS

BASILIQUE DE ST-DENIS

1, r. de la Légion d'Honneur and 2, r. de Strasbourg. From the métro, head toward the town square down r. Jean Jaurès and turn left at the tourist office on r. de la République. ☎01 48 09 83 54. ***Open*** *Apr.-Sept. M-Sa 10am-6:30pm, Su noon-6:30pm; Oct.-Mar. M-Sa 10am-4:30pm, Su noon-4:30pm.* ***Admission*** *to nave, side aisles and chapels free. Admission to transept, ambulatory, and crypt €5.50, seniors and students 18-25 €3.50, under 18 free. Enter to the right of the basilica and go to the ticket kiosk (last entry 30min. before closing).* ***Audioguide*** *in various languages €4 for 1 person, €5.50 for 2.* ***Tours*** *in French daily at 12:15 and 3pm.*

Surrounded by modern buildings, markets, and non-Christian communities, the Basilique de St-Denis stands as an odd, archaic symbol of the long-dead French monarchy. Buried in the transept, crevet, and crypt are the remains of three royal families, 41 kings, 32 queens, 63 princes and princesses, 10 dignitaries, and the relics of three saints. During the height of the French monarchy, the basilica was, in effect, the national church of France; it became synonymous with the crown as the protector of the country's most valuable political artifacts: the *Oriflamme* (the royal banner) and coronation paraphernalia.

The first church on this site was built on top of an existing Gallo-Roman cemetery, in honor of Paris's first bishop, St-Denis. St-Denis was martyred by the Romans in AD 260 for trying to Christianize the city. After being beheaded on Mount Mercury, which was renamed Montmartre (Mount of the Martyr; see p. 119) in his honor, he allegedly picked up his head and walked north with it to the sight of this church, where he collapsed. His tragic tale is told in stained glass on the northern side of the nave. In 475, a small church was built to mark St-Denis's grave. King Pepin the Short built a larger basilica to accommodate the many pilgrimages to this site and was buried here in 768. The more famous monarchs buried here include Clovis, François I, Anne d'Autriche, Louis XIV, Louis XVI, and Marie-Antoinette.

The basilica's 12th-century ambulatory was the first instance of Gothic architecture in Europe (the scornful term "Gothic" was coined by Italian critics to describe St-Denis's extravagant style). Nicknamed "Lucerna" (Latin for "lantern") for its luminosity, the basilica features enormous stained-glass windows, high vaults, and exceptionally wide, airy transepts. These and other innovations were ordered by St-Denis's great patron, **Abbot Suger** (1122-1151), the influential clergyman and politician who had grown dissatisfied with the dark interiors of Romanesque churches and who famously began rebuilding the basilica in 1136 to open it to the "uninterrupted light of the divine." The vaulted arches and flying buttresses outside freed the walls from the burden of supporting the roof, and enabled the architects to replace them with huge stained-glass windows that became the trademark of Gothic style.

Suger's shocked contemporaries worked to outdo him in technical brilliance, building ever more intricate interiors, larger stained-glass windows, and loftier vaults. But few were able to rival the luminous pyrotechnics of the eastern end of the church: Suger's celebrated, color-flooded **crevet.** Dubbed the "manifesto" of the new Gothic style, the crevet was originally built to displace the crowds of pilgrims who flooded into the crypt to view the reliquaries. The crowds got so immense at times that women, rumor has it, would faint and even suffocate to death in the tiny, air-deprived vault. Despite all their screaming female fans, the terrified monks worried that the reliquaries would be stolen and had taken to jumping out the windows with the saintly remains in their arms. The crevet is still home to some of the finest stained glass around Paris, with wall-to-wall ripple effects and intricate patterns. But the price tag for innovation is high: according to Suger himself, the windows cost more money than the entire building. Almost all of the original stained glass was replaced during the 19th century after the originals were shattered during the Revolution. Some of the 12th-century windows can still be seen, however, in the center of the ambulatory. Abbot Suger ensured his immortality by having his likeness—a small monk prostrate before the Virgin Mother—added to the design.

Suger died in 1151, well before the basilica was finished, but having firmly established it as France's seat of theological power. Several queens were crowned here, and in 1593, underneath the nave, Henri IV converted to Catholicism (see **Life & Times,** p. 41). With such a royalist pedigree, it is no wonder that St-Denis was a prime target for the wrath of the Revolution. Tombs were destroyed, windows were shattered, and the remains of the Bourbon family were thrown into a ditch. With the restoration of the monarchy in 1815, Louis XVIII ordered that the necropolis be re-established, and Louis XVI and Marie-Antoinette were buried here with great pomp in 1819. The remains of the Bourbons were dug up and placed in a small **ossuary** inside the crypt, and tombs and funerary monuments were relocated and replaced.

MUSÉE D'ART ET D'HISTOIRE

22bis, r. Gabriel Péri. ☎01 42 43 05 10; musee.saint-denis@wanadoo.fr. ***Open*** *M and W-F 10am-5:30pm, Th 10am-8pm, Sa-Su 2-6:30pm.* ***Admission*** *€4, students and seniors €2, under 16 free.*

Located in a former convent (the nuns' cells are still intact), the Musée d'Art et d'Histoire features exhibits on daily life in medieval St-Denis and on the convent's most famous resident, Madame Louise, beloved daughter of Louis XV, who spent her life here in quiet devotion. The interesting array of religious paraphernalia, archaeological finds, and historical artifacts is especially notable for the impressive collection of documents from the Paris Commune of 1871. An immense collection that will take you several hours to completely absorb, the museum also hosts temporary exhibits on its top floor and has a peaceful inner courtyard.

INSIDE

Museums

If you're going to be doing the museum circuit (as opposed to just eating and shopping) while in Paris—and you have no excuse not to—you may want to invest in a **Carte Musées et Monuments,** which offers admission to 70 museums in greater Paris. This card will probably save you money if you are planning to visit more than three museums/sights every day and will enable you to sail past all of the frustrated tourists standing in line. The card is available at major museums and in almost all métro stations. Ask for a brochure listing participating museums and monuments. A pass for one day is €22; for three consecutive days €38; for five consecutive days €52. For more information, call **Association InterMusées,** 4, r. Brantôme, *3ème* (☎01 44 61 96 60; fax 01 44 61 96 69; www.intermusees.com). Most museums, including the Musée d'Orsay, are closed on Mondays, while the Louvre is closed on Tuesdays.

MAJOR MUSEUMS

MUSÉE DU LOUVRE

1er. M: Palais-Royal-Musée du Louvre. ☎01 40 20 51 51; www.louvre.fr. ***Open*** *M and W 9am-9:30pm, Th-Su 9am-5:30pm.* ***Closed Tu.*** *Last entry 45min. before closing, but people are asked to leave 15-30min. before closing.* ***Admission*** *M and W-Sa 9am-3pm €7.50, M and W-Sa 3pm-close and Su €5, under 18 and first Su of the month free. Prices include both the permanent and most tempo-*

Louvre Oeuvre

Beyond the grand trio (Mona, Venus, and Victory), the following masterworks are just a few of those that await you in the halls of the Louvre.

Dutch Painting:
Jan van Eyck's *Madonna of Chancellor Rolin*
Bosch's *Ship of Fools*
Rubens's *Médicis Cycle*
Vermeer's *Lacemaker*

French Painting:
David's *Oath of the Horatii*
Gericault's *Raft of the Medusa*
Delacroix's *Liberty Leading the People*
Ingres's *Le Bain Turc*

Italian Painting:
Cimabue's *Virgin & Child in Majesty*
Giotto's *Saint Francis of Assisi*
Botticelli's *Venus & the Graces Offering Gifts to a Maiden*
Raphael's *Portrait of Balthazar Castiglione*
Caravaggio's *Death of the Virgin*

Greek, Etruscan, & Roman Antiquities:
Greek vases
Sarcophagus of a Married Couple
Sleeping Hermaphrodite

Other Collections include:
Oriental Antiquities
Islamic Art
objets d'art
Sculpture
Napoleon III Apartments

rary collections. ***Temporary exhibits*** *in the Cour Napoléon open at 9am. Sign up for the English* ***tours*** *at information desk; M and W-Sa at 11am, 2, 3:45pm; €3.* ***Bookstore*** *and* ***cafés*** *open same hours as the museum on M and W, Th-Su close at 7pm.*

Built on the foundations of a medieval castle that housed French kings for four centuries; restructured by a 20th-century Socialist politician and a Chinese-American architect; and filled with priceless objects from the tombs of Egyptian pharaohs, the halls of Roman emperors, the studios of French painters, and the walls of Italian churches, the Louvre is an intersection of time, space, and national boundaries. Explore the endless exhibition halls, witness new generations of artists at work on easels in the galleries, and see the Louvre's most famous residents: the **Mona Lisa,** the **Venus de Milo,** and the **Winged Victory of Samothrace.**

PRACTICAL INFORMATION

The **surface entrance** to the Louvre is through I.M. Pei's glass pyramid, where an escalator descends into the Cour Napoléon, the museum's enormous lobby. **Tickets** for the museums are sold in the Cour Napoléon. Lines can be brutal; see **Essential Information** on p. 137 for time and sanity saving tricks.

Due to constant renovations and conservation efforts, no guidebook can offer a completely accurate walking tour of the museum—which is why we don't even try; check out our list of highlights (**Louvre Oeuvre,** at left), but let the museum, and its very informative materials speak for themselves. To find out which rooms will be open on your visit, check the home page, ask the info desk, or call museum info (☎01 40 20 51 51). Indispensable **updated maps** are available at the circular info desk in the center of the Cour Napoléon. Whatever your visiting pace, consider *Destination Louvre* (€7.50), a book (in English) available in the bookstore of the Cour Napoléon. **Audioguides,** available at the top of both the Denon and Sully escalators (rental €5; deposit of driver's license, passport, or credit card), describe over 350 of the museum's highlights. **Tours** fill up quickly. The plastic info cards *(feuillets)* found in gallery corners provide detailed commentary and historical context.

The Louvre is fully **wheelchair-accessible.** You can borrow a wheelchair for free at the central information desk (passport deposit required); call information for disabled visitors (☎01 40 20 59 90). The Louvre has begun a series of workshops for **children** ages 4-13 in English (classes on subjects ranging from hieroglyphics to painting in perspective; see the info desk in the Cour

Napoléon). The auditorium in the Cour Napoléon hosts concerts (€10-23), films, lectures, and colloquia (all €3.81). For more information on these sorts of events, call ☎01 40 20 53 17. There is also a small theater in the hall with free 1hr. films in French relating to the museum (call ☎01 40 20 53 17 for more info; films M-F every hr. 10am-6pm, Sa-Su every 1½hr. 10am-6pm).

The **Carte Louvre Jeunes,** an amazing deal at just €15.25, entitles its holder to one year's unlimited entrance to the permanent collection and temporary exhibits, visits with a guest on Monday nights 6-9:45pm, and discounts on all books, tours, concerts, movies, and classes. Only visitors who are teachers or under 26 are eligible for the card. Call ☎01 40 20 51 04 or inquire at the main desk for more information.

When visiting the Louvre, strategy is everything. Think like a four-star general: the goal is to come and see without being conquered. The museum is organized into three different, sprawling wings—**Sully, Richelieu,** and **Denon**—each leading off the Cour Napoléon. Each wing is divided into different sections according to the art's period, national origin, and medium. The collection itself is divided into seven departments: Oriental Antiquities; Egyptian Antiquities; Greek, Etruscan, and Roman Antiquities; Painting; Sculpture; Decorative Arts; and Graphic Arts. The color-coding and room numbers on the Louvre's free maps correspond to the colors and numbers on the plaques at the entrances to every room. Getting lost is an inevitable part of the Louvre-going experience, but there are plenty of docents who can point you in the right direction.

ESSENTIAL INFORMATION

STRAIGHT TO THE ART

The lines stretching across the courtyard at the Louvre can be a disheartening sight. To sail right past those poor suckers, try the following strategies:

–Don't enter through the glass pyramid; instead, follow the signs from the métro to the **Carrousel du Louvre.**

–Either the **Carte Musée et Monuments** (see p. 135) or **Carte Louvre Jeunes** (see p. 137) will let you skip ticket lines.

–Use coins or a credit card in one of the **automatic ticket machines** in the Cour Napoléon, or buy **tickets online** (valid to the end of the calendar year).

–Visit on a weekday afternoon or on **Monday or Wednesday evening,** when the museum is open until 9:45pm. You'll cut down on waiting time, and get up close and personal with Mona.

HISTORY

Construction of the Louvre began in 1190, and it still isn't finished. **King Philippe-Auguste** built the original structure as a fortress to defend Paris while he was away on a crusade. In the 14th century, **Charles V** converted the fortress into a residential château. The monarchs of the 15th century avoided the narrow, dank, and rat-infested building but **François I** returned to the Louvre in 1528 in an attempt to flatter the Parisian bourgeoisie. François razed Charles's palace and commissioned **Pierre Lescot** to build a new palace in the open style of the Renaissance. All that remains of the original Louvre are its foundations, unearthed in the early stages of Mitterrand's renovations and displayed in an underground exhibit called **Medieval Louvre** on the ground floor of the Sully wing (admission included in museum ticket).

François I was succeeded by Henri II, whose widow, **Catherine de Médicis,** had the Tuileries Palace built looking out on an Italian-style garden to give herself a little privacy (it was burned by the *communards* in 1871; see **Life & Times,** p. 45). **Henri IV** embarked on what he called the **Grand Design**—linking the Louvre and the Tuileries with the two large wings you see today in a "royal city." He oversaw completion of only a fraction of the project before his death in 1610.

After fleeing the Palais-Royal in 1650, **Louis XIV** moved into the Louvre. The **Cour Carrée** owes its classicism to Louis XIV, who hired a trio of architects—**Le Vau, Le Brun,** and **Perrault**—to transform the Louvre into the grandest palace in Europe.

A Day at Orsay

Presenting French art from 1848 to 1914:

Classicism & Romanticism:
Carpeaux's *Ugolin*
Ingres's *La Source*
Delacroix's *La Chasse aux Lions*

Realism:
Millet's *Angelus*
Courbet's *Un Enterrement à Ornans*
Manet's *Olympia* and *Dejeuner sur l'herbe*
Caillebotte's *The Floor Planers*

Belle Epoque & Art Nouveau:
Salle des Fêtes
Rodin's *Portes de l'Enfer*
Charpentier, Bigot, and Fontaine's Belle Epoque Dining Room

Impressionism & Post-Impressionism:
Monet's *La Gare St-Lazare* & *Cathédrale de Rouen* series
Renoir's *Le Bal du Moulin de la Galette*
Degas' *La classe de Danse* and *Petite danseuse de quatorze ans*
Van Gogh's *Portrait de l'Artiste*
Gaugin's *Belle Angèle*
Whistler's *Portrait of the Artist's Mother*
Cézanne's *Pommes et Oranges*
Seurat's *Cirque*

Louis XIV eventually abandoned the Louvre for Versailles, and construction did not get past the Cour Carrée.

In 1725, after years of relative abandonment, the Academy of Painting inaugurated annual **salons** in the halls to show the work of its members. In 1793, the Revolution made the exhibit permanent, thus creating the **Musée du Louvre.** For over a century, French painting would revolve around the Louvre salons. **Napoleon** filled the Louvre with plundered art from continental Europe and Egypt (much of which had to be returned after his defeat at Waterloo). More durably, he built the **Arc de Triomphe du Carrousel,** a copy of Rome's Arch of Septimus Severus, to commemorate his victories. Continuing Henri IV's Grand Design, he extended the Louvre's two wings to the Tuileries palace and remodeled the facades of the older buildings.

For most of the 20th century, the Louvre was a confusing maze of government offices and inaccessible galleries. **Mitterrand's** *Grands Projets* campaign (see **Life & Times,** p. 63) transformed the Louvre into a well-organized museum. Internationally renowned American architect **I.M. Pei** came up with the idea of moving the museum's entrance to an underground level in the Cour Napoléon, surmounted by his stunning **glass pyramid.** At first, Pei's proposal met with intense controversy: some saw it as sacrilege, others as a stroke of genius. Today, the Cour Napoléon glows in the sun streaming through the 666 panes of glass—each one seeming to contribute one more degree of intense heat in summer.

MUSÉE D'ORSAY

62, r. de Lille. 7ème. M: Solférino; RER: Musée d'Orsay. ☎01 40 49 48 14; www.musee-orsay.fr. ***Open*** *June 20-Sept. 20 Tu-W and F-Su 9am-6pm, Th 9am-9:45pm; Sept. 21-June 19 Tu-W and F-Su 10am-6pm, Th 10am-9:45pm.* ***Closed M.*** *Last ticket sales 45min. before closing.* ***Admission*** *€7, ages 18-25 and all on Su €5, under 18 free. Free 1st Su of every month. English* ***tours*** *Tu-Sa 11:30am, 2:30pm, 1½hr., €5.50.* ***Bookstore*** *open Tu-W and F-Su 9am-6:30pm, Th 9am-9:30pm. MC/V. Wheelchair- accessible.*

If only the unimaginative Académiciens who turned the Impressionists away from the Louvre salon could see the Musée d'Orsay today, with visitors from around the world lining up year-round to see these famous rejects (see **Life & Times**, p. 61). Housed in a former railway station, the Musée presents paintings, sculpture, decorative arts, architecture, photography, and cinema, with works spanning the period from 1848 until the onset of World War I (1914).

PRACTICAL INFORMATION

For all its size and bustle, the Orsay delights art lovers as one of the friendliest museums in Paris. A clearly marked escalator at the far end of the building ascends directly to the Impressionist level, and maps and English-language information are available at the entrance.

The museum is least crowded on Sunday mornings and on Thursday evenings when it is open late. Almost everything in the collections is worth a visit; check out our list of the highlights (**A Day at Orsay,** p. 138), get a map, and consider splurging on the excellent *Guide to the Musée d'Orsay* by Caroline Mathieu, the museum's director (€14.50). Also available is the practical *Musée d'Orsay Pocket Guide* (€5.50). Hand-held **audioguides,** available in English and other languages, provide anecdotal histories and analyses of 60 masterpieces throughout the museum.The recording lasts two hours, but you should set aside at least three to visit all the rooms (€5; driver's license, passport, credit card, or €76 deposit required). **Tours** leave every 1½hr. from the group reception area. In addition to the permanent collection, seven **temporary exhibition** spaces, called *dossiers*, are scattered throughout the building. Call or pick up a free copy of *Nouvelles du Musée d'Orsay* to find out which temporary exhibitions are currently installed. The museum also hosts conferences, special tours (including children's tours), and concerts.

The **Café des Hauteurs** sits on the 5th floor behind one of the train station's huge iron clocks (open Tu-W, F-Su 10am-5pm, Th 10am-9pm). There is also a self-serve food stand directly above the café (open Tu-Su 11am-5pm). The **Restaurant du Musée d'Orsay** on the middle floor is a museum piece all its own, and worthy of a visit (lunch Tu-Su 11:30am-2:30pm, tea 3:30pm-5:30pm except Th; dinner Th 7pm-9.30pm). A Belle Epoque artifact designed by Gabriel Ferrier, the restaurant offers a view of the Seine and magnificent chandeliers in addition to pricey dining options (averaging €9-15 per *plat*).

HISTORY

Built for the 1900 Universal Exposition, the **Gare d'Orsay's** industrial function was carefully masked by architect **Victor Laloux** behind glass, stucco, and a 370-room luxury hotel, so as not to mar the elegance of the *7ème.* For several decades it was the main departure point for southwest-bound trains, but newer trains were too long for its platforms, and it closed in 1939. After WWII, the station served as the main French repatriation center, receiving thousands of concentration camp survivors and refugees. Orson Welles filmed *The Trial* here in 1962. The Musée d'Orsay opened in 1986 as one of Mitterrand's *Grands Projets*, taking works from the Louvre, Jeu de Paume, Palais de Tokyo, Musée de Luxembourg, provincial museums, and private collections.

CENTRE POMPIDOU

Pl. Georges-Pompidou, r. Beaubourg, 4ème. M: Rambuteau or Hôtel-de-Ville; RER: Châtelet-Les-Halles. ☎01 44 78 12 33, wheelchair info ☎01 44 78 49 54; www.centrepompidou.fr. ***Centre open*** *M and W-Su 11am-10pm;* ***museum open*** *M and W-Su 11am-9pm, last ticket sales 8pm;* ***library open*** *M and W-F noon-10pm, Sa-Su 11am-10pm.* ***Library*** *and* ***Forum*** *free. Museum* ***admission*** *prices differ depending on how much of the centre you want to see: permanent collection €5.50, students and over 60 €3.50, under 18 free, first Su of month free for all visitors; current exhibition €6.50, students and over 60 €4.50, under 13 free; permanent collection, current exposition, and Atelier Brancus €10, students and seniors €8.* ***Audio guides*** *€4.50. 160-page visitor's guide €12.*

Often called the Beaubourg, the **Centre National d'Art et de Culture Georges Pompidou** has inspired architectural controversy ever since its inauguration in 1977. Named after French president Georges Pompidou, it fulfills his desire for Paris to have a cultural center embracing music, cinema, books, and the graphic arts. Chosen from 681 competing designs, Richard Rogers and Renzo Piano's building-turned-inside-out bares its circulatory system to all. Piping and ventilation ducts in various colors run up, down, and sideways along the outside (blue for air, green for water, yellow for electricity, red for heating). Framing the building like a cage, huge steel bars support its weight. The Centre Pompidou attracts more visitors per year than any other museum or monument in France—8 million to the Louvre's 3 million. Not surprisingly, then, long lines greet visitors, no matter the time of day (different exhibits have different ticket lines; be sure you're waiting in the right one). The Center rewards visitors for their pains with amazing views of Paris.

And the art's not bad, either. The **Musée National d'Art Moderne,** the Pompidou's main attraction, houses a rich selection of 20th-century art, from the Fauvists and Cubists to Pop and Conceptual Art. Most of the works were contributed by the artists themselves or by their estates; **Joan Miró** and **Wassily Kandinsky's** wife number among the museum's founding members. The Salle Garance hosts an adventurous film series, and the Bibliothèque Publique d'Information is a free, non-circulating library. Located in a separate building is the Institut de la Recherche et de la Coordination Acoustique/Musique (IRCAM), an institute and laboratory where scientists and musicians develop new technologies. IRCAM also holds occasional concerts.

MUSÉE RODIN

77, r. de Varenne, 7ème. M: Varenne. ☎01 44 18 61 10; www.musee-rodin.fr. ***Open*** *Tu-Su Apr.-Sept. 9:30am-5:45pm; Oct.-Mar. 9:30am-4:45pm. Last admission 30min. before closing.* ***Admission*** *€5; seniors, 18-25, and all on Su €3.* ***Park*** *open Tu-Su Apr.-Sept. 9:30am-6:45pm; Oct.-Mar. 9:30am-5pm. Admission to park alone €1.* ***Audio tour*** *€4.* ***Temporary exhibits*** *housed in the chapel, to your right as you enter. Persons who are blind or vision-impaired may obtain advance permission to touch the sculptures.* ***Café*** *open Tu-Sa Apr.-Oct. 10am-5:45pm; Nov.-Jan. 10am-5:30pm. MC/V. Ground floor and gardens wheelchair-accessible.*

The museum is located in the elegant 18th-century **Hôtel Biron,** where Auguste Rodin lived and worked at the end of his life, sharing it with the likes of **Isadora Duncan, Cocteau, Matisse,** and **Rilke**. During his lifetime (1840-1917), Rodin was among the country's most controversial artists, classified by many as Impressionism's sculptor (Monet, incidentally, was a close friend and admirer). Today, he is almost universally acknowledged as the father of modern sculpture.

Many Parisians say the Musée Rodin is one of the best museums in Paris (they're right). Besides housing many of Rodin's better known sculptures (including *Le Baiser* and *L'Homme au Nez Cassé*), the *hôtel* and its interior are worthy of close inspection themselves. Chairs are plentiful, allowing time for thoughtful contemplation, or perhaps amazement. Many of the sculptures rest on lovely antiques that are labeled for their own merits, and the walls are adorned with beautiful paintings and photographs by artists like Renoir, Munch, Van Gogh, Gericault, and Steichen, including some of Rodin in his *atelier*. Rodin's sculptures are everywhere, decorating the staircase and doorways, and there are entire rooms devoted to large works like *Balzac* and *Les Bourgeois de Calais*, including various studies and versions. In addition, the museum has several works by **Camille Claudel,** Rodin's muse, collaborator, and lover. Claudel's striking *L'Age Mûr* has been read as her response to Rodin's decision to leave her for another woman, here depicted as an angel of death leading a man away from a woman pleading on her knees for him to stay.

The *hôtel's* expansive garden displays Rodin's work amongst rose trees and fountains, including the collection's star: *Le Penseur (The Thinker)*, situated on the right side of the garden as you enter. *Balzac*, to the left of *Le Penseur*, was commissioned in 1891 by the Société des Gens de Lettres. A battle over Rodin's design and his inability to meet deadlines raged for years. Eventually, Rodin canceled the commission and kept the statue himself. Later in his life, he noted, "Nothing that I made satisfied me as much, because nothing had cost me as much; nothing else sums up so profoundly that which I believe to be the secret law of my art." On the other side of the garden stands one version of Rodin's largest and most intricate sculpture, the unfinished *Portes de l'Enfer* (*The Gates of Hell*, 1880-1917), inspired by Dante's *Inferno.* Viewing machines placed in front of the sculpture allow visitors to look more closely at the anguished faces of these damned souls and at other fine details of the work (note also that on the second floor of the museum is a cabinet of miniature studies of the figures which eventually came together as this sculpture). Originally commissioned as the entrance doors for the new Ecole des Arts Décoratifs, the sculpture was never finished. To his critics, the master of French sculpture countered, "Were the cathedrals ever finished?"

INVALIDES MUSEUMS

Esplanades des Invalides, 7ème; ***Musée de l'Ordre de la Libération*** *at 51bis, bd. de Latour-Maubourg. M: Invalides. ☎01 47 05 04 10,* ***Musée des Plans-Reliefs*** *☎01 45 51 92 45,* ***Musée de l'Armée*** *☎01 44 42 37 72; www.invalides.org.* ***All open*** *daily Apr.-Sept. 10am-6pm; Oct.-Mar. 10am-5pm. Last ticket sales 30min. before closing.* ***Admission*** *to all 3 museums €7, students under 26 €5, under 18 free. MC/V.*

In 1670, Louis XIV decided to "construct a royal home, grand and spacious enough to receive all old or wounded officers and soldiers." Architect Libéral Bruand's building accepted its first wounded in 1674, and veterans still live in the Invalides today. For all his beneficence toward the wounded soldiers, Louis XIV requested the Dome Church have two separate entrances so that he could attend mass without mingling with, well, the masses. Jules Hardouin-Mansart provided the final design for the double chapel within the Invalides complex, the Royal Dome church adjacent to a long hall dubbed St-Louis des Invalides where the soldiers could hear the priest but had to enter through a separate, inner courtyard. The restoration monarch, Louis Philippe, had Napoleon's remains returned to the French as a political move in 1840, but it wasn't until the reign of Napoleon's nephew, Louis-Napoleon, that the mosaic floor of the Dome Church was destroyed to build the huge, circular crypt for Napoleon I. Completed in 1861, Napoleon's tomb consists of six concentric coffins, made of materials ranging from mahogany to lead. The tomb is viewed first from a round balcony above it, forcing everyone who visits to bow down to the emperor even in his death (delighting Adolf Hitler on his visit to Paris in 1940). Names of significant battles are engraved in the marble surrounding the coffins; oddly enough, Waterloo isn't there. Bas-reliefs recall Napoleon's institutional reforms of law and education; Napoleon himself is depicted as a Roman emperor in toga and laurels. Six chapels dedicated to different saints lie off the main room and harbor the tombs of French Marshals. In 1989, the 107m high Eglise du Dôme was regilded using 12kg of gold, making it the glorious Hôtel des Invalides, the only monument in Paris glinting with real gold.

MUSÉE DE L'ARMÉE. The Musée de l'Armée celebrates French military history. The museum lies in two wings on opposite sides of the Invalides's cobblestone main courtyard, the Cour d'Honneur. If swords and armor interest you, then the **West Wing** *(Aile Occident)*, which is filled almost exclusively with armor (including that of the pint-sized variety) from Medieval times onward, along with some Oriental metal and a 20th-century exhibit, is sure to please. The **East Wing** *(Aile Orient)* is more well-rounded, with uniforms, maps, royal ordinances, medals, and portraits in addition to armor, focusing on the 17th, 18th, and 19th centuries.

MUSÉE DES PLANS-RELIEFS. The Musée des Plans-Reliefs on the fourth floor is a collection of about 100 models of fortified cities from 1668 to 1870. Citadels, chateaus, and entire areas of the French countryside are intricately modeled, displayed beside aerial photographs of the land today to show interesting comparisons.

MUSÉE DE L'ORDRE DE LA LIBÉRATION. Just beyond the West Wing of the Musée de l'Armée, this museum tells the story of those who fought for the liberation of France during WWII. A diverse collection of de Gaulle-related paraphernalia is complemented by tributes to the Résistance fighters of Free France. Radio broadcasts, video footage, and newspapers clippings help to place the visitor in the era. On the top floor, sketches of concentration camp prisoners provide a moving glimpse into their lives and personalities.

MUSÉE PICASSO

5, r. de Thorigny, 3ème. M: Chemin Vert. ☎01 42 71 63 15, 01 42 71 70 84, or 01 42 71 25 21. ***Open*** *Apr.-Sept. M and W-Su 9:30am-6pm; Oct.-Mar. 9:30am-5:30pm; last entrance 30min. before closing.* ***Admission*** *€5.50, Su and ages 18-25 €4, under 18 free.*

When Picasso died in 1973, his family paid the French inheritance tax in artwork. The French government put this collection on display in 1985 in the 17th-century **Hôtel Salé,** creating a catalogue of the life and 70-year career of one of the most prolific and inventive artists of the 20th century. Arranged chronologically, the museum leads the viewer through the evolution of Picasso's artistic and personal life. From his earliest work in Barcelona to his Cubist and Surrealist years in Paris, and later his Neoclassical work on the French Riviera, each room situates his art within the context of different events and periods in his life: his many mistresses, his reactions to the two World Wars, etc. This chronological arrangement has provoked interest and some criticism. You can follow the *Sens de Visite* arrows around the building and little numbers on each of the works—or, if you don't believe an artist's work should be defined by his time, go your own way.

Born in Málaga, Spain in 1881, Picasso loved Paris and moved to the studios of the Bateau-Lavoir in Montmartre (see **Sights,** p. 120) in 1904. There he painted one of his masterpieces, *Les Demoiselles d'Avignon* (1907), which resides in the New York Museum of Modern Art but is represented in this museum by various preliminary studies. In the late 1920s, Picasso moved to Montparnasse (see **Sights,** p. 113), where he frequented the Café Sélect and La Closerie des Lilas along with Jean Cocteau and Surrealist guru André Breton. Unable to return to Spain during the Franco regime, Picasso adopted France as his permanent home. Later, he moved to the French Riviera, where he died in Cannes in 1973.

Highlights of the collection include: the haunting blue *Autoportrait*, *Le violon et la musique (Violin with Sheet Music)*, the post-Cubist *Deux femmes courant sur la plage (Two Women Running on the Beach)*, and sculptures from the 1930 that play games with human morphology. Picasso's experiments with abstraction often went hand-in-hand with his love affairs: witness *La femme qui lit (Woman Reading)*, a portrait of his lover Marie-Thérèse Walter; *La femme qui pleure (Woman Crying)*, inspired by the surrealist photographer Dora Maar; and *The Kiss*, painted later in his life while he was married to Jacqueline Roque. By the time of their wedding, Clouzot's film *Le Mystère Picasso* and retrospectives at the Petit Palais were already celebrating his life's work.

MUSÉE DE CLUNY

6, pl. Paul Painlevé, 5ème. M: Cluny-La Sorbonne. ☎01 53 73 78 00. ***Open*** *M and W-Sa 9:15am-5:45pm; last ticket sold at 5:15pm.* ***Admission*** *€6.70; students, under 25, over 60, and Su €5.20; under 18 free.* ***Garden*** *open 8 or 9am (depending on the day) to 5:30pm in winter or 9:30pm in summer; free. Call for information on weekly* ***concerts*** *☎01 53 73 78 16; prices and schedule vary.*

The **Hôtel de Cluny** houses the **Musée National du Moyen Âge,** one of the world's finest collections of medieval art, jewelry, sculpture, and tapestries. The *hôtel* itself is a flamboyant 14th-century medieval manor built on top of first-century Roman ruins. One of three ancient *thermae* (public baths) in Roman Lutèce (see **Life & Times,** p. 39), the baths were purchased in 1330 by the Abbot of Cluny, who built his residence upon them. In the 15th century, the *hôtel* became home to the monastic Order of Cluny, led by the powerful Amboise family. In 1843, the state converted the *hôtel* into the medieval museum; excavations after WWII unearthed the baths.

The museum's collection includes art from Paris's most important medieval structures: Ste-Chapelle, Notre Dame, and St-Denis. Panels of brilliant stained glass in ruby reds and royal blues from Ste-Chapelle line the ground floor. The brightly lit *Galerie des Rois* contains sculptures from Notre Dame—among which are a series of marble heads of the kings of Juda, severed during the Revolution. A collection of medieval jewelry includes royal crowns, brooches, and daggers. Perhaps the most impressive work of goldsmithing is the exquisite 14th-century **Gold Rose,** found on the first floor. And tucked away among gilded reliquaries and ornate illuminated manuscripts, there is even a gruesome sculpture of the head of St. John the Baptist on a platter. But the museum's star is the marvelous series of allegorical tapestries **La Dame et la Licorne** *(The Lady and the Unicorn)*, which visually depict the five senses. The centerpiece of the museum's collection of 15th- and 16th-century Belgian weaving, this complete cycle was made famous by George Sand, who discovered the tapestries hanging in the Château Broussac in Chantelle, south of Paris.

Outside, cowslips, primroses, and foxgloves line the Jardin Médiéval, a 5000 sq. m replica of a medieval pleasure garden. The grounds are divided into four sections: the Forest of the Unicorn, which contains plants used in daily life; *Le Chemin Creux*, dedicated to the Virgin Mary; a *terrasse* of potted plants used for medicinal and aromatic purposes; and *Le Tapis de Mille Fleurs* (Carpet of a Thousand Flowers), which is supposedly something of an aphrodisiac. The museum sponsors chamber music concerts in its Roman and medieval spaces.

LA VILLETTE

La Villette is the product of a successful urban renewal project. Once a meat-packing district that provided Paris with much of its pork and beef, the area became outmoded after the advent of refrigerated trucks. A decision was made to replace the neighborhood slaughterhouses with a neighborhood park, and *voilà:* what President Mitterrand inaugurated in 1985 as "the place of intelligent leisure" was born.

The park's lines of sight are sliced by the angles of funny-shaped red buildings foolish enough to be called *folies;* and joining them in architect Bernard Tschumi's rebuttal of right angles are squiggly metal canopies. The **Cité des Sciences et de l'Industrie** makes for an intriguing visit, but stay away if you don't like the feeling of screeching *gosses* (little kids) running through your legs or the overwhelming sound of giggling and wailing.

PARC DE LA VILLETTE

*General info including **Grande Halle** ☎01 40 03 75 03; **Trabendo** info ☎01 42 01 12 12, reservations ☎01 49 25 89 99; Zénith ☎01 42 08 60 00, but call FNAC to buy tickets. **Info office** open daily 10am-7pm. **Promenade des Jardins** open 24hr. Free.*

Cut in the middle by the **Canal de l'Ourcq** and the **Canal St-Denis,** the **Parc de la Villette** separates the Cité des Sciences from the Cité de la Musique and is dominated by the steel-and-glass **Grande Halle,** which features frequent plays, concerts, temporary exhibits, and films. The red *folies* which surround the Grand Halle give the park a structural unity, and at least one offers hamburgers—from an outpost of Le Quick, the French version of McDonald's.

Every July and August, La Villette hosts a free open-air **film festival** that shows foreign, art, and generally funky movies next to the Folie de Charolais Tuesday through Sunday at sundown (usually around 10pm). The **Zénith** concert hall hosts major rock bands. Directly behind Zénith is the **Trabendo** jazz and modern music club; the park's excellent yearly jazz festival is extraordinarily popular (see **Discover,** p. 18).

Finally, the **Promenade des Jardins** links several thematic gardens, such as the **Garden of Dunes and Wind,** which looks like a very tricky mini-golf course; the **Garden of Childhood Fears,** which winds through a wooded grove resonant with spooky sounds; and the roller coaster **Dragon Garden.** If you can bypass the height requirement, and pass yourself off as under 12, then you too can join a gaggle of moppets leaping on trampolines, running on rolling hills, and zooming down slides.

CITÉ DES SCIENCES ET DE L'INDUSTRIE

M: Porte de la Villette. ☎01 40 05 70 00, in French; www.cite-sciences.fr.

EXPLORA SCIENCE MUSEUM

***Museum** open Su 10am-7pm, Tu-Sa 10am-6pm. €7.50, under 25 or those accompanying children €5.50, under 7 free. **Planetarium** €2.50, under 7 free. **Médiathèque** open Su and W-Sa noon-6:45 pm, Tu noon-7:45pm. Free. **Cité des Enfants** programs about every 2hr. Su and Tu-Sa; 1½hr. long. €5.*

Dedicated to bringing science to young people, the Explora science museum is La Villette's star attraction. The futuristic, ramp-heavy architecture of the buildings rocks on its own, but the displays inside are fantastic, and kids will love them (adult visitors will find their inner children equally hooked). There are close to 300 exhibits, ranging from astronomy and mathematics to computer science and sound. Dare to ask "What is a hunter-killer submarine used for?" or "When will the sun burn out?" The museum also features a **planetarium** (Floor 2), the **Cinéma Louis Lumière** with 3D movies, a modest **aquarium** (Floor S2), and the **Médiathèque,** a multimedia scientific and technical library that has over 4000 films. If you're traveling with children, the Explora's **Cité des Enfants** offers one set of programs for kids ages 3-5 and another for ages 5-12. Both require adult accompaniment, but no more than two adults per family are admitted. Although programs are in French, the interactive exhibits are just as fun for English-speaking explorers. The *vestiaire* on the ground floor rents strollers and wheelchairs.

GÉODE

*☎01 40 05 79 99. **Open** Su 10:30am-7:30pm, Tu-Sa 10:30am-9:30pm, M variable hours. Shows every hour. **Tickets** €8.75, for 2 consecutive films €11.*

Outside the Cité, the enormous Géode is a huge mirrored sphere mounted on a water basin, like a disco ball in a birdbath. The exterior is coated with 6433 polished, stainless-steel triangles that reflect every detail of the surroundings. Inside, **Omnimax movies** on volcanoes, glaciers, and other natural phenomena are shown on a 1000 sq. m hemispheric screen.

ARGONAUTE

***Open** Sa-Su 11am-6:30pm., Tu-F 10:30am-5:30pm. **Admission** €3, under 7 free. Audioguide **tour** of the submarine, in English or French, is included.*

To the right of the Géode, the Argonaute submarine details the history of submersibles from Jules Verne to present-day nuclear-powered subs. This 400-ton, 50m-long fighter submarine was designed in 1950 as part of the French national fleet.

CINAXE

*☎01 40 05 12 12. **Open** Tu-Su 11am-6pm; shows every 15min. **Admission** €4.50, €4.24 if bought with another exhibition ticket.*

Between the Canal St-Denis and the Cité, Cinaxe features inventive movies filmed in first-person perspective from vehicles like Formula One cars, low-flying planes, and Mars land rovers, while hydraulic pumps simulate every curve and bump. Lunch beforehand is not recommended.

CITÉ DE LA MUSIQUE

*M: Porte de Pantin. ☎01 44 84 44 84, info 01 44 84 45 45; médiathèque ☎01 44 84 46 77; www.cite-musique.fr. **Info center** open Su and Tu-Sa noon-6pm. **Musée de la Musique** open Su 10am-6pm, Tu-Sa noon-6pm. **Admission** €6.10, students €4.60, children 6-18 €2.30, under 6 free; €2.30 more for temporary exhibits. **Guided tours** in French; call the info office for times. €10, reduced €7.60, under 18 €4.60. **Médiathèque** open Tu-Su noon-6pm. Free.*

At the opposite end of La Villette from the Cité des Sciences is the Cité de la Musique. Designed by Franck Hammoutène and completed in 1990, the complex of buildings is visually stunning, full of curves and glass ceilings. The highlight for classical music lovers is the **Musée de la Musique,** a handful of paintings and sculptures, and 900 antique instruments. Visitors don a pair of headphones that tune in to musical excerpts and explanations of each instrument. The Cité de la Musique's two per-

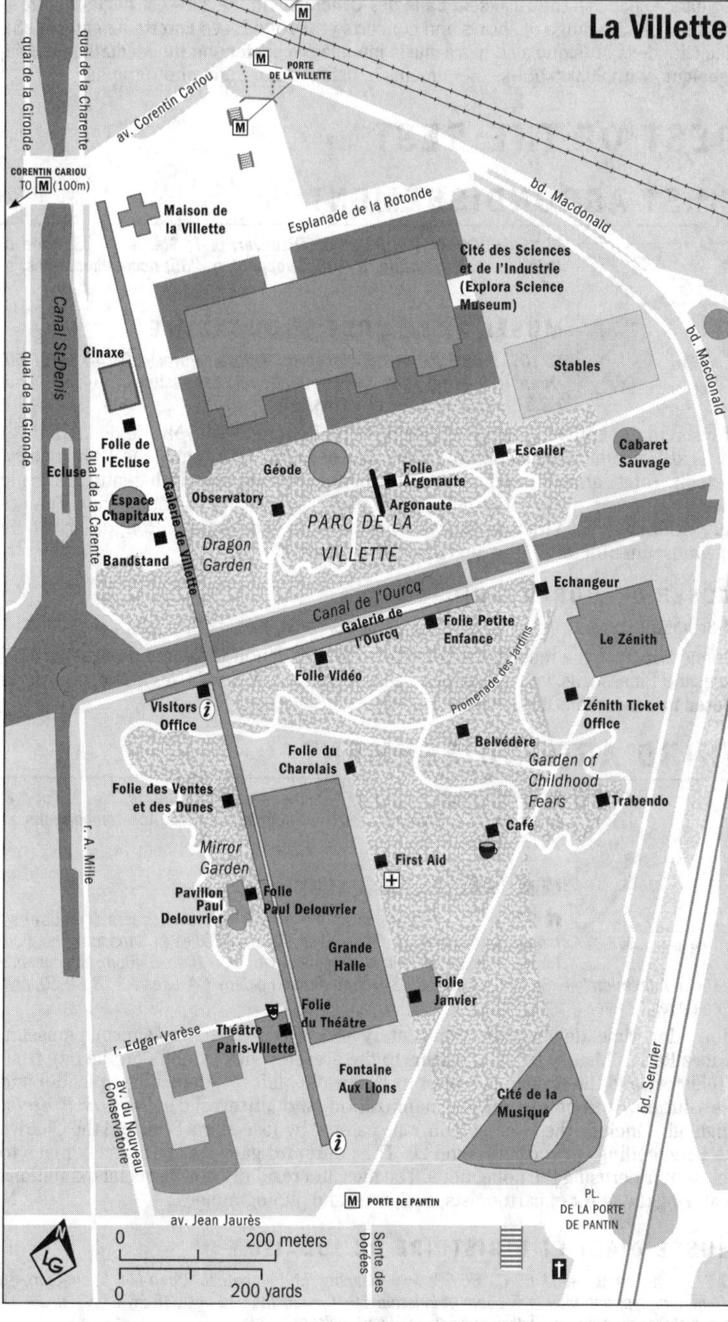

La Villette
PORTE DE LA VILLETTE
av. Corentin Cariou
quai de la Gironde
quai de la Charente
CORENTIN CARIOU TO M (100m)
Maison de la Villette
Esplanade de la Rotonde
bd. Macdonald
Cité des Sciences et de l'Industrie (Explora Science Museum)
Canal St-Denis
Cinaxe
Stables
Folie de l'Ecluse
Ecluse
Escalier
Cabaret Sauvage
Géode
Folie Argonaute
Argonaute
Observatory
Espace Chapiteaux
PARC DE LA VILLETTE
Dragon Garden
Bandstand
Galerie de Villette
quai de la Carente
Echangeur
Canal de l'Ourcq
Galerie de l'Ourcq
Folie Petite Enfance
Le Zénith
Promenade des Jardins
Folie Vidéo
Visitors Office
Zénith Ticket Office
Belvédère
Folie du Charolais
Garden of Childhood Fears
Folie des Ventes et des Dunes
Trabendo
Café
r. A. Mille
Mirror Garden
First Aid
Pavillon Paul Delouvrier
Folie Paul Delouvrier
Grande Halle
Folie Janvier
Folie du Théâtre
r. Edgar Varèse
Théâtre Paris-Villette
Fontaine Aux Lions
av. du Nouveau Conservatoire
Cité de la Musique
bd. Serurier
PORTE DE PANTIN
PL. DE LA PORTE DE PANTIN
av. Jean Jaurès
0 200 meters
0 200 yards
Sente des Dorées

formance spaces—the 1200-seat **Salle des Concerts** and the 230-seat **Amphithéâtre**—host an eclectic range of shows and concerts year-round (see **Entertainment,** p. 228). The Cité de la Musique also has a **music information center** and the **Médiathèque Pédagogique,** with 90,000 books, documents, music journals, and photographs.

BEST OF THE REST

FIRST ARRONDISSEMENT

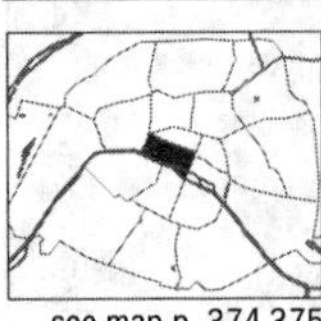
see map p. 374-375

NEIGHBORHOOD QUICKFIND: ***Discover,*** *p. 7;* ***Sights,*** *p. 73;* ***Food & Drink,*** *p. 171;* ***Nightlife,*** *p. 206;* ***Shopping,*** *p. 235;* ***Accommodations,*** *p. 254.*

MUSÉE DE LA MODE ET DU TEXTILE

107, r. de Rivoli, Palais du Louvre. M: Palais-Royal. ☎01 44 55 57 50. ***Open*** *Tu-F 11am-6pm, Sa-Su 10am-6pm.* ***Admission*** *€5.34, students €3.81. MC/V. Wheelchair-accessible.*

Housed in the Louvre with the Musée des Arts Décoratifs, the Musée de la Mode et du Textile is a huge collection of all that has been *en vogue* since the 18th century. Exhibits rotate annually and trace the history of costume from 17th-century brocade evening dresses to the wild runway fashions of Chanel and Christian Dior. Temporary exhibits in 2004 include the fashions of Dutch duo Viktor & Rolf, described by one museum official as "the next Jean-Paul Gaultier."

MUSÉE DE L'ORANGERIE

Southwest corner of the Jardin des Tuileries. M: Concorde. ☎01 42 97 48 16.

Opened in 1927, the museum is home to works by Renoir, Cézanne, Rousseau, Matisse, and Picasso, as well as Monet's *Les Nymphéas (Water Lilies)*. The museum is **closed for renovations** until 2004.

THIRD ARRONDISSEMENT

see map p. 376-377

NEIGHBORHOOD QUICKFIND: ***Discover,*** *p. 8;* ***Sights,*** *p. 79;* ***Food & Drink,*** *p. 174;* ***Nightlife,*** *p. 207;* ***Shopping,*** *p. 237;* ***Accommodations,*** *p. 257.*

MUSÉE CARNAVALET

23, r. de Sévigné. ☎01 44 59 58 58; www.paris.fr/musees/musee_carnavalet. M: Chemin Vert. Take r. St-Gilles (it turns into r. de Parc Royal), and turn left on r. de Sévigné. ***Open*** *Tu-Su 10am-5:40pm; last entrance 5:15pm.* ***Admission*** *free. Special exhibits €5.50, students and elderly €4, ages 13-18 €2.50, children under 12 free.*

Housed in Mme. de Sévigné's 16th-century *hôtel particulier*, this amazing museum traces Paris's history from its origins to the present, with exhibits on the city from prehistory and the Roman conquest to Medieval politics, 18th-century splendor and Revolution, 19th-century Haussmannization, and Mitterrand's *Grands Projets*. Highlights include the Wendel Ballroom, painted by Jose-Maria Sert, and the Charles Le Brun ceilings in rooms 19 and 20. The courtyard gardens are a lovely place to relax after perusing the collections. The museum regularly hosts special exhibitions featuring the work of cartoonists, sculptors, and photographers.

MUSÉE D'ART ET D'HISTOIRE DU JUDAÏSME

71, r. de Temple. ☎01 53 01 86 60; www.mahj.org. M: Rambuteau. ***Open*** *M-F 11am-6pm, Su 10am-6pm; last entrance at 5:15pm.* ***Admission*** *€6.10, students and ages 18-26 €3.80, under 18 free; includes an excellent English audioguide. Wheelchair-accessible.*

Newly renovated and housed in the grand **Hôtel de St-Aignan,** once a tenement for Jews fleeing Eastern Europe, this museum displays a history of Jews in Europe, France, and North Africa. Highlights include an ornate 15th-century Italian ark, letters written to wrongly accused French general Dreyfus, a small collection of Chagall and Modigliani paintings, Lissitzky lithographs, and modern art collections looted by the Nazis from Jewish homes.

MUSÉE COGNACQ-JAY

8, r. Elzévir. ☎01 40 27 07 21. M: St-Paul. Walk up r. Pavée and take a left on r. des Francs-Bourgeois and a right on r. Elzévir. ***Open*** *Tu-Su 10am-5:40pm; last entrance 5:10pm.* ***Admission*** *free.*

The 16th-century Hôtel Donon houses Enlightenment art and furniture, including minor works by Rembrandt, Ingres, Rubens, Greuze, Canaletto, and Fragonard. While the museum offers a good impression of what a house of the time would have looked like, the numerous paintings of cherubic girls in lace dresses get redundant.

MUSÉE DE L'HISTOIRE DE FRANCE

60, r. des Francs-Bourgeois. ☎01 40 27 60 96. M: Rambuteau. Walk up r. Rambuteau, which becomes r. des Francs-Bourgeois. ***Open*** *M and W-F 10am-12:30pm and 2-5:30pm, Sa-Su 2-5:30pm.* ***Admission*** *€3, ages 18-25 and seniors €2.30, under 18 free, Su €2.30.*

Housed in the Hôtel de Soubise, this museum is the main exhibition space of the Archives Nationales, featuring historically significant documents, including an edict drafted by Richard the Lionheart, an extract from Louis XVI's diary the day he was arrested by the Revolutionaries, and a letter from Napoleon to Josephine. Call for information regarding current exhibits.

MUSÉE DE LA POUPÉE

Impasse Berthaud. ☎01 42 72 73 11. M: Rambuteau. ***Open*** *Tu-Su 10am-6pm.* ***Admission*** *€6, students €4, under 18 €3.*

This small, out-of-the-way museum is devoted to dolls from the 1800s to the present. Dolls are literally everywhere, posed in scenes that recreate past games. A great place to bring the kids, though the non-doll-obsessed may find it slightly creepy.

FOURTH ARRONDISSEMENT

NEIGHBORHOOD QUICKFIND: ***Discover,*** *p. 8;* ***Sights,*** *p. 79;* ***Food & Drink,*** *p. 175;* ***Nightlife,*** *p. 209;* ***Shopping,*** *p. 237;* ***Accommodations,*** *p. 258.*

see map p. 376-377

MAISON DE VICTOR HUGO

6, pl. des Vosges. ☎01 42 72 10 16. M: Chemin-Vert or Bastille. ***Open*** *Tu-Su 10am-5:40pm.* ***Admission*** *free except during special exhibits (€3-5).*

Dedicated to the father of the French Romantics and housed in the building where he lived from 1832 to 1848, the museum displays Hugo memorabilia, including little-known paintings by the artist. One room is devoted to paintings of scenes from *Les Misérables*, another to *Notre Dame de Paris*. Other rooms, such as the *chambre chinoise*, reveal Hugo's flamboyant interior decorating skills.

MUSÉE ADAM MICKIEWICZ

6, quai d'Orléans. On the Île-St-Louis. ☎01 55 42 83 83. M: Pont Marie.

Located in the **Bibliothèque Polonaise de Paris,** the museum is dedicated to Polish poet Adam Mickiewicz and includes letters from Goethe and Hugo as well as a sketch by Delacroix on George Sand's letterhead. In the same building are the **Musée Boleslas Bregas** and the **Salon Chopin,** with more of Mickiewicz's manuscripts, letters, and his death mask. The Bibliothèque and the three museums are under renovation and will **reopen in January 2004** (call to confirm).

FIFTH ARRONDISSEMENT

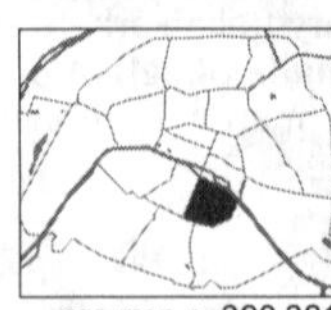
see map p. 380-381

NEIGHBORHOOD QUICKFIND: ***Discover,*** *p. 3;* ***Sights,*** *p. 86;* ***Food & Drink,*** *p. 177;* ***Nightlife,*** *p. 211;* ***Shopping,*** *p. 239;* ***Accommodations,*** *p. 259.*

MUSÉE D'HISTOIRE NATURELLE

57, r. Cuvier, in the Jardin des Plantes. ☎01 40 79 30 00; www.mnhn.fr. M: Gare d'Austerlitz. ***Grande Galerie de l'Evolution*** *open M and W-Su 10am-6pm, Th 10am-10pm. €6.10, students €4.57.* ***Musée de Minéralogie*** *open M and W-Su 10am-6pm. €4.57, students €3.05.* ***Galeries d'Anatomie Comparée et de Paléontologie,*** *open M and W-Su 10am-5pm, Apr.-Oct. Sa-Su until 6pm. €4.57, students €3.05.*

Three science museums in one, all beautifully situated within the greenery of the Jardin des Plantes. The hyper-modern, four-floor **Grand Galérie d'Evolution** tells the story of evolution with an ironically Genesis-like parade of naturalistic stuffed animals and lots of multimedia tools. Endangered and extinct species are given special attention on the third floor of the building, evidence of the rich collection (75 million specimens) that the museum holds. A section of the permanent exhibit is dedicated to human interaction with the environment—farming, sustainable development, and a frightening world population counter which estimates our numbers into the future. The Grand Galerie hosts temporary exhibitions in its basement, so give yourself at least two hours to absorb all of the fun, facts, and beauty in this museum.

Next door, the **Musée de Minéralogie,** surrounded by luscious rose trellises, contains some lovely diamonds, rubies, and sapphires, in addition to lesser-known minerals which just might astound you with their beauty. Look toward the back of the main hall to find gems glowing eerily under blacklighting.

The **Galeries d'Anatomie Comparée et de Paléontologie** is at the far end of the garden, with an exterior that looks like a Victorian house of horrors. Inside, the museum is a fittingly ghastly cavalcade of fibias, rib-cages, and vertebrae formed into historic and pre-historic animals. Despite some snazzy new placards, the place doesn't seem to have changed much since its 1898 opening; it's almost more notable as a museum of 19th-century *grotesquerie* than as a catalogue of anatomy. Check out the first floor to see fossils, which are less explicit than the body-parts-in-jars of the main hall.

INSTITUT DU MONDE ARABE

1, r. des Fossés St-Bernard. ☎01 40 51 38 38; www.imarabe.org. M: Jussieu. From the métro, walk down r. Jussieu away from the Jardin des Plantes; make your first right onto r. des Fossés St-Bernard. ***Museum*** *open Tu-Su 10am-7pm;* ***library*** *open Tu-Sa 1-8pm. Museum* ***admission*** *€4, ages 12-18 €3, under 12 free. Cinema €4, reduced rate €3.*

This beautiful, spacious museum assembles 3rd- to 18th-century art from three Arab regions: the Maghreb, the Near East, and the Middle East. Level 4 is devoted entirely to contemporary Arab art. An extensive **public library** houses over 50,000 works as well as an audio-visual center, and provides internet access for research purposes. From September to June, the auditorium hosts Arabic movies (subtitled in English and French), music, theater, and activities for kids. Check out the IMA's website, or pick up their monthly IMAInfo brochure for more details. The **rooftop terrace** has a fabulous and free view of Montmartre, Sacré Coeur, the Seine, and Île de la Cité.

SIXTH ARRONDISSEMENT

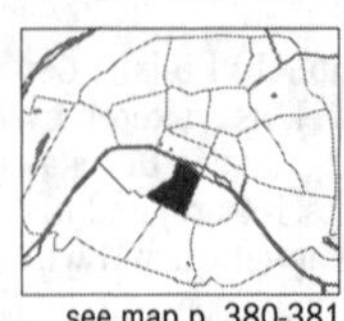
see map p. 380-381

NEIGHBORHOOD QUICKFIND: ***Discover,*** *p. 3;* ***Sights,*** *p. 91;* ***Food & Drink,*** *p. 181;* ***Nightlife,*** *p. 212;* ***Shopping,*** *p. 239;* ***Accommodations,*** *p. 261.*

MUSÉE ZADKINE

100bis, r. d'Assas. M: Vavin; RER: Port-Royal. Just south of the Jardin du Luxembourg. From the métro, cross bd. Raspail on bd. Montparnasse and turn left on r. de la Grande Chaumière; turn right on r. Notre Dame des

Champs, left on r. Joseph Bara, and left on r. d'Assas. ☎*01 43 26 91 90.* ***Open*** *Tu-Su 10am-5:30pm.* ***Admission*** *€3.60, seniors and students €2.20, under 26 €1.60.*

Installed in 1982 in the house and studio where he worked, the Zadkine Museum highlights the work of Russian sculptor Ossip Zadkine (1890-1967). Zadkine, who emigrated to Paris in 1909, worked with influences from Primitivism to Neo-Classicism to Cubism; as such, the collection represents all twelve of his creative periods. In addition to its regular collection and tiny sculpture garden, the museum also holds temporary exhibits by contemporary artists, and is exactly the tourist-free artspace you might be looking for.

MUSÉE DELACROIX

6, r. de Furstenberg. M: St-Germain-des-Prés. Behind the Eglise St-Germain, off r. de l'Abbaye. At the courtyard, follow the sign to the atelier Delacroix. ☎*01 44 41 86 50.* ***Open*** *M and W-Sa 9:30am-5pm; last entry 4:30pm.* ***Admission*** *€4, ages 18-25, students, and over 60 €2.60, under 18 free; entrance at reduced price every Sunday. MC/V.*

Delacroix is perhaps most famous for his huge, Romantic painting *Liberty Leading the People*, which hangs in the Louvre (see **Musée du Louvre,** p. 135), but the Musée Delacroix, in the refurbished three-room apartment and *atelier* in which the artist lived and worked for much of his life, offers a surprisingly intimate, manageable, and scholarly glimpse of the master. Sketches, watercolors, engravings, and letters to Théophile Gautier and George Sand are part of the permanent holdings, while sporadic traveling exhibitions showcase significant achievements in Delacroix scholarship. Between the *atelier* (which is wonderfully equipped with Delacroix's original palettes and studies) and the artist's private apartment, there is also a lovely enclosed garden in which to relax.

MUSÉE DE LA MONNAIE

11, quai de Conti. M: Pont Neuf. From the métro, cross the Pont Neuf and turn right on quai de Conti. ☎*01 40 46 55 35 or 01 40 46 58 55; www.monnaideparis.fr.* ***Open*** *Tu-F 11am-5:30pm, Sa-Su noon-5:30pm.* ***Admission*** *with audioguide €8, under 16 free. AmEx/MC/V.*

Cooler than it sounds, the Musée de la Monnaie (Currency Museum)—housed in the Hôtel des Monnaies, where coins were minted until 1973—is not just for coin-collectors. A veritable cultural history lesson of France and Paris written in the language of commerce, the museum displays the history of French coinage from Roman times to the present. The museum has everything, from answers to every question you've ever had about the Euro to some medieval coins the size of dinner plates. Note that only the main floor is wheelchair-accessible.

SEVENTH ARRONDISSEMENT

NEIGHBORHOOD QUICKFIND: ***Discover,*** *p. 4;* ***Sights,*** *p. 96;* ***Food & Drink,*** *p. 183;* ***Nightlife,*** *p. 213;* ***Shopping,*** *p. 242;* ***Accommodations,*** *p. 262.*

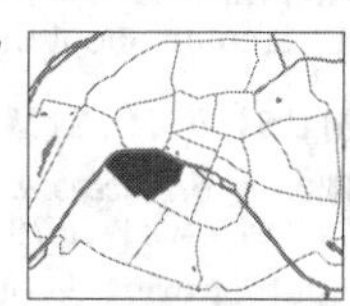

see map pp. 382-383

MUSÉE DES EGOUTS DE PARIS (MUSEUM OF THE SEWERS OF PARIS)

Across from 93, quai d'Orsay. M: Alma-Marceau. ☎*01 53 68 27 81.* ***Open*** *May-Sept. Sa-W 11am-6pm; Oct.-Apr. 11am-5pm. Last tickets sold 1hr. before closing. Closed 2 weeks in Jan.* ***Admission*** *€3.80; students, over 60, and under 10 €3.05; under 5 free.*

From 1892 to 1920, a brave and curious few observed the bowels of the city of Paris via subterranean boats. Luckily, today's tourists get to travel on foot through tunnels that are only slightly moist and smelly, at times particularly so (don't worry, the tour guide will warn you before you enter the more fragrant tunnels). The detailed displays showing Paris' struggle for potable water and a clean Seine are definitely worth the slightly uncomfortable journey.

MUSÉE NATIONAL DE LA LÉGION D'HONNEUR ET DES ORDRES DE CHEVALERIE

2, r. de la Légion d'Honneur. R. de Bellechasse is named r. de la Légion d'Honneur for this block; the museum is at r. de Lille, opposite the Musée d'Orsay's west side. M: Solférino. ☎01 40 62 84 25. **Open** *Tu-Su 11am-5pm.* **Admission** *€3.81; students, ages 18-25, and seniors €2.29; free for students the first Su of the month.*

Housed in the 18th-century Palais de la Légion d'Honneur (see **Sights,** p. 99), this museum mostly displays medals of the French Legion of Honor, made of everything from enamel to precious stones, as well as medals and uniforms from other European countries. Both the Palais and museum are **closed for renovations until 2005.**

EIGHTH ARRONDISSEMENT

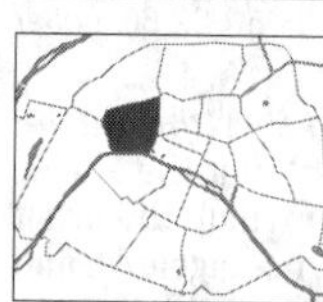

see map pp. 384-385

NEIGHBORHOOD QUICKFIND: **Discover,** *p. 9;* **Sights,** *p. 100;* **Food & Drink,** *p. 184;* **Nightlife,** *p. 213;* **Shopping,** *p. 243;* **Accommodations,** *p. 263.*

MUSÉE JACQUEMART-ANDRÉ

158, bd. Haussmann. ☎01 45 62 11 59. M: Miromesnil. **Open** *daily 10am-6pm; last entrance at 5:30pm.* **Admission** *€8, students and 7-17 €6, under 7 free. English headsets free with admission.*

Nelie Jacquemart and her husband liked to impress: during their lifetime, everyone had a chance to admire their double-corniced marble and iron staircase, but only very special friends saw their precious collection of Renaissance artwork, including a *Madonna and Child* by Botticelli and *St. George and the Dragon* by Ucello. Now, in a relaxed and intimate setting, you can peruse the opulent, late 19th-century home at your leisure and appreciate a collection worthy of the most prestigious museums. Do your best to absorb the beauty and extravagance of each room while also taking in the artwork. The frescoed stairwell, with twin marble staircases and gilded railing, is worth a good few minutes of incredulous reflection. Visitors can also eat a light lunch in the tearoom under a fresco by Tiepolo or admire the museum's impressive facade while resting in the courtyard.

PALAIS DE LA DÉCOUVERTE

In the Grand Palais, entrance on av. Franklin D. Roosevelt. ☎01 56 43 20 20, planetarium 01 40 74 81 73; www.palais-decouverte.fr. M: Franklin D. Roosevelt or Champs-Elysées-Clemenceau. **Open** *Tu-Sa 9:30am-6pm, Su 10am-7pm.* **Admission** *€5.60, students, seniors and under 18 €3.65, under 5 free.* **Planetarium** *entrance €3.05. Family entrance €12.20 for 2 adults and 2 children over 5. AmEx/MC/V.*

Kids tear around the Palais's interactive science exhibits, pressing buttons that start comets on celestial trajectories, spinning on seats to investigate angular motion, and glaring at all kinds of creepy-crawlies. Grown-up kids will have just as much fun exploring the colorful displays and exhibits of the museum, and will learn a surprising amount about the world. The **planetarium** has shows four times per day.

MUSÉE NISSIM DE CAMONDO

63, r. de Monceau. ☎01 53 89 06 40. From M: Villiers, walk down r. de Monceau; the museum is on the right. **Open** *W-Su 10am-5pm.* **Admission** *€4.60, ages 18-25 €3.10, under 18 free. MC/V.*

Another private collection gone public, the museum was dedicated by a Turkish count to the Musée des Arts Décoratifs, in memory of his son who died in the Great War. This collection of Chinese vases, Svonnerie carpets, and Sèvres porcelain is impressive, but less ornate (and easier to digest) than the Jacquemart-André's.

MUSÉE CERNUSCHI

7, av. Velasquez, outside the gates of Parc Monceau. ☎01 45 63 50 75. M: Villiers or Monceau. **Open** *Tu-Su 10am-5:30pm.* **Admission** *€5.38, under 26 free; during exhibits €5.38, under 26 €3.81.*

A magnificent collection of ancient to 18th-century Asian art, including a three-ton Japanese buddha. **Closed for renovations** until 2004.

GRAND PALAIS

3, av. du Général Eisenhower. ☎01 44 13 17 30 or 01 44 13 17 17. M: Champs-Elysées-Clemenceau. Follow av. W. Churchill towards the river; the museum is on your right. ***Open*** *M and Th-Su 10am-8pm, W 10am-10pm; last entry 45min. before closing.* ***Admission*** *varies by exhibit and some require reservations; approximately €8, ages 13-26 €5.50, under 13 free.*

Designed for the 1900 Universal Exposition, most of the building houses the Palais de la Découverte (see above), but the Grand Palais also hosts temporary exhibits. **Main hall closed for renovations indefinitely;** call for updated information.

PETIT PALAIS

av. Winston Churchill. ☎01 42 65 12 73. M: Champs-Elysées-Clemenceau or FDR.

Also called the Palais des Beaux-Arts de la Ville de Paris. Built for the 1900 Universal Exposition, the Palais houses 17th- to 20th-century Flemish, French, and Dutch painting and sculpture, but will be **closed for renovations** until winter 2004-05.

NINTH ARRONDISSEMENT

NEIGHBORHOOD QUICKFIND: ***Discover,*** *p. 9;* ***Sights,*** *p. 105;* ***Food & Drink,*** *p. 186;* ***Nightlife,*** *p. 214;* ***Accommodations,*** *p. 264.*

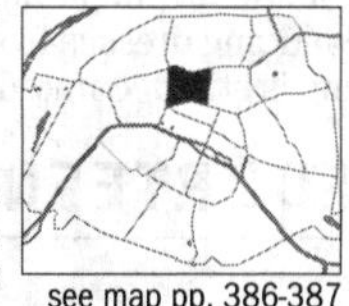

see map pp. 386-387

MUSÉE GRÉVIN

10, bd. Montmartre. ☎01 47 70 85 05. M: Grands Boulevards. From the métro, walk west on bd. Montmartre. ***Open*** *daily 10am-7pm, last entry 6:30pm.* ***Admission*** *€16, students and seniors €13.80, ages 6-14 €9. AmEx/MC/V for charges over €15.25.*

In the garish, mirrored, and disorienting halls of Paris's surreal wax museum, visitors can lose all sense of reality while studying the lifelike figures of everyone from Molière to Harrison Ford. Some of the figures, such as the puzzled-looking George Bush and extremely well-endowed Madonna, seem more like caricatures than realistic likenesses. Some gruesome scenarios with Black Plague victims and a pre-execution Joan of Arc are also on display.

MUSÉE GUSTAVE MOREAU

14, r. de la Rochefoucauld. M: Trinité. From the métro, make a right on r. St-Lazare and then a left onto r. de la Rochefoucauld. ☎01 48 74 38 50. ***Open*** *M and Th-Sa 10am-12:45pm and 2-5:15pm, W 11am-5:15pm.* ***Admission*** *€4, students, over 60, and Su €2.60, under 18 and the first Su of every month free. MC/V.*

This monograph museum, housed in Gustave Moreau's home and *atelier*, was opened in 1898, just two years before the artist's death. Symbolist master, professor at the Ecole des Beaux-Arts, and teacher of Matisse and Roualt, Moreau created a fantastical body of work. The museum is virtually overflowing with his more than 6000 drawings, maquettes, watercolors, sculptures, and paintings (many unfinished), organized according to the artist's wishes. At the top of the celebrated flamboyant Victorian staircase is the famous *L'Apparition*, an opium-inspired vision of Salomé dancing before the severed head of John the Baptist.

TENTH ARRONDISSEMENT

NEIGHBORHOOD: ***Discover,*** *p. 11;* ***Sights,*** *p. 107;* ***Food & Drink,*** *p. 187;* ***Accommodations,*** *p. 265.*

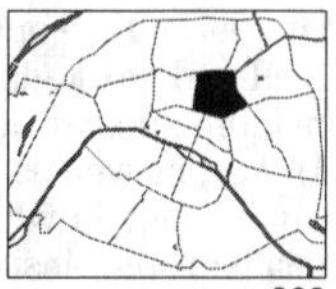

see map p. 388

CRISTALLERIES BACCARAT

30bis, r. de Paradis. M: Gare de l'Est. Walk against traffic on bd. Strasbourg and turn right on r. de la Fidelité, which becomes r. de Paradis. Enter on 2nd fl. ☎01 47 70 64 30. www.baccarat.fr. ***Open*** *M-Sa 10am-6pm.* ***Admission*** *€3.*

Since its founding in 1764 by Louis XV, Baccarat has been the most prestigious of crystal makers, patronized by kings, tsars, and shahs. Now you, too, can glimpse wares fit for royalty. Inordinately expensive bowls and goblets fill the showroom. The museum displays crystal objects from the 18th century on. The **Baccarat Jewelry Shop** at 17, r. de la Paix, *2ème* (☎01 42 44 18 45), which could be a museum itself, sells exquisite jewelry at not-so-pretty prices. Open M-Sa 10am-7pm. MC/V.

TWELFTH ARRONDISSEMENT

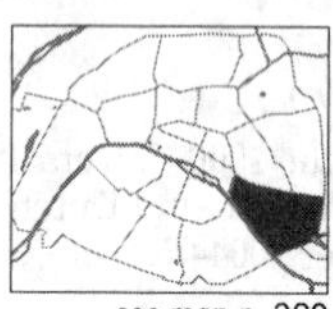

see map p. 389

NEIGHBORHOOD QUICKFIND: ***Discover,*** *p. 12;* ***Sights,*** *p. 110;* ***Food & Drink,*** *p. 189;* ***Nightlife,*** *p. 215;* ***Shopping,*** *p. 243;* ***Accommodations,*** *p. 267.*

MUSÉE DES ARTS D'AFRIQUE ET D'OCÉANIE

293, av. Daumesnil. M: Porte Dorée. On the western edge of the Bois de Vincennes. ☎01 43 46 51 61. ***Open*** *M and W-Su 10am-5:30pm, last entry 4:45pm.* ***Admission*** *€5, 18-26 and everyone on Su €4, under 18 and first Su of every month free.*

This museum is home to a stunning collection of several millennia of African and Pacific art, including an impressive display of African statues, masks, jewelry, and wedding dresses from the Maghreb. Built for the 1931 Colonial Exposition, the building is still decorated with its original murals and friezes.

FOURTEENTH ARRONDISSEMENT

see map pp. 395-396

NEIGHBORHOOD QUICKFIND: ***Discover,*** *p. 4;* ***Sights,*** *p. 113;* ***Food & Drink,*** *p. 191;* ***Nightlife,*** *p. 216;* ***Accommodations,*** *p. 269.*

FONDATION CARTIER POUR L'ART CONTEMPORAIN

261, bd. Raspail. M: Raspail or Denfert-Rochereau. ☎01 42 18 56 51; www.fondation.cartier.fr. ***Open*** *Tu-Su noon-8pm.* ***Admission*** *€5, students and seniors €3.50, under 10 free. Soirées Nomades (Nomadic Nights) Sept.-June Th 8:30pm; check web site for specific performances. Reserve ahead ☎01 42 18 56 72.*

A stunning modern glass facade surrounds the natural wildlife and local flora of the *fondation*'s grounds, creating the appearance of an avant-garde indoor forest. Inside the main building, the gallery hosts contemporary art exhibits on everything from Andy Warhol to African folk art. On Thursdays, art-hounds can scope out an eclectic set of dance, music, and performance art at the *Soirées Nomades*.

FIFTEENTH ARRONDISSEMENT

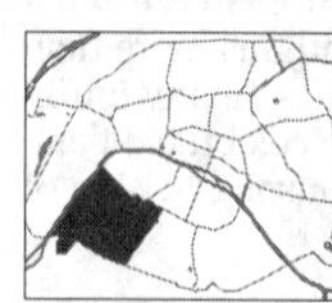

see map p. 393

NEIGHBORHOOD QUICKFIND: ***Discover,*** *p. 5;* ***Sights,*** *p. 114;* ***Food & Drink,*** *p. 192;* ***Accommodations,*** *p. 270.*

MUSÉE BOURDELLE

18, r. Antoine Bourdelle. M: Montparnasse-Bienvenüe. From Place Bienvenüe, take av. du Maine, turn left onto r. Antoine Bourdelle. ☎01 49 54 73 73. ***Open*** *Tu-Su 10am-5:40pm; last entry 5:15pm. Free.*

A pupil of Rodin and a mentor of Giacometti, Emile-Antoine Bourdelle (1861-1929) sculpted the reliefs that adorn the Théâtre des Champs-Elysées and the opera house in Marseilles. Housed in the studios where the sculptor lived and worked, the museum displays 500 works in marble, plaster, and bronze, including the work considered by most to be Bourdelle's masterpiece, *Heracles as Archer*, as well as a series of 40 busts of Beethoven. The sculpture gardens provide much space in which to admire the sculptor's massive works, but don't miss the smaller rooms inside the museum, which feature not only his finished works but displays of his studies and casts.

MÉMORIAL DE LA LIBÉRATION DE PARIS

23, allée de la 2ème D.B., Jardin Atlantique. M: Montparnasse-Bienvenüe. On the roof above the tracks of the Gare Montparnasse. Follow signs to the Jardin Atlantique from the train station, pl. du Pont des Cinq Martyrs du Lycée Buffon, or r. Commandant René Mouchotte. ☎01 40 64 39 44. ***Open*** *Tu-Su 10am-5:40pm; last entry 5:15pm.* ***Admission*** *to permanent collection free; exhibitions €4, students and seniors €3, age 14-26 €2 . Wheelchair-accessible.*

These two museums were opened jointly in 1994 to commemorate the 50th anniversary of the French Resistance. One is a memorial to Maréchal Leclerc, a French Commander who fought in North Africa and led his small army to liberate Paris from the Germans in August of 1944. The other is a museum commemorating the founder, president, and martyr of the French Resistance, Jean Moulin. The museums, both of which are filled with official documents and letters relating to the Liberation, present a comprehensive timeline of WWII France.

SIXTEENTH ARRONDISSEMENT

NEIGHBORHOOD QUICKFIND: ***Discover,*** *p. 12;* ***Sights,*** *p. 116;* ***Food & Drink,*** *p. 193;* ***Nightlife,*** *p. 217;* ***Accommodations,*** *p. 272.*

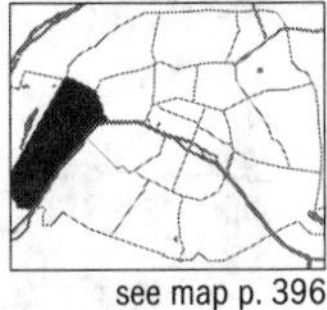
see map p. 396

SITE DE CREATION CONTEMPORAINE

Palais de Tokyo, 13, av. du Président Wilson. M: Iéna. From the métro, follow av. du Président Wilson with the Seine on your right. ☎01 47 23 54 01; www.palaisdetokyo.com. ***Open*** *Tu-Su noon-midnight.* ***Admission*** *varies with exhibit, expect approximately €5, with reduced student/youth/senior prices. Free admission for art students.*

In a warehouse-like setting inside the Palais de Tokyo, with rough-hewn concrete floors and fencing around the bookshop, the *site de creation contemporaine* houses several exhibits a year, all guaranteed to challenge your conceptions of art. Showing off exciting, controversial international work, usually by a number of different artists, the large, open space of the *site* accommodates massive abstract sculpture, video displays and other creative forms of media. Don't forget to pick up some free souvenirs on your way out: poster-sized advertisements for past exhibitions, piled on the coffee table beneath the staircase.

MUSÉE D'ART MODERNE DE LA VILLE DE PARIS

Palais de Tokyo, 11, av. du Président Wilson. M: Iéna. From the métro, follow av. du Président Wilson with the Seine on your right. ☎01 53 67 40 00. Wheelchair-accessible. ***Open*** *Tu-F 10am-5:30pm, Sa-Su 10am-6:45pm.* ***Admission*** *to permanent exhibitions free; special exhibits admission varies, expect approximately €5, students €2.20-3.*

Housed in the magnificent Palais de Tokyo (see **Sights,** p. 116), this museum contains one of the world's foremost collections of 20th-century art, but on a smaller scale than that of the Centre Pompidou. Matisse's *La Danse Inachêvée,* which was executed with the help of a brush attached to a bamboo stick, dominates its own room, but there are also formidable gatherings of Modiglianis, Vuillards, and Braques. The final room on the circuit contains the more recent works and is a veritable playground of modernity, with lots of lights and colorful plastics. Upstairs houses temporary exhibitions, often more experimental than the permanent work.

MUSÉE MARMOTTAN MONET

2, r. Louis-Boilly. M: La Muette. Follow Chaussée de la Muette, which becomes av. Ranelagh, through the Jardin du Ranelagh park. ☎01 44 96 50 33; www.marmottan.com. Wheelchair-accessible. ***Open*** *Tu-Su 10am-6pm.* ***Admission*** *€6.50, students €4, under 8 free.*

This Empire-style house became a lucrative shrine to Impressionism following the generous familial donations of Monet and others. The ground floor showcases many of the house's original furnishings and hangings, while the top floor dazzles with works by Monet's peers, with an emphasis on the paintings of Berthe Morisot. The basement is the real draw, with large, late Monets, including his famed water lilies.

Musée d'Orsay

Musée Picasso

Gallery of Comparative Anatomy

MUSÉE NATIONAL DES ARTS ASIATIQUES (MUSÉE GUIMET)

6, pl. d'Iéna. M: Iéna. ☎ 01 56 52 53 00; www.musee-guimet.fr. Wheelchair-accessible. **Open** *M and W-Sa 10am-6pm; last entrance 5:45pm.* **Admission** *€5.50, ages 18-25 and all visitors on Su €4, under 18 and all visitors on the first Su of the month free.*

With four floors of Asian art, from 17 different countries, the clean grey and white lines of this architectural marvel display a beautiful collection. Over 45,000 works of art, in stone, metal, paper, and canvas dazzle in a maze of rooms organized by country, from Afghanistan to Vietnam. Just around the corner, the **Panthéon Bouddhique** (on av. d'Iéna; free) packs in more art, and a tranquil garden out back.

MAISON DE BALZAC

47, r. Raynouard. M: Passy. ☎ 01 55 74 41 80. **Open** *Tu-Su 10am-6pm, last entrance 5:40pm.* **Admission** *to permanent collection €3.30, reduced admission €2.20, ages 14-26 €1.60, under 14 free.*

This *maison*, home of Honoré de Balzac from 1840-47, was where the author hid from bill collectors (under the pseudonym M. de Breugnol) and wrote a substantial part of *La Comédie Humaine*. Visitors can see the desk where he wrote and edited for a reported 17 hours a day and, in the fantastic "Manuscript Room," appreciate his excruciating editing process. Check out more than 400 printing block portraits of his characters, organized into genealogical sequences, in one of the final rooms.

MUSÉE HENRI BOUCHARD

25, r. de l'Yvette. M: Jasmin. ☎ 01 46 47 63 46; www.musee-bouchard.com. **Open** *July-Sept. 15, Oct.-Dec. 15, Jan. 2-Mar. 15, and Apr.-June 15 W and Sa 2-7pm.* **Admission** *€4, students 26 and under €2.50.*

Housed in the workshop of Henri Bouchard (1875-1960), sculptor of the Palais de Chaillot's *Apollo* as well as 1200 other pieces. The workshop has been left in its original state with the largest collection of Bouchard's *maquettes* and sculptures in existence, alongside the plasters, tools, and moulds used to make them. Bouchard's son and daughter-in-law are the curators of this charming memorial museum, and are available to explain his style and technique with reverential exuberance.

MUSÉE GEORGES CLEMENCEAU

8, r. Benjamin Franklin. M: Passy. ☎ 01 45 20 53 41. **Open** *Tu, Th, Sa-Su 2-5pm; closed Aug.* **Admission** *€3.05, students and seniors €2.29.*

The museum thoroughly documents the life of revered and vilified journalist and statesman Georges Clemenceau (1841-1929). Publisher of Emile Zola's *J'accuse*, Prime Minister of France, and much-criticized negotiator of the Treaty of Versailles, Clemenceau lived here from 1895 until his death in 1929.

FONDATION LE CORBUSIER

Villa la Roche 8-10, sq. du Docteur Blanche. M: Jasmin. Walk up r. de l'Yvette and turn left on r. du Docteur-Blanche and left again at no. 55 into pl. du Docteur-Blanche; go down to the cul-de-sac and ring the bell at your right. ☎01 42 88 41 53; www.fondationlecorbusier.asso.fr. ***Open*** *M 1:30-6pm, Tu-Th 10am-12:30pm and 1:30-6pm, F 10am-12:30pm and 1:30-5pm.* ***Admission*** *€2.40, students €1.60.* ***Library*** *in Villa Jeanneret open after 1:30pm by appointment only. Free.*

The foundation is located in Villas **La Roche** and **Jeanneret,** both designed and furnished by the Swiss architectural master Le Corbusier (1887-1965). Villa Jeanneret houses the foundation's scholarly library, but the real attraction is the reduced geometry, the understated curvature, and the dignified spaciousness of Villa La Roche's interiors. A small collection of prints and drawings is on display (the building was originally intended to house La Roche's collection of Modernist art), but the Villa itself is clearly the collection's masterpiece. The bizarre curving ramps and narrow stairwells reflect the architect's maxim that "a house is a machine one lives in!"

MUSÉE DE L'HOMME (MUSEUM OF MAN)

17, pl. du Trocadéro. M: Trocadéro. In the Palais de Chaillot, on the right-hand side if you're facing the Eiffel Tower. ☎01 44 05 72 72; recorded message 01 44 05 72 00; www.mnhn.fr. ***Open*** *M and W-Sa 9:45am-5:15pm, last entry 4:45pm.* ***Admission*** *€5, under 27 and seniors €3, under 4 free.* ***Films*** *in the afternoon Tu-Su; for info on showtimes and events, call ☎01 44 05 72 59.*

Visit this anthropology museum, with its displays on world cultures from 250,000 BC to the present, while you still can; there is talk of shutting it down and dispersing its collections to other sites. Those who make it in time will see a more-than-healthy dose of dioramas and a variety of ethnological artifacts, including prehistoric tools, Eskimo fishing boats, and hats from Cameroon. The displays on birth control and medicine over the years will make you joyful to be living in the 21st century.

MUSÉE DE LA MARINE (MUSEUM OF THE NAVY)

17, pl. du Trocadéro. M: Trocadéro. In the Palais de Chaillot, immediately to the right of Musée de l'Homme. ☎01 53 65 69 69. ***Open*** *M and W-Sa 10am-6pm; last entry 5:30pm.* ***Admission*** *€7, students and seniors €5.40, under 18 €3.85. Audioguide in English €4. AmEx/MC/V.*

A dream come true for aquaphiles of all ages, this museum exhibits swaths of rope two feet in diameter and model ships of astounding detail. A few real boats from the 17th to 19th centuries are anchored here, including a lavish golden dinghy built for Napoleon in 1810. Oil paintings of stormy sea battles round out the collection.

MUSÉE DE LA MODE ET DU COSTUME (MUSEUM OF FASHION & CLOTHING)

In the Palais Galliera, 10, av. Pierre 1er de Serbie, in the pl. de Tokyo. M: Iéna. From the métro, walk down either av. du Président Wilson or av. Pierre 1er de Serbie with the Eiffel Tower to your right. The museum entrance is in the center of the Palais and can be reached from the pl. de Rochambeau side. ☎01 56 52 86 00. ***Open*** *Tu-Su 10am-6pm; last entrance 5:30pm.* ***Admission*** *€7, students and seniors €5.50, children €3.50.* ***Audio tour*** *in French free. MC/V for charges over €7.*

With 30,000 outfits, 70,000 accessories, and a relatively small space, the museum rotates exhibitions to showcase fashions of the past three centuries. This is *the* place to go to see the history of Parisian high fashion and high society.

MAISON DE RADIO FRANCE

116, av. du Président Kennedy. RER: av. du Pt. Kennedy/Maison de Radio France. Head for the Seine, go right, and enter through Door A (directly across from the Seine) of the big, white, cylin-

drical building. ☎01 56 40 21 80. ***Tours*** *M-F 10:30am and 2:30 pm, or by reservation for 11am and 4pm.* ***Admission*** *€5, students and seniors €3.*

The museum, open only to guided tours, presents the history of communications at the headquarters of France's public radio stations. Attractions range from ancient radio specimens to a concert hall.

MUSÉE DU VIN

r. des Eaux, or 5-7, pl. Charles Dickens. M: Passy. Go down the stairs, turn right on pl. Alboni, and then turn right on r. des Eaux; the museum is facing you at the end of the street. ☎01 45 25 63 26; www.museeduvinparis.com. ***Open*** *Tu-Su 10am-6pm.* ***Admission*** *(includes 1 glass of wine) €6.50, seniors €5.90, students €5.70. MC/V.*

In the dank corridors of this renovated 15th-century cellar, visitors learn all about the difference between Alsatian wine and Burgundy wine, and then wash all that learnin' down with a bottle of Chardonnay, available for purchase in the gift shop. The *cave* is peopled with wax models in the process of wine making and drinking, as well as displays of wine containers dating to the 18th century. After the tour, you may have to remind the receptionist to give you your free tasting of red, *rosé*, or white. If that whets your appetite for more, a wine-heavy lunch is available in the fine restaurant (see **Food & Drink,** p. 194).

SEVENTEENTH ARRONDISSEMENT

see map p. 397

NEIGHBORHOOD QUICKFIND: ***Discover,*** *p. 13;* ***Sights,*** *p. 118;* ***Food & Drink,*** *p. 194;* ***Nightlife,*** *p. 217;* ***Accommodations,*** *p. 273.*

MUSÉE JEAN-JACQUES HENNER

43, av. de Villiers. Across av. de Villiers from M: Malesherbes. ☎01 47 63 42 73. ***Open*** *Tu-Su 10am-12:30pm and 2-5pm.* ***Admission*** *free.*

Three full floors display the works of Alsatian artist Jean-Jacques Henner (1829-1905). The exhibits include lots of landscapes, nymphs, and soft-focus subjects. The museum is under renovation and is scheduled to **reopen in March 2004.**

EIGHTEENTH ARRONDISSEMENT

see map pp. 386-387

NEIGHBORHOOD QUICKFIND: ***Discover,*** *p. 13;* ***Sights,*** *p. 119;* ***Food & Drink,*** *p. 195;* ***Nightlife,*** *p. 218;* ***Shopping,*** *p. 245;* ***Accommodations,*** *p. 273.*

HALLE ST-PIERRE

2, r. Ronsard. M: Anvers. Walk up r. de Steinkerque, turn right at pl. St-Pierre, then left onto r. Ronsard. ☎01 42 58 72 89; www.hallesaintpierre.org. ***Open*** *daily 10am-6pm.* ***Admission*** *€6.50, students €5. Children's art workshops (ages 3-14) W and Sa-Su 3-4pm. €6. Wheelchair-accessible.*

Within a former 19th-century marketplace, this gallery and cultural center holds temporary exhibits of "outsider, naïve, and folk" contemporary drawing, painting and sculpture from France to Haiti to North America. In addition to a library, café (see **Food & Drink,** p. 197), community auditorium, and various children's art workshops (call ahead for information), the space is home to the **Musée d'Art Naïf Max Fourny,** a one-room permanent collection of folk art from around the world.

MUSÉE DE L'EROTISME

72, bd. de Clichy. M: Blanche. ☎01 42 58 28 73. www.eroticmuseum.net. ***Open*** *daily 10am-2am.* ***Admission*** *€7, students and over 60 €5.*

Bronze statues in the missionary position, Japanimation sex cartoons, vagina-shaped puppets—7 floors of these sexy creations await visitors at Paris's Museum of Erotic Art. This shrine to sex celebrates erotic art across all mediums (including painting, sculpture, and video) and is sure to stimulate both artistically and erotically. While Hindus, Americans, Aborigines, and Pygmies may have their differences, this museum unites them through the universal language of sex. After all, the 2000-item collection is intended to commemorate "art in all its forms, throughout time and different world cultures," not simply to make people hot under the collar.

MUSÉE DU VIEUX MONTMARTRE

12, r. Cortot. M: Lamarck-Caulaincourt. Turn right on r. Lamarck, right again up steep r. des Saules, then left onto r. Cortot. ☎ *01 46 06 61 11.* ***Open*** *Tu-Su 11am-6pm.* ***Admission*** *€4.50, students and seniors €3. MC/V.*

Located in a charming 17th-century apartment building which Raoul Dufy, Renoir, Utrillo, and conductor Claude Charpentier once called home, the museum is dedicated to the political, artistic, cultural, and religious past of the *village* Montmartre. Letters, cabaret posters, journals, and mediocre paintings by celebrated Montmartre residents line the walls. Don't miss the view of the *butte* from the garden.

TWENTIETH ARRONDISSEMENT

NEIGHBORHOOD QUICKFIND: ***Discover,*** *p. 14;* ***Sights,*** *p. 123;* ***Food & Drink,*** *p. 197;* ***Nightlife,*** *p. 218;* ***Accommodations,*** *p. 275.*

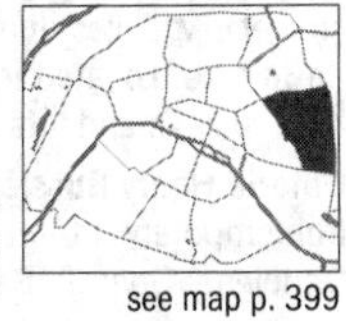
see map p. 399

LA MAISON DE L'AIR

27, r. Piat. ☎ *01 43 28 47 63. M: Pyrénées. Walk down the sloping r. de Belleville and turn left on r. Piat.* ***Open*** *Apr.-Sept. Tu-F 1:30-5:30pm, Sa-Su 1:30-6:30pm; Oct.-Mar. Tu-Su 1:30-5pm.* ***Admission*** *€2, ages 7-25 and over 60 €1, under 7 free.*

This kid-friendly museum allows you to touch, hear, and smell your way into a broader understanding of the air around you. Exhibits investigate the wonders of flight, the atmosphere, meteorology, and the evils of air pollution (a serious problem in Paris). Parc de Belleville surrounds the museum and provides amazing views.

GALLERIES

The highest concentration of contemporary art galleries is in the Marais and in the *6ème's* St-Germain-/des-Prés area. These galleries exhibit primarily contemporary art. The *8ème*, on the other hand, is loaded with Old Masters. Those near M: Franklin D. Roosevelt on the Champs-Elysées, av. Matignon, r. du Faubourg St-Honoré, and r. de Miromesnil focus on Impressionism and post-Impressionism. The *Portes Ouvertes* festival allows visitors to witness artists in action in their studios (see **Discover,** p. 18). Almost all galleries close in August.

THIRD ARRONDISSEMENT

The swank galleries in the Marais, concentrated in the *3ème*, display some of Paris's most exciting and avant-garde art. Cutting-edge paintings, sculptures, and photography peek out of store-front windows along **rue de Perche, rue Debellyme, rue Vieille-du-Temple, rue Quincampoix, rue des Coutures St-Gervais, rue de Poitou,** and **rue Beaubourg.** Most are closed Sundays and Mondays, along with the entire month of August.

Fait & Cause, 58, r. Quincampoix (☎ 01 42 74 26 36). M: Rambuteau or Etienne-Marcel. Art (mostly photos) aimed at spreading humanist and humanitarian consciousness. Exhibits draw large crowds, and past artists have included Jacob Riis, Jane Evelyn Atwood, and Robert Doisneau. Open Tu-Sa 1:30-6:30pm.

Galerie Thullier, 13, r. de Thorigny (☎ 01 42 77 33 24; www.galeriethuillier.com). M: St-Sébastien-Froissart, behind the Picasso Museum. Featuring over 1500 pieces of art each year at 21 annual expositions, this is among the city's most active galleries. Exhibition (and free refreshments) Tu evening from 7pm. Open Tu-Sa noon-7pm.

Galerie Daniel Templon, 30, r. Beaubourg (☎01 42 72 14 10). M: Rambuteau. From the métro, walk north on r. Beaubourg. Enter at no. 30; the gallery is at the back of the courtyard. Tucked away from the chaos near the Centre Pompidou, this is one of Paris's most respected contemporary galleries. 20th-century painting and sculpture and an impressive roster of artists, including Ross Bleckner, Arman, and Jim Dine. Open M-Sa 10am-7pm. Closed Aug.

Galerie Michèle Chomette, 24, r. Beaubourg (☎01 42 78 05 62). M: Rambuteau. From the métro, walk north on r. Beaubourg. Ring the buzzer at no. 24 and proceed upstairs. 6-8 exhibitions per year of contemporary and historic photography. Open Tu-Sa 2-7pm. Closed Aug.

Gilles Peyroulet & Cie, 80, r. Quincampoix (☎01 42 78 85 11). M: Rambuteau. Showcases contemporary photographers like Waplington; design across the street in Espace #2. Open Tu-F 2-7pm, Sa 11am-7pm.

Galerie Nathalie Obadia, 5, r. du Grenier St-Lazare (☎01 42 74 67 68). M: Rambuteau. A variety of installations, mostly by female artists. Open M-Sa 11am-7pm.

Galerie Birthe Laursen, 56-58 r. Vieille-du-Temple (☎01 44 54 04 07). M: Rambuteau. Recent artists include Anne Tholstrup, Kirsten Klein, and Anders Moseholm. Open Tu-Sa 2-7pm and by appointment. Closed Aug.

Galerie Sabine Puget, 108, r. Vieille-du-Temple (☎01 42 71 04 20; www.od-arts.com/spuget). M: Filles du Calvaire. Walk down r. des Filles du Calvaire, which becomes r. Vieille-du-Temple. Located in the heart of the Marais; features contemporary artists in a space with high ceilings and lots of natural light. Open Tu-Sa noon-7pm. Closed July-Aug.

Galerie Henry Bussière, 21/21bis, r. Michel le Comte (☎01 42 74 64 90). M: Rambuteau. Contemporary art in all forms. Recent exhibit of charcoal sketches and sculpture by Eugène Dodeigne. Open Tu-Sa 10:30am-12:30pm and 2-7pm.

Galerie Zürcher, 56, r. Chapon (☎01 42 72 82 20). M: Arts et Métiers. From the métro, walk south on r. Beaubourg and turn right on r. Chapon; enter at no. 56; gallery is at back of courtyard. Young, abstract, European artists. Open Tu-Sa 11am-7pm, Su 2-6pm.

Galerie Askéo, 19, r. Debellyme (☎01 42 77 17 77). M: Filles du Calvaire. This 3-story gallery displays installation art and sculpture on a grand scale. Open W-Sa 2:30-7pm.

Polaris, 8, r. St-Claude (☎01 42 72 21 27). M: St-Sébastien-Froissart. Promising new artists, especially in photography. Open Tu-F 1-7:30pm, Sa 11am-1pm and 2-7:30pm.

Galerie Denise René, 22, r. Charlot (☎01 48 87 73 94). M: St-Sébastien-Froissart. Presents primarily abstract art and has had an exhibition at the Centre Pompidou. Open Tu-Sa 2-7pm.

Galerie DeBelleyme, 112, r. Vieille-du-Temple (☎01 42 71 14 02). M: Filles du Calvaire. Abstract paintings by artists like Grataloup and Zabov. Open Tu-Sa 11am-7pm. Closed Aug.

Galerie Florence Arnaud, 10, r. de Saintonge (☎01 42 77 01 79). M: Filles du Calvaire. Mixture of modern art and historical documents; featured artists include Nemours, Brandt, and Michaux. Open Tu-Sa 2:30-7pm. MC/V.

FOURTH ARRONDISSEMENT

Galerie Rachlin & Lemaire Beaubourg, 23, r. de Renard (☎01 44 59 27 25). M: Rambuteau or Châtelet. Adventurous contemporary art. Mainly showcases paintings, but expositions often include sculptures. Open M-Sa 10:30am-1pm and 2:30-7pm.

galerie du jour agnès b., 44, r. Quincampoix (☎ 01 44 54 55 90). M: Rambuteau. This highly praised contemporary photo gallery also doubles as an interesting bookstore. Open Tu-Sa noon-7pm. Closed Aug. 5-20.

Galerie de France, 54, r. de la Verrerie (☎01 42 74 38 00). M: Hôtel-de-Ville. One of the Marais's best-established galleries. Known for showing the work of prominent artists like Richard Avedon, Pier Paolo Calzolari, and Patrick Faigenbaum. Open Tu-Sa 11am-7pm.

Galerie Gana-Beaubourg, 3, r. Pierre au Lard (☎01 42 71 00 45). M: Rambuteau. Spacious, split-level international contemporary art space, showcasing many Asian artists. Open Tu-Sa 10am-12:30pm and 2-7pm.

Galerie Nelson, 40, r. Quincampoix (☎01 42 71 74 56; www.galerie-nelson.com). M: Rambuteau. Interesting work in ceramics, mostly by French artists, but other European countries are also represented. Open Tu-Sa 2-7pm.

SIXTH ARRONDISSEMENT

North of bd. St-Germain, back-to-back galleries cluster on **rue de Seine, rue Mazarine, rue Bonaparte, rue Jacques Callot, rue Dauphine,** and **rue des Beaux-Arts.** Most are marked with colorful "Art of St. Germain des Pres" flags. Just don't go at lunchtime (usually 1-2:30pm), or on a Monday, as most galleries will be closed.

Galerie Patrice Trigano, 4bis, r. des Beaux-Arts (☎01 46 34 15 01; www.od-arts.com/patricetrigano). Just down the street from the Ecole des Beaux-Arts, Trigano is one of the most stellar spaces in the *6ème,* with excellent contemporary sculpture, painting, and mixed media in several rooms (don't forget to check out their basement). Ask to see the small sculpture garden in the back. Open Tu-Sa 10am-1pm and 2:30-6:30pm.

Galerie Loevenbruck, 2, r. de L'Echaude (☎01 53 10 85 68; www.loevenbruck.com). Enter off r. Jacob. An outstanding gallery, specializing in politically engaged Dada- and Pop-inspired contemporary sculpture, video, photography, and painting—most of it with a sense of humor. Pick up free postcards advertising exciting art events in Paris. Open Tu-Sa 11am-7pm.

Kamel Mennour, 60, r. Mazarine (☎01 56 24 03 63; www.galeriemennour.com). A hip gallery with high quality exhibits by stars like Annie Leibovitz and Larry Clark. Friendly, young staff with some of the best contemporary photography, video, and painting that the *6ème's* up-and-comers, as well as the world famous, have to offer. Open M-Sa 11am-7:30pm.

Galerie Seine 51, 51, r. de Seine (☎01 43 26 91 10; www.seine51.com). With one of the flashiest collections of contemporary artists on the Left Bank and some of the most innovative curatorial projects (including occasional pink walls and astroturf), Seine 51 is a funny, melodramatic, and garish treat. Exhibits range from pop-inspired installations, photography, and furniture to more standard works. Open Tu-Sa 10:30am-1pm and 2:30-7pm.

Galerie Loft, 3, r. des Beaux-Arts (☎01 46 33 18 90; www.galerieloft.com). Enter the courtyard at no. 3 and climb the stairs. Expressive and politically oriented Chinese avant-garde art, unlike anything else you'll find in St-Germain. Open Tu-Sa 10am-1pm and 2-7pm.

Claude Bernard, 7-9, r. des Beaux-Arts (☎01 43 26 97 07; www.claude-bernard.com). An expansive and modern art space, Claude Bernard has perhaps the most prestigious gallery of r. des Beaux-Arts. The space holds a mix of traditionally beautiful photographs and off-the-wall collages and modern art. Has exhibited such greats as Dubuffet, Balthus, David Levine, and Henri Cartier-Bresson. Open Tu-Sa 9:30am-12:30pm and 2:30-6:30pm.

Galerie Di Meo, 9, r. des Beaux-Arts (☎01 43 54 10 98; contact@dimeo.fr). This gallery specializes in multimedia painting and sculpture, with a fabulous retinue of neo-pop and abstract-expressionist contemporary artists. Open Tu-Sa 10am-1pm and 2:30-7pm.

Galerie Laurent Herschtritt, 5, r. Jacques Callot (☎01 56 24 34 74; laurent.herschtritt@libertysurf.fr). A highly stylish gallery specializing in photography from the 19th and 20th centuries. Open Tu-Sa 2:30-7pm.

Galerie Lelia Mordoch, 50, r. Mazarine (☎01 53 10 88 52; www.galerieleliamordoch.com). Holds superior individual and group shows of Pop- and minimalist-inspired sculpture, painting, photography, and installation—all done with a very clean aesthetic. Open Tu-Sa 1-7pm.

JGM, 8bis, r. Jacques Callot (☎01 43 26 12 05; jgm@free.fr). Some of the best sculptures (modern and contemporary) on the Left Bank in a friendly, 2-storied space. Open Tu-F 10am-1pm and 2-7pm, Sa 11am-7pm.

EIGHTH ARRONDISSEMENT

Galerie Lelong, 13, r. de Téhéran (☎01 45 63 13 19). M: Miromesnil. A popular gallery with a standard display of famous 20th-century art, including some works by Miró. Good selection of art books. Open Tu-F 10:30am-6pm, Sa 2-6:30pm. Closed July 27-Sept. 30.

Galerie Louis Carré et Cie, 10 av. de Messine (☎01 45 62 57 07). M: Miromesnil. A satisfying, novel array of contemporary French painting and sculpture presented in a fresh and welcoming space with leather couches. About 4 exhibitions per year. Open M-F 10am-12:30pm and 1:30-6:30pm, Sa 10am-12:30pm and 1:30-6:30pm.

NINTH ARRONDISSEMENT

Fondation Taylor, 1, r. la Bruyère (☎01 48 74 85 24). M: St-Georges. From the métro, walk up r. Notre Dame de Lorette away from pl. St-Georges and turn left onto r. la Bruyère. Run as a not-for-profit art space and serving the Parisian and international artistic community with annual prizes in painting, sculpture, and engraving, and year-round exhibitions ranging from figurative to non-objective work. Open Tu-Sa 1-7pm.

ELEVENTH ARRONDISSEMENT

Espace d'Art Yvonamor Palix, 13, r. Keller (☎01 48 06 36 70; yapalix@aol.com). M: Ledru-Rollin. Walk up av. Ledru-Rollin, turn left on r. de Charonne and right on r. Keller. Small gallery displays contemporary works by international artists from countries including Switzerland, Mexico, Argentina, and the United States. White gravel covers the ground floor. Expositions change monthly. Open Tu-F 2-5pm and Sa 2-7pm.

Glassbox, 113bis, r. Oberkampf (☎01 43 38 02 82; glassbox@hotmail.com). M: Oberkampf. Located below the post office; walk down the staircase in front of the post office entrance. Independently run by volunteers, this all-but-conventional gallery displays the work—some of it installation art, some of it sculpture, some of it defying characterization—of young international artists. Open Th-Sa 2-6pm.

TWELFTH ARRONDISSEMENT

The **Viaduc des Arts,** with its intimate artisan workshops and gallery spaces, runs through the 12*ème* (see **Sights,** p. 110; M: Bastille). And the fabulous **Jean-Paul Gaultier** has a gallery at **no. 30, r. du Faubourg St-Antoine.** Establishments on r. Daumesnil offer strollers a funky but swanky artisan's haven in the heart of the Bastille.

Malhia Kent, 19, av. Daumesnil (☎01 53 44 76 76). Watch amazing artisans weaving the fabric that becomes the *haute couture* clothing for houses like Dior and Chanel. Also sells clothing and accessories; scarves €30. Open M-F 9am-6pm, Sa-Su 11am-7pm.

55-57, av. Daumesnil (☎01 43 45 98 98). These gallery spaces are rented out every month by a variety of artists and craftsmen—usually a good place for international contemporary art.

Vertical, 63, av. Daumesnil (☎01 43 40 26 26; www.vertical.fr). A very Zen gallery filled with streamlined wooden sculptures that are probably beyond your budget and aesthetic understanding, but pre

tty decorative pieces made of palm leaves and treated roses on twisting metal rods (last up to a year!) start at an affordable €35. Open M 3-8pm, Tu-F 10am-1pm and 2:30-7:30pm, Sa 11am-1:30pm and 3-7:30pm.

Galerie Claude Samuel, 69, av. Daumesnil (☎01 53 17 01 11; www.claude-samuel.com). The only fixed contemporary art gallery in the Viaduc—but the artists change every 6 weeks. Open Tu-F 10am-1pm and 2:30-7pm, Sa 11am-7pm.

Poupées Automates, 97, av. Daumesnil (☎01 43 42 22 33). Dolls, dolls, and more dolls—Poupées Automates offers restorations as well as an incredible selection for purchase. Open Tu-Sa 10:30am-6:30pm.

THIRTEENTH ARRONDISSEMENT

The 13*ème* has a coterie of new galleries along **rue Louise-Weisse** (M: Chevarelet) and the perpendicular **rue Duchefdelaville.** Expect glossy, colorful photos, loopy (and looping) videos, and gleefully bold installations. Any one of the show spaces can provide you with the *Louise* pamphlet, which gives descriptions of each gallery and plots them on a mini-map. One good place to start is **Galerie Jennifer Flay** (20, r. Louise Weiss; ☎01 44 06 73 60; open Tu-Sa 2-7pm), which in recent years had an uncanny ability to pick and showcase up-and-comers like John Currin and Claud Closky.

FOURTEENTH ARRONDISSEMENT

Galerie 213, 213, bd. Raspail (☎01 43 22 83 23; fax 01 43 22 03 31; www.galerie213.com). M: Vavin or Raspail. Founded by an ex-fashion mogul, this lavish gallery is a mixture of postmodern chic and *fin-de-siècle* largesse (check out the adjoining Art Nouveau photography shop and lavish bathroom, complete with Japanese drapery and smoking corner). The stylish rooms upstairs overlook bd. Raspail and host exhibitions by hip young photographers. Openings draw luminaries of the Paris fashion world. Open Tu-Sa 11am-7pm.

Galerie Camera Obscura, 12, r. Ernest Cresson (☎01 45 45 67 08; cameraobscura@claranet.fr). M: Denfert-Rochereau. With your back to the pl. Denfert-Rochereau, walk down av. du Général Leclerc and turn right on r. Ernest Cresson; the gallery is on the right. This elegant, upscale gallery exhibits the works of classical and contemporary international photographers. Open Tu-Sa 2-7pm or by appointment.

19 F 95

INSIDE

Food & Drink

DINING IN PARIS

French cooking is renowned—and its influence has spread—worldwide, setting for many the standard by which *cuisine* itself is defined. The preparation and consumption of food are integral to French daily life, and food establishments of all kinds—elegant restaurants with six-course meals and as many forks, street markets where old women haggle for fresh produce, sidewalk cafés where intellectuals brood and sip espresso and smoke endless cigarettes, *pâtisseries* displaying desserts that look like works of art—provide the setting for scenes of Parisian life imagined, filmed, written, touristed, and lived.

Don't approach French dining with the assumption that chic equals *cher;* while world-famous chefs and their five-star restaurants are a valued Parisian institution, you don't have to pay their prices for excellent cuisine, either classic or adventurous. Join locals in celebrating the return of the *bistro,* a more informal, less expensive restaurant. Even more casual are *brasseries;* often crowded and action-packed, *brasseries* are best for large groups and high spirits. The least expensive option is usually a *crêperie,* a restaurant specializing in the thin Breton pancakes filled with meats, cheeses, chocolates, fruits, and condiments, where you can often eat for the price of a fast-food chain. The offerings of specialty food shops, including *boulangeries* (bakeries), *pâtisseries* (pastry shops), and *traiteurs* (prepared food shops), make delicious and inexpensive snacks and picnic supplies. A number of North African restaurants serve affordable couscous dishes. At *nouveaux bistros,* French, Mediterranean, Asian, and Spanish flavors converge in a setting that is usually modern and artsy. Eating and drinking can easily be the most memorable part of any visit to Paris—and our guide will help you make it so. *Bon appetit!*

ON THE MENU

Your Daily Bread

The loaf of baguette is one of those icons of Paris which, like the sidewalk café, is as apparent on the living streets of the city as in the imagination of the tourist. Though the average Parisian today consumes only around 5½ oz. of bread per day, down from around 2 lb. in 1900, it is still eaten with almost every meal, and you'll rarely walk down a street without seeing a few people sneaking bites off the loaves they are carrying home for dinner. Soon, you'll be forgetting that low-carb diet altogether.

But with 1300 *boulangeries* in Paris to choose from, how to separate the wheat from the chaff? Start with the definition. According to the craft, a baguette must weigh 250-300g, measuring about 70cm in length and 6cm in diameter. The crust must be smooth and golden, ready to crackle under moderate finger-pressure (ask for it *"bien cuit"*). The underside, or "sole," should never be charred; beware also a honeycomb imprint, indicating accelerated cooking in a rotating oven–the taste will be cut short as well. The inside ("mie") should be light, with large air holes. The bread should have a full, salty taste and a soft, subtly doughy texture. Look for *boulangeries* that have won the "Grand Prix de la Baguette," which is awarded yearly by the city hall of Paris.

A BRIEF HISTORY

In the 16th century, Italian monarch Catherine de Médicis brought the tradition of **haute cuisine,** the elegantly prepared foods now thought of as typically "French," from Florence, along with her cooks, who taught the French to appreciate the finer aspects of sauces and seasonings. Great 19th-century chefs made fine food an essential art of civilized life, and much of their wisdom on sauces and glazes is collected in the voluminous *Larousse Gastronomique*, a standard reference for French chefs today. The style made famous in the US by Julia Child is **cuisine bourgeoise,** quality home-cooking. A glance through her *Mastering the Art of French Cooking I & II* will give you ideas for dishes to try in France. Both *haute cuisine* and *cuisine bourgeoise* rely heavily on the **cuisine de province** (also called *cuisine campagnarde*), since they are basically sophisticated versions of this regional cuisine. Trendy and health-conscious **nouvelle cuisine**—tiny portions of delicately cooked, artfully arranged ingredients with light sauces—became popular in the 1970s. Immigrant communities have shaken up the traditional French culinary scene. In addition to ubiquitous Greek *gyro* sandwiches, there are outstanding Moroccan, Algerian, Tunisian, Senegalese, Ivory Coast, and Caribbean restaurants in Paris. Many bistros have menus with foreign dishes or visiting chefs. North African couscous is the most assimilated foreign dish. Chinese, Thai, Vietnamese, Cambodian, Korean, Tibetan, Japanese, Indian, and Pakistani restaurants, especially in the "Chinatowns" of the *9ème*, *13ème*, and *19ème*, have brought vegetarian options to the traditionally meat-heavy Paris dining experience.

MEALTIMES

BREAKFAST. *Le petit déjeuner* is usually light, consisting of bread, croissants, or *brioches* (buttery breads) with jam and butter, plus an espresso with hot milk or cream *(café au lait* or the more currently trendy *café creme)* or a hot chocolate (*le chocolat*, often served in a bowl).

LUNCH. *Le déjeuner*, traditionally the largest meal of the day, is served between noon and 2:30pm, although some cafés and restaurants in tourist areas stay open throughout the day. Restaurants are most crowded from 1-3pm, when all of Paris takes an extended lunch break. During lunch, some shops, businesses, and government offices close; linger over a two-hour lunch a few times and you'll be hooked, too.

DINNER. *Le dîner* begins quite late. Most restaurants open at 7pm, with 8:30pm the typical time to dine; revelers sometimes extend their meals into the early morning. A complete French dinner includes an *apéritif*, an *entrée* (appetizer), *plat* (main course), salad, cheese, dessert, fruit, coffee, and a *digestif* (after-dinner drink, typically a cognac or other local brandy). The French usually take wine with their restaurant meals. You might hear the story of the famous director who dared to order a Coke with his 1500F meal; he was promptly kicked out of the restaurant. Of him it was said, *"Il manque de savoir vivre"*—"He doesn't know how to live."

ETIQUETTE

HOW TO ORDER. Always greet your server by looking him or her attentively in the eye and saying, *"Bonjour, Monsieur,"* or *"Bonjour, Mademoiselle"* as appropriate. In the evening,, brush off your smartest *"Bon soir."* Failure to employ these simple phrases (even if you plan to order in English) will be rewarded with cool treatment and melodramatic, reprimanding glares. In Paris, the position of waiter or waitress is not a temporary job; it's a career. Your server will appreciate acknowledgement of her services with a gracious *"s'il vous plaît"* or *"merci beaucoup."* Also, do not ask for any unfinished food to go, and do not ask to split a dish with your dining partner. And to ask for the bill say (again, with a deep current of *politesse* in your voice), *"L'addition, s'il vous plaît."* The bill will rarely come without your requesting it.

TIPPING. You will usually see the words *service compris* (service included) on a menu, which means the tip is automatically added to the check (if not, you should tip 15-20%). Bear in mind, however, that the included "tip" is spread over the entire staff of the restaurant and goes to pay their fixed salary. If you are particularly pleased with the service, feel free to leave a small cash tip in addition to what is normally expected (anywhere from €0.50 to 10% of the check), but don't feel obligated. Most Parisians do not leave a tip at lunch but do so consistently at dinner.

THE MENU

Most restaurants offer *un menu à prix fixe* (fixed-price meal) that costs less than ordering *à la carte* (when you pick individual items out). Importantly, lunch *menus* are often cheaper than dinner *menus*—if there is a pricier restaurant that you'd particularly like to try, consider going for lunch. A *menu* will usually include an *entrée* (appetizer), a main course *(plat)*, cheese *(fromage)*, and dessert. Some also include wine or coffee. For lighter fare, try a *brasserie*, which has a fuller menu than a café but is more casual than a restaurant.

DRINKS

Mineral water is everywhere; order sparkling water *(eau pétillante* or *gazeuse)* or flat mineral water *(eau plate)*. Ice cubes *(glaçons)* won't come with your drink; you'll have to ask for them. To order a pitcher of tap water, ask for *une carafe d'eau fraîche*. There are five major *apéritifs* (pre-meal drinks): *kir*, a blend of white wine with *cassis*, black currant liqueur (*kir royale* substitutes champagne for the wine); *pastis*, a licorice liqueur; *suze*, which is fermented *gentiane*, a sweet-smelling mountain flower that yields a wickedly bitter brew; *picon-bière*, beer mixed with a sweet liqueur; and the martini. Finish the meal with an espresso *(un café)*, which comes in lethal little cups with blocks of sugar. *Café au lait* and *café crème* are generally considered only breakfast drinks, so if you must have your nighttime coffee with milk, try a *noisette*, which is espresso with just a dash of milk. When *boisson compris* is written on the menu, you are entitled to a free drink (usually wine) with the meal. In cafés, drinks are usually cheaper at the counter than seated.

ON THE MENU

Pitcher This

Foreign visitors to France have an understandable fear of ordering the cheapest wine on the menu. In many countries, the cheapest wine is cheap for a reason: it is grainy and has a faint hint of vinegar, better suited for putting on a salad than in a glass. The same cannot be said of the lower-priced wines you find on menus in Paris, including the cheapest of the cheap–*vin en pichet*. Often poured straight from the barrel into the *pichet* brought to your table, these wines offer great taste at a significant savings compared to bottled wine. The only true sacrifice is the loss of the *presentation du vin*, but unless you are trying to impress a date with your oenophilic savvy, this isn't much of a sacrifice at all. And whereas soft drinks are the beverage of choice for those on a budget in the US, in Paris splitting a half carafe of wine between a few people can be much cheaper than four Cokes. Restaurants make it easy for you, carrying one red, one white and one rosé in pitchers. The most common sizes you'll see on the menu are 12cl (1 glass), 50cl (4 glasses) and 1L (a party).

If you want to live large and sample expensive wines without breaking your budget, head to a **wine bar**, where they are available by the glass for remarkably low prices. For a list of wine bars, see **Nightlife,** p. 221.

WINE

In France, wine is not a luxury; it's an everyday institution. During World War I, French infantrymen pinned down in the trenches by heavy shellfire subsisted on the barest of rations: bread and wine. When the French sent their first citizen into orbit aboard a Soviet space craft, he took some *vin* with him.

WINE-PRODUCING REGIONS. The **Loire Valley** of France produces a number of whites, with the major vineyards at Angers, Chinon, Saumur, Anjou, Tours, and Sancerre. **Cognac,** farther south on the Atlantic coast, is famous for the double-distilled spirit that carries the same name. Centered on the Dordogne and Garonne Rivers, the classic **Bordeaux** region produces red and white Pomerol, Graves, and sweet Sauternes. The spirit *armagnac*, similar to cognac, comes from **Gascony,** while Jurançon wines come from vineyards higher up the slopes of the **Pyrénées.** Southern wines include those of **Languedoc and Roussillon** on the coast and **Limoux and Gaillac** inland. The vineyards of **Provence** on the coast near Toulon are recognized for their rosés. The **Côtes du Rhône** from Valence to Lyon in the Rhône Valley are home to some of the most celebrated wines produced in France, including Beaujolais. **Burgundy** is especially famous for its reds, from the wines of Chablis and the Côte d'Or in the north to the Mâconnais in the south. The white whines produced in **Alsace** tend to be much spicier and more pungent than others. Many areas of France produce sparkling wines, but the only one that can legally be called "Champagne" is, appropriately enough, distilled in the **Champagne** region of the country, surrounding Reims.

SELECTING WINE. There is a specific wine for every occasion and every type of meal, with pairings dictated by draconian rules. Don't worry too much about these rules; go with your own tastes. **White wines** tend to be lighter, drier, and fruitier. They go with fish, and many of the white dessert wines, like Barsac, Sauternes, or Coteaux du Layon, are great with fruit. **Red wines** tend to be heavier, more fragrant, and considerably older. Red meat and red wine is a fine combination. When confused about which wine to choose, just ask. Most waiters in restaurants and employees in wine shops will be more than happy to recommend their favorites to you. Or, fall back on the *vin de maison* (house wine), served in pitchers at reduced prices (see **Pitcher This,** p. 166, for more on this).

BY TYPE

ALL-YOU-CAN-EAT
Restaurant Natacha (195) 17ème ❸

AMERICAN
Coffee Parisien (181) 6ème ❷
Café du Marché (184) 7ème ❸
Bagel &Co. (185) 8ème ❸
Haynes Restaurant (186) 9ème ❸

BASQUE
Le Caveau du Palais (169) Île de la Cité ❸
Chez Gladines (190) 13ème ❷
Le Troquet (193) 15ème ❹

BISTRO
Le Rouge et Blanc (169) Île de la Cité ❸
Les Fous de l'Île (171) Île St-Louis ❸
Café Med (170) Île St-Louis ❷
Les Noces de Jeannette (173) 2ème ❹
Le Grizzli (176) 4ème ❷
Le Divin (176) 4ème ❸
Le Perraudin (180) 5ème ❸
Le Bistro d'Henri (181) 6ème ❹
Le Bistro Ernest (183) 6ème ❷
Le Petit Vatel (181) 6ème ❷
Au Pied de Fouet (184) 7ème ❷
Le Bistro de Gala (186) 9ème ❹
Cantine d'Antoine et Lili (187) 10ème ❶
Chez Paul (188) 11ème ❷
Le Bistrot du Peintre (188) 11ème ❷
Le Bistro de Théo (195) 17ème ❹
Va et Vient (195) 17ème ❷
Le Zéphyr (198) 20ème ❹

BRUNCH
Le Soleil d'Or (170) Île de la Cité ❶
Le Fumoir (172) 1er ❸
Au Rocher de Cancale (174) 2ème ❷
Le Loup Blanc (173) 2ème ❸
En Attendant Pablo (175) 3ème ❷
L'Appartement Café (175) 3ème ❷
Café Beaubourg (177) 4ème ❹
Les Enfants Gâté (177) 4ème ❸
Mariage Frères (198) 4ème ❷
Le Loir Dans la Thélère (199) 4ème ❷
Café des Lettres (184) 7ème ❷
Ladurée (198) 8ème ❹
Le Troisième Bureau (189) 11ème ❷
Café du Commerce (190) 13ème ❷
Phinéas (191) 14ème ❷
L'Endroit (195) 17ème ❷
The James Joyce Pub (195) 17ème ❷
Le Sancerre (197) 18ème ❶
Café Flèche d'Or (198) 20ème ❷

CAMBODIAN, THAI & VIETNAMESE
Le Lotus Blanc (183) 7ème ❸
Bangkok Café (185) 8ème ❷

CAMBODIAN, THAI & VIETNAMESE, CONT'D
Tricotin (190) 13ème ❶
La Lune (190) 13ème ❶
Thai Phetburi (192) 15ème ❷
Wassana (196) 18ème ❷
Lao Siam (197) 19ème ❷

CARIBBEAN
Babylone Bis (173) 2ème ❸

CLASSIC CAFÉ
Café Vavin (182) 6ème ❷
Le Comptoir du Relais (183) 6ème ❷
Café de Flore (182) 6ème ❸
Les Deux Magots (182) 6ème ❷
Le Paris (185) 8ème ❷
Café de la Paix (186) 9ème ❹
Au Général La Fayette (186) 9ème ❷
La Terrasse du Musée 16ème ❷
Les Hortensias (195) 17ème ❷
Halle St-Pierre (197) 18ème ❶
La Kaskad' (197) 19ème ❷

CRÊPERIE
La Crêpe en l'Île (170) Île St-Louis ❶
La Crêpe Rit du Clown (181) 6ème ❶
Crêperie Saint Germain (182) 6ème ❷
Objectifs Crêpes (185) 8ème ❶
Jours de Fête (188) 11ème ❶
Ty Breiz (193) 15ème ❶
La Bolée Belgrand (198) 20ème ❷

FUSION/ECLECTIC
Le Réconfort (174) 3ème ❸
Grannie (184) 4ème ❹
Paris-Dakar (187) 10ème ❸
Le Kitch (188) 11ème ❷

HISTORIC
Au Rocher de Cancale (174) 2ème ❷
Le Sélect (182) 6ème ❷
Café de Flore (182) 6ème ❸
Les Deux Magots (182) 6ème ❷
Le Procope (182) 6ème ❹
Fouquet's (185) 8ème ❹
Café de la Paix (186) 9ème ❹
La Coupole (192) 14ème ❹

ICE CREAM
Amorino (170) Île St-Louis ❶
Berthillon (170) Île St-Louis ❶
Octave (177) 5ème ❶

INDIAN
Anarkali Sarangui (186) 9ème ❸
Pooja (188) 10ème ❹

IRISH
The James Joyce Pub (195) 17ème ❷

ITALIAN
Little Italy Tratoria 4ème ❷
Le Jardin des Pâtés 5ème ❷
Rital & Courts 20ème ❷

JAPANESE
Furu Sato 2ème ❷
Lamen Kintaro 2ème ❷

KOSHER
L'As du Falafel (176) 4ème ❶
Sasha Finkelsztajn (176) 4ème ❶
Bagel & Co. (185) 8ème ❶

LATE NIGHT FOOD (1AM OR LATER)
Brasserie de l'Île St-Louis (171) Île St-Louis ❷
Le Fumoir (172) 1er ❸
Le Café Marly (172) 1er ❹
Taxi Club (171) 1er ❶
Babylone Bis (173) 2ème ❸
Au Petit Fer à Cheval (175) 4ème ❷
Café Beaubourg (177) 4ème ❹
Café Delmas (180) 5ème ❷
Les Editeurs (182) 6ème ❷
Café de Flore (182) 6ème ❸
Les Deux Magots (182) 6ème ❷
Le Sélect (182) 6ème ❷
Fouquet's (185) 8ème ❹
Latina Café 8ème ❸
Le Paris (185) 8ème ❷
Au Général La Fayette (186) 9ème ❷
Café de la Paix (186) 9ème ❹
Cantine d'Antoine et Lili (187) 10ème ❶
Paris-Dakar (187) 10ème ❸
Le Kitch (188) 11ème ❷
Le Bistrot du Peintre (188) 11ème ❷
Café de l'Industrie (189) 11ème ❶
Pause Café (189) 11ème ❷
Le Troisième Bureau (189) 11ème ❷
Papagallo 13ème ❷
Chez Papa (191) 14ème ❷
La Coupole 14ème ❹
Mozlef 15ème ❶
Casa Tina 16ème ❸
L'Endroit (195) 17ème ❷
Chez Ginette (196) 18ème ❸
Refuge des Fondues (196) 18ème ❸
Le Sancerre (197) 18ème ❶

MALAYSIAN
Chez Foong (192) 15ème ❷

MEXICAN
La Cucaracha (173) 2ème ❷
Ay, Caramba! (197) 19ème ❸

MIDDLE EASTERN
Chez Omar (174) 3ème ❸
Chez Marianne (176) 4ème ❷
L'As du Falafel (176) 4ème ❶
Comptoir Méditerranée (177) 5ème ❷

MIDDLE EASTERN, CONT'D
Savannah Café (177) 5ème ❹
Mozlef (193) 15ème ❶
Samaya (193) 15ème ❷
Byblos Café (193) 16ème ❷

NORTH AFRICAN
404 (174) 3ème ❸
Café de la Mosquée (180) 5ème ❷
Paris-Dakar (187) 10ème ❸
Café Cannelle (188) 11ème ❷
Chez Guichi (196) 18ème ❷
Café Flèche d'Or (198) 20ème ❷

PROVENÇALE
Le Divin (176) 4ème ❸
L'Aimant du Sud (190) 13ème ❸
Le Troquet (193) 15ème ❹
Le Patio Provençal (194) 17ème ❷
Le Soleil Gourmand (196) 18ème ❷
Aux Arts et Sciences Réunis (197) 19ème ❸

SANDWICHERIE/DELI
Sasha Finkelsztajn (176) 4ème ❶
Così (181) 6ème ❶
Guen-maï (181) 6ème ❷
Bagel & Co. (185) 8ème ❶
Vitamine (185) 8ème ❷

SCANDINAVIAN
Café des Lettres (184) 7ème ❷

SPANISH
Papagallo (190) 13ème ❷
Casa Tina (193) 16ème ❸

TRADITIONAL & MODERN FRENCH
Au Rendez-Vous des Camionneurs (170) Île de la Cité ❸
Au Vieux Paris d'Arcole (170) Île de la Cité ❺
Brasserie de l'Île St-Louis (171) Île St-Louis ❷
Au Chien qui Fume (172) 1er ❺
Jules (172) 1er ❹
Le Grillardin (172) 1er ❸
Nemo's Café (172) 1er ❸
L'Homosapiens (173) 2ème ❸
Taxi Jaune (174) 3ème ❷
Au Petit Fer à Cheval (175) 4ème ❷
Bofinger (176) 4ème ❹
Pain, Vin, Fromage (175) 4ème ❷
Au Port Salut (177) 5ème ❸
L'Auberge Bressane (183) 7ème ❺
Escrouzailles (185) 8ème ❸
Le Bistro de Gala (186) 9ème ❺
Chartier (186) 9ème ❷
La 25ème Image (187) 10ème ❷
Au Bon Café (187) 10ème ❷
Les Broches à l'Ancienne (189) 12ème ❷
La Connivence (189) 12ème ❸
L'Ebauchoir (189) 12ème ❸

TRADITIONAL & MODERN FRENCH, CONT'D.

Les Grandes Marchés (190) 12ème ❹
Paul Sud (189) 12ème ❷
Café du Commerce (190) 13ème ❷
Le Temps des Cerises (191) 13ème ❷
L'Amuse Bouche (192) 14ème ❹
Phinéas (191) 14ème ❷
Chez Papa (191) 14ème ❷
Au Rendez-Vous Des Camionneurs (192) 14ème ❷
Aux Artistes (193) 15ème ❸
Le Tire Bouchon (192) 15ème ❸
Le Troquet (193) 15ème ❹
Musée du Vin Restaurant (194) 16ème ❺
Au Vieux Logis (195) 17ème ❷
Chez Ginette (196) 18ème ❸
Refuge des Fondues (196) 18ème ❸
La Kaskad' (197) 19ème ❷
Café Flèche d'Or (198) 20ème ❷

TRENDY/INTELLIGENTSIA

Le Café Marly (172) 1er ❹
Le Fumoir (172) 1er ❸
Chez Omar (174) 3ème ❸
L'Apparemment Café (175) 3ème ❸
Chez Janou (174) 3ème ❷
Les Arts et Métiers (175) 3ème ❸
Georges (176) 4ème ❸
Café Beaubourg (177) 4ème ❸
Les Enfants Gâtés (177) 4ème ❹
Café de Flore (182) 6ème ❸
Le Sélect (182) 6ème ❷
Les Editeurs (182) 6ème ❷
buddha-bar (184) 8ème ❺
Chez Paul (188) 11ème ❷

TRENDY/INTELLIGENTSIA, CONT'D

Café de l'Industrie (189) 11ème ❶
Pause Café (189) 11ème ❷
Le Troisième Bureau (189) 11ème ❷
Aux Artistes (193) 15ème ❸
La Rotunde de la Muette (194) 16ème ❶
L'Endroit (195) 17ème ❷
Le Sancerre 18ème ❶
Café Flèche d'Or 20ème ❷

TURKISH

Restaurant Assoce (188) 11ème ❷
Le Cheval de Troie (189) 12ème ❷

VEGETARIAN & VEGAN/DETOX

La Victoire Suprême du Coeur (172) 1er ❷
Furu Sato 2ème ❷
La Verte Tige (175) 3ème ❷
Aquarius (176) 4ème ❷
Piccolo Teatro (175) 4ème ❷
Le Jardin des Pâtés (180) 5ème ❷
Le Grenier de Notre Dame (177) 5ème ❷
Guen-maï (181) 6ème ❷
Le Petit Vatel (181) 6ème ❷
Le Lotus Blanc (183) 7ème ❸
Escrouzailles (185) 8ème ❸
Le Kitch (188) 11ème ❷
Phinéas (191) 14ème ❷
Aquarius Café (192) 14ème ❷
Au Grain de Folie (196) 18ème ❷
Le Soleil Gourmand (196) 18ème ❷

WEST & EAST AFRICAN

Babylone Bis (173) 2ème ❸
La Banane Ivoirienne (188) 11ème ❷

BY LOCATION

The *arrondissement* listings rank restaurants in order of value; the top entry may not be the cheapest, but it will be the best value in its price range and area.

SEINE ISLANDS

NEIGHBORHOOD QUICKFIND: ***Discover,*** *p. 2;* ***Sights,*** *p. 67,* ***Accommodations,*** *p. 254.*

ÎLE DE LA CITÉ

see map p. 380-381

Le Caveau du Palais, 19, pl. Dauphine (☎01 43 26 04 28). M: Cité. Le Caveau is a chic, intimate restaurant serving traditional, hearty French food from an old-style brick oven. The proprietor serves up Basque specialties, which include lots of steak (€16-25) and fish (€20-25) on the sidewalk or in an intimate dining area. Prices are high, but then so is the level of ambience; this one's a favorite with the locals. Reservations encouraged. Open daily noon-3pm and 7-10:30pm. MC/V. ❸

Le Rouge et Blanc, 26, pl. Dauphine (☎01 43 29 52 34). M: Cité. This simple, *provençale* bar and bistro is the creation of proprietor Rigis Tillet, a friendly young man who is proud of his southern roots and treats his customers like old friends. *Menus* €17 and €22; a la carte

the BIG $plurge

Offshore Dining

Maybe it's because of the exorbitant costs associated with shipping food from the mainland, or maybe it's all those tourists—dining on the islands is expensive. Budget travelers in search of bargain menus should shop around—but **Au Vieux Paris d'Arcole** on the Île de la Cité is worth the extra cash. As if its 16th-century style building weren't enough, this traditional French restaurant features antique furniture in its elegant, red-silk-everything dining room. The mouthwatering recipes come direct from owner Odette's childhood and will spoil even the most finicky of taste buds. Customers choose wine from the cellar below and watch Odette prepare their meals from farm- and ocean-fresh ingredients. While almost all the food at Au Vieux Paris is amazing, it is most famous for its *foie-gras, coquilles,* and *coufidou.*

Au Vieux Paris d'Arcole, 24, r. Chanoinesse (☎01 40 46 06 81; www.auvieuxparis.fr), on the Île de la Cité. Entrées *€9-14,* plats *€18-30. Open M-Su noon-3pm and 7-11pm. MC/V.* ❺

plats €14-20. On sunny days, tables are set out along the sidewalk. Open M-Sa 11am-3pm and 7-10:30pm. Closed when it rains. MC/V. ❸

Au Rendez-Vous des Camionneurs, 72, quai d'Orfèvres (☎01 43 54 88 74). M: Cité. On the outside corner of pl. Dauphine, this charming restaurant has Italianate decorations, French food, scores of recommendations, and a €16 *menu. Formule* meal €22.50. Serves a luscious lamb curry with rice. Open F-W noon-11:30 pm, Th 6-11:30pm. AmEx/MC/V. ❸

Le Soleil d'Or, 15, bd. du Palais (☎01 43 54 22 22). M: Cité. Don't let the posh, faux-velvet chairs scare you: this classy-looking brasserie is a real bargain. Eclectic menu offers delicious crepes (€4.50, with ice cream €5.50), milkshakes (€5.50), and Sunday brunch (€10). Pizza and sandwiches from €7. Open daily 9am-10pm. MC/V.❶

ÎLE ST-LOUIS

Berthillon, 31, r. St-Louis-en-l'Île (☎43 54 31 61). M: Cité or Pont Marie. Okay, technically not a restaurant, but who needs dinner when there's dessert, especially when it's the best ice cream and sorbet in Paris? Choose from dozens of *parfums* (flavors), ranging from passionfruit and gingerbread to the standard chocolate. Look for stores nearby that sell Berthillon indulgences; the wait is shorter and they're open in late July and Aug., when the main outfit is closed. Singles €1.80; doubles €3; triples €4. Open Sept.-July 14. Take-out W-Su 10am-8pm; eat-in W-F 1-8pm, Sa-Su 2-8pm. Closed 2 weeks in Feb. and Apr. ❶

La Crêpe en l'Île, 13, r. des Deux Ponts (☎01 43 26 28 68). M: Pont Marie. A *crêperie* just off of the main drag and a bit less crowded than its island siblings. Choose from among 20 options, including the indulgent *La Super* (chocolate, ice cream, whipped cream, and nuts). *La Provençale* (ratatouille, egg, and roasted pepper) is a meal in itself. Incredible selection of unique and flavorful teas enhances the friendly atmosphere. Prices range from €2.50 to €7.20; 3-course *menu* €8.40. Open M-Su high-season 11:30am-midnight; low-season 11:30am-11pm. ❶

Amorino, 47, r. St-Louis-en-l'Île (☎01 44 07 48 08) M: Pont Marie. Cross the Pont Marie and turn right on r. St-Louis-en-l'Île. With a selection of 18 gelati, Amorino serves amazing concoctions in any combination. Your cone (€3-5.50) will look like a work of art when you ask for the popular green pistachio or the red fruit flavors mixed with creams and chocolates. ❶

Café Med, 79, r. St-Louis-en-l'Île (☎01 43 29 73 17). M: Pont Marie. Cross the Pont Marie and make a right on r. St-Louis-en-l'Île; the restaurant is on the left. This cute little bistro serves up both French (crêpes €4.75-7.95) and Italian (pasta €6-9.50) food in a cheerful blue and yellow room right on the island's main street. Its prices are hard to beat on either island, as are its ultimate *crêpes*: "greedy pancakes" covered in dessert combinations to make any mouth water. *Menus* range from €9.90 (only on weekdays) to €18.60. MC/V. ❷

Brasserie de l'Île St-Louis, 55, quai de Bourbon (☎01 43 54 02 59). M: Pont Marie. Cross the Pont Marie and turn right on r. St-Louis-en-l'Île; continue on to the end of the island. This old-fashioned *brasserie* is known for its delectable Alsatian specialities, such as *choucroute garnie* (a mixture of sausages and pork on a bed of sauerkraut; €16), but also features an array of omelettes and other typical café fare (€7-10). Open M-Tu and F-Su noon-1am, Th 5pm-1am. AmEx/MC/V. ❷

Les Fous de l'Île, 33, r. des Deux Ponts (☎01 43 25 76 67). M: Pont Marie. A mellow bistro for the neighborhood crowd. Displays the work of local artists and has evening concerts (jazz, Brazilian, *chansons françaises*) every Tu and W except in Aug. Appetizers €3-7. *Plats* €10.50-14. €13 lunch *menu* is a delicious value with changing specials like roast pork in a *Bordelaise* sauce. Open Tu-F noon-11pm, Sa 3-11pm, Su noon-7pm. MC/V. ❸

FIRST ARRONDISSEMENT

NEIGHBORHOOD QUICKFIND: ***Discover,*** *p. 7;* ***Sights,*** *p. 73;* ***Museums,*** *p. 146;* ***Nightlife,*** *p. 206;* ***Shopping,*** *p. 235;* ***Accommodations,*** *p. 254.*

see map p. 374-375

The arcades overlooking the Louvre along **r. de Rivoli** are filled with everything chic and expensive, but tea and *chocolat chaud* at one of the many *salons de thé* (see p. 198) are still quite affordable. **Les Halles** has louder, crowded eateries, serving everything from fast-food to four-course Italian feasts. Diverse lunch and dinner options are also available along **rue Jean-Jacques Rousseau.** Those in search of a quieter meal should head to the many restaurants located along **rue du Marché St-Honoré** or behind the **Palais Royal.**

Papou Lounge, 74, r. Jean-Jacques Rousseau (☎01 44 76 00 03). M: Les Halles. From the métro, take the Rambuteau exit, walk toward Eglise St-Eustache, turn left onto r. Coquillère, then right on r. Jean-Jacques Rousseau. Food, glorious food. Papou's delicious cuisine is both flavorful (rumpsteak €13) and inventive (tuna tartare with strawberries €13.50). The menu changes monthly, so trust yourself (or your server) to suggest the right dish. With world music,

the hidden deal

Cab Fare

When it comes to grabbing a late night snack in Paris, the options are pretty limited. The paucity of after-hours dining options exists for good reason: past 2am, perhaps the only people awake are club-goers and taxi-drivers. While the former group stumbles home, the latter group can be found chowing down at a club all their own, known as the **Taxi Club** (look for the taxis). While far from gourmet, this quirky cafe attracts taxi-drivers with its cheap beer (€2.10-2.30) and cheaper coffee (€1). Customers dig in to breakfast served round-the-clock (*omelette paysanne* €4), a wide variety of meats (grilled chicken €4.20), and the most expensive item on the menu: the *plat du jour*, a whopping €7. As if the cheap grub weren't appealing enough, the club has perfected the tacky-chic look: white Christmas lights, picnic tablecloths, and mounted objects that were once attached to taxis.

Taxi Club, 8, r. Etienne Marcel, 1er (☎ 01 42 36 28 30), at r. de Turbigo. Open daily 11am-2am and 4am-6am. ❶ black-and-white tile floors, and photographs of tribal warriors, your other senses will be happy, too. Lunch special €10. Beer €3.30. Open daily 10am-2am; food served noon-4:30pm and 7pm-midnight. MC/V. ❷

Jules, 62, r. Jean-Jacques Rousseau (☎ 01 40 28 99 04). Take the r. Rambuteau exit from M: Les Halles, walk toward St-Eustache, then take a left onto r. Coquillère and a right on r. Jean-Jacques Rousseau. Named after award-winning chef and owner Eric Teyant's son, this restaurant feels like home, with a mantelpiece and blinds on the windows. Subtle blend of modern and traditional French cooking; selections change by season. 4-course *menu* €21-29 includes terrific cheese course. Open M-Sa noon-2:30pm and 7-10:30pm. AmEx/MC/V. ❹

La Victoire Suprême du Coeur, 41, r. des Bourdonnais (☎01 40 41 93 95). M: Châtelet. From the métro, take the r. des Halles exit. Follow traffic on r. des Halles; turn left on r. des Bourdonnais. Run by the devotees of guru Sri Chinmoy, who have both body and soul in mind when creating dishes like *escalope de seitan a la sauce champignon* (€8.50). Never mind the weird photos of their Yul Brynner-esque guru up to his elbows in dough. It's all vegetarian, and very tasty. Meals marked with a "V" can be made vegan. 2-course lunch *menu* (€10.80). Open M-F 11:45am-3pm and 6:40-10pm, Sa noon-3pm and 6:40-10pm. MC/V. ❷

Le Grillardin, 52, r. de Richelieu (☎01 42 97 54 40). M: Louvre. This French restaurant has been serving customers since 1827. In an excellent location (behind the Palais-Royal) for those needing rest after the Louvre. *Menu* (lunch €14, dinner €22) includes adventurous specialities like rabbit pâté with pink hen livers and thyme flowers and pan-fried frog's legs in chive sauce. Open M-F noon-3pm and 7-11pm, Sa 7-11pm. AmEx/MC/V. ❸

Au Chien qui Fume, 33, r. du Pont Neuf (☎01 42 36 07 42). M: Châtelet-Les Halles. Even passersby who aren't hungry stop at this popular restaurant just to see the cooks arrange beautiful plates of shellfish at its famous oyster bar. The Agathe *menu* (€33) includes only main dishes consisting of oysters, guaranteed to liven up any date. Excellent starters and desserts €8. With the check, the friendly waitstaff present diners with a handful of meringue cookies. Between courses, patrons can amuse themselves with the pictures of dogs dancing, eating and, of course, smoking, that grace almost every wall. Open daily noon-midnight. ❹

CAFÉS

Le Fumoir, 6, r. de l'Amiral Coligny (☎01 42 92 05 05). M: Louvre. On r. du Louvre, cross r. de Rivoli and r. du Louvre will become r. de l'Amiral Coligny. Conveniently close to the Louvre. Decidedly untouristy types drink their chosen beverage in deep leather sofas. Part bar, part tea house in feel. Serves the one of the best brunches in Paris (€20), Su midnight-3pm; coffee €2.50. Open daily 11am-2am. AmEx/MC/V. ❸

Le Café Marly, Cour Napoleon (☎01 49 26 06 60). M: Palais-Royal. One of Paris's classiest cafés; located in the Richelieu wing of the Louvre. With a terrace facing the famed I.M. Pei pyramids and others overlooking the Louvre's Cour Napoleon, this is a prime spot for tourists and locals alike. Enjoy a full meal or sit back with a glass of wine and watch the sunset. Breakfast (pastry, toast, jam, juice, and coffee or hot chocolate; €12.50) served from 8-11am. Main dishes €16-28. Omelettes €10. Open daily 8am-2am. AmEx/DC/MC/V. ❹

Nemo's Café, 36, pl. du Marché St-Honoré (☎01 42 60 36 67). From M: Tuileries, walk down r. du 29 Juillet; it turns into r. du Marché St-Honoré. Suits on their lunchbreaks dine on standard French food. Try the hard-to-find *steak hache* (€12.50) and tiramisu (€5.80) for dessert. Open daily noon-1am; food served until midnight. MC/V. ❷

SECOND ARRONDISSEMENT

see map p. 374-375

NEIGHBORHOOD QUICKFIND: ***Discover,*** *p. 7;* ***Sights,*** *p. 77;* ***Nightlife,*** *p. 206;* ***Shopping,*** *p. 235;* ***Accommodations,*** *p. 255.*

The *2ème* has many inexpensive dining options. **Rue Montorgueil** is lined with excellent bakeries, fruit stands, and specialty stores (see p. 199). Side streets like **rue Marie Stuart** and **rue Mandar** are also worthwhile. You'll find fast, cheap food on **passage des Panoramas** and **passage des Italiens** (see **Sights,** p. 77).

Les Noces de Jeannette, 14, r. Favart, and 9, r. d'Amboise (☎01 42 96 36 89). M: Richelieu-Drouot. Exit onto bd. des Italiens, turn left, and go left onto r. Favart. Named after a 19th century *opéra comique* playing across the street at the time of the restaurant's founding, Jeanette's elegance and wonderfully diverse clientele will impress your date. *Menu du Bistro* (€27.50) includes large salad *entrées;* roasted fish, duck, and grilled meat *plats;* and desserts to make you faint with delight. Free *kir* with meal. Reservations recommended. Open daily noon-1:30pm and 7-9:30pm. ❹

La Cucaracha, 31, r. Tiquetonne, (01 40 26 68 36). M: Etienne-Marcel. Walk against traffic on r. de Turbigo and go left on r. Tiquetonne. At this small, Mexican-run restaurant, flavorful dishes like *enchiladas verde* or *fajitas* will run you a reasonable €11-15. The *mole* sauce used in a number of dishes is made with 39 different spices. The portions are moderate, the flavors intense (but not too hot) and the crowd mostly French (but very hot). You'll find a bit of Mexican kitsch inside the restaurant if you can't get a table outside on the pedestrian r. Tiquetonne. Open daily 7-11:30pm. MC/V ❷

L'Homosapiens, 29, r. Tiquetonne (01 40 26 94 85) M: Etienne-Marcel. Walk against traffic on r. de Turbigo and go left on r. Tiquetonne. Great service at this cozy eatery. Try the *mignon de porc* or *filets de canard*. If you don't need to people-watch on r. Tiquetonne, ask for a table in the hip cave-like *sous sol*. Total steal of a lunch *menu* starting at €10.50. Immense dinner *menu* including wine and cheese €25. Open Tu-F noon-2pm and 7:30-10:30pm, Sa 7:30-10:30pm. MC/V. ❸

Lamen Kintaro, 24, r. St-Augustin (☎01 47 42 13 14). M: Opéra. Walk down Ave. de l'Opéra and turn left on r. St-Augustin. Delicious and popular Japanese restaurant. With no sushi in sight, Kintaro offers great noodle bowls (€7.80) and an array of menu combinations (€8-13). Sapporo €4.30. Open M-Sa 11:30am-10pm. MC/V. ❷

Le Loup Blanc, 42, r. Tiquetonne (☎01 40 13 08 35). M: Etienne-Marcel. Walk against traffic on r. de Turbigo and go left on r. Tiquetonne. Mixed grille has samples of 4 kinds of meats (mmm...cardamom filets of duck) and sides (€13-15.50). Vegetarian *salade mosaïque* includes salad and 4-6 sides (€10-12.50). Homemade yogurt €3.50. Su brunch €16. Open M-Sa 7:30pm-midnight, Su 11am-4:30pm and 7:30pm-1am. MC/V. ❸

Babylone Bis, 34, r. Tiquetonne (☎01 42 33 48 35). M: Etienne-Marcel. From the métro, walk against traffic on r. de Turbigo and turn left onto r. Tiquetonne. Babylone Bis specializes in Antillean and African cuisine. With zebra skin on the walls, banana leaves on the ceiling, and incredibly loud *zouk* music playing,

Café de l'Olympia

Au Hasard Balthazar (Café)

Café de la Mosquée

this place gets wild. Don't miss such dishes as *aloko* (flambéed bananas; €5.50) and *poulet braisé* (lime-marinated chicken; €13). Cocktails €8-13. Dinner served all night. Open daily 8pm-8am. MC/V. ❸

Furu Sato, 60, r. Montorgueil (☎01 42 33 49 61). M: Sentier. Follow r. Réaumur and turn right on r. des Petits-Carreaux, which becomes r. Montorgueil. Tranquil Japanese restaurant on a market street. Grill *menus* €10.50. Sushi/sashimi *menus* €11.44-18.30. Vegetarian *menu* €10.52. Open daily noon-2:30pm and 7-10:45pm. MC/V. ❷

CAFÉS

Au Rocher de Cancale, 78, r. Montorgueil (☎01 42 33 50 29). M: Etienne-Marcel. From r. Etienne Marcel make a right onto r. Montorgueil. This historic café has occupied this spot for over 200 years and is proud of it. Most places on r. Montorgueil are closed for Su brunch, but at this one it's very pleasant and only €9. The terrace is good for cappuccino-sipping (€3.50). Open M-Sa 8am-2am, Su 8am-7pm. AmEx/MC/V. ❷

THIRD ARRONDISSEMENT

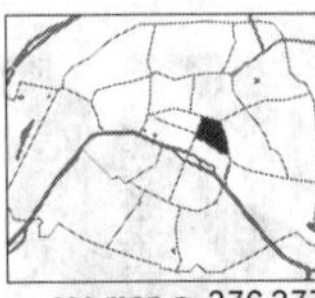

see map p. 376-377

NEIGHBORHOOD QUICKFIND: ***Discover,*** *p. 8;* ***Sights,*** *p. 79;* ***Museums,*** *p. 146;* ***Nightlife,*** *p. 207;* ***Shopping,*** *p. 237;* ***Accommodations,*** *p. 257.*

The restaurants of the upper Marais offer an array of Peruvian, Tibetan, Middle Eastern, and French cuisine. Numerous charming bistros line **rue St-Martin.** A number of kosher food stands and restaurants are located around **rue du Vertbois** and **rue Volta.** Dinner in the Marais can be pricey, but lunchtime *menus* often offer good deals.

Chez Janou, 2, r. Roger Verlomme (☎01 42 72 28 41). M: Chemin-Vert. From the métro, take r. St-Gilles and turn left almost immediately on r. des Tournelles. The restaurant is on the corner of r. Roger Verlomme. Tucked into a relatively quiet corner of the 3*ème*, this hip and friendly restaurant is lauded for its reasonably priced gourmet food. No menus; instead, the dishes are listed on blackboards scattered throughout the restaurant. The *ratatouille* (€8.50) and the goat cheese and spinach salad (€8.50) are both delicious. Main courses such as *thon à la provençale* (€14) are delightful, as are the desserts (€6). Open daily noon-3pm and 8pm-midnight. ❷

404, 69, r. des Gravilliers (☎ 01 42 74 57 81). M: Arts et Métiers. Walk down r. Beaubourg and take a right on r. des Gravilliers. Metal hanging lights and rich red curtains create an almost mystical world behind the plain stone facade of this classy but comfortable North African restaurant. Features mouth-watering couscous (€13-23) and *tagines* (€13-19). Lunch *menu* €17. Open daily noon-2:30pm and 8pm-midnight. AmEx/MC/V. ❸

Chez Omar, 47, r. de Bretagne (☎01 42 72 36 26). M: Arts et Métiers. Walk along r. Réamur, away from r. St-Martin. R. Réamur turns into r. de Bretagne. One of the better Middle Eastern places in town; packed past 8:30pm. Come at 7:30pm for peace and quiet, later to see the intelligentsia in action. Couscous with vegetables €9. The *steak au poivre* (€14) is served in a spectacular sauce. Other specialties like *brochettes* and *ratatouille* €11-22. Open M-Sa noon-2:30pm and 7pm-midnight, Su 7:30-11:30pm. ❸

Le Réconfort, 37, r. de Poitou (☎01 42 76 06 36; reservations 01 49 96 09 60). M: St-Sébastien-Froissart. Walk along r. du Pt-Aux-Choux to r. de Poitou. Hyper-eclectic, swank eating experience. French, Indian, and Middle Eastern tastes fuse in creations like the chicken with honey and spices (€14). Lunch *menu* €12-15. Main courses €14-17, but the lunchtime *plat du jour* is only €9.50. Open M-Th noon-2pm and 8-11pm, F-Sa 8-11:30pm. MC/V. ❸

Taxi Jaune, 13, r. Chapon (☎01 42 76 00 40). M: Arts et Métiers. Walk along r. Beaubourg and turn left onto r. Chapon. Adhering to a fry-as-little-as-possible policy, Taxi Jaune is a comfy joint more than makes up for its slightly bizarre taxi fetish. Menu changes daily. *Entrées* €5.50-6.50. *Plats* €14. Lunch *menu* €12-13. Open M-F 8:30am-2am, food served noon-2pm and 8-10:30pm. MC/V. ❷

La Verte Tige, 13, r. Ste-Anastase (☎01 42 77 22 15). M: St-Sébastien-Froissart. From the métro, walk down r. Pt-Aux-Choux and turn left on r. de Turenne. Rue Ste-Anastase is 3 blocks down on the right. Here's something you don't come across every day in Paris: a delightful, healthy vegetarian eatery. *Salade verte tige* (€8) mixes hearts of palm with tofu sausage, olives, and coriander, along with other creative ingredients. Vegan options available. Open Tu-Sa noon-2:30pm and 7:30-10:30pm, Su 12:30-4pm. MC/V. ❷

En Attendant Pablo, 78, r. Vieille-du-Temple (☎01 42 74 34 65). M: Hôtel-de-Ville. From r. de Rivoli, turn left on r. Vieille-du-Temple. While waiting for Pablo, this friendly *pâtisserie*-lunch café serves enormous salads (€8.90) and *tartines* (€8.90). Lunch *menu* €8.60. Su brunch €14.40. Large selection of fruit juices (€4-5) and killer chocolate pastries (€4.60). Open Su and Tu-Th 11am-6pm, F-Sa 11am-8pm. MC/V. ❷

CAFÉS

L'Apparemment Café, 18, r. des Coutures St-Gervais (☎01 48 87 12 22). M: St-Paul. Behind the Picasso Museum, this hip café offers coffee (€1.60), make-your-own salads (€7.60-10), and choose-your-own Su brunch (€15) in comfortable cushioned chairs. Come to chat or to play ping pong in the game room. Open M-F noon-2am, Sa 4pm-2am, Su 12:30pm-midnight. MC/V. (Also see **Nightlife,** p. 208.) ❸

Les Arts et Métiers, 51, r. de Turbigo (☎01 48 87 83 25). M: Arts et Métiers. Yet another Paris café-of-the-moment–you should at least make an appearance. The terrace overlooks a busy intersection, but the quiet, harem-esque couch interior is a favorite for the local brooding types. Delicious milkshakes €6.40. Happy Hour (5-9pm) features a cocktail of the day for a mere €5. Open daily 6:30am-midnight. MC/V. ❸

FOURTH ARRONDISSEMENT

NEIGHBORHOOD QUICKFIND: ***Discover,*** *p. 8;* ***Sights,*** *p. 81;* ***Museums,*** *p. 147;* ***Nightlife,*** *p. 209;* ***Shopping,*** *p. 237;* ***Accommodations,*** *p. 258.*

see map p. 376-377

In the *4ème,* food is more about where you're eating, how well you can see everyone else, and how good you look doing it. Food in this *arrondissement* isn't exactly cheap, but living off salads and sandwiches from the many café/bar/restaurants or grabbing an Eastern European snack *à emporter* from **rue des Rosiers** can get you through the day without breaking the bank. Besides, Sunday brunch is your chance to eat as much as you can at one of the many buffets. So splurge: go somewhere happening, get as little food as possible, and revel in the chic Marais atmosphere.

Au Petit Fer à Cheval, 30, r. Vieille-du-Temple (☎01 42 72 47 47). M: Hôtel-de-Ville or St-Paul. From St-Paul, go with the traffic on r. de Rivoli and turn right; the restaurant will be on your right. An oasis of *chèvre, kir,* and *Gauloises,* and a local crowd that knows a good thing when they find it. Invisible from the front, a few tables huddle behind the bar, where you can order *filet mignon de veau* (€15) or any of the excellent house salads (€3.50-10). Desserts €4-7. Open daily 10am-2am; food served noon-1:15am. MC/V. (If the outdoor seating is full–and it will be–try the neighboring **Les Philosophes** or **La Chaise au Plafond**, all owned by the same charming, lucky fellow). ❷

Piccolo Teatro, 6, r. des Ecouffes (☎01 42 72 17 79). M: St-Paul. From the métro, walk with the traffic down r. de Rivoli and take a right on r. des Ecouffes. A romantic vegetarian hideout. Weekday lunch *menus* at €8.20, €9.90, or €13.30. *Entrées* €3.60-7.10. *Plats* €7.70-12.50. Open Tu-Sa noon-3pm and 7-11:30pm. AmEx/MC/V. ❷

Pain, Vin, Fromage, 3, r. Geoffrey L'Angevin (☎01 42 74 07 52). On a small side street rigt near the Centre Pompidou, this Parisian classic (complete with seating in the basement wine cellar) serves France's three culinary specialties (you guessed 'em) in countless combinations. Fondues (€14), salads (€4-8), and more are accompanied by a winning wine list. Open M-Sa 7-11pm. ❷

the hidden deal

Falafel (& more) in the Fourth

L'As du Falafel, 34, r. des Rosiers (☎01 48 87 63 60). M: St-Paul. This kosher falafel stand and restaurant displays pictures of Lenny Kravitz, who credited it with "the best falafel in the world, particularly the special eggplant falafel with hot sauce." Go his way. Falafel special €5. Thimble-sized (but damn good) lemonade €3.50 per glass. Open Su-F 11:30am-11:30pm. MC/V. ❶

Chez Marianne, 2, r. des Hospitalières-St-Gervais (☎01 42 72 18 86). M: St-Paul. Pick 4 (€10), 5 (€11.50), or 6 (€13) specialties including *tzatziki* and *brick farci à la viande de boeuf* (delicious spiced meat in a flaky pastry). Reservations recommended after 9pm. Take-out falafel available. Open daily noon-midnight. AmEx/MC/V. ❷

Sacha Finkelsztajn, 27, r. des Rosiers (☎01 42 72 78 91). M: St-Paul. This Jewish deli makes sandwiches for around €5.50-7.50. Go with an open mind, leave the ingredients up to the friendly owners, and come away with delicious combos like smoked salmon and green olive paste. Open M and W-Th 10am-2pm and 3-7pm, F-Su 10am-7:30pm. ❶

Little Italy Trattoria, 13, r. Rambuteau (☎01 42 74 32 46). M: Rambuteau. Walk along r. Rambuteau in the direction of traffic; it's on the right, you'll see people waiting outside. An enticing *salumeria* with tables both indoors and out. Amazing *antipasti* selection for two €21.50, delicate fresh pastas €8-13. Pitcher of wine €7-7.50. Open daily 8:30am-11:30pm, food served noon-4pm and 7-11pm. MC/V. ❷

Le Divin, 41, r. Ste-Croix-de-la-Bretonnerie (☎01 42 77 10 20). M: Hôtel-de-Ville. Walk away from Hôtel-de-Ville on r. Vieille-du-Temple and go right on r. Ste-Croix-de-la-Bretonnerie. Go South, where sun and cheer (in the form of friendly service and nude paintings) bounce off the walls as fab *Provençal* fare gets passed around. Vegetarian options available. *Menus* €16 and €21. Open Tu-Su 7-11:30pm. MC/V. ❸

Aquarius, 54, r. Ste-Croix-de-la-Bretonnerie (☎01 48 87 48 71). M: Hôtel-de-Ville. Walk away from the Hôtel-de-Ville on r. du Temple and turn right on r. Ste-Croix-de-la-Bretonnerie. A happy, no-smoking, vegetarian zone; vegans will also leave satisfied. Try the house specialty, *assiette paysanne* (€11). Lunch *menu* €10.65, dinner *menus* €15.40. Open M-Sa noon-10:30pm. AmEx/MC/V. **Also** at 40, r. de Gergovie, 14*ème* (☎01 45 41 36 88). ❷

Bofinger, 6, r. de la Bastille (☎01 42 72 87 82). M: Bastille. R. de la Bastille runs directly off pl. de la Bastille. Somewhat affordable, totally classic cuisine. *Prix fixe* at €30.50 is perhaps a bit much, but the lunch *menu* at €21.50 is a steal. Go for the dressy atmosphere as much as the heavenly food. Open daily noon-1am; food served noon-3pm and 6:30pm-1am. AmEx/MC/V. For a slightly dressed-down version, try **Petit Bofinger** across the street. ❹

Le Grizzli, 7, r. St-Martin (☎01 48 87 77 56). M: Châtelet. Walk along quai de Gesvres and turn left onto r. St-Martin. Near the Centre Pompidou, this cool bistro serves meticulously prepared salads (€13.50-14) and pastas (€11-15.50). Outdoor seating. Open M-Sa noon-2am; food served noon-2:30pm and 7:30-11pm. MC/V. ❷

CAFÉS

Georges, Centre Pompidou, 6th fl. (☎01 44 78 47 99). Enter via the center or an elevator to the left of the Pompidou's r. Beaubourg entrance. M: Rambuteau. Even if you miss the museum, stop by this ultra-sleek, Zen-cool, in-the-spotlight café, especially for the terrace. Its minimalist design is even exhibited in the museum. Come for a glass of wine or Champagne (€8-10), a snack (gazpacho €8, fruit salad €9.50), or (if you can afford it) a pricey *plat* (filet of lamb €28, crispy duck €27), or just to take a peek at the menu—supposedly designed by Dior menswear creator Hedi Slimane. Open M and W-Su noon-2am. ❸

Café Beaubourg, 100, r. St-Merri (☎01 48 87 63 96). M: Rambuteau or Hôtel-de-Ville. Facing Centre Pompidou. A clientele wearing everything from the newest Lagerfeld to dockers to green hair. This is *the* spot to see and be seen during the day. Coffee €2.70, steamed vanilla milk €5, grog with rum or honey €5.50. Breakfast €12.50. Brunch €22. Open M-Th and Su 8am-1am, F-Sa 8am-2am. AmEx/MC/V. ❹

Les Enfants Gâtés, 43, r. des Francs-Bourgeois (☎01 42 77 07 63). M: St-Paul. Walk against traffic on r. de Rivoli, turn left onto r. Pavée and right on r. des Francs-Bourgeois. "Spoiled children" is a sexy spot to brood, linger, and of course, people-watch. Coffee €2.10. Brunch €14.50-26. Berthillon ice cream €3.20-6.40. It also sells chic leather purses (from €60). Open daily 11am-8pm, food served until 4:30pm. MC/V. ❸

FIFTH ARRONDISSEMENT

NEIGHBORHOOD QUICKFIND: ***Discover,*** *p. 3;* ***Sights,*** *p. 86;* ***Museums,*** *p. 148;* ***Nightlife,*** *p. 211;* ***Shopping,*** *p. 239;* ***Accommodations,*** *p. 259.*

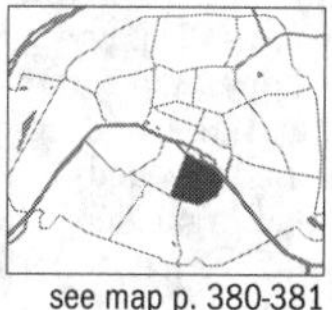

see map p. 380-381

A particularly diverse area of Paris, the *5ème* is home to a score of inexpensive traditional bistros as well as Tibetan, Vietnamese, and Middle Eastern fare. All the way down **rue Mouffetard,** back-to-back restaurants with high-quality food, old-fashioned charm, and surpassingly low prices (expect a *menu* from €9.50 to €14) crowd the streets. Hordes of lovely sidewalk bistros are crowded together along **rue de la Montagne Ste-Geneviève** and continue north of the Panthéon, onto **rue Descartes** and into **place de la Contrescarpe.** Cheap, touristy Greek and Middle Eastern restaurants also line **rue de la Huchette** and **rue Galande.**

Octave, 138, r. Mouffetard, *5éme* (01 45 35 20 56). M: Censier-Daubenton. If heaven ever froze over, it would be served in a cone at Octave. Quite simply the best ice cream you will ever eat. With no preservatives or coloring (unlike better-known rival Berthillon), all you taste in each lovely scoop is fresh melon, rich chocolate, soothing cinnamon or one of their many other *parfums*. The ingredients are held to such standards that Octave doesn't serve strawberry or raspberry ice cream in winter when those fruits are out of season. Be sure to try the pistachio and the banana ice creams–both of which are a light brown given their natural color when mashed into the ice cream. One scoop €2, two scoops €3. Open Tu-Su 10am-11:30pm, M 2-7:30pm. ❶

Savannah Café, 27, r. Descartes (☎01 43 29 45 77). M: Cardinal Lemoine. Follow Cardinal Lemoine uphill, turn right on r. Clovis, and walk 1 block. Decorated with eclectic knick-knacks, this cheerful yellow restaurant prides itself on its Lebanese food and other "selections from around the world." Dishes include eggplant caviar, taboule, and traditional French and Italian cuisine, including an extensive pasta selection (€12.50). Try the perfectly composed starter sampler (€14) so that you don't miss out on any fabulous flavours. *Entrées* €7-12.50. *Formule* €23. Open M-Sa 7-11pm. MC/V. ❹

Comptoir Méditerranée, 42, r. du Cardinal Lemoine (☎01 43 25 29 08). Savannah Café's little sister, run by the same welcoming owner. Similar tastes, from Lebanon and elsewhere, presented in a fresh and colorful array of ingredients. Select from 20 hot and cold dishes to make your own plate (€5.34), sandwich (€3.05) or thyme pizza (€3.05). You won't find a more satisfying deal anywhere. Open M-Sa 11am-10pm. ❷

Le Grenier de Notre-Dame, 18, r. de la Bucherie (☎01 43 29 98 29; www.legrenierdenotredame.com). M: St-Michel. Walk along quai St-Michel to quai de Montebello; turn right on r. Lagrange and left on r. de la Bucherie. Sunflowers and organic plants decorate the patio and interior of this eclectic café. Macrobiotic and vegetarian specialties with a contemporary French spin, all delicious. A haven for vegans in this *fromage*-loving city. 3-course *formule zen* (€12.50) might help you reach Nirvana. Salads €10-11. Open M-Th noon-2:30pm and 7:30-11pm, F-Sa noon-2:30pm and 7:30-11:30pm, Su noon-3pm and 7:30-11:30pm. MC/V. ❷

Au Port Salut, 163bis, r. St-Jacques (☎01 46 33 63 21). M: Luxembourg. Exit onto bd. St-Michel, turn right onto r. Soufflot, then right on r. des Fossés St-Jacques at pl. de l'Estrapade; on the corner of r. St-Jacques. Behind its iron portcullis, this old stone building (once a

The Postwar Years

World War II and the Nazi occupation of France between 1940 and 1944 polarized Parisian intellectuals. While some (Robert Brasillach [1909-1945], Pierre Drieu La Rochelle [1893-1945]) chose to collaborate with the enemy, most joined the Resistance to fight actively or by writing, often at the price of their lives, clandestine tracts that denounced the enemy and urged the population to resist. With the liberation of Paris in August 1944, intellectual freedom returns. The postwar years were under the sign of hope associated with ideals from the Resistance and soon of decolonization. Most postwar intellectuals tended to the left. The Communist Party had organized much of the resistance during the war. After Liberation, it retained its influence through the "Comité national des écrivains" (National Committee of Writers), founded in 1942 and composed of writers and artists of different political stripes. With the escalation of the Cold War and the rise of McCarthyism in the US, many intellectuals turned to the Soviet Union, which since the 30s had been a symbol of peace. Dominated by the fear of nuclear war, the late 1940s and early fifties were for intellectuals a time of mass manifestations and international Peace Movements. Writers and artist signed countless appeals. They defended Henri Martin, a French sailor condemned for distributing anti-colonialist tracts (1951) and the Rosenbergs, a Jewish-American couple executed in the US for supposedly selling atomic secrets to Russia (1952-53). These years of militancy coincided with political, economic, and social instability in France. The death of Stalin (1952), revelations about gulags and repression in satellite states like Hungary (1945), and growing economic prosperity in France led to the loss of unity among intellectuals.

The postwar Parisian intellectual scene was dominated by a neo-Hegelianism of Marxist and existential signature. While intellectuals who stayed with the Communist Party lost influence amids ebbing postwar euphoria, existentialisms centered around various philosopher-writers thrived. Jean-Paul Sartre (1905-1980) and Simone de Beauvoir (1908-1986) were known for their writings and anti-bourgeois "bohemian lifestyle." It was rumored that they wrote treatises on tables at the Café de Flore and frequented dimly lit jazz cellars in hip areas of St-Germain. Sartre's pronouncement on the importance of existence above and beyond human essence, his insistence on the necessity of action, personal responsibility, and *engagement* (commitment) not only in life but in writing, molded a generation. Next to his arduous *L'Être et le Néant* (1943; *Being and Nothingness*, 1956), Sartre popularized his thought in novels, short stories, and plays. He drew readers and viewers into existential experiences (*La Nausée* [1938; *Nausea*, 1939]), made them ponder the mixtures of courage, chance, and fate in war times (*Le Mur* [1939; The Wall, 1948]), and reflect on human self-deception and fear of action (*Huis Clos* [1945; *No Exit*, 1946]).

Simone de Beauvoir quit teaching to further her career as a writer. In *Le Deuxieme Sexe* (1949; *The Second Sex*, 1953), a book taking on the condition of women, she coined the famous aphorism "one is not born woman, one becomes woman." Her novels (*Le Sang des autres*, [1945; *The Blood of Others*, 1948]), plays, and autobiographies (*Memoires d'une fille rangée* [1958; *Memoires of a Dutiful Daughter*, 1958]) address the question of our responsibility to others and of living one's life in an open-ended way without accepting the living death imposed by institutional norms (family, church, or schools).

Born in Algeria, Albert Camus (1913-1960) represented another strain of existentialism. *L'étranger* (1942; *The Stranger*, 1946) became influential in the postwar era. Camus's critique of bourgeois institutions, insistence on living according to one's bodily rhythms and pleasures, and his will to reject false moral values engaged debate. His theater of the absurd dealt with life's unexpected twists, with misunderstandings, impossible situations, chance, fate, and power (*Le Malentendu* [1944; *Cross Purpose*, 1947]; *Caligula* [1944; 1947]). In his Nobel Prize (1957) acceptance speech, he declared that the artist needed to be "in the arena," involved in universal human dilemmas but without realism or dogmatism. He intrigued the public with his brooding image of a solitary soul wearing a trench coat à la Humphrey Bogart, an omnipresent cigarette hanging from his lips. In 1960, Camus was the victim of an accident that took place when the car driven by his editor smashed into a tree. When it was revealed that Camus had a train ticket in his pocket, his untimely and absurd death seemed to come out of one of his own plays.

Yet the 1950s were for Camus not only a time of hedonism, existential humanism, and the absurd but also a time of politics. While he lived in Algeria, Camus had worked as a journalist. Early on he had decried the human misery of a mountainous region of Algeria known as Kabylia ("Chro niques algériennes, 1939-1958" in *Actuelles* III, 1958). Though appalled by the poverty of the indigenous population, Camus took on the subject of Algeria a position opposed to the position of Sartre, which led to a permanent rift between the two. Until his death, two years before Algerian independence, Camus was convinced compromise was possible, with French settlers—"pied-noirs"—remaining side-by-side with natives in an independent Algeria. Sartre, as shown in his preface to Frantz Fanon's *Les Damnés de la terre* (1961; *The Wretched of the Earth*, 1963) took a far more radical stand, arguing for independence and an evacuation of all settlers from native soil.

Slightly older, André Malraux (1901-1976) had been known for dramatic pre-war novels about the human condition in a transforming world, be it that of the Chinese revolution (*La condition humaine* [1933; *Man's Fate*, 1938]) or the Spanish civil war (*L'espoir* [1938; *Man's Hope*, 1953]). After the war, he wrote about art (*Les Voix du silence* [1951; *The Voices of Silence*, 1953]) and became Minister of Culture (1959) under de Gaulle. He undertook to bring art to the people by building Maisons de la Culture (Houses of Culture) all over France and ordered the preservation and restoration of Paris's historic buildings. Malraux's elegance and good looks—whether in aviator garb or black-tie—were legendary. As a cultural envoy, he traveled to India, China, and to the US on the invitation of Jackie Kennedy (1963), who was charmed by what she saw as Malraux's talent for furthering the arts.

If the postwar years were the time when tourists hoped to find a quaint Paris of painters, writers, and musicians (as romanticized in Vincent Minelli's musical *An American in Paris*; 1951), major changes were under way. With the Marshall plan, industrialization and "Americanization" of both the city and the country took place. In the films of Jacques Tati (1909-1982), Paris was seen losing its gallic quaintness (*Mon Oncle*, 1958), becoming a postmodern nightmare or simulacrum for tourists (*Playtime*, 1967). Intellectuals saw their lives threatened by consumerism. Despite rising consumer culture, the intellectual aura of Sartre, Beauvoir, Camus, and Malraux continued to radiate beyond the City of Lights.

The late 1950s and 60s, marked by prosperity, the Algerian War's end and decolonization, the waning of Resistance memories, and a lessening of Cold War tensions, saw the rise of a new intellectual breed. "New novelists" like Michel Butor (1926-) and Alain Robbe-Grillet (1922-) launch experimental writings. A young generation of intellectual, poetic "new wave" filmmakers defied studio rules to deal with human dilemmas in a modernizing city (François Truffaut, *Les Quatre Centes Coups* [1959; 400 Blows]); Jean-Luc Godard, *A Bout de soufflé* [1961; *Breathless*]; *Deux ou trois choses que je sais d'elle* [1967; *Two or Three Things I Know About Her*]).

In 1960, criticizing their elders for militant leftism and concepts of historical self, Philippe Sollers (1936-) and others founded interdisciplinary journal *Tel Quel*. Editors touted textual Marxism based on psychoanalysis and argued that true liberation is that of desire. The journal published rising stars like Julia Kristeva (1941-)—soon to be Sollers' wife—and Jacques Derrida (1930-). A decade of intellectual effervescence under the aegis of structuralism and, later, poststructuralism culminated with the 1968 uprisings. From Claude Lévi-Strauss's (1908-) "savage thought," to Louis Althusser's (1918-1990) reading of Marx, Michel Foucault's (1925-1984) history as discourse, Jacques Lacan's (1901-1981) French Freud, Gilles Deleuzes (1925-1995) and Félix Guattari's (1930-1992) rhizomes, Derrida's (1930-) deconstruction of oppositions and Hélène Cixous's (1937-) textual feminism, the sixties are rife with talent. Tourists report sightings at the Coupole and the Hotel Lutetia.

After 1968, the values inherited from the Resistance were resolutely passé. Decolonization had been largely achieved and new problems arose in its wake. The ideals of 1968—promising transformations of oppositions into an endless play of sexual, racial, and cultural differences—ran afoul when a rising market economy, a sense of acceleration under the impact of new technologies, and massive migrations transformed Paris and France. With the disappearance of the countryside, the gentrification of old neighborhoods, and the emergence of squalid suburban living conditions, the very concept of the city was re-evaluated (Henri Lefebvre, *La Révolution Urbaine* [1970; The Urban Revolution, 2003]). Paris is now comprised of many histories and cultures. New intellectuals, writers, and artists are reevaluating the recent past and discussing a present (Etienne Balibar, *Nous, citoyens d'Europe? Les frontières, l'Etat, le peuple* [2001; *We, Citizens of Europe? Borders, the State, the People*]) that, with the arrival in Paris of people from all over the world, promises to be increasingly diverse.

Verena Andermatt Conley *teaches Romance Languages and Literatures at Harvard University. She has published extensively; a book on postwar Parisian intellectuals is forthcoming.*

Don't Call Them Pancakes

Upon arrival in Paris, the crêpe will seem like an incredibly cheap meal substitute. The ubiquitous crêpe stand serves up sweet and tasty delights from around €2, but be warned: your stomach can only take so much nutella and banana. When you've reached your limit, *galettes* will come to the rescue.

The more sophisticated sibling in the crêpe family, *galettes* are often advertised as crêpe *sarrassin*. The *galette* is made from a savory buck-wheat *(sarrassin)* batter, cooked in the same manner as the familiar crêpe, but ending up a dark, crispy masterpiece. *Galettes* are no paltry excuse for a meal; they are a feast in themselves, and many restaurants specialize in them. Everything from cheese to potatoes and vegetables can fill a *galette*, and the proportions can vary depending on appetite.

Cooked on a round *billig*, with a *rozell* twisted deftly in the chef's hand, *galettes* were consumed in place of bread in ancient Brittany. The first crêpe recipe in France dates to about 1390, and hungry late-night clubbers and budget travelers have benefited from it since.

cabaret of the same name) houses 3 floors of traditional French gastronomic joy: geraniums decorate the quiet, non-smoking dining room upstairs; the *rez-de-chaussée* is a popular bar with a piano and an often boisterous crowd. Roman-esque frescoes cover the walls of the outrageous cave downstairs, which recalls the cabaret history of the restaurant. The restaurant specializes in fabulous 3-course *menus* that change with the season (€12.40 and €21.90). Salads €8.90-9.30. Open Tu-Sa noon-2:30pm and 7-11:30pm. MC/V. ❸

Le Jardin des Pâtés, 4, r. Lacépède (☎01 43 31 50 71). M: Jussieu. From the métro, walk up r. Linné and turn right on r. Lacépède. As calming and pleasant as the Jardin des Plantes around the corner. As its name implies, Le Jardin's menu of organic food is heavy on the pâté (€7-12.50), pasta, and vegetables. Appetizers €3.30-8.80. Open daily noon-2:30pm and 7-11pm. MC/V. ❷

Le Perraudin, 157, r. St-Jacques (☎01 46 33 15 75). M: Cluny-La Sorbonne. Exit the métro and walk down bd. St-Michel, turn left on r. Soufflot, and then turn right on r. St-Jacques; the restaurant is right on the corner. With a deep red exterior, an intimate little garden, and *tartes* lining the wooden counter, Le Perraudin has the inviting look and feel of a traditional French bistro. Simple, elegant, and *pas trop cher*, Le Perraudin serves up countless old Parisian favorites like *confit de canard* and *boeuf bourguignon* to a boisterous crowd of regulars, mostly students and hungry locals. Plates of the day €9-12. Lunch *menu* €18, *menu gastronomique* €28. Open M-F noon-2:30pm and 7-11pm. ❸

CAFÉS

Café de la Mosquée, 39, r. Geoffrey St-Hilaire (☎01 43 31 38 20). M: Censier-Daubenton. In the Mosquée de Paris. With porphyr fountains, white marble floors, and an exquisite multi-level terrace, this café deserves a visit whether a trip to the Mosquée is on your itinerary or not. Rest under the shady fig and olive trees and savor some Persian mint tea (€2) and *maghrébin* pastries (€2). Or, eat couscous (€9.25) off a copper platter in the richly decorated restaurant. Tea room open daily 9am-11:30pm; restaurant daily noon-3pm and 7:30-10:30pm. ❷

Café Delmas, 2, pl. de la Contrescarpe (☎01 43 26 51 26). M: Cardinal Lemoine. From the métro, walk up r. du Cardinal Lemoine straight into pl. de la Contrescarpe. In this happening area, Delmas is the place to while away the hours in style. Black-clad waiters serve trendy food like an Asian-inflected niçoise salad (€12) and cocktails from a lengthy drink menu to glamorous people-watchers. Café €2.40. Open Su-Th 8am-2am, F-Sa 8am-4am. MC/V. ❷

SIXTH ARRONDISSEMENT

NEIGHBORHOOD QUICKFIND: **Discover,** p. 3; **Sights,** p. 91; **Museums,** p. 148; **Nightlife,** p. 212; **Shopping,** p. 239; **Accommodations,** p. 261.

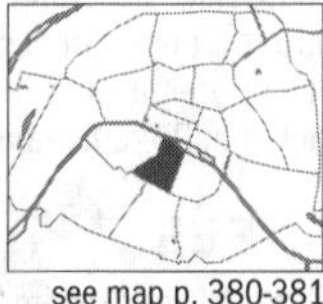
see map p. 380-381

Tiny restaurants with rock-bottom prices jockey for space and customers in the streets enclosed by **boulevard St-Germain, boulevard St-Michel, rue de Seine,** and the river **Seine.** Within the tangle, **rue de Buci** harbors bargain Greek restaurants and a rambling street market, while **rue Grégoire de Tours** has the highest density of cheap, greasy and tourist-themed restaurants and **rue St-Andre-des-Arts** is lined with *crêperies* and purveyors of *panini.* More options are near Odéon; the **Carrefour d'Odéon** has several traditional bistros, while **rue Princesse, rue Guisarde,** and **rue des Canettes** are jam-packed with cheap and pedestrian-friendly *crêperies* and bistros.

Le Petit Vatel, 5, r. Lobineau (☎01 43 54 28 49). M: Mabillon. From the métro, follow traffic on bd. St-Germain, turn right on r. de Seine, and then take the second right onto r. Lobineau. This charming little home-run bistro with sunny yellow walls and movie posters serves up a fresh menu of Mediterranean-French specialties like *catalan pamboli* (bread with puréed tomatoes, ham, and cheese), all a very reasonable €10. Perhaps most impressive is the 100% non-smoking environment in which you can enjoy it all. €11 lunch menu. Vegetarian option always available. Open Tu-Sa noon-2:30pm and 7-10:30pm. ❷

Le Bistro d'Henri, 16, r. Princesse. M: Mabillon. From the métro, walk down r. du Four and left onto r. Princesse. This Left Bank bistro serves classic (read: delicious but heart attack-inducing) food made with fresh ingredients. Their *gratin dauphinois* (layered potatoes and cheese) and *gigot d'agneau* are rumored to be the best in Paris. Appetizers €6-7. *Plats* €12-14. Dinner *menu* €26. Open daily noon-2:30pm and 7-11:30pm. MC/V. Around the corner is **Le Machon d'Henri,** 8, r. Guisarde (☎01 43 29 08 70), with the same *menus* in a slightly smaller, white-stone alcove. Also in the 5*ème,* the same restaurant done with a bit more elegance: **Chez Henri,** 9, r. de la Montagne-Ste-Geneviève (☎01 43 29 12 12). ❹

La Crêpe Rit du Clown, 6, r. des Canettes (☎01 46 34 01 02). M: Mabillon. From the métro, walk down r. du Four and turn left on r. des Canettes. The clown-heavy decorations may be the makings of a horror movie, but the food is very tasty, and very cheap. *Formule* €10. Savory crêpes €5.50-8. The *kir* is even less expensive–just €2.50 a glass. *Salut* to Bozo. Open M-Sa noon-11:30pm. MC/ V. ❶

Così, 54, r. de Seine (☎01 46 33 35 36). M: Mabillon. From the métro, walk down bd. St-Germain and make a left onto r. de Seine. Named for the Mozart opera, this hip *sandwicherie* sells enormous, tasty, inexpensive sandwiches on fresh, brick-oven bread. Don't be deterred by the long lines. Sandwiches €5.20-7.60 depending on number of ingredients. Desserts €2.80-3.40. Open daily noon-11pm. ❶

Coffee Parisien, 4, r. Princesse (☎01 43 54 18 18). M: Mabillon. From the métro, walk down r. du Four and go left on r. Princesse. Walls are covered with loopy Americana and placemats bearing the likenesses of American presidents. The place to go for homesick American travelers craving a bagel with lox and a schmear (€12.50), a hot fudge sundae (€7), or a bacon cheeseburger (€13). Open daily noon-midnight. AmEx/MC/V. **Also** in the 16*ème* at 7, r. Gustave Courbet (☎01 45 53 17 17). ❷

Guen-maï, 2bis, r. de l'Abbaye, entrance at 6, r. Cardinale (☎01 43 26 03 24). M: Mabillon. From the métro, walk against traffic on bd. St-Germain and go right on r. de la Petite Boucherie, then left on r. de l'Abbaye. This place might be have more appeal for vegetarians and vegans than for their carnivorous friends (though they do have fish, and everyone can use the occasional detox in this hedonistic city), but for those who crave seitan and soy, it's like finding a little piece of macrobiotic heaven. The lunch counter doubles as a *salon de thé* and bookstore, as well as a vitamin boutique. Choices include miso soup (€4.50), agar fruit salad (€5), *poisson crudités* (€9.50), and other daily specials like *gratin de tofu* and *tempura de légumes* (€10.50). Lunch served M-Sa 11:45am-3:30pm; store open M-Sa 9am-8:30pm. MC/V. ❷

Crêperie Saint Germain, 33, r. St-André-des-Arts (☎01 43 54 24 41). M: St-Michel. From the métro, cross pl. St-Michel, and walk down r. St-André-des-Arts. Filling wheat-flour *crêpes noirs,* like the Chihuahua (chicken, peppers, tomato, onion, banana; €8.60) or Manhattan (ground beef, cheese, tomatoes, and egg; €9.20), and sweet dessert *crêpes* (€2.80-7.60). Funky tiles and painted splotches lend a mellow artsiness. €8.10 *menu* (M-F noon-3pm) includes 2 crêpes and *cidre.* Open daily noon-midnight. AmEx/MC/V. ❷

CAFÉS

Forget fine dining; cafés are the heart and soul (and stomach) of the *6ème's* culture of consumption. Ordering a *café express* will guarantee you a seat and a place to while away the hours with your *confrères.* While the big boys like **Le Sélect** and **Café de Flore** still hold court along the **boulevard Montparnasse** and **boulevard St-Germain-des-Prés,** a lot of new blood on the café circuit clusters around **Carrefour d'Odéon** and north of bd. St-Germain near the galleries.

Les Editeurs, 4, carrefour d'Odéon (☎01 43 26 67 76). The newest and classiest café on the block, Les Editeurs pays homage to St-Germain's literary pedigree with books—on everything from Marilyn Monroe to Brassaï—overflowing its plush red and gold dining rooms, and outlets for struggling, laptop-toting young writers. Jazz music and a piano upstairs. Café €2.50, *pressions* €4.50, cocktails €9. *Croque Monsieur* €9.50. Ice creams like *mandarine des montagnes* or pistachio €7.50. Happy Hour daily 6-8pm (cocktails €6-8, and delicious complementary olives!). Open daily 8am-2am. AmEx/MC/V. ❷

Café Vavin, 18, rue Vavin (☎01 43 26 67 47). The elusive creature: a café with personality, location, and delicious food. Vavin inhabits a delightful pocket of the 6*ème*, and is surrounded by small boutiques (including an outpost of *Petite Bateau*). Come for the funky tiling on the walls, stay for a tasty smoked duck salad (€7.65), chicken with *bernaise* sauce (€11.30), or just café (€2.30). Open M-F 7am-midnight, Sa 7am-6pm. MC/V. ❷

Café de Flore, 172, bd. St-Germain (☎01 45 48 55 26). M: St-Germain-des-Prés. From the métro, walk against traffic on bd. St-Germain. Sartre composed *Being and Nothingness* here; Apollinaire, Camus, Artaud, Picasso, Breton, and Thurber sipped brew, and in the contemporary feud between Café de Flore and Les Deux Magots, Flore reportedly snags more of the local intellectuals—possibly by offering a well-respected literary prize. Brigitte Bardot drinks on the *terrasse*, but the close seating upstairs, with its beige booths, Art Deco simplicity, and serious chain-smoking Parisians is still the coolest (check out Sartre and de Beauvoir's booth on the left). Espresso €4. *Salade Flore* €12.20. Pastries €6.10-10.40. Open daily 7:30am-1:30am. AmEx/MC/V. ❸

Les Deux Magots, 6, pl. St-Germain-des-Prés (☎01 45 48 55 25). M: St-Germain-des-Prés. Just down the street from the Eglise St-Germain-des-Prés. The cloistered area behind the famous high hedges has been home to literati (from Mallarmé to Hemingway) since 1885, but is now favored mostly by Left Bank residents and tourists. Named after 2 Chinese porcelain figures (the originals are still inside), *not* after fly larvae. Coffee €3.80, hot chocolate €6, pastries €6.70. Sandwiches €6.10-7.60. Breakfast *menu* €15. Open daily 7:30am-1:30am. AmEx/V. ❷

Le Sélect, 99, bd. du Montparnasse (☎01 45 48 38 24). M: Vavin. Walk west on bd. du Montparnasse; across the street from La Coupole. Trotsky, Satie, Breton, Cocteau, and Picasso all frequented this huge Art Deco café which advertises itself as an "American Bar." Have the bartender mix you a classic cocktail (€10.40-11) as the surprisingly local crowd carries on gregariously. Café €1.20-3 depending on the time of day. *Menus* and dinner, too *(plats* start at €12). Open daily 7am-3am. MC/V. ❷

Le Procope, 13, r. de l'Ancienne Comédie (☎01 40 46 79 00). M: Odéon. Walk against traffic on bd. St-Germain and go right on r. de l'Ancienne Comédie. Founded in 1686, making it the first café in the world. Voltaire reportedly drank 40 cups per day here while writing *Candide;* his table remains what the owners call "a testimony of permanence." Marat came here to plot the Revolution. Now a seafood restaurant, or, history with a price: €30 *menu*. Coffee (€2.60) and beer (€7.40-8.90) are more affordable. Open daily 11am-2am. AmEx/MC/V. ❹

Le Comptoir du Relais, 5-7, carrefour de l'Odéon (☎01 43 29 12 05). M: Odéon. Once a working class haunt, but now draws a regular crowd of neighborhood residents, who come to gossip over tea while admiring their reflections in the wall-to-wall mirrors and watching the people-watchers across the street at Les Editeurs (above). Homemade *tartes* and other *pâtisseries* are displayed on the Art Deco counter. Quiches €7.40. *Salades* €8.40. Homemade desserts €6. Sangria €3.80, wines €2.80-8.50. Open daily noon-midnight. ❷

Le Bistro Ernest, 21, r. de Seine (☎01 56 24 47 47). Gallery owners, artists, students, filmmakers, musicians, and other Left Bank riff-raff gather in this small café-bar lined with gallery posters and manned by a friendly bartender from Martinique. A calm alternative to the bustle of St-Germain. Jazz music. In the heart of the gallery district. Café €1.10 at the bar, beer €1.35-2.60, punch €4.30. AmEx/MC/V. ❷

St-Germain-des-Prés

SEVENTH ARRONDISSEMENT

NEIGHBORHOOD QUICKFIND: ***Discover,*** *p. 4;* ***Sights,*** *p. 96;* ***Museums,*** *p. 149;* ***Nightlife,*** *p. 213;* ***Shopping,*** *p. 242;* ***Accommodations,*** *p. 262.*

see map pp. 382-383

The 7*ème* is not budget-friendly, but ubiquitous bakeries and markets offer sandwiches or quiche at reasonable prices. The restaurants below are worth the splurge.

Ceci n'est pas un café

Le Lotus Blanc, 45, r. de Bourgogne (☎01 45 55 18 89). M: Varenne. Walk on bd. des Invalides, toward the Invalides; turn left onto r. de Varenne and then left again onto r. de Bourgogne. Chef Pham-Nam Nghia has been creating Vietnamese specialties for over 25 years. Lunch and all-day *menus* €9-29. Perpetually hungry (in Paris, anyway) vegetarians will appreciate the great veggie *menu* (€6.50-12.50), which should also keep vegans happy. Reservations encouraged. Open M-Sa noon-2:30pm and 7-10:30pm. Closed 2 weeks in Aug. AmEx/MC/V. ❸

L'Auberge Bressane, 16, av. de la Motte Picquet (☎01 47 05 98 37). M: Ecole Militaire or Tour Maubourg. Worth the higher price, this small and luxuriously decorated restaurant is bouncing with regular patrons enjoying dishes like butter-soft artichoke hearts in a light vinaigrette (€9) and their famous *poulet à la crème et aux morilles* (€19). Three-course lunch *menu* M-F €15-24. Reservations are a must any day of the week. Open daily noon-2:30pm and 8-10:30pm, but happy patrons stay as late as 2am, drinking and chatting with the friendly, multi-lingual waitstaff. Closed Sa during lunch. ❺

Café Contrescarpe

the BIG $plurge

Dine Like The Gods

Tucked between historic hotels and the American embassy lies the **buddha-bar,** two floors of pure delight where you can spend a few hours living like the rich and famous (which just might be worth a few days' budget). Swanky, candlelit, and expensive, yet surprisingly welcoming, buddha will seduce you with its stunning atmosphere, food, and clientele. The afternoon *menu degustation* is a (comparative) steal at €32. Wine, café, and 3 courses are included as, of course, is the flawless yet friendly service. The adventurous *menu* treats you to appetizers that range from raw meat to crispy springrolls, and a main dish that frames rice with fish, steak, and a spring salad. For dessert, expect something that looks like artwork and awakens new tastebuds.

Gawk at the drink menu, which lists a particular bottle of cognac at over €1000 (you could just take a 2cl shot for €122!). For ordinary humans, the fantastically original cocktails are around €12. So that you can relive the experience at home, a line of buddha-bar CDs, chopsticks, and other items are for sale at reception.

buddha-bar, 8, r. Boissy d'Anglais, 8ème (☎01 53 05 90 00). M: Concorde or Madeleine. Lunch M-F noon-3pm. Open nightly 6pm-2am. ❺

Grannie, 27, r. Pierre Leroux (☎01 43 34 94 14). M: Vaneau. Walk west on r. de Sèvres and make a right onto r. Pierre Leroux. French fare with a subtle Japanese twist served in an atmosphere both cozy and classy. *Menus* €17 or €24. Wine €4.50-5. Open M-F noon-2:30pm and 7:30-10:30pm, Sa 7:30-10:30pm. MC/V. ❹

Au Pied de Fouet, 45, r. de Babylone (☎01 47 05 12 27). M: Vaneau. Take r. Vaneau and turn left onto r. de Babylone. Small, bustling bistro that attracts both cigarette-puffing locals and tourists. Straightforward French home-cooking at bargain prices. Cheeses, wines, and main dishes change regularly. Appetizers €2-3. Main dishes €7-11. Desserts (try the *crème caramel*) €2.75. Open M-F noon-2:30pm and 7-9:30pm, Sa noon-2pm. ❷

CAFÉS

Café des Lettres, 53, r. de Verneuil (☎01 42 22 52 17). M: Solférino. Exit the métro onto pl. J. Blainville and take r. de Villersexel; turn right onto r. de l'Université, make a left onto r. de Poitiers, and another right onto r. de Verneuil. Hidden in the sidestreets of the 7*ème*, this Scandinavian café offers unique tastes in a fantastic atmosphere. Sharing a sun-blessed courtyard with the *Maison des Ecrivains*, patrons enjoy platters of smoked salmon and *blindis* (€16) and other Danish seafood dishes (€12.50-19.50). Su features a Scandinavian-style brunch buffet (€25); reservations are recommended. Coffee €2.50, beer €5.00-6.00. Open M noon-3pm, Tu-F noon-11pm, Sa noon-7pm. ❷

Café du Marché, 38, r. Cler (☎01 47 05 51 27). M: Ecole Militaire. From the métro, walk up r. de la Motte Piquet and turn left onto r. Cler. Watch the chic residents of the 7*ème* doing their errands from this beautiful terrace on a bustling street. Enjoy good, American-style food like a Caesar salad (€8) and the customary French dishes (fish or meat tartar €9.50). Open M-Sa 7am-1am (food served until 11pm), Su 7am-3pm. MC/V. ❷

EIGHTH ARRONDISSEMENT

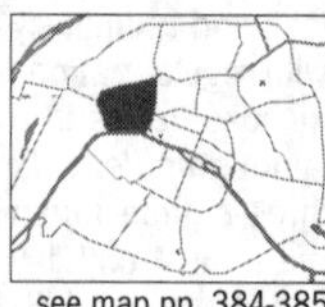
see map pp. 384-385

NEIGHBORHOOD QUICKFIND: ***Discover,*** *p. 9;* ***Sights,*** *p. 100;* ***Museums,*** *p. 150;* ***Nightlife,*** *p. 213;* ***Shopping,*** *p. 243;* ***Accommodations,*** *p. 263.*

The eighth *arrondissement* is as glamorous and expensive as it gets in the city of Paris. In a way, the charm of the 8*ème* lies in its gratuitous, over-the-top extravagance. Those who are not interested in such materialistic overindulgence need not fear: there are some affordable restaurants in the *8ème*, most of them located on the side streets around **rue la Boétie.**

Objectifs Crêpes, 10, r. de Constantinople (☎01 40 08 00 17). M: Europe. From the métro, walk up r. de Rome and take a left on r. de Constantinople. This intimate and rustic *crêperie* with cheerful colored walls serves up inventive gourmet crêpes and *galettes*. Create your own meal from a list of ingredients (*galettes* €5.10-5.90, crêpes €3.10-4.30) or try the intriguing house specialties. Ciders €2.50-9. Lunch *menu* €11. Open M-F noon-2pm and 7-10:30pm, Sa 7-10:30pm. ❶

Escrouzailles, 36, r. du Colisée (☎01 45 62 94 00). M: Franklin D. Roosevelt. Take av. Franklin D. Roosevelt and turn right on r. du Colisée. This intimate restaurant has several comfortable yellow-walled dining rooms. Perhaps the best place to enjoy fine yet relaxed dining after a day wandering the Champs. Choose from lists of *entrées* (€8) such as *foie gras, plats* (€12) such as the rack of lamb with zucchini, and delicious desserts (€6). Plenty of vegetarian options. Open M-Sa noon-2:30pm and 7:30-10:30pm. MC/V. ❸

Bagel & Co., 31, r. de Ponthieu (☎01 42 89 44 20). M: Franklin D. Roosevelt. From the métro, walk toward the Arc de Triomphe on the Champs-Elysées, then go right on av. Franklin D. Roosevelt and left on r. de Ponthieu. This bright, modern, New York-inspired deli lets customers choose from a large array of creative bagel and specialty sandwiches (€3-5) named after American cities, such as the New York (cream cheese and smoked salmon, of course!). All natural ingredients; no GMOs. Choose from the intimate upstairs eating area or the cafeteria-bar. Create your own salad for €3.50-6.50 and then reward yourself with dessert (homemade goodies €2-3). Lots of vegetarian and kosher options. Open M-F 7:30am-9pm, Sa 10am-8pm. AmEx/MC/V. ❶

Bangkok Café, 28, r. de Moscou (☎01 43 87 62 56). M: Rome. From the métro, take a right onto r. Moscou. A talented Thai chef and her French husband serve inventive seafood salads and soups (€8-10) and a choice of meats cooked in coconut milk, curry, or satay sauce (€12-18). Plenty of vegetarian options. *Menus* €15-21. Open M-F noon-2:30pm and 7-11:30pm, Sa 7-11:30pm. AmEx/MC/V. ❷

Vitamine, 20, r. de Bucarest (☎01 45 22 28 02). M: Liège. From the métro, walk up r. de Moscou. Sandwich bar is on the first corner on the right. Overlooking the lively pl. Dublin with both outdoor and indoor seating, this minimalistic restaurant serves mostly stuff that's good for you. Hot plates around €7. Sandwiches on excellent bread €2-3. Salads €3-7. Coffee €0.90! What city are we in again? Open M-F 8am-5pm. ❷

CAFÉS

Latina Café, 114, av. des Champs-Elysées (☎01 42 89 98 89). M: George V. Drawing one of the largest nightclub crowds on the glitzy Champs-Elysées (see **Nightlife,** p. 214), Latina Café doubles as a café during the evening. Drinks €6. Café open daily 7:30pm-2am. ❸

Le Paris, 93, av. des Champs-Elysées (☎01 47 23 54 37). M: George V. Rivalled in snobbery only by Fouquet's, Le Paris does have some selling points, beginning with the unique decor: a deep purple and turquoise melange, with plasma screens playing anime above the bar. Simple yet elegant, it is one of the few reasonably affordable cafés on the Champs, and the terrace is the ideal space for people-watching and sipping tea. At night, the café turns into a bar with a live DJ. Coffee €3.50, tea €5.50, glass of wine €5.50-7. Sandwiches €10-12.50. Soup €7. Open daily 8am-6am. ❷

Fouquet's, 99, av. des Champs-Elysées (☎01 47 23 70 60). M: George V. Filled with French stars, but mostly on the walls in frames. Beneath its red awning reside stagey grandeur and snobbery so "French" that the place seems like a caricature of itself. The restaurant is a designated historical monument, which might be an excuse for the red velvet furniture that overpowers the senses. Love that bank-breaking coffee (€4.60)! Main dishes €10-34. *Menus* €39-54. Food served all day in the café, while the restaurant serves noon-3pm and 7pm-midnight. Open daily 8am-2am. AmEx/MC/V. ❹

NINTH ARRONDISSEMENT

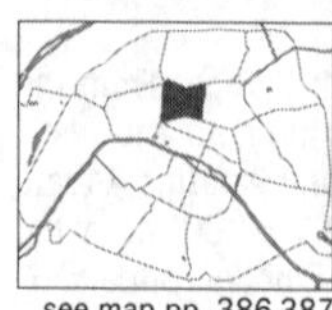
see map pp. 386-387

NEIGHBORHOOD QUICKFIND: ***Discover,*** *p. 9;* ***Sights,*** *p. 105;* ***Museums,*** *p. 151;* ***Nightlife,*** *p. 214;* ***Accommodations,*** *p. 264.*

Except for a few gems, restaurants and eateries close to the Opéra cater to the after-theater and movie crowd; meals here can be quite expensive. For cheaper deals, head farther north in the *9ème*. **Rue du Faubourg-Montmartre** is crammed with countless cheap sandwich and pizza places, though the general area is of dubious cleanliness.

Haynes Restaurant Américain, 3, r. Clauzel (☎01 48 78 40 63). M: St-Georges. From the métro, head uphill on r. Notre Dame de Lorette and turn right on r. H. Monnier, then right on r. Clauzel to the end of the block. The first African-American owned restaurant in Paris (it opened in 1949), a center for expatriates, and a former hangout of such legendary Africam American figures as Louis Armstrong, James Baldwin, and Richard Wright, Haynes is famous for its "original American Soul Food" and its complimentary cornbread with meat sauce. You won't find any other place like it in Paris. The portions here are very generous, and most of them are under €16. Ma Sutton's fried chicken with honey €14. Sister Lena's BBQ spare ribs €14. Vocal jazz concerts F nights; funk and groove Sa nights (€6 cover). Open Tu-Sa 7pm-12:30am. AmEx/MC/ V. ❸

Anarkali Sarangui, 4, pl. Gustave Toudouze (☎01 48 78 39 84). M: St-Georges. From the métro, walk uphill on r. Notre Dame de Lorette and turn right onto r. H. Monnier. This rare North Indian restaurant has a pleasant outdoor seating area out front. The interior, filled with many lovely Indian paintings, is a classy and comfortable alternative. Tandoori and curries €7.50-12.50. Vegetarian dinner *menu* €22. Open M 7-11:30pm, Tu-Su noon-2:30pm and 7-11:30pm. MC/V. ❸

Le Bistro de Gala, 45, r. du Faubourg-Montmartre (☎01 40 22 90 50). M: Grands Boulevards. The commercial noise and neon lights of Faubourg-Montmartre fade away as you enter this spacious bistro lined with film posters, the reputed hangout of some of Paris's theater elite. The food, with favorites like *foie gras* and *confit de canard,* is likewise a departure from the surrounding fast-food *sandwicheries.* The price of the *menu* is predictably high (€26-36), but definitely worth it. Reservations recommended. Open M-F noon-2:30pm and 7-11:30pm, Sa 7-11:30pm. AmEx/MC/V. ❹

Chartier, 7, r. du Faubourg-Montmartre (☎01 47 70 86 29). M: Grands Boulevards. This Parisian fixture has been serving well-priced French cuisine since 1896. Come to Chartier for the busy, train-station atmosphere, not for the late-night diner-quality food. The restaurant has very high ceilings and is in a large, open space. As tradition dictates, the quick waitstaff still add up the bill on the paper tablecloth at your table. Affordable traditional main dishes like *steak au poivre* run €7.50-9.50. Side dishes €2.20. Open daily 11:30am-3pm and 7-10pm. MC/V. ❷

CAFÉS

Café de la Paix, 12, bd. des Capucines (☎01 40 07 36 36). M: Opéra. On the left as you face the Opéra. This café just off r. de la Paix (the most expensive property on French Monopoly) has drawn a classy crowd since it opened in 1862 and has been frequented by the likes of Oscar Wilde. Now filled mostly by tourists drinking expensive coffees (€4.58 per cup!). Croissants €2. Cocktails €8.15. Lunch *menu* €24. Dinner *menu* €28. Open daily 10am-1:30am. AmEx/MC/V. ❹

Au Général La Fayette, 52, r. la Fayette (☎01 47 70 59 08). M: Le Peletier. With intricate Art Nouveau lamps and mirrors, and walls covered from top to bottom in Klimt-esque Belle Epoque exoterie, Au Général is one of the few classy café-bars in the area. The restaurant features a newspaper and magazine reading room as well as a laid-back atmosphere. Salads €3.90-10.80. Wine €3.70-4.20, beer (at the bar) €2.80-3.50, cocktails €9. Open daily 10am-4am. AmEx/MC/V. ❷

TENTH ARRONDISSEMENT

NEIGHBORHOOD QUICKFIND: ***Discover,*** *p. 11;* ***Sights,*** *p. 107;* ***Museums,*** *p. 151;* ***Accommodations,*** *p. 265.*

see map p. 388

While many tourists never see more of the 10*ème* than their Gare du Nord layover allows, those who venture out will find French, Indian, and African restaurants with reasonable prices, as well as neighborhood cafés and brasseries on every corner.

Cantine d'Antoine et Lili, 95, quai de Valmy (☎01 40 37 34 86). M: Gare de l'Est. From the métro, go down r. Faubourg St-Martin and make a left on r. Récollets; Cantine is on the corner of quai de Valmy. This canal-side café-bistro is one third of the Antoine and Lili operation, which also includes a neighboring furniture store (selling everything you see in the cafe), and a clothing boutique. The counter staff and the vibrant decor are very welcoming, and the tasty food consists mostly of light café fare: pasta salads €6, salads €6.50, and quiches €7.50. Prices are less for takeout. Open Su-Tu 11am-8pm, W-Sa 11am-1am. AmEx/MC/V. ❶

La 25ème Image, 9, r. des Récollets (☎01 40 35 80 88). M: Gare de l'Est. From the *gare*, go down r. Faubourg St-Martin and make a left on r. Recollets. Right near the Canal St-Martin, this funky little café, with colorful walls and patrons, offers a lovely selection of light food. Try one of the salads, or feast on a *plat* like grilled salmon (€10). Make sure to leave room for dessert—the berry-centric tarts and crumbles are divine (€3-4.30). Dinner is slightly more elaborate and pricey. M-F 10am-3pm and 6:45pm-12:30am Sa 6:45pm-12:30am. MC/V. ❷

Paris-Dakar, 95, r. du Faubourg St-Martin (☎01 42 08 16 64). M: Gare de l'Est. With your back to the *gare,* take r. du Faubourg St-Martin ahead of you. This place has been much-lauded for its Franco-Senegalese cuisine. Features *tiébou dieune* (fish with rice and veggies, €15) and the addictively refreshing house drink *bissap (*€5.34), made from African flowers and fresh mint. Vegetarians will have difficulty finding a main course but should be able to make a meal out of appetizers (€6) like roasted plantains. Lunch *menu* €9. Dinner *menu* €22.72. African *menu* €30.35. Open Sa-Su and Tu-Th noon-3pm and 7pm-2am, F 7pm-2am. AmEx/MC/V. ❸

Au Bon Café, 2, bd. St-Martin (☎01 42 00 21 45). M: République. The café is just to the right of pl. de la République if you exit the station facing the statue.

the hidden deal

Buck-A-Brick

For one shiny euro, **Du Pain et des Idées,** an ambitiously-named bakery in the 10*ème*, will furnish you with perhaps the tastiest and certainly the easiest to eat snack Paris has to offer: a *pavé garné* (brick). Flavors include blue cheese with dried apricots, bell peppers with goat cheese, *lardon et reblochon* (ham and cheese), and, for your sweet tooth, banana and chocolate. The unique ingredients are folded into the center of the dough then baked (think Italian *calzone* minus the grease), producing a light snack you can throw in your backpack and forget about until it's time for a *pause*. Two or three of them make a meal.

Open continuously since 1889, the bakery's new young English-speaking owners are dedicated to offering a *boulangerie* experience *a l'ancienne*. Their baguettes (€0.90) are made the old-fashioned way—without yeast—producing a unique taste and a longer freshness. Don't miss the heirloom ceiling decorations.

*Du Pain et des Idées, 34, r. Yves Toudic, 10*ème *(☎01 42 40 44 52). M: République. Walk against traffic on r. du Fauborg du Temple then left on r. Yves Toudic. Bricks €1, tartelettes €2.10. Open M-F 7:30am-2:30pm and 3:30-8pm.*

This delightful eatery is a haven from the frenzy of the pl. de la République, and a nice alternative to the *place's* McDonald's and pizza chain stores. Grab one of its wooden tables and sample a crisp salad with such creative ingredients as *coquilles*, grapefruit, pear, avocado and tomato. Salads €9-10. Quiches €6-8. AmEx/MC/V. ❷

Pooja, passage Brady (☎01 48 24 00 83). M: Strasbourg-St-Denis. Passage Brady is located between nos. 33 and 35, bd. de Strasbourg. Pooja's Indian cuisine is best enjoyed at night, when the passageway (which also houses many other Indian restaurants) is charmingly lit with hanging lanterns. The area surrounding the restaurant may be unsafe at night, so don't have *too* many of the delicious green Cocktail Pooja's (€4) before you depart. Lunch *menu* €7.50. Several vegetarian options. Open Su and Tu-Sa 11:30am-2pm and 6-11:30pm. ❷

ELEVENTH ARRONDISSEMENT

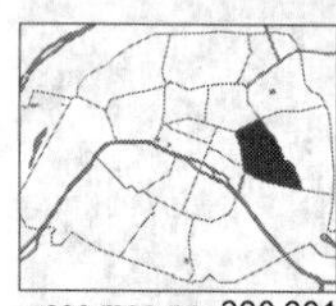

see map pp. 390-391

NEIGHBORHOOD QUICKFIND: ***Discover,*** *p. 11;* ***Sights,*** *p. 108;* ***Nightlife,*** *p. 214;* ***Accommodations,*** *p. 266.*

Although Bastille swells with fast-food joints, this increasingly diverse neighborhood offers (among others) Spanish, African, and Asian cuisines, with the most popular haunts lining the bustling **rues de Charonne, Keller, de Lappe,** and **Oberkampf.**

Chez Paul, 13, r. de Charonne (☎01 47 00 34 57). M: Bastille. Go east on r. du Faubourg St-Antoine and turn left on r. de Charonne. Downstairs has a classic bistro feel; upstairs has a cozy, romantic atmosphere. Paul's fun staff serves a menu to make your palate sing. Extensive appetizer list; great *steak au poivre* with *au gratin* potatoes (€13). Reservations are a must during peak hours. Open daily noon-2:30pm and 7pm-2am; food served until 12:30am. AmEx/MC/V. ❷

Le Kitch, 10, r. Oberkampf (☎01 40 21 94 14). M: Oberkampf or Filles-du-Calvaire. Amusingly guarded by Oscar, the owner's bull terrier, this hip restaurant-bar has food just as eclectic as the pleasingly mismatched tableware and wall decorations. Dishes come from various culinary traditions and include honey sauce chicken with couscous (€10), penne with gorgonzola (€8), and chocolate *soufflé* (€5). Vegetarian options available. Bottled beer €4. Open daily 5:30pm-2am. ❷

Café Cannelle, 1bis, r. de la Forge Royale (☎01 43 70 48 25). M: Ledru-Rollin. From the métro, walk away from pl. de la Bastille on r. du Faubourg St-Antoine and turn left on r. de la Forge. Moroccan restaurants crowd the 11*ème*, but few have Cannelle's atmosphere. The open kitchen serves up delicious *tajine* (couscous) meals (€13-15). Great vegetarian options. Open Tu-Su 8pm-midnight. AmEx/MC/V. ❷

Jours de Fête, 115, r. Oberkampf (☎01 40 21 70 34). M: Oberkampf. With almost every inch of wallspace covered in a mix of children's toys and vintage movie posters, this *crêperie* is colorful and upbeat. The sign hanging over the entrance reads "Queen of the Crêpe," and the queen is sure to please with delicious and inexpensive crêpes both *sucré* (€2-5) and *salé* (€5-8). Take-out also available. Open Su-Th 11:30am-3pm and 7pm-midnight, F-Sa 11:30am-2pm and 6:30pm-2am. ❶

La Banane Ivoirienne, 10, r. de la Forge-Royale (☎01 43 70 49 90). M: Faidherbe-Chaligny. Walk west on r. du Faubourg St-Antoine and turn right on r. de la Forge-Royale. Ivory Coast prints, palm trees, and African cuisine like *brochettes* of shrimp (€15.25) and cooked plantains (for parties of 3 or more; €15 per person). Come for the ambience as much as the food. *Plats* €8.50-15.25. Veggie *menu* €11. Live African music F 10pm. Open Tu-Sa 7pm-midnight. AmEx/MC/V. ❷

Restaurant Assoce, 48bis, r. St-Maur (☎01 43 55 73 82). M: St-Maur. A bit out of the way, this restaurant offers delicious and inexpensive Turkish cuisine. Enjoy lentil soup or lamb with garlic yogurt and tomato sauce. Lunch *menu* €8.39. Dinner *menu* €16.62. Veggie options available. Open M-Sa noon-3pm and 7-11pm, Su 7-11pm. AmEx/MC/V. ❷

Le Bistrot du Peintre, 116, av. Ledru-Rollin (☎01 47 00 34 39). M: Ledru-Rollin. Walk up av. Ledru-Rollin directly from the métro. Le Bistrot du Peintre sticks to its Art Nouveau roots, sporting rich dark wood, curvy mirrors, and ornate floral tiles. An outdoor table here is just the place to watch the 11*ème* whirl, clang, and honk by. The classic menu includes *foie gras* (€12) and *confit de canard* (€12). Entrees €10-13. Desserts €2.70-6.10. Open M-Sa 7am-2am, Su 10am-1am. MC/V. ❷

CAFÉS

Café de l'Industrie, 16, r. St-Sabin (☎01 47 00 13 53). M: Breguet-Sabin. This happening café could double as a museum of French colonial history, with its photos of natives, palm trees, and weapons on the walls. With the recent acquisition of a neighbor, l'Industrie may be the only restaurant in Paris to straddle a street. Both serve the same quality food, including a €9 lunch *menu*. Coffee €2, *vin chaud* €4. Salads €7-7.50. After 10pm, add €0.61. Open Su-F 10am-2am; lunch served noon-2pm. ❶

Pause Café, 41, r. de Charonne (☎01 48 06 80 33). M: Ledru-Rollin. Walk along av. Ledru-Rollin and turn left onto r. de Charonne. Always a good place to be part of a hip crowd, Pause is now all the cooler for having starred in the film *Chacun Cherche Son Chat*. Generous portions. Salads €8-10. Beer €2.80. The menu changes regularly—trust your server's recommendation. Open M-Sa 8am-2am, Su 8:30am-8pm. MC/V. ❷

Le Troisième Bureau, 74, r. de la Folie-Méricourt (☎01 43 55 87 65). M: Oberkampf. Take r. de Crussol across bd. Richard Lenoir and turn left on r. de la Folie-Méricourt. A trendy café-bar with a fresh artistic edge gets lively in the evenings to the sound of drum 'n' bass and acid funk. Try the ginger- or rose-flavored Absolut shots (€5.50). Coffee €1.50. 2-course *menu* €10.52. Sunday brunch. Lunch served noon-3pm; dinner served 7-11:30pm. Open M-F 7am-2am, Sa-Su 10am-2am. MC/V. ❷

TWELFTH ARRONDISSEMENT

NEIGHBORHOOD QUICKFIND: ***Discover,*** *p. 12;* ***Sights,*** *p. 110;* ***Museums,*** *p. 152;* ***Nightlife,*** *p. 215;* ***Shopping,*** *p. 243;* ***Accommodations,*** *p. 267.*

see map p. 389

L'Ebauchoir, 45, r. de Citeaux (☎01 43 42 49 31). M: Faidherbe-Chaligny. Walk down r. du Faubourg St-Antoine, turn left on r. de Citeaux. L'Ebauchoir has something of a dressed-up diner feel, but the dressing—a mix of funky and Frenchie—works. €13 lunch *menu* includes drink, and *à la carte plats* start at €11. All-day *menu* €23. Open M-Th noon-2:30pm and 8-10:30pm, F-Sa noon-2:30pm and 8-11pm. MC/V. ❸

La Connivence, 1, r. de Cotte (☎01 46 28 49 01). M: Ledru-Rollin. Take r. Rollin to r. de Charenton and turn left. R. de Cotte is on your left. An elegant and intimate restaurant with deep orange walls and mint-green tablecloths. High-class food without high-class prices. Lunch *menus* €13-16. Dinner *menus* €17-22. Choose from main courses such as veal cooked in white chocolate sauce (€13.50) and desserts like *crêpes suzettes* (€5.80). Wine €14-38 per bottle, cocktails €3-6. Open M-Sa noon-2:40pm and 7:40-11pm. MC/V. ❸

Le Cheval de Troie, 71, r. de Charenton (☎01 43 44 24 44). M: Bastille. As you're facing the Opéra, r. de Charenton is the street just to the left; the restaurant is on your left. Savory Turkish food in an appealing setting. Lunch *formule* €10.30. Feast on appetizers like *çoban salatası* (€4.70), with fresh cucumbers, tomatoes, and feta; a main course like *imambayıldı* (stuffed eggplant, €5.50); and dessert like *balli yogurt* (the house yogurt with honey and almonds, €3.90). Dinner *menu* €16. Open M-Sa noon-2:30pm and 7-11:30pm. MC/V. ❷

Les Broches à l'Ancienne, 21, r. St-Nicolas (☎01 43 43 26 16). M: Ledru-Rollin. Walk along r. du Faubourg St-Antoine away from the Bastille column and turn right onto r. St-Nicolas. Then follow your nose: the high-quality meats here are slow-cooked over flames in a stone oven. Succulent shoulder of lamb with *frites* €15. Appetizers €4.40-10.40. Photography displays in basement. Jazz F nights; dinner and performance €23-26; reservations recommended. Open M noon-2:30pm, Tu-Sa noon-2:30pm and 7:30-10:30. AmEx/MC/V. ❷

Paul Sud, 47, r. de Charenton (☎01 43 47 55 47). M: Bastille. As you're facing the Opéra, r. de Charenton is the street just to the left of you. Simple, good food at excellent, affordable prices, speedy table service, and a cheery and informal setting make Paul Sud an excellent choice for lunch, dinner, or a snack in the 12*ème*. 2-course lunch *menu* €11. Typical French *plats* like *brochette de poulet* start at €9. Salads €9-10. Also serves breakfast. Open M-F 9am-midnight. ❷

Les Grandes Marchés, 6, pl. de la Bastille (☎01 43 42 90 32). M: Bastille. Adjacent to the Opéra. Sleek, air-conditioned, and expensive (but worth it), this is among the area's nicest restaurants. Ample €22-€33 lunch *menu* includes a half-bottle of wine per person. Feast on such delicious *entrées* as creamy risotto with truffles (€13.80; most *entrées* run €12-19) before savoring one of the countless meat or fish dishes (€22.30-28.80). Open daily noon-1am. MC/V. ❹

THIRTEENTH ARRONDISSEMENT

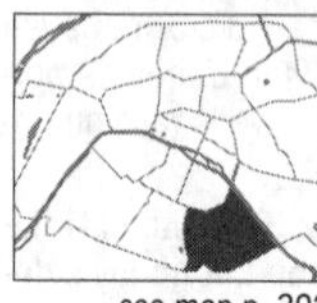

see map p. 392

NEIGHBORHOOD QUICKFIND: ***Discover,*** *p. 4;* ***Sights,*** *p. 111;* ***Nightlife,*** *p. 216;* ***Accommodations,*** *p. 268.*

The 13*ème* is a budget gourmand's dream. The **Butte-aux-Cailles's** high-spirited restaurants and bars fill to capacity with locals most nights of the weeks. Scores of Asian restaurants cluster in Paris's **"Chinatown,"** located just south of pl. d'Italie on av. de Choisy, and a number of North African restaurants crowd in near the St-Marcel métro.

Tricotin, 15, av. de Choisy (☎01 45 84 74 44). M: Porte de Choisy. This Asian eatery, one of the best in Chinatown, serves delicious food from Cambodia, Thailand, and Vietnam in two incredibly noisy but appealing cafeteria-style rooms. Patrons indulge in mild Vietnamese soups (from €6) while those who like it hot partake in spicy Thai curries (€6-6.60). The food is beautifully presented. The *vapeur* foods are specialties here—see if you can eat just one order of steamed shrimp ravioli (€3.40). Open daily 9:30am-11:30pm. MC/V. ❶

Café du Commerce, 39, r. des Cinq Diamants (☎01 53 62 91 04). M: Place d'Italie. Take bd. Auguste Blanqui and turn left onto r. des Cinq Diamants; it will be on your left. This funky and relaxed establishment serves traditional food with a twist. Dinner (€15.50) and lunch (€10.50) *menus* both feature options like *boudin antillais* (spiced bloodwurst), steak with strawberries, and *fromage blanc aux kiwis*. Open daily noon-3pm and 7pm-2am, Sa and Su brunch noon-4pm. Reservations recommended for dinner. AmEx/MC/V. ❷

L'Aimant du Sud, 40, bd. Arago (☎01 47 07 33 57). M: Les Gobelins. Walk down av. des Gobelins, then turn right onto bd. Arago. This delightful restaurant with many a sunny accolade posted in the window serves tasty food from the South of France, including a delicious *scallop de foie gras*, for a young (or young-at-heart) clientele. The emphasis of the main dishes is on steaks and fish (€13.50-18). Lunch *menu* €16. Open Sept.-Mar. Tu-Sa noon-2:30pm, 7:30-10:30pm; Apr.-Aug. M-Sa noon-2:30pm, 7:30-10:30pm. AmEx/MC/V. ❸

La Lune, 36, av. de Choisy (☎01 44 24 38 70). M: Port de Choisy. An enormous selection of Vietnamese, Thai, Cambodian, and Chinese food. All of the photographed dishes are the owner's specialties; if you're still lost, you can depend on the *banh coun* (a sort of slippery ravioli filled with spiced beef; €5). Classic soups like Vietnamese *pho* €4.25-6.25; other dishes €3.25-11.25. Open M-Tu and Th-Su 7:30am-10:30pm. MC/V. ❶

Chez Gladines, 30, r. des Cinq Diamants (☎01 45 80 70 10). M: Place d'Italie. Take bd. Auguste Blanqui and turn left onto r. des Cinq Diamants; on the corner of r. Jonas. Serves southwestern French and Basque specialties to carnivorous locals with whom you may find yourself getting cozy, given the intimate seating. 3-course lunch *menu* €9.15. Popular large salads (featuring seemingly every part of poultry intestine) €6.10-8.70. Wines by the glass €2.30. Open daily noon-3pm and 7pm-midnight. ❷

Papagallo, 25, r. des Cinq Diamants (☎01 45 80 53 20). M: Place d'Italie. Take bd. Auguste Blanqui and turn left onto r. des Cinq Diamants. The colorful facade and Spanish menu barely prepare you for the reggae ambience of this tiny restaurant/bar. Small assortment of tapas like guacamole or omelette (€4.50-6.50), main dishes for €7-10, and a *menu* for €9, but the locals come for the rum cocktails (€7). Reservations for dinner. Open M 6pm-2am, Tu-Su noon-3pm and 6pm-2am. ❷

Le Temps des Cerises, 18, r. de la Butte-aux-Cailles (☎01 45 89 69 48). M: Place d'Italie. Take r. Bobillot and turn right on r. de la Butte-aux-Cailles. A local restaurant cooperative, Le Temps has been in shared ownership between all its workers (from cook to bartender) since 1976. Classic French food like *andouillette.* Lunch €9.15, anytime *menus* €12 and €20.15. Open M-F 11:45am-2:15pm and 7:30-11:45pm, Sa 7:30-11:45pm. AmEx/MC/V. ❷

FOURTEENTH ARRONDISSEMENT

NEIGHBORHOOD QUICKFIND: ***Discover,*** *p. 4;* ***Sights,*** *p. 113;* ***Museums,*** *p. 152;* ***Nightlife,*** *p. 216;* ***Accommodations,*** *p. 269.*

see map pp. 395-396

The 14*ème* is bordered at the top by the busy **boulevard du Montparnasse,** which is lined with various restaurants, ranging from Tex-Mex chains to classic Parisian cafés. **Rue du Montparnasse,** which intersects with the boulevard, teems with delicious and reasonably priced Breton *crêperies.* The central **rue Daguerre** is a haven of vegetarian-friendly restaurants. Inexpensive restaurants cluster on **rue Didot,** and fabulously priced ethnic take-out spots and couscous restaurants line **avenue du Maine.**

Chez Papa, 6, r. Gassendi (☎01 43 22 41 19). M: Denfert-Rochereau. Walk down Froidevaux along the cemetery; the restaurant will be on the left at the intersection with Gassendi. Many of Chez Papa's delicious, generous dishes are served straight from the pot in which they were cooked. Feast on the massive *salade boyarde,* which has lettuce, potatoes, ham, cantal, and *bleu de brebis* (€6.40). Hearty *menu* (€9.15) served M-F until 4pm (the eggs poached in melted blue cheese are divine). Satisfied mostly 30-something clientele. **Also** in the 8*ème* (29, r. de l'Arcade; ☎01 42 65 43 68), 10*ème* (206, r. Lafayette; ☎01 42 09 53 87), and 15*ème* (101, r. de la Croix Nivert; ☎01 48 28 31 88). Open daily 10am-1am. AmEx/MC/V. ❷

Phinéas, 99, r. de l'Ouest (☎01 45 41 33 50). M: Pernety. Follow the traffic on r. Pernety and turn left on r. de l'Ouest. The restaurant is on your left. Wild ferns, hand-painted stained-glass windows, and one oversized crown cover the pink walls of this restaurant's two dining rooms, while in the open kitchen the chef makes *tartes salées* (€6.50-8) and *tartes sucrées* (€6-6.50) right before your eyes. The restaurant (named after a 1970s comic book character) also doubles as a comic book shrine: the menus are pasted into old comic books, and the *patronne* is

ON THE MENU

The Raw Deal

Meat-eating travelers in France will commonly encounter the "undercooked" steak problem. It's a cultural shock to realize just how rare the French like their meat, and those accustomed to dining on medium-rare or rare steak might want to reconsider when ordering red meat in France.

Some helpful vocabulary: *bien cuit* is well done, *à point* is medium-rare, *saignant* is rare (literally "bleeding"), and *bleu* is very, very rare. Expect meat to come less cooked than you imagined—"well done" in a French restaurant is like medium-rare. Only the daring would order their beef *saignant*, while truly adventurous diners might try the slightly warmed over *bleu*.

Those who develop a taste for moist red meat might delve into *steak tartare*, a raw ground beef kneaded with onions, capers, and herbs, and topped with raw egg. If planning to dine on *tartare,* choose a reputable restaurant (some prepare it at your table)—these chefs, after all, will have their hands all over your raw meat.

So how French is this recipe? It's said that the dish actually comes from the ancient clans of the Baltic states, but don't tell that to any of the Parisian restaurants that proudly list their range of *tartars* on their chalkboard menus.

famous for her extravagant comic book cakes (€5.50 per serving, minimum 6 servings; order 2 days in advance). Vegetarian options. Su brunch 11am-3pm. Open Tu-Sa 9am-noon for take-out, noon-11:30pm for dine-in. AmEx/MC/V. ❷

L'Amuse Bouche, 188, r. du Château (☎01 43 35 31 61). M: Alésia. Take av. du Maine to r. du Château. The cheery atmosphere and staff of this classy restaurant more than make up for the obscure location. The €29 dinner *menu* offers, among other things, escargots with mushrooms and lamb fondant with couscous, plus one of the delightful desserts. Reservations strongly recommended. Open Tu-Sa noon-2pm and 7:30-10:15pm. MC/V. ❹

Au Rendez-Vous Des Camionneurs, 34, r. des Plantes (☎01 45 40 43 36). M: Alésia. From the métro, walk up av. du Maine with the church St-Pierre de Montrouge to your right, turn left onto r. du Moulin Vert and right onto r. des Plantes. Bottlecaps line the bar and red lights decorate the facade of this vibrant local spot, whose patrons have included cartoonist Reiser, artist Giacommetti (whose drawing hangs proudly on the back wall), as well as a bevy of local models who flock here every weekday from a nearby modelling agency for lunch (do Parisian models actually eat?). The *menus* consist of simple, country-style dishes (€12). Reservations required. Open M-F noon-2:30pm and 7:30-9:30pm. Closed Aug. ❷

Aquarius Café, 40, r. de Gergovie (☎01 45 41 36 88). M: Pernety. Walk against traffic on r. Raymond Losserand and turn right on r. de Gergovie. A vegetarian oasis and celebrated local favorite. Their desserts are light and feel almost healthy (€3-7), and they even have organic wines. Open M-Sa noon-2:15pm and 7-10:30pm. AmEx/MC/V. ❷

CAFÉS

La Coupole, 102, bd. du Montparnasse (☎01 43 20 14 20). M: Vavin. Half-café, half-restaurant, La Coupole's Art Deco chambers have hosted Lenin, Stravinsky, Hemingway, and Einstein. Though fairly touristy and overpriced, it's still worth the nostalgic splurge on coffee (€2), hot chocolate (€3), or a *croque monsieur* (€5). The food itself, though unabashedly expensive, is considered to be among the best in Paris. Come for the dancing Tu and Th-Sa (salsa, hip-hop, garage, and R&B, respectively) 10pm-5am; cover €16. Open M-F 8:30am-1am, Sa-Su 8:30am-1:30am. AmEx/MC/V. ❹

FIFTEENTH ARRONDISSEMENT

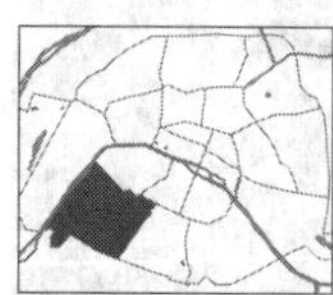

see map p. 393

NEIGHBORHOOD QUICKFIND: ***Discover,*** *p. 5;* ***Sights,*** *p. 114;* ***Museums,*** *p. 152;* ***Accommodations,*** *p. 270.*

The 15*ème* offers a diverse selection of restaurants, with traditional French cuisine alongside Middle Eastern and Asian specialities. Cheap eateries crowd **rue du Commerce, rue de Vaugirard, boulevard de Grenelle,** and **Gare Montparnasse.**

Thai Phetburi, 31, bd. de Grenelle (☎01 41 58 14 88; www.phetburi-paris.com). M: Bir-Hakeim. From the métro, walk away from the river on bd. de Grenelle; the restaurant is on your left. Award-winning food, friendly service, low prices, and a relaxing atmosphere, just minutes from the Eiffel Tower. The *tom yam koung* (shrimp soup flavoured with lemongrass; €7) and the *lab kai* (chicken in thai grass; €8.80) are both favorites. Open M-Sa noon-2:30pm and 7-10:30pm. AmEx/MC/V. ❷

Le Tire Bouchon, 62, r. des Entrepreneurs (☎01 40 59 09 27). M: Charles Michels. Run by a charming couple, Tire Bouchon serves classic French cuisine with a creative touch to a mixed crowd of Parisians and Americans. The flawless service makes up for the somewhat unexceptional decor. €20 *menu* (M-Th nights), or choose your own dishes (starters €7, main dishes €18.50). For dessert, a number of inventive departures from the standard mousse or caramel are offered, including a carrot, cumin and orange cake (€6.50). Open M and Sa 7:30-11pm, Tu-F noon-2:30pm and 7:30-11pm. MC/V. ❸

Chez Foong, 32, r. Frémicourt (☎01 45 67 36 99). M: Cambronne. From the métro, walk across pl. Cambronne, then turn left onto r. Frémicourt. At this Malaysian restaurant, the meals are superb (though the small portions may leave you hungry). Try the grilled fish in banana leaves with coconut (€11), mango and shrimp salad (€9.50), and exquisite pastries (€6). 3-course lunch *menu* €9.90 and dinner *menus* €14.50-15 (M-F). Open M-Sa noon-2:30pm and 7-11pm. MC/V. ❷

Samaya, 31, bd. de Grenelle (☎01 45 77 44 44). M: Bir-Hakeim. From the métro, walk away from the river on bd. de Grenelle; adjacent to Thai Phetburi (see above). Samaya serves traditional Lebanese food at reasonable prices. Dinner *menu* €11.50; take-away sandwiches €3.50. Vegetarians rejoice: falafel for €3. Open daily until midnight. ❷

Le Troquet, 21, r. François Bonvin (☎01 45 66 89 00). M: Sèvres-Lecourbe. From the métro, walk down r. Lecourbe and turn right on r. François Bonvin. Run by a husband-and-wife team, this hidden-away restaurant entices diners with a cuisine that blends Basque, Provençal, and Parisian flavors. *Menu* (4 plates for €28–lots of money but well spent) changes daily. Open Tu-Sa noon-2pm and 7:30-10:30pm. MC/V. ❹

Ty Breiz, 52, bd. de Vaugirard (☎01 43 20 83 72). M: Pasteur. This classic Breton *crêperie* brings a taste of Northern France to the 15*ème*, from fine and filling crêpes to clogs on the wall. Dinner crêpes €3.40-9.50. They're serious about their crêpes here: use the "p" word ("pancake!") and you may be forced to read educational pamphlets on crêpe vocabulary and the definition of a *galette.* Dessert crêpes €3.40-10.50. Open Tu-Sa 11:45am-2:45pm and 7-10:45pm. MC/V. ❶

Mozlef, 18, r. de l'Arrivé (☎ 01 45 44 77 63). M: Montparnasse-Bienvenüe. From r. Montparnasse, walk up r. de l'Arrivé; the restaurant is on your right. Mozlef serves inexpensive Middle Eastern cuisine, with no dish over €15. Take-away menu has sandwiches; more extensive meals inside. *Kebabe, salade,* and french fries €6.50. Open M-Su noon-2am. Cash only. ❶

CAFÉS

Aux Artistes, 63, r. Falguière (☎01 43 22 05 39). M: Pasteur. Follow Pasteur away from the rails and make a left onto r. Falguière. One of the 15*ème's* coolest spots, this lively café draws a mix of professionals, students, and artists. Modigliani was supposedly a regular. The chaotic decor will charm you, as will the friendly waitstaff. Lunch *menu* €9.20, dinner *menu* €12.50. Open M-F noon-2:30pm and 7:30pm-midnight, Sa 7:30pm-midnight. ❷

SIXTEENTH ARRONDISSEMENT

NEIGHBORHOOD QUICKFIND: ***Discover,*** *p. 12;* ***Sights,*** *p. 116;* ***Museums,*** *p. 153;* ***Nightlife,*** *p. 217;* ***Accommodations,*** *p. 272.*

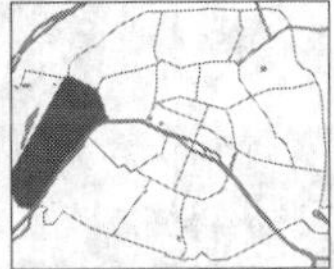

see map p. 396

A good greasy spoon (or even a cheap bistro) is hard to find in the wealthy 16*ème*, particularly in its lower half. However, there is a crowd of more budget-friendly restaurants along **rue de Lauriston,** as well as a number of picnic-friendly *traiteurs* on **rue Passy** and **avenue Mozart,** at the *marchés* on av. du Président Wilson, r. St-Didier, and at the intersection of r. Gros and r. La Fontaine (see p. 202).

Byblos Café, 6, r. Guichard (☎01 42 30 99 99). M: La Muette. Walk down r. Passy one block and turn left on r. Guichard. This airy, modern, Lebanese restaurant serves cold *mezzes* (think Middle Eastern *tapas*) that are good for pita-dipping; taboule, moutabal, moussaka, and a variety of hummus dishes, all €5.80-8. Warm *mezzes* include hot Lebanese sausages and falafel (€6.50). *Menu* €15. Takeout 15-20% less than eating in. Vegetarian options available. Open daily 11am-3pm and 5-11pm. AmEx/MC/V. ❷

Casa Tina, 18, r. Lauriston (☎01 40 67 19 24; www.casa-tina.com). M: Charles de Gaulle-Etoile. Walk down av. Victor Hugo, turn left on r. Presbourg and right on r. Lauriston going uphill. Spanish tiles, edge-to-edge tables, and dried peppers hanging from the ceiling. The food and the sangria (€5) are both divine, but expect to sacrifice leg and elbow room. €14 lunch *menu* on weekdays includes tapas, paella, and sangria. Dinner *menu* €19. Open daily 11:30am-3pm and 6pm-1am. Reservations recommended. AmEx/MC/V. In the same neighborhood is **Casa Paco,** a twin version of Casa Tina, 13, r. Bassano (☎01 47 20 98 15). ❸

the hidden deal

University Restaurants

When school is in session (Sept.-June), most of the following offer a cafeteria-style choice of sandwiches, regional and international dishes, grilled meats, and drinks for around €2.30 to those with a student ID: all listed places are open for lunch 11:30am-2pm, and Bullier, Châtelet, Citeaux, Mabillon, and Dauphine are also open for dinner 6:30-8pm. **Bullier,** 39, av. Georges Bernanos, 5*ème* (RER: Port-Royal); **Cuvier-Jussieu,** 8bis, r. Cuvier, 5*ème* (M: Cuvier-Jussieu); **Censier,** 31, r. Geoffroy St-Hilaire, 5*ème* (M: Censier-Daubenton); **Châtelet,** 10, r. Jean Calvin, 5*ème* (M: Censier-Daubenton); **Assas,** 92, r. d'Assas, 6*ème* (M: Notre-Dame-des-Champs); **Mabillon,** 3, r. Mabillon, 6*ème* (M: Mabillon); **Citeaux,** 45, bd. Diderot, 12*ème* (M: Gare de Lyon); **Tolbiac,** 17, r. de Tolbiac, 13*ème*; **Dareau,** 13-17, r. Dareau, 14*ème* (M: St-Jacques); **Necker,** 156, r. de Vaugirard, 15*ème* (M: Pasteur); **Dauphine,** av. de Pologne, 16*ème* (M: Porte Dauphine); **Bichat**, 16, r. Henri Huchard, 18*ème*.

Musée du Vin Restaurant, r. des Eaux, or 5-7, pl. Charles Dickens. M: Passy. Go down the stairs, turn right on Square Alboni, and then turn right on r. des Eaux. In the musty air of ancient wine caves, enjoy a lunch *menu* (€40) with specialized wines for each plate you choose. Smoked cheeses, foie gras, and other French delicacies will distract you from the wax monks that overlook the eating area, and you're sure not to find a more picturesquely "French" dining experience in Paris. Open M-F noon-3pm. MC/V. ❺

CAFÉS

La Rotunde de la Muette, 12, Chaussée de la Muette (☎01 45 24 45 45). M: La Muette. 2min. from the métro down Chaussée de la Muette; head towards the Jardin de Ranelagh. Located in a beautiful fin-de-siècle building overlooking the tree-lined Chaussée de la Muette. Indoors, the stylish red and yellow lamps, hip music, and plush Burgundy seats take a sleek spin on the patio's classic feel—but the outdoor seating is best. A good place for a sandwich (€5-9.60) or salad (€4-9.15) before heading to the excellent Musée Marmottan. Open daily noon-11pm. AmEx/MC/V. ❶

La Terrasse du Musée (☎01 53 67 40 47). M: Iéna or Alma Marceau. Follow directions to the Palais de Tokyo (see **Sights**, p. 116). This lively café is located directly in the porticoed, Neoclassical *terrasse* of the Musée de l'Art Moderne de la Ville de Paris. After an afternoon of High Modernism, you just may need a fig tart (€7.50) or a plate of tapenades (€8). View of the Eiffel Tower and the Seine. Salads €10.50. Open Tu-Su 10am-9pm. Cash only. ❷

SEVENTEENTH ARRONDISSEMENT

see map p. 397

NEIGHBORHOOD QUICKFIND: ***Discover,*** *p. 13;* ***Sights,*** *p. 118;* ***Museums,*** *p. 156;* ***Nightlife,*** *p. 217;* ***Accommodations,*** *p. 273.*

Far away from tourists, no restaurant in the 17*ème* can survive without strong local support. Fortunately, the variety of neighborhoods here yields an equal variety in cuisine. The best area to look for cheap, high-quality, country-style eats is in the **Village Batignolles,** around r. des Batignolles, north of r. des Dames.

Le Patio Provençal, 116, r. des Dames (☎01 42 93 73 73). M: Villiers. Follow r. de Lévis away from the intersection and go right on r. des Dames. Le Patio Provençal is a quality rustic restaurant that serves staples of southern French fare, such as *filet* *de rascasse* (€14.50). Glass of wine €2. Three course formule €24. This place is frequently super-busy, making service often a bit slow and reservations a must. Open M-F noon-2:30pm and 7-11pm. MC/V. ❷

The James Joyce Pub, 71, bd. Gouvion St-Cyr (☎01 44 09 70 32; www.kittyosheas.com). M: Porte Maillot (exit at Palais de Congrès). Take bd. Gouvion St-Cyr past Palais de Congrès. Upstairs from the pub is a restaurant with stained-glass windows depicting scenes from Joyce's novels. Spectacular Su brunch (noon-3pm) is a full Irish fry: eggs, bacon, sausage, black and white puddings, beans, chips, and coffee (€13.84). Downstairs, the pub pulls pints of what Joyce called "...Ghinis. Foamous bomely brew bebattled by bottle gagerne de guergerre..." An informal tourist office for middle-aged and younger Anglophone ex-pats. Televised sporting events; consult their weekly advertisement in *Pariscope* for times. Traditional Irish meals like stew with bacon and cabbage (€9.15). Pub open M-Th 9pm-1:30am, F-Su 10am-2am; restaurant M-Sa noon-3pm and 7:30-10:30pm, Su noon-5pm. AmEx/MC/V. ❷

Restaurant Natacha, 35, r. Guersant (☎01 45 74 23 86). M: Porte Maillot. Take bd. Gouvion St-Cyr past the Palais de Congrès and turn right on r. Guersant. This traditional French country-style *grillade* prides itself on its *pavé de boeuf* and is especially great for lunch, with an all-you-can-eat buffet for €13.50. Dinner *menu* €17.50. Open M-Th noon-2:30pm and 7:30-10:30pm, F noon-2:30pm and 7:30-11:30pm, Sa 7:30-11:30pm. Reservations recommended. MC/V. ❸

Le Bistrot de Théo, 90, r. des Dames (☎01 43 87 08 08). M: Villiers. From the métro, take r. de Lévis and turn right on r. des Dames. This classy bistro tempts with *plats* like roast duck and prunes garnished with apple and mango chutney. Lunch *menu* €12.20; dinner *menu* €22.50 or €27. Open M-Sa noon-2:30pm and 7:30-11:30pm. AmEx/MC/V. ❹

Au Vieux Logis, 68, r. des Dames (☎01 43 87 77 27). M: Rome. Take r. Boursault to r. des Dames; the restaurant is on the corner. An acclaimed but friendly local spot, this bar-restaurant features a simple and traditional 3-course lunch *menu* (€11) that changes daily. Open M-F noon-2:30pm and 8-10:45pm, Sa 8-10:45pm. AmEx/MC/V. ❷

Va et Vient, 8, r. des Batignolles (☎01 45 22 54 22). M: Rome. On the corner of r. des Batignolles and r. Caroline. Located in the heart of the Village Batignolles, this charming sidewalk bistro serves up inventive salads (€12.20) with ingredients like chicken, mango, and pineapple. Lots of meat dishes, such as the jumbo steak for two (€33). Open M-F 8am-11:30pm, Sa 10am-11:30pm. MC/V. ❷

CAFÉS

L'Endroit, 67, pl. du Dr. Félix Lobligeois (☎01 42 29 50 00). M: Rome. Follow r. Boursault to r. Legendre, and turn right. Look for the blue exterior. As cool during the day as it is at night, L'Endroit must be, well, *the place* to go in the 17ème. 4-course Su brunch (noon-3:30pm; €16) heads a long menu packed with things like melon and *jambon* (€10.80), salads (€10.70), and toasted sandwiches (€9.90). Open daily noon-2am. MC/V. ❷

Les Hortensias, 4, pl. du Maréchal de Juin (☎01 47 63 43 39 or 01 46 22 69 84). M: Pereire. In the idyllic rotunda around the park in this bustling intersection near l'Etoile. Light, airy, and busy. *Menu* includes *croque monsieur* (€5), gazpacho (€9), and salads (€9). Beer €4, *apéritifs* €4.50-5. Open daily 11am-11:30pm. MC/V. ❷

EIGHTEENTH ARRONDISSEMENT

NEIGHBORHOOD QUICKFIND: ***Discover,*** *p. 13;* ***Sights,*** *p. 119;* ***Museums,*** *p. 156;* ***Nightlife,*** *p. 218;* ***Shopping,*** *p. 245;* ***Accommodations,*** *p. 273.*

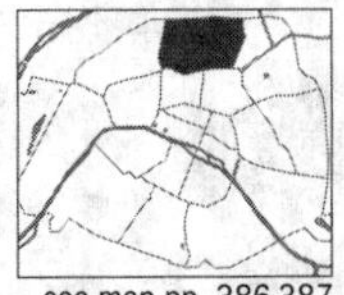

see map pp. 386-387

During the siege of Paris in 1814, Russian cossacks occupied Montmartre. They called the restaurants, where they grabbed quick bites between battles "*bistro*" (Russian for "quick"). The Russians are gone, but the tourists are here in full force, particularly around the kitschy pl. du Tertre and pl. St-Pierre. Lovely bistros and cafés are common between **rue des Abbesses** and **rue Lepic,** along **rue des Trois Frères,** and touristy (but charming) piano bars can be found

the hidden deal

Dining on the Green

In a city not known for its culinary friendliness towards vegetarianism, there are at least a few diamonds in the rough. **Au Grain de Folie,** in the 18*ème*, is one such gem. Both vegetarians and vegans (and maybe even those ever-suspicious carnivores) will leave this small, unassuming vegetarian hide-out on a quiet side street happy. The friendly staff serves delightful veggie treats at great prices. Try the *grain de folie* plate (€11), which includes grilled goat cheese, lentils, grains, grilled vegetables and fresh salad. Also gracing the menu are *entrées* like fresh guacamole (€6), salads (€9-10), and delicious desserts (including frozen bananas doused in chocolate; €5). Vegan options are available.

*Au Grain de Folie, 24, r. Lavieuville, 18*ème *(☎01 42 58 15 57). From M: Abbesses, take r. Lavieuville; the restaurant is near the intersection with r. des Trois Frères. Coffee €2, wine €2-3, beer €3.50. Open M-Sa 12:30-2:30pm and 7:30-11pm, Su 12:30-11pm.* ❷

around **Place du Tertre.** In addition to the listings below, **Chez Louisette** and **Au Baryton,** which are within the **Puces de St-Ouen** (flea market) just north of the 18*ème*, offer *moules marinière*, *frites*, and live French *chanson* entertainment (see **Shopping,** p. 248).

Le Soleil Gourmand, 10, r. Ravignan (☎01 42 51 00 50). M: Abbesses. Facing the church in Place des Abbesses, head right down r. des Abbesses and go right (uphill) on r. Ravignan. This local favorite with funky artistic flare serves inventive and refreshingly light *Provençale* fare. Try the specialty *bricks* (grilled stuffed filo dough; €11), 5-cheese *tartes* with salad (€10), and house-baked cakes (€4.50-7). The menu is rounded out with vegetarian options like the *assiette sud* (€12), a generous collection of grilled and marinated vegetables. Evening reservations a must. Open daily 12:30-2:30pm and 8:30-11pm. ❷

Refuge des Fondues, 17, r. des Trois Frères (☎01 42 55 22 65). M: Abbesses. Walk down r. Yvonne le Tac and take a left on r. des Trois Frères. Only 2 main dishes: *fondue bourguignonne* (meat fondue) and *fondue savoyarde* (cheese fondue). The wine (2 choices: red or white) is served in baby bottles with rubber nipples; leave your Freudian hang-ups at home and join the family-style party at the 2 long tables. *Menu* with *apéritif,* wine, appetizer, fondue, and dessert €15. Reserve a table or show up early. Open daily 6:30pm-2am (but they don't accept new diners after 12:30am). Closed Aug. ❸

Chez Ginette, 101, r. Caulaincourt (☎01 46 06 01 49). M: Lamarck-Caulaincourt. Upstairs from the métro. This unspoiled slice of Montmartre attracts locals with inventive French dishes, like filet with foie gras sauce (€20.80). Omelettes €7.50. Open daily 9am-2am. Closed Aug. AmEx/MC/V. ❸

Chez Guichi, 76, r. Myrha (☎01 42 23 77 99). M: Barbès-Rochechouart. From the métro, walk up bd. Barbès and turn right onto r. Myrha. Guichi's owners opened this local watering hole in order to provide cheap North African cuisine to local merchants. Don't let the oppressively bright fluorescent lights or floor-to-ceiling mirrors fool you; Parisians come from all over the city to sample Guichi's specialty, *brochette foie gras* (€10). Sandwiches €4-7.50. *Plats* €6-10.50. A little desolate at night so aim for lunch here. Open Su-Th noon-4pm and 7-11pm, F noon-4pm. ❷

Wassana, 10, r. Ganneron (☎01 44 70 08 54). M: Place de Clichy. Walk up av. de Clichy; make the fifth right. Pink dining room and delicious Thai food 5min. from the corpse of Stendhal (in the Cimitière Montmartre). Lunch *menus* (€10.40 and €13.45) include fish and lemon soup, chicken in coconut milk, and sautéed beef with ginger and mushrooms. *Entrées* €5.40-10.40. *Plats* €7.60-13.50. Open M-F noon-2:30pm and 7-11:30pm, Sa 7-11:30pm. AmEx/V. ❷

CAFÉS

Le Sancerre, 35, r. des Abbesses (☎01 42 58 08 20 or 01 42 58 47 05). M: Abbesses. Facing the church in pl. des Abbesses, head right on r. des Abbesses. Classic Montmartre café with a scruffy bohemian crowd, topless mermaids on the ceiling, and interesting dishes like *bruschettas* (€7.70-8.50) and *chili con carne* (€10). Hip 20-somethings congregate at night on the terrace. Beer €3.20-4.20, *apéritifs* €3.90-7, wines €3.40-5.40. Sa-Su brunch €11. Open daily 7am-2am. MC/V. ❶

Halle St-Pierre, 2, r. Ronsard (☎01 42 58 72 89). M: Anvers. Walk up r. de Steinkerque, turn right at pl. St-Pierre, then left onto r. Ronsard. A quiet café in the gallery of the same name (see **Museums,** p. 156), with assorted coffee and tea (€1.30-3.20), cookies, brownies, and cakes (€2.50-3), and the major French newspapers. A pleasant setting, relatively free from the tourists outside. Open Tu-Su 10am-6pm. ❶

NINETEENTH ARRONDISSEMENT

NEIGHBORHOOD QUICKFIND: ***Discover,*** *p. 14;* ***Sights,*** *p. 123;* ***Accommodations,*** *p. 274.*

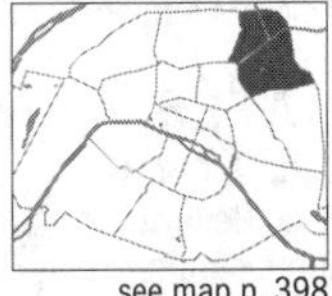
see map p. 398

The ethnically diverse 19*ème* offers its finest budget dining in **Little Chinatown,** where Chinese, Vietnamese, Thai, and Malaysian restaurants cluster along **rue de Belleville** (M: Belleville). Greek sandwich shops line **avenue Jean Jaurès** and **rue de Crimée.** The **Parc des Buttes-Chaumont** is a winning spot for a picnic.

Lao Siam, 49, r. de Belleville (☎01 40 40 09 68). M: Belleville. With a wall full of articles touting the Thai and Chinese cuisine served up at this local favorite, it's no surprise that every bite is worth writing about. A unique dried calamari salad (€8.40) makes for a light preamble to the *Poulet Royal au curry* (€8.40) or *boef piquant au basilic* (€7.60). Wash it down with a *citron presse* (€2.30) and finish it off with kumquats (€2.80) and you'll forget that you came so far out of your way. Non-smokers get the front of the restaurant (for once), though the decor is pleasant throughout. Open daily noon-3pm, 6:30-11:30pm. MC/V. ❷

Aux Arts et Sciences Réunis, 161, av. Jean-Jaurès (☎01 42 40 53 18). M: Ourcq. A short stroll away after a day at La Villette. Serving up hearty southwestern meals family-style, Aux Arts brings in a local crowd. *Plats* like salmon with hollandaise sauce €12.90-21.50. Lunch *menu* €9.50. French piano music during dinner Sa. Open M-Sa 7:30am-10:30pm. Food served noon-2:30pm and 7:30-10:30pm. MC/V. ❸

Ay, Caramba!, 59, r. de Mouzaïa (☎01 42 41 23 80). M: Pré-St-Gervais. From the métro, turn right on r. de Mouzaïa. With nightly Mariachi music and sombreros on the wall, Ay, Caramba! stands out in its quiet, residential neighborhood. Pricey but generous fajitas and tacos €16. *Nachos paisa* €6.90. Margaritas €7. Open daily 7:30pm-11pm, open for lunch F-Su noon-2:30pm. AmEx/MC/V. ❸

CAFÉS

La Kaskad', 2, pl. Armand-Carrel (☎01 40 40 08 10). M: Laumière. Wander into La Kaskad' after a morning in the Parc des Buttes-Chaumont, for a big, creative salad (€11), a dessert (€6) or coffee (€2). Open daily 8am-2am. MC/V. ❷

TWENTIETH ARRONDISSEMENT

NEIGHBORHOOD QUICKFIND: ***Discover,*** *p. 14;* ***Sights,*** *p. 123;* ***Museums,*** *p. 157;* ***Nightlife,*** *p. 218;* ***Shopping,*** *p. 245;* ***Accommodations,*** *p. 275.*

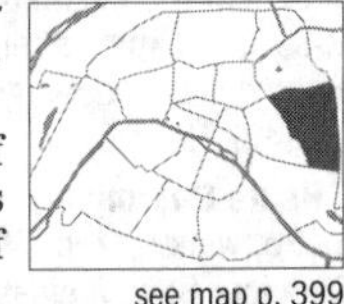
see map p. 399

A traditional meal amid Belleville's cobblestones is a breath of fresh air after Paris's crowded center. A number of trendy cafés and bistros line **rue St-Blaise** in the south. Come for lunch if you're in the neighborhood, or just plain lost.

Café Flèche d'Or, 102, r. de Bagnolet (☎01 43 72 04 23; www.flechedor.com). M: Alexandre Dumas. Follow r. de Bagnolet until it crosses r. des Pyrénées; the café is on the right. Near Porte de la Réunion at Père Lachaise. In a defunct train station, this bar/café/performance space serves North African, French, Caribbean, and South American cuisine with nightly jazz, ska, folk, salsa, and samba (cover €5-6). Political cafés the first Sa morning of every month and political debates every other Su morning. Dinner *menus* €12-15. How's that for eclectic? Su brunch *menu* €11. Bar/café open daily 10am-2am; dinner daily 8pm-1am. MC/V for charges over €15.25. ❷

La Bolée Belgrand, 19, r. Belgrand (☎01 43 64 04 03). M: Porte de Bagnolet. Take the Hôpital Tenon exit from the métro and the restaurant will be across the street. In cramped but friendly quarters, this *petite crêperie* serves up delicious crêpes to a local crowd of families and couples. Make sure you order a bottle of *cidre* (€3.50-7.50) with your meal. Lunch *menu* €10. Crêpes €3-8.50. Salads €3-7. Open Tu-Sa noon-2pm and 7-11pm. MC/V. ❷

Le Zéphyr, 1, r. Jourdain (☎01 46 36 65 81). M: Jourdain. Walk along Belleville toward the church and turn left onto r. Jourdain. A classic Parisian bistro with unique dishes and snappy 1930s decor. 4-course dinner *menu* €26. Lunch *menu* €12.50. Reservations recommended. Open M-F noon-2pm and 8-11pm, Sa 8-11pm. MC/V. ❹

CAFÉS

Rital & Courts, 1, r. des Envierges (☎01 47 97 08 40). M: Pyrénées. Walk down the sloping r. de Belleville, turn left on r. Piat, and turn left on r. des Envierges. This pleasantly funky Italian restaurant/café/bar perches on a corner across from Parc de Belleville and offers spectacular views along with delicious meals. Lasagne €11. Lunch *menu* €10.50 or €13. Open daily 11am-midnight; lunch noon-2pm, dinner 8-10pm, crowded bar 10pm-midnight. ❷

SALONS DE THÉ

Parisian *salons de thé* (tea rooms) fall into three categories: those stately salons straight out of the last century and piled high with macaroons, Seattle-style joints for pseudo-intellectuals, and cafés that simply want to signal that they also serve tea.

Ladurée, 16, r. Royale, *8ème* (☎01 42 60 21 79). M: Concorde. Ever wondered what it would be like to dine inside a Fabergé egg? The rococo decor of this classic tea salon attracts the well-groomed shoppers that frequent the pricey boutiques in the area. Famous for the mini macaroons stacked in the window (€5). Pastry counter for take-away. Specialty tea *Ladurée mélange* €6.50. Su brunch €29. Open daily 8:30am-7pm; lunch served until 3pm. AmEx/MC/V. Also at 75, av. des Champs-Elysées, *8ème* (☎01 40 75 08 75). M: FDR.

Angelina's, 226, r. de Rivoli, *1er* (☎01 42 60 82 00). M: Concorde or Tuileries. Audrey Hepburn's old favorite. Little has changed here since the *salon*'s 1903 opening.; the frescoes, mirrored walls and marble tables are all original. *Chocolat africain* (hot chocolate; €6.20) and *Mont Blanc* (meringue with chestnut nougat; €6) are the dangerous house specialties. Tea €6. Open daily 9am-7pm. AmEx/MC/V.

Mariage Frères, 30, r. du Bourg-Tibourg, *4ème* (☎01 42 72 28 11). M: Hôtel-de-Ville. Started by 2 brothers who found British tea shoddy, this salon offers 500 varieties of tea (€7-15), from Russian to Vietnamese. The subtle, white-suited waiters and the sophisticated clientele make this a classic French institution. Tea *menu* includes sandwich, pastry, and tea (€25). Classic brunch *menu* is excellent (brioche, eggs, tea, cakes; €25). Reserve for brunch. After eating, exit through the impressive tea store which sells a wide variety of books (such as *The Art of French Tea*), pots of tea, and tea kettles (metallic €75, glass €160, and purely ornamental porcelain with Chinese calligraphy €230). Open daily 10:30am-7:30pm; lunch M-Sa noon-3pm; afternoon tea 3-6:30pm; Su brunch 12:30-6:30pm. AmEx/MC/V. **Also** at 13, r. des Grands Augustins, *6ème* (☎01 40 51 82 50). M: St-Michel; and at 260, r. du Faubourg St-Honoré, *8ème* (☎01 46 22 18 54).

L'Heure Gourmand, 22, passage Dauphine, *6ème* (☎01 46 34 00 40). M: Odéon. From the métro, walk up r. de l'Ancienne Comédie and turn right onto the passage Dauphine after the Carrefour Buci. A classy, quiet little *salon de thé* that has a terrace on a beautiful side street.

The inside, with its magenta carpets, jazz music, and romantic balcony upstairs, is a lovely setting for sipping tea. First Su of every month, they host a tribute to French song with covers of Jacques Brel and Georges Brassens, 5-7pm. All teas €4.50, Berthillon ice cream €7-8, pastries €3-6. Open M-Sa noon-9pm, Su noon-7pm. MC/V.

Le Loir Dans la Théière, 3, r. des Rosiers, *4ème* (☎01 42 72 90 61). M: St-Paul. From the métro, cross r. de Rivoli, follow r. Pavée, and take a right on r. des Rosiers. The door mouse from *Alice in Wonderland* (after whom the tea shop is named) drowns in his teapot on the mural gracing this laid-back, artsy salon. Serves curious caramel tea (€4) and curiouser coffees (€2-4.50). Sa-Su brunch (€14.50-20). Open M-Sa 11am-7pm, Su 10am-7pm. MC/V.

Muscade, 36, r. de Montpensier, *1er* (☎01 42 97 51 36). M: Palais-Royal. In the Palais-Royal's northwest corner, Muscade has mirrored walls and art by Cocteau. *Le Chocolat a l'Ancienne* (€5) is a melted chocolate bar parading as a liquid. An assortment of pastries (€6) and 26 kinds of tea (€4). Terrace open in summer; reservations recommended. Open Tu-Su for tea 10-11:30am and 3-6pm; lunch 12:15-3pm; dinner 7:15-10:30pm. Closes 7pm Su. AmEx/MC/V.

FOOD SHOPS & MARKETS

Restaurants and cafés are well and good, but you will not have had a complete French eating experience if you don't forego fine dining at least once and strike out on your own. Trust us, Parisians can often be found with hamper and baguette, munching in parks or crunching on *quais*. One tour of some choice food stores, and you'll be ready to join them; picnic ingredients are generally cheap and always delectable. Here's a guide to the different types of specialty shops around Paris.

A **charcuterie** is the French version of a delicatessen, a *crémerie* sells dairy products, and the corner **fromagerie** may stock over 100 kinds of cheese. **Boulangeries** will supply you with your daily bread—they're usually best visited in the early morning or right before mealtimes, when the baguettes are steaming hot. **Pâtisseries** sell pastries, and **confiseries** sell candy; both often vend ice cream as well. You can buy your produce at a **primeur,** your meat and poultry at a **boucherie,** and all manner of prepared foods at a **traiteur. Epiceries** (grocery stores) have staples, wine, and produce. A **marché,** an open-air market (held weekly; see p. 202), is the best places to buy fresh produce, fish, and meat. Finally, you

Le pain

Pâtisserie

Au marché

in recent news

How the Cheese Crumbles

According to legend, the creation of camembert cheese coincides with that of the French Republic. In 1791, a milkmaid from Normandy combined a local recipe with the process used to make brie and *voilà*: a national symbol was born.

But while the French still consume more cheese than any other nation–25kg per person annually–camembert is no longer the nation's *fromage préféré*. Camembert now accounts for a mere 10% of cheese sales.

Producers blame the decline in popularity on a changing economy subject to the rules of the EU. Farmers now sell their cheeses to large industrial groups rather than directly to picky *fromageries*. Additionally, the EU's obsession with cleanliness has led to stringent regulations, forcing cheese makers to leave behind their stone-walled buildings and the natural yeasts that accumulated on their walls and equipment and gave camemberts their distinct flavor. Producers also claim that ultra-clean milk demanded by the EU leads to tasteless cheese.

Camembert is also falling victim to supermarket culture. Less pungent, pre-wrapped cheeses are taking up more shelf space. For camembert, made from full-fat milk, convenience has replaced convention.

can grab an array of simple food items, cigarettes, and lotto tickets at any corner **dépaneur** (convenience store).

Supermarchés (supermarkets) are, of course, also an option, but they're no fun. Do capitalize on the one-stop shopping at the **Monoprix** and **Prisunics** that litter the city (48 in all). They carry men's and women's clothing and have photocopiers, telephone cards, and a supermarket. They are usually open during the week until 9pm; the Prisunic at 52, av. Champs-Elysées is open until midnight. Starving students swear by the ubiquitous **Ed l'Epicier** and **Leader Price.** At both you can buy in bulk and save a good amount of money. **Picard Surgelés,** with 50 locations in the city, stocks every food ever frozen—from *crêpes* to calamari.

One more piece of advice: French storeowners are very touchy about people touching their fruits and vegetables; unless there's a sign that says *libre service*, ask inside before you start handling the goods displayed.

SPECIALTY SHOPS

Food shops, particularly *boulangeries* and *pâtisseries*, can be found on virtually every street in Paris, and most of them are very good. The following listings, arranged by *arrondissement*, are among the best specialty food shops that Paris has to offer; all deserve a ☒.

BOULANGERIES

Julien, 75 r. St-Honoré, 1*er* (☎01 42 36 24 83). The best of everything: breads, sandwiches, pastries, cakes. For an indulgent breakfast, try the *pain au chocolat* (a flaky, buttery chocolate croissant) or the very different but equally delicious *pain chocolat* (a small loaf of bread with chocolat chips). The lines at lunch get quite long.

Poujauran, 20, r. Jean-Nicot, 7*ème* (☎01 47 05 80 88). M: La Tour-Maubourg. A taster's delight, selling a wide range of *petit pains*, or miniature breads, alongside their bigger brothers (and sisters). Try bread studded with olives, herbs, figs, or sesame seeds, or dive right into dessert with one of several kinds of hearty tarts and cookies. 2 *petit pains* average €1.50. Open Tu-Sa 8:30am-8:30pm.

Au Coin du Pétrin, 96, r. des Entrepreneurs, 15*ème* (☎01 45 79 36 67). M: Felix Faure. Walk against traffic on the left side of the church; turn left onto r. des Entrepreneurs. Devotees gladly make the trek to this bakery, home to an award-winning *baguette traditionnelle* and a hard-working staff. One bit of your favorite indulgence will have you coming back for more. Try their sandwiches (€3-5). Open M-Sa 7am-9pm.

CHOCOLATERIES

Jadis et Gourmande, 39, r. des Archives, *4ème* (☎01 48 04 08 03). M: Rambuteau. Offers up delightful chocolates, and some of the richest ice cream in town. 1 scoop €2. Open M 1-7:30pm, Tu-F 10am-7:30pm, Sa 10:30am-7:30pm.

La Maison du Chocolat, 8, bd. de la Madeleine, *9ème* (☎01 47 42 86 52). M: Madeleine. A whole range of exquisite chocolates, from milk to dark, and, for those tired of the usual consumption of solid chocolates, a mysterious distilled chocolate essence drink. Box of 2 chocolates €3.30. **Also** at other locations, including 19, r. de Sèvres, *6ème* (☎01 45 44 20 40). Open M-Sa 10am-7pm. MC/V.

CONFISERIES

La Cure Gourmande, 88, r. St-Martin, *3éme* (☎01 42 71 26 18; www.la-cure-gourmande.com). M: Rambuteau. This one-of-a-kind candy shop prepares its original treats using only natural ingredients. Indulge in the amazing almond-olive chocolates (€3.60 per 100g) and the scrumptious house bon-bons (€16.50 per can), or play it cheap with €0.80 lollipops. Open daily 10am-7:30pm, June-Aug. until 9:30pm. MC/V.

Confiserie Rivoli, 17, r. de Rivoli, *4ème* (☎01 42 72 80 90). M: St-Paul. While far from gourmet, this warehouse of reasonably-priced goodies will tempt even the sweetest sweet tooth. Caramel coated camembert and chocolate Eiffel Towers (both €2.50). Haribo gummy bears by the tub (€8.80). Open M-Sa 10am-6:30pm. AmEx/MC/V.

EPICERIES

L'Epicerie, 51, r. St-Louis-en-l'Île, Île St-Louis (☎01 43 25 2014). A condiment mecca. Homemade jams, sweets, mustards, olive oil, vinegar, and even flavored sugar are found inside this shop. Perhaps the tastiest souvenirs you could bring home from Paris.

Izrael, 30, r. François Miron, *4ème* (☎01 42 72 66 23). M: St-Paul. Barrels of nuts and dried fruits jostle with fresh pesto, bottles of HP Sauce bump up against pricey exotic alcohols, and classic French tins and plate-ware abound, all in one amazing gourmet-food bazaar. American favorites like peanut butter and instant oatmeal available. Open Tu-F 9:30am-1pm and 2:30-7pm, Sa 9am-7pm. MC/V.

Fauchon, 26, pl. de la Madeleine, *8ème* (☎01 47 42 60 11). M: Madeleine. Paris's favorite gourmet food shop (complete with gourmet prices), this *traiteur/pâtisserie/épicerie/charcuterie* has it all. Go home with a prettily packaged tin of *madeleines*, or browse their wine cellar, one of the finest in Paris. Open M-Sa 10am-7pm. MC/V.

Tang Frères, 48, av. d'Ivry, *13ème* (☎01 45 70 80 00). M: Porte d'Ivry. Look for no. 44 and go down a few steps, or look for no. 48 and follow the sign through a parking lot. Chinatown's answer to Wal-Mart, this huge shopping center in the heart of Chinatown contains a grocery store, flower store, bakery, and porcelain shop. Rice, spices, teas, soups, and noodles in bulk. Also a sassy selection of exotic fruit (durian, €5 per kg), cheap Asian beers (Sapporo and Kirin €1.19), rice wines, and sake. Open Tu-Sa 11am-7:30pm.

O&CO, locations throughout Paris. Sells high-quality olive oils made in France. Olives are harvested from farms in Provence and other regions throughout the Mediterranean, like Italy, Spain, and Tunisia. Gifts can be wrapped to make it safely home. Bottles range from €5.80-11.90. Also sells olive, fruit, and herb spreads, along with other gourmet food products and olive oil-related cooking accessories. Most branches open M-Sa 10am-8pm.

FROMAGERIES

Fromages...ou Desserts, 13, r. Rambuteau, *3ème* (☎01 42 72 73 56). M: Rambuteau. Follow the scent of cheese. Any type of cheese you can imagine and then some can be found at this cheese-lover's paradise. Open Su and Tu-Sa noon-2:30pm and 4:30-8pm.

Androuët, 19, r. Daguerre, *14ème* (☎01 43 21 19 09). Amid the many food stores that decorate Androuët's street, this little cheese shop is notable for its beautiful decorated cheeses, many of which are patterned with leaves or studded with raisins. Open Tu-Th 9am-1pm and 4-8pm, F-Sa 9am-8pm.

MARCHAND DE VIN

Nicolas, locations throughout Paris. Super-friendly English-speaking staff is happy to help you pick the perfect Burgundy. They will even pack it up in travel boxes with handles. Most branches open M-F 10am-8pm. AmEx/MC/V.

PÂTISSERIES

Au Panetier, 10, pl. des Petits Pères, 2*ème* (☎01 42 60 90 23). M: Bourse. Known for its wide selection of sweet pastries. Experiment with whatever you see for the first time here—you won't go wrong. The beautifully tiled Au Panetier—one of the oldest pastry shops in Paris—also creates delectable sandwiches (€2.30-3.35) and savory tarts. Open M-F 8am-7pm.

Gérard Mulot, 76, r. de Seine, 6*ème* (☎01 43 26 85 11). M: Odéon or St-Sulpice. Outrageous selection of painstakingly crafted pastries, from flan to marzipan with virtually any kind of fruit. The *macaron* is heaven on earth (€4.19). Tarts from €2.50; éclairs €2; mousse chocolat noisettes €6.10. Open Tu and Th-Su 7am-8pm.

MARKETS (MARCHÉS)

In the 5th century, ancient Lutèce held the first market on what is now Île de la Cité. More than a millennium and a half later, markets exude conviviality and neighborliness in every *arrondissement*, despite the ongoing growth of the *supermarché*. Most are open two to six days per week (always on Sunday). The freshest products are often sold by noon, when many stalls start to close. Quality and price can vary significantly from one stall to the next, making it a good idea to stroll through the entire market before buying.

Marché r. Montorgueil, 2*ème*. M: Etienne-Marcel. From métro, walk along r. Etienne Marcel away from the river. R. Montorgueil is the 2nd street on your right. A center of food commerce and gastronomy since the 13th century, the marble Mount Pride Market is comprised of wine, cheese, meat, and produce shops. Open Tu-Su 8am-7:30pm.

Marché Monge, 5*ème*. M: Monge. In pl. Monge at the métro exit. A bustling, friendly, and easy-to-navigate market. You'll find everything from cheese to shoes to jewelry and flowers in these stalls. Look for the very popular prepared foods (perfect for a lunch picnic at the Arènes de Lutèce). Open W, F, and Su 8am-1:30pm.

Marché Port Royal, 5*ème*. M: Les Gobelins. Walk downhill to the major intersection, turn left onto bd. de Port Royal, look for the stalls in front of the hospital (about 10 min.). Sells mostly fresh vegetables, fruit, meat and cheese, mostly to locals. Some clothes and housewares also for sale. Open Tu, Th, and Sa 7am-2:30pm.

Marché Mouffetard, 5*ème*. M: Monge. Walk through pl. Monge and follow r. Ortolan to r. Mouffetard. Cheese, meat, fish, produce, and housewares sold here. The bakeries are reputed to be some of the best of all the markets, and don't miss the ice cream at Octave near the far end of the market. Open Tu-Su 8am-1:30pm.

Marché Biologique, on bd. Raspail between r. du Cherche-Midi and r. de Rennes, 6*ème*. M: Rennes. French new-agers peddle everything from organic produce to 7-grain bread and tofu patties. Open Su 7am-1:30pm.

Marché St-Quentin, 85bis, bd. de Magenta, 10*ème*. M: Gare de l'Est or Gare du Nord. Outside: a massive construction of iron and glass, built in the 1880s, renovated in 1982, and covered by a glorious glass ceiling. Inside: stalls of all varieties of produce, meat, cheese, seafood, and wine. A small bar in the center for those in need of a break. Open Tu-Sa 8am-1pm and 2:30-7:30pm, Su 8am-1pm.

Marché Bastille, on bd. Richard-Lenoir from pl. de la Bastille north to r. St-Sabin, 11*ème*. M: Bastille. Produce, cheese, exotic mushrooms, bread, meat, and housewares stretch all the way from M: Richard Lenoir to M: Bastille. Popular Su morning family outing. Open Th and Su 7am-1:30pm.

Marché Popincourt, on bd. Richard-Lenoir between r. Oberkampf and r. de Jean-Pierre Timbaud, 11*ème*. M: Oberkampf. Fresh, well-priced fruits, vegetables, meat and fish. A smattering of vendors selling essentials you may need to restock before your next European stop—

socks, sunglasses, shoes, shirts and underwear. A DJ in the center of the market announces special deals while he spins all the latest Edith Piaf jams. Open Tu and F 7am-2:30pm.

Marché Beauvau St-Antoine, on r. d'Aligre between r. de Charenton and r. Crozatier, 12*ème*. M: Ledru-Rollin. One of the largest Parisian markets, lined with Muslim *halal* butcher shops and restaurants. Busiest on weekends. Quality of produce varies between stands. Produce market open Tu-Sa 8am-1pm and 4-7:30pm, Su 8am-1pm. Tag sale daily 8am-1pm.

Marché Président-Wilson, on av. Président-Wilson between r. Debrousse and pl. d'Iéna, 16*ème*. M: Iéna or Alma-Marceau. An alternative to the 16*ème's* exorbitantly priced restaurants. Agricultural and dairy products, meat, and fish. Flower stalls, clothing, table linens, and other household goods. Open W and Sa 7am-2:30pm.

Marché Berthier, on bd. de Reims between r. de Courcelles and r. du Marquis d'Arlandes, along pl. Ulmann, 17*ème*. M: Porte de Champerret. Turn left off bd. Berthier onto r. de Courcelles, then right on bd. de Reims. Follow the scent of produce—the cheapest in Paris. North African and Middle Eastern specialties like fresh mint, Turkish bread, and baklava. Open W and Sa 7am-2:30pm.

INSIDE

Nightlife

AN OVERVIEW

BARS & PUBS. Bars in Paris are either nighttime cafés bursting with Parisian people-watching potential or more laid-back Anglo havens. In the *5ème* and *6ème*, bars cater to French and foreign students, while the Bastille and Marais teem with Paris's young and hip, gay and straight. Les Halles and surroundings draw a slightly older set, while the outer *arrondissements* cater to the full range of locals in tobacco-stained bungalows and yuppie drinking holes.

CLUBS. Clubbing is less about hip DJs and cutting-edge beats, and more about dressing up, getting in, and being seen. Drinks are expensive and people drink little. Many clubs accept reservations, which means that on busy nights, there will be no available seating. It is advisable to dress well, to come early, to be confident but not aggressive about getting in, and to come in a couple if you can. Clubs are usually busiest between 2 and 4am.

BISEXUAL, GAY, & LESBIAN NIGHTLIFE. The Marais is the center of gay and lesbian life in Paris. Most gay bars and clubs cluster around r. du Temple, r. Ste-Croix de la Bretonnerie, r. des Archives, and r. Vieille-du-Temple in the *4ème* (see p. 209). A number of lesbian bars can be found in the *3ème* (see p. 207). For the most comprehensive listing of gay and lesbian restaurants, clubs, hotels, organizations, and services, consult *Illico* (free at gay bars and restaurants), *Gai Pied's* annually updated book *Guide Gai* (€13 at kiosks and bookstores), or weekly magazine Zurban's annual *Paris Gay and Lesbian Guide* (€5 at any kiosk). **Les Mots à la Bouche,** Paris's largest gay and lesbian bookstore, serves as an unofficial information center for queer life; they can tell you what's hot now (see **Shopping,** p. 239).

BY ARRONDISSEMENT

FIRST ARRONDISSEMENT

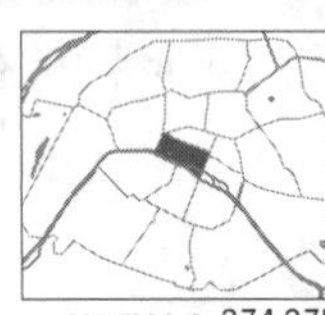
see map p. 374-375

NEIGHBORHOOD QUICKFIND: ***Discover,*** *p. 7;* ***Sights,*** *p. 73;* ***Museums,*** *p. 146;* ***Food & Drink,*** *p. 171;* ***Shopping,*** *p. 235;* ***Accommodations,*** *p. 254.*

Banana Café, 13-15, r. de la Ferronerie (☎01 42 33 35 31). M: Châtelet. From the métro, take r. Pierre Lescot to r. de la Ferronerie. This *très branché* (way cool) evening arena is the most popular gay bar in the 1*er*, and draws an extremely mixed group; head downstairs for a more exclusively male crowd. Legendary theme nights. The "Go-Go Boys" W-Sa midnight-dawn. During Happy Hour (6-9pm) drinks are 2 for 1, except cocktails. Beer M-F €5.18, Sa-Su €6.71. Open daily 4pm-dawn. AmEx/MC/V.

Le Fumoir, 6, r. de l'Amiral Coligny (☎01 42 92 05 05). M: Louvre. As cool and ritzy by night as it is by day. Extra dry martini €10.40-11.40; champagne €11.00. Happy Hour 6-8pm with €6 cocktails. See full listing in **Food & Drink,** p. 172.

Café Oz, 18, r. St-Denis (☎01 40 39 00 18). M: Châtelet. From the métro take the r. de Rivoli exit, walk down r. de Rivoli, and make a left onto r. St-Denis. **Also** 1, rue de Bruxelles 9*ème* (01 40 16 11 16) M: Blanche. Huge, friendly Australian bar with pine benches, big tables, and happy-to-be-of-service bartenders. DJ W-Sa spinning brand new retro during the week and dance music on weekends. Pint €6. Happy Hour daily 6-8pm with cocktails €5. Open Su-Th 3pm-2am, F 3pm-3am, Sa noon-3am. MC/V.

The Flann O'Brien, 6, r. Bailleul (☎01 42 60 13 58). M: Louvre-Rivoli. From the métro, walk away from the Seine on r. du Louvre and make the first right after crossing r. de Rivoli. Arguably the best Irish bar in Paris, Flann is often packed, especially on live music nights (F-Su). Go for the Guinness and stay for the reportedly good "crack" downstairs (that's Irish for good fun). Demi €4, full pint €6. Open daily 6pm-5am.

SECOND ARRONDISSEMENT

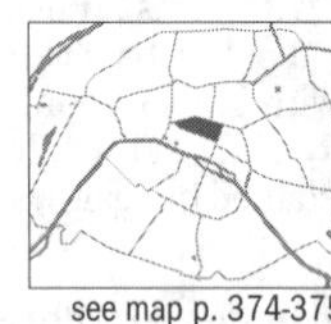
see map p. 374-375

NEIGHBORHOOD QUICKFIND: ***Discover,*** *p. 7;* ***Sights,*** *p. 77;* ***Food & Drink,*** *p. 172;* ***Shopping,*** *p. 235;* ***Accommodations,*** *p. 255.*

Le Champmeslé, 4, r. Chabanais (☎01 42 96 85 20; lachampmesle.no-ip.com). M: Pyramides or Quatre Septembre. From the métro, walk down av. de l'Opéra and make a right on r. des Petits Champs, and make another right onto r. Chabanais. This welcoming lesbian bar is Paris's oldest and most famous. Mixed crowd in the front, but women-only in back. Beer €4. Cocktails (€8) garnished with a glow stick. Popular cabaret show Th 10pm (first drink is €8). Enjoy a free drink during the month of your birthday. Monthly art exhibits. No cover. Open M-Th 2pm-2am, F-Sa 2pm-2am. MC/V.

Le Café Noir, 65, r. Montmartre (☎01 40 39 07 36). M: Sentier. From the métro, walk down r. Réaumur and make a left onto r. Montmartre. Plastic creatures hanging from the ceiling, crazy tiling on the floor, and bartenders leaping onto the bar to perform comedy. A true mix of locals and Anglophones: patrons gladly overcome language barriers to meet one another. Beer €2-3. Open M-F 8am-2am and Sa 2pm-2am. AmEx/MC/V.

Harry's New York Bar, 5, r. Daunou (☎01 42 61 71 14). M: Opéra. Walk down r. de la Paix and turn left onto r. Daunou. The kitsch birthplace of the Bloody Mary (€10) hosts businessmen, tourists, and couples in their 30s and 40s. Claiming to be the "oldest cocktail bar in

Europe," Harry's tries to make international students feel at home with college flags and foreign currencies on the walls. Beer €5.40 Open daily 11am-4am. Downstairs 1920's style piano bar. Tu-Sa 10pm-2am. Slightly higher drink prices. AmEx/MC/V.

Frog & Rosbif, 116, r. St-Denis (☎01 42 36 34 73). M: Etienne-Marcel. At the corner of r. St-Denis and r. Tiquetonne. As if a slice of High Street had been plugged in next to the peep shows. Live rugby and football broadcasts, house ales, and the typical entourage of Englishmen. Happy Hour 6-8pm, but for students it's all night long on Thursday (€4.20 beer and cocktails). Otherwise beer €5.80 cocktails €5.50. Open daily noon-2am. MC/V.

DANCE CLUBS

Le Pulp, 25, bd. Poissonnière (☎01 40 26 01 93). Internet: pulp.xroot.fr M: Grands Boulevards. This legendary lesbian club has an old school movie theater feel with red couches and drapes, and an intimately low ceiling. House and techno are the mainstays. Drinks €6-10.50. Crowd tends to be quite mixed, except on Sa when it is mostly women; men welcome if accompanied by women. Cover Th free; F-Sa €8 (includes first drink). Open Th-Sa midnight-5am.

Rex Club, 5, bd. Poissonnière (☎01 42 36 10 96). M: Bonne-Nouvelle. A non-selective club which presents the most selective of DJ line-ups. Very young clubbers crowd this casual venue to hear cutting-edge techno, jungle and house fusion from international DJs on one of the best sound systems in Paris. Large dance floor and lots of seats as well. Shots €4-5, beer €5-7. Cover €8-13. Open Th-Sa 11:30pm-6am.

Le Scorp, 25, bd. Poissonnière (☎01 40 26 01 93). M: Grands Boulevards. A casual gay dance club located underneath the famed Le Pulp. Women may come, but very few do. Big dance floor with raised seating areas on either side and black paint (and black lights) throughout. W disco, Th Oh là là (French songs), weekends vary. Drinks €5-10.50. Cover (includes first drink) Th €9, weekends €12, W Free. Open W-Sa midnight-5am.

THIRD ARRONDISSEMENT

NEIGHBORHOOD QUICKFIND: ***Discover,*** *p. 8,* ***Sights,*** *p. 79;* ***Museums,*** *p. 146;* ***Food & Drink,*** *p. 174;* ***Shopping,*** *p. 237;* ***Accommodations,*** *p. 257.*

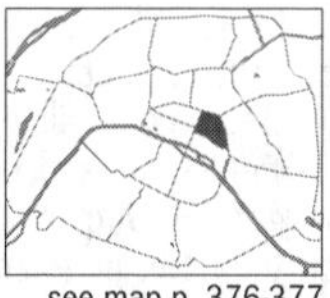
see map p. 376-377

Nightlife in the *3ème* is more subdued than the scene found in the neighboring *4ème*—for the most part, women (and men, too) can leave their stiletto heels at home. There

Le Fumoir

Au Duc des Lombards

Le Piano Vache

from the road

Sketch in the City

Some time past 2am, as smoke pumped onto the dance floor (and alcohol pumped through my veins), I watched the over-60-bar-prowler giving the you-can't-touch-me-twink. A fresh-out-of-the-closet wallflower was hiding in his corner, gawking at shirtless muscle queens. Here, at one of Paris's most popular gay clubs, the usual cast of characters was present. But though the players were wearing the same clothes and dancing to the same music as anywhere else, the game, I found out, was completely different.

When a friend and I entered the club (in the name of research, I assure you), sultry neon signs presented us with two options: "clubbing" or "cruising." Feeling a bit uptight, I decided to claim my complimentary drink at the bar. As I sat sipping my vodka tonic, I felt a hand on my left thigh, and then on my right. Two buff boys were groping me. "Are you innocent?" they asked. Of course I am. "Do you want to come with us to our chateau tomorrow?" Dream on.

Less inhibited after a second drink, I ventured into the designated "cruising" area. Stepping through fake vines, I entered a labyrinth of dark rooms and darker corridors,

are a number of gay and lesbian bars in the area on and around **rue aux Ours, rue St-Martin,** and **rue Michel Le Comte.**

L'Apparemment Café, 18, r. des Coutures St-Gervais. M: St-Paul. Beautiful wood and red lounge with games and a calm, young crowd. Late-night meals €10-13, served until closing. (See **Food & Drink,** p. 175, for full listing.)

Villa Keops, 58, bd. Sébastopol (☎01 40 27 99 92). M: Etienne-Marcel. Walk east on r. Etienne Marcel; Villa Keops is on the corner with bd. Sébastopol. Stylish, candlelit couch bar where the boy-toy waiters are as beautiful as the designer drinks. *The* place to show your face (before doing the same at Les Bains). Divine Rose du Nile €8.50, caramelized vodka €7.50. Happy Hour 8-10pm. Open M-Th noon-2am, F-Sa noon-4am, Su 4pm-3am. AmEx/MC/V.

Boobs Bourg, 26, r. de Montmorency (☎01 42 74 04 82). M: Rambuteau. Walk against traffic on r. Beaubourg and turn right onto r. de Montmorency. This is where the well-spiked, stylishly punk girls go to find each other. Always lively at night, occasional daytime lectures and discussions. Boys can come accompanied by women, but this is a girls' bar all the way. Beer on tap €3.80, mixed drinks €7. Open Tu-Su 5:30pm-2am. MC/V.

Le Duplex, 25, r. Michel Le Comte (☎01 42 72 80 86) M: Rambuteau. A great place to make friends instead of trouble. Small and intimate atmosphere features a computer where patrons can snap photos to remember their evening. Not an exclusively male bar, and anyone is welcome, but few women hang out here. Beer €2.60 until 10pm, €3.50 after. Cocktails €7.30. Open Su-Th 8pm-2am, F-Sa 8pm-4am.

Utopia, 15, r. Michel Le Comte (☎06 17 11 90 13). M: Rambuteau. With the slogan *"Parlez-moi d'amour, faites moi connaitre!"*, Utopia comes complete with house beats, pool, pinball, and a club downstairs Sa. Older women dominate the supposedly "mixed" crowd. Beer €3.20. Open M-Sa 5pm-2am. Cash only.

DANCE CLUBS

Les Bains, 7, r. du Bourg l'Abbé (☎01 48 87 01 80). From M: Etienne-Marcel or Réaumur-Sébastopol, take r. Etienne Marcel east, turn left onto bd. Sébastopol, and take the next right. Look for the long line of people. Ultra-selective, super-crowded, and expensive. It used to be a public bath, visited at least once by Marcel Proust. More recently, Mike Tyson, Madonna, Mick Jagger, and Jack Nicholson have stopped in. Models on the floor; mirrored bar upstairs. Funky house and garage grunge; W hip hop. Cover (includes first drink) Su-Th €16, F-Sa €19. Drinks €11. Open daily 11pm-6am. AmEx/MC/V.

Le Dépôt, 10, r. aux Ours (☎01 44 54 96 96; www.ledepot.com). M: Etienne-Marcel. Take r. Etienne Marcel east; it becomes r. aux Ours. A veritable pleasure complex for gay men. Dance for inspiration, but don't waste time on small talk; just take your boy toy of the night to one of the rooms in the downstairs labyrinth. Find said boy toy in the designated "cruising" area while watching porno on mounted TVs. Women welcome after 11pm on the upstairs dance floor. The post-Su-brunch Gay Tea Dance is especially popular. Disco M, House/Techno W, Queer Mother Night Th, visiting DJ F, House Sa (called "*Putas* at Work"). Cover includes first drink; M-Th €7.50, F €10, Sa €12, Su €10. Open daily 2pm-8am. V.

FOURTH ARRONDISSEMENT

NEIGHBORHOOD QUICKFIND: ***Discover,*** *p. 8;* ***Sights,*** *p. 81;* ***Museums,*** *p. 147;* ***Food & Drink,*** *p. 175;* ***Shopping,*** *p. 237;* ***Accommodations,*** *p. 258.*

see map p. 376-377

No matter where you are in the *4ème*, a bar is close by. With the exception of Les Enfants Gâtés, all the **cafés** listed on p. 176 also double as bars. Spots with outdoor seating are piled on top of one another on **rue Vieille-du-Temple,** from r. des Francs-Bourgeois to r. de Rivoli. Gay bars crowd **rue Ste-Croix-de-la-Bretonnerie.** The bars on **rue des Lombards** have a more frat-house atmosphere.

Chez Richard, 37, r. Vieille-du-Temple (☎01 42 74 31 65). M: Hôtel-de-Ville. Inside a courtyard off r. Vieille-du-Temple, this bar's stone interior, hidden balcony, yellow lighting, slowly spinning ceiling fan, and shadow-casting palm leaves are reminiscent of Casablanca. A hot spot to people-watch on weekends, but ideal for chilling on weekdays, with hip bartenders and smooth beats. Happy Hour 6-8pm. Beer €4-6, cocktails €9. Open daily 6pm-2am. AmEx/MC/V.

Lizard Lounge, 18, r. du Bourg-Tibourg (☎01 42 72 81 34). M: Hôtel-de-Ville. A happening, split-level space for American Anglo/Franco college kids. Underground cellar has DJs every night from 10pm; M open DJ night, Tu and Th Drum and Bass, W and F House and Techno, Sa German House. Happy Hour upstairs 6-8pm, throughout bar 8-10pm (pints and cocktails €4.60). "Lizard Juice" €7.50. Open daily noon-2am. Food served noon-3pm and 7-10:30pm, brunch Sa-Su noon-4pm. MC/V.

Les Etages, 35, r. Vieille-du-Temple (☎01 42 78 72 00). M: St-Paul. Set in an 18th-century hotel-turned-bar. Its 3 floors are filled with neither the super-chic

the only light coming from pornographic films playing on mounted TVs. All around me, shadowy figures entered cell-like rooms together. I didn't hear any talking—just the opening and closing of doors. In each room, a lubricant dispenser was visible on the wall. Condoms could be purchased from vending machines in the hall.

Walking through the corridor, I saw men lined up against the wall. By watching the men in front of me, I learned the rules of engagement. A walker expresses his desire for a rendez-vous by staring at a man against the wall. After a five to ten second confirmation stare, the two go on their merry way.

Knowledge of this simple courting technique is critical to preventing misunderstandings. Searching for a clock, I found one on the cruising wall. Little did I know that a man's eyes were in my line of vision. I wanted the time (3:45am), not a cheap thrill. He stared back, assuming that the mating ritual was underway; a prompt *"Non, merci!"* ended his advance.

After unsuccessfully searching for my friend, I decided that he had succumbed to temptation, and I left the club. Watching strangers stumble home together, I realized that the French *joie de vivre* can take scintillating forms. At Le Dépôt, the desire for pleasure streamlines social foreplay. Bluntness replaces pretense and talk is unnecessary. The players here know the rules of this game—and before you decide to play in their arena, you should, too.

—William Lee Adams

nor scary-sketch. This non-threatening crowd basks in dim orange-red lighting. €4 cocktails during Happy Hour (3:30-9pm)—they'll bring it to you with a side of nuts. Su 11am-4pm. Open daily 3:30pm-2am. MC/V.

Amnésia Café, 42, r. Vieille-du-Temple (☎01 42 72 16 94). M: Hôtel-de-Ville. A largely gay crowd comes to lounge on plush sofas in Amnésia's classy wood-paneled interior. This is one of the top see-and-be-seen spots in the Marais, especially on Sa nights. Espresso €2; *kir* €4. Open daily 10:30am-2am. MC/V.

Cox, 15, r. des Archives (☎01 42 72 08 00). M: Hôtel-de-Ville. As the name suggests, this is a buns-to-the-wall men's bar with bulging and beautiful boys. So crowded that the guys who gather here block traffic on the street. Cruisy and hypersexualized; not place for a quiet weekend cocktail. Happy Hour (beer half-off) daily 6-9pm. Beer €3.30. Open daily noon-2am.

Mixer Bar, 23, r. Ste-Croix de la Brettonerie (☎01 48 87 55 44). M: St-Paul. Boys, boys, and more boys, but this is a "mixed" bar, or so they say. Packed even early in the night, with Marais crawlers soaking in the beer and 3 nightly DJs above the doorway (from 6pm). Happy hour 6-8pm. Beer €2.80-3.50; mixed drinks €7. Open daily 5pm-2am. AmEx/MC/V.

Les Scandaleuses, 8, r. des Ecouffes (☎01 48 87 39 26). M: St-Paul. Walk with traffic along r. de Rivoli and turn right onto r. des Ecouffes. The Marais's hippest, best-known lesbian bar set to techno beats. Men welcome accompanied by women. Downstairs club with DJ F-Sa. Beer €4-6, *cocktail scandaleux* €7.20. Happy Hour 6-8pm. Open daily 6pm-2am. MC/V.

Le Café du Trésor, 5, r. du Trésor (☎01 42 74 35 17). M: St-Paul. Walk along r. de Rivoli in the direction of traffic, turn right onto r. Vieille-du-Temple and right onto the pedestrian r. du Trésor. This newly redone restaurant/bar/club complex takes up most of the block. Classy and minimalist, it's ultra-sophisticated white interior (complete with glass chandeliers) draws crowds. Beer €4-5, frozen margaritas €9. Open daily 9am-2am; food served M-F 12:30-3pm and 8-11:30pm, Sa-Su 12:30-11:30pm. MC/V.

Café Klein Holland, 36, r. du Roi de Sicile (☎01 42 71 43 13). M: St-Paul. From St-Paul, take r. Pavée and turn left onto r. du Roi de Sicile. An easy-going, stylish Dutch bar with friendly bartenders and a lively atmosphere. The candy-sweet vodka banana is €6, beer €2.75. Dishes like the Kip Sate €10. Open daily 5pm-2am; food served 6:30-10:30pm, but lip-smacking, deep fried Dutch snacks served all night long (€2.50-10). MC/V.

Open Café, 17, r. des Archives (☎01 42 72 26 18). M: Hôtel-de-Ville. The most popular of the Marais gay bars, often drawing a large crowd of loiterers to its corner. Women welcome, but most patrons are men. Bring your sassiest attitude and wear your tightest pants. Beer €3.30, cocktails €6.90. Open daily 11am-2am. Happy Hour 6-9pm. AmEx/MC/V.

La Belle Hortense, 31, r. Vieille-du-Temple (☎01 48 04 71 60). M: St-Paul. Walk with traffic along r. de Rivoli and turn right onto r. Vieille-du-Temple. A breath of fresh air for those worn out by the *hyper-chic* scene along the rest of the *rue,* but you still need to fit in here; these are *intellectuels.* Varied wine selection from €3 a glass, €20-36 a bottle. Coffee €1.30-2. Walls and walls of books (literature, art, philosophy) and (shocker!) some really mellow music to go with your merlot. Frequent exhibits, readings, lectures, signatures, and discussions in the small leather-couch-filled back room. Open daily 5pm-2am. MC/V.

Au Petit Fer à Cheval, 30, r. Vieille-du-Temple (☎01 42 72 47 47; www.cafeine.com). M: Hôtel-de-Ville. A Marais institution with a horseshoe bar, sidewalk terrace, and small restaurant in the back. Serves up the best mojito in Paris (€7.50-8.50). Beer €2.50-10, cocktails €7.5-8.50. For more on their food, see **Food & Drink,** p. 175. Open daily 10am-2am. MC/V.

Le Quetzal, 10, r. de la Verrerie (☎01 48 87 99 07). M: Hôtel-de-Ville. Nicknamed *l'Incontournable* (it's been around for over 15 years!), this spacious black-lit men's bar plays everything from rap to techno and runs the gamut from stylish to shady. The cruisy Quetzal is opposite the r. des Mauvais Garçons (Bad Boys). Beer €3.20, mixed drinks €6.25. Happy Hour 5-9pm and Su-Th 11pm-midnight. Open daily 5pm-5am. MC/V.

Bliss Kfé, 30, r. du Roi de Sicile (☎ 01 42 78 49 36). M: St. Paul. This "sensitive lounge bar" takes the edge off with comfy leather chairs, dim lighting, and (surprise) mellow lounge music. A mixed crowd of young things gather here, but cute-ish women rule the terrain. Cocktails €7.70. Try a *Charmer* and then drown in *Bliss*. Open daily 5pm-2am.

Le Masque Rouge, 49, r. des Blancs Manteaux (☎01 40 27 97 42). M: Rambuteau. Walk east on r. Rambuteau, turn right onto r. du Temple, and make a left onto r. des Blancs Manteaux (at this corner you may already hear the bouncer calling out to invite you in). Energetic crowd and hysterical bar staff. Piano bar F-Sa featuring local musicians and sassy drag queen Blanche. Not the place for a quiet drink; come to revel in the campiness of it all. Happy Hour 6-9pm (beer €2.75). Beer €3.20-5, cocktails €4-6.50. Open daily 5pm-2am. MC/V.

Stolly's, 16, r. Cloche-Perce (☎01 42 76 06 76). M: St-Paul. On a dead-end street off r. du Roi de Sicile. This small Anglophone hangout pulls off "dive-bar cool" with ease. Crowd usually overflowing into the street. Friendly bartenders and bar-goers make you feel at home, as do the €12 pitchers of cheap blonde and lifesize papier-mâché animals. Happy Hour 5-8pm (€10 pitchers). Cocktails €6-8. Open daily 4:30pm-2am (but last call comes early).

L'Unity, 176-178, r. St-Martin (☎01 42 72 70 59). M: Rambuteau. Walk down r. Rambuteau and turn right on r. St-Martin. This women's club features a pool table, cards and boardgames at the bar, and a soundtrack of reggae, folk, rock, and techno. Men welcome if accompanied by women. Happy Hour M-F 4-8pm. Beer €3.60-7, cocktails €3.50-7. Open daily 4pm-2am.

Le Bar du Palmier, 16, r. des Lombards (☎01 42 78 53 53). M: Châtelet. Walk north on bd. de Sébastopol and turn right on r. des Lombards. With a mixed crowd and a nice terrace for people-watching, the Palmier is fun if you need a place to go after 2am. Ignore or indulge the tropical theme. Happy Hour 6-8pm, 15% off everything. Beer €3.50-5. Serves food all the time. Salads €6-9. Sandwiches €3.50-6.50. Open daily 5pm-5am. AmEx/MC/V.

FIFTH ARRONDISSEMENT

NEIGHBORHOOD QUICKFIND: ***Discover,*** *p. 3;* ***Sights,*** *p. 86;* ***Museums,*** *p. 148;* ***Food & Drink,*** *p. 177;* ***Shopping,*** *p. 239;* ***Accommodations,*** *p. 259.*

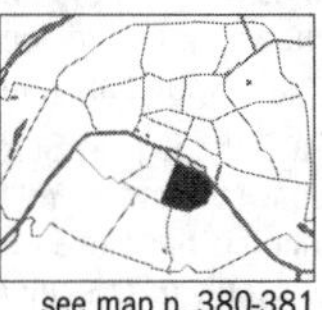

see map p. 380-381

Le Caveau des Oubliettes, 52, r. Galande (☎01 46 34 23 09). M: St-Michel. Walk from pl. St-Michel on quai de Montebello and turn right on r. Petit Pont, then left onto r. Galande. Three scenes in one, all with a mellow, funky atmosphere: the upstairs bar ("La Guillotine") has sod carpeting, ferns, and a real guillotine; the downstairs cellar is an outstanding jazz club; beneath the club, you can romp through the narrow "*caveau des oubliettes*" (cave of the forgotten ones), where criminals were locked up and forgotten. Free *soirée boeuf* (jam session) Su-Th 10:30pm-1:30am; F-Sa concerts €7.50. Beer €3.70-4.10. Rum Cocktail €3.80. Happy Hour daily 5-9pm. Open daily 5pm-2am.

Le Reflet, 6, r. Champollion (☎01 43 29 97 27). M: Cluny-La Sorbonne. Walk away from the river on bd. St-Michel, turn left on r. des Ecoles, then right. Small, low-key, and crowded with students and workers stopping by for a post-cinema drink (it's opposite 3 theatres). Beer €1.90-2.70, cocktails €5, salads €7-9. Open M-Sa 10am-2am, Su noon-2am. MC/V.

Who's Bar, 13, r. Petit Pont (☎01 43 54 80 71) M: St-Michel. Walk away from pl. St-Michel on quai Montebello, and make a right onto r. Petit Pont. This hopping bar is right in the swing of things, by r. de la Huchette and the Seine. Live music, some of it not too terrible, starting nightly at 10:30pm, and a dance club in the basement on weekends. Beer €4.50-5, cocktails €9. Happy Hour daily 6-10pm, all drinks half-price. Open Su-Th 6pm-4am, F-Sa 6pm-6am.

Finnegan's Wake, 9, r. des Boulangers (☎01 46 34 23 65). M: Cardinal Lemoine. An Irish pub set in a renovated ancient wine cellar with low, black-beamed ceilings. Have a pint (€3.50) with the boisterous crowd of students and soak up some Irish culture. F night concerts of traditional Irish music, jazz, rhythm and blues, and rock in the *cave* from 5pm on. Happy Hour daily 6-8pm. Open M-F 11am-2am, Sa-Su 6pm-2am.

Le Piano Vache, 8, r. Laplace (☎01 46 33 75 03). M: Cardinal Lemoine or Maubert-Mutualité. From the métro, walk up r. de la Montagne Ste-Geneviève and make a right on r. Laplace. Once a butcher-shop, now an extremely dark, poster-plastered bar hidden behind the Panthéon and full of cow paraphernalia. Not for those scared of the dark (or of loud music), but the more goth-oriented will love it. Happy Hour 6-9pm. Beer €2-3.50, cocktails €6.10. Goth night W 8pm-2am; Celtic night first Tu of every month. Open July-Aug. M-F 6pm-2am, Sa-Su 9pm-2am; Sept.-June M-F noon-2am, Sa-Su 9pm-2am.

SIXTH ARRONDISSEMENT

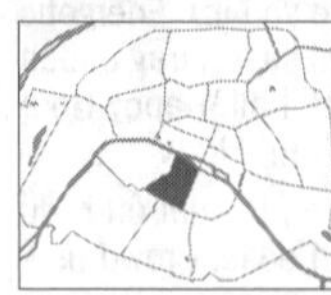
see map p. 380-381

NEIGHBORHOOD QUICKFIND: ***Discover,*** *p. 3;* ***Sights,*** *p. 91;* ***Museums,*** *p. 148;* ***Food & Drink,*** *p. 181;* ***Shopping,*** *p. 239;* ***Accommodations,*** *p. 261.*

Le Bar Dix, 10, r. de l'Odéon (☎01 43 26 66 83). M: Odéon. From the métro, walk against traffic on bd. St-Germain and make a left on r. de l'Odéon. Le Bar Dix is a classic student hangout where you might overhear existentialist discussions in the downstairs cellar area. After several glasses of their famous sangria (€3), you might just feel inspired to join in. The bar's great jukebox plays everything from Edith Piaf to Aretha Franklin. Open daily 5:30pm-2am.

Bob Cool, 15, r. des Grands Augustins (☎01 46 33 33 77). M: Odéon. From the métro, walk up r. de l'Ancienne Comédie, turn right on r. St-André-des-Arts, and turn left on to the small r. des Grands Augustins. Bob Cool has laid-back clientele, a friendly vibe, and a reputation among those in the know for being one of the best bars in the entire city. The music is at the discretion of the bartender and veers all over the spectrum, from salsa to The Corrs. Ask for sweeties with your drinks and you'll be pleasantly surprised. Mexican *mezcal* €8.50, wine €4. Open daily 5pm-2am.

Le Crocodile, 6, r. Royer-Collard (☎01 43 54 32 37). M: Cluny-La Sorbonne. From the métro, walk up bd. St-Michel 7 blocks and make a left onto r. Royer Collard (10min.). A lively, rowdy crowd of twentysomethings packs into this unassuming little bar on a quiet side street in the heart of the 6*ème*. With the some 238 tasty cocktails (€8, before midnight M-Th €6) to choose from, this local place is not for the beer-swigging crowd; nevertheless, the remarkable (and remarkably potent) concoctions are sure to delight. Open M-Sa 10:30pm-4am.

Fu Bar, 5, r. St-Sulpice (☎01 40 51 82 00). M: Odéon. Take Carrefour d'Odeon to r. de Condé; then turn right on r. St-Sulpice. A multilevel haven for a boisterous Anglophone crowd, this hip bar serves an astounding array of tantalizing martinis (€6-8) along with the regular bar fare. Tu is student night, when martinis are half-off all night long and students pack the place almost to bursting. Happy Hour daily 4-9pm. Open daily 4pm-2am.

Moosehead, 16, r. des Quatre Vents (☎01 46 33 77 00; www.mooseheadparis.com). M: Odeon. From the métro, walk towards r. d'Odeon, and take a right onto r. des Quatre Vents. Moosehead is frequented by a welcoming crowd of expats and French-speakers, this creatively decorated Canadian bar feeds the masses with Su brunch and a restaurant open until 11pm—its burgers are said to be among Paris's best. Those yearning for a glass (or pitcher) of Canadian beer will be delighted with the selection (€4.80-6.20). Others can choose from Australia, New Zealand, Chile, and France (bottle €15-26). Ladies' Night Tu. Happy Hour daily 4-9pm. Restaurant open M-F 4-11pm, Sa-Su 11:30am-11pm. Bar open M-Sa noon-2am, Su 11:30-2am.

Chez Georges, 11, r. des Canettes (☎01 43 26 79 15). M: Mabillon. Walk down r. du Four and turn left on r. des Cannettes. Upstairs, Chez Georges is an elegant wine bar with a mixed crowd; downstairs it's a smoky, candlelit cellar rampant with students. Beer €3.50-4.50, wine €1.30-3.20. Upstairs open Tu-Sa noon-2am, cellar open 10pm-2am. Closed Aug.

Café Mabillon, 164, bd. St-Germain (☎01 43 26 62 93). M: Mabillon. This hyper fast-track café-bar with lavender lights, hard techno, and snappy attitude draws the area's Gucci-wearing glamor girls and black-clad "it" boys. Drinks are pricey (fancy cocktails €10.20-11.50), but maybe it's worth it for a late-night glimpse of St-Germain's in-crowd in action. Happy Hour daily 7-9pm. Open daily 8am-6am. MC/V.

L'Assignat, 7, r. Guénégaud (☎01 43 54 87 68). M: Mabillon or Odéon. From the métro, walk down r. Mazarine off bv. St-Germain and make a right on r. Guénégaud. Very neighborhood-oriented and very cheap (beer €1.60, wine €1.90, and warm milk €1.25 at the counter), this little pub named after a Revolutionary bank note is quite popular with the student crowd, in part because of its busy foosball table. Irregular jazz happenings. Open M-Sa 9am-11pm. Closed July.

SEVENTH ARRONDISSEMENT

NEIGHBORHOOD QUICKFIND: ***Discover,*** *p. 4;* ***Sights,*** *p. 96;* ***Museums,*** *p. 149;* ***Food & Drink,*** *p. 183;* ***Shopping,*** *p. 242;* ***Accommodations,*** *p. 262.*

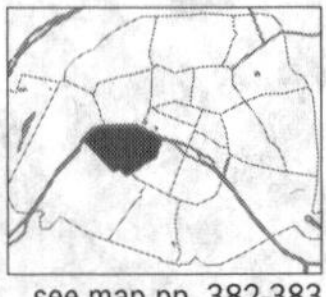

see map pp. 382-383

Le Club des Poètes, 30, r. de Bourgogne (☎01 47 05 06 03; www.poesie.net). M: Varenne. Walk up bd. des Invalides with the Invalides behind you and to your left; go right on r. de Grenelle and left onto r. de Bourgogne. Since 1961, Jean-Pierre Rosnay has been making "poetry contagious and inevitable—*vive la poésie!*" A restaurant by day, Le Club des Poètes is transformed at 10pm each night when a troupe of readers and comedians, including Rosnay's family, bewitch the audience with poetry from Villon, Michaux, Rimbaud, and others. If you arrive after 10pm, wait to enter until you hear clapping or a break in the performance. Not cheap (dinner without wine €20), but come for a drink after 10pm to be part of the fun. Lunch *menu* €15. Drinks €9, for students €5-7. Open M-Sa noon-2:30pm and 8pm-1am; food served until 10pm. AmEx/MC/V.

Malone's, 64, av. Bosquet (☎01 45 51 08 99). M: Ecole Militaire. Chic mahogany decor and warm candlelight create a surprisingly easy-going atmosphere, enhanced by the friendly waitstaff. Jazz downstairs several nights a week. Cocktails (try the grasshopper) €8. Beer €5. Tasty snacks like *croques* and *tartines* served until closing, €4.90-5.90. Open M-Sa 5pm-2am, Su 5pm-1am. MC/V.

O'Brien's, 77, r. St-Dominique (☎01 45 51 75 87). M: La Tour Maubourg. Follow traffic along bd. de La Tour Maubourg. A bustling Irish pub with a horseshoe-shaped bar. TV plays sports matches in the evenings (everything from darts to soccer). Happy Hour M-F from opening time until 8pm, pints €5. Otherwise, 25cl beer €4-5, 50cl beer €6-7, cocktails €7. Open M-Th 6pm-2am, F-Su 4pm-2am. MC/V.

EIGHTH ARRONDISSEMENT

NEIGHBORHOOD QUICKFIND: ***Discover,*** *p. 9;* ***Sights,*** *p. 100;* ***Museums,*** *p. 150;* ***Food & Drink,*** *p. 184;* ***Shopping,*** *p. 243;* ***Accommodations,*** *p. 263.*

see map pp. 384-385

buddha-bar, 8, r. Boissy d'Anglas (☎01 53 05 90 00; www.buddha-bar.com). M: Madeleine or Concorde. An experience you won't soon forget. If you're going to break the bank, this is the place to do it. The legendary buddha-bar is in fact an elegant bar and restaurant that combines candlelight and music (buddha-bar cd compilations are big sellers) to create an evening so close to perfect, you won't notice the difference. A jolly, giant buddha keeps watch over those really important (and often really famous) people eating on the ground floor; the upstairs has a more relaxed atmosphere. See **The Big Splurge**, p. 184, for more on the restaurant. Mixed drinks and martinis €12; the mysterious Delight (€12.50) is indeed that. Weekday lunch menu €32 includes wine and café. Open M-F noon-3pm and daily 6pm-2am.

House of Live, 124, r. La Boétie (☎01 42 25 18 06) M: Franklin D. Roosevelt. Walk toward the Arc on the Champs; r. La Boétie will be the second street on your right. Formerly the Chesterfield Café. This friendly and happening American bar has first-class live music, scheduled most nights of the week, and usually free. Americans and Francophones mix happily inside the red-brick walls. Snack bar has good ol' Yankee fare: hamburgers €11, brownies €5.50, key lime pie €5.90. Cocktails €6.80, beer €6, coffee €2-4. No cover Su-Th. Open daily 9am-5am. AmEx/MC/V.

Asian Bar-Restaurant, 30, av. Georges V (☎01 56 89 11 00; www.asian.fr). M: George V. Large plush chairs, smooth lounge music, and a truly impressive menu of cocktails attract many travelers, primarily of the wealthy European and Asian business magnate types. This versatile venue goes from restaurant to tearoom to bar depending on the time of day. Champagne €11, cocktails €10-11, Beer €7.50. Happy Hour 6-8pm. *Menus* €23-58. Open Su-F noon-2am, Sa 5pm-2am.

Green Party

Degas's painting *L'absinthe* (1875) features the green concoction **absinthe** being downed at a Pigalle café. Some think Van Gogh owed much of his inspiration—and madness—to it. Ernest Hemingway wrote: "that opaque, bitter, tongue-numbing, brain-warming, stomach-warming, idea-changing liquid alchemy." Picasso, Toulouse-Lautrec, and hordes of Parisians once drank it fanatically.

First distilled in 1792 from the wormwood plant *(Artemisia absinthium)* and chlorophyll, which makes it green, the 120-proof, licorice-like drink was first used by French soldiers in Algeria to foil dysentery. They returned to France in the 1830s with a taste for the stuff, and soon all of Paris was riding the green wave. Bars had *l'heure vert* (green hour), where water was poured onto a sugar cube and into the green liquor. Some spoke of the *fée verte* (green fairy) that stole the drinker's soul, while others warned of *le péril vert.* In 1915, it was outlawed in France. *Pernod* tastes similar, but for the real thing, most of us will probably have to settle for anecdotes—maybe for the best. "After the first glass," wrote Oscar Wilde, "you see things as you wish they were. After the second, you see things as they are not. Finally you see things as they really are, and that is the most horrible thing in the world."

DANCE CLUBS

Latina Café, 114, av. des Champs-Elysées (☎01 42 89 98 89). M: George V. Drawing one of the largest nightclub crowds on the Champs, Latina Café plays an energetic world music mix, including salsa, Cuban, and hip hop. Basement club, 1st fl. café, 2nd fl. restaurant. Drinks €9-11. Women Su-Th, men pay €7 cover which includes a drink. €16 cover F-Sa includes first 2 drinks. Café open daily 7:30pm-2am, club open daily 11:30am-6:30am.

Le Queen, 102, av. des Champs-Elysées (☎01 53 89 08 90). M: George V. Where drag queens, superstars, models, moguls, and go-go boys get down to the mainstream rhythms of a 10,000-gigawatt sound system. Her Majesty is one of the cheapest and most fashionable gay clubs in town, but caters to a mix of tastes. Girls welcome! Some nights are rumored to end in a wild foam bath. M disco; Th-Sa house; Su 80s. Cover Su-Th €12, includes 1 drink. F-Sa €18. All drinks €9. Open daily midnight to dawn. AmEx/MC/V.

NINTH ARRONDISSEMENT

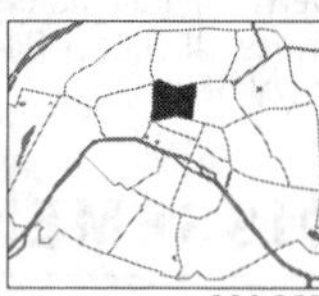
see map pp. 386-387

NEIGHBORHOOD QUICKFIND: ***Discover,*** *p. 9;* ***Sights,*** *p. 105;* ***Museums,*** *p. 151;* ***Food & Drink,*** *p. 186;* ***Accommodations,*** *p. 264.*

Folies Pigalle, 11, pl. Pigalle (☎01 48 78 55 25). M: Pigalle. Largest, wildest club in the sleazy Pigalle *quartier*—not for the faint of heart. A former strip joint, the Folies is popular with both gay and straight clubbers. Mostly house and techno. Always crowded. Open Su 5pm-6am, Tu-Th midnight-6am, F-Sa midnight-noon. €20 cover includes first drink. Drinks €10. AmEx/MC/V.

Bus Palladium, 6, r. Fontaine (☎01 53 21 07 33). From M: Pigalle, walk down r. Jean-Baptiste Pigalle, turn right on r. Fontaine, and look for the blue and silver facade. Getting past the bouncers can be tough—look hot. A trendy, beautiful crowd rocks this rock 'n' roll club, which still sports vintage posters and faded gilded decor. Cover €16. Tu free cover and drinks for ladies. Drinks €13. Open Tu-Sa 11pm-6am. AmEx/V.

ELEVENTH ARRONDISSEMENT

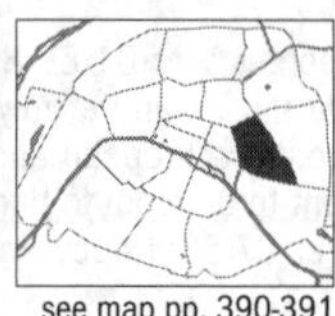
see map pp. 390-391

NEIGHBORHOOD QUICKFIND: ***Discover,*** *p. 11;* ***Sights,*** *p. 108;* ***Food & Drink,*** *p. 188;* ***Accommodations,*** *p. 266.*

Nightlife in the 11*ème* is a tale of two scenes. With a few exceptions, **rue de Lappe** and its neighbors offer a big, raucous night on the town, while **rue Oberkampf** is more eclectic and local. Both streets are definitely well worth your time, even if you have only one night in the area.

Boteco, 131, r. Oberkampf (☎01 43 57 15 47). M: Parmentier. A popular Brazilian bar-restaurant (its name is Portuguese for..."bar-restaurant") with trendy waitstaff, jungle decor, and avant-garde art. The flip-up benches often transforms the small space into a spontaneous late-night dance floor. Munch on free homemade thick-cut potato chips while you sip a delicious Boteco (€6.50), made with the traditional Brazilian rum *cachaça,* pineapple juice, and vanilla extract. Beer €3.10. Open daily 9am-2am.

Le Bar Sans Nom, 49, r. de Lappe (☎01 48 05 59 36). M: Bastille. From the métro, walk down r. de la Roquette and make a right onto r. de Lappe. A laid back oasis amid the noise of r. de Lappe, the No-Name bar is a great place to decompress. Dim, seductive lounge famous for its inventive cocktails, posted on oversized wooden menus, some even *flambé.* Don't leave Paris without trying their mojito (€8.50). Free tarot-card reading Tu 7-9pm, when the bar is mobbed by young Parisian women in search of their future. Beer €5-6.20, shots €6.20, cocktails €8.50. Open M-Sa 7pm-2am. MC/V.

Café Charbon, 109, r. Oberkampf (☎01 43 57 55 13). M: Parmentier or Ménilmontant. Proudly bears traces of its *fin-de-siècle* dance hall days. The crowd varies with the act playing at the attached Nouveau Casino (see below). A house specialty at Café Charbon is sweet beer with *cassis* (€2.30). *Salades* €6-8.50. Beer €2.80. Happy Hour daily 5-7pm. Open 9am-2am. MC/V.

Sanz Sans, 49, r. du Faubourg St-Antoine (☎01 44 75 78 78). M: Bastille. Popular, upbeat bar/club/restaurant with severe bouncer control (during peak hours there must be a female in your group) but thankfully no cover. For the voyeur in each of us: a large, baroque-framed screen projects scenes from the bar like a black-and-white movie. DJs spin hip-hop and house. Outdoor seating; indoor A/C. Drink prices go up after 9pm. Open Su-M 9am-1am, Tu-Sa 9am-5am. MC/V.

Bar bat, 23, r. de Lappe (☎01 43 14 26 06). M: Bastille. A busy bar and restaurant that attracts all sorts of 20-somethings. Chill-out area with sofas near the entrance seems more like café than bar. Restaurant serves a Corsican menu to you in your leopard-print seat. *Plats* €11-16. Long mirrored bar with friendly waiters; Happy Hour daily 5-8pm in the back. Beer €3.50-4. DJ plays house. Open daily 5pm-2am; food served 7:30pm-1am. MC/V.

DANCE CLUBS

Wax, 15, r. Daval (☎01 48 05 88 33). M: Bastille. From the métro, walk north on bd. Richard Lenoir and make a right on r. Daval. One of those rare Parisian miracles: a place that is always free and fun. Set up in a concrete bunker, with retro orange, red and white couches, this bar/club has DJ competitions and its own magazine. Funk and electronic music. Open M-Su 6pm-2am; closed Su in summer months. Drinks €4-9.50. AmEx/MC/V.

Nouveau Casino, 109, r. Oberkampf (☎01 43 57 57 40; www.nouveaucasino.net). M: Parmentier or Ménilmontant. A "nouveau" face on r. Oberkampf, this latest hot-spot is drawing in the crowds of the 11*ème.* Each night offers a different form of entertainment, ranging from concerts (rock, electronic, house, or drum and bass), clubbing, video shows, and modern art exhibits. Call ahead or check the web site for a weekly schedule of events and times.

TWELFTH ARRONDISSEMENT

NEIGHBORHOOD QUICKFIND: ***Discover,*** *p. 12;* ***Sights,*** *p. 110;* ***Museums,*** *p. 152;* ***Food & Drink,*** *p. 189;* ***Shopping,*** *p. 243;* ***Accommodations,*** *p. 267.*

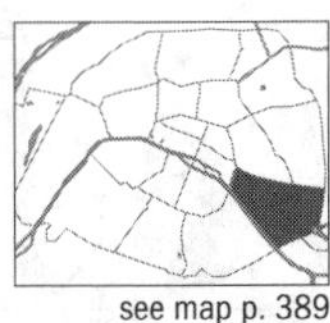
see map p. 389

Barrio Latino, 46/48, r. du Faubourg St-Antoine (☎01 55 78 84 75). M: Bastille. Take r. du Faubourg St-Antoine from the métro; it's on the right. No wallflowers on this hot Latin dance floor, and not an empty barstool on weekends. Sneakers and jeans will get you in, but the clientele here prefers to salsa in style. Strawberry margarita €10. Open daily noon-2am; the DJ arrives at 10pm. AmEx/MC/V.

China Club, 50, r. de Charenton (☎01 43 43 82 02). M: Ledru-Rollin or Bastille. Swank, red-lit club with a *fumoir chinois* look. High-class prices, but a Chinatown (gin fizz with mint; €10.50) is worth it. Feeling adventurous? Sip on Naughty Nuts (cocktails €7.50-11). Weekend jazz after 10pm. Games and a bar upstairs. Happy Hour daily 7-9pm; drinks €6. Downstairs club closes for 3 weeks at the end of July and in early August. Call ahead. Dinner reservations recommended. Open M-Th 7pm-2am, F-Sa 7pm-3am. AmEx/MC/V.

Factory Café, 20 r. du Faubourg St-Antoine (☎01 44 74 68 74). M: Bastille. Heading down r. du Faubourg St-Antoine from the Place de la Bastille, the club is on your right. Hip hopping every night, and a cinch to get into. Cover Su-Th €8, F-Sa €12.50 includes first drink; subsequent drinks €8. Open Su-Th 11pm-4am, F-Sa 10pm-6am. AmEx/DC/MC/V.

THIRTEENTH ARRONDISSEMENT

see map p. 392

NEIGHBORHOOD QUICKFIND: ***Discover,*** *p. 4;* ***Sights,*** *p. 111;* ***Food & Drink,*** *p. 190;* ***Accommodations,*** *p. 268.*

Rue de la Butte-aux-Cailles has a few local bars that are perfect for kicking back. If kicking up your heels sounds better, head for the new boat bars along the **Quai de la Gare.**

La Folie en Tête, 33, r. de la Butte-aux-Cailles (☎01 45 80 65 99). M: Corvisart. *The* artsy axis mundi of the 13*ème*. World music and exotic instruments line the walls. Crowded concerts on Sa nights, usually Afro-Caribbean music (€8); no concerts July-Aug. Beer €2.40; Ti punch €4.50. Happy Hour 6-8pm (*kir* €1.50). Open M-Sa 6pm-2am. MC/V.

Bateau El Alamein, Port de la Gare (☎01 45 86 41 60). M: Quai-de-la-Gare. This docked boat is like a floating Eden, with everything from orange trees to morning glories blooming on its pleasant deck. The stage downstairs features local performers nightly, with an emphasis on vocals, but call ahead to be sure. Entrance €5-8. Popular drinks include a mean Mojito and the TGV (tequila, git, vodka), both €8. Open daily 7pm-2am.

Le Merle Moqueur, 11, r. de la Butte-aux-Cailles. M: Corvisart. Take r. Bobillot south until r. de la Butte-aux-Cailles branches right. Bamboo walls, African music, and a shabby-cool ambiance in the back room. Cheap drinks beer €2.50, *kir* €3); try your luck in a "rum race"–6 to 25 different-flavored shots of rum (€15-45). Happy Hour 5-8pm. Open daily 5pm-2am.

La Guinguette Pirate, Porte de la Gare (☎01 43 49 68 68). This casual outdoor bar is a favorite of locals who sip cheap booze at picnic tables. The "pirate ship" behind the bar features live music. Drink specials nightly. Cover €8. Open M-Sa 6pm-2am, Su 4pm-midnight.

DANCE CLUBS

Batofar, facing 11, quai François-Mauriac (☎01 56 29 10 33). M: Quai-de-la-Gare. Facing the river, walk right along the quai–Batofar has the red lights. This barge/bar/club has made it big with the electronic music crowd but maintains a friendly vibe. The "Batofar Otocar," a double-decker bus parked outside, provides music for the many who come to get down right on the quai until the early morning. Open Tu-Th 9pm-3am, F-Sa until 4am; hours change for special film and DJ events. Cover €6.50-9.50, which usually includes first drink. "Electronic brunch" on Sunday afternoon. MC/V.

FOURTEENTH ARRONDISSEMENT

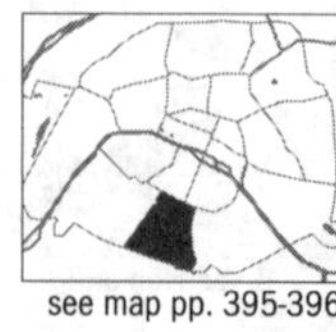

see map pp. 395-396

NEIGHBORHOOD QUICKFIND: ***Discover,*** *p. 4;* ***Sights,*** *p. 113;* ***Museums,*** *p. 152;* ***Food & Drink,*** *p. 191;* ***Accommodations,*** *p. 269.*

L'Entrepôt, 7-9, r. Francis de Pressensé (☎01 45 40 07 50; film schedule 08 36 68 05 87; restaurant reservations ☎01 45 40 07 50; www.lentrepot.fr). M: Pernety. From the métro, turn right, walk down r. Raymond Losserand and turn right onto r. Francis de Pressensé. Proving that intellectualism and good times go together, this savvy establishment offers a quadruple combo: a 3-screen cinema, a fancy ivy-decked restaurant with garden patio, and an art gallery and a trendy bar that features live jazz, latin, and world music. You may need to (and should!) come a few times to see it all. Poetry readings (Tu 7pm) and jazz (Th 7pm). Ciné-Philo, a screening, lecture, and discussion café, is held 2 Sa per month at 2pm; check the monthly schedule in the main foyer. Concerts F-Sa; usually around €5. Beer €2.50. Su brunch 11:30am-4:30pm (€15). Open M-Sa 9am-midnight (though usually stays open later), Su 11:30am-midnight; food served noon-3pm and 7:30-11:30pm.

Smoke Bar, 29, r. Delambre (☎01 43 20 61 73). M: Vavin. From the métro, walk down r. Delambre past sq. Delambre; the bar is to the left. A place where you might be able to strike up a conversation with a stranger without feeling like an outsider. Or come with a couple friends and calmly drink the night away. Jazz and blues posters line the dark wood walls. Cocktails €5-7; beer €2.50-3; enourmous mug of beer €7.50. Open M-Sa 5pm-2am. MC/V.

Café Tournesol, 9, r. de la Gaîté (☎01 43 27 65 72). M: Edgar Quinet. From the métro, turn left on r. de la Gaîté; the bar is on the left, at the corner of impasse de la Gaîté and r. de la Gaîté. At this ultra-Mod café-bar some of the 14*ème's* most stylish come out to drink, read, and mingle. The chic clientele praise the easy-going, open atmosphere. Maybe it's the piped-in techno and industrial-chic decor with great artwork; the alcohol can't hurt, either (beers €2.30-6; wines €2-3). Open M-Sa 8:30am-1:30am, Su 9:30am-1:30am. MC/V.

Mustang Café, 84, bd. du Montparnasse (☎01 43 35 36 12). M: Montparnasse-Bienvenüe. From the métro, take the r. d'Odessa exit and head straight down bd. du Montparnasse to the corner of r. du Montparnasse. Looking for a party after 2am? Head to Mustang, where €3.50 beers and all-American good times flow freely all night. Thumping juke box, hordes of Anglophones, and the occasional wet T-shirt contest. Happy Hour M-F 4-8pm. American brunch Sa-Su noon-5pm. Open daily 9am-5am. Food served until 2am. MC/V.

SIXTEENTH ARRONDISSEMENT

NEIGHBORHOOD QUICKFIND: ***Discover,*** *p. 12;* ***Sights,*** *p. 116;* ***Museums,*** *p. 153;* ***Food & Drink,*** *p. 193;* ***Accommodations,*** *p. 272.*

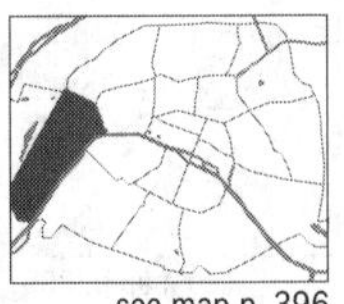
see map p. 396

Duplex, 2bis, av. Foch (☎01 45 00 45 00). M: Charles de Gaulle-Etoile. Walk around the Arc; a blue-awninged entrance leads to the underground nightclub. A crowd of wealthy glamorazzi mix with tourists and dance to techno-fied pop, funk, and R&B. On weekends, businessmen display their arm-candy here. Also houses an expensive restaurant (open Tu-Su 9pm-1am). Tu students; W airline night; F "mucho-much"; Su Asian night. Cover and first drink Su and Tu-Th €15, F-Sa €19. Women free before midnight Tu-Th and Su. All drinks €9.15. Open Tu-Su 11:00pm-dawn. Closed July 30-Aug. 25.

SEVENTEENTH ARRONDISSEMENT

NEIGHBORHOOD QUICKFIND: ***Discover,*** *p. 13;* ***Sights,*** *p. 118;* ***Museums,*** *p. 156;* ***Food & Drink,*** *p. 194;* ***Accommodations,*** *p. 273*

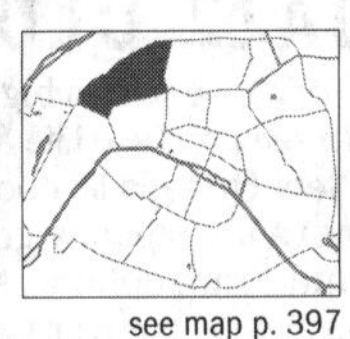
see map p. 397

L'Endroit, 67, pl. du Dr. Félix Lobligeois (☎01 42 29 50 00). M: Rome. Follow r. Boursault to r. Legendre, and make a right. Hip, young 17*èmers* come for the snazzy bar and idyllic location. Beer €4.50-5.10, wine €3.50-4, and cocktails €6. Try the Pearl Harbor (vodka, melon liquor, and pineapple nectar) or down the mysterious and fruity "Bitch." Open daily noon-2am. MC/V. See also **Food & Drink,** p. 195.

La Main Jaune, pl. de la Porte de Champerret (☎01 47 63 26 47). M: Porte de Champerret. The métro lets you out right in the middle of the *place*. A fun roller disco with regular dancing as well. Open W and Su 2:30-7pm, F 10:30pm-6am, Sa 2:30-7pm and 10:30pm-6am. Admission W and Sa-Su afternoons €8 (includes a drink), skate rental €1.50; F-Sa becomes a disco with Portuguese music and skating (€11; ladies free).

EIGHTEENTH ARRONDISSEMENT

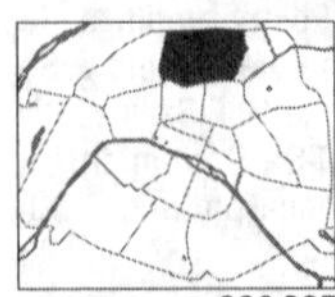
see map pp. 386-387

NEIGHBORHOOD QUICKFIND: ***Discover,*** *p. 13;* ***Sights,*** *p. 119;* ***Museums,*** *p. 156;* ***Food & Drink,*** *p. 195;* ***Shopping,*** *p. 245;* ***Accommodations,*** *p. 273.*

Much of the 18*ème's* nightlife lies in the sleazy southernmost end of the *butte,* around the red-light district near **Place Pigalle** and **boulevard Rochechouart.** The streets are lined with aggressive peep-show hawkers and prowling drug dealers; stay near well-lit, heavily trafficked areas. Tourists traveling alone, especially women, should avoid the areas around M: Pigalle, M: Anvers and M: Barbès-Rochechouart at night. For live music clubs in Montmartre, see **Entertainment,** p. 228.

Chez Camille, 8, r. Ravignan (☎01 46 06 05 78). M: Abbesses. From the métro, walk down r. de la Veuville and make a left on r. Drevet and another left on r. Gabrielle, which becomes r. Ravignan. Small, trendy, bright yellow bar on the safer upper slopes of Montmartre, with funky charm and a pretty terrace looking down the *butte* to the Invalides dome (especially dramatic at night). Cheap coffee (€1.20) and tea (€2.80). Beer €2.20-3.30, wine from €2.80, cocktails €6.50. Open M 11am-2pm, Tu-Sa 9am-2am, Su 9am-8pm.

La Fourmi, 74, r. des Martyrs (☎01 42 64 70 35). M: Pigalle. From the métro, walk east on bd. Rochechouart and make a left on r. des Martyrs. An artsy atmosphere with a large zinc bar and industrial-chic decor, complete with a chandelier made of green chianti bottles and urban b&w photography. A hyper-hip, energetic, and scrappy young crowd takes refuge in the back room from the sleazy surroundings of bd. Rochechouart. Beer €2.30-3.20, wine €2.50-2.60, cocktails €5.40-10. Open M-Th 8:30am-2am, F-Sa 8:30am-4am, Su 10am-2am. V.

TWENTIETH ARRONDISSEMENT

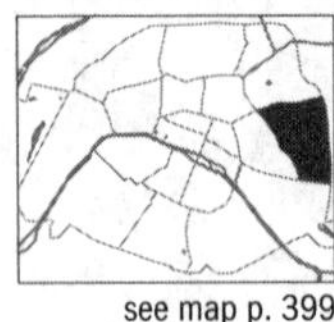
see map p. 399

NEIGHBORHOOD QUICKFIND: ***Discover,*** *p. 14;* ***Sights,*** *p. 123;* ***Museums,*** *p. 157;* ***Food & Drink,*** *p. 197;* ***Accommodations,*** *p. 275.*

Café Flèche d'Or, 102bis, r. de Bagnolet. Live music nightly, from reggae to hip-hop to Celtic rock. Art videos, dance classes, Su *bals,* and crazy theater on the tracks below the terrace. North African, French, Caribbean, and South American food with nightly jazz, ska, folk, salsa, samba (cover €5-6; no cover if you eat dinner). Beer €4-5, cocktails €4-7. Open daily 10am-2am. MC/V. See also **Food & Drink,** p. 198.

Lou Pascalou, 14, r. des Panoyaux (☎01 46 36 78 10). M: Ménilmontant. Follow bd. de Ménilmontant and make a left on r. des Panayaux. Features open-air terrace seating, a pool table, occasional concerts, and art displays. A bit out of the way; attracts mostly a local crowd. Beer €2-€3, cocktails €3.50-6; add €0.30 after 10pm. Open daily 9am-2am. MC.

JAZZ CLUBS

For those with a big travel budget (or a corporate credit card), Paris is a great place to see jazz (see **Life & Times,** p. 64). Nearly every type of jazz is represented here, from New Orleans to cool, from acid to hip hop and fusion. Brazilian samba and bossa nova are steadily growing in popularity together with music from the West Indies and Francophone Africa. Paris's jazz clubs charge either through inflated drink prices or a cover charge. Once you have paid your cover, you are not required to drink, though you should brace yourself for a disapproving look every time the server passes your table. You will likely not be disturbed should you choose to nurse one drink for the rest of the night. Frequent summer festivals sponsor free or nearly free jazz concerts. The **Fête du Marais** often features free Big Band, while the **La Villette Jazz Festival** has very big names and a few free shows (see **Discover,** p. 19). In the fall, the **Jazz Festival of Paris** comes to town as venues open their doors to celebrity and up-and-coming artists. French mags *Jazz Hot* (€7) and *Jazz Magazine* (€5.50) are great sources, as is the bimonthly *LYLO* (*Les Yeux, Les Oreilles;* free). *Pariscope* and *l'Officiel des Spectacles* (both available at any *tabac*) also have jazz listings.

Au Duc des Lombards, 42, r. des Lombards, 1*er* (☎01 42 33 22 88; www.jazzvalley.com /duc). M: Châtelet. From r. des Halles, walk down r. de la Ferronerie and make a right on r. St-Denis and another right on r. des Lombards. Murals of Ellington and Coltrane cover the exterior of this premier jazz joint. Still the best in French jazz, with occasional American soloists, and hot items in world music. Three sets each night—you pay less cover if you only catch the last set. Cover €12-23, music students €8-19. Beer €5-8, cocktails €9. Music 9:30pm-1:30am. Open M-Sa 8pm-2am. MC/V.

Le Baiser Salé, 58, r. des Lombards, 1*er* (☎01 42 33 37 71). M: Châtelet. From r. des Halles, walk down r. de la Ferronerie and make a right on r. St-Denis and another right on r. des Lombards. This club features Cuban, African, and Antillean music featured together with modern jazz and funk in a welcoming, mellow space. Month-long African music festival (month varies). Concerts start at 10pm, music until 3am (typically 3 sets). Cover €6-18, depending on performers; mainly new talent. Free M jam sessions at 9:30pm with 1 drink minimum. Beer €4.80, cocktails €9. Happy Hour 5-7:15pm. Bar and club open daily 5pm-6am. AmEx/MC/V.

Le Petit Opportun, 15, r. des Lavandières-Ste-Opportune, 1*er* (☎01 42 36 01 36). M: Châtelet. From the métro, walk down r. des Halles and make a right onto r. des Lavandières-Ste-Opportune. Tiny basement venue in 3 rooms; show up early for a spot in the front room. Some of the best modern jazz around, including Americans. Cover €13-16 depending on act. Drinks €5-9. Open Aug.-June Tu-Sa 9pm-5am; music begins between 9:30 and 10:30pm.

Le Slow Club, 130, r. de Rivoli, 1*er* (☎01 42 33 84 30). M: Châtelet. In a cellar that used to be a banana-ripening warehouse. An old favorite of Miles Davis. Big Band, Dixieland, and rock 'n' roll. Expect dancing and a crowd in their 30s. Weekday cover €10, students €9; weekend cover from €13. Drinks from €4. Open Tu-Th 10pm-3am, F-Sa 10pm-4am.

Le Sunset, 60, r. des Lombards, 1*er* (☎01 40 26 46 60; sunset@jazzvalley.com). M: Châtelet. From r. des Halles, walk down r. de la Ferronerie and make a right on r. St-Denis and another right on r. des Lombards. An easy-going club with an old and widespread reputation, Le Sunset is where musicians come to unwind and jam into the wee hours after their gigs. Mostly French and European acts. Cover €8-25 with a €2 student discount; drinks €4.30+. Concerts M-Sa 8:30pm-2am. Regular jam sessions after 2am. MC/V.

Latin Quarter by Night

Le Sunset

Le Bar Dix

NO WORK ALL PLAY

Night Musique

While the **Fête de la Musique** is celebrated nationwide, it should be no surprise that Paris brings in the biggest crowds. We'd love to tell you which part of the city serves as the epicenter for this huge, crazy festival, but there isn't one: the entire city of Paris is engulfed.

While you can catch a few acts as early as noon, it isn't until about 8pm that the city gets humming. Head to one of the major *places* to see big international acts—2003's lineup included Robbie Williams and Simply Red. After the big shows end, wander whatever area you find yourself in. Every café and bar stays open through the night, pumping music into the street. Musicians of all sorts can be found on every corner. Everything is free—including entry into normally pricey venues—and vendors blanket the city with hot dogs and *shish kebab* sandwiches (€4) and beer (€2). Some subway lines stay open and night buses run on more regular schedules. For €2.50, you can buy an unlimited métro pass good from the evening of June 21 through the morning of June 22, but you may have a tough time getting home between midnight and 6am. Consider doing what the Parisians do—stay out until the sun comes up. You'll be glad you did.

June 21. ☎01 40 03 94 70.

Le Petit Journal St-Michel, 71, bd. St-Michel, 5*ème* (☎01 43 26 28 59; www.petitjournalsaint-michel.com). M: St-Michel. From the métro, walk down bd. St-Michel away from the Seine. Le Petit is another of the early jazz strongholds, though it's now more traditional and more popular with an older crowd (40s-50s). First-class New Orleans and Big Band performers frequently perform here. Obligatory 1st drink €15.25, subsequent drinks €6.10. M-Sa 9pm-1:15am. Closed Aug.

Le Caveau de la Huchette, 5, r. de la Huchette, 5*ème* (☎01 43 26 65 05). M: St-Michel. From bd. St-Michel, make a right onto r. de la Huchette. Come prepared to listen, watch, and dance the jitterbug, swing, and jive in this extremely popular, if somewhat touristy, club. Bebop dance lessons at 9:30pm (call ☎01 42 71 09 09). Widely varied age group. Crowded on weekends. Cover Su-Th €10.50, F-Sa €13. Students €9. Dance School €8. Drinks €5.50-8.50. Open daily 9:30pm-2:30am, F till 3:30am, Sa till 4am. AmEx/MC/V.

Aux Trois Mailletz, 56, r. Galande, 5*ème* (☎01 43 54 00 79; before 5pm 01 43 25 96 86). M: St-Michel. From the métro, walk along the Seine on the Quai St-Michel, make a right on r. du Petit Pont and a left on r. Galande. What you'd expect a cool jazz club to look like. The basement houses a crowded café featuring world music and jazz vocals. The upper floor is packed with a strange mix of well-dressed students and well-dressed forty-somethings. €12.20-18.30 admission to club on weekends; admission to bar is free. Grog €9 at bar, cocktails €12.50 at bar. Bar open daily 5pm-dawn; *cave* 10pm-dawn.

New Morning, 7-9, r. des Petites-Ecuries, 10*ème* (☎01 45 23 51 41; www.newmorning.com). M: Château d'Eau. This 400-seat former printing plant now plays host to some of the biggest American headliners in the city. Dark, smoky, and crowded, New Morning is everything a jazz club should be. The venue's best acoustics are in the lower front section or near the wings of the stage. All the greatsest names in jazz music have played here—from Chet Baker to Stan Getz and Miles Davis. These days it continues to attracts big names like Wynton Marsalis, Betty Carter, and John Scofield. Tickets can be purchased from the box office, any branch of FNAC, or the Virgin Megastore; they average €16-20. Drinks €6-10. Open Sept.-July from 8pm, though exact times vary; concerts begin at 9pm. MC/V.

Café Universel, 267, r. St-Jacques, 6*ème* (☎01 43 25 74 20). M: Luxembourg. From the métro, walk up r. Soufflot and turn right onto r. St-Jacques. A student-populated, very Latin Quarter hangout with free and easy jazz, and an emphasis on vocals. Concerts at 9:30pm. No cover. Beer €4, wine €4.50. Bar open M-Sa 9pm-2am. MC/V.

WINE BARS

Although wine bistros have existed since the early 19th century, the budget-friendly, wine-by-the-glass bar emerged with the invention of a machine that pumps nitrogen into the open bottle, protecting wine from oxidation. Rare wines have become remarkably affordable. The owners carefully select the wines that fill their *caves* (cellars) and are available to help out less knowledgeable patrons. For a crash course on French wine, see **Food & Drink,** p. 166.

Jacques Mélac, 42, r. Léon Frot, 11*ème* (☎01 43 70 59 27). M: Charonne. From the métro, walk down r. Charonne, and turn left onto r. Léon Frot. A cozy, family-owned wine bar and bistro open since 1938. In mid-Sept., Mélac lets children harvest, tread upon, and extract wine from grapes grown in vines hanging from the bar's storefront. Wine €3.70-4 per glass; bottle €15-38. Open Sept.-July Tu-Sa 9am-3pm and 7:30-midnight. V.

La Belle Hortense, 31, r. Vieille-du-Temple, 4*ème* (☎01 48 04 71 60). M: St-Paul. Walk in the direction of traffic along r. de Rivoli and turn right onto r. Vieille-du-Temple. A popular intellectual hangout, this wine bar/bookstore has a wide wine selection, from €3 a glass and €15 a bottle. Open daily 5pm-2am. MC/V. See listing in **Nightlife,** p. 210.

Le Clown Bar, 114, r. Amelot, 11*ème* (☎01 43 55 87 35). M: Filles du Calvaire. Cross bd. du Filles du Calvaire to r. Amelot; across from the Cirque d'Hiver. Those afraid of clowns should stay far, far away—clown paintings, posters, and sculptures adorn every surface. Wines by the glass from €3. Dinner *menu* €18. Open M-Sa noon-3:30pm and 7pm-1am.

Willie's Wine Bar, 13, r. des Petits Champs, 1*er* (☎01 42 61 05 09). M: Palais-Royal. Behind the Palais. Popular since its opening in 1980, this place is fancier than its name suggests. Exposed wood beams, chic decor, and huge windows looking out onto the Palais and apartment of author Colette. Friendly staff and international clientele. Huge selection of French wines €4-12.20 a glass. Open M-Sa noon-midnight. MC/V.

Le Baron Rouge, 1, r. Théophile-Roussel, 12*ème* (☎01 43 43 14 32). M: Ledru-Rollin. Follow the r. du Faubourg St-Antoine away from the Opéra and take a right on r. Charles Baudelaire. Théophile-Roussel is your first left. The boisterous bartender will suggest one of the dozens of wines on the menu (a steal at €1-3 a glass). Light snacks €4.50. Open Tu-F 10am-2pm and 5-10pm, Sa 10am-2pm, Su 10am-3pm. MC/V.

INSIDE

Entertainment

When it comes to entertainment, Paris can satisfy all tastes. When looking for something to do, consult the bibles of Paris entertainment, the weekly bulletins **Pariscope** (€0.40) and **Officiel des Spectacles** (€0.30), both on sale at newsstands. Even if you don't understand French, you should be able to decipher the listings of times and locations. Contact **Info-Loisirs,** a recording that keeps tabs on what's on in Paris (English/French, ☎08 92 68 31 12; €0.40 per min.).

You don't need to speak fluent French to enjoy the theater scene. Paris's theaters present productions whose music, physical comedy, and experimental abstraction lend themselves to any audience. The comedy-oriented **café-théâtres** and the music-oriented **cabarets** perpetuate the ambience of 1930s Paris. Paris's ballet and modern dance companies often host performances by visiting companies, including the Kirov Ballet, the Alvin Ailey Dance Company, and the Dance Theater of Harlem. Paris's new **Stade de France** and other athletic venues offer spectator and participatory sports galore.

Among Paris's many treasures, music and film top the list. West African music, Caribbean calypso and reggae, Latin American salsa, North African *raï*, European house, techno, and rap are fused by the hippest of DJs in the coolest of Paris's **clubs** (see **Nightlife,** p. 205). Classical concerts are staged in both expensive concert halls and churches, particularly during the summer. Parisians are inveterate film-goers, greedy for movies from all over the world. Frequent English-language film series and festivals make Parisian cinema accessible, inventive, challenging, and entertaining.

Circus Maximus

In Paris, the circus is not just for children; it's high art, of the kind popularized worldwide by Cirque du Soleil. Try these cutting-edge establishments for a unique blend of techno music, acrobatics, and totally wild costumes:

Espace Chapiteaux (☎01 40 03 75 75) in La Villette (see p. 123). M: Porte-de-la-Villette. Holds circuses of all varieties year-round in its giant tent, with tickets ranging from €14-17, depending upon your age and willingness to put your head in a lion's mouth.

Cirque Alexandra Franconi (☎01 43 24 33 18), in the Parc de St-Cloud, porte du Musée de la Céramique de Sèvres. M: Pont de Sèvres. Performs W and all school vacation days at 2:30pm, Sa-Su 3pm, from €10-24.

Cirque Diana Moreno Borman, 9, bd. du Bois Lepretre, 17*ème* (☎01 47 39 44 71; reservations 06 10 71 83 50). M: Porte de Clichy. Performances W and Sa-Su fall to spring and daily in summer at 3pm; tickets €10-30.

Cirque Tzigane Romanes, 12, av. de Clichy, 18*ème* (☎01 43 87 16 38). M: Place de Clichy. Performance times vary. This "gypsy circus" has drawn lots of attention for its minimalist style and mystique. Prices vary.

THEATER

Fortunately for the non-fluent, much of Parisian theater is highly accessible, thanks in part to its dependence on the classics and in part to its love of a grand spectacle. Four of France's five **national theaters,** those bastions of traditional French drama, are located in Paris (the fifth is in Strasbourg). Unless you're banking on last-minute rush tickets, make reservations 14 days in advance. Paris's **private theaters,** though less celebrated than their state-run counterparts, often stage outstanding productions. Most theaters have shows every day except Monday and are closed for July and August. *Pariscope* (€0.40 at any newsstand) and *l'Officiel des Spectacles* (€0.35) provide listings of current shows, as well as information on one of the best ways to see theater in Paris: **half-price previews.** Many theatres offer student tickets at discounted prices. For **Ticket Services,** see **Service Directory,** p. 345.

La Comédie Française, 2, r. de Richelieu, 1*er* (☎01 44 58 15 15; www.comedie-francaise.fr). M: Palais-Royal. Founded by Molière, now the granddaddy of all French theaters. Expect wildly gesticulated slapstick farce; you don't need to speak French to understand the jokes. Performances take place in the 896-seat Salle Richelieu. This season: canonized plays by French greats Copi and Duras (established foreigners like Werner Schwab and Gao Xingjianare also represented). Box office open daily 11am-6pm. Tickets €4.50-30, under 27 €4.50-7.50 (no category A seating available). Rush tickets for students (€9) available 1hr. before show. Handicapped patrons and their guests are asked to make reservations in advance (tickets €11). If you plan to stay in Paris for a long time, you may want to invest in the **Passeport Comédie-Française,** which allows you to make reservations at reduced prices. The *comédiens français* also mount the same sort of plays in the 330-seat **Théâtre du Vieux Colombier,** 21, r. des Vieux Colombiers, 6*ème* (☎01 44 39 87 00 or 01 44 39 87 01). M: St-Sulpice or Sèvres-Babylone. Tickets €25, over 60 €17.50; student rush tickets (€9-13) sold 45min. before performances. AmEx/MC/V.

Bouffes du Nord, 37bis, bd. de la Chapelle, 10*ème* (☎01 46 07 34 50; www.bouffesdunord.com). M: La Chapelle. Bouffes du Nord is an experimental theater (headed by British director Peter Brook and Stephen Lissner) that produces cutting-edge performances and concerts and offers occasional productions in English. Closed Aug. Box office open M-Sa 11am-6pm. Concerts €18.50, under 26 and over 60 €12; plays €14-24.50. Wheelchair-accessible, but you must call in advance.

Comédie Italienne, 17-19, r. de la Gaîté, 14*ème* (☎01 43 21 22 22). M: Edgar Quinet. Exit the métro and r. de la Gaîté will be the one to your left. Features the never-ending adventures of Arlequin, Europe's favorite rapscallion, in this 100-seat theater decorated with exquisite costumes, masks, and *trompe-l'oeil* murals. Box office open M-Sa 11am-7pm, Su noon-3pm. Tickets €30, seniors €25, students under 26 €25, under 15 €20.

Odéon Théâtre de l'Europe, 1, pl. Odéon, 6*ème* (☎01 44 85 40 00; www.theatre-odeon.fr). M: Odéon. Programs in this elegant Neoclassical building range from classics to avant-garde, but the Odéon specializes in foreign plays in their original language. 1042 seats. The 2003-2004 season includes Sophocles' *Antigone* and Shakespeare's *Othello.* Box office open daily 11am-7pm. Tickets €5-28 for most shows; under 27 rush tickets (€7.50) available 1½hr. before performance; cheaper rates available Th and Su; call ahead. Also **Petit Odéon,** an affiliate with 82 seats. Tickets €10. Call ahead for wheelchair access. MC/V.

Théâtre de la Huchette, 23, r. de la Huchette, 5*ème* (☎01 43 26 38 99). M: St-Michel. 100-seat theater where Ionesco's *La cantatrice chauve (The Bald Soprano)* and *La leçon (The Lesson)* premiered 43 years ago and continue to play today. A bastion of Left Bank intellectualism; high-school French will suffice. Shows M-Sa. *La cantatrice chauve* starts at 7pm, *La leçon* at 8pm. No one admitted after curtain. Box office open M-Sa 4:30-9pm. Tickets €16, students under 25 M-F €12.50; both shows €25, students M-F €19. Also a rotating third show, around €24, €12 for students. Wheelchair-accessible.

Théâtre National de Chaillot, 1, pl. du Trocadéro, 16*ème* (☎01 53 65 30 00; www.theatre-chaillot.fr). M: Trocadéro. In the Palais de Chaillot. Innovative plays, music, and dance concerts take place in 2 rooms, one with 1250 and the other with 418 seats. 2003-4 season includes Valletti's *Le Negre Au Sang*, and Jean Genet's *Les Paravents.* Box office open M-Sa 11am-7pm, Su 11am-5pm. Tickets €25, under 25 and seniors €19.50. Handicapped and hearing impaired individuals should call in advance to request special seating and headsets.

CABARET

Au Lapin Agile, 22, r. des Saules, 18*ème* (☎01 46 06 85 87). M: Lamarck-Coulaincourt. Turn right on r. Lamarck, then right again up r. des Saules. Picasso, Verlaine, Renoir, and Apollinaire hung out here during Montmartre's heyday; now a mainly tourist audience crowds in for comical poems and songs. Originally called the *Cabaret des Assassins,* it came to be known as *le lapin à Gill* (Gill's Rabbit) in 1875, when the artist André Gill painted a rabbit on the facade.

People's Theater

La Cartoucherie translates as "the cartridge factory," and a 19th-century weapons factory may seem like an unlikely space for theater. However, since 1970, *La Cartoucherie* has housed cutting-edge, socially conscious, and refreshingly democratic theatre. The internationally renowned theater (located just beyond the periphery of the 12*ème*) is home to 5 collectives, 2 studios, and 7 performance spaces.

Art Nouveau lettering welcomes you to the quiet, forested group of buildings. Fantastically decorated interiors with immense, well-managed backstage and performance spaces contrast sharply with brick exteriors. Prior to many performances, theater troupes offer meals (of meat or veggie dishes) at picnic tables. After washing your dishes, you may watch actors and technicians apply make-up, search for costumes, or prepare soundboards prior to the performance. "Backstage" is open to the public eye. Technicians, musicians, and actors are all given equal billing of at *La Cartoucherie.*

It's easy to see how the spirit of the '68 uprisings has lived on here. The cooperating troupes adapt and reinvent their craft while maintaining a space that welcomes new work, young talent, and daring subject matter. It makes for a remarkable show.

Most shows €15-20. For more information, visit www.la-tempete.fr/theatre/cartoucherie.html, or check Pariscope. M: Château de Vincennes; a free shuttle departs every 15min. beginning 1hr. before performance, from the station.

Champs-Elysées Cinéma

La Villette

Le foot

The name eventually morphed into *Le lapin agile* (the nimble rabbit). The *chansonnier* inspired Steve Martin's 1996 hit play *Picasso at the Lapin Agile.* Shows Tu-Su at 9pm-2am. Admission and first drink €25, Su-F students €18 Subsequent drinks €6-7.

Caveau de la République, 1, bd. St-Martin, *3ème* (☎01 42 78 44 45). M: République. A Parisian crowd fills the 482 seats of this 100 year-old venue for political satire. The *tour de champs* (tour of the field) consists of 6 separate comedy and song acts. Solid French skills and knowledge of French politics are a must to get the gags. Tickets sold up to 6 days in advance, M noon-6pm, Tu-Sa noon-7pm, Su noon-4pm. Shows mid-Sept. to June Tu-Sa 9pm, Su 3:30pm. Admission Su and Tu-Th €24, F-Sa €30, Tu-F and Su under 25 €15. MC/V.

CINEMA

Every night, swarms of Parisians populate the city's cafés after a night at the movies, continuing Paris's century-long love affair with the cinema (see **Life & Times**, p. 64). You'll find scores of cinemas throughout the city, particularly in the *Quartier Latin* and on the Champs-Elysées. You may not notices them at first, but take a wander around Place St. Michel and La Sorbonne, especially the sidestreets, and you'll see theatres playing everything from the latest from Iran to Lars Von Trier retrospectives. Many theaters in Paris specialize in programs featuring classic European film, current independent film, Asian classics, American classics, and Hollywood blockbusters. The two big theater chains—**Gaumont** and **UGC**—offer *cartes privilèges* discounts for five visits or more, and student discounts for shows before 7pm, Sunday through Thursday. In late June, the wonderful three-day **Fête du Cinéma** offers great discounts and great films (see **Discover,** p. 19).

Check the publications **Pariscope** or **L'Officiel des Spectacles** (available at any newsstand, €0.40) for weekly film schedules, prices, and reviews (cinemas will be listed quite conveniently by *arrondissement*). The notation V.O. (*version originale*) after a non-French movie listing means that the film is being shown in its original language with French subtitles; watching an English-language film with French subtitles is a great way to pick up new vocabulary. V.F. *(version française)* means that the film has been dubbed—an increasingly rare phenomenon. Like most European and American cinemas, Paris's cinemas offer student, senior, and family discounts. On Monday and Wednesday, prices drop by about €1.50 for everyone.

Musée du Louvre, 1*er* (info ☎01 40 20 53 17; schedules and reservations ☎01 40 20 52 99; www.louvre.fr). M: Louvre. Art films, films on art, silent movies. Open Sept.-June. Free.

Les Trois Luxembourg, 67, r. Monsieur-le-Prince, 6*ème* (☎01 46 33 97 77). M: Cluny. Turn left onto bd. St-Michel, right onto r. Racine, and left onto r. M-le-Prince. High-quality independent, classic, and foreign films, all in V.O. €6.40, students and seniors €5.

Action Christine, 4, r. Christine, 6*ème* (☎01 43 29 11 30). M: Odéon. Off r. Dauphine. International selection of art and classic films from the 40s and 50s. Many famous Hollywood pics. Always V.O. €7; early show (usually 6 or 7pm), M, and students €5.50. 1-year pass for 10 movies €40 .

L'Arlequin, 76, r. de Rennes, 6*ème* (☎01 45 44 28 80). M: St-Sulpice. A revival cinema with occasional visits from European directors and first-run previews. Some films V.O., others dubbed. Buy tickets in advance. €7.50, students M-F and all tickets W €5.50, Su matinee €4.50. 6-month pass for 10 movies €50. MC/V.

Saint André des Arts, 30, r. de St-André des Arts. 6*ème* (☎01 43 26 48 18). M: St-Michel. A revival theatre with the typical French fondness for Woody Allen. Past retrospectives also include movies by Swedish directors. All movies V.O. €7.30, students €5.80.

La Pagode, 57bis, r. de Babylone, 7*ème* (☎01 45 55 48 48). M: St-François-Xavier. A pseudo-Japanese pagoda built in 1895 and reopened as a cinema in 2000, La Pagode screens foreign and independent films, and the occasional American film. (See **Sights,** p. 99.) Stop in at the café in between shows. Tickets €7.30; over 60, under 21, students, and M and W €5.80. MC/V.

Cinémathèque Française, pl. du Trocadéro, 16*ème* (☎01 45 53 21 86, recorded info 01 47 04 24 24 lists all shows; www.cinemathequefrancaise.com). M: Trocadéro. At the Musée du Cinéma in the Palais de Chaillot; enter through the Jardins du Trocadéro. **Also** 42, Boulevard Bonne Nouvelle, 10eme. M: Bonne Nouvelle. A must for film buffs. 2-3 classics, near-classics, or soon-to-be classics per day. Foreign films usually in V.O. Buy tickets 20min. early. Open W-Su 5-9:45pm. €4.70, students €3.

MUSIC, OPERA, & DANCE

Acclaimed foreign and provincial dance companies visit Paris frequently; watch for posters and check the listings in *Pariscope.* Connoisseurs will find the thick and indexed *Programme des*

Musique

Au Lapin Agile

L'Opéra Garnier

Piscine The Day Away

If you're feeling worn down by the hectic pace of sightseeing, take a break in one of the many pools sprinkled around the city. One of the most popular is **Club Quartier Latin,** which offers its guests a unique, reasonably priced experience. For €3.80 you can take a dip in the 33m pool with lap lanes for those in search of a workout as well as space for just relaxing. The building truly merits its historical monument status. High above the giant pool, a glass roof lets in all the sunlight but none of the unpredictable Paris weather. For €0.45 you get your own private changing room that looks onto the pool area, a pleasant departure from the sometimes awkward communal rooms found in the US. If you feel like a workout, for another €11 you can use their individual and group fitness rooms. For other fitness clubs in Paris, see **Service Directory,** p. 343.

19, r. de Pontoise, 5ème (☎01 55 42 77 88; www.clubquartierlatin.com). M: Maubert-Mutualite. ***Pool*** *open year round: June-Aug. M-F 7-8:30am and 11:30am-8:45pm, Sa 10am-7pm, Su 8am-7pm. Sept.-May same hours except also closed M-T and Th-F 1:30-4:30pm.* ***Gym*** *open M-F 9am-midnight, Sa-Su 9:30am-midnight.*

Festivals (free at tourist offices) an indispensable guide to seasonal music, dance series, and celebrations. Beware of rock-bottom prices to performances, as seats are often obstructed (like at **Opéra Garnier**) or the venue's acoustics are bad (like at **Opéra Bastille**). For seasonal events, consult **Festivals,** p. 18.

FREE CONCERTS. For listings of free concerts, check the free magazine *Paris Selection*, available at tourist offices throughout the city. Free concerts are often held in churches and parks, especially during summer festivals, and are extremely popular, so plan to arrive at the host venue early. The **American Church in Paris,** 65, quai d'Orsay, *7ème*, sponsors free concerts (Sept.-May Su 6pm; ☎01 40 62 05 00; M: Invalides or Alma Marceau). **Eglise St-Germain-des-Prés** (see **Sights,** p. 95) also has free concerts; check the information booth just inside the door for times. **Eglise St-Merri,** 78, r. St-Martin, *4ème*, is also known for its free concerts (Sept.-July Sa 9pm, Su 4pm; M: Hôtel-de-Ville); contact Accueil Musical St-Merri, 76, r. de la Verrerie, *4ème* (☎01 42 71 40 75 or 01 42 71 93 93; M: Châtelet). Concerts take place W-Su in the **Jardin du Luxembourg's** band shell, *6ème* (☎01 42 34 20 23); show up early for a seat or be prepared to stand. Occasional free concerts are held in the **Musée d'Orsay,** 1, r. Bellechasse, *7ème* (☎01 40 49 49 66; M: Solférino).

VENUES & COMPANIES

Le Bataclan, 50, bd. Voltaire, 11*ème* (☎01 43 14 35 35). M: Oberkampf. An 800-person concert space and café-bar that hosts the likes of Metallica, Oasis, Blur, and Prince, as well as indie rock bands. Tickets start at €15 and vary with show. Call for schedules and reservations. Open Sept.-July. MC/V.

La Cigale, 120, bd. Rochechouart, 18*ème* (☎01 49 25 89 99). M: Pigalle. One of the 2 large rock clubs in Pigalle, seating 2000 for international indie, punk, and hard-core bands. Also stages modern dance shows. Music starts 8:30pm, box office open M-Sa noon-showtime. Concerts €15-35. MC/V.

Cité de la Musique, La Villette, 19*ème* (☎01 44 84 44 84; www.cite-musique.fr). M: Porte de Pantin. Opened in 1995 as one of Mitterrand's *grand projets,* this modern venue hosts everything from lute concerts to American gospel in its enormous *salle des concerts* and smaller *amphithéâtre*. Shows at 8pm; box office open M-Sa noon-6pm, Su 10am-6pm; open until 8pm on performance nights. Ticket prices vary.

Elysée Montmartre, 72, bd. Rochechouart, 18*ème* (☎01 44 92 45 42; www.elyseemontmartre.com). M: Anvers. The biggest-name rock, reggae, and rap venue in Paris. An historic building dating from the First Empire, which served as a revolutionary club during the *Commune*. Featuring well-known British and American groups in addition to young, home-grown talent, and a large dance floor for disco, techno, and salsa nights. Drinks €5-8, shows €15-35. AmEx/MC/V.

L'Etoile du Nord, 16, r. Georgette Agutte, 18*ème* (☎01 42 26 47 47; www.etoiledunord.org). M: Guy Môquet. An independent dance space with impressive modern choreographers. Tickets €7-19, students and over 60 €13. MC/V.

L'Olympia, 28, bd. des Capucines, 9*ème* (☎01 55 27 10 00; www.www.olympiahall.com). M: Opéra. The oldest music hall in Paris. The Beatles and Sinatra played here, and it's still going strong and drawing big-name acts. You, too, can get in on the stomping and the teeny-bopper swooning. Box office open M-Sa 9am-7pm. Tickets €25-60. MC/V.

Opéra de la Bastille, pl. de la Bastille, 12*ème* (☎08 92 69 78 68; www.opera-de-paris.fr). M: Bastille. Opera and ballet with a modern spin. Because of acoustical problems, it's not the place to go all-out for front row seats. Subtitles in French. Call, write, or stop by for a free brochure of the season's events. Tickets can be purchased by Internet, mail, fax, phone (M-Sa 9am-7pm), or in person (M-Sa 11am-6:30pm). Rush tickets for students under 25 and over 65 15min. before show. For wheelchair access, call 2 weeks ahead (☎01 40 01 18 08). Tickets €60-105. MC/V.

Opéra Comique, 5, r. Favart, 2*ème* (☎01 42 44 45 46; www.opera-comique.com). M: Richelieu-Drouot. Operas on a lighter scale—from Rossini to Offenbach. The 2003-2004 season includes *L'Amour Masqué* and *Rita (ou le mari battu)*. Box office open M-Sa 11am-7pm. Tickets €29-112. Student rush tickets available 15min. before show.

Opéra Garnier, pl. de l'Opéra, 9*ème* (☎ 08 92 89 90 90; www.opera-de-paris.fr). M: Opéra. Hosts symphonies, chamber music, and Ballet de l'Opéra de Paris. Tickets available 2 weeks before shows. Box office open M-Sa 11am-6pm. Last-minute discount tickets available 1hr. before showtime. For wheelchair access, call 2 weeks ahead (☎01 40 01 18 08). Tickets usually €19-64. AmEx/MC/V.

Orchestre de Paris, 252, r. du Faubourg St-Honoré, 8*ème* (☎01 45 61 65 60; www.orchestredeparis.com). M: Ternes. This internationally renowned orchestra may be headed in bold directions under a new artistic director. Season runs Oct.-June; call or stop by for concert calendar. 2003-2004 season includes various works by the likes of Copland, Mozart, and Tchiakovsky. Box office open M-Sa 11am-6pm. Shows at 8pm. Tickets €9.15-57.95. Student tickets (€7.63) for some shows can be reserved in advance. MC/V.

The Local LEGEND

Tour de Force

101 years old this July, the 3500km **Tour de France** (www.letour.fr) is an adrenaline rush for anyone who can catch a glimpse as the race winds its way around the country. In 2003, its centennial year, the Tour began in Paris for the first time since 1963, and passed through the original sixth city of the race: Lyon, Marseille, Toulouse, Bordeaux, Nantes and Paris. Close to 200 cyclists on 22 teams participate in the grueling three-week ordeal, ending last Sunday in July. After putting their mettle to the pedal in a mix of wind, rain, and scorching heat, athletes enter Paris and arrive on the Champs-Elysées for their final laps. Having rested for only two days throughout the race, some ride toward the Arc de Triomphe toasting their achievement with a glass of champagne.

Those interested in camping out to cheer for their favorite cyclist should ask locals for tips—when to arrive and claim a road-side spot, how to travel, where to stay. The mountainous stages, when cyclists climb at slower speeds, make for some of the best spectator material, and die-hard fans will have prime viewing spots claimed days ahead. Book well in advance for accommodation in the Tour towns, and prepare yourself with water, rain gear, sunblock, and a camera to remember the occasion.

Beyond Pinocchio

In 2001, Paris hosted the first biennial international puppet festival, **Biennale Internationale des Arts de la Marionnette,** sponsored jointly by the Parc de la Villette and the Puppet Theatre of Paris. A huge success, the festival returns in early summer every two years, hosting puppeteering groups from all over the world. Chile, Italy, Laos, Belgium, Australia, Spain, and of course, France, were all represented at the 2003 festival.

The festival prides itself on an eclectic collection of performers, ranging from video and choreographed dance to traditional ("pure") puppeteering techniques. On stage, performances show the evolution of the marionette while incorporating other arts, including writing and music (accompaniment is sometimes live). While certain groups incorporate political and social messages into their puppeteering, it's difficult not to sit back and simply enjoy with child-like wonder.

☎01 40 03 75 75; www.biam2003.com or www.villette.com. M: Porte de Pantin. Tickets range from free to €22.

Palais Omnisports de Paris-Bercy, 8, bd. de Bercy, 12*ème* (☎08 92 69 23 00; www.bercy.fr). M: Bercy. The acoustics vary, but the popularity of the performers doesn't—after all, it's tough to fill a stadium. Box office open M-Sa 11am-6pm. Tickets €22-90. MC/V.

Théâtre des Champs-Elysées, 15, av. Montaigne, 8*ème* (☎01 53 23 99 19; www.theatrechampselysees.fr). M: Alma- Marceau. Top international dance companies and orchestras, from world music to chamber music, as well as opera. Season runs Sept.-June. 2003-2004 season includes Mozart's *The Marriage of Figaro*. Buy tickets 3 weeks in advance. Reserve by phone M-F 10am-noon and 2-6pm; box office open M-Sa 1-7pm. Call ahead for wheelchair access. Tickets €5-110. AmEx/MC/V.

Théâtre Musical de Paris, pl. du Châtelet, 1*er* (☎01 40 28 28 40; www.chatelet-theatre.com). M: Châtelet. A superb 2300-seat theater featuring orchestras, ballet companies, opera, and dance. Magnificent acoustics. Season runs Oct.-June. 2003-2004 includes *De Berlioz et Broadway* and *Fosse 2004*. Call ahead for wheelchair access. Tickets €8-10. Last-minute discount tickets available 15min. before show. AmEx/MC/V.

Théâtre de la Ville, 2, pl. du Châtelet, 4*ème* (☎01 42 74 22 77; www.theatredelaville-paris.com). M: Châtelet. Primarily known for its innovative dance productions, this venue also offers a selection of classical and world music concerts. Season runs Sept.-June. Call for program and discounts. Tickets sold by phone M-Sa 11am-7pm; box office open M 11am-7pm, Tu-Sa 11am-8pm. Call ahead for wheelchair access. Tickets €15-22. AmEx/MC/V.

Zénith, 211, av. Jean-Jaures, 19*ème* (☎01 42 08 60 00; www.le-zenith.com). M: Porte de Pantin. This loud, large venue on the edge of the city hosts major rap and rock artists. Tickets start at €16 and are available only from ticket agencies; try FNAC. MC/V.

GUIGNOLS

Grand guignol is a traditional Parisian marionette theater featuring the *guignol*, its classic stock character. It's like Punch and Judy, but without the domestic violence. Although the puppets speak French, they're very urbane, and you'll have no trouble understanding the slapstick, child-geared humor. Nearly all parks have *guignols;* check *Pariscope* for more info. During the months of July and August, all guignols switch to a daily schedule to accommodate the French *vacances scholaires*.

Marionnettes du Luxembourg, in the Jardin du Luxembourg (see **Sights,** p. 91), 6*ème* (☎01 43 26 46 47 or 01 43 29 50 97). M: Vavin. The best *guignol* in

Paris. This theater plays the same classics it has since its opening in 1933, including Little Red Riding Hood, The Three Little Pigs, and others. Running time 45min. Arrive 30min. early for good seats. Performances W 11am, Sa-Su 11am and 4pm. €3.90.

Marionnettes du Champ-de-Mars, on the Champs de Mars (see **Sights,** p. 97), 7*ème* (☎01 48 56 01 44). M: Ecole Militaire. Performances W, Sa-Su 3:15 and 4:15pm. €2.80.

Théâtre Guignol Lyonnais du Parc de Choisy, enter across from 149, av. de Choisy, 13*ème* (☎01 43 66 72 39). M: Place d'Italie or Tolbiac. Performances M, Sa-Su 3:30pm. €1.83.

Marionnettes de Montsouris, in the Parc Montsouris, entrance at av. Reille and r. Gazan, 14*ème* (☎01 46 63 08 09). RER: Cité Universitaire. Performances W, Sa-Su 3:30 and 4:30pm. €2.73.

Marionnettes du Parc Georges Brassens, enter the park across from 86, r. Brancion, 15*ème* (☎01 48 42 51 80). M: Porte de Vanves. Performances W, Sa-Su 4 and 5pm. €2.80.

Théâtre Guignol du Square St-Lambert, 15*ème* (☎01 56 23 10 87). M: Commerce or Vaugirard. Performances W 4 and 5pm; Sa-Su 4, 5, 5:30pm. €2.70.

Guignol du Jardin d'Acclimatation, in the Bois de Boulogne (see **Sights,** p. 125), 16*ème* (☎01 45 01 53 52). M: Sablons. Performances W, Sa-Su 3 and 4pm. €2.50.

Marionnettes du Ranelagh, Jardins du Ranelagh, av. Ingres, 16*ème* (☎01 45 83 51 75). M: La Muette. Performances W, Sa-Su 3:15 and 4:15pm. €2.45.

Guignol de Paris, in the Parc des Buttes-Chaumont (see **Sights,** p. 123), enter from the corner of av. Simon Bolivar and r. Botzaris, 19*ème* (☎01 43 64 24 29). M: Buttes-Chaumont. Performances W, Sa-Su 4pm. €2.50.

Théâtre Guignol Anatole, Parc des Buttes-Chaumont, 19*ème* (☎01 40 30 97 60; www.petits-buffons.com). M: Laumière. Performances W and Su 3:30 and 4:45pm, Sa 4:45pm. €3.

Christian
Dior

INSIDE

Shopping

Fashion is born by small facts, trends, or even politics, never by trying to make little pleats and furbelows, by trinkets, by clothes easy to copy, or by the shortening or lengthening of a skirt.
—Elsa Schiaparelli

In a city where Hermès scarves function as slings for broken arms and department store history stretches back to the mid-19th century, shopping in Paris is nothing less than an art form. Be prepared to expend every ounce of available energy and patience while out in the boutique battlefield, but take comfort in the knowledge that your efforts will pay off. Almost everything in this city, from the world's most expensive dresses to the newest in trendy clubwear to kitchen appliances, is astoundingly stylish. The brave and experimental, willing to splurge on the independent designs of off-the-beaten path boutiques in the 18*ème* or the Marais, will be especially rewarded with one-of-a-kind pieces—wearable evidence of your exploits in the fashion capital of the world.

A BRIEF HISTORY OF PARISIAN FASHION

Paris has been at the vanguard of fashion since the Romans got tunic-making tips from the Gauls. Or at least since the 17th century, when the ever more extravagant costumes of royals and aristocrats inspired the envy of both the wealthy and the lowly, who eventually got so fed up with those five-foot high wigs and ten-foot wide skirts that they started a

Couture Culture

Every year, in January and July, the stars collide: models, designers, actresses, and heireses descend on Paris for the *haute couture* fashion shows. Journalists and groupies follow in their wake–and the world, or at least the part of it that cares about fashion, watches.

Haute couture (high fashion) is a strictly defined business, subject to regulations of French Department of Industry. Only 18 houses qualify as *haute couturiers* today, employing 4500 designers and craftspeople. Every *haute couture* garment is made entirely by hand and fitted precisely to the body of the model or client. Due to the astronomical price tags–a dress can cost up to $100,000–there are only 1500 *couture* clients in the world today (there were 15,000 in 1947). Many of the designs are totally unwearable, made only for the spectacle of the runway. *Couture* houses gain most of their profit from the (somewhat) less expensive **prêt-a-porter** (ready-to-wear) lines (what you see in stores), and from the overpriced fragrances and cosmetics that commoners can afford, purchasing a little bit of glamor with their lipsticks.

Recently, some have claimed that due to dwindling profits and supposedly lessening creativity, *haute couture* will soon die out. But it continues to be defended by designers and scholars, who see it as the space where fashion forgets practicality and becomes art, and by the government, which sees it as a part of French cultural heritage–and to influence, however indirectly, what the world wears.

Revolution. Post-Revolutionary **Empire** style, perhaps aware of its mistakes in the previous century, was all about a "simple" Neoclassical ideal. But fashion as we know it today came into being in the 1800s, when the first department stores were built (see p. 246), the *bourgeoisie* became consummate consumers, artists like **Edouard Manet** and writers like **Charles Baudelaire** began to represent fashion as a signifier of modernity—a unique expression of the "the moral and aesthetic feeling" of the era—and the *couturier* (designer; see **Couture Culture,** at left) was born.

The first modern *couturier* was **Charles Frederick Worth,** whose House of Worth opened in Paris in 1858; he invented the fashion show, the designer as celebrity (clothing-makers had previously been considered lowly artisans), and the label as status-symbol. In the early 20th century, designers like **Madeliene Vionnet** and **Paul Poiret,** influenced by Art Nouveau and Orientalist trends, "liberated" women out of the corsets and heavy petticoats and into whimsical shapes and flowing bias-cut dresses. In the 1920s **Coco Chanel** revolutionized women's dress forever with her boyish elegance, insistence on comfort, invention of the "little black dress," and legendary suits. Meanwhile, the designs of innovators like **Elsa Schiaparelli** echoed radical art movements like Surrealism and Cubism (Salvador Dali designed the fabric for some of her dresses). During WWII, strict regulations were enforced on fabric and design, and patriotic self-denial came into fashion. But in 1947, **Christian Dior** aroused shock, anger, and delight with the cinched waists and outlandishly full skirts of his New Look, reestablishing Paris as the center of the fashion world and, once again, reinventing the way the female form was idealized. In the 1960s, **André Courreges** and **Paco Rabanne** moved fashion in ever more fantastically futuristic directions, employing bold shapes and radical new materials. **Yves Saint Laurent** dominated Parisian fashion throughout the second half of the 20th century with his unconventional embrace of androgynous style and Left Bank beatnik chic.

Today, designers like **Jean-Paul Gaultier** and **Christian Lacroix** create clothing that fascinates fashionistas and inspires imitation the world over, displaying it in extravagant bi-annual spectacles. As it always has, fashion continues to exist at the crossroads of art and consumerism; to inspire loathing and obsession; to reinvent the past and imagine the future; and to shape—and be shaped by—the way we perceive our desires, bodies, and eras. And Paris is where it happens. Prepare to be amazed.

BY ARRONDISSEMENT

ÎLE ST-LOUIS

NEIGHBORHOOD QUICKFIND: ***Discover,*** *p. 2;* ***Sights,*** *p. 67;* ***Food & Drink,*** *p. 170.*

Shopping on Île St-Louis is not for the faint of heart—you can spend a fortune on antiques or rare books, both of which abound on this historical piece of land. Unique boutiques can be found all over the island, however, and you might find that one-of-a-kind hat (or toaster) that you've been looking for. Most stores cluster on **rue St-Louis-en-l'Île.**

CLOTHING & ACCESSORIES

Pylones, 57, r. St-Louis-en-l'Île (☎01 46 34 05 02). M: Pont Marie. **Also** at 13, r. Ste-Croix de la Brettonnerie, 4*ème.* All the crazy items that you'll never really need (but will certainly want) are housed in this boutique. Liquid-filled mousepads, decorated crockery, toys, puppets, cut-out-postcards, and cartoonish toasters (€44) fill the shelves and windows of this colorful shop. Open daily 10:30am-7:30pm. AmEx/MC/V/Travelers checks.

Le Grain de Sable, 79, r. St-Louis-en-l'Île (☎01 46 33 67 27; www. grain.de.sable.free.fr). M: Pont Marie. Dozens of hats are displayed throughout the shop, in every color, shape and size imaginable (beginning at €60). *Parisiennes* bring in dresses to match colors when ordering their latest piece, and staff are more than willing to spend hours with each customer. Open daily 11am-7pm. MC/V.

Blaspheme, 37, r. St-Louis-en-l'Île (☎01 43 54 17 30; www.blaspheme.fr). M: Pont Marie. From extravagant charm bracelets to unique handbags, the accessories-obsessed among us will be delighted with finds inside this enticing shop. Also look out for stylish clocks and watches. Open daily 11am-7pm. AmEx/MC/V.

La Boutique Suedoise, 10, r. Jean du Bellay (☎01 56 24 09 09). M: Cite or Pont Marie. Who can resist a little bit of Sweden while in Paris? Clogs, striped socks and tights, sweaters and housewares, all from the north, can be found in this very friendly boutique that charms with the colorful, simple style of Swedish goods. Open Su 1pm-7pm, T-Sa 10am-7pm,

78, 78, r. St-Louis-en-l'Île (☎01 40 46 06 36; www.78-79ilesaintlouis.com). M: Pont Marie. Check out the mirrors and jewelry boxes decorated with colorful ornaments and beads. A fantastic collection of clocks hangs on the walls. If this place whets your appetite, check out the more feminine **79,** at 79, r. St-Louis-en-l'Île. Open daily 11am-7pm. MC/V.

ESSENTIAL INFORMATION

GOING ONCE, GOING TWICE... SOLDES!

Twice a year, Parisians and tourists alike hit the pavement for what is the shopper's version of the Tour de France. As during the famed bicycle race, Paris's semi-annual sales will take you down winding roads and through superstores to find that last pair of beaded mules at a quarter of their original price in your size.

The two great *soldes* (sales) of the year start right after New Year's and at the very end of June. If you don't mind slimmer pickings, the best prices are at the beginning of February and the end of July. And if at any time of the word *braderie* (clearance sale) appears in a store window, that is your signal to enter said store without hesitation.

FIRST & SECOND ARRONDISSEMENTS

NEIGHBORHOOD QUICKFIND: ***Discover,*** *p. 7;* ***Sights,*** *p. 73;* ***Museums,*** *p. 146;* ***Food & Drink,*** *p. 171;* ***Nightlife,*** *p. 206;* ***Accommodations,*** *p. 254.*

Sugar and spice, and all things naughty. In these two tourist-packed *arrondissements*, the fabrics are a little cheaper and the style is younger, especially around **rue Tiquetonne**. A stroll down **rue Etienne-Marcel** will delight shoe fetishists. The popular **Forum Les Halles** (see p. 247) and the streets that surround it offer everything you'll need for a full urban warrior aesthetic.

the local story

Antique Chic

Eric Chocki knows fashion. As proprietor of the *4ème*'s **Les Antiquaires de la Mode** (see p. 238)—one of Paris's hottest spots for vintage fashion—he is fluent in Dior, Pucci, and his mother tongue, Chanel. *Let's Go* spoke with Chocki about his passion for clothes.

LG: When did you open this boutique?
EC: We just opened this shop one year and three months ago [in March 2002].

LG: Has fashion always been important to you?
EC: Yes, I started as a designer and then I started to collect clothes....A lot of friends came in to my flat and said 'Eric, you have such nice things....Why don't you open a shop and sell vintage things?' So I decided to open this shop. I want this shop [to be] very fun.

LG: Where are the most fashionable places in Paris?
EC: This area, the *4ème* is a really nice area of fashion. There are a lot of designer shops and a lot of creative shops here....There are two areas in Paris that are very famous: the *4ème* and the *6ème* are both very nice areas for fashionable people.

LG: If I had €1000, how would you make me sexy?
EC: If you want to be sexy I would propose a Thierry Mugler dress....Also, we sell

MEN'S & WOMEN'S CLOTHING

Le Shop, 3, r. d'Argout, *2ème* (☎01 40 28 95 94). M: Etienne-Marcel. Whatever you buy here, you'll be the only one with it back home. 2 levels, 1200 sq. m and 24 "corners" of sleek Asian-inspired club wear plus a live DJ. Shirts and pants start at around €50. Open M 1-7pm, Tu-Sa 11am-7pm. AmEx/MC/V.

Espace Kiliwatch, 64, r. Tiquetonne, *2ème* (☎01 42 21 17 37). M: Etienne-Marcel. Walk against traffic on r. de Turbigo and go left on r. Tiquetonne. One of the most popular, fun shops in Paris. Pre-owned *(fripe)* shirts from €19, pants from €30. New, pricier clothes, books, furnishings and other funky stuff also for sale. MC/V.

SHOES & ACCESSORIES

Jacques Le Corre, 193, r. St-Honoré, *1er* (☎01 42 96 97 40). Stunning high-end women's shoes, handbags and hats. Jacques only makes 4 pairs of each shoe model, and only sells them at this small boutique and one in New York City (at much higher prices). Staff is friendly—even if you don't look like you could buy the whole store. Shoes €350, hats €140, handbags €300 (but, like the rest of Paris, everything is about half-price in June and July). All handmade in France. Open M-Sa 10am-7pm. AmEx/MC/V.

Longchamp, 404, r. St-Honoré, *1er* (☎01 43 16 00 18). **Also** at 21, r. du Vieux-Colombier, *6ème* (☎01 42 22 74 75). The classic leather-strapped canvas totes that fold up into painfully cute and glaringly useless little bundles. Basic bags start at €45. Open M-Sa 10am-7pm. AmEx/MC/V

Colette, 213, r. St-Honoré, *1er* (☎01 55 35 33 90; www.colette.fr). M: Concorde. An "anti-department store" whose bare display tables feature an eclectic selection of art books, scuba watches, Japanese vases, and Dean & DeLuca pasta sauce—you'll surely find something affordable. Second floor has high-priced clubwear. Downstairs café has free (temperamental) Internet for Macs equipped with AirPort. Open M-Sa 11am-7pm. AmEx/MC/V.

La Droguerie, 9-11 r. du Jour, *1er* (01 45 08 93 27). M: Etienne Marcel. What seems like every button, ribbon or yarn ever made. Everything you would need to do anything from patch a hole in your backpack to create a ball gown (except the fabric). Open M 2-6:45pm, Tu-Sa 10:30am-6:45pm.

BOOKS & MUSIC

W.H. Smith, 248, r. de Rivoli, *1er* (☎01 44 77 88 99; www.whsmith.fr). M: Concorde. Large general selection includes many scholarly works. A good selection of magazines and tourist guidebooks. Sunday *New York Times* available by M after 2pm. Open M-Sa 9am-7:30pm, Su 1-7:30pm. AmEx/MC/V.

Brentano's, 37, av. de l'Opéra, *2ème* (☎01 42 61 52 50; www.brentanos.fr). M: Opéra. An American and French bookstore with an extensive selection of English literature, guidebooks, and greeting cards in English. Paperbacks €8-16. Open M-Sa 10am-7:45pm. AmEx/MC/V.

Monster Melodies, 9, r. des Déchargeurs, *1er* (☎01 42 33 25 72). M: Les Halles. Downstairs supplies the used CDs, while the upstairs overflows with records. Mostly American pop and rock, but some techno and indie rock. CDs €€8-22. Open M-Sa 11am-7pm.

THIRD & FOURTH ARRONDISSEMENTS

NEIGHBORHOOD QUICKFIND: ***Discover,*** *p. 8;* ***Sights,*** *p. 79;* ***Museums,*** *p. 146;* ***Food & Drink,*** *p. 174;* ***Nightlife,*** *p. 207;* ***Accommodations,*** *p. 257.*

Shopping in the Marais is a complete aesthetic experience: boutiques of all colors and flavors pop out along medieval streets and among welcoming, tree-shaded cafés (M: St-Paul or Hôtel-de-Ville). What the Marais does best is independent designer shops selling truly unique creations, as well as vintage stores that line **rue Vieille-du-Temple, rue de Sévigné, rue Roi de Sicile** and **rue des Rosiers.** The best selection of affordable-chic menswear in Paris can be found here, especially along **rue Ste-Croix-de-la-Bretonnerie,** in stores catering to a largely gay clientele—but anyone, queer or otherwise, who wants to absorb a bit of metrosexual Euro-style should check them out. Most stores are open Sundays.

MEN'S & WOMEN'S CLOTHING

Free 'P' Star, 8 r. Ste-Croix-de-la-Bretonnerie, *4ème* (☎ 01 42 76 03 72). M: Hôtel-de-Ville. Enter as Plain Jane and leave as a star. Start with a sexy sailor top (€20), add a velvet blazer (€50) and a trendy bag (€20), finish off with sizzling hot pants (€20). P is for porn (of course!). Open Su 2-11pm, Tu-Sa noon-11pm.

WOMEN'S CLOTHING

Culotte, 7, r. Malher, *4ème* (☎01 42 71 58 89). M: St-Paul. Japanese designs ranging from ripped printed tees to 40s-style dresses, all handmade and reasonably priced. Funky vintage jewelry, especially of the mod and 80s variety. Most items under €100. Open Su 1-7pm, Tu-Sa 11am-7pm. AmEx/MC/V.

Plein Sud, 21, r. des Francs-Bourgeois, *4ème* (☎01 42 72 10 60). M: St-Paul. A sweep of delicate, shimmering tops (starting at €100) and dead-sexy dresses (from €200) that will add a spark to any wardrobe—and take it away from any wallet. Open M-Sa 11am-7pm, Su 2-7pm. AmEx/MC/V.

a lot of Pucci dress[es] for young people. We want to be very 1970s looking. So very Pucci...It's about €500-700 to have a nice dress from all those companies.

LG: Do you have to be skinny to buy clothes here?
EC: We have clothes for every body type....People who are big in size don't want to look older. They want to be young looking, very stylish, very vintage. It's possible. In the shop we get sizes 6-12 currently, but if I have people who want a size bigger I can get it.

LG: What is the one article of clothing you absolutely couldn't live without?
EC: Chanel....I have a big collection of Chanel things. I don't sell many Chanel things in the shop because the look of Chanel is very *ladies*. Chanel is very womanlike, a Jackie Kennedy, a woman who wants to be very *woman*.

LG: Is there any aspect of American fashion that you hate?
EC: I think Americans have nice style....It's very new in France to get a vintage shop because it's not in the personality of French people to get things from the past and use it. This is very English and American....Americans are very stylish. They use a lot of vintage things.

LG: Besides Chanel, who is the best designer?
EC: After Chanel, I have so many....I like to mix designers....I hate to have a complete look from a designer....It depends on how you are feeling when you get up in the morning. Sometimes you want to be dressy and sometimes you want to be happy....You have to feel well in your head to feel well in your clothes.

Bernie X, 12, r. de Sévigné, *4ème* (☎01 44 59 35 88). M: St-Paul. A tiny boutique filled to the brim with everything from centerpiece candles to lacy 50s-style underwear to tailored pants to slipper-shoes. Bags €100-160. Open M 2-7:30pm, Tu-Sa noon-7:30pm, Su 3-7:30pm. MC/V.

Bel'Air, 2, r. des Rosiers, *4ème* (☎01 48 04 82 16). M: St-Paul. At the intersection with r. Malher. Beads, lace, sequins and appliqué flowers abound here. Flirty, feminine clothes with an experimental edge (€50-100). Open M-Sa 10:30am-7:30pm, Su 2-7:30pm. AmEx/MC/V.

Abou d'abi Bazar, 10, r. des Francs-Bourgeois, *3ème* (☎01 42 77 96 98). M: St-Paul. Fun and flirty French fashion with all the newest trends at affordable prices. Most items under €100. Features labels like Tara Jarmon, Les Petites, and Vanessa Bruno. The accessories are not to be missed. Open Su-M 2-7pm, Tu-Sa 10:30am-7:15pm. AmEx/MC/V.

MEN'S CLOTHING

Loft Design By Paris, 12, r. de Sévigné, *4ème* (☎01 48 87 13 07). **Also** at 12, r. du Faubourg-St-Honoré, *8ème* (☎01 42 65 59 65). M: Concorde or Madeleine. Mostly men's clothing, including well-tailored shirts and casual sweaters and pants. Loft's selling points are refinement and style rather than innovation. Open M-Sa 11am-7pm. AmEx/MC/V.

Boy'z Bazaar, 5, r. Ste-Croix-de-la-Bretonnerie, *4ème* (☎01 42 71 94 00). M: Hôtel-de-Ville. A large selection of all that's elegant and trendy in casual menswear from Energie to Paul Smith. Caters largely to a gay clientele, though straight men would do well to follow their fashion lead. Jeans €100-200. Nipple-piercing t-shirts €40-50. Athletic-wear branch down the street at no. 38. Open M-Th noon-9pm, F-Sa noon-midnight, and Su 2-8pm. AmEx/MC/V.

Fabien Nobile, 7, r. Ferdinand Duval (☎01 42 78 51 12). M: St-Paul. With brands like Be Ice Be, Desize, Phard, and Free, this campy boutique is the place to expand your *club couture*. Bad-ass rhinestone-studded Ts (€35-60), tight trousers (€80-110), and an impressive selection of denim jackets (around €150). Open daily noon-8pm, Th until 9pm.

IEM, 16, r. Ste-Croix-de-la-Bretonnerie, *4ème* (☎01 42 74 01 61; www.iem.fr). M: Hôtel-de-Ville. This sexy boutique flies the rainbow flag but is popular with a mixed crowd seeking naughty leather bracelets (€11-13) and naughtier iron dog collars (€129). Like to play dress up? Police and military uniforms from €60. Open Su 2-9pm, Tu-Th 1-8pm, F-Sa 1-10pm.

VINTAGE & CONSIGNMENT CLOTHING

Les Antiquaires de la Mode, 11, r. d'Ormesson (☎01 42 78 05 45). M: St-Paul. Eric and Jaques, the friendly "antique dealers of fashion" who run this vintage-trendy boutique (see **The Local Story: Antique Chic,** p. 236), offer reincarnated Jackie O.-style dresses (€100), Chanel suits (€150), and the latest in Playboy Bunny handbags (€60-70). Open Su and Th-Sa 2-7:30pm. MC/V.

Alternatives, 18, r. de Roi de Sicile, *4ème* (☎01 42 78 31 50). M: St-Paul. This upscale second-hand shop sells an eclectic collection of quality clothes, including many designers at reasonable (if not exactly cheap) prices. Most items over €100. Prada boots €84, Yves St-Laurent gowns €300. Open Tu-Sa 11am-1pm and 2:30-7pm. MC/V.

Vertiges, 85, r. St-Martin, *3ème* (☎01 48 87 36 64). M: Rambuteau. A consignment shopper's heaven—racks and racks of shirts (€5), skirts, dresses, pants (€10), and fabulous leather jackets (€60-65). Lacoste polos €15. Open M-Sa 10am-8pm, Su noon-8pm.

SHOES & ACCESSORIES

Karine Dupont Boutique, 22, r. de Poitou, *3ème* (☎01 40 27 84 94). M: St-Sébastien Froissart. Mostly from unassuming, waterproof tent material, Karine Dupont makes ingenious bags in every shape imaginable. Most bags €40-80. Open M-Sa noon-7:30pm. MC/V.

Sentimental, 14, r. du Roi de Sicile, *4ème* (☎01 42 78 84 04). M: St-Paul. Always wanted a pair of shoes made to order? All of the models on the floor can be made in your size and of whatever material you desire—if you're willing to pay. Men from €206; women from €428. Open Tu-Sa 2-7pm. AmEx/MC/V.

Monic, 5, r. des Francs-Bourgeois, *4ème* (☎01 42 72 39 15). M: Chemin Vert or St-Paul. **Also** at 14, r. de l'Ancienne-Comedie, *6ème* (☎01 43 25 36 61). M: Odéon. Jewelry of all types abounds at this fantastic boutique. Silver, gold, precious and semi-precious stones anywhere from €1-300; mostly under €50. Jewels for your pierced belly-button from €6. Open Su-M 2:30-7pm, Tu-Sa 10am-7pm. AmEx/MC/V.

Brontibay, 3, r. de Sevigné, *4ème* (☎01 42 76 90 80). M: St-Paul. Beautiful, bright, and fun bags come in all shapes and sizes, with materials ranging from canvas to leather to delicate silk. Prices start at €25; most bags go for around €75-€175. Open M 11am-8pm, Tu-Sa 1-8pm, Su 1-6pm. MC/V.

Lollipops, 2, r. des Rosiers, *4ème* (☎01 42 77 43 75; www.lollipops.fr). M: St-Paul. Sugar 'n spice at just the right price. This boutique specializes in bags and purses (€30-60) but dabbles in sandals, bathing suits, and beaded jewelry. Tawdry army and go-go-esque belts from €10. Open M-Sa noon-6pm. MC/V.

Tokyoite, 12, r. du Roi de Sicile, *4ème* (☎01 42 77 87 01). M: St-Paul. A large selection of vintage and new Nike and Converse sneakers—spend the €100 for the ultimate sporty chic. Sleek, Japanimation-style motorcycle helmets €200-600 (pricey, yes, but oh-so-necessary). Open Su and Tu-Sa 1-7pm. MC/V.

BOOKS

Les Mots à la Bouche, 6, r. Ste-Croix de la Bretonnerie, *4ème* (☎01 42 78 88 30; librairie@motsbouche.com; www.motsbouche.com). M: Hôtel-de-Ville. From the métro, walk with traffic along r. du Temple and turn right onto r. Ste-Croix de la Bretonnerie. A 2-story bookstore offering queer literature, essays, photography, magazines, and art. Don't miss the video collection (with videos that are somewhere between art and porn) in the corner of the bottom level. Open M-Sa 11am-11pm, Su 2-8pm. MC/V.

Galeries Lafayette

Chapeaux

FIFTH & SIXTH ARRONDISSEMENTS

NEIGHBORHOOD QUICKFIND: ***Discover,*** *p. 3;* ***Sights,*** *p. 86;* ***Museums,*** *p. 148;* ***Food & Drink,*** *p. 177;* ***Nightlife,*** *p. 211;* ***Accommodations,*** *p. 259.*

While you'll find plenty of chain clothing and shoe stores around **boulevard St-Michel** and numerous little boutiques selling chic scarves and jewelry, bookstores of all kinds are where the *5éme* really stands out.

Post-intellectual, materialistic St-Germain-des-Prés, meanwhile, particularly the triangle bordered by **boulevard St-Germain, rue St-Sulpice and rue des Sts-Pères,** is saturated with high-budget names. **Rue du Four** (M: St-Germain-des-Prés) has fun and affordable designers likes **Paul and Joe** (men's; no. 40; ☎01 45 44 97 70; open daily 11am-7:30pm) and **Sinéquanone** (women's, no. 16; ☎01 56 24 27 74; open M-Sa 10am-7:30pm).

Shakespeare & Co.

MEN'S & WOMEN'S CLOTHING

Bill Tornade, 32 r. du Four, 6*ème* (☎01 45 48 73 88). M: St-Germain-des-Prés. This *super-chic* clothing boutique for fashion-plates-in-training sells the latest runway styles sized down for toddlers and small children. Open M-Sa 10:30-7pm. AmEx/MC/V.

WOMEN'S CLOTHING

Moloko, 53, r. du Cherche-Midi, 6*ème* (☎01 45 48 46 79). M: Sèvres-Babylone, St-Sulpice, or Rennes. Simple, Asian-inspired women's clothing with creative twists: surprising colors, shapes, and unique closures. Buy a piece here and wear it for life, and the compliments will keep coming. Dresses from €120. 2 other boutiques in the 4*ème* and Forum des Halles. Open Tu-Sa 11am-1pm and 2-7pm; closed Aug. MC/V.

Tara Jarmon, 18, r. du Four, 6*ème* (☎01 46 33 26 60) and 51, r. de Passy (01 45 24 65 20). **Also** at 73, av. des Champs-Elysées, 8*ème* (☎01 45 63 45 41). Classic feminine styles in lovely fabrics. A relaxed and clean shopping experience that will deliver items you'll wear for years to come. Open M-Sa 10:30am-7:30pm.

Vanessa Bruno, 25, r. St-Sulpice, 6*ème* (☎01 43 54 41 04). M: St-Sulpice. Chic, trendy, simple, exotic, conservative, wild...all describe Vanessa Bruno's beautiful, well-cut clothing creations. Color schemes and fabrics that will fit any wardrobe—if not prices that will fit any budget. Blazers €150, skirts €160, belts €90. Open M-Sa 10:30am-7:30pm. AmEx/MC/V.

SHOES & ACCESSORIES

Om Kashi, 7, r. de la Montagne Ste-Geneviève, 5*ème* (☎01 46 33 46 07). M: Maubert-Mutualité. Imported boxes of henna, incense (more than 300 kinds), and shelves of clothing and jewelry mix with 18th-century furniture in this welcoming store. Also carries the unusual scarves and fabrics that Parisians love to accessorize with. Open M 2-7pm, Tu-Sa 10am-7pm.

Muji, 27 and 30, r. St-Sulpice, 6*ème* (☎01 46 34 01 10). M: Odéon. Made in Japan, this bric-à-brac is affordable, modern, and minimalist. Everything from bathroom candles to magazine racks and bathrobes. Lots under €10. Open M-Sa 10am-8pm. AmEx/MC/V.

No Name, 8, r. des Canettes, 6*ème* (☎01 44 41 66 46). M: St-Sulpice. Smooth sneakers in every color, fabric, and shade of glitter possible. Sandals €53-61, sneakers €60-90. Open M-Tu 10am-1pm and 2-7:30pm, W-Sa 10am-7:30pm. AmEx/MC/V.

Free Lance, 30, r. du Four, 6*ème* (☎01 45 48 14 78). M: St-Germain-des-Prés or Mabillon. You'll wish you had the appropriately quirky style, courage, and budget to wear these shoes. It's hard not to love a pair of *très cher* slick rainbow stilettos or patterned knee-high leather boots. Some more basic merchandise falls just below the €200 mark. Come for the sales. Open M-Sa 10am-7pm. AmEx/MC/V.

BOOKS & MUSIC

Abbey Bookshop, 29, r. de la Parchiminerie, 5*ème* (☎01 46 33 16 24; www.abbeybookshop.com). M: St-Michel or Cluny. This laid-back shop overflows with new and used English-language titles and Canadian pride, furnished by its friendly expat owner. A good selection of travel books (including *How to Survive at the North Pole*). Impressive basement collection of anthropology, sociology, history and literary criticism titles. Also carries French Canadian work and much English language fiction, and happy to take special orders. Ask about author events and Su hikes, or get your name on their email list. Open M-Sa 10am-7pm.

Shakespeare & Co., 37, r. de la Bûcherie, 5*ème*. M: St-Michel. Across the Seine from Notre-Dame. Run by *bon vivant* George Whitman (alleged great-grandson of Walt), this shop seeks to reproduce the atmosphere of Sylvia Beach's 1920s expat hangout at no. 8, r. Dupuytren. The current location has accumulated a quirky and wide selection of new and used books (and a quirky and wide selection of kids, who crash in the back room). Bargain bins outside include French classics in English (€2.50). Open daily noon-midnight. Credit cards accepted for purchases above €15. See listing in **Sights,** p. 90.

Gibert Jeune, 5, pl. St-Michel, 5*ème* (☎01 56 81 22 22). M: St-Michel. Main branch plus 6 specialized branches clustered around the Fontaine St-Michel (you can't miss the yellow canopies). The main place for books in all languages including lots of reduced-price choices.

Very extensive stationery department downstairs. University text **branch,** 27, quai St-Michel (☎01 56 81 22 22). M: St-Michel. Open M-Sa 10am-7pm. General books **branch,** 15bis, bd. St-Denis, 2*ème* (☎01 55 34 75 75). Open M-Sa 10am-7pm. Main branch open M-Sa 9:30am-7:30pm. AmEx/MC/V.

L'Harmattan, 16 and 21bis, r. des Ecoles. 5*ème* (☎01 46 34 13 71; www.editions-harmattan.fr). M: Cluny-La Sorbonne. From the métro, walk with traffic down bd. St-Germain, make a right on r. St-Jacques, and a left onto r. des Ecoles. Over 90,000 titles of Francophone literature from Africa, the Indian Ocean, Antilles, the Middle East, Asia, and Latin America. A good place to go for classic novels. So packed with books that it's hard to navigate. Free General Catalogue available at the entrance to simplify your search or ask any sales staff for help. Open M-Sa 10am-12:30pm and 1:30-7pm. MC/V.

Présence Africain, 25bis, r. des Ecoles, 5*ème* (☎01 43 25 96 67). M: Cluny-La Sorbonne. Both a publisher and a bookstore, this was the first bookstore in Paris to specialize in African literature, history, and social science. The well-organized shelves have everything from contemporary political analysis to children's stories from Francophone African countries. Open M-F 10:30am-7pm, Sa 10:30am-1pm and 2-7pm.

The Village Voice, 6, r. Princesse, 6*ème* (☎01 46 33 36 47; voice.village@wanadoo.fr). M: Mabillon. Takes its name less from the Manhattan paper than from the Parisian neighborhood that was known as *"le village de St-Germain-des-Prés."* An excellent Anglophone bookstore and the locus of the city's English literary life, featuring 3-4 readings, lectures, and discussions every month (Sept.-June). A good selection of English language travel books. Paperbacks €7-14. Open M 2-8pm, Tu-Sa 10am-8pm, Su 2-7pm (closed Su in Aug.). AmEx/MC/V.

San Francisco Book Co., 17, r. Monsieur le Prince, 6*ème* (☎01 43 29 15 70). M: Odéon. The towering shelves of this old bookshop hold scads of second-hand English-language books, both literary and pulp—including some rare and out of print titles. This is a great place to trade in used paperbacks. Open M-W 11am-9pm, Th 11am-8:30pm, F 11am-9pm, Su 2-7:30pm.

Tea and Tattered Pages, 24, r. Mayet, 6*ème* (☎01 40 65 94 35; tandtp@hotmail.com). M: Duroc. This place's funky collection of second-hand English-language books is a lot of fun to browse through. Sell books at €0.30-0.80 per paperback and get a 10% discount on your next purchase. Books €3-11. If they don't have what you want, sign the wish list and you'll be called if it comes in. Tea room serves root beer floats, brownies, and American coffee with free refills. Occasional poetry readings, and lots of

the insider's CITY

r. du Four
r. Canettes
r. Princesse
r. Mabillon
r. Clement
r. Félebion
r. de Siene
r. Toustain
r. Guisarde
1 2 3 4 5
r. Lobineau
TO M St. Sulpice
r. St-Sulpice
ST-SULPICE
r. Tournon
r. Jouvenel
r. Palatine
r. Garancière

LÈCHE-VITRINES

Translation: window-shopping, or, literally, "window-licking." The long streets of the 6ème hold an amazing array of clothing shops, but the smaller streets surrounding St-Sulpice showcase truly drool-worthy window displays and minimalist clothing collections. Go to discover what money really can buy.

1 Yves Saint Laurent. Famous for their handbags and haughty clientele (☎01 43 29 43 00).

2 Lola. Browse among feminine dresses and soft sweaters (☎01 46 33 60 21).

3 Christian Lacroix. See what the golf-club set will be wearing to this year's benefit ball (☎01 42 68 79 00).

4 Tabula Rasa. Try on that pink, tut-skirted cocktail number—the next Little Black Dress? (☎01 3 10 80 74).

5 Nannini. Accessorize with these sleek and shiny handbags (☎01 42 89 14 70).

information for English speakers in Paris. Particularly useful is the free *Insider's Guide,* available in a box just inside the store's door. Open M-Sa 11am-7pm, Su noon-6pm. MC/V for purchases over €15.25.

Gibert Joseph, 26-34, bd. St-Michel, 6*ème* (☎01 44 41 88 88). M: Odéon or Cluny-La Sorbonne. A gigantic *librairie* and music store, with new and used selections. Frequent sidewalk sales with crates of books and notebooks from €2. Good selection of used dictionaries and guidebooks. Open M-Sa 10am-7:30pm; used books open M-Sa 9:30am-7pm. MC/V.

La Chaumière à Musique, 5, r. de Vaugirard, 6*ème* (☎01 43 54 07 25). M: Odéon. As if attending a concert, the sophisticated patrons at this classical music store move quietly and speak softly. Knowledgeable and friendly staff. Bargain bin CDs start at €4. Will buy back and trade used CDs. Open M-F 11am-8pm, Sa 10am-8pm, Su 2-8pm.

Crocodisc, 40-42, r. des Ecoles, 5*ème* (☎01 43 54 47 95 or 01 43 54 33 22). M: Maubert-Mutualité. Music from the big, yellow speakers entertains patrons browsing through 2 rooms of used CDs, tapes, and records. Mainly stocks rock, pop, techno, reggae, and classical. Buys CDs for €2-5. Nearby **Crocojazz,** 64, r. de la Montagne-Ste-Geneviève (☎01 46 34 78 38) stocks jazz and blues. Both stores open Tu-Sa 11am-7pm. MC/V.

SEVENTH ARRONDISSEMENT

NEIGHBORHOOD QUICKFIND: ***Discover,*** *p. 4;* ***Sights,*** *p. 96;* ***Museums,*** *p. 149;* ***Food & Drink,*** *p. 183;* ***Nightlife,*** *p. 213;* ***Accommodations,*** *p. 262.*

Affordable luxury goods are not to be found in the 7*ème*, but that shouldn't stop you from looking. Specialty shops abound, and it's easy to spend an entire day window-shopping. Begin your trek along **rue du Bac** (entire guidebooks have been written about the shops on this street), taking in everything from specialty pens to baby clothes, until you arrive at **Au Bon Marché** (see p. 246) at r. de Sèvres. Stroll down **rue de Sevres,** and if you're tired and hungry, pop into one of the many cafés to recharge.

CLOTHING & ACCESSORIES

La Femme Ecarlaté, 42, av. Bosquet (☎01 45 51 08 44). M: Ecole Militaire. Forgot that $3000 evening gown? Owners Monique and Katie will help you select a Lacroix, Azzarro, Scherre, Balmain, or other designer evening gown for around 10% of the original price. Also rents bridal gowns. 1-night rentals €92-€275. No deposit required. Cash only.

Durand, 77, r. du Bac, 7*ème* (☎01 42 22 63 86). Socks, tights, and fishnets like you've never seen them before. This 3-generation family-run shop sells accessories that you never even knew you needed. Gloves (€15-90), toe-socks (€13), and other cozy footwear for women and men. Such a selection, the Durands often supply theatre and film companies with costume stock. Open M-Sa 9am-7pm.

BOOKS ETC.

Ciné-Images, 68, r. de Babylone (☎01 47 05 60 25; fax 01 45 51 27 50; www.cine-images.com). A cinephile's paradise, this boutique has endless catalogues of stock: original movie posters from the beginning of film history to the late 1970s. Prices range from €23 to as high as €15,250, but it's worth a browse through the shelves even if you can't afford a thing. The kind, English-speaking owner also does amazing restorations and mounting work *(entoilage)* for about €100. Open Tu-F 10am-1pm and 2-7pm, Sa 2-7pm.

Florent Monestier, 47bis, av Bosquet (☎ 01 45 55 03 01) A stroll through the narrow aisles of this shop brings back memories of childhood and, well, adulthood. A mix of traditional wood-carved children's toys and all funky things household, you're sure to find that quintessentially Parisian gift among this quiet boutique's colorful clutter.

Librairie Gallimard, 15, bd. Raspail, 7*ème* (☎01 45 48 24 84; www.librairie-gallimard.com). M: Rue du Bac. The main store of this famed publisher of French classics features a huge selection of pricey Gallimard books. Basement filled with folio paperbacks. Open M-Sa 10am-7pm. AmEx/MC/V.

EIGHTH ARRONDISSEMENT

NEIGHBORHOOD QUICKFIND: ***Discover,*** *p. 9;* ***Sights,*** *p. 100;* ***Museums,*** *p. 150;* ***Food & Drink,*** *p. 184;* ***Nightlife,*** *p. 213;* ***Accommodations,*** *p. 263.*

The *8ème* is not exactly wallet-friendly, but it is perfect for a day of window shopping. Take a break from the exhausting Champs-Elysées and walk along **avenue Montaigne** to admire the great couture houses; their collections change every season, but are always innovative, gorgeous, and jaw-droppingly expensive—and the window displays won't disappoint. Check out **Chanel** at no. 42, **Christian Dior** at no. 30, **Emanuel Ungaro** at no. 2, and **Nina Ricci** at no. 39. **Rue du Faubourg Saint-Honoré** is home to **Lanvin** at no. 22, **Jean-Paul Gaultier** at no. 30, and other boutiques. Around the **Madeleine,** you'll find **Burberry** and some big American names. Keep in mind that many of these shops might as well have a dress code, and you'll find it difficult to browse their collections if you don't look like you can afford them. A more accessible way to peruse *couture* collections is in the major department stores (see p. 246).

Back on the **Champs-Elysées,** you can purchase everything from CDs (check out the **Virgin Megastore,** open until midnight) to perfumes to chocolates, usually until a much later hour than in the rest of Paris. Sale season on the Champs is a great time to pillage the collections and come home with money to spare.

Sephora, 70-72, av. des Champs-Elysées (☎01 53 93 22 50). M: Charles de Gaulle-Etoile. An enormous array of cosmetic products that will awaken your secret (or not-so-secret) vanity. The welcoming carpeted corridor is lined with almost every eau-de-toilette on the market, both for men and women. The perfect place to go wild and transform yourself before a night at the clubs. Prices run the gamut from reasonable to absurd. Open daily 10am-midnight. AmEx/MC/V.

ELEVENTH & TWELFTH ARRONDISSEMENTS

NEIGHBORHOOD QUICKFIND: ***Discover,*** *p. 11;* ***Sights,*** *p. 108;* ***Food & Drink,*** *p. 188;* ***Nightlife,*** *p. 214;* ***Accommodations,*** *p. 266.*

The *12ème* has a surprising number of funky little boutiques, mostly in the northwestern part of the *arrondissement,* around **rue de la Roquette.**

WOMEN'S CLOTHING

Incognito, 41, r. de la Roquette, 12*ème* (☎01 40 21 86 55). M: Bastille. With provocative barely-there dresses (€125), scintillating shear tops (€40), and super-tight jeans (from €60), this popular boutique lets you look hot and pay little. Open daily 11am-8pm. AmEx/MC/V.

Planisphere, 19, r. de la Roquette, 12*ème* (☎01 43 57 69 90). M: Bastille. A large selection of women's jeans (€120-200) with names like Miss Sixty, Killah, and Diesel. Belts (from ordinary to original to over-the-top) €30-50. Open daily 11am-8pm. AmEx/MC/V. **Men's location** at 78, r. de la Roquette (☎01 48 05 10 55).

Nikita, 7, r. de la Roquette, 12*ème* (☎01 47 00 56 81). M: Bastille. Be *that* girl at the party by sporting Nikita's sexy, silky designs. Attention-grabbing pants, skirts, and tops all start at €60. Original bags and shoes. Open M-Sa 11am-8:30pm, Su 2pm-8pm. MC/V.

Atelier 33, 33, r. du Faubourg Ste-Antoine, 12*ème* (☎01 43 40 61 63). M: Bastille. If you can flash the cash, choose from over 200 designs, wait one month, and take home a glamorous gown (€300-2200) in any fabric imaginable. All clothes can be tailored, including the ready-made jackets (€200), pants (€85), and sexy 2-piece Brazilian bathing suits (€70). Prices negotiable. Open daily 10:30am-7:30pm. AmEx/MC/V.

Les Nuits d'Alizée, 21, r. de la Roquette, 12*ème* (☎01 47 00 56 81). M: Bastille. Victoria may have her secret, but Alizée takes the night. The store features intimate offerings by Aubade, Lise Charmel, and Antigel, among others. Bras (€15-35), lingerie ensembles (from €50), and see-through bustiers (€80-100) are sure to make it a late night. Open daily 10am-7:30pm. AmEx/MC/V.

A La Page

Paris is heaven for bibliophiles, who search back alleys and hidden doors, hunting for arcane treasures and obscure whimsies. The true *flâneur* might browse American comic books at **Arkham Comics** (15, r. Soufflot, 5*ème*), old sheet music at the **Librairie Musicale** (☎01 40 28 18 18; 68bis, r. de Réaumur, 3*ème*), bibles of style at **Mode Information** (67, bd. Sébastopol, 2*ème*), or esoteric travelogues at **Ulysse** (☎01 43 25 17 35; 26, r. St-Louis-en-l'Île, Île St-Louis). You might get down with the proletariat at the **Bibliothèque Marxiste** (☎01 40 40 11 18; 21, r. Barrault, 13*ème*), sip wine with your Proust at **La Belle Hortense** (31, r. Vielle-du-Temple, 4*ème*), browse soft-core porn at the trendy **Taschen** showroom (☎01 40 51 70 93; 2, r. de Buci, 6*ème*), get your manuscript critiqued at **La Maroquinerie** (☎01 40 33 30 60; 23, r. Boyer, 20*ème*), or read the Swahili news at the **Bibliothèque Publique d'Information** at the Centre Pompidou, 4*ème*.

And that's only indoors. Collectors and locals spend pleasant, if intense, hours scouring the collections at the **Marchés des Livres Anciens** (part of the Puces de St-Ouen; see p. 248), or in the **Parc Georges Brassens** (r. Brancion, 15*ème*). And, with some exceptions, the Seine-side **bouquinistes** cater more to bibliophiles than tourists. Stalls specialize in anything from ancient Gaul to 1950s kitsch to military history and offer bargain bins where the romantic can find a tattered copy of Voltaire for a euro.

—Maryanthe Malliaris

MEN'S CLOTHING

Stone Company, 6, r. Bréguet, 12*ème* (☎01 47 00 56 81). M: Bastille. Swiss owned and operated but specializing in all things Italian. Shoes (€180), shirts (€60), and leather jackets (up to €2500) by Alkis, Portland, and others. No wardrobe is complete without a cheetah-print belt (€78). Open M 1-8pm, Tu-Su 10am-noon and 1-8pm. MC/V.

ACCESSORIES

Total Eclipse, 40, r. de la Roquette, 12*ème* (☎01 48 07 88 04). M: Bastille. It's time to accessorize. Purchase you-can't-find-me-anywhere-else jewelry in bright colors (from €20), one-of-a-kind necklaces (€56), and a "where-did-you-get-that" bracelet (€30-50). Then shove them in your trendy new bag (€20-160). Open M-Sa 11am-7:30pm. AmEx/MC/V.

La Baleine, 11, r. Boulle, 12*ème* (☎01 43 14 94 94). M: Bastille. Classic toys and accessories by Hello Kitty and Groovy Girls, animal and food shaped lamps (penguin, rabbit, *champignon*...) €39-70, and porcelain figurines €4. Check out the remote-controlled mobiles €30-69. Open M-Sa noon-8pm. MC/V.

BOOKS & MUSIC

Les Soeurs Lumière, 18, r. St-Nicolas, 12*ème* (☎01 43 43 13 15; www.soeurslumiere.fr). M: Ledru Rollin. With the motto "Un livre, un film," this cinema-centered bookstore sells DVDs and the books that they are based on. The selection includes classics like *The Importance of Being Earnest* and more recent works such as *Harry Potter*. Open M-Sa 11am-7pm. MC/V.

L'arbre à Lettres, 62, r. du Faubourg St-Antoine 12*ème* (☎01 53 33 83 23). M: Bastille. A vast selection of French literature. Regular readings and lectures. Consult store for details. Open Su 2-7pm, Tu-Sa 10am-7pm. MC/V.

Vibe Station, 57, r. du Faubourg Ste-Antoine, 12*ème* (☎01 44 74 64 18; www.vibe-station.fr). M: Bastille. House, garage, techno, disco, hip hop, jazz, and R & B on tape, CD, and vinyl. Learn to spin records by buying "The Art of Turntablism" (€34) or just go ahead and buy your turntables (€600). Open M noon-8pm, Tu-Sa 11:30am-8pm. AmEx/MC/V.

Wave, 36, r. Keller, 11*ème* (☎01 40 21 86 98). M: Bastille. This tiny store packs a great selection of techno, house, electronic, jungle, and ambient music. Record and CD players for those who want to listen before buying. Also has a board with posters and flyers listing upcoming shows and other events. Open Tu-F 1-7:30pm and Sa 11am-7:30pm. MC/V.

Born Bad Record Shop, 17, r. Keller, 12*ème* (☎01 43 38 41 78). M: Bastille. Vintage records from all genres, including surf, 60s, disco, and more. Open M-Sa noon-8pm. **Born Bad Exotica** sells clothing and accessories. MC/V.

EIGHTEENTH ARRONDISSEMENT

NEIGHBORHOOD QUICKFIND: ***Discover,*** *p. 13;* ***Sights,*** *p. 119;* ***Museums,*** *p. 156;* ***Food & Drink,*** *p. 195;* ***Nightlife,*** *p. 218;* ***Accommodations,*** *p. 273.*

The 18*ème* has some of the city's most eclectic shopping: stroll around **rue de Lavieuville** for funky independent designer wares. In the **Goutte d'Or** area, meanwhile, cheap fabric and clothing stores abound.

WOMEN'S CLOTHING

Spree, 16, r. de Lavieuville (☎01 42 23 41 40). M: Abbesses. A colorful mix of fabrics and styles, Spree carries some of the cutest and most original girl's wear in Paris. Don't miss the baskets of patterned underwear and socks! Skirts around €70, screen-printed t-shirts €30. Open Tu-Sa 11am-7pm.

Lili Perpink, 22, r. de Lavieuville (☎01 42 52 37 24). M: Abbesses. This cool white space displays shoes and clothing from independent designers alongside Japanese flavored housewares. Racks of skirts, t-shirts, jackets, and trousers are at the back of the shop. Clothing ranges from €30-400. Open Tu-Sa noon-7pm.

CHAIN STORES

MEN'S & WOMEN'S CLOTHING

agnès b., 6-12, r. du Vieux-Colombier (☎01 44 39 02 60). M: St-Sulpice. Men's at 12, women's at 6, plus several other locations throughout the city. No matter what the current trend in fashion may be, you can always depend on agnès b's classic separates. Often features some original and stylish pieces. A staple of Parisian casual fashion. Open daily 10am-7pm. AmEx/MC/V.

H&M, 120 r. de Rivoli, 1*er* (☎01 55 34 96 86). M: Châtelet. Other locations throughout the city. This fabulous Swedish chain sells stylish and inexpensive, if not particularly well-made, clothes for the whole family. Open M-Sa 10am-8pm. AmEx/MC/V.

Esprit, 72bis, r. Bonaparte. M: St-Germain-des-Prés or Mabillon. Other locations throughout the city. Men's and women's classics and basics done cheaply with a sporty turn. Women's turtleneck sweater €50; short-sleeve blouse €39.50. AmEx/MC/V.

WOMEN'S CLOTHING

Petit Bateau, 26, r. Vavin, *6ème* (☎01 55 42 02 53). M: Vavin or Notre-Dame-des-Champs. Other locations throughout the city. T-shirts, tanks, undies, and pajamas in the softest of cottons. A children's store, but the stylish Parisian mothers are not there for their kids—the size for age 16 is about the same as an American 6; sizes go up to age 18. Tees and tanks €6.50. Open M-Sa 10am-7pm; Aug. M 2-7pm, T-Sa 10am-7pm. AmEx/MC/V.

Mango, 3, pl. du 18 Juin, 6*ème* (☎01 45 48 04 96). **Also** at 82, r. de Rivoli, 4*ème* and 6, bd. des Capucines, 9*ème* (☎01 53 30 82 70). This Spanish chain delivers fun and fashionable European styles at reasonable prices. Open M-Sa 10am-8pm. AmEx/MC/V.

Naf Naf, 25, bd. St- Michel, 5*ème* (☎01 43 29 36 45). **Also** at 52, av. des Champs-Elysées, 8*ème* (☎01 45 62 03 08), 34, r. du Faubourg St-Antoine, 12*ème* (☎01 53 33 80 12), and ten and other locations throughout the city. One of the two big French chains (along with Kookaï), Naf Naf sells consistently affordable and usually fashionable clothes to teens and 20-somethings. Open M-Sa noon-7pm. MC/V.

Kookaï, Place Carrée, Forum des Halles, 1*èr* (☎01 40 26 40 30). **Also** at 155, r. de Rennes, 6*ème* (☎01 45 48 26 36), 66, bd. de Montparnasse, 15*ème* (☎01 45 38 74 30), and 15 other locations throughout the city. Quintessential French clothing chain with fabulous and fashionable (if not terribly durable) items. Open M-Sa 10:30am-7:30pm.MC/V.

Zara, 128, r. de Rivoli, *1er* (☎ 01 44 82 64 00). **Also** at 140bis, r. de Rennes, *6ème* (☎01 42 84 44 60) and 38 and 44, av. des Champs-Elysées, *8ème* (☎01 45 61 52 80). An immense Spanish chain with upscale but reasonably-priced clothing. Also has great shoes, lingerie and accessories. Shirts start at €20, skirts at €30. Some men's and children's apparel. Open M-Sa 10am-8pm. AmEx/MC/V.

Zadig & Voltaire, 15, r. du Jour, *1er* (☎01 42 21 88 70). M: Etienne-Marcel. 6 other locations around Paris. Funky, sleek, and expensive women's designs by Paul & Jack, Holly, etc. Their own label does soft, feminine designs. A big selection of handbags. Shirts from €80, pants from €150. Opening hours vary by branch. Main branch open M 1-7:30pm, Tu-Sa 10:30am-7:30pm. AmEx/MC/V.

Cacharel, 64, r. Bonaparte, *6ème* (☎01 40 46 00 45). M: St-Germain-des-Prés. Other locations throughout the city. The house of Cacharel has gone upscale, more mature, and ultra-stylish of late. Emphasis is on bold patterns and bright colors. T-shirts start at €60, but dresses can get up to €500. Open M-F 10:30am-7pm, Sa 10:30am-7:30pm. AmEx/MC/V.n

MEN'S CLOTHING

Celio, 60, r. de Rivoli, *1er* (☎01 42 21 18 04). M: Palais-Royal. Other locations throughout the city. Exhaustive collection of shirts, jeans, pants, and sweaters of all styles. The Celio Sport section of the store carries basic athletic wear. And everything is more than reasonably priced (tees €15, shirts €25, jeans €40). Most stores open M-Sa 11am-7pm. AmEx/MC/V.

BOOKS & MUSIC

FNAC (Fédération Nationale des Achats et Cadres), is the big Kahuna of music chains in Paris and has 10 locations throughout the city. The Champs-Elysées (74, av. des Champs-Elysées, ☎01 53 53 64 64), Bastille (4, pl. de la Bastille, ☎01 43 42 04 04), Italiens (24, bd. des Italiens,☎01 48 01 02 03), and Etoile (26-30, av. des Ternes, ☎01 44 09 18 00) branches are the largest, with a comprehensive selection of music, stereo equipment, and, in some cases, books. Use scanners to listen to any CD in the store. Tickets to nearly any concert and many theater shows can be purchased at the FNAC ticket desk located on the ground level of the store. For detailed and helpful information (for French speakers, anyway), visit the web site at www.fnac.com. All branches open at 10am, and most close at 7:30 or 8pm. The Champs-Elysées and Italiens branches close at midnight. MC/V.

DEPARTMENT STORES

Au Bon Marché, 22, r. de Sèvres, *7ème* (☎01 44 39 80 00). M: Sèvres-Babylone. Paris's oldest department store, Bon Marché has it all, from scarves to smoking accessories, designer clothes to home furnishings. Look out for the shoes on the top floor, which get their own display cases, lights, and guards! Across the street is *La Grande Epicerie de Paris,* Bon Marché's celebrated (and reasonably priced) gourmet food annex. Open M-W and F 9:30am-7pm, Th 10am-9pm, Sa 9:30am-8pm. AmEx/MC/V.

Au Printemps, 64, bd. Haussmann, *9ème* (☎01 42 82 50 00). M: Chaussée d'Antin-Lafayette or Havre-Caumartin. **Also** at 30, pl. d'Italie, *13ème* (☎01 40 78 17 17), M: Place d'Italie; and 21-25, cours de Vincennes, *20ème* (☎01 43 71 12 41), M: Porte de Vincennes. One of the two biggies in the Parisian department store scene. Oo-la-la your way through endless *couture* (more women's fashion than men's). Most hotels have 10% discounts for use in the store. Haussmann open M-W and F-Sa 9:35am-7pm, Th 9:35am-10pm. Other locations open M-Sa 10am-8pm. AmEx/MC/V.

BHV, 52-64, r. de Rivoli across from the Hôtel-de-Ville, *4ème* (☎01 42 74 90 00). M: Hôtel-de-Ville. Dior, Lacoste, and John Deere? An immense, all-encompassing and completely unpretentious department store. Clothes, accessories, books, home furnishings and the biggest and best hardware store in the heart of Paris. Classy and inexpensive 6th floor café; access to roof and a stellar view of the city. Open M-Tu and Th-Sa 9:30am-7:30pm, W 9:30am-8:30pm. AmEx/MC/V.

Forum des Halles, M: Les Halles or RER: Châtelet-Les Halles, 2*ème* (☎01 44 76 96 56). Subterranean shopping at its best. The four main entrances lead down to over 200 boutiques, including FNAC music and CD store, the cosmetics wonderland Sephora, boutiques featuring independent designers, and a 4-story H&M. Take a break from shopping at the movie theater or swimming pool. All stores open M-Sa 10am-7:30pm.

Galeries Lafayette, 40, bd. Haussmann, 9*ème* (☎01 42 82 34 56). M: Chaussée d'Antin. **Also** at 22, r. du Départ, 14*ème* (☎01 45 38 52 87), M: Montparnasse. Chaotic (the equivalent of Paris's entire population visits here each month), but carries it all, including mini-boutiques of Kookaï, agnès b., French Connection, and Cacharel. The astounding gourmet food annex, *Lafayette Gourmet,* on the first floor, has everything from a sushi counter to a mini-*boulangerie* to its own security guards. Haussmann open M-W and F-Sa 9:30am-7:30pm, Th 9:30-9pm; Montparnasse open M-Sa 9:45am-7:30pm. AmEx/MC/V.

Monoprix, locations throughout Paris. Monoprix means "one price"–a cheap one. Everything from *pâté* to bathing suits to wine glasses. Most locations open daily 9:30am-7:30pm, but some open until 10pm. MC/V.

Samaritaine, 67, r. de Rivoli, on the quai du Louvre, 1*er* (☎01 40 41 20 20). M: Pont Neuf, Châtelet-Les Halles, or Louvre-Rivoli. 4 large, historic Art Deco buildings between r. de Rivoli and the Seine, connected by tunnels and bridges. Not as chic as Galeries Lafayette or Bon Marché, as it dares to sell souvenirs (gasp!) and merchandise at down-to-earth prices (the horror!), but a calmer, pleasant shopping experience. The rooftop observation deck provides one of the best views of the city; take the elevator to the 9th floor and climb the short, spiral staircase. Most hotels offer 10% discount coupons for the store. Open M-W and F-Sa 9:30am-7pm, Th 9:30am-10pm. AmEx/MC/V.

Tati, 13, pl. de la République, 3*ème* (☎01 48 87 72 81). M: République. **Also** at 106, r. Faubourg du Temple, 11*ème* (☎01 43 57 92 80), M: Belleville; and 4, bd. de Rochechouart, 18*ème* (☎01 55 29 50 00), M: Barbès-Rochechouart. A fabulously kitschy, chaotic, crowded, and cheap department store. Generally low-end, but worth rummaging through. Get your sales slip made out by one of the clerks (who stand around for just that purpose) before heading to the cashier. All branches open M-F 10am-7pm, Sa 9:15am-7pm. AmEx/MC/V.

OUTLET STORES

CENTRAL PARIS

Stock is French for outlet store, with big name clothes for less—often because they have small imperfections or are from last season. Many are on r. d'Alésia in the 14*ème* (M: Alésia), including **Cacharel Stock,** no. 114 (☎01 45 42 53 04; open M-Sa 10am-7pm; AmEx/MC/V); **Stock Chevignon,** no. 122 (☎01 45 43 40 25; open M-Sa 10am-7pm; AmEx/MC/V); **S.R. Store** (Sonia Rykiel) at nos. 110-112 and no. 64 (☎01 43 95 06 13; open Tu 11am-7pm, W-Sa 10am-7pm; MC/V); **Stock Patrick Gerard,** no. 113 (☎01 40 44 07 40). A large **Stock Kookaï** bustles at 82, r. Réamur, 2*ème* (☎01 45 08 93 69; open M 11:30am-7:30pm, Tu-Sa 10:30am-7pm); **Apara Stock** sits at 16, r. Etienne Marcel (☎01 40 26 70 04); and **Haut-de-Gomme Stock,** with names like Armani, Khanh, and Dolce & Gabbana, has two locations, at 9, r. Scribe, 9*ème* (☎01 40 07 10 20; open M-Sa 10am-7pm; M: Opéra) and 190, r. de Rivoli, 1*er* (☎01 42 96 97 47; open daily 11am-7pm; M: Louvre-Rivoli).

LA VALLÉE OUTLET SHOPPING VILLAGE

3, cours de la Garonne. Serris (Marne-la-Vallée). ☎*01 60 42 35 00. Take RER A from Châtelet to Val d'Europe (35min. from Châtelet; €10.40 one-way). Exit by Serris Centre Commercial and turn right out of the station. Go through the modern shopping mall until you reach FNAC and the food court. Exit to your right through the food court. Open M-Sa 10am-8pm (7pm in winter), Su 11am-7pm. AmEx/MC/V.*

the insider's CITY

MARCHÉ ST-OUEN

Here are some of the Puces de St-Ouen's gems.

1 Trésors de Perse, stall #41. Start high class, with this stall's ivory-inlaid chairs and Persian carpets.

2 Stalls #51 & #100. These two gallery-esque stalls sell paintings from Provence and bright, abstract canvasses.

3 Stall #128. Feathered hats, oodles of buttons, ribbons, and shells. You can even buy fabric off the spool here.

4 Les Nuits de Satin, #284-85. Victoria's ultimate secret: 19th- and 20th-century vintage lingerie, as well as vintage hats and dresses.

5 Les Verres de Nos Grand-mères, Stall #2. Shelf upon shelf of antique glassware—tread carefully.

6 M. Emberger, Stall #25. Ever wonder what happened when the fair was taken down each summer? The castaway carousel horses and signs came here.

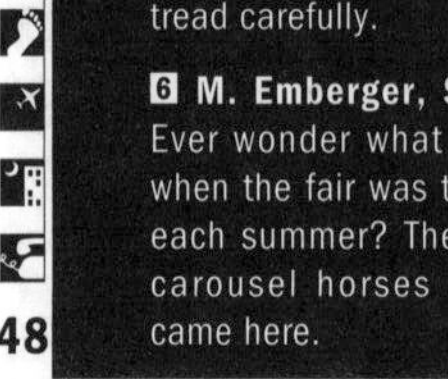

Thirty-five minutes outside of Paris by RER and a 3min. train ride from Disneyland Paris, the Val d'Europe is the most recent in a series of American-style designer outlet malls (complete with playground to keep the kids happy) that have invaded the European shopping scene. Located on the outskirts of other big cities like London, Madrid, and Brussels, the Paris take on the "outlet village" houses *couture* in quaint awninged houses set along a pedestrian "main street." Instead of hot pretzels, vendors tempt weary shoppers with *gauffres* (waffles). European names like **Versace, Apara, Diesel, Camper,** and **MaxMara,** along with American ones like **Tommy Hilfiger** and **Ralph Lauren,** sell last season's collections at slashed prices (at least 33% off regular prices, plus the usual 50% off sales in June). Check out **Coat Concept** for the ultimate polka-dot rain slicker or lambswool winter jacket (€60-200), or stock up on stylish **Bodum** coffee makers and teacups at prices so low you'll buy several kitchens worth. For a complete listing of shops and labels, pick up a map at the visitor's welcome center at the opposite side of the shopping strip. The Vallée remains relatively uncrowded for the time being (especially during the week). But when serious shoppers catch on to this new phenomenon, that's sure to be a thing of the past.

MARCHÉ AUX PUCES

PUCES DE ST-OUEN

Located in St-Ouen, a town just north of the 18ème. M: Porte-de-Clignancourt. ***Open*** *Sa-M 7am-7:30pm (although most stalls open between 9am-10am); most vendors only open between 9am-6pm on M; many of the official stalls close early, but renegade vendors may open at 5am and stay open until 9pm.*

The granddaddy of all flea markets, the Puces de St-Ouen is an overwhelming smorgasbord of stuff. It opens early and shuts down late, and serious hunters should allow themselves the better part of a day in order to cover significant ground. In general, merchandise is either dirt-cheap and shoddy or expensive and antique, but those with patience might find incredible deals in the mix. The market began during the Middle Ages, when merchants resold the cast-off clothing of aristocrats (crawling with fleas—*puces*—hence the name) to peasant-folk. At today's market, while aristocratic clothing might be hard to come by, you can still find style at prices that can't be matched anywhere else in Paris.

RENEGADE MARKET

The 10min. walk along av. de la Porte de Clignancourt, under the highway, and left on r. Jean Henri Fabre to the official market is jammed with tiny **unofficial stalls.** From the moment you exit the metro, you will be surrounded—and hassled—by sellers. These stalls sell flimsy new clothes, African masks, and cheap, colorful jewelry. It's a tourist trap and the pickpockets know it, so keep a close watch on your belongings. If this renegade bazaar turns you off, continue on to the official market, where you'll be able to browse leisurely in a much less crowded setting.

Prepare yourself for a day of selective shopping, and the Puces de St-Ouen will reward.

OFFICIAL MARKET

Located on r. des Rosiers and r. Jules Vallès, the regular market is officially divided into a number of sub-markets, each specializing in a certain type of item. Don't try to follow a set path or worry about hitting every *marché*, as they all generally have the same eclectic collection of everything antique you could ever think of—your best bet is to get lost and then keep browsing. Most of the official markets have posted maps of their layout and stalls which are very helpful once inside.

From r. Jean Henri Fabre, slip into the **Marché Malik,** a warehouse filled with discount and vintage clothing, leather jackets, sneakers, and a tattoo parlor. Exiting onto r. Jules Vallès, and walking away from the bongo drums and hard-sell banter of r. Fabre, you'll encounter the indoor **Marché Jules Vallès** with its overwhelming collection of old trinkets and antique miscellany. **Marché Paul Bert,** on r. Paul Bert, has more antiques as well as a large collection of furniture. Next door at the more posh **Marché Serpette,** specialized antique Art Deco furniture stores reign side-by-side with shops dealing in antique firearms. **Marché Biron,** on r. des Rosiers, has home furnishings for those willing and able to pay a fortune for them (it even has its own specialized worldwide shipping agency). **Marché Dauphine,** also on r. des Rosiers, is home to 300 dealers on two levels and has stalls specializing in leather armchairs, costume dresses, jewelry, and antique kitchenware. **Marché Vernaison,** located between r. des Rosiers and av. Michelet, has more upper-class tchotchkes and furniture, prints, beads, buttons, and musical instruments. The **Marché des Rosiers,** r. Paul Bert (lamps, vases, and 20th-century art) and the **Marché Autica,** r. des Rosiers (paintings, furniture), are smaller, paler shadows of the larger markets. The **Marché Malassis** sells vintage cameras, perfume bottles, *couture*, and furniture.

i ESSENTIAL INFORMATION

COMMENT DIT-ON "RIP-OFF"?

First-time flea market visitors should note some important tips.

–There are no €1 diamond rings here. If you find the Hope Diamond in a pile of schlock jewelry, the vendor planted it there.

–Be prepared to bargain; sellers at flea markets don't expect to get their starting price.

–Pickpockets love crowded areas, especially the one around the unofficial stalls.

–Three Card Monte con artists proliferate. Don't be pulled into the game by seeing someone win lots of money: he's part of the con, planted to attract suckers.

–If you are a savvy rock 'n' roll connoisseur with a sense of patience, this is the place to find rare records. Record peddlers seem not to know what they have, and if you look long enough, you might just find a priceless LP for next to nothing.

INSIDE

Accommodations

TYPES OF ACCOMMODATIONS

HOTELS

Small hotels have long been an institution in the city of Paris; they almost all proudly flaunt their eccentric character. Hotels offer total privacy and (usually) concerned managers. Most importantly, they routinely accept advance reservations. Groups of two or more may find it more economical to stay in a hotel than a hostel, since hotels charge by the room and not by the body. Double rooms can be made into triples with the use of a *lit supplementaire* (pull-out bed, €8-20 extra)—especially useful for families with small children. *Mansarde* rooms are on the top floor; they have sloping ceilings, charm, and more space for extra beds.

The French government rates hotels with zero to four stars depending on the services offered, the percentage of rooms with bath, and other amenities. Most hotels listed here are zero, one- or two-star, with a smattering of inexpensive three-stars. At the absolute minimum, expect to pay €25 for a single room and €30 for a double.

If you want a room with twin beds, make sure to ask for *une chambre avec deux lits* (a room with two beds); otherwise you may find yourself in *une chambre avec un grand lit* (room with a double bed). In our listings, the term "doubles" refers to rooms with one full-size bed; "two-bed doubles" refer to the rare room with two separate (usually twin) beds. Rooms in cheap hotels normally don't have private showers or toilets, but share both with other guests on the same floor. Occasionally, you will have to pay extra for a hot shower (€2-4). Otherwise, hotel rooms may come with a variety of add-ons: *avec bidet-lavabo* means a sink and a bidet, but no toilet; *avec WC* or *avec cabinet* means with sink and toilet; *avec douche* means with shower; and *avec salle de bain* is with a full bathroom. All French hotels display a list on the back of each room's door of the prices of rooms, breakfast, and any residency tax. It is illegal for a hotel to charge a guest more than is shown on this list, although you can try to bargain for a lower rate if you are staying in the hotel for more than a few days.

HOSTELS & FOYERS

Many of Paris's **hostels** don't bother with the restrictions that characterize most international hostels, such as sleepsheets. They do have maximum stays, age restrictions, and lockouts, but these are often flexible. According to French law, all hostels must have a curfew of 2am, although some are more flexible than others. Accommodations in hostels usually consist of single-sex rooms with two to eight beds, but you may be asked whether or not you are willing to stay in a co-ed room. Most rooms are simply furnished with metal or wood frame bunkbeds, thin sheets, and cheap blankets. Most hostel rooms have sinks and mirrors; showers and toilets are in a courtyard or communal hallway.

Foyers are simple accommodations intended for university students or workers during the academic year and are available for short- or long-term stays during the summer. They offer the security and privacy of a hotel and the lower prices and camaraderie of a hostel.

Hostels of Europe cards cost €15, and many independent hostels are members. These cards are not obligatory, but usually offer 5% off your bill; you can order online at www.hostelseurope.com. Despite the hype, there are only six official **Hostelling International (HI)** hostels in Paris. Most of the hostels and *foyers* in the city are privately run organizations, usually with services comparable to those at HI and often preferable to the HI hostels because of their more central locations. To stay in a Hostelling International hostel, you must be a member.

RESERVATIONS

A good rule of thumb is to make hotel reservations two weeks ahead of time, up to two months ahead in summer. The staff at smaller hotels may not speak English, but most proprietors are used to receiving calls from non-French-speakers. Let's Go has tried to include useful phrases for getting around the language barrier (see **Appendix,** p. 347). In order to reserve a room you may be asked to either read your credit card number over the phone, or to fax it to the hotel. Ask about your hotel's cancellation policy before giving out your credit card number, and find out if your credit card is going to be billed. If you can, avoid leaving a credit card number; either say you don't have a credit card or ask to send written confirmation instead. If you decide to leave Paris early, or if you want to switch hotels, don't expect to get back all of your deposit. Most hotels don't hold rooms without prior notice, so if you plan to arrive late, call and ask a hotel to hold your room. Once in Paris, the **Office du Tourisme** on the Champs-Elysées or one of its other bureaus should be able to find you a room, although the lines at such offices may extend to the horizon and the selections are not necessarily the cheapest (see **Tourist Offices,** p. 345). For accommodation agencies, see the **Service Directory,** p. 341.

BY PRICE

Accommodation prices are based on the cost of the least expensive rooming option available at each hotel or hostel (including dorm-beds, singles, or doubles) and are ranked in five groups, as noted below..

€51-75 (❸), CONT'D.		€76-95 (❹), CONT'D.	
Pacific Hôtel (270)	15ème	Hôtel Eiffel Rive Gauche (262)	7ème
Paris Nord Hôtel (265)	10ème	Hôtel Favart (256)	2ème
Touring Hotel Magendie (268)	13ème	Hôtel de France (262)	7ème
€76-95 (❹)		Hôtel de Nice (258)	4ème
Castex Hôtel (258)	4ème	Hôtel du Lys (262)	6ème
Grand Hôtel Jeanne d'Arc (258)	4ème	Hôtel de la Paix (262)	7ème
Hôtel Amélie (263)	7ème	**€96 & UP (❺)**	
Hôtel Beaumarchais (266)	11ème	Hôt'l Madeleine Haussmann (263)	8ème
Hôtel Belidor (273)	17ème	Hôtel du Midi (269)	14ème
Hôt'l Bellevue & du Chariot d'Or (257)	3ème	Hôtel de la Place des Vosges (258)	4ème
		Timhotel Le Louvre (255)	1er

BY NEIGHBORHOOD

SEINE ISLANDS: ÎLE DE LA CITÉ

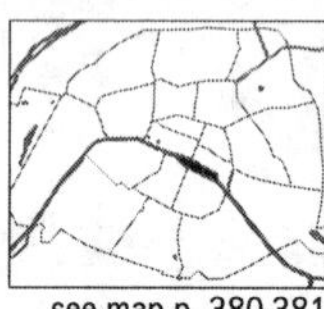
see map p. 380-381

NEIGHBORHOOD QUICKFIND: ***Discover,*** *p. 2;* ***Sights,*** *p. 67;* ***Food & Drink,*** *p. 254.*

Hôtel Henri IV, 25, pl. Dauphine (☎01 43 54 44 53). M: Pont Neuf. Henri IV is one of Paris's best located and least expensive hotels. Named in honor of Henri IV's printing presses, which once occupied the 400-year-old building, this hotel has big windows and charming views of the tree-lined pl. Dauphine. The spacious rooms have sturdy, mismatched furnishings. Showers €2.50. Reserve one month in advance, earlier in the summer. Singles €23; doubles €30, with shower and toilet €54; triples €41, with shower €48; quads €48. ❶

FIRST ARRONDISSEMENT

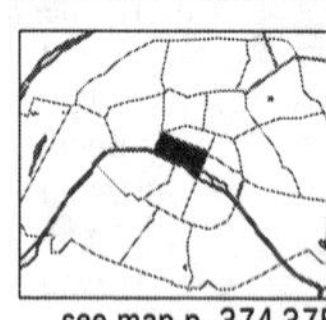
see map p. 374-375

NEIGHBORHOOD QUICKFIND: ***Discover,*** *p. 7;* ***Sights,*** *p. 73;* ***Museums,*** *p. 146;* ***Food & Drink,*** *p. 171;* ***Nightlife,*** *p. 206;* ***Shopping,*** *p. 235.*

Hôtel Montpensier, 12, r. de Richelieu (☎01 42 96 28 50; fax 01 42 86 02 70). M: Palais-Royal. Walk around the left side of the Palais-Royal to r. de Richelieu. Clean rooms, lofty ceilings, bright decor. Its good taste distinguishes it from most hotels in this area and price range. English-speaking staff welcome the clientele. Small elevator. TVs in rooms with shower or bath. Internet access €1 per 4min. Breakfast €7. Shower €4. Reserve 2 months in advance in high season. Singles and doubles with toilet €57, with toilet and shower €76, with toilet, bath, and sink €89. Extra bed €12. AmEx/DC/MC/V. ❸

Hôtel Lion d'Or, 5, r. de la Sourdière (☎01 42 60 79 04; fax 01 42 60 09 14). M: Tuileries or Pyramides. From M: Tuileries, walk down r. du 29 Juillet away from the park and turn right on r. St-Honoré, then left on r. de la Sourdière. Clean and carpeted, in a quiet area. Phone and TV in most rooms. Friendly, English-speaking staff. Breakfast €6.10. 20 rooms; reserve 1 month in advance in high season. 5% discount for stays of more than 3 nights. Singles with shower, toilet, and double bed €58-74, with bath €68-80; doubles €74-85/€80-95; triples €84-95/€90-105. Extra bed €10. AmEx/MC/V. ❸

Hôtel St-Honoré, 85, r. St-Honoré (☎01 42 36 20 38 or 01 42 21 46 96; fax 01 42 21 44 08; paris@hotelsainthonore.com). M: Louvre, Châtelet, or Les Halles. From M: Louvre, cross r. de Rivoli onto r. du Louvre and turn right on r. St-Honoré. Friendly, English-speaking staff and young clientele. Recently renovated, with breakfast area and sizable modern rooms. Refrigerator access. Internet €6 per hr. All rooms have shower, toilet, and TV. Breakfast €5. Reserve by fax, phone, or email 3 weeks ahead and confirm the night before. Singles €59; 1-bed doubles €74, with bathtub €83; 2-bed doubles €83; triples and quads €92. AmEx/MC/V. ❸

Hôtel Louvre-Richelieu, 51, r. de Richelieu (☎01 42 97 46 20; www.louvre-richelieu.com). M: Palais-Royal. See directions for Hôtel Montpensier, above. 14 simple but large, comfortable, clean rooms. English spoken. Internet access €2 per 15min. Breakfast €6. Reserve 3 weeks ahead in high season. Singles €55, with shower €82; doubles €70/82; triples with shower and toilet €105. MC/V. ❸

Timhotel Le Louvre, 4, r. Croix des Petits-Champs (☎01 42 60 34 86; fax 01 42 60 10 39). M: Palais-Royal. From the métro, cross r. de Rivoli to r. St-Honoré; take a left onto r. Croix des Petits-Champs. Although more expensive, this recently renovated 2-star chain hotel has the only wheelchair-accessible rooms at reasonable prices in the 1*er*. Clean, modern rooms with bath, shower, and cable TV. Great location next to the Louvre. Small garden. Breakfast €8.50. Singles and doubles €125; 1 triple €165; 1 quad suite €205. AmEx/DC/MC/V. ❺

> **ESSENTIAL INFORMATION**
>
> **PAY FOR WHAT YOU GET...**
>
> You should be aware that the city of Paris has a **Taxe de Séjour** of approximately €1.50 flat-rate per person per night: this does not have to be included in advertised or quoted prices, but must be listed along with the room price on the price list posted on the back of the hotel room door.
>
> It is advisable to check for other add-on expenses such as **direct telephone service** (some hotels will even charge you for collect calls) before making your reservation.
>
> Also, **always insist on seeing a room first,** before you settle in, even if the proprietor is not amenable to the request.

HOSTELS & FOYERS

Centre International de Paris (BVJ): Paris Louvre, 20, r. Jean-Jacques Rousseau (☎01 53 00 90 90). M: Louvre or Palais-Royal. From M: Louvre, take r. du Louvre away from the river, turn left on r. St-Honoré and right on r. J.J. Rousseau. Large hostel that draws a very international crowd. Courtyard hung with brass lanterns and strewn with *brasserie* chairs. 200 beds. Bright, dorm-style rooms with 2-10 beds per room. English spoken. Internet €1 per 10min. Breakfast and showers included. Lockers €2. Reception 24hr. Weekend reservations up to 1 week in advance; reserve by phone only. Rooms held for only 5-10min. after your expected check-in time; call if you'll be late. Doubles €28 per person; other rooms €25 per person. ❶

SECOND ARRONDISSEMENT

NEIGHBORHOOD QUICKFIND: ***Discover,*** *p. 7;* ***Sights,*** *p. 77;* ***Food & Drink,*** *p. 172;* ***Nightlife,*** *p. 206;* ***Shopping,*** *p. 235.*

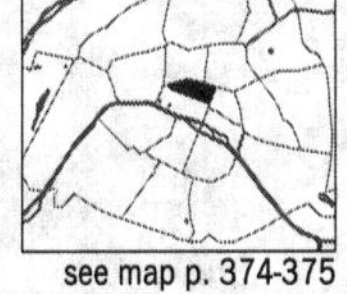

see map p. 374-375

Hôtel Tiquetonne, 6, r. Tiquetonne (☎01 42 36 94 58; fax 01 42 36 02 94). M: Etienne-Marcel. Walk against traffic on r. de Turbigo; turn left on r. Tiquetonne. Near Marché Montorgueil, some tasty eateries on r. Tiquetonne, the rowdy English bars near Etienne-Marcel, and r. St-Denis's sex shops—what more could you want in a location? This affordable 7-story hotel is a study in faux finishes: from fake-marble corridors to "I-can't-believe-it's-not-wood" doors. But the (friendly) giant German Shepherd is real. Elevator. Breakfast €5. Hall showers €5. Closed Aug. and 1 week at Christmas. Reserve 2 weeks in advance. Singles €28, with toilet €38; doubles with shower and toilet €46. AmEx/MC/V. ❶

Hôtel Vivienne, 40, r. Vivienne (☎01 42 33 13 26; fax 01 40 41 98 19; paris@hotel-vivienne.com). M: Grands Boulevards. Follow the traffic on bd. Montmartre, pass the Théâtre des Variétés, and turn left on r. Vivienne. From the hardwood floors in its reception area to its spacious rooms with armoires, this hotel adds a touch of refinement to budget digs. Some rooms with balconies. Elevator. Breakfast €6. Singles with shower €50, with shower and toilet €78; doubles €65/80, 3rd person under age 10 free, over 10 add 30%. MC/V. ❸

the local story

"You Feel High"

Lucy Lelong, a 21-year-old Parisian, is about to embark on student life abroad, far from the city in which she grew up. Before leaving the sights and sounds of Paris, she wanted to share some of the secrets of the city with Let's Go travelers.

LG: What is it like to grow up in a city that the world romanticizes?

LL: On one hand living in Paris is not always a romantic experience: Parisian people keep moaning all the time about anything, they are very rude when they drive, winter here is gray and disheartening and it's polluted in the summer time. On the other hand, it is true that now and again, through glimpses, you realize that it's a privilege to live in such a beautiful and glamorous city, for instance when you walk across the Seine river on one of its bridges, no matter what the weather is like and your mood, you feel high. [Living here] doesn't mean that we cannot fantasize, the way tourists do, about certain places, because we too superimpose famous pictures or photos on reality.

LG: What's an experience that every visitor to Paris should not miss?

LL: I think one should not

Hôtel Favart, 5, r. Marivaux (☎01 42 97 59 83; fax 01 40 15 95 58; favart.hotel@wanadoo.fr). M: Richelieu Drouot. From the métro, turn left down bd. des Italiens, then take another left onto r. Marivaux. This handsome hotel on a quiet, well-located street was once the home of controversial Spanish painter Francisco Goya. Rooms are a cut above those of most hotels, in that they are sizable, spacious, and very comfortable. Some even have satin wallpaper, mirrored ceilings, and excellent views of the Théâtre Musicale. All rooms come with cable TV, phone, shower, toilet, and hair dryer. There is 1 wheelchair-accessible room on the first floor with a very large bathroom. Large elevator. Breakfast included. The hotel offers substantial discounts for *Let's Go*-toting travelers, so be sure to mention this guide. Discounted prices: singles €85; doubles €108. Extra bed €15.25. AmEx/MC/V. ❹

Hôtel des Boulevards, 10, r. de la Ville Neuve (☎01 42 36 02 29; fax 01 42 36 15 39). M: Bonne Nouvelle. From the métro, walk against traffic on av. Poissonnière and make a right on r. de la Ville Neuve. In a funky but slightly run-down neighborhood, this hotel features quiet, simple rooms with TVs, phones, wooden wardrobes, and new carpets. The higher the room, the brighter it gets. Friendly reception. Breakfast included. Reserve at least 2 weeks ahead and confirm with a credit card deposit. 10% *Let's Go* discount. Prices without discount: singles and doubles €39, with shower €49, with bath €53-55. Extra bed €10. AmEx/MC/V. ❸

Hôtel La Marmotte, 6, r. Léopold Bellan (☎01 40 26 26 51; fax 01 21 42 96 20). M: Sentier. From the métro, take r. Petit Carreaux (the street market) and then turn right at r. Léopold Bellan. The hotel reception is located in the cheerful ground-floor bar. Rooms are quiet and come equipped with TVs, phones, and free safe-boxes. Breakfast €4. Shower €3. Reserve at least 2 weeks in advance. Singles and 1-bed doubles €28-35, with shower €42-54; 2-bed doubles €60. Extra bed €12. ❷

Hôtel Bonne Nouvelle, 17, r. Beauregard (☎01 45 08 42 42; fax 01 40 26 05 81; www.hotel-bonne-nouvelle.com). M: Bonne Nouvelle. From the métro, follow traffic down r. Poissonnière and turn left on r. Beauregard. On an old medieval street in a less than elegant neighborhood, the Hôtel Bonne Nouvelle is a fun mix of kitschy Swiss chalet and 70s motel. All the rooms in the hotel have TVs, hair dryers, and private bathrooms equipped with toilet, shower, or bath. Elevator. Breakfast €5-6. Room service available. Reserve at least 1 week in advance with a credit card. Prices vary by room size (the larger rooms also have cooler decor and much more light). Singles €55-65; doubles €59-72; triples €87-105; quads €105-120. MC/V. ❸

THIRD ARRONDISSEMENT

NEIGHBORHOOD QUICKFIND: ***Discover,*** *p. 8;* ***Sights,*** *p. 79;* ***Museums,*** *p. 257;* ***Food & Drink,*** *p. 174;* ***Nightlife,*** *p. 207;* ***Shopping,*** *p. 237.*

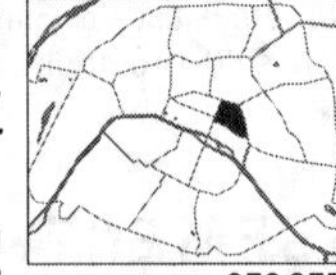

see map p. 376-377

Hôtel du Séjour, 36, r. du Grenier St-Lazare (☎/fax 01 48 87 40 36). From M: Etienne-Marcel, follow traffic on r. Etienne-Marcel, which becomes r. du Grenier St-Lazare. One block from Les Halles and the Centre Pompidou, this family-run hotel offers clean, bright rooms and a warm welcome. Reserve in advance. 20 rooms. Showers €4. Reception 7am-10:30pm. Singles €31; doubles €43, with shower and toilet €55, third person €23. ❷

Hôtel de Roubaix, 6, r. Greneta (☎01 42 72 89 91). From M: Réaumur-Sébastopol, walk opposite traffic on bd. de Sébastopol; turn left on r. Greneta. Helpful staff, clean rooms with flowered wallpaper, carpet, soundproof windows, and new baths. All rooms have shower, toilet, phone, locker, and TV. Some with balconies. Breakfast included. Reserve 1 week in advance. Singles €54-60; doubles €65-84; triples €74-83; quads €89; quints €95. MC/V. ❸

Hôtel Picard, 26, r. de Picardie (☎01 48 87 53 82). M: République. Follow bd. du Temple and turn right on r. Charlot. Take the first right on r. de Franche Comte, which becomes r. de Picardie. Superb location with a friendly, helpful staff. TVs in rooms with showers. Elevator. Breakfast €4.50. Hall showers €3. Reserve 2 weeks ahead Apr.-Sept. Singles €33, with shower €41, with shower and toilet €51; doubles €40-43, with shower €52, with bath €63; triples €59-82. 5% discount if you flash your *Let's Go*. Wheelchair-accessible. MC/V. ❷

Hôtel Bellevue et du Chariot d'Or, 39, r. de Turbigo (☎01 48 87 45 60; chariotdor@wanadoo.fr). M: Etienne-Marcel. A Belle Epoque lobby, with bar and breakfast room. Clean rooms with phones, TVs, toilets, and baths. Quiet courtyard. Breakfast €5.25. Reserve in advance. Singles €54; doubles €59; triples €75; quads €92. AmEx/MC/V. ❹

Hôtel du Marais, 16, r. de Beauce (☎01 42 72 30 26; hotelmarais@voila.fr). M: Temple or Filles-de-Calvaire. From M: Temple, follow r. du Temple south; take a left on r. de Bretagne and a right on r. de Beauce. Dirt cheap without the dirt. This small hotel offers very simple but spotless rooms in a great location near an open air market. Ideal for students. Take the small stairs above the café owned by the same friendly man. Curfew 2am. 3rd fl. showers €3. Singles with sink €25; doubles €33. ❷

leave Paris without having tasted an ice cream in the Jardins du Luxembourg, a glass of Champagne on the Pont des Arts at midnight. Another thing not to miss out is cycling around Paris, buying Jewish delicatessen food on the rue des Rosiers to be eaten nicely seated on the lawns of the Place des Vosges. If you are in Paris in the summer, don't miss its special events!

LG: Do you really eat French bread?
LL: Yes, everyday. But French bread is a multi-part experience: my favorite is the *flûte à l'ancienne* and the *pain au pavot.* Very important is its freshness, so you have to buy it before every meal. Anyway, you can't resist the lovely smells outside each boulangerie—one in particular comes to my mind: La Flûte Gana, on rue des Pyrénées (M: Gambetta).

LG: What's your favorite thing about living in Paris?
LL: My favorite thing about living in Paris is actually living in Paris! I mean experiencing the city on a daily basis, being able to occasionally visit it as tourists do without having to plan, without having to think about it.

LG: What will you miss the most when you move away to school? Do you think you'll come back to Paris?
LL: Certainly not the accordionists in the subway! But I'll miss the atmosphere, the color of the stones in the fall, the feeling of belonging when you walk along the streets. And yes, of course I'll come back.

Hôtel Paris France, 72, r. de Turbigo (☎01 42 78 00 04; fax 01 42 71 99 43; resa@paris-france-hotel.com). M: République or Temple. From M: République, take r. de Turbigo. Clean, bright and welcoming, this newly renovated hotel has a lovely café-like breakfast room and an 18th century-style lobby with leather sofas, mosaic-tiled floors, and a big TV. All rooms have TV, phone, hair dryer, and locker. Elevator. Breakfast €6. Singles €62-72, with shower €69-84; doubles with shower €72-86, with bath €86-146; triples with bath €109-144; extra bed €23. AmEx/MC/V. ❸

FOURTH ARRONDISSEMENT

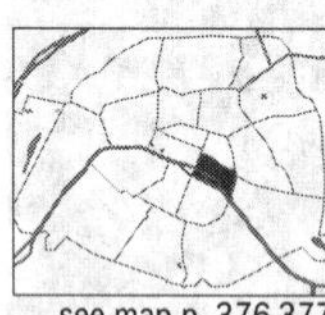

see map p. 376-377

NEIGHBORHOOD QUICKFIND: ***Discover,*** *p. 8;* ***Sights,*** *p. 81;* ***Museums,*** *p. 258;* ***Food & Drink,*** *p. 175;* ***Nightlife,*** *p. 209;* ***Shopping,*** *p. 237.*

Grand Hôtel Jeanne d'Arc, 3, r. de Jarente (☎01 48 87 62 11; fax 01 48 87 37 31; www.hoteljeannedarc.com). From M: St-Paul walk opposite traffic on r. de Rivoli and turn left on r. de Sévigné, then right on r. de Jarente. This bright, clean hotel on a quiet side-street features a pleasant lounge and breakfast area. Recently renovated rooms with showers, toilets, and TVs. 2 wheelchair-accessible rooms on the ground floor. Elevator. Breakfast €5.80. Reserve 2-3 months in advance. Singles €55-64; doubles €67-92; triples €107; quads €122. Extra bed €12. MC/V. ❹

Hôtel de la Place des Vosges, 12, r. de Birague (☎01 42 72 60 46; fax 01 42 72 02 64; hotel.place.des.vosges@gofornet.com). M: Bastille. Take r. St-Antoine; r. de Birague is the third right. Only steps away from pl. des Vosges. Beautiful interior with exposed beams and stone walls; once a stable for horses. TVs and full baths in all rooms. Elevator from the first floor. Breakfast €6. Reserve by fax 2 months ahead with 1 night's deposit. Singles or doubles €101-120; triples €120-140; family suite €120. AmEx/MC/V. ❺

Hôtel de Nice, 42bis, r. de Rivoli (☎01 42 78 55 29; fax 01 42 78 36 07). M: Hôtel-de-Ville. Walk opposite traffic on r. de Rivoli for about 4 blocks; the hotel is on the left. Friendly hotel with bright rooms featuring vintage catalogue illustrations, TVs, toilets, showers, and phones. A few have balconies with great views. Hot in the summer (fans provided). Elevator. Breakfast €6. For summer, reserve by fax or phone with 1 night's deposit 1 month ahead. Singles €65; doubles €100; triples €120; quads €135. Extra bed €20. MC/V. ❹

Hôtel Practic, 9, r. d'Ormesson (☎01 48 87 80 47; fax 01 48 87 40 04; www.hotel.pratic.com). M: St-Paul. Walk opposite traffic on r. de Rivoli, turn left on r. de Sévigné and right on r. d'Ormesson. A clean hotel on a cobblestone square in the heart of the Marais; plenty of restaurants nearby. Rooms are modest but bright, and all have TVs and hair dryers. English spoken. Breakfast included. Reserve by fax or email 2-3 weeks in advance. Book online for a 15% discount. Singles with toilet €59, with shower €87, with both €102; doubles €74/€98/€117; triples €135. Extra bed €12. MC/V. ❸

Hôtel du 7ème Art, 20, r. St-Paul (☎01 44 54 85 00; fax 01 42 77 69 10; hotel7art@wanadoo.fr). Covered in framed movie posters and pictures of favorites like Bogie and "Charlot." Even the bathroom tiles have a movie motif. Breakfast €7. Cable TV, telephones, and safes in all rooms. Singles with shower and bath in the hall €59; rooms for 1 or 2 people with full bath €75-130; rooms with 2 twin beds and full baths €85-130. Extra bed €20. AmEx/MC/V. ❸

Castex Hôtel, 5, r. Castex (☎01 42 72 31 52; fax 01 42 72 57 91; www.castexhotel.com). M: Bastille or Sully-Morland. Exit M: Bastille on bd. Henri IV and take the 3rd right on r. Castex. Completely renovated in 2003, this modern and uber-comfortable hotel boasts A/C, cable TV, and full baths in every room. Decorated in a gorgeous "Louis XIII style." Breakfast €8. Reserve by sending a fax with a credit card number at least 1 month in advance. Singles €95; doubles €120; triples and quads €190. AmEx/MC/V. ❹

Hôtel Andréa, 3, r. St-Bon (☎01 42 78 43 93; fax 01 44 61 28 36). M: Hôtel-de-Ville. From the métro, follow traffic down r. de Rivoli and then turn right on r. St-Bon. This hotel is on a quiet street 2 blocks from Châtelet. Recently renovated, with plenty of amenities. Clean rooms come with comfortable mattresses, plus phones, toilets, showers, TVs, A/C; some even have Internet connections. Elevator. Top floor rooms have balconies. Breakfast €6. Reserve at least 1 month in advance with a credit card number. Singles €58-64; doubles €78-92; triples €95-120. MC/V. ❸

Hôtel Rivoli, 44, r. de Rivoli/2, r. des Mauvais Garçons (☎01 42 72 08 41). M: Hôtel-de-Ville. Walk against traffic on r. de Rivoli. Small with basic rooms, but extremely well situated. No entrance from 2-7am. Reserve 1 month in advance. Singles €27, with shower €35; doubles €35, with shower €39, with bath and toilet €49; triple €54. Extra bed €9. ❷

Hôtel de la Herse d'Or, 20, r. St-Antoine (☎01 48 87 84 09; fax 01 48 87 94 01). M: Bastille. Take r. St-Antoine from the métro; the hotel will be about a block down on the right. The rooms are clean, but old, small and a bit dark. Breakfast €4. Rooms for 1 or 2 people €30, with toilet €35, with full bath €54, with TV €56. AmEx/MC/V. ❶

Sully Hôtel, 48, r. Saint-Antoine (☎01 42 78 49 32; fax 01 44 61 76 50). M: St. Paul or Bastille. All rooms come equipped with shower, toilet, and cable TV. The rooms are clean, but some of the carpets could use a good scrub. An eager staff prepares breakfast made-to-order (€3.50). Doubles €52-55; triples €70-72. MC/V. ❷

HOSTELS & FOYERS

Hôtel des Jeunes (MIJE) (☎01 42 74 23 45; fax 01 40 27 81 64; accueil@mije.com; www.mije.com). Books beds in Le Fourcy, Le Fauconnier, and Maubuisson (see below), 3 small hostels on cobblestone streets in beautiful old Marais residences. No smoking. English spoken. The restaurant (at Le Fourcy) offers a main course with drink (€8.50) and 3-course "hosteler special" (€10.50). Internet €0.15 per min. Public phones and free lockers (with a €1 deposit). Ages 18-30 only. 7-day max. stay. Reception 7am-1am. Lockout noon-3pm. Curfew 1am. Quiet after 10pm. Breakfast, shower, and sheets included. Arrive before noon the first day of reservation (call in advance if you'll be late). Groups (of 10 or more people) may reserve a year in advance. Individuals should reserve at least 1 week in advance. 5-bed (or more) dorms €24-26; singles €40-47; doubles €30-36; triples €26-31; quads €25-27. ❶

Le Fourcy, 6, r. de Fourcy. M: St-Paul or Pont Marie. From M: St-Paul, walk opposite the traffic for a few meters down r. François-Miron and turn left on r. de Fourcy. Hostel surrounds a large courtyard ideal for meeting travelers or for open-air picnicking. Light sleepers should avoid rooms on the social courtyard. Elevator.

Le Fauconnier, 11, r. du Fauconnier. M: St-Paul or Pont Marie. From M: St-Paul, take r. du Prevôt, turn left on r. Charlemagne, and turn right on r. du Fauconnier. Ivy-covered building steps away from the Seine and Île St-Louis.

Maubuisson, 12, r. des Barres. M: Hôtel-de-Ville or Pont Marie. From M: Pont Marie, walk opposite traffic on r. de l'Hôtel-de-Ville and turn right on r. des Barres. A half-timbered former girls' convent on a silent street by the St-Gervais monastery. Elevator.

FIFTH ARRONDISSEMENT

NEIGHBORHOOD QUICKFIND: ***Discover,*** *p. 3;* ***Sights,*** *p. 86;* ***Museums,*** *p. 259;* ***Food & Drink,*** *p. 177;* ***Nightlife,*** *p. 211;* ***Shopping,*** *p. 239.*

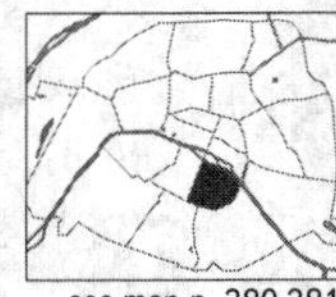

see map p. 380-381

To stay in the *5ème*, **reserve well in advance**—from one week in the winter to two months in the summer. If foresight eludes you, don't despair: there are same-day vacancies at even the most popular hotels. In the fall, the return of students means more competition for *foyers*.

Hôtel St-Jacques, 35, r. des Ecoles (☎01 44 07 45 45; fax 01 43 25 65 50; hotelstjacques@wanadoo.fr). M: Maubert-Mutualité; RER: Cluny-La Sorbonne. Turn left on r. des Carmes, then left on r. des Ecoles. Jim Morrison may have bummed around Hôtel de Médicis, but Cary Grant filmed *Charade* here—a telling difference. Spacious, faux-elegant rooms at reasonable rates, with balconies, renovated bathrooms, and TVs. Chandeliers and walls decorated with *trompe-l'oeil* designs give it a regal feel. English spoken. Elevator. Internet access. Breakfast €7. Singles €49, with toilet and shower €75; doubles with toilet and shower €85, some with baths €112. AmEx/MC/V. ❸

from the road

A Long Shot

My girlfriend, Yvonne, and I had to get innoculations in Paris for a trip to Thailand. Anxiously, I called the **Centre Medical Europe** (44, r. Amsterdam, ☎01 42 81 93 33). I was braced for the worst of infamous French bureaucracy: long waits, complex procedures, maybe a strike here or there—but I was pleasantly surprised.

We got an appointment 1hr. hence, and arrived just in time. After divulging only our names and birthdates, we paid our €20 *consultation.* A few minutes after our appointed time, Dr. Benoilid emerged and took us to her office. She walked us through the vaccination list I had, wrote prescriptions for the appropriate one, and sent us across the street to a pharmacy. We bought the shots there (€50 per person)—the pharmacist was surprised to see cash and not a *securité social* card—and returned to the doctor's office, where she administered them. I wouldn't say the day was painless (we did get shots, after all), but we were impressed with the French health care system, and happily surprised that our stereotypes about French bureaucracy were not infallible. Let's hope the inoculations are.

—Brendan McGeever

Hôtel Marignan, 13, r. du Sommerard (☎01 43 54 63 81; fax 01 43 25 16 69; www.hotel-marignan.com). From M: Maubert-Mutualité, turn left on r. des Carmes, then right on r. du Sommerard. Clean, freshly decorated, amenable rooms that can sleep up to 5—almost an impossibility in the rest of Paris. Over half of the hotel is set up to sleep 3-4 people, in various combinations of double and twin beds. Tremendously friendly English-speaking owner welcomes backpackers and families to a place with the privacy of a hotel and the welcoming atmosphere of a hostel. Free laundry and kitchen access. TVs in every room upon request (free of charge). Hall showers open until 11pm. Breakfast €3. Internet access. Reserve 2 months in advance with credit card or check deposit. Singles €42-45; doubles €60, with shower and toilet €80-86; triples €90-110; quads €100-130. 15% discount from mid-Sept. to Mar. AmEx/MC/V accepted for stays longer than 5 nights. ❷

Hôtel d'Esmeralda, 4, r. St-Julien-le-Pauvre (☎01 43 54 19 20; fax 01 40 51 00 68). M: St-Michel. Walk along the Seine on quai St-Michel toward Notre Dame, then turn right at Parc Viviani. Rooms here are clean but creaky, and tend to have an ancient, professorial feel about them. Antique wallpapers, ceiling beams, and red velvet make each room a step back into the Parisian past—made all the more appealing by a great location by a small park, views of the Seine, and the pealing of Notre Dame's bells. Breakfast €6. Singles €35, with shower and toilet €65; doubles €90; triples €110; quads €120. ❷

Hôtel des Argonauts, 12, r. de la Huchette (☎01 43 54 09 82; fax 01 44 07 18 84). M: St-Michel. With your back to the Seine, take the first left off bd. St-Michel onto r. de la Huchette. Above a Greek restaurant of the same name. Ideally located in a bustling, antique pedestrian quarter (a stone's throw from the Seine), this hotel's clean rooms flaunt a cheerful Mediterranean motif. Leopard-print chairs in the lobby bar, photographs of idyllic Greek islands, and mirrors on every floor. Breakfast €4. Reserve 3-4 weeks in advance in high season. Singles with shower €44; doubles with bath and toilet €63-71. AmEx/MC/V. ❷

Hôtel Gay-Lussac, 29, r. Gay-Lussac (☎01 43 54 23 96; fax 01 40 51 79 49). M: Luxembourg. Friendly owner and clean, stately old rooms, some with fireplaces. It can get a bit noisy from neighborhood traffic, but the peaceful shade of the Luxembourg gardens is just a few blocks away. Elevator. Discounts during the winter. Reserve by fax at least 2 weeks in advance (1 month in the summer). Breakfast included. Singles €38, with toilet €50, with shower and toilet €64; doubles with toilet €65, with shower and toilet €74; triples with shower €83, with shower and toilet €74; quads €100. ❷

Hôtel des Médicis, 214, r. St-Jacques (☎01 43 54 14 66). From RER: Luxembourg, turn right on r. Gay-Lussac and left on r. St-Jacques. Rickety old place that shuns right-angle geometry; perhaps that's why Jim Morrison slummed here (room #4) for 3 weeks in 1971. 1 shower and toilet per floor. Laundromat next door. English spoken. Reception 9am-11pm. Singles €16; larger singles €20; doubles €31; triples €45. ❶Hostels & Foyers

Hôtel le Central, 6, r. Descartes (☎01 46 33 57 93). M: Maubert-Mutualité. From the métro, walk up r. de la Montaigne Ste-Geneviève. Great location near r. Mouffetard and the Panthéon. Carpeted but uneven stairs (watch out!) lead to well-priced rooms. While not the pinnacle of spotless perfection, Le Central does offer inexpensive rooms with views of the Right Bank. All rooms have showers. All rooms €28-44. Cash only. ❷

HOSTELS & FOYERS

Young and Happy (Y&H) Hostel, 80, r. Mouffetard (☎01 45 35 09 53; fax 01 47 07 22 24; www.youngandhappy.fr). M: Monge. From the métro, cross r. Gracieuse and take r. Ortolan to r. Mouffetard. A funky, lively hostel located on r. Mouffetard, the emblematic street of the hopping student quarter. The laid-back staff, clean rooms, and commission-free currency exchange make this a perfect place for college-age and 20-something adventurers to crash for a few weeks–though the bathrooms can get a bit dirty. Kitchen and Internet access (€1 per 10min.). English spoken. Breakfast included. Sheets €2.50. Towels €1. Laundry nearby. Lockout 11am-4pm. Curfew 2am. 25 rooms, a few with showers and toilets. Dorms from €20 per person; doubles from €23 per person; low-season (Jan.-Mar.) prices €2 less per night. ❶

Centre International de Paris (BVJ): Paris Quartier Latin, 44, r. des Bernardins (☎01 43 29 34 80; fax 01 53 00 90 91). M: Maubert-Mutualité. Walk with traffic on bd. St-Germain and turn right on r. des Bernardins. Boisterous, generic, and only slightly dingy hostel with large cafeteria. English spoken. Internet €1 per 10min. Breakfast included. Microwave, TV, and message service. Showers in rooms. Lockers €2. Reception 24hr. Reserve at least 1 week in advance and confirm, or arrive at 9am to check for availability. 97 beds. 5- and 6-person dorms €25; singles €30; doubles and triples €27 per person. ❷

Foyer International des Etudiantes, 93, bd. St-Michel (☎01 43 54 49 63). RER: Luxembourg. Across from the Jardin du Luxembourg. Marbled reception area, library, laundry facilities, and TV lounge. Kitchenettes, showers, and toilets on hallways. Rooms are elegant (if faintly musty smelling), with wood paneling and furnishings and some with balconies. 3 night minimum. Breakfast included in summer. July-Sept. foyer is coed, and open 24hr. Reserve in writing as early as Jan. for summer months; €35 deposit. Singles €27.50; 2-bed dorms €20 per person. Oct.-June foyer is women only, and rooms are available for rent by the month (inquire at desk for prices). Singles €23.50 per night; doubles €16 per person per night. ❶

SIXTH ARRONDISSEMENT

NEIGHBORHOOD QUICKFIND: ***Discover,*** *p. 3;* ***Sights,*** *p. 91;* ***Museums,*** *p. 148;* ***Food & Drink,*** *p. 212;* ***Nightlife,*** *p. 212;* ***Shopping,*** *p. 239.*

see map p. 380-381

Hôtel de Nesle, 7, r. du Nesle (☎01 43 54 62 41; www.hoteldenesle.com). M: Odéon. Walk up r. de l'Ancienne Comédie, take a right onto r. Dauphine and then take a left on r. du Nesle. Fantastic, friendly, and absolutely sparkling, the Nesle (pronounced "Nell") stands out in a sea of nondescript budget hotels. Every room is unique, representing a particular time-period or locale. The lobby's ceiling is made of bouquets of dried flowers. Garden with terrace and duck pond, laundry room. Singles €50-69; doubles €69-99. Extra bed €12. Reserve by telephone, confirm 2 days in advance with arrival time. AmEx/MC/V. ❸

Hôtel St-André des Arts, 66, r. St-André-des-Arts (☎01 43 26 96 16; fax 01 43 29 73 34; hsaintand@minitel.net). From M: Odéon, take r. de l'Ancienne Comédie, then turn right on r. St-André-des-Arts. Stone walls, high ceilings and exposed beams give this hotel a country inn feeling, though it's in the heart of St-Germain. The new bathrooms (all have showers or baths, sinks and toilets), free breakfast, and very friendly owner are added perks. Reservations recommended. Singles €63; doubles €80-85; triples €100; quads €110. MC/V.❸

Hôtel Stella, 41, r. Monsieur-le-Prince (☎01 40 51 00 25; http://site.voila.fr/hotel_stella). From M: Odéon, walk against traffic on bd. St-Germain and make a left on r. Monsieur-le-Prince. Takes the exposed beam look to a whole new level, with woodwork reportedly centuries old. Gigantic triples have pianos. All rooms have shower, toilet and character. Reserve in advance with deposit. Singles €45; doubles €55; triples €75; quads €85. ❷

Hôtel du Lys, 23, r. Serpente (☎01 43 26 97 57; fax 01 44 07 34 90; www.hoteldulys.com). M: Odéon or St-Michel. Take r. Serpent just off bd. St. Michel. This splurge is well worth it. Floral wall-prints, rustic beams, and antique porcelain tiles give this spotless hotel a sublime French country feel. All 22 rooms include bath or shower, TV, phone, and hair dryer. Breakfast and taxes also included. Reserve one month in advance in summer. Singles €95; doubles €110; triples €125. MC/V. ❹

Delhy's Hôtel, 22, r. de l'Hirondelle (☎01 43 26 58 25; fax 01 43 26 51 06; delhys@wanadoo.fr). M: St-Michel. Just steps from pl. St-Michel and the Seine on a cobblestone way. Wood paneling, flower boxes, modern facilities, and quiet location. TV with satellite dish and phone in rooms. Breakfast and tax included. Hall showers €4. Toilets in the hallways. Each night must be paid in advance. Reserve 15-20 days ahead with deposit. Singles €40-52, with shower €66-73; doubles €58-64/€72-79; triples €94-116. Extra bed €15. MC/V. ❸

Hôtel de Chevreuse, 3, r. de Chevreuse (☎01 43 20 93 16; fax 01 43 21 43 72). M: Vavin. Walk up bd. du Montparnasse away from the Tour and turn left on r. de Chevreuse. Small, clean, quiet rooms with TV and Ikea-style furniture. Breakfast €6. Reserve 1 month in advance and confirm by fax. Singles €38, with shower and toilet €62, with bath €68; doubles with shower, TV, and toilet €62/€68; triples with shower, TV, and toilet €88. MC/V. ❸

SEVENTH ARRONDISSEMENT

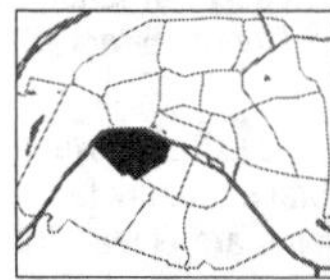
see map pp. 382-383

NEIGHBORHOOD QUICKFIND: ***Discover,*** *p. 4;* ***Sights,*** *p. 96;* ***Museums,*** *p. 149;* ***Food & Drink,*** *p. 183;* ***Nightlife,*** *p. 213;* ***Shopping,*** *p. 242.*

Hôtel du Champs de Mars, 7, r. du Champ de Mars (☎01 45 51 52 30; www.hotel-du-champs-de-mars.com). M: Ecole Militaire. More pricey, but beats its competitors in quality and elegance. Rooms, each named after a particular flower and decorated accordingly, have phone and satellite TV. Home-made breakfast with fresh orange juice €6.50. Reserve 1 month ahead and confirm with a credit card number. Small elevator. Singles and doubles with shower €68-74; triples with bath €94. MC/V. ❸

Hôtel Eiffel Rive Gauche, 6, r. du Gros Caillou (☎01 45 51 24 56; fax 01 45 51 11 77; www.hotel-eiffel.com). M: Ecole Militaire. Walk up av. de la Bourdonnais, turn right on r. de la Grenelle, then left on Gros-Caillou. Located on a quiet street, this family-run hotel is a favorite of Anglophone travelers. With a bright courtyard and cheerful staff, the Hôtel Eiffel couldn't be more welcoming. Rooms have cable TV, phone, and full baths. Dogs allowed. Breakfast buffet €9. Rooms €69-89 (double bed must be requested upon booking). Extra bed €14. MC/V. ❹

Hôtel Montebello, 18, r. Pierre Leroux (☎01 47 34 41 18; fax 01 47 34 46 71). A bit far from the *7ème*'s sights, but amazing prices for this upscale neighborhood. Behind the unremarkable facade are clean, cheery rooms with full baths. Reserve at least 2 weeks in advance. Breakfast served 7:30-9:30am, €3.50. 1 person €37; 2 people €42-45. ❸

Hôtel de France, 102, bd. de la Tour Maubourg (☎01 47 05 40 49; fax 01 45 56 96 78; www.hoteldefrance.com). M: Ecole Militaire. Directly across from the Hôtel des Invalides. Clean rooms and amazing views, particularly from fifth floor balconies. Staff offers advice on Paris in English, Spanish, German, and Italian. Two wheelchair accessible rooms (€76.25). All rooms with phone, cable, minibar, and full bath. Reserve 1 month in advance. Breakfast €7. Singles €69; doubles €85; connecting rooms for 4-5 people available. AmEx/MC/V. ❹

Hôtel de la Paix, 19, r. du Gros-Caillou (☎01 45 51 86 17; fax 01 45 55 93 28 hotel.de.la.paix@wanadoo.fr). M: Ecole Militaire. Opposite Hôtel Eiffel Rive Gauche (above). Freshly decorated, clean, and friendly. Breakfast in a charming dining room, €7. Reserve 1 week ahead. Singles with shower €61; doubles with shower and toilet €91-100; triple €111. One room with wheelchair access. ❹

Grand Hôtel Lévêque, 29, r. Cler (☎01 47 05 49 15; fax 01 45 50 49 36; www.hotel-leveque.com). M: Ecole Militaire. Take av. de la Motte-Picquet to cobbled and colorful r. Cler. Cheery and clean, although the lobby has a disinfected quality (which is good and bad). Small elevator. Baggage storage. English spoken. Satellite TV, safe (€3), private telephone line, A/C in all rooms. Breakfast €7. Reserve 6 months ahead. Singles €53; doubles with shower and toilet €84, with twin beds, shower, and toilet €85-91; triples with shower and toilet €114. The only showers for singles are on the 5th floor. AmEx/MC/V. ❸

Hôtel de Turenne, 20, av. de Tourville (☎01 47 05 99 92; fax 01 45 56 06 04; hotel.turenne.paris7@wanadoo.fr). M: Ecole Militaire. 34 rooms with A/C, full bath, and satellite TV. Spotless bathrooms and convenient location. Breakfast €6.20. Reserve 3 weeks in advance. Singles €61; doubles €71-82; triples with roll-out bed €98. AmEx/MC/V. ❸

Hôtel Amélie, 5, r. Amélie (☎01 45 51 74 75; fax 01 45 56 93 55; www.123france.com). M: La Tour-Maubourg. Walk in the direction of traffic on bd. de la Tour Maubourg, make a left onto r. de Grenelle, then a right onto r. Amélie. On a picturesque back street, Amélie is tiny but charmingly decorated and has a friendly owner. Minibar and full bath in all rooms. Breakfast €6.10. Reserve 2 weeks in advance. Singles €61-72; doubles €71-82. AmEx/MC/V. ❹

EIGHTH ARRONDISSEMENT

NEIGHBORHOOD QUICKFIND: ***Discover,*** *p. 9;* ***Sights,*** *p. 100;* ***Museums,*** *p. 150;* ***Food & Drink,*** *p. 184;* ***Nightlife,*** *p. 213;* ***Shopping,*** *p. 243.*

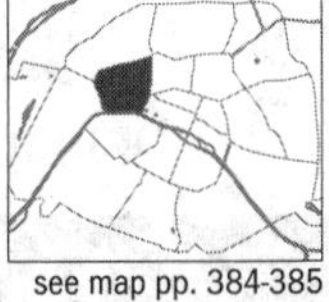

see map pp. 384-385

Hôtel Europe-Liège, 8, r. de Moscou (☎01 42 94 01 51; fax 01 43 87 42 18). M: Liège. From the métro, walk down r. d'Amsterdam and turn left on r. de Moscou. Very pleasant, quiet, and reasonably priced (for the 8*ème*) hotel with clean and fresh rooms, a friendly staff, and a lovely interior courtyard. Many restaurants nearby. Reserve 15 days in advance. All rooms have TV, hair dryer, phone, and shower or bath. 2 wheelchair-accessible rooms on the ground floor. Breakfast €7. Singles €68; doubles €84. AmEx/MC/V. ❸

Hôtel Madeleine Haussmann, 10, r. Pasquier (☎01 42 65 90 11; fax 01 42 68 07 93; www.3hotels.com). M: Madeleine. From the métro, walk up bd. Malesherbes and turn right on r. Pasquier. Worth the high prices: centrally located, comfortable, and professional, with a bathroom, hair dryer, TV, safe box, and minibar in every cheery room. 1 small room on the ground floor is wheelchair-accessible. Breakfast €7, €9 in the room. Reserve 1 month in advance. Singles €100-120; doubles €120-130; quads €180. AmEx/MC/V. ❺

HOSTELS & FOYERS

Foyer de Chaillot, 28, av. George V (☎01 47 23 35 32; fax 01 47 23 77 16; www.ufjt.org). M: George V. From the métro, turn right onto av. George V and walk about 3 blocks (on the opposite side of the street) until you see a high-rise silver office building called Centre Chaillot Galliera. Take the elevator to the foyer on the 3rd fl. Cheerful, well-equipped rooms in an upscale dorm-like environment; for **women only.** Residents must be working or holding an internship and be between the ages of 18-25; 1-month min. stay, 2-year max. stay. Singles each have a sink, while doubles have shower and sink. Toilets and additional showers in each hall. Large common rooms equipped with stereo and TV. Fully equipped kitchen. *Salle informatique* with Internet access. Small gym with exercise bikes. Guests permitted until 10pm. Bulletin boards advertise apartments for rent, theatre outings, and other activities. €337 deposit required to reserve a room, along with an application or a fax that states your age, the duration of your stay, and a description of your activities in Paris. Breakfast and dinner included M-F. Doubles €495 per month per person; after a stay of 2 months, singles available for €565 per month. ❶

Union Chrétienne de Jeunes Filles (UCJF/YWCA), 22, r. Naples (☎01 53 04 37 47; fax 01 53 04 37 54). M: Europe. From the métro, take r. de Constantinople and turn left onto r. de Naples. **Also** at 168, r. Blomet, 15*ème* (☎01 56 56 63 00; fax 01 56 56 63 12). M: Convention. For **women only;** men should contact the YMCA Foyer **Union Chrétienne de Jeunes**

Gens, 14, r. de Trévise, *9ème* (☎01 47 70 90 94). The UCJF has spacious and quiet (if a bit worn) rooms with hardwood floors, sinks, and large desks. Large oak-paneled common room with fireplace, TV, VCR, books, theater space, and family-style dining room. June-Aug. 3-day min. stay; Sept.-May longer stays for women ages 18-26. All guests pay €4.58 YWCA membership fee, as well as €7.63 (for 1-week stays) or €15.25 (for stays of 1 month or more) processing fee. Reception M-F 8am-12:25am, Sa 8:30am-12:25pm, Su 9am-12:25pm and 1:30pm-12:30am. Guests permitted until 10pm; men not allowed in bedrooms. Curfew 12:30am (ask for key). Kitchen, laundry. Breakfast included, evening meal €7.15. Singles €27, €162 per week, €511-527 per month; shared rooms (doubles or dorms) €24/€130/€416-466 per person. ❶

NINTH ARRONDISSEMENT

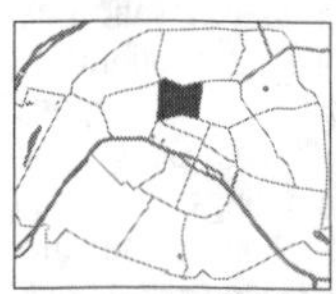

see map pp. 386-387

NEIGHBORHOOD QUICKFIND: ***Discover,*** *p. 9;* ***Sights,*** *p. 105;* ***Museums,*** *p. 151;* ***Food & Drink,*** *p. 186;* ***Nightlife,*** *p. 214.*

Unless you reserve one of the more popular hotels along the southern border, staying in the *9ème* will provide for a quieter stay than most.

Hôtel Chopin, 10, bd. Montmartre, or 46, passage Jouffroy (☎01 47 70 58 10; fax 01 42 47 00 70). M: Grands Boulevards. Walk west on bd. Montmartre and make a right into passage Jouffroy. Inside a spectacular old *passage* lined with shops. Very clean, new rooms decorated in a tasteful style a cut above most budget hotels. Some rooms have views of the Musée Grévin's wax studio (see **Museums,** p. 151). All rooms have TV, phone, and fans by request. Elevator. Breakfast €7. Singles with shower €57, with shower and toilet €64-72; doubles with shower and toilet €73-84; triples with shower and toilet €97. AmEx/MC/V. ❸

Perfect Hôtel, 39, r. Rodier (☎01 42 81 18 86 or 01 42 81 26 19; fax 01 42 85 01 38; perfecthotel@hotmail.com). Across from the Woodstock Hostel, see directions below. This hotel almost lives up to its name, with hotel-quality rooms at hostel prices. Some with balconies, and the upper floors have a beautiful view. Phones, communal refrigerator and kitchen access, free coffee, beer vending machine (€1.50), and a concerned, English-speaking staff. Elevator. Breakfast free for *Let's Go* users. Singles €30, with shower and toilet €50; doubles €36/€50; triples €53/€65. MC/V. ❷

Modial Hôtel Européen, 21, r. Notre Dame de Lorette (☎01 48 78 60 47; fax 01 42 81 95 58). M: St-Georges. Safely removed from the grimy debauchery of Pigalle, this charming hotel has spotless and comfortable rooms. All come with direct telephone line, color TV, and either bath and toilet or shower and toilet. Reservations recommended 2 weeks in advance. Singles €60; doubles €65; triples €98; quads €114. MC/V. ❸

Hôtel des Arts, 7, Cité Bergère (☎01 42 46 73 30; fax 01 48 00 94 42). M: Grands Boulevards. Walk uphill on r. du Faubourg-Montmartre, turn right on Cité Bergère (at 6, r. du Faubourg-Montmartre; there is a large sign outside the alleyway). A family hotel with small but clean and comfortable rooms on a very quiet pedestrian street lined with other hotels. All rooms have toilet, TV, and hair dryer. Elevator. Breakfast €6. Singles €64, with shower €66; doubles €68/€70; triples €88/€90. AmEx/MC/V. ❸

HOSTELS & FOYERS

Woodstock Hostel, 48, r. Rodier (☎01 48 78 87 76; fax 01 48 78 01 63; www.woodstock.fr). M: Anvers. From the métro, walk against traffic on pl. Anvers, turn right on av. Trudaine and left on r. Rodier. With ubiquitous incense, reggae music, tie-dye paraphernalia, and a Beatles-decorated VW Bug hanging from the ceiling. The nicest rooms are off the courtyard. Communal kitchen, safe deposit box, Internet access (€1 per 10min.), and fax. International staff; English spoken. Breakfast included. Sheets €2.50, towels €1. Showers on every floor are free (and clean). Call ahead to reserve a room. Max. stay 1 week. Curfew 2am. Lockout 11am-4pm. 4- to 8-person dorms €20; doubles €23; max. 8 people per room. ❶

TENTH ARRONDISSEMENT

NEIGHBORHOOD QUICKFIND: ***Discover,*** *p. 11;* ***Sights,*** *p. 107;* ***Museums,*** *p. 151;* ***Food & Drink,*** *p. 187.*

Don't count the 10*ème* out for budget accommodations; there is a glut of cheap hotels around the Gares du Nord and de l'Est. If those below are full, there is probably an adequate one nearby.

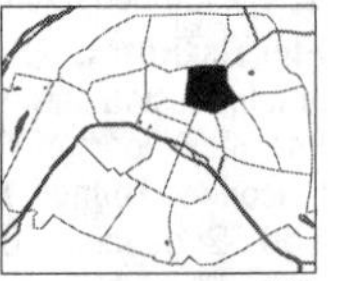

see map p. 388

Cambrai Hôtel, 129bis, bd. de Magenta (☎01 48 78 32 13; www.hotel-cambrai.com). M: Gare du Nord. Follow traffic on r. de Dunkerque to pl. de Roubaix and turn right on bd. de Magenta. A family-owned hotel close to the Gare du Nord. Clean, 50s-style rooms with high ceilings and TVs. Breakfast €5.34. Showers €3. Singles €30, with toilet €35, with shower €41, with full bath €48; doubles with shower €46, with full bath €54, with twin beds and full bath €60; triples €80; 4-person family suite €90; 5-person family suite €110(wheelchair-accessible). AmEx/MC/V. ❷

Hôtel Palace, 9, r. Bouchardon (☎01 42 06 59 32; hotel.palace@club-internet.fr). M: Strasbourg-St-Denis. Walk against traffic on bd. St-Denis until the small arch; follow r. René Boulanger on the left, then turn left on r. Bouchardon. A private, clean, centrally located (for the 10*ème*, anyway) hotel with the rates of a hostel. Laundromat next door and supermarket across the street. Breakfast €3.50. Shower €3.50. Reserve 2 weeks ahead. Singles €17-21, with shower €31; doubles €26/€36; triples €48; quads €58; quints €68. AmEx/MC/V. ❶

Paris Nord Hôtel, 4, r. de Dunkerque (☎01 40 35 81 70; fax 01 40 35 09 30). M: Gare du Nord. Facing the Gare du Nord, take r. Dunkerque to the right. Hardwood floors and walls, and clean, well-decorated rooms conveniently located between both train stations. Elevator. Reserve 1 week in advance. Breakfast €5. All rooms are identical, with king-sized beds and full bathrooms. €60 for one person, €65 for two people, €10 more for third person and extra bed. AmEx/MC/V. ❸

Hôtel de Milan, 17, r. de St-Quentin (☎01 40 37 88 50; fax 01 46 07 89 48). M: Gare du Nord. From the métro, follow r. de St-Quentin from outside Gare du Nord; the hotel is on the right-hand corner of the 3rd block. This hotel's location is incredibly convenient, and the concierge is extremely friendly. Breakfast €4. Hall showers €4. Singles €27-30; doubles €34-41, with full bath €47-52, with twin beds and full bath €59; triples with full bath €69; extra person €17. MC/V. ❷

Hôtel Montana La Fayette, 164, r. La Fayette (☎01 40 35 80 80; fax 01 40 35 08 73). M: Gare du Nord. Walk up r. La Fayette in the direction of Gare de l'Est. The hotel is on the right. Conveniently close to the Gare du Nord, yet still quiet. Enjoy the clean rooms with generous bathrooms. Breakfast €5. Most rooms have shower, toilet, and TV. Singles €46; doubles €65. AmEx/MC/V. ❷

ELEVENTH ARRONDISSEMENT

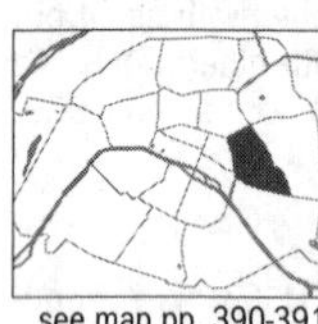

see map pp. 390-391

NEIGHBORHOOD QUICKFIND: ***Discover,*** *p. 11;* ***Sights,*** *p. 108;* ***Food & Drink,*** *p. 188;* ***Nightlife,*** *p. 214.*

Modern Hôtel, 121, r. de Chemin-Vert (☎01 47 00 54 05; fax 01 47 00 08 31; www.modern-hotel.fr). M: Père Lachaise. A few blocks from the métro on r. de Chemin-Vert, on the right. Newly renovated, with modern furnishings, pastel color scheme, and spotless marble bathrooms. All rooms have a hair dryer, modem connection, and safe-deposit box. 6 floors of rooms but no elevator (ask for a low floor). Breakfast €5. Singles €60; doubles €70-75; triples €85; quads €95. Extra bed €15. AmEx/DC/MC/V. ❸

Hôtel Beaumarchais, 3, r. Oberkampf (☎01 53 36 86 86; fax 01 43 38 32 86; www.hotel-beaumarchais.com). M: Oberkampf. Exit on r. de Malte and turn right on r. Oberkampf. Newly renovated, with colorful, modern furniture, clean baths, and TVs, this hotel is worth the extra money. Each room's decor has different artistic influences, including Calder and Gaudi. Suites include TV room with desk and breakfast table. Elevator. A/C. Breakfast €7. Reserve 2 weeks in advance. Singles €69-85; doubles €99; suites €140. Baby beds €16. No adult-sized extra beds. AmEx/MC/V. ❹

Plessis Hôtel, 25, r. du Grand Prieuré (☎01 47 00 13 38; fax 01 43 57 97 87; hotel.plessis@club_internet.fr). M: Oberkampf. From the métro, walk north on r. du Grand Prieuré. 5 floors of clean, bright rooms. Rooms with showers have hair dryers, fans, TVs, and balconies. Lounge with TV and vending machines. Breakfast €6. Open Sept.-July. Singles €50-52; doubles €62. AmEx/MC/V. ❷

Hôtel Notre-Dame, 51, r. de Malte (☎01 47 00 78 76; fax 01 43 55 32 31; hotelnotre-dame@wanadoo.fr). M: République. Walk down av. de la République and go right on r. de Malte. Rooms are basic but upbeat; those facing the street have big windows and the 6th fl. has balconies. Elevator. Showers €3.50. Breakfast €6. Reserve 10 days ahead. Requires credit card and email or fax to hold reservation. Singles and doubles €36, with shower €43, with shower and toilet €58-69; triples €79-83. AmEx/MC/V. ❷

Hôtel Rhetia, 3, r. du Général Blaise (☎01 47 00 47 18; fax 01 48 06 01 73). M: Voltaire or St-Ambroise. From the Voltaire métro, take av. Parmentier and turn right on r. Rochebrune, then left on r. du Général Blaise. In a calm, out-of-the-way neighborhood. Moderately clean, with simple furnishings and narrow single beds. Small public garden across the street. Breakfast €3. Reception 7:30am-10pm. Reserve 15 days in advance. Singles €25, with shower €37; doubles €41-43; triples €52. Extra bed €8. ❷

Hôtel de Belfort, 37, r. Servan (☎01 47 00 67 33; fax 01 43 57 97 98). M: Père-Lachaise, St-Maur, or Voltaire. From M: Père-Lachaise, take r. de Chemin-Vert and turn left on r. Servan. 15min. from Bastille. Dim corridors and clean, functional rooms. Draws a young crowd; popular with schools and tour groups, but the layout of the hotel prevents noise from resonating throughout. All rooms with shower, toilet, TV, and phone. Elevator. Reserve 1 week in advance. Breakfast (€5) served 8:30-9:30am. Singles €49; doubles €35, with shower €52; triples €77. Extra bed €23. MC/V. ❸

HOSTELS & FOYERS

Auberge de Jeunesse "Jules Ferry" (HI), 8, bd. Jules Ferry (☎01 43 57 55 60; auberge@easynet.fr). M: République. Walk east on r. du Faubourg du Temple and turn right on the far side of bd. Jules Ferry. Wonderful location in front of a park and next to pl. de la République. 100 beds. Clean rooms with sinks, mirrors, and tiled floors. Doubles with big beds. Party atmosphere. Breakfast and showers included. Lockers €1.55. Sheets free. Laundry €3.05 wash, €1.55 dry. 1 week max. stay. Internet access in lobby €0.15 per min. Lockout 10am-2pm. Reception and dining room 24hr. No reservations; arrive by 8am. If there are no vacancies, they will try to book you in one of the other nearby hostels. 4- to 6-bed dorms €19.50; doubles €19.50 per person. MC/V. ❶

Maison Internationale des Jeunes pour la Culture et pour la Paix, 4, r. Titon (☎01 43 71 99 21). M: Faidherbe-Chaligny. Walk along r. de Montreuil and make a left onto r. Titon. A bit out of the way. Rooms are spare but clean and have 2-8 cot-like beds. The 2nd fl. has quaint lofts. Breakfast and showers included. Sheets €2.30. Internet access in lobby with your Telecarte. Guests w/o children must be 18-30 years. Reception 8am-2pm. Lockout 10am-5pm. Curfew 2am. 5 night max. stay. Reserve 2 weeks in advance, sooner for large groups. €20 per night. ❶

TWELFTH ARRONDISSEMENT

NEIGHBORHOOD QUICKFIND: ***Discover,*** *p. 12;* ***Sights,*** *p. 110;* ***Museums,*** *p. 152;* ***Food & Drink,*** *p. 189;* ***Nightlife,*** *p. 215;* ***Shopping,*** *p. 243.*

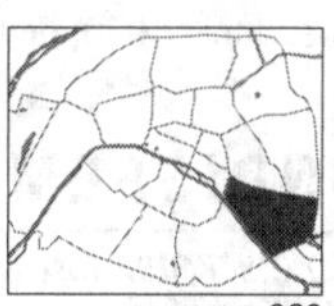

see map p. 389

Hôtel Printania, 91, av. du Dr. Netter (☎01 43 07 65 13). M: Porte de Vincennes. Walk west on the cours de Vincennes and turn left on av. du Dr. Netter. 25 rooms with mini-fridges, large soundproof windows, and faux-marble floors. Breakfast €4.60. In high season you may need a credit card number as deposit. Reserve 2 weeks in advance; confirm by fax. Doubles with sink and *bidet* €39, with shower and bath €48, with TV €54; triples with shower, bath, and TV €61. AmEx/MC/V. ❷

Nièvre-Hôtel, 18, r. d'Austerlitz (☎01 43 43 81 51). M: Gare de Lyon or Quai de la Rapée. From Gare de Lyon, walk away from the train station on r. de Bercy and turn right on r. d'Austerlitz. Centrally located but quiet, this recently redone hotel has a friendly atmosphere and rooms with high ceilings and spotless baths. Breakfast €4. Singles €31; doubles €37, with shower €46, with toilet €54. MC/V. ❷

the BIG $plurge

Finding Your Centre

Sometimes this city's blatant materialism and unstoppable hedonism can get exhausting. You might find yourself wanting somewhere where you can get away from it all, somewhere you can have time to think and, of course, meditate. You're in luck. Whether you're trying to reach Nirvana, looking to detox, or just need time to think, Dharma-masters Grazyna and Jacob Perl's **Centre Parisien de Zen** can take you there! The *centre*'s weekly apartment rentals feature six spotless, attractive rooms with private bath, kitchenette, and views of a serene garden and courtyard. The center helps guests forget modern-day hang-ups with a soothing meditation room (no experience necessary) and a strict policy of no shoes, no smoking, and no TVs or phones in the rooms (there is a common phone and answering machine for residents).

Centre Parisien de Zen, 35, r. de Lyon, 12ème (☎01 44 87 08 13; www.maisonzen.com). M: Bastille or Gare de Lyon, near the Opéra. 1 week for 1 person €315; for 2 people sharing a studio €420. Deluxe suites with bedroom and living room €385/€490. Reserve far in advance, especially Apr.-July. ❸

Nouvel Hôtel, 9, r. d'Austerlitz (☎01 43 42 15 79; fax 01 43 42 31 11). M: Gare de Lyon. Walk away from the train station on r. de Bercy and take a right on r. d'Austerlitz. Bright, clean rooms with big windows and big baths. Elevator. Singles €61, with shower €63.50, with bath €69; doubles €69-74; triples €91.50. AmEx/DC/MC/V. ❸

Mistral Hôtel, 3, r. Chaligny (☎01 46 28 10 20; fax 01 46 28 69 66). M: Reuilly-Diderot. Walk west on bd. Diderot and turn left onto r. Chaligny. Clean and reasonably priced. All rooms have TV and phone. Breakfast €5.50. Hall showers €2.30. Call 7am-midnight to reserve 2 weeks in advance and confirm in writing or by fax. Free storage. Singles €39, with shower €46; 1-bed doubles with shower €46; 2-bed doubles with shower €49; triples with shower and toilet €59; quads with shower and toilet €69. MC/V. ❷

Hôtel de l'Aveyron, 5, r. d'Austerlitz (☎01 43 07 86 86; fax 01 43 07 85 20). M: Gare de Lyon. Walk away from the train station on r. de Bercy and take a right on r. d'Austerlitz. On a quiet street, with clean, unpretentious rooms. Downstairs lounge with TV. English-speaking staff is eager to make suggestions. 26 rooms. Breakfast €5. Reserve 1 month in advance. Singles and doubles €32, with shower €42; triples €39/€49. MC/V. ❷

Hôtel de Reims, 26, r. Hector Malot (☎01 43 07 46 18; fax 01 43 07 56 62). M: Gare de Lyon. Take bd. Diderot away from the tall buildings and make a left onto r. Hector Malot. Stay at this hotel for its central location, just off av. Daumesnil near Opéra Bastille and the Gare de Lyon. 27 clean rooms. Reserve by phone 1 week in advance and confirm in writing or by fax. Singles €29, with shower €40, with shower and toilet €43; doubles €36/€42/€45; triples with shower €48. MC/V. ❷

HOSTELS & FOYERS

Centre International du Séjour de Paris: CISP "Ravel," 6, av. Maurice Ravel (☎01 44 75 60 00; fax 01 43 44 45 30; www.cisp.asso.fr). M: Porte de Vincennes. Walk east on cours de Vincennes then take the first right on bd. Soult, left on r. Jules Lemaître, and right on av. Maurice Ravel. Large, clean rooms (most with fewer than 4 beds), art exhibited all around, auditorium, and outdoor public pool (€3.40). Cafeteria open daily 7:30-9:30am, noon-1:30pm, and 7-8:30pm. Restaurant open noon-1:30pm. Internet €1.50 per 10min. Breakfast, sheets, and towels included. 5-day max. stay (but you can renew at the end). Reception 6:30am-1:30am; you can arrange to have the night guard let you in after 1:30am. Reserve at least a month ahead by phone or email. 8-bed dorm with shower and toilet in hall €15.50; 2-to 4-bed dorm €19.50; singles with shower and toilet €30; doubles with shower and toilet €24 per person. AmEx/MC/V. ❶

THIRTEENTH ARRONDISSEMENT

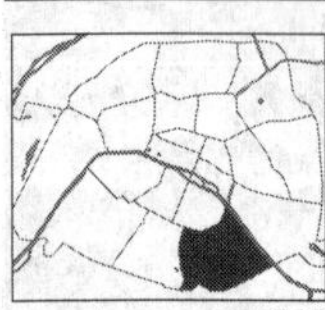

see map p. 392

NEIGHBORHOOD QUICKFIND: ***Discover,*** *p. 4;* ***Sights,*** *p. 111;* ***Food & Drink,*** *p. 190;* ***Nightlife,*** *p. 216.*

Touring Hôtel Magendie, 2, r. Magendie (☎01 43 36 13 61; www.touring-hotel.com). From M: Glacière, follow rue de la Glacière to rue Magendie. Offers a quiet stay in a bustling area and a helpful staff. Breakfast buffet €6. Reservations suggested at least 1 week in advance. Singles €58, doubles €68, triples €84. Special weekend rates Jan.-June and Sept.-Dec. (€46-69). MC/V. ❸

HOSTELS & FOYERS

Centre International du Séjour de Paris: CISP "Kellerman," 17, bd. Kellerman (☎01 44 16 37 38; fax 01 44 16 37 39; www.cisp.asso.fr). M: Porte d'Italie. Cross the street and turn right onto bd. Kellerman. This large, 396-bed hostel resembles a spaceship on stilts from the outside. Inside, its rooms are clean and adequate, if a bit nondescript. Close to Cité Universitaire and the métro. TV room, laundry, and cafeteria (open daily noon-1:30pm and 6:30-9:30pm). Breakfast included (7-9am). Free showers on floors with dorms. No reception 1:30-6:30am. Wheelchair-accessible. Reserve 2-3 weeks in advance. 8-bed dorms €15.40; 2- to 4-bed dorms €19.21; singles with shower and toilet €30; doubles with shower and toilet €24. AmEx/MC/V. ❶

Association des Foyers de Jeunes: Foyer des Jeunes Filles, 234, r. de Tolbiac (☎01 44 16 22 22; fax 01 45 88 61 84; www.foyer-tolbiac.com). M: Glacière. Walk east on bd. Auguste Blanqui, turn right on r. de Glacière, then left on r. de Tolbiac. It's the unfortunately colored salmon and white building. Large, modern foyer **for women** ages 18-26 from outside of France—with an emphasis on non-students (the number of students is kept down by a quota). Excellent facilities include kitchen, TV, laundry, gym, library, and cafeteria. 278 rooms. Linens included. Vacancies in summer, but reserve as far in advance as possible, especially for June and July. €5 registration fee (good for 1 year). Sunny singles €394.50 per month; doubles €285 per month. MC/V. ❶

FOURTEENTH ARRONDISSEMENT

NEIGHBORHOOD QUICKFIND: ***Discover,*** *p. 4;* ***Sights,*** *p. 113;* ***Museums,*** *p. 269;* ***Food & Drink,*** *p. 191;* ***Nightlife,*** *p. 216.*

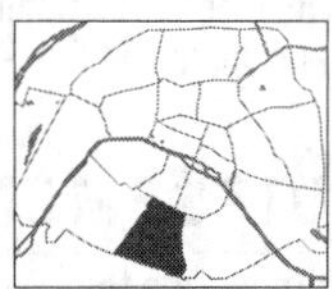
see map pp. 395-396

Hôtel de Blois, 5, r. des Plantes (☎01 45 40 99 48; fax 01 45 40 45 62). M: Mouton-Duvernet. From the métro, turn left on r. Mouton Duvernet then left on r. des Plantes. One of the best deals in Paris. Glossy wallpaper, ornate ceiling carvings, and velvet chairs. Send the very welcoming owner a thank-you note afterwards and she'll put it in the scrapbook that she proudly displays to all guests. TVs, phones, hair dryers, and big, clean baths. Laundromat across the street, public pool next door. 25 rooms. Breakfast €5. Reserve 10 days ahead. Singles €39, with shower €43, with shower and toilet €45, with bath and toilet €51; doubles €41/€45/€47/€56; triples €61. Free hall showers. AmEx/MC/V. ❷

Ouest Hôtel, 27, r. de Gergovie (☎01 45 42 64 99; fax 01 45 42 46 65). M: Pernety. Walk against traffic on r. Raymond Losserand and turn right on r. de Gergovie. A clean hotel with modest furnishings, outstanding rates, friendly staff, and *brasserie*-style walls in the lobby. A small library and a charming dining room perfect for munching on *panini* and chatting it up with fellow travelers. Breakfast €5. Hall shower €5 (sometimes long waits). Singles with small bed €22, with larger bed €28; 1-bed doubles €28, with shower; €37; 2-bed doubles €34/€39. MC/V. ❷

Hôtel du Midi, 4, av. René-Coty (☎01 43 27 23 25; fax 01 43 21 24 58). M: Denfert-Rochereau. From the métro, take the "av. du G. Leclerc côté du Nos. Impairs" exit; turn right at the corner, and onto av. René-Coty. Popular with business travelers, but serves

in recent news

The French (Wi-Fi) Revolution

With the end of the Concorde's reign over high-speed commercial travel, it's only fitting that Paris take the lead in another sort of high-speed travel: Wireless Internet. With a pilot program completed in the summer of 2003, Paris took one step towards the realization of a plan to make the entire city one big "hot-spot" that would allow anyone with a computer equipped with Wi-Fi technology to get on the Internet—whether at home, at a café, or on the bus.

As of June 2003, a dozen antennae had already been installed along the route of bus no. 38. By the end of the year, there may be two or more antennae installed outside each of the city's 72 métro stations, linked through a fiber optics network that would allow uninterrupted access all over the city. The project will cost up to €10 million, and subscribers will have to pay an as-yet undecided fee. The project's leaders still need to overcome a number of hurdles, both technological and bureaucratic—but it looks like this latest revolution is well under way.

other travelers looking for a few extra amenities: marble baths, hair dryers, TVs, fridges, and jacuzzis in some rooms. All have shower and toilet. Some feature steam showers and A/C. Breakfast €6. Parking €9. Reserve at least 15 days in advance. Prices vary with whimsically defined seasons. Singles €68-88; doubles €78-98; large suite €128 AmEx/JCB/MC/V. ❺

Hôtel du Parc, 6, r. Jolivet (☎01 43 20 95 542; www.hotelduparc.com). M: Edgar Quinet. Facing the Tour Montparnasse, turn left on r. de la Gaîté, right on r. du Maine, then right on r. Jolivet. Well-lit rooms with cable TVs, phones, hair dryers. Does not accept big groups. Breakfast €5.50. Singles €46, with shower €55, with shower and toilet €63; doubles with shower and bath €68-75; triples with shower and bath €83-90 AmEx/DC/MC/V. ❸

HOSTELS & FOYERS

FIAP Jean-Monnet, 30, r. Cabanis (☎01 43 13 17 00; reservations ☎01 43 13 17 17; fax 01 45 81 63 91; www.fiap.asso.fr). M: Glacière. From the métro, walk straight down bd. Auguste-Blanqui, turn left on r. de la Santé and then right on r. Cabanis. With a high-end, prefab feel, this 500-bed student center offers spotless rooms with phone, toilet, and shower. The fabulous concrete complex has a game room, TV rooms, laundry, sunlit piano bar, restaurant, outdoor terrace, and disco. Breakfast included; add €1.60 for buffet. Curfew 2am. Reserve 2-4 weeks in advance. Be sure to specify if you want a dorm bed or you will be booked for a single. €15 deposit per person per night by check or credit card. Wheelchair-accessible. Rooms cleaned daily. Check-in after 2:30pm. Check-out 9am. 3-month maximum stay. Singles €49.50; doubles €32 per person; quads €27.40 per person; 6-bed rooms €22 per person. MC/V. ❷

FIFTEENTH ARRONDISSEMENT

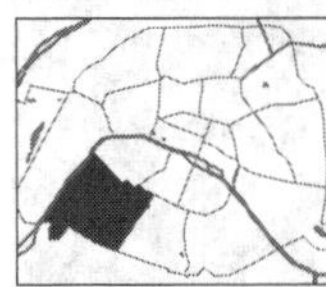

see map p. 393

NEIGHBORHOOD QUICKFIND: ***Discover,*** *p. 5;* ***Sights,*** *p. 114;* ***Museums,*** *p. 152;* ***Food & Drink,*** *p. 192.*

Practic Hôtel, 20, r. de l'Ingénieur Keller (☎01 45 77 70 58; www.practichotel.fr). M: Charles Michels. From pl. Charles Michels, walk up r. Linois, turn left on r. des 4-Frères Peignot, then turn right on r. de l'Ingénieur Keller. Small hotel run by a meticulous owner. Obsessively clean, with incredibly spacious bathrooms and bedrooms, excellent for families. Close to movie theatres, shopping centres, and métro. Breakfast €7.50. Make reservations at least 2 weeks ahead in summer. Single or double with toilet €48, with shower or bath €66; triples and quads €98-110. AmEx/MC/V. ❷

Hôtel Printemps, 31, r. du Commerce (☎01 45 79 83 36; hotel.printemps.15e@wanadoo.fr). M: La Motte-Picquet-Grenelle. In a busy neighborhood, surrounded by shops (including Monoprix) and budget restaurants, this 53 room hotel is pleasant, clean, and cheap. Breakfast €4. Hall showers €3. Reserve 3-4 weeks ahead. Singles and doubles with sink €30, with shower €39, with shower and toilet €43. MC/V. ❷

Pacific Hôtel, 11, r. Fondary (☎01 45 75 20 49; fax 01 45 77 70 73; www.pacifichotel-paris.com). M: Dupleix or av. Emile Zola. A little bit out of the way, but easily the most elegant of the 15*ème's* budget offerings. Spacious rooms with desks. Breakfast €6. Reserve at least 2 weeks in advance. Singles and doubles with shower €56; doubles €62-64. MC/V. ❸

Hôtel Camélia, 24, bd. Pasteur (☎01 47 83 76 35 or 01 47 83 69 91; fax 01 40 65 94 98). M: Pasteur. On a main boulevard next to the métro and surrounded by shops and cafés. In a convenient location, with double windows that block the rooms from the noise of the bustle below. Nice, big baths. Breakfast €5. Renovations until April 2004, but the hotel will remain open and prices won't increase when the new rooms are unveiled. Singles or doubles €35-65, with shower and TV €48-65; extra bed €11. AmEx/MC/V. ❸

HOSTELS & FOYERS

Three Ducks Hostel, 6, pl. Etienne Pernet (☎01 48 42 04 05; fax 01 48 42 99 99; www.3ducks.fr). M: Félix Faure. Walk against traffic on the left side of the church; the hostel is on the left. With palm trees in the courtyard and bizarre beach-style shower shacks, this

hostel is aimed at Anglo fun-seekers. Enjoy the in-house bar (open only to residents) until the 2am curfew; this is probably the best late-night option in the 15*ème*. Kitchen, lockers, and small 2- to 8-bed dorm rooms. Laundry and groceries are both nearby. Internet access in lobby. Shower and breakfast included. Reception daily 8am-2am. Lockout daily 11am-5pm. 1 week max. stay. Sheets €2.29; towels €0.76. Reserve with credit card a week ahead. Mar.-Oct. dorm beds €22; doubles €25 per person. Nov.-Feb. brings special low-season rates; call for details. MC/V. ❶

Aloha Hostel, 1, r. Borromée (☎01 42 73 03 03; fax 01 42 73 14 14; www.friends@aloha.fr). M: Volontaires. From the métro, walk against traffic on r. de Vaugirard then turn right on r. Borromée. More tranquil than the raucous Three Ducks (see above) nearby, but still a quite lively mix of international backpackers. Music and drinks are available in the café. No outside alcohol on premises. Breakfast included. Safety deposit boxes and security cameras. Sheets €3, towels €3–but you get to keep them (because you should never travel without a towel). Reception 8am-2am. Lockout 11am-5pm. Curfew 2am. Reserve a week ahead. Apr. to mid-Sept. dorms €21; doubles €25. Mid-Sept. to Nov. €17/€22. Apr.-June €21/€25. ❶

La Maison Hostel, 67bis, r. Dutot (☎01 42 73 10 10; www.mamaison.fr). M: Volontaires. Cross r. de Vaugirard on r. des Volontaires, take the second right (r. Dutot), and go 2 blocks. Doubles and clean 3- or 4-bed dorms in a quiet neighborhood; an excellent choice for families. All rooms have shower and toilet. Internet €1 per 10min. Kitchen open to residents. Breakfast included. Doubles come with sheets; otherwise, sheets €2.50, towels €1, plus deposit. Reception 8am-2am. Lockout 11am-4pm. Curfew 2am. Reserve 1 month in advance. High-season 2- and 3-bed dorms €21, doubles €24. Low-season (starts Nov. 1) dorms €19; doubles €22.50. ❶

SIXTEENTH ARRONDISSEMENT

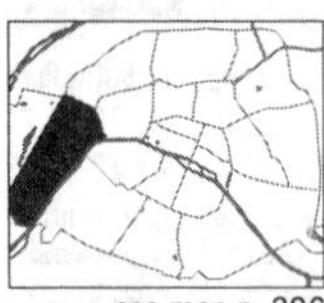

see map p. 396

NEIGHBORHOOD QUICKFIND: ***Discover,*** *p. 12;* ***Sights,*** *p. 116;* ***Museums,*** *p. 153;* ***Food & Drink,*** *p. 193;* ***Nightlife,*** *p. 217.*

Hôtel Boileau, 81, r. Boileau (☎01 42 88 83 74; fax 01 45 27 62 98; www.cofrase.com/boileau). M: Exelmans. From the métro, walk down bd. Exelmans in the direction of the Seine and turn right on r. Boileau. This charming hotel features marble busts, Oriental rugs, vintage cashboxes, a sunny breakfast room, and an equally sunny staff. Cable TV, Internet access, and clean rooms to boot. Breakfast €6. Singles €69; doubles €77-86; triples €109. AmEx/MC/V. ❸

Hôtel Keppler, 12, r. Keppler (☎01 47 20 65 05; fax 01 47 23 02 29). M: George V or Kléber. From the George V métro, turn left on r. Bassano and take the fourth right onto r. Keppler. This delightful hotel has a very friendly staff and is just 5min. from the Arc de Triomphe. As such, it's ideal for those who want to rev up for the Champs-Elysées club circuit somewhere quiet and tastefully decorated. Spacious breakfast room and lobby with small bar. Breakfast €5.40. 2 single beds with bath or shower €76, with balcony €84; 3 single beds €98.50. AmEx/MC/V. ❸

Villa d'Auteuil, 28, r. Poussin (☎01 42 88 30 37; fax 01 45 20 74 70). M: Michel-Ange Auteuil. Walk up r. Girodet and turn left on r. Poussin. At the edge of the Bois de Boulogne, on a peaceful street is the Parisian Fawlty Towers, with eccentric staff members and (of course) a parrot. Rooms have wood-frame beds, shower, toilet, phone, and TV. High rooms have you working off those croissants–there's no elevator. Breakfast €5. Singles €48-52; doubles €56-60; triples €68. MC/V. ❷

Hôtel Ribera, 66, r. La Fontaine (☎01 42 88 29 50; fax 01 42 24 91 33). M: Jasmin. Walk down r. Ribera to its intersection with r. La Fontaine; hotel on your left. The cheerful, colorful rooms match the personnel's charm. Some rooms come with faux sculpture or marble fireplaces. Pull-out beds in doubles are perfect for a small child. Excellent location in the heart of Auteuil. Safe and television in every room. Breakfast €5. Rooms €43-54. 10% discount July 15-Aug. 15. AmEx/MC/V. ❷

SEVENTEENTH ARRONDISSEMENT

NEIGHBORHOOD QUICKFIND: ***Discover,*** *p. 13;* ***Sights,*** *p. 118;* ***Museums,*** *p. 156;* ***Food & Drink,*** *p. 194;* ***Nightlife,*** *p. 217.*

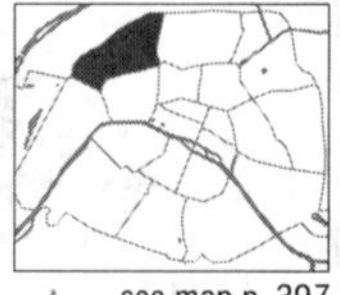
see map p. 397

Hôtel Prince Albert Wagram, 28, passage Cardinet (☎01 47 54 06 00; fax 01 47 63 83 12; www.hotelprincealbert.com). M: Malesherbes. Follow r. Cardinet across bd. Malesherbes and r. de Tocqueville and turn left into passage Cardinet. In a quiet neighborhood 10min. from the métro. Newly renovated, with clean and bright rooms and an elevator. Small dogs welcome. All rooms with shower, toilet, TV, and safety box. Breakfast free for *Let's Go* users. Singles €63-67; doubles €82. AmEx/MC/V. ❸

Hôtel Champerret Héliopolis, 13, r. d'Héliopolis (☎01 47 64 92 56; fax 01 47 64 50 44). M: Porte de Champerret. Turn left off av. de Villiers. 22 brilliant and sparkling blue-and-white rooms, some with little wooden balconies opening onto a palm-lined terrace. In a beautiful location, close to the métro, with many pleasant eateries nearby. Welcoming and helpful staff. All rooms have showers, TVs, phones, hair dryers. One wheelchair-accessible room. Breakfast €7. Reserve 15 days in advance. Singles €65; doubles €77, with bath €84; triples with bath €91. AmEx/DC/MC/V. ❸

Hôtel Riviera, 55, r. des Acacias (☎01 43 80 45 31; fax 01 40 54 84 08). M: Charles de Gaulle-Etoile. Walk north on av. MacMahon, then turn left on r. des Acacias. Close to the Arc de Triomphe, this hotel wins on location. Modern, quiet rooms have comfortable beds, TVs, telephones, hair dryers. Some have A/C. Elevator. Breakfast €6. Reservations 2-3 weeks in advance. Singles with shower €48, with toilet €61-71; doubles with toilet and bath or shower €65-81; triples with toilet and bath or shower €90-96; quads €98-103. AmEx/MC/V. ❷

Hôtel Belidor, 5, r. Belidor (☎01 45 74 49 91; fax 01 45 72 54 22). M: Porte Maillot. From the métro, go north on bd. Gouvion St-Cyr and turn right on r. Belidor. The hotel's slightly dingy halls give way to quiet, clean, and spacious rooms. Some with tubs. Most rooms face a quiet, tiled courtyard. Breakfast included. Reserve 10-15 days in advance. Open Sept.-July. Singles €42, with shower €52, with shower and toilet €59; doubles €63.50; 2-bed doubles with toilet €82. MC/V. ❷

EIGHTEENTH ARRONDISSEMENT

NEIGHBORHOOD QUICKFIND: ***Discover,*** *p. 13;* ***Sights,*** *p. 119;* ***Museums,*** *p. 156;* ***Food & Drink,*** *p. 195;* ***Nightlife,*** *p. 218;* ***Shopping,*** *p. 245.*

see map pp. 386-387

Hôtel Caulaincourt, 2, sq. Caulaincourt (☎01 46 06 46 06; fax 01 46 06 46 16; bienvenue@caulaincourt.com). M: Lamarck-Caulaincourt. Walk up the stairs to r. Caulaincourt and proceed to your right, between nos. 63 and 65. Half hotel, half hostel, this friendly establishment is located in a pleasant, quiet area of the picturesque Montmartre. Formerly used as artists' studios, these large, simple rooms have great light and wonderful views of Montmartre and the Paris skyline. One of the best values around. TVs and phones in every room. Breakfast €5.50. Reserve up to 1 month in advance. Singles €33, with shower €42, with shower and toilet €50; doubles €44-74; triples with shower €60-75. MC/V. ❷

Style Hôtel, 8, r. Ganneron (☎01 45 22 37 59; fax 01 45 22 81 03). M: Place de Clichy. Walk up av. de Clichy and turn right onto r. Ganneron. Next to the cemetery. Two buildings; the newer is recently renovated in Art Deco style, with larger rooms, wood floors, and armoires, while the older building is quieter and slightly worn but charming. Hall bathrooms and showers. Breakfast €5. Reserve at least 3 weeks in advance. Singles €34, with shower and toilet €43; doubles €34/€48; triples with bath and toilet €55; quads with bath and toilet €65. Extra bed €5. AmEx/MC/V. ❷

Hôtel André Gill, 4, r. André Gill (☎01 42 62 48 48; fax 01 42 62 77 92). M: Abbesses. Walk downhill on r. des Abbesses and turn right on r. des Martyrs and left on r. André Gill. In a tiny courtyard, André Gill provides refuge from the noise and seediness of bd. de Clichy; just be careful when walking through the nearby sex district at night. Elevator. Breakfast €4. Hall showers €4. Telephone €0.42. Reserve 1 week in advance. Singles €39; doubles €55, with shower or bath €79. Dorms €25 (breakfast included). MC/V. ❷

HOSTELS & FOYERS

Village Hostel, 20, r. d'Orsel (☎01 42 64 22 02; fax 01 42 64 22 04; www.villiagehostel.fr). M: Anvers. Go uphill on r. Steinkerque and turn right on r. d'Orsel. In the midst of the heavy Sacré-Coeur tourist traffic, but clean and cheap. Doubles and 3- to 5-bed dorms, some with a view of Sacré-Coeur, some off a spacious patio, and some facing the noisy street (make sure to specify). Kitchen, beer dispenser, TV, stereo, telephones, and Internet access in the lounge. Toilet and shower in every room. Breakfast included. Sheets €2.50; towel €1. Curfew 2am. Lockout 11am-4pm. 7-day max. stay. Reservations by fax or email. Same-day telephone reservations accepted—call at 8am when reception opens. 4-bed dorms €21.50; 1-bed or 2-bed double €50; triples €69. Cash only. ❶

NINETEENTH ARRONDISSEMENT

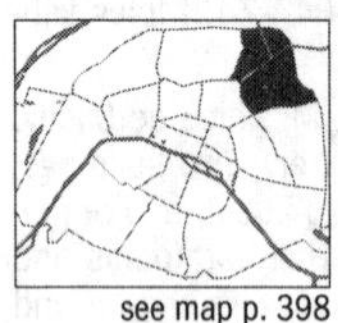
see map p. 398

NEIGHBORHOOD QUICKFIND: ***Discover,*** *p. 14;* ***Sights,*** *p. 123;* ***Museums,*** *p. 274;* ***Food & Drink,*** *p. 197.*

Rhin et Danube, 3, pl. Rhin et Danube (☎01 42 45 10 13; fax 01 42 06 88 82). M: Danube; or bus #75 from M: Châtelet (30 min). Just steps from the métro, the R&D is a real deal for the budget traveler. The suites don't sparkle, but they are spacious, and many look onto a quaint *place*. Each room has kitchen, fridge, dishes, coffeemaker, hair dryer, shower, toilet, direct phone, and color TV with satellite. Singles €46; doubles €61; triples €73; quads €83; quints €92. MC/V. ❷

Crimée Hôtel, 188, r. de Crimée (☎01 40 36 75 29 or 01 40 35 19 57; fax 01 40 36 29 57). M: Crimée. By the métro at the corner of r. de Flandre. In the northern, commercial 19*ème*, relatively close to La Villette. This place has a business conference feel. The rooms, though a bit sterile, are spotless. Some rooms have hair dryer, TV, A/C, toilet, and shower. Elevator. Breakfast €6. Singles €52-54; doubles €60-62; triples €67; quads €75. 10% discount for *Let's Go* readers on weekends in July and Aug. AmEx/MC/V. ❸

La Perdrix Rouge, 5, r. Lassus (☎01 42 06 09 53; fax 01 42 06 88 70). M: Jourdain. Steps from the metro, a bank, a grocery store, a laundromat, and a few restaurants, this is a great spot if you're looking for a little peace away from the clamor of central Paris. No-nonsense staff welcomes you to a no-nonsense hostel. Spartan rooms are a little dark, but each has TV, toilet, and bath or shower. Breakfast €5.50. Reserve by fax. Singles €50; doubles €55-60; triples €80. AmEx/MC/V. ❷

TWENTIETH ARRONDISSEMENT

NEIGHBORHOOD QUICKFIND: ***Discover,*** *p. 14;* ***Sights,*** *p. 123;* ***Museums,*** *p. 157;* ***Food & Drink,*** *p. 197;* ***Nightlife,*** *p. 218.*

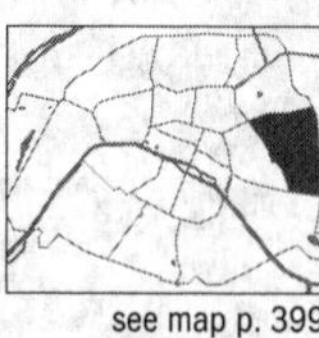

see map p. 399

Eden Hôtel, 7, r. Jean-Baptiste Dumay (☎01 46 36 64 22; fax 01 46 36 01 11). M: Pyrénées. Turn right from the métro; off r. de Belleville. An oasis of hospitality, with good value for its 2 stars. Clean rooms with TVs and toilets. Elevator. Breakfast €4.50. Bath or shower €4. Reserve rooms by fax 1 week in advance. Singles €36, with shower €49; doubles with shower €51-54, 1 double with bath €54. Extra bed €10. MC/V. ❷

L'Ermitage, 42bis, r. de l'Ermitage (☎01 46 36 23 44; 01 46 36 89 13; hotelermitage@aol.com). M: Jourdain. Walk down r. Jourdain, turn left onto r. des Pyrénées, and left on r. de l'Ermitage. Welcoming, family-run establishment with clean, simple rooms. Breakfast €4.50. Singles €30, with TV and shower €40; doubles with TV and shower €45. MC/V. ❷

HOSTELS & FOYERS

Auberge de Jeunesse "Le D'Artagnan" (HI), 80, r. Vitruve (☎01 40 32 34 56; fax 01 40 32 34 55; www.hostels-in.com). M: Porte de Bagnolet or Porte de Montreuil. From Porte de Bagnolet, walk south on bd. Davout and make a right on r. Vitruve. A massive Martian outpost standing watch over the remote 20*ème*. Neon lights and funky decorations in every color welcome legions of boisterous young backpackers as well as older single travelers and families. 435 beds. Restaurant (open 6:30-9:30pm), bar (open 9pm-2am; Happy Hour 8-9pm), and a small cinema (free films nightly 6pm). Breakfast (served 7am-11am) and sheets included. Lockers €2-4 per day. Laundry €3 per wash, €1 per dry. 6 night max. stay. Reception 8am-1am. Lockout noon-3pm. Reservations by fax or email a must. 3-, 4-, and 8-bed dorms €20.60 per person; children under 10 €10.30. ❶

LONG-TERM ACCOMMODATIONS

Almost every *arrondissement* in Paris contains some form of affordable housing and is well connected to the city by the city's extensive public transportation system. You will probably find the cheapest housing in peripheral *arrondissements.* Try the 12*ème*, 13*ème*, the northern half of the 17*ème* (near La Fourche), 18*ème*, 19*ème*, or 20*ème*. If you are set on a central location, the more commercial parts of the 2*ème* may have something within your price range. During August, even ritzier locales can provide affordable housing, as the entire city empties out for the greatest Parisian vacation of them all, the *grandes vacances*. For more information on specific neighborhoods, see **Discover,** p. 2.

STUDENTS

For travelers planning a summer, semester, or academic year visit to Paris, student housing is available in the dormitories of most French universities. Contact the **Centre Régional des Oeuvres Universitaires (CROUS)** for more information (see **Service Directory,** p. 341). Lodging is available on a month-to-month basis at the **Cité Universi-**

One of the Family

A viable alternative to being in a hostel or hotel, for both short- and long-term stays in Paris, is to live with a family. It's fairly inexpensive, and can be a great way to experience Parisian life. The following agencies match guests with host families.

3,2,1...Mondialoca, 11, av. Charles de Gaulle, Roissy en France 95700 (☎03 23 71 61 40; www.mondialoca.net). Offers rooms in Paris for 2-night min. stay. Singles from €40 per night; doubles from €50.

Alcove & Agapes—Paris Bed & Breakfast, 8bis, r. Coysevox, 18*ème* (☎01 44 85 06 05; www.bed-and-breakfast-in-paris.com). Host rooms in Paris. €49-114 per night.

France Lodge Locations, 41, r. La Fayette, 9*ème* (☎01 53 20 02 54). 160 rooms in and around Paris. €15 membership fee lasts up to 1 year. 1 person €44-50 per night.

France Accommodation & Culture, 53, r. Boissière, 16*ème* (☎01 45 00 45 51; www.fac-paris.com). For professionals and foreigners studying French. 1-week min. €212 per week.

Good Morning Paris, 43, r. Lacépède, 5*ème* (☎01 47 07 28 29). Host rooms from 2 nights to 2 weeks. Single room with breakfast €46 per night.

taire, 15, bd. Jourdan, 14*ème* (☎01 44 16 64 45; www.ciup.fr); M: Cité Universitaire. For information, write to M. le Délégué Général de Cité Universitaire de Paris, 19, bd. Jourdan, 75690 Paris Cedex 14. Over 30 different nations maintain dormitories at the Cité Universitaire, where they board their citizens studying in Paris. In summer, dorms lodge students and academics in Paris for short-term stays; an application is required. Some kitchens are available (summer singles €16-23 per night.) To stay in the **American House,** write to Fondation des Etats-Unis, 15, bd. Jourdan, 75690 Paris Cedex 14. (☎01 53 80 68 80; fax 01 53 80 68 99. Rates vary according to demand: summer €440 per month; cheaper low season. Office open M-F 9am-5pm.)

RENTING AN APARTMENT

For help renting an apartment in France, call, fax, write, or visit **Allô Logement Temporaire** (see **Service Directory,** p. 341). This helpful, English-speaking association charges a membership fee of €50 if they succeed in finding an apartment for you, which is followed by an additional charge of €35 per month up to a year; maximum fee €470. The company suggests writing or calling before you leave for France.

Alternatively, the French Department at local universities may be able to connect you with students abroad who want to sublet their apartments. Short-term rentals, more expensive per month than longer rentals, are difficult to procure, especially in winter months. **New York Habitat** (www.nyhabitat.com) finds furnished short- and long-term rentals for its clients. The web site has photos of most apartments, but be aware that a photograph can make any shoebox look like a palace.

If possible, stay in a hotel or hostel your first week in Paris and find an apartment while you're there. Among the best places to look are the bulletin boards in the **American Church** (see **Service Directory,** p. 345). Those upstairs tend to advertise long-term rentals, while those downstairs list short-term, cheaper arrangements. A smaller list of apartments to rent or share can be found at the bookstore **Shakespeare & Co.** (see **Shopping,** p. 240). Check listings in any of the English-French newsletters like **Paris Free Voice** or **France-USA Contacts (FUSAC),** a free publication found in English bookstores and restaurants throughout Paris. FUSAC is also distributed in the US. (FUSAC, P.O. Box 115, Cooper Station, New York, NY 10276; ☎212-777-5553; fax 777-

5554, www.fusac.com; in Paris, 26, r. Bernard, 14*ème*, 75014 Paris; ☎01 56 53 54 54; fax 01 56 53 54 55; www.fusac.fr; M: Pernety.) It includes classified ads, in which Anglophones offer apartments for rent or sublet. The Paris office also has a bulletin board with apartment and job listings. ***De Particulier à Particulier*** is a French publication that comes out on Thursdays with listings, as does the Tuesday **Le Figaro.** *De Particulier à Particulier* also has an excellent web site with a number of apartment listings in Paris (www.pap.fr).

Subletting is technically illegal, but it is common. Subletters should work out a written agreement with the landlord, defining all of their mutual expectations. The original renter may require cash payments to avoid paying heavy taxes, and utilities and mailbox are likely to remain under the renter's name. The subletter may need to tell the building superintendent or *concierge* that he or she is a guest of the renter.

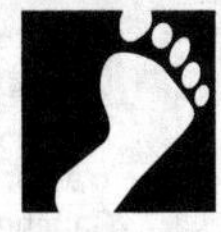

INSIDE

Daytripping

TRIP	TRAVEL TIME
Versailles	40-60 minutes
Fontainebleau	55-65 minutes
Chartres	65-75 minutes
Vaux-le-Vicomte	1¼-2 hours
Chantilly	45-75 minutes
Giverny	1-1¼ hours
Auvers-sur-Oise	1-1½ hours
Disneyland Paris	45-50 minutes

VERSAILLES

By sheer force of ego, the Sun King converted a simple hunting lodge into the world's most famous palace. The sprawling château and bombastic gardens (see p. 284) stand as a testament to the despotic playboy-king, Louis XIV, who lived, entertained, and governed here on the grandest of scales. A century later, while Louis XVI and Marie-Antoinette entertained in lavish style, the peasants of Paris starved. The opulence of Versailles makes it clear why they lost their heads (see **Life & Times,** p. 43).

PRACTICAL INFORMATION

Trains: The **RER** runs from M: Invalides or any stop on RER Line C5 to the Versailles Rive Gauche station (30-40min., departs every 15min, €4.90 round-trip). From the Invalides or other RER Line C stop, take trains with labels beginning with "V." Buy your RER ticket before going through the turnstile to the platform; although a métro ticket will get you through these turnstiles, it will not get you through RER turnstiles at Versailles and could get you fined by the *contrôleurs*. From the RER Versailles train station, turn right down av. de Général de Gaulle, walk 200m, and turn left at the first big intersection on av. de Paris; the entrance to the château is straight ahead.

Tourist Office: Office de Tourisme de Versailles, 2bis, av. de Paris (☎01 39 24 88 88; fax 01 39 24 88 89; www.versailles-tourisme.fr). From the RER Versailles train station, follow directions to the château; the office will be on your left on av. de Paris before you reach the courtyard of the château. A great place to get a calm explanation of your options in Versailles from a human being before reaching the tourist mayhem in the palace. The office sells tickets for château events like the Fêtes de Nuit, and provides brochures on accommodations, restaurants, and events in town. Open daily summer 9am-7pm; winter 9am-6pm.

Food: While there are a number of tourist dining options (including McDo) along the walk from the train station to the palace, perhaps your best warm weather bet is to bring a picnic (and a blanket) to enjoy by the canal in the gardens after you tour the palace. On the weekends you'll be in good company among the many French who do the same–minus the palace visit. Should you forget your *piquenique*, there are reasonably priced snack bars tucked in various corners of the gardens.

SIGHTS

PALACE

HISTORY

A child during the aristocratic insurgency called the Fronde, Louis XIV is said to have entered his father's bedchamber one night only to find (and frighten away) an assassin. Fearing noble conspiracy the rest of his life, Louis chose to move the center of royal power out of Paris and away from potential aristocratic insubordination. In 1661, the Sun King renovated the small hunting lodge in Versailles and enlisted the help of architect Louis Le Vau, painter Charles Le Brun, and landscape architect André Le Nôtre (of Vaux-le-Vicomte fame) just months after their previous patron, Jean Fouquet, had been sentenced to lifetime imprisonment (see **Vaux-le-Vicomte,** p. 293). Indeed, Versailles's Vaux-esque fountains and grandiloquent scale smack of supreme royal one-upmanship. The court at Versailles became the nucleus of noble life, where France's aristocrats vied for the king's favor (see **Gardens,** p. 283).

No one knows just how much it cost to build Versailles; Louis XIV burned the accounts to keep the price a mystery. Though every aspect of life was a minutely choreographed public spectacle, things there was less luxurious than one might imagine: courtiers wore rented swords and urinated behind statues in the parlors, wine froze in the drafty dining rooms, and dressmakers invented the color *puce* (literally, "flea") to camouflage the insects crawling on the noblewomen. Louis XIV died on September 1, 1715 and was succeeded by his great-grandson Louis XV in 1722. He commissioned the Opéra, in the North Wing, for the marriage of Marie-Antoinette and Louis XVI. The newlyweds inherited the throne and Versailles when Louis XV died of smallpox at the château in 1774. The Dauphin and Marie-Antoinette changed little of the château's exterior, but did create Marie-Antoinette's personal pretend playland, the *Hameau*. On October 5, 1789, 15,000 Parisian fishwives and National Guardsmen marched out to the palace and brought the royal family back to Paris, where they were guillotined in 1793.

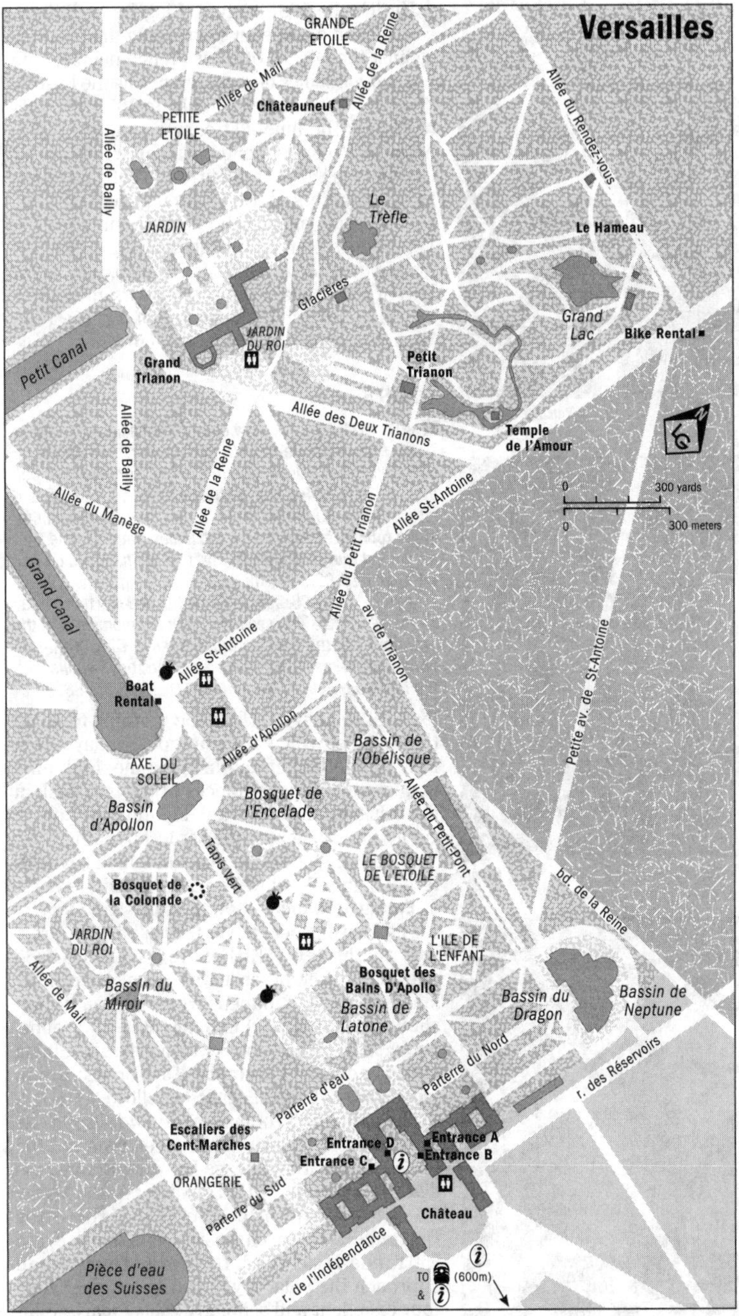

Versailles

GRANDE ETOILE
Allée de la Reine
Allée de Mail
Châteauneuf
PETITE ETOILE
Allée de Bailly
Allée du Rendez-vous
Le Trèfle
JARDIN
Le Hameau
Glacières
Grand Lac
Bike Rental
JARDIN DU ROI
Petit Canal
Grand Trianon
Petit Trianon
Allée des Deux Trianons
Temple de l'Amour
Allée de Bailly
Allée de la Reine
Allée St-Antoine
Allée du Manège
Allée du Petit Trianon
0 300 yards
0 300 meters
Grand Canal
av. de Trianon
Petite av. de St-Antoine
Allée St-Antoine
Boat Rental
Allée d'Apollon
Bassin de l'Obélisque
AXE. DU SOLEIL
Bassin d'Apollon
Bosquet de l'Encelade
Allée du Petit-Pont
LE BOSQUET DE L'ETOILE
Tapis Vert
Bosquet de la Colonade
bd. de la Reine
JARDIN DU ROI
L'ILE DE L'ENFANT
Allée de Mail
Bosquet des Bains D'Apollo
Bassin du Miroir
Bassin de Latone
Bassin du Dragon
Bassin de Neptune
Parterre du Nord
r. des Réservoirs
Parterre d'eau
Escaliers des Cent-Marches
Entrance D
Entrance A
Entrance B
Entrance C
ORANGERIE
Parterre du Sud
Château
r. de l'Indépendance
Pièce d'eau des Suisses
TO & (600m)

Versailles Gardens

Hall of Mirrors

Inside the Palace

During the 19th century, King Louis-Philippe established a museum to preserve the château, against the wishes of most French people, who wanted Versailles demolished just as the Bastille had been (see **Sights,** p. 110). In 1871, the château took the limelight once again, when Wilhelm of Prussia became Kaiser Wilhelm I of Germany in the Hall of Mirrors. That same year, as headquarters of the Thiers regime, Versailles sent an army against the Paris Commune. The *Versaillais* pierced the city walls and crushed the *communards.* On June 28, 1919, the Hall of Mirrors was again the setting for an historic occasion, this time the signing of the Treaty of Versailles, which brought an end to WWI.

TOURS

☎01 30 83 76 79; www.chateauversailles.com. ***Open*** *Tu-Su May-Sept. 9am-6:30pm; Oct.-Apr. 9am-5:30pm. Last admission 30min. before closing.* ***Admission*** *to palace and* ***self-guided tour, entrance A:*** *€7.50, over 60 and after 3:30pm €5.30, under 18 always free. Supplement for* ***audio tour, entrance C:*** *1hr.; €4, under 7 free. Supplement for* ***guided tour, entrance D:*** *1hr. tour of Chambres du Roi, €4, under 18 €2.70; 1½hr. tour of the apartments of Louis XV and the opéra €6, ages 7-17 €4.20.* ***Full-day tour*** *"A Day at Versailles" (2 1½hr. segments, 1 in the morning, 1 in the afternoon) is the most comprehensive; €20.* ***Sign-language tours*** *available; make advance reservations with the Bureau d'Action Culturelle, ☎01 30 83 77 88.*

It's best to arrive early in the morning to avoid the crowds, which are worst on Sundays from May to September and in late June. Pick up a map at one of the entrances or the info desk in the center of the courtyard. Figuring out how to get into the château is the hardest part; there are half a dozen entrances, many of which have different sights. Most of Versailles's visitors enter at **Entrance A,** located on the right-hand side in the north wing, or **Entrance C,** located in the archway to the left. (Either ticket allows free entrance to the other; native speakers of Russian, Chinese, Japanese, Spanish, or Italian should start from C.) **Entrance B** is for groups, **Entrance D** is where tours with a living, breathing guide begin, and **Entrance H** is for visitors in wheelchairs. **General admission** allows entrance to the following rooms: the *grands appartements*, where the king and queen received the public; the War and Peace Drawing Rooms; the *Galerie des Glaces* (Hall of Mirrors); and Marie-Antoinette's public apartment. Head for Entrance C to purchase an **audioguide.** From Entrance D, at the left-hand corner as you approach the palace, you can choose between four excellent and scholarly **guided tours** of different parts of the château. The best is the 1½hr.

tour of the Louis XV apartments and opéra. After the tour, you'll be able to explore the rest of Versailles on your own, without waiting in the general admission line. To avoid an excessive wait for guided tours, arrive before 11am.

SELF-GUIDED TOUR. Begin at **Entrance A.** The general admission ticket starts your visit in the **Musée de l'Histoire de France,** created in 1837 by Louis-Philippe to celebrate his country's glory. Along its textured walls hang portraits of men and women who shaped the course of French history. The 21 rooms (arranged in chronological order) seek to construct a historical context for the château, which is helpful for those not taking an audio or guided tour.

Up the staircase to the right is the dual-level **royal chapel,** constructed by architect Hardouin-Mansart from 1699-1710, where the king heard mass. Back toward the staircase and to the left is a series of gilded **drawing rooms** in the **State Apartments** that are dedicated to Hercules, Mars, and the ever-present Apollo (the Sun King identified with the sun god). The ornate **Salon d'Apollo** was Louis XIV's throne room. Framed by the **War and Peace Drawing Rooms** is the **Hall of Mirrors,** which was originally a terrace until Mansart added a series of mirrored panels and windows to double the light in the room and reflect the gardens outside. These mirrors were the largest that 17th-century technology could produce and were an unthinkable extravagance. Le Brun's ceiling paintings (1679-1686) tell the history of Louis XIV's heroism, culminating with *The King Governs Alone.* The Treaty of Versailles was ratified here, effectively ending WWI.

The **Queen's Bedchamber,** where royal births were public events, is now furnished as it was on October 6, 1789, when Marie-Antoinette left the palace for the last time. A version of the David painting depicting Napoleon's self-coronation dominates the **Salle du Sacré** (also known as the Coronation Room). The **Hall of Battles,** installed by Louis-Philippe, is a monument to 14 centuries of France's military.

GARDENS

Open *daily sunrise-sundown. Apr.-Oct. M-F €3, ages under 18 and after 6pm free.* ***Fountains*** *turned on for special displays, such as the* ***Grandes Eaux Musicales,*** *Apr.-Oct. Sa-Su 11am-noon and 3:30-5:30pm. €6. Though the most convenient place for* ***bike rentals*** *is across from the base of the canal, there are 2 other locations: one to the north of the Parterre Nord by the Grille de la Reine, and another by the Trianons at Porte St-Antoine. ☎01 39 66 97 66. Open Feb.-Nov Sa-Su 10am-closing and M-F 1pm-closing. 1hr. €5, ½hr. €3.30. Rent* ***boats*** *for 4 at the boathouse to the right side of the base of the canal. ☎01 39 66 97*

"Let Them Steal Furniture!"

October 5, 1789 was a good day for the French Revolution and a very bad one for Versailles. Taking their cue from the large crowd that stormed the Bastille prison, another, even larger one made their way to Versailles, unceremoniously grabbed the King and Queen, and headed back to Paris.

After those shenanigans, the Revolutionaries, penniless from all their rabble-rousing, were forced to auction off many of the chests, chairs, and tables that filled the palace. All of the palace's artwork was transported to the Louvre for safekeeping. Many of the rooms and buildings at Versailles were later returned to their pre-Revolutionary glory, with reproductions put in place of the original furnishings. Of the roughly 17,000 items sold off at public auction, the majority are lost forever.

But not all. Gerald van Kemp, a French curator who died in January 2002, made it his life's work to track down missing pieces and return them to their rightful place. Nicknamed "The Man Who Gave Us Back Versailles," he retrieved some Riesener commodes made for Marie-Antoinette and a Savonniere carpet, items that must be important judging by the millions of dollars the museum shelled out to bring them home. Versailles's most prized former possession is Leonardo da Vinci's *Mona Lisa,* but let's hope she doesn't leave the Louvre anytime soon—the lines at Versailles are long enough already.

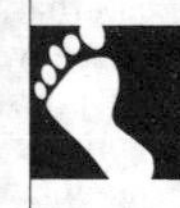

Nature as Social Theater in 18th-Century Paris

You don't have to be a Francophile to know that, when it came to Versailles, Louis XIV was something of a control freak. After assuming sole leadership of the French state upon the death of Cardinal Mazarin in 1661, the 22-year-old king quickly set about re-fashioning all of France into an integrated symbol of his new regime. At the top of the list was the establishment of a centralized court, and to that end Louis hired scores of artists to refurbish his father's old hunting pavilion and transform it into what would become Versailles, epicenter of courtly culture for the next hundred years and emblem of the Sun King's reign for hundreds more.

Although Louis left his mark throughout the palace, from the grand Hall of Mirrors to the small solar motifs that adorn the walls, perhaps the best evidence for Versailles as a manifestation of the king's power is the garden designs by Le Nôtre. Appearing to extend infinitely from the main building, the Versailles garden represents a triumph of engineering, a marshaling of immense resources, and, in its rigid geometry and strict bilateral symmetry, an image of nature brought under man's control. Not only is nature tamed, but it's served up for the gaze of the king: recalling the one-point perspective system of Renaissance painting, the "vanishing point" of the garden is perfectly on axis with the king's bedroom. Like Louis's famous statement, "I am the state," the Versailles garden testifies to the fact that careful management of one's image is not just a product of our own media-saturated age.

To ensure that this carefully calibrated message was clear, Louis penned a guidebook, the *Maniére de montrer les jardins de Versailles* (1689), which required that all visitors follow in the king's footsteps while touring his gardens. Although Versailles would remain for many the paragon of French garden design in the one hundred years between the publication of the *Maniére* and the outbreak of the Revolution, there appeared in the 18th century a number of alternatives to the formal garden system, just as there were an increasing number of alternative proposals to the ideology of absolutism. Whereas courtiers had formerly spent a great deal of time ambulating through the gardens at Versailles and performing their loyalty to the king, during the Regency period (1715-23) certain members of the court avoided Versailles in favor of more intimate rendezvous at their country houses outside of Paris. We can observe them today in the delightfully ambiguous paintings of Antoine Watteau (many of which reside in the Louvre), where aristocrats mix with wealthy financiers, and it's never quite clear whether the courtiers are watching a play, mingling with actors, or donning theatrical costumes and playing the roles themselves. What is clear in these improvisational gatherings is that the idea of the garden as a space of self-representation not only survives Louis XIV's reign but emerges as a crucial means of expression—personal and political—in the waning days of the Old Regime.

Far from the politically neutral spaces that we think of today, gardens in France in this period comprised quite a contested terrain. One major controversy was the debate between France and England over who had invented the more "naturalistic" style of gardening that became popular around the middle of the 18th century. Across the Channel, the Prime Minister's son Horace Walpole published a treatise on garden design, insisting that the new preference for untamed nature, serpentine walkways, and meandering streams was an indisputably English phenomenon, and reflected his government's ties to liberty and free expression. French writers similarly praised this new trend but argued not only that *they* had developed the style independently of the English, but that whatever devices the English were exhibiting in their gardens had been cribbed from the Chinese. No one went so far as to point out that this "natural" style was built upon a paradox—the idea that one would spend an enormous amount of money transforming a piece of nature into a garden that, in its painstaking attempt at informality, recalled a piece of nature.

Whether they admitted it or not, wealthy Frenchmen and Frenchwomen of the second half of the 18th century closely monitored developments in England before commissioning artists to transform their Louis XIV-style gardens into landscapes that embraced the new taste for the "natural." In Paris, three projects from the 1770s indicate the immense popularity of the new style as well as its relative diversity in contrast to Versailles. Two gardens were constructed in the Bois de Boulogne, which at that time served as a quasi-public space to promenade, duel, see and be seen, and engage in illicit sexual activity (that this last association persists today is evidenced by the recent publication of Catherine Millet's scandalous memoir *The Sexual Life of Catherine M*). One sight belonged to the king's rakish younger brother, the Comte d'Artois, and was the result of a bet he made with Marie-Antoinette that he could entertain her in a sparkling new Parisian pavilion constructed in three months' time. Luckily for Artois, his land was located near a major thoroughfare entering Paris from the west, allowing him to commandeer all building supplies headed toward the city and redirect them toward his own building site. Artois took a keen interest in every aspect of the design, devising a decorating scheme for his bedroom along the lines of an extended military metaphor, which spoke both to his prowess in the armed forces and his famed erotic conquests. Ultimately the pavilion, named "Bagatelle," was completed in just 64 days. It still stands in the Bois de Boulogne, and is best visited in June, when the site's famous roses are in full bloom.

Bagatelle's gardens were attacked by architect François Bélanger and his Scottish collaborator Thomas Blaikie with the same militaristic zeal. Following the latest "Anglo-Chinese" fashion, the gardens contained the requisite winding walkways studded with small buildings knows as "follies," which reference previous eras and other cultures, like an encyclopedia in three dimensions (recalling the ambitious Encyclopedic publishing project of Diderot and d'Alembert). Among the structures were an Egyptian obelisk, rustic hermitage, and Gothic-style philosopher's pavilion, the windows of which allowed visitors to view the garden through different-colored panes of glass, depending on one's mood. Overall, the gardens represented a shift from the idea of nature reconstituted in one man's image—the king's—to nature as an infinitely diverse yet private experience of individual contemplation. Of course, one still had to write to Artois's secretary to obtain permission to visit Bagatelle, a fact later redressed by the Revolutionary government, which in 1793 declared the gardens open to *all* members of the French citizenry.

Bagatelle's designers created an even more elaborate Anglo-Chinese garden adjacent to it for Charles Baudard de Saint-James, the wealthy financier and newly appointed treasurer of the American colonies. In addition to the more conventional follies, the gardens of the "Folie Saint-James" contained a mock dairy for the banker's daughter to entertain in—suggesting that Marie-Antoinette's obsession with playing milkmaid was not an isolated phenomenon—as well as a structure known as the *Grand Rocher*, referred to by contemporaries as the "Eighth Wonder of the World." This great rock (all that remains of the garden today) consisted of an enormous grotto surrounding a Doric portico that stood as the facade for the luxuriously appointed rooms behind it. The structure recalled an ancient archaeological ruin, signifying an interest in origins as well as a desire on the part of the *arriviste* Saint-James to "naturalize" his connection to the land and to the social position that ownership of such an estate implied. The public responded favorably to his garden by visiting it in droves, but Artois was less than pleased and, rumor has it, instructed Bélanger to ruin Saint-James financially by proposing ever-more elaborate building schemes. The plan apparently worked: Saint-James declared bankruptcy in 1787.

The final example, the Parc Monceau, was also constructed in the western part of the city, near the Champs-Elysées. Although many of Monceau's follies were destroyed in the Revolution, several remain, and the site is now a public park and jogging track (but don't be surprised if you draw stares from incredulous Parisians while attempting to run there). In the early 1770s King Louis XVI's cousin, the Duc de Chartres (later the Duc d'Orléans), commissioned the designer Carmontelle to lay out a garden which loosely followed the Anglo-Chinese program, complete with hermitage, obelisk, and decorative farm, where cows were tended by servants dressed in "Turkish" costume. Some commentators have declared Monceau to be the anti-Versailles, an emblem of the duke's self-professed Anglomania as well as his public criticism of the monarchy: during the Revolution the duke voted to have Louis XVI beheaded and, in 1793, ended up losing his own head as well. But one should not be too quick to ascribe a political message to Monceau, for, as its designer insisted, it followed no particular formula but was rather a "landscape of illusion," where visitors could "change the scenes in a garden like the stage sets at the Opéra." Carmontelle's statement adequately captures the status of Old Regime gardens as pieces of social theater, where aristocrats and their hangers-on eagerly performed for an audience of the King, as much as for themselves. In addition, it also speaks to the climate of unreality that surrounded these 18th-century spaces and their inhabitants, who despite such fertile imagination could scarcely have dreamed up what would befall their nation in 1789.

Meredith Martin *is a Ph.D. candidate in the Department of the History of Art and Architecture at Harvard University.*

66. Open Tu-F noon-5:30pm, Sa-Su 11am-6pm. €11 per hr., €8 per 30min.; €7.63 refundable deposit. ***Horse-drawn carriages*** *run Tu-Su, departing from right of the main terrace.* ☎ *01 30 97 04 40.*

Numerous artists—Le Brun, Mansart, Coysevox—executed statues and fountains for Versailles's gardens, but master gardener André Le Nôtre provided the overall plan. Louis XIV wrote the first guide to the gardens, entitled the *Manner of Presenting the Gardens at Versailles*, and today they remain a spectacular example of obsessive-compulsive landscaping: neatly trimmed rectangular hedges line the geometric *bosquets* (groves), as if proving Louis XIV's mastery over nature. The Sun King even proved his control over his visitors' vision: the cross-shaped canal is wider on the westernmost end, creating a perspective-defying illusion when viewed from the terrace. For more on Versailles garden design, see **Garden Party,** p. 284.

Though the château offers a decent 2hr. **Discovering Groves Tour** of the gardens (covering Le Nôtre's work with an emphasis on Greco-Roman mythology), the best way to visit the park is during the spectacular summer festival, **Les Grandes Eaux Musicales,** when the fountains are turned on and chamber music groups fill the garden's groves with glorious period music (see **Festivals,** p. 18). Any self-guided tour of the gardens must begin, as the Sun King commanded, on the terrace. Start by heading down the left-hand aisle from the terrace and working your way to the right. To the left of the terrace, the **Parterre Sud** graces the area in front of Mansart's **Orangerie,** once home to 2000 orange trees; the temperature inside still never drops below 6°C (43°F). In the center of the terrace lie the fountains of the **Parterre d'Eau,** while the **Bassin de Latone** fountain down the steps features Latona, the mother of Diana and Apollo, shielding her children as Jupiter turns villains into frogs.

Past the fountain and to the left is one of the Versailles Gardens' undisputed gems: the fragrant, flower-lined, exotic sanctuary of the **Jardin du Roi,** accessible only from the easternmost side facing the **Bassin du Miroir.** Still near the south gate of the grove is the magnificent **Bassin de Bacchus,** one of four seasonal fountains depicting the Greek god of wine crowned in vine branches reclining on a bunch of grapes. Working your way north toward the center of the garden you can see where the king used to take light meals amid the exquisite **Bosquet de la Colonnade's** 32 violet and blue marble columns, sculptures, and white marble basins, just east of the Jardin du Roi. The north gate to the Colonnade exits onto the 330m long **Tapis Vert** (Green Carpet), the central mall linking the château to the garden's conspicuously central fountain, the **Bassin d'Apollon,** whose charioted Apollo rises, youthful and god-like, out of the water to enlighten the world.

On the north side of the garden is Marsy's incredible **Bosquet de l'Encelade.** When the fountains are turned on, a 25m high jet bursts from Titan's enormous mouth, which is plated with shimmering gold and half buried under rocks. Flora reclines on a bed of flowers in the **Bassin de Flore,** while a gilded Ceres luxuriates in sheaves of wheat in the **Bassin de Cérès.** The **Parterre Nord,** full of flowers, lawns, and trees, overlooks some of the garden's most spectacular fountains. The **Allée d'Eau,** a fountain-lined walkway, provides the best view of the **Bassin des Nymphes de Diane.** The path slopes toward the sculpted **Bassin du Dragon,** where a beast slain by Apollo spurts water 27m high into the air. Ninety-nine jets of water attached to urns and seahorns surround Neptune in the **Bassin de Neptune,** the gardens' largest fountain.

Beyond Le Nôtre's classical gardens stretch wilder woods, meadows, and farmland perfect for a *picque-nique* away from the manicured perfection of Versailles. Stroll along the **Grand Canal,** a rectangular pond beyond the Bassin d'Apollon that measures an impressive 1535m long. To explore destinations farther afield around Versailles, rent a **bike** or a **boat,** or go for a **horse-drawn carriage** ride.

TRIANONS & MARIE-ANTOINETTE'S HAMEAU

Shuttle trams *from the palace to the Trianons and the Hameau leave from behind the palace facing the canals; head right. Round-trip €5, ages 3-12 €3. The walk takes 15min. Both Trianons:* ***Open*** *Nov.-Mar. Tu-Sa noon-5:30pm; Apr.-Oct. noon-6:30pm; last entrance 30min. before closing.* ***Admission*** *to the Trianons €5, after 3:30pm €3, under 18 free.*

The Trianons and particularly Marie-Antoinette's Hameau provide a racier and more rustic counterpoint to the château: this is where kings trysted with lovers, and Marie-Antoinette pretended to live like the peasant she wasn't.

PETIT TRIANON

On the right down the wooded path from the château is the **Petit Trianon,** built between 1762 and 1768 for Louis XV and his mistress Madame de Pompadour. Marie-Antoinette took control of the Petit Trianon in 1774, and it soon earned the nickname "Little Vienna." The Petit Trianon was later inhabited by Napoleon's sister and the Empress Marie-Louise. In 1867, the Empress Eugénie, who worshiped Marie-Antoinette, turned it into a museum.

Exit the Petit Trianon, turn left, and follow the marked path to the libidinous **Temple of Love,** a domed rotunda with 12 white marble columns and swans. Marie-Antoinette held many intimate nighttime parties in the small space, during which thousands of torches would be illuminated in the surrounding ditch. The Queen was perhaps at her happiest and most ludicrous when spending time at the **Hameau,** her own pseudo-peasant "hamlet" down the path from the Temple of Love. Inspired by Jean-Jacques Rousseau's theories on the goodness of nature and the *hameau* at **Chantilly** (see p. 295), the Queen aspired fashionably to a so-called "simple" life. She commissioned Richard Mique to build a compound of 12 buildings (including a mill, dairy, and gardener's house, all surrounding a quaint artificial lake) in which she could play at country life, though the result is something of a cross between English Romanticism and Euro Disney. At the center of the complex is the **Queen's Cottage.** Any illusions of country-style slumming disappear after crossing through her cottage doors. The rooms are filled to the brim with ornate furniture, sparkling marble fireplaces, and walk-in closets for all those monogrammed linens and silverware, plus Marie-Antoinette's numerous footmen.

GRAND TRIANON

The single-story, stone-and-pink-marble Grand Trianon was intended as a château-away-from-château for Louis XIV. Here the King could be reached only by a short boat trip along the **Grand Canal.** The palace, which consists of two wings joined together by a large central porch, was designed by Mansart and erected in 1687 (work was not completed until 1688). Lovely and simple **formal gardens** located behind the colonnaded porch are a relief from the rest of Versailles's showy *bosquets.* The mini-château was stripped of its furniture during the Revolution, but was later restored and inhabited by Napoleon and his second wife. President Charles de Gaulle installed presidential apartments and rooms for visiting heads of state here, and the constitutional amendment for Maastricht was also written here.

FONTAINEBLEAU

More digestible than Versailles, the Château de Fontainebleau achieves nearly the same grandeur, while preserving a charm unique among the great châteaux. With lush surrounding gardens, the estate ranks among the best daytrips from Paris.

Kings of France have hunted on these grounds since the 12th century, when the exiled Thomas à Becket consecrated Louis VII's manor chapel. In 1528, François I rebuilt the castle to be closer to the game he loved to hunt. Italian artists designed and decorated the palace, and their paintings, including the *Mona Lisa,* filled François's private collections. Subsequent kings commissioned magnificent new rooms and wings. Louis XIII was born here in 1601, Louis XIV revoked the Edict of Nantes here in 1685, and Louis XV was married here in 1725. Napoleon, who visited frequently, called it "*la Maison des Siècles*" (the House of Centuries). In 1814, Napoleon bid goodbye to the Empire from the central courtyard, now called the **Cour des Adieux** in his honor.

Rowing at Fontainebleau

Chantilly Gardens

Ah...les fleurs

PRACTICAL INFORMATION

Trains: Hourly trains from **Gare de Lyon,** *banlieue* level (45min., €14.60 round-trip). From the station, **Connex** (☎01 63 22 23 88) runs buses (€1.40) after each train arrival from Paris; take the bus in direction "Château-Lilas" and get off at the Château stop. The château is a 30min. walk away, through the small towns of Avon and Fontainebleau.

Tourist Office: 4, r. Royal (☎01 60 74 99 99; fax 01 60 74 80 22; fontainebleau-tourisme@wanadoo.fr). Across from the château. Organizes tours of the village, finds accommodations, sells audio tours of the exterior of the château, and has maps of Fontainebleau and Barbizon. Open M-Sa 10am-6pm, Su 10am-12:30pm and 3-5pm.

SIGHTS

CHÂTEAU DE FONTAINEBLEAU

☎01 60 71 50 60; www.musee-chateau-fontainebleau.fr. ***Open*** *May-Sept. M and W-Su 9:30am-6pm; Oct.-Apr. M and W-Su 9:30am-5pm. Last entry 1hr. before closing.* ***Admission*** *€5.50, under 18 free, first Su of the month free. Invest in a printed guide (€7.50), available down the hall from the ticket booth. 60min.* ***audio tours*** *€4.60. 1hr.* ***tours*** *in French €3, ages 15-25 €2.30. Call ahead for tour schedule. Admission to* ***Musée Chinois de l'Impératrice Eugénie*** *is included. Usually closed due to low staffing, so call ahead.*

GRANDS & PETITS APPARTEMENTS

The Grands Appartements provide a lesson on the history of French architecture and decoration. Dubreuil's **Gallery of Plates** represents the history of Fontainebleau on a remarkable series of 128 porcelain plates fitted into the woodwork. In the long **Galerie de François I,** muscular figures by Il Rosso (known in French as Maître Roux) tell mythological tales of heroism, brilliantly illuminated by windows that look out onto the **Fountain Courtyard.** Similarly, the Ball Room's magnificent octagonal ceiling, heavy wood paneling, and bay windows face out onto the **Oval Courtyard.** The **King's Cabinet** (also known as the Louis XIII Salon because Louis XIII was born there) was the site of *le débotter*, the king's post-hunt boot removal. Napoleon pored over the volumes in the sunlit **Diana Gallery.** Since the 17th century, every queen and empress of France has slept in the gold and green **Queen's Bed Chamber;** the gilded wood bed was built for Marie-Antoinette. The N on the red and gold velvet throne of the **Throne Room** is a testament to Napoleon's humility in what is today the only existing throne room in France. Sandwiched between two mirrors, Napoleon's Bed Chamber is a monument to either narcissism or eroticism (or both), while his austere Small Bed Chamber contains a narrow military bed. In the Emperor's Private Room, known today as the Abdication Chamber, Napoleon signed off his empire in 1814. The tour ends with the 16th-century, Italian-frescoed **Trinity Chapel.**

Parts of the château can be seen only by guided tour. The tour of the **Petits Appartements** features the private rooms of Napoleon and the Empress Josephine, as well as the impressive **map room** and **Galerie des Cerfs.**

MUSÉE NAPOLEON

☎01 60 71 50 60. Around 6 1hr. ***tours*** *in French per day. €3, under 25 €2.30, under 18 free. Call ahead for tour schedule.*

The Musée Napoleon features an extensive collection of the Emperor's personal effects: his wee toothbrush, his tiny shoes, his field tent, his son's toys, and gifts from European monarchs.

GARDENS

Fontainebleau's serene Jardin Anglais and Jardin de Diane shelter quiet grottoes guarded by statues of huntress Diana and the Etang des Carpes, a carp-filled pond that can be explored by rowboat. *(Boat rental June-Aug. daily 10am-7pm; Sept. Sa-Su 2-6pm. €9 per 30min., €15 per hr.)* The Forêt de Fontainebleau is a thickly wooded 20,000-hectare preserve with hiking trails, bike paths, and sandstone rock-climbing. The tourist office provides maps.

FOOD

The bistros immediately surrounding the château are not the only dining options when visiting Fontainebleau. Walk a couple of minutes into town, following r. de Ferrare, and you'll find several serving up traditional French cuisine.

Le Caveau des Ducs, 24, r. de Ferrare (☎01 64 22 05 05; www.lecaveaudesducs.com). At this medieval-style bistro, the €20 *menu* includes either *entrée* and *plat* or *plat* and *dessert.* Taller patrons at the Duke's Cave should keep a heads up for the arches and hanging candles. Open daily 9am-1pm and 6-11pm. AmEx/MC/V. ❸

La Petite Alsace, 26, r. de Ferrare (☎01 64 23 45 45). Warm yellow walls, lace curtains, and flowery tablecloths welcome you to this traditional restaurant with *menus* from €11. If it's nice out, the terrace is lovely. Open daily noon-2pm and 7-10:30pm. AmEx/MC/V. ❷

CHARTRES

Nothing compares to Chartres. It is the thinking of the Middle Ages itself made visible.
—Emile Male

Were it not for a piece of fabric, the cathedral and town of Chartres might be only a sleepy hamlet. But because of a sacred relic—the cloth the Virgin Mary supposedly wore when she gave birth to Jesus—Chartres became a major medieval pilgrimage center. The spectacular cathedral that towers over the city isn't the only reason to visit: the *vieille ville* (old town) is also a masterpiece of medieval architecture, and will almost let you forget the zooming highways that have encroached upon it.

Founded as the Roman city *Autricum*, Chartres is an old hill-top village at heart. Its oldest streets are clustered around the cathedral and are still named for the trades once practiced there. There is even an old "Salmon House" on the walking tour (map available at tourist office), right by the pl. Poissonnière. These winding paths offer some of the best views of the cathedral and are navigable using the well-marked tourist office circuit. Chartres's medieval tangle of streets can be confusing, but getting lost here can only be enjoyable.

Timing is important if you want to fully enjoy your visit to Chartres, as everything closes during lunch time, casual visits to the cathedral are not permitted during mass, and English tours are only given twice a day. For an ideal daytrip, arrive around 10 or 10:30am, pick up the invaluable walking tour map of the *vieille ville* from the tourist office, and head straight for the **Musée des Beaux-Arts** to catch it before it closes at noon (those particularly interested in stained glass can walk through the smaller **Centre International du Vitrail** afterwards, as it closes at 12:30pm). You can start your walking tour in the northward direction after visiting the museum and stop en route for lunch at the beautiful **Moulin de Poneau,** on the bank of the stream (be sure to make reservations the day before). A visit to the **Maison Picassiette** makes for an enjoyable detour. Finish with a visit to some of the beautiful smaller churches, and make it back to the cathedral in time for **Malcolm Miller's English tour,** or just for your own afternoon visit. Rest at any of the cafés surrounding the cathedral or in the streets neighboring it, and then finish the day with brief visits to any of the small museums.

PRACTICAL INFORMATION

Trains: Chartres is accessible by frequent trains from **Gare Montparnasse, Grandes Lignes.** At least 1 train per hr. during the summer; call ahead for winter schedule. Trains take 50-75 min.; round-trip €23.60, under 26 and groups of 2-4 €17.80, over 60 €17.60). To reach the cathedral from the train station, walk straight along r. Jehan de Beauce to pl. de Châtelet and turn left into the *place,* right onto r. Ste-Même, and left onto r. Jean Moulin (or just head toward the massive spires).

Tourist Office: (☎02 37 18 26 26; fax 02 37 21 51 91; info@otchartres.fr). In front of the cathedral's main entrance at pl. de la Cathédrale, the tourist office helps find accommodations (€9.15 surcharge, €7.63 of which is put toward your hotel bill) and supplies visitors with a very helpful map guide that includes a walking tour and a list of restaurants, hotels, and additional sights. Open Apr.-Sept. M-Sa 9am-7pm, Su and holidays 9:30am-5:30pm; Oct.-Mar. M-Sa 10am-6pm, Su and holidays 10am-1pm and 2:30-4:30pm. Closed Jan. 1, Nov. 1 and 11, and Dec. 25. For those with difficulty walking or who want a relaxed tour of the town, *Le petit train Chart'train* runs late Mar.-early Nov. with 35min. narrated tours (in French only) of the old city (☎02 37 21 87 60. Tours begin in front of the tourist office every hour starting at 10:30am. €5.50, under 12 €3).

SIGHTS

THE CATHEDRAL

☎02 37 21 75 02; www.cathedrale-chartres.com. ***Open*** *Easter through Oct. daily 8am-8pm, Nov. through Easter daily 8:30am-7pm. No casual visits during mass.* ***Masses*** *M-F 11:45am and 6:15pm; Sa 11:45am and 6pm; Su 9:15am (Latin), 11am, 6pm (in the crypt). Call the tourist office for info on concerts in the cathedral, the annual student pilgrimage in late May, and other pilgrimages and festivals throughout the year.* ***North Tower*** *open May-Aug. M-Sa 9:30am-noon and 2-5:30pm, Su 2-5:30pm; Sept.-Apr. M-Sa 9:30am-noon and 2-4:30pm, Su 2-4:30pm; Tower closed on Jan. 1 and 5 and Dec. 25.* ***Tower admission*** *€4, ages 18-25 €2.50, under 18 and some Su free. English audioguides available at the gift shop (€2.90, €3.80, or €5.65, depending on tour) and require a piece identification as a deposit.* ***English tours of the cathedral by Malcolm Miller*** *(see p. 292) begin outside the gift shop in the cathedral and last 1¼hr. Easter to early Nov. M-Sa noon and 2:45pm, call ☎02 37 28 15 58 for tour availability during winter months. €8, students €5.* ***French tours of the crypt*** *leave from the inside of the cathedral. ☎02 37 21 75 02. Tours 30min. Apr.-Oct. M-Sa 11am, 2:15, 3:30, 4:30pm; Nov.-Mar. 11am and 4:15pm; additional 5:15pm tour June 22-Sept. 21; no 11am tours anytime during the year on Su. €2.50 students €1.70, under 7 free.*

The Cathédrale de Chartres is the best-preserved medieval church in Europe, having miraculously escaped major damage during the French Revolution and WWII. A patchwork masterpiece of Romanesque and Gothic design, the cathedral was constructed by generations of unknown masons, architects, and artisans. Its grand scale dominates the town, with spires visible from most locations, and its history is strongly bound to that of France—it was here, for example, that Henri IV was coronated in 1594. Approaching from the pl. de la Cathedrale, you'll be able to see the discrepancy between the two towers: the one on the left, finished in 1513, is flamboyantly Gothic; the one on the right, built just before an 1194 fire, is sedately Romanesque and octagonal (the tallest in its style still standing). The 12th-century statues of the Portale Royale present an assembly of Old Testament figures. The 13th-century *Porche du Nord* depicts the life of Mary, while the *Porche du Sud* depicts the life of Christ.

SANCTA CAMISIA

The year after he became emperor in 875, Charlemagne's grandson, Charles the Bald, donated to Chartres the Sancta Camisia, the cloth believed to be worn by the Virgin Mary when she gave birth to Christ. Although a church dedicated to Mary had existed on the site as early as the mid-700s, the emperor's bequest required a new cathedral to accommodate the growing number of pilgrims. In the hope that the sacred relic would heal and answer prayers, thousands flocked to the church on their knees. The sick were nursed in the crypt below the sanctuary. The powers of the relic were confirmed in AD 911 when the cloth supposedly saved the city when it came under attack from invading Goths and Vikings; the Viking leader Rollon converted to Christianity, becoming the first Duke of Normandy. Today, the relic is preserved behind glass and is on display in the back of the church on the left-hand side.

STAINED GLASS

At a time when books were rare and the vast majority of people illiterate, the cathedral served as a multimedia teaching tool. Most of the 172 stained glass windows date from the 13th century and were preserved through both World Wars by heroic town authorities, who dismantled over 2000 sq. m and stored the windows pane by pane in Dordogne. The famous **Blue Virgin, Tree of Jesse,** and **Passion and Resurrection of Christ** windows are among the surviving 13th-century stained glass. The medieval merchants who paid for the windows are represented in the lower panels, which provide a record of daily life in the 13th century. The windows are characterized by the stunning blue color known as "Chartres blue." The center window depicts the story of Christ from the Annunciation to the ride into Jerusalem. Binoculars are useful for viewing the high windows. Stories read from bottom to top, left to right.

LABYRINTH

The windows of Chartres often distract visitors from a treasure below their feet: a winding labyrinth pattern that is carved into the floor in the rear of the nave. Designed in the 13th century, the labyrinth was laid out for pilgrims as a substitute for a journey to the Holy Land. By following this symbolic journey on their hands and knees, the devout would enact a voyage to heavenly Jerusalem.

TOUR JEHAN-DE-BEAUCE

The adventurous, the athletic, and the non-claustrophobic can climb the cathedral's narrow-staircased north tower, Tour Jehan-de-Beauce (named after its architect) for a stellar view of the cathedral roof, the flying buttresses, and the city below. If you don't make it all the way to the top, the first viewing platform offers a slightly obstructed but nonetheless impressive sight.

CRYPT

Parts of Chartres's **crypt,** including a well down which Vikings tossed the bodies of their victims during raids, date back to the 9th century. Visitors may enter the 110m long subterranean crypt only as part of a tour that leaves from La Crypte (the store opposite the cathedral's south entrance). The tour is in French, but information sheets are available in English near the entrance to the crypt.

ELSEWHERE IN THE CATHEDRAL

Inside the church, the Renaissance choir screen, begun by Jehan de Beauce in 1514, depicts the Virgin Mary's life. The lovely, candlelit shrine to "*Notre Dame de Pilier*" is near the Sancta Camista. Both are worth a visit.

The only English-language **tours** of the cathedral are given by tour-guide **Malcolm Miller,** an authority on Gothic architecture who has been leading visitors through the church for the past 40 years. His presentations on the cathedral's history and symbolism are intelligent, witty, and enjoyable for all ages. If you can, take both his morning and afternoon tour—no two are alike.

OTHER SIGHTS

MUSÉE DES BEAUX-ARTS

29, r. du Cloître Notre-Dame. Next to the cathedral. ☎02 37 36 41 39. Open May-Oct. M and W-Sa 10am-noon and 2-6pm, Su 2-6pm; Nov.-Apr. M and W-Sa 10am-noon and 2-5pm, Su 2-5pm. €2.45, students and over 60 €1.20.

The Musée des Beaux-Arts is housed in the former Bishop's Palace, which is itself an impressive sight. Built mainly in the 17th and 18th centuries (on a site occupied by bishops since the 11th century), the palace houses a wildly eclectic collection of painting, sculpture, and furniture, including works by Vlaminck, Navarre, and Soutine. A harpsichord collection dating back to the 17th century and an impressive collection of Oceanic art is also on display. After you are done art-gazing, go grazing, and hit the grass of the pretty park, which includes a miniature labyrinth.

OTHER MUSEUMS

Chartres offers a number of small museums that cater to specific interests. The small **Centre International du Vitrail,** 5, r. du Cardinal Pie (facing the cathedral), housed in a small 13th-century barn once used by the clergy, hosts two temporary exhibitions on stained glass a year (☎02 37 36 15 34; www.centre-vitrail.org. Open M-F 9:30am-12:30pm and 1:30-6pm, Sa-Su 10am-12:30pm and 2:30-6pm. €4, students €3.) The **Maison Picassiette,** 22, r. du Repos, is an extraordinary house covered entirely in mosaic tiles, inside and out. (☎02 37 34 10 78. Open Apr.-Oct. M and W-Sa 10am-noon and 2-6pm, Tu and Su 2-6pm. €2.40, students €1.20; combination ticket with the Musée des Beaux-Arts €5.40, students €2.70.) There is also a substantial natural history museum, the **Muséum des Sciences Naturelles et de Préhistoire,** 5bis, bd. de la Courtille (☎02 37 28 36 09. Open July to mid-Sept. Su-F 2-6pm, mid-Sept. to June Su and W 2-5pm. Free). The **Maison de l'Archéologie,** 16, r. St-Pierre, offers an impressive collection of archaeological finds (☎02 37 30 99 38. Open July-Sept. Su and W-Sa 2-6pm, Oct.-May Su and W 2-6pm, closed Dec. 21-Jan. 3. €1.50, under 16 free.) The **Musée Départemental de l'Ecole,** 1, r. du 14 Juillet, is a replica of a turn-of-the-century village classroom (☎02 37 30 07 69. Open M-F 10am-noon and 2-6pm except holidays. €3, under 16 €2, under 6 free). And the **Conservatoire de l'Agriculture COMPA,** Pont de Mainvilliers, the largest agricultural museum in France, has on display a huge array of tractors and other machinery, as well as one temporary exhibition at a time, on subjects like horses and farm life. (☎02 37 84 15 00; www.lecompa.com. Open Tu-F 9am-12:30pm and 1:30-6pm, Sa-Su 10am-12:30pm and 1:30-7pm. €3.80, students €3, ages 6-18 €1.50, under 6 free.)

CHURCHES

Rebuilt in the 16th century, the feudal **Eglise St-Aignan,** on r. des Greniers, offers summer concerts. (Open daily 9am-noon and 2-6pm.) The 12th-century Romanesque **Eglise St-André** sits on r. St-André on the banks of the Eure River. (Open daily 10am-noon and 2-6pm.) Once part of a Benedictine monastery, the **Eglise St-Pierre,** on pl. St-Pierre, is a 13th-century Gothic masterpiece. (Open daily 9am-noon and 2-6pm.) All three churches are on the tourist office's walking tour.

MONUMENT TO JEAN MOULIN

A monument to famous WWII Resistance hero Jean Moulin stands on r. Jean Moulin, off bd. de la Résistance. It consists of a giant stone hand gripping the hilt of a broken sword. Prefect of Chartres before the war, Moulin attempted suicide rather than sign a Nazi document accusing French troops of atrocities. Tortured and killed by the Gestapo in 1943, he was eventually buried in the Panthéon. The monument is plotted on the tourist office's walking tour.

FOOD

Le Moulin de Ponneau, 21/23, r. de la Tannerie (☎02 37 35 30 05). Located on one of the lower medieval stone landings along the town's beautiful stream, this classic French restaurant is worth every penny. 3-course weekday lunch *menu* (€20) includes wine and coffee. Make reservations before you visit Chartres—you'll regret it if you don't. Open M-F noon-2pm and 7:30-9pm, Sa 7:30-9pm, and Su noon-2pm. ❸

Les Trois Lys, 3, r. Porte Guillame (☎01 37 28 42 02). This casual *crêperie* right by the river is just off the walking tour, and offers a formidable assortment of savory and sweet crêpes for a most delicious price (€2.30-8). Open daily noon-3pm and 7pm-midnight. No lunch on M. AmEx/MC/V. ❶

Crousty Poulets, 26, r. Saint Même (☎02 37 21 29 56), just before the cathedral. A tiny sandwicherie on the ground floor and a cozy restaurant upstairs, this local favorite serves sandwiches (€3.50-5) like the *crousty chêvre* (goat cheese, emmental, and tomatoes), *plats du jours* (from €6.10) like *andouillette grillee* and *jarret de porc*, and of course *crousty poulet* (whole chicken €11). Open M-Sa 11am-3pm and 6-9pm. ❶

VAUX-LE-VICOMTE

Nicolas Fouquet, Louis XIV's Minister of Finance, assembled the triumvirate of Le Vau, Le Brun, and Le Nôtre (architect, artist, and landscaper) to build Vaux in 1641. On August 17, 1661, upon the completion of what was then France's most beautiful château, Fouquet threw an extravagant 6000-guest party in honor of Louis XIV. The King and Anne d'Autriche were but two of the witnesses to a regal bacchanalia that premiered poetry by Jean de la Fontaine and a comedy-ballet, *Les Fâcheux*, by Molière. After novelties like elephants in crystal jewelry and whales in the canal, the evening concluded in a "Chinese" fireworks extravaganza featuring the King and Queen's coat of arms and pyrotechnic squirrels (squirrels were Fouquet's family symbol). But the housewarming bash was the beginning of the end for Fouquet. Shortly thereafter, young Louis XIV—supposedly furious at having been upstaged—ordered Fouquet arrested. Once he was in custody, it came to light that he had been embezzling state funds. As Voltaire wrote: "At six in the evening, Fouquet was king of France; at two the next morning, he was nothing." In a trial that lasted three years, the judges voted narrowly for banishment over death. Louis XIV overturned the judgement in favor of life imprisonment—the only time in French history that the head of state overruled the court's decision in favor of a more severe sentence. Fouquet was to remain imprisoned at Pignerol, in the French Alps, until his death in 1680. Many suspected that Fouquet was the legendary man in the iron mask, including Alexandre Dumas, who fictionalized the story in *Le Vicomte de Bragelonne*.

PRACTICAL INFORMATION

Vaux is one of the most exquisite of French châteaux (and less crowded than Versailles, whose construction it reputedly inspired). Getting there can be an ordeal, as there is no shuttle service from the train station in Melun to the château 7km away, but the trek is well worth it.

Tour Groups: Several tourist groups run trips to the château with varying frequencies and prices; call ahead to book a trip. Services with regularly scheduled trips are **ParisVision** (☎01 42 60 30 01; www.parisvision.com) and **Cityrama** (01 44 55 61 00; www.cityrama.fr).

Driving: The château is 50km out of Paris. Take Autoroute A4 or A6 from Paris and exit at Troyes-Nancy by N104. Head toward Meaux on N36 and follow the signs.

By Train: Take the **RER** to Melun from Châtelet-Les Halles or Gare de Lyon (45min.; round-trip €13.40). Then take a taxi (at least €15) to the château (be sure to ask the driver to meet you back at the chateau at a certain time, or pay 20 centimes for the staff at the exit to phone for you). You can walk, but it is a perilous trek–on the highway. Follow av. de Thiers to highway 36, direction "Meaux," and follow signs to Vaux-Le-Vicomte. It will take you 1½-2hr.

Tourist Office: 2, av. Gallieni (☎01 64 37 11 31). By the train station in Melun. Information on accommodations and sight-seeing, plus free maps. Open Tu-Sa 10am-noon and 2-6pm.

SIGHTS

☎01 64 14 41 90; www.vaux-le-vicomte.com. ***Open*** *Mar. 23-Nov. 11 daily 10am-6pm; visits by appointment for groups of 20 or more the rest of the year.* ***Admission*** *to château, gardens, and carriage museum €12; students, seniors, and ages 6-16 €9.50; under 6 free. On Sa evenings from May to the beginning of Oct., and F in July and Aug., the château is open for* ***visites aux chandelles*** *(candlelight visits) 8pm-midnight. €15; ages 6-16, students, and seniors €13.* ***Fountains*** *on Apr.-Oct., 2nd and last Sa of each month 3-6pm. Château* ***audiotour*** *includes good historical presentation in English; €2.50.* ***Club cars*** *station to the right of the garden from the entrance; €13 for 45min. ride; €125 deposit. First floor only of the château is wheelchair-accessible. MC/V.*

CHÂTEAU

The château seems rather plain when viewed from the front, but cross the threshold or go out back, and you will find something quite different—a kind of baroque celebration. The building is covered with ornate scripted "F"s and squirrels (Fouquet's symbol) and the family motto *"Quo non ascendit"* ("what heights might he not reach"); the tower with three battlements has his second wife's crest engraved on it. **Madame Fouquet's Closet** once had walls lined with small mirrors, the decorative forerunner of Versailles's Hall of Mirrors. Over the fireplace of the **Square Room** hangs Le Brun's portrait of Fouquet. Le Brun's **Room of the Muses** is one of his most famous decorative schemes. The artist had planned to crown the cavernous, Neoclassical **Oval Room** (or **Grand Salon**) with a fresco entitled *The Palace of the Sun*, but Fouquet's arrest halted all decorating activity, and only a single eagle and a patch of sky were completed. The tapestries once bore Fouquet's menacing squirrels, but Colbert seized them and replaced the rodents with his own adders. The ornate **King's Bedchamber** boasts an orgy of cherubs and lions fluttering around the centerpiece, Le Brun's *Time Bearing Truth Heavenward.*

GARDENS

At Vaux, Le Nôtre gave birth to the classical French garden—shrubs were trimmed, lawns shaved, bushes sculpted, and pools strategically placed (see **Garden Party,** p. 284). Vaux's multilevel terraces, fountained walkways, and fantastical *parterres* (literally "on the ground": the low-cut hedges and crushed stone in arabesque patterns) are still the most exquisite example of 17th-century French gardens. The collaboration of Le Nôtre with Le Vau and Le Brun ensured that the same patterns and motifs were repeated with astonishing harmony in the gardens, château, and tapestries inside. Vaux owes its most impressive *trompe l'oeil* (fools the eye) effect to Le Nôtre's whimsical and adroit use of the laws of perspective. From the back steps of the château, it looks as if you can see the entire landscape at a glance. The grottoes at the far end of the garden appear directly behind the large pool of water. Yet, as you approach the other end, the grottoes seem to recede, revealing a sunken canal known as **La Poêle** (the Frying Pan), which is invisible from the château. The **Round Pool** and its surrounding 17th-century statues mark an important intersection; to the left, down the east walkway, are the **Water Gates,** the backdrop for Molière's performance of *Les Fâcheux*. The **Water Mirror,** farther down the central walkway, was designed to reflect the château perfectly, but you may have some trouble positioning yourself to enjoy the effect. A climb to the **Farnese Hercules** provides the best vista of the grounds. The tremendous Hercules sculpture at the top was at the center of Fouquet's trial; in an age when kings enjoyed divine rights to their royalty, the beleaguered Fouquet had to justify why he had likened himself to Hercules, the only mortal to become a god. The old stables, **Les Equipages,** also house a fantastic **carriage museum.** But by far the best way to see Vaux's gardens is during the **visites aux chandelles,** when the château and grounds are lit up by thousands of candles, and classical music plays through the gardens in imitation of Fouquet's legendary party; arrive around dusk to see the grounds in all their glory.

CHANTILLY

The name should sound familiar—*crème chantilly* is the French term for "whipped cream." The place where the creamy delight was first concocted is much less well known, which is good news for those looking for a great day-trip from Paris that isn't overrun with tour buses and souvenir salesmen. The 14th- to 19th-century **Château de Chantilly** is a whimsically baroque amalgam of Gothic extravagance, Renaissance geometry, and flashy Victorian ornamentalism. The triangular-shaped château (a dolled-up hunting lodge) is surrounded by a moat, lakes, canals, and the simple, elegant Le Nôtre gardens (no Versailles fireworks here). With the architecturally masterful **Grandes Ecuries** (stables) and world-class **Musée Condé,** it's a wonder that this lovely château has stayed a hidden treasure for so long.

A Roman citizen named Cantilius originally built his villa here, and a succession of medieval lords constructed elaborate fortifications. In the 17th century, Louis XIV's cousin, the Grand Condé, commissioned a château and asked André Le Nôtre to create the gardens. The Grand Château was razed during the Revolution. In the 1870s, the château was rebuilt under the Duc d'Aumale, fifth son of King Louis-Philippe, complete with the eclectic facade, modern wrought-iron grillwork, copies of Michelangelo marbles, lush greenery, and extravagant entrance hall you see today.

PRACTICAL INFORMATION

Trains: Take the **train** from the Gare du Nord (Grandes Lignes) to Chantilly Gouvieux (35min., approximately every hr. 5am-midnight, round-trip €11.40). Free and frequent **navettes** (shuttles) to the château; catch one just to the left as you exit the train station; take direction Senlis. Otherwise, the château is a 30min. walk from the station—your only option Su when the shuttle is not running.

Tourist Office: 60, av. du Maréchal Joffre (☎03 44 67 37 37; www.chantilly-tourisme.com). From the train station, go straight up r. des Otages about 50m. Offers brochures, maps, and a schedule of the free shuttle buses running to and from the château. The tourist office can also call a taxi (€6). Open May-Sept. M-Th 9am-12:30pm and 1:30-6pm, F 9am-12:30pm and 1:30-5pm, Sa 10am-12:30pm and 1:30-5pm, Su 10am-1:30pm; Oct.-Apr. M-Th 9am-12:30pm and 2-6pm, F 9am-12:30pm and 2-5pm, Sa 10am-12:30pm and 2-5pm. To continue to the stables and château, turn left on av. Maréchal Joffe, and then right on r. de Connetable, the town's main street (2km), or take a more scenic route straight through the forest.

SIGHTS

CHÂTEAU, GARDENS, & MUSÉE CONDÉ

☎*03 44 62 62 62; www.institut-de-france.fr/patrimoine/chantilly/chantilly.htm.* ***Open*** *Mar-Oct. M and W-Su 10am-6pm; Nov.-Feb. M and W-Su 10:30am-12:45pm and 2-5pm. (last entrance 1hr. before closing). Admission to* ***gardens*** *€3, students and children €2; to* ***gardens and château*** *€7,* *students €6, children €2.80. Various* ***ticket packages*** *available: gardens and boat or train ride €8.50, students €7.50, children €5; gardens, château, and boat or train ride €13/€11/€7; gardens, train and boat ride €13/€11/€7; gardens, chateau, boat and train ride €15/€13/€9. Miniature trains offer 30min. tours of the gardens and grounds in French and English. Frequent free 45min.* ***tours*** *of the château's appartements in French. AmEx/MC/V.*

Maps of the **gardens** (€1 at the information office) offer a suggested walking tour of the grounds, but wandering is just as effective. A bike can help you explore the château's 115 hectares of parks and grounds. Directly in front of the château, the gardens' central expanse is designed in the French formal style, with neat rows of carefully pruned trees, calm statues, and geometric pools. To the left, hidden within a forest, the Romantic English garden attempts to re-create untamed nature. Here, paths meander around pools where lone swans glide elegantly. Windows carved into the foliage allow you to see fountains in the formal garden as you stroll. To the right the gardens hide a play village **hameau** (hamlet), the somewhat less corny inspiration for Marie-Antoinette's hamlet at Versailles. Farther in, a statue of Cupid reigns over the "Island of Love." A 2003 addition is the kangaroo enclosure. These 15 or so wallabies represent the park's first hop towards recreating the *menagerie* that existed during the chateau's heyday.

But Chantilly's biggest attraction lies inside the château: the spectacular **Musée Condé** houses the Duc d'Aumale's private collection of pre-modern paintings, and is one of only two museums in France to boast three Raphaels (the other is the Louvre). The skylit picture galleries contain 800 paintings, 3000 drawings, and hundreds of engravings, sculptures, and tapestries, among them works by Titian, Corot, Botticelli, Delacroix, and Ingres. Bronze basset hounds, deer antlers, and huge Gobelin tapestries depicting hunting scenes all confirm the château's ribald and gamey past. Following the Duke's will, the paintings and furniture are arranged as they were over a century ago, in the distinctively 19th-century frame-to-frame ("academic") style. The absolute gem, however, is the tiny **sanctuario.** This hidden gallery contains what the Duke himself considered the finest works in his collection: illuminated manuscripts by Jean Fouquet, a painting by Fra Filippo Lippi, and two Raphaels. Alas, the museum's two most valuable pieces, a Gutenberg Bible and the illuminated manuscripts of the *Très Riches Heures* (1410), are too fragile to be kept in public view—but a near-perfect facsimile of the latter can be seen by the entrance. The illustrious **library** (second only to the Bibliothèque Nationale in prestige) is filled with enough centuries-old books to make any bibliophile drool. The rest of the château's **appartements** can be visited only by taking a free guided tour in French.

GRANDES ECURIES

☎03 44 57 13 13 or ☎03 44 57 40 40; reservations ☎03 44 57 91 79; www.musee-vivant-du-cheval.fr. ***Open*** *Apr.-Oct. M and W-F 10:30am-5:30pm, Sa-Su 10:30am-6pm; Nov.-Mar. M and W-F 2-5pm, Sa-Su 10:30am-5:30pm.* ***Museum*** *€8; children, students, and seniors €7.50.* ***Equestrian show*** *on the first Su of each month, 3:30pm. €17, children €16.* ***Hippodrome*** *matches daily in June 11am, 12:30, 2, 3:15, 4:30pm. ☎03 44 57 13 13. Open Apr.-Oct. M and W-F 10:30am-6:30pm, Sa-Su 10:30am-7pm; May-Aug. also open Tu 10:30am-5:30pm.*

The other great draw to the château is the Grandes Ecuries (stables), whose immense marble corridors, courtyards, and facades are masterpieces of 18th-century French architecture. Originally commissioned by Louis-Henri Bourbon, who hoped to live here when he was reborn as a horse, the Ecuries' extravagant fountains, domed rotundas, and sculptured patios are enough to make even the most cynical believe in reincarnation. From 1719 to the Revolution, the stables housed 240 horses and hundreds of hunting dogs, and now are home to the **Musée Vivant du Cheval,** an extensive collection (supposedly the largest in the world) of all things equine (beware the rather graphic horse biology exhibit near the end of the museum tour). In addition to the stables' 30 live horses, donkeys, and ponies, on display are saddles, horseshoes, international merry-go-rounds, and a horse statue featured in a James Bond film. On the first Sunday of every month and Christmas, equestrian shows, such as "Horses, Dream, and Poetry" and "Horse Gospel" are a fanciful highlight. The Hippodrome (or racetrack) on the premises is the Kentucky Derby of France: two of France's premier horse races are held here in June. In mid-September, polo at the Hippodrome is free to the public.

FOOD

R. de Connetable runs through the middle of the town of Chantilly to the Grandes Ecuries, offering a number of reasonable dining options—cafés, *crêperies*, and *boulangeries*. Near the entrance to the château grounds, you'll find ice cream and sandwich stands. The chateau itself has a pricey restaurant. In the gardens, have a dessert or meal at **Les Gouters Champetres** (below). Whatever you do, don't miss the small strawberry patch behind the snack shop in Le Hameau. The berries are yours for the picking while they're in season.

Les Gouters Champetres, Le Hameau, Parc Chantilly (☎03 44 57 46 21). From the château, bear left and walk along le Canal des Morfondus. Cross the canal using the large, woodplanked bridge and you'll see the restaurant on you right once you clear the woods. Only a few feet from the site of the invention of whipped cream, this garden restaurant takes *creme chantilly* very, very seriously. You can have it straight up (€3.60) or with strawberries (€6.50). Also offers full *menus* starting at €16.20. Beer €4. Open daily mid-Mar. to mid-Nov. noon-6pm. MC/V. ❸

GIVERNY

Drawn to the verdant hills, haystacks, and lily pads on the Epte river, painter Claude Monet and his eight children settled in Giverny in 1883. By 1887, John Singer Sargent, Paul Cézanne, and Mary Cassatt had placed their easels beside Monet's and turned the village into an artists' colony. Today, the vistas depicted by these artists remain undisturbed: the cobblestone street that was the setting for Monet's *Wedding March*, for instance, is instantly recognizable. In spite of the tourists, who come in droves to retrace the steps of the now-famous Impressionists (see **Life & Times,** p. 61) who found inspiration here, Giverny retains its rustic tranquility.

PRACTICAL INFORMATION

From Paris to Vernon: The **SNCF** runs trains regularly from Paris **Gare St-Lazare** to **Vernon,** the station nearest to Giverny. To get to the Gare St-Lazare, take the métro to St-Lazare and follow the signs to the *Grandes Lignes*. From there, proceed to any ticket line marked "France." To schedule a trip ahead of time, call the SNCF (☎08 36 35 35 35) or look up the schedule on the web at www.voyages-sncf.com. Round trip €21, ages 18-25 €16.

From Vernon to Giverny: Take a bus (☎02 32 71 06 39; 10min.; Tu-Su 4 buses per day leave from Vernon to Giverny 15min. after the train arrives in Vernon. 3 buses daily go from Giverny to Vernon; look for the schedule inside the information office in the train station; €2, round-trip €4). You can rent a bike from **Café du Chemin de Fer,** opposite the Vernon station (☎02 32 51 01 72). €12 per day, plus driver's license/ID deposit. MC/V. The 6km, 1½hr. hike from the Vernon station to Giverny along a pedestrian and cyclist path is unmarked: it begins as the dirt road that intersects r. de la Ravine above the highway (free map at Vernon tourist office). Taxis (☎06 08 63 04 85) run from the train station for a flat rate (M-F €10, Sa-Su and holidays €13).

SIGHTS

FONDATION CLAUDE MONET

84, r. Claude Monet. ☎02 32 51 28 21; www.fondation-monet.com. ***Open*** *Apr.-Oct. Tu-Su 9:30am-6:30pm.* ***Admission*** *€5.50, students and ages 12-18 €4, ages 7-12 €3. Gardens €4.*

From 1883 until 1926, Claude Monet—the leader of the Impressionist movement—resided in Giverny. His home, with its pink, crushed brick facade, was surrounded by ponds and immense gardens, two subjects central to his art. Today, Monet's house and gardens are maintained by the Fondation Claude Monet. From April to July, the gardens overflow with wild roses, hollyhocks, poppies, and the scent of honeysuckle. The water lilies, Japanese bridge, and weeping willows of the Orientalist Water Gardens look like—well, like *Monets*. Strolling through the elaborate and well-landscaped gardens is like flipping through a series of Monet paintings. To avoid the rush, go early in the morning and, if possible, early in the season. In Monet's thatched-roof home, big windows, solid furniture, and pale blue walls house his collection of 18th- and 19th-century Japanese prints. It also houses the only aerial view of the Gardens, from Monet's bedroom window.

MUSÉE D'ART AMÉRICAIN

99, r. Claude Monet. ☎02 32 51 94 65; www.maag.org. ***Open*** *Apr.-Oct. Tu-Su 9:30am-6:30pm.* ***Admission*** *€5.50; students, seniors, and teachers €4; 12-18 years €3. Free the first Sunday of each month. Audioguides available for €1.*

Near the Fondation is the incongruously modern Musée d'Art Américain, sister institution to the Museum of American Art in Chicago. It houses a small number of works by American expatriates, such as Theodore Butler and John Leslie Breck, who came to Giverny to learn how to paint in the style of the Impressionists. Outside, an impressive garden designed by landscape architect Mark Rudkin features an array of flowers separated by large, rectangular hedges. While not nearly as impressive as Monet's garden, this smaller labyrinth is worth a visit. If nothing else, it offers a scenic view of Giverny Hill, the inspiration for many Impressionist paintings.

FOOD

Ancien Hôtel Baudy, 81, r. Claude Monet (☎ 02 32 21 10 03). From the Fondation, walk up the r. Claude Monet 300m. In addition to its delicious Normandie-style cuisine, this renovated hotel (once frequented by Monet, Cézanne, and Cassatt) has an exquisitely terraced hillside garden. Also on the premises is a reconstructed ivy-covered artist's atelier. *Menus* €18.50. Salads €6.90-11.40. Open Tu-Su 10am-9pm. Closed Su evening. MC/V.

Les Nymphéas, r. Claude Monet (☎02 32 21 20 31). Adjacent to the parking lot of the *Fondation.* After a day of roses and honeybees, hungry pilgrims to the temple *à* Monet gorge the rest of their senses at Les Nymphéas, named after those famous waterlilies. The building was actually part of Monet's farm. Decorated with Toulouse-Lautrec posters, the indoor terrace is a picturesque setting for sampling the *nouvelle-Normandie* cuisine (*menu* €21.50, wine €3). The *salade Monet* (€10.50) is a masterpiece: mixed greens with mushrooms, smoked salmon, crab, and avocado. Open Apr.-Oct. Tu-Su 9:30am-6pm. MC/V.

AUVERS-SUR-OISE

I am entirely absorbed by these plains of wheat on a vast expanse of hills—like an ocean of tender yellow, pale green, and soft mauve.

—Vincent van Gogh, 1890

The 70 canvases van Gogh produced during his ten-week stay in Auvers bear testimony to what he called the "medicinal effect" of this bit of countryside, only 30km northwest of Paris. Fleeing Provence, where he had been diagnosed with depression and possible epilepsy, van Gogh arrived at Auvers-sur-Oise in May 1890, where he would be treated by a Dr. Gachet. But neither the doctor nor the countryside were enough to lift his depression. On the afternoon of July 27, he set off with his paints to the fields above the village, crawling back into his room that evening with a bullet lodged deep in his chest. Gachet, van Gogh's brother Theo, and even the police had a chance to demand an explanation from the painter as he lay smoking his pipe and bleeding for two days. "Sadness goes on forever," he told his brother, and died.

PRACTICAL INFORMATION

Trains: Take the **SNCF train** from Gare St-Lazare (☎01 30 36 70 61) or Gare du Nord to Pontoise (this may involve intermediate changes; consult the station's information desk), then switch to the Persau-Creil line and get off at Gare d'Auvers-sur-Oise. The connection can take up to 1hr. (1-1½hr., every hr., €9 roundtrip). Go to ticket desks marked "Paris Banlieue;" ask about the departure time and platform of your connecting train when you buy your tickets. Should you hit the afternoon lull in return train service, catch the **bus** to Pontoise. Or you can take the **RER** express 'A' line from Châtelet-Les Halles or Etoile toward Cergy-le-Haut (€9 round-trip). Get off at Cergy-Prefecture and take bus #95-07 toward Parmain. The connection can take from 20min.-1½hr. Ask to stop at "Auvers-sur-Oise-Mairie." The bus ride takes about 30min. and costs €1.20 each way.

Tourist Office: Manoir des Colombières, r. de la Sansonne (☎01 30 36 10 06; www.auvers-sur-oise.com/francais/index.htm). Helpful free walking maps. **Open** Apr.-Oct. daily 9:30am-12:30pm and 2-6pm; Nov.-Mar. M-F 9:30am-12:30pm and 2-5pm, Sa-Su 2-5:30pm. 1½hr. guided **tours** in French Apr.-Sept. Su 3pm; €5, under 14 €2. Free and informative audiovisual guide (15 min.).

SIGHTS

The following walk should take around 2hr. Whether you are at the train station or bus stop, begin facing uphill and turn left.

As you begin, on your right you will find the **Auberge Ravoux** where van Gogh stayed while in Auvers-sur-Oise and where he ultimately killed himself. While the **Maison de van Gogh,** 8, r. de la Sansonne, is just around the corner and a good place to start your tour, it has little to offer beyond a glimpse of van Gogh's bare room and a pretty (and pretty uninformative) slide show. However, the cost of admission includes an elegant souvenir "passport" to Auvers-sur-Oise that details the history of the *auberge* and van Gogh's sojourn here. A booklet about the town that is also available here gives information on the other museums and self-guided walking tours in the region, as well as offering discounts to four of the museums. (☎01 30 36 60 60. Open daily 10am-6pm. €5, family ticket €10.)

A visit to the **Cimetière d'Auvers,** where van Gogh and his brother Théo are buried, is worth the 10min. walk from the Maison de van Gogh. To get the cemetery, follow the small path behind the museum as it curves to the right onto r. Daubigny. Along r. Daubigny, you will reach a narrow staircase on your left. Follow the steps to the elegant **Notre Dame d'Auvers** (open daily 9am-6pm), which served as the 12th-century subject of Van Gogh's 1890 *Eglise d'Auvers*, which hangs in the Musée d'Orsay (see **Museums,** p. 138).

Continue walking along r. Daubigny, up a little hill, until you reach the cemetery. Behind the cemetery, the *chemin du cimetière* leads through the fields where van Gogh painted his *Champs de blé aux corbeaux* (*Wheatfields with Crows*, 1890). Circle up and to your left on the dirt path through the fields; after a 10min. walk, it emerges near the **Atelier de Daubigny,** 61, r. Daubigny, once the home and studio of pre-Impressionist painter Charles-François Daubigny. (☎01 34 48 03 03. Open Apr. 10.-Nov. 1 Su and Tu-Sa 2-6:30pm. €4.50, under 12 free.) Climb r. Daubigny and turn left onto r. de Léry. On a side street off r. de Léry, is the **Musée de l'Absinthe,** 44, r. Callé, a tribute to the potent green liqueur (see **The Green Party,** p. 214) immortalized in various paintings by Degas and Manet. Samples of a legal but much less toxic (read: less fun) version of the supposedly psychedelic drink that van Gogh liked so much are on sale at the museum's small gift shop. (☎01 30 36 83 26. Open Oct.-May Sa-Su 11am-6pm; June-Sept. W 2-6pm, Th-Su 11am-6pm. €4.50, students €3.80, under 14 free.) Follow r. de Léry up to the **Château d'Auvers,** which houses a modest collection of engaging Impressionist paintings. (☎01 34 48 48 31; www.chateau-auvers.fr. Open Apr.-Sep. M 2-6pm, Tu-Th 10:30am-6pm, F-Su 10:30am-6:30pm; Oct.-Mar. 10:30am-4:30pm. Free.)

FOOD

Small cafés and panini stands can be found throughout the town, but those willing to splurge will be rewarded with gourmet cuisine and impressive ambience.

Auberge Ravoux, 52, r. de Général-de-Gaulle (☎01 30 36 60 60). For the ultimate van Gogh experience, dine in style at the same auberge where the painter took his life 100 years ago. The elaborate glasswork and lace curtains almost let you forget the prices of the €19-38 *menu* (which are worth every Euro). Reservations a must. Open daily noon-2pm and 7-10pm. Closed Jan. and Tu Oct.-Mar. AmEx/MC/V. ❹

Hostellerie du Nord, 6, r. de Général-de-Gaulle (☎01 30 36 70 74). *Menus* include an *entrée,* a *plat* (like *cuisse de lapin*), dessert, and a half bottle of wine (€40-59). If the prices give you a headache (and even if they don't), dine on the relaxing terrace for the fresh air and spectacular garden. Open M-Sa noon-2:30pm and 7-10pm. Closed Tu Oct.-Mar. MC/V. ❺

DISNEYLAND RESORT PARIS

It's a small, small world, and Disney is hell-bent on making it even smaller. When Euro-Disney opened on April 12, 1992, Mickey Mouse, Cinderella, and Snow White were met by the jeers of French intellectuals and the popular press, who called the Disney theme park a "cultural Chernobyl." Resistance seems to have subsided since Walt & Co. renamed it Disneyland Paris and started serving wine. Pre-construction press touted the complex as a vast entertainment and resort center covering an area one-fifth the size of Paris. In truth, the current theme park doesn't even rank the size of an *arrondissement,* though Disney owns (and may eventually develop) 600 hectares. But this Disney park is the most technologically advanced yet, and the special effects on some rides will blow you away. If you have bottomless pockets, indulging in one of the park's seven world-class hotels (like the palatial Disneyland Hotel—a "lavish Victorian fantasy") may be worth the extra euros. For the more frugal (and those with a low tolerance for toddlers), however, a daytrip will more than suffice.

PRACTICAL INFORMATION

Everything in Disneyland Paris is in English and French. The detailed guide called the *Park Guide Book* (free at Disney City Hall to the left of the entrance) has a map and information on everything from restaurants and attractions to bathrooms and first aid. The *Guests' Special Services Guide* has info on wheelchair accessibility. For more info on Disneyland Paris, call ☎01 60 30 60 81 (from the US) or 01 60 30 63 53 from all other countries, or visit their web site at www.disneylandparis.com.

Trains: Take RER A4 from either M: Gare de Lyon or Châtelet-Les Halles (dir. Marne-la-Vallée) to the last stop, M: Marne-la-Vallée-Chessy. Before boarding the train, check the boards hanging above the platform to make sure there's a light next to the Marne-la-Vallée stop and not the Boissy-Saint-Leger stop (40min., departs every 30min., round-trip €11). The last train to Paris leaves Disney at 12:22am, but the métro closes at midnight, so you'll have to catch an earlier train to make it to the métro in time. **TGV** service from de Gaulle reaches the park in a mere 15min., making Disneyland Paris easily accessible for travelers with Eurail passes. Certain **Eurostar** trains now run directly between Waterloo Station in London and Disneyland. (☎08 36 35 35 39. Departure usually around 9:15am returning at 7:30pm. Prices from €135-375. Reserve far in advance.)

Car: Take the A4 highway from Paris and get off at Exit 14, marked "Parc Disneyland Paris," about 30min. from the city. Parking €8 per day; 11,000 spaces in all.

Bus: Disneyland Paris buses make the rounds between the terminals of both Orly and de Gaulle and the bus station near the Marne-la-Vallée RER. (40min.; departs every 45-60min. 8:30am-7:30pm, 8:30am-9:30pm at CDG on F and Su; round-trip €14; ages 3-11 €11.50.)

Tickets: Instead of selling tickets, Disneyland Paris issues **passeports,** valid for 1 day and available at the ground floor of the Disneyland Hotel. *Passeports* are also sold at the Paris tourist office on the Champs-Elysées (see **Service Directory,** p. 345), FNAC, Virgin Megastores, the Galeries Lafayette, any Disney store, many hotels in Paris, or at any of the major stations on RER line A, such as Châtelet-Les Halles, Gare de Lyon, or Charles de Gaulle-Etoile. Any of these options beats buying tickets at the park, as ticket lines can be very long.

Admission: A 1-day ticket allows entry to either Disneyland Park or Walt Disney Studios. For an extra €10, you can visit both theme parks. Nov.-Jan. €38, ages 3-11 €29; Jan.-Apr. €29/€25; Apr.-Nov. €39/€29. 2- and 3-day *passeports* also available. **Fastpasses** allow guests to make reservations to ride attractions, shaving 45min. off of the wait to ride a roller coaster. Inquire at the Fastpass counters outside of each attraction.

Hours: Apr.-Sept. daily 9am-11pm; Oct.-Apr. M-F 10am-9pm, Sa-Su 10am-10pm. Hours subject to change, especially during winter; call ahead for details.

DISNEYLAND PARK

Divided into five areas, each overcrowded with screaming children and their parents, Disneyland Park showcases American cultural imperialism in action. "Main Street, U.S.A." attempts to recreate "the charm of a small American town at the turn of the 20th century." Horse-drawn streetcars and the Main Street Railroad Station are employed in this venture. Each day at 6pm the **Princess Parade**—a parade of Disney characters marching to a loud fanfare of Disney tunes—takes place on Main Street. At 10:30pm each evening, the street is home to the **Fantillusion Parade** where "imagination flows and glows" in an impressive (albeit overblown) display of pyrotechnic lighting and lasers featuring (go figure) Disney characters. Finally, at 11:15pm, Disney caps off the night with Tinker Bell's **fireworks.** In addition to Main Street, Frontierland, Adventureland, Fantasyland, and Discoveryland circle around the park's central plaza—a flowery garden in front of Sleeping Beauty Castle.

The park's main draws, of course, are its 41 **rides** and attractions. For children, slow-moving and colorful attractions like **Pinocchio's Fantastic Journey** (through a toyshop) and **Peter Pan's Flight** (through the Isle of Never Land) are perennial favorites. For guests seeking more action, or those simply hoping to feel nauseous, **Indiana Jones and the Temple of Peril: Backwards!** and **Space Mountain** are sure to thrill. The latter is the more modern and technologically savvy counterpart of Space Mountain at DisneyWorld (USA). Passengers ride on a turbulent "rocket-powered" spaceship that loops, twists, drops, and climbs through complete darkness. If that doesn't scare you, check out **Phantom Manor**—a mansion haunted by 999 ghosts and witches.

WALT DISNEY STUDIOS

Less child-oriented and more technical than Disneyland Park, Walt Disney Studios features motor stunt shows (daily 11:45am, 2:30, 4:30pm), an Armageddon special effects exhibit, and an entire building dedicated to the art of Disney animation. Coaster-enthusiasts fret not! The **Rock 'N' Roll Roller Coaster with Aerosmith** is a thrilling indoor coaster with loud music, strobe lights, and loops. Each day at 11am, noon, 1, 2, 4:15, and 5pm, children can enjoy an Animagique show with Mickey, Donald, and the rest of the gang. Daily cinema parades at 3:30pm.

INSIDE

Planning Your Trip

WHEN TO GO

PARIS BY SEASON

Everyone loves Paris in the **springtime.** Well, almost everyone, almost all of the time. The weather in spring is fickle, with rainy and sunny days in about equal numbers. In **summer,** the heat does nothing to soften the blow of Paris's pollution. June is notoriously rainy, and high temperatures usually hit in July. In August, tourists move in and (partly for that very reason) Parisians move out for vacation. Smaller hotels, shops, and services close for the month, resulting in a run on the remaining ones and frustration for all involved. Still, parts of Paris can be remarkably calm in the summertime (avoid the Champs-Elysées, Versailles, and the Eiffel Tower), and a number of the city's best festivals are held during the summer months (see **Discover,** p. 18, for details). In the **fall,** the tourist madness begins to calm down. Despite **winter** cold and rain, there isn't much snow. In the off season, airfares and hotel rates drop, travel is less congested, and the museum lines are shorter. For a list of Paris's best festivals and national holidays, see **Discover,** p. 18.

AVG TEMP (LOW/HI)	JANUARY		APRIL		JULY		OCTOBER	
	°C	°F	°C	°F	°C	°F	°C	°F
PARIS	0/7	32/45	4/15	40/59	13/25	56/77	10/22	51/71

DOCUMENTS & FORMALITIES

EMBASSIES & CONSULATES

FRENCH CONSULAR SERVICES ABROAD

The web site **www.embassyworld.com** has a complete, up-to-date list of consulates. For a list of foreign consular services in Paris, see **Once in Paris,** p. 30.

Australia, Consulate General, Level 26, St. Martin Tower, 31 Market St., Sydney NSW 2000 (☎02 9261 5779; fax 9283 1210; www.consulfrance-sydney.org). Open M-F 9am-1pm.

Canada, Consulat Général de France à Montréal, 1 pl. Ville-Marie, Ste. 2601, Montréal, QC H3B 4S3 (☎514-878-4385; fax 878-3981; www.consulfrance-montreal.org). Open M-F 8:30am-noon. Consulat Général de France à Québec, Maison Kent, 25, r. St-Louis, Québec, QC G1R 3Y8 (☎418-694-2294; fax 694-1678; www.consulfrance-quebec.org). Open M-F 9am-12:00pm. Consulat Général de France à Toronto, 130 Bloor St. W., Ste. 400, Toronto, ON M5S 1N5 (☎416-925-8041; fax 925-3076; www.consulfrance-toronto.org). Open M-F 9am-1pm.

Ireland, French Embassy, Consulate Section, 36 Ailesbury Rd., Ballsbridge, Dublin 4 (☎01 277 5000; fax 283 01 78; www.ambafrance.ie). Open M-F 9:30am-12:30pm.

New Zealand, New Zealand Embassy and Consulate, 34-42 Manners St., P.O. Box 11-343, Wellington (☎04 384 2555; fax 384 2577). Open M-F 9am-1pm. French Honorary Consulate in Auckland, P.O. Box 1433, Auckland (☎09 379 58 50; fax 09 358 70 68; www.ambafrance-nz.org).

South Africa, Consulate General at Johannesburg (for residents of Gauteng, Kwazulu-Natal, Free State, Mpumalanga, Northern Province, North West Province, or Lesotho), 191 Jan Smuts Ave., Rosebank. Mailing address: P.O. Box 1027, Parklands 2121 (☎011 778 56 00; visas 778 56 05; fax 778 56 01). Open M-F 8:30am-1pm. Consulate General at Cape Town (for residents of the Northern Cape, Eastern Cape or Western Cape), 2 Dean St., Gardens. Mailing address: P.O. Box 1702 Cape Town 8000 (☎021 423 15 75; fax 424 84 70). Both consulates on the web at www.consulfrance.co.za. Open M-F 9am-12:30pm.

United Kingdom, Consulate General at London (for residents of England, Wales, and Northern Ireland), P.O. Box 520, 21 Cromwell Rd., London SW7 2EN. ☎020 7073 1200; fax 020 7073 1201; www.ambafrance-uk.org. Open M 8:45am-2pm, T-Th 8:45am-noon, F 8:45-11:30am. Visa service: P.O. Box 57, 6a Cromwell Pl., London SW7 2EW. ☎020 7073 1250. Open M-F 8:45-11:30am. Consulate General at Edinburgh (for residents of Scotland), 21 Randolph Crescent, Edinburgh EH37TT (☎0131 225 7954; fax 0131 225 8975; www.consulfrance-edimbourg.org). Open M-F 9:30am-1pm.

United States, Consulate General, 4101 Reservoir Rd. NW, Washington, DC 20007 (☎202-944-6195, fax 944-6148; visa service 944-6200, fax 944-6212; www.consulfrance-washington.org). Open M-F 8:45am-12:45pm. Consulates also located in Atlanta, Boston, Chicago, Houston, Los Angeles, Miami, New Orleans, New York, and San Francisco. See www.info-france-usa.org/intheus/consulates.asp for more info.

PASSPORTS

REQUIREMENTS. Citizens of Australia, Canada, New Zealand, South Africa, Ireland, the United Kingdom, and the US need valid passports to enter France and to re-enter their own country. France does not allow entrance if the holder's passport expires in under three months after the expected date of departure; returning home with an expired passport is illegal and may result in a fine.

PHOTOCOPIES. Be sure to photocopy the page of your passport with your photo, passport number, and other identifying information, as well as any visas, travel insurance policies, plane tickets, or traveler's check serial numbers. Carry one set of copies in a safe place, apart from the originals, and leave another set at home. Consulates also recommend that travelers carry an expired passport or an official copy of your birth certificate in a part of your baggage separate from other documents.

LOST PASSPORTS. If you lose your passport in France, immediately notify the local police and the nearest embassy or consulate of your home government. To expedite replacement, you will need to know all information contained in the lost passport and show identification and proof of citizenship. US embassies and consulates will no longer issue American passports abroad. Applying for a passport from the French consulate will now take longer, because the passport must be printed in the US. Any visas stamped in your old passport will be irretrievably lost. In an emergency, ask for temporary traveling papers that will permit you to re-enter your home country. Your passport is a public document belonging to your nation's government. You may have to surrender it to a foreign government official; if you don't get the document back in a reasonable amount of time, inform the nearest mission of your home country.

NEW PASSPORTS. Citizens of Australia, Canada, New Zealand, Ireland, the United Kingdom, and the United States can apply for a passport at the nearest post office, passport office, or court of law. Citizens of South Africa can apply for a passport at the nearest Home Affairs Office. Any new passport or renewal applications must be filed well in advance of the departure date, although most passport offices offer rush services for a very steep fee. Citizens living abroad who need a passport or renewal services should contact the nearest consular service of their home country.

VISAS & WORK PERMITS

French visas are valid for travel in any of the states of the EU common travel area (the entire Union except the UK and Ireland, plus Iceland and Norway); however, if the primary object of your visit is a country other than France you should apply to their consulate for a visa. Visitors to France are required to register their presence with the police in the town in which they are staying; this is normally done automatically by hotels and hostels or when signing a lease with a landlord. Double-check on entrance requirements at the nearest French Embassy or Consulate (listed under **Embassies & Consulates,**

ESSENTIAL INFORMATION

ONE EUROPE

The idea of European unity has come a long way since 1958, when the European Economic Community (EEC) was created in order to promote solidarity and cooperation among its six founding states. The EEC has become the European Union (EU), with political, legal, and economic institutions spanning 15 member states: Austria, Belgium, Denmark, Finland, France, Germany, Greece, Ireland, Italy, Luxembourg, the Netherlands, Portugal, Spain, Sweden, and the UK.

What does this have to do with the average non-EU tourist? In 1999 the EU established **freedom of movement** across 14 European countries—the entire EU minus Ireland and the UK, but plus Iceland and Norway. This means that border controls between participating countries have been abolished, and visa policies harmonized. While you're still required to carry a passport (or government-issued ID card for EU citizens) when crossing an internal border, once you've been admitted into one country, you're free to travel to all participating states. Britain and Ireland have also formed a **common travel area,** abolishing passport controls between the UK and the Republic of Ireland. The only times you'll see a border guard within the EU are when traveling between the British Isles and the Continent.

There are also no customs controls at internal EU borders; you can freely transport any legal substances for non-commercial use between EU countries.

p. 304) for up-to-date information before departure. Citizens of the United States can also consult the informational web site at www.pueblo.gsa.gov/cic_text/travel/foreign/foreignentryreqs.html.

VISITS OF UNDER 90 DAYS. Most travelers need only their passport to reside in France for under 90 days. Citizens of South Africa, however, need a **short-stay visa** *(court séjour)*. To apply, your passport must be valid for three months past the date you intend to leave France. In addition, you must submit two passport-sized photos, proof of a hotel reservation or an organized tour, or, if you intend to stay with relatives or friends, a certificate of accommodation stamped by the police station or town hall (2 copies), or, if you intend to work, a letter from your employer, a return ticket and proof of medical insurance. A transit visa (1 or 2 entries of 1 or 2 days) costs ZAR86.74; single/multiple entry visa for 30 days or under costs ZAR216.79; for 31-90 days, the cost is ZAR260.21, for single entry, or ZAR303.53 for multiple entries. Apply for a visa at your nearest French consulate; short-stay visas for South African nationals can take up to two weeks to process.

VISITS OF OVER 90 DAYS. All non-EU citizens need a **long-stay visa** *(long séjour)* for stays of over 90 days. Requirements vary according to the nature of your stay; contact your French consulate. The visa itself can take two months to process and costs about €100. US Citizens can take advantage of the Center for International Business and Travel (☎617-354-7755), which will secure visas for travel to almost all countries for a service charge. Within 60 days of their arrival, all foreigners (including EU citizens) who plan to stay over 90 days must apply for a **temporary residence permit** *(carte de séjour temporaire)*. For more information on long-term stays in Paris, see **Alternatives to Tourism,** p. 336.

STUDY & WORK PERMITS. Only EU citizens have the right to work and study in France without a visa. Others wishing to study in France must apply for a special student visa. For more information, see **Alternatives to Tourism,** p. 336.

IDENTIFICATION

French law requires that all people carry a form of official identification at all times—either a passport or an EU government-issued identity card. The police have the right to demand to see identification at any time. Minority travelers, especially black and Arab travelers, should be especially careful to carry proof that they are in France legally. Never carry all of your IDs together; split them up in case of theft or loss, and keep photocopies of them in your luggage and at home.

For more information on all the forms of identification listed below, contact the organization that provides the service, the **International Student Travel Confederation (ISTC),** Herengracht 479, 1017 BS Amsterdam, Netherlands (☎20 421 28 00; fax 421 28 10; www.istc.org).

TEACHER, STUDENT & YOUTH IDENTIFICATION. The **International Student Identity Card (ISIC),** the most widely accepted form of student ID, provides discounts on sights, accommodations, food, and transport; access to 24hr. emergency helpline (☎44 20 8762 8110); and insurance benefits for US cardholders. The ISIC is preferable to an institution-specific card (such as a university ID) because it is more likely to be recognized abroad. Applicants must be degree-seeking students of a secondary or post-secondary school and must be of at least 12 years of age. Because of the proliferation of fake ISICs, some services (particularly airlines) require additional proof of student identity.

The **International Teacher Identity Card (ITIC)** offers teachers the same insurance coverage as well as similar but limited discounts. For travelers who are 25 years old or under but are not students, the **International Youth Travel Card (IYTC;** formerly the **GO 25** Card) also offers many of the same benefits as the ISIC. Similarly, the **International Student Exchange ID Card (ISE)** provides discounts, medical benefits, and the ability to purchase student airfares.

Each of these identity cards costs US$22 or equivalent. ISIC and ITIC cards are valid for roughly one-and-a-half academic years; IYTC cards are valid for one year from the date of issue. Many student travel agencies (see p. 312) issue the cards; for a list of issuing agencies, or for more information, contact the **Internationa Student Travel Confederation (ISTC),** Herengracht 479, 1017 BS Amsterdam, The Netherlands (☎31 20 421 28 00; fax 421 28 10; www.istc.org).

CUSTOMS

Upon entering France, you must declare certain items from abroad and pay a duty on the value of those articles that exceeds the allowance established by France's customs service. Note that goods and gifts purchased at **duty-free** shops abroad are not exempt from duty or sales tax at your point of return and thus must be declared as well; "duty-free" merely means that you need not pay a tax in the country of purchase. Duty-free allowances have been abolished for travel between EU member states, but still exist for those arriving from outside the EU. Upon returning home, you must declare all articles acquired abroad and pay a duty on the value of articles in excess of your home country's allowance. To expedite your return, you should make a list of any valuables brought from home and register them with customs before traveling abroad. Also be sure to keep receipts for all goods acquired abroad.

RECLAIMING VALUE-ADDED TAX. Most purchases in France include a 19.6% value-added tax (TVA). Non-EU residents (including EU citizens who reside outside the EU) can in principle reclaim the tax on purchases for export worth over €175 made in one store. Only certain stores participate in this *vente en détaxe* refund process; ask before you pay. You must show a non-EU passport or proof of non-EU residence at the time of purchase, and ask the vendor for a tripartite form called a *bordereau de vente à l'exportation;* make sure that they fill it out, including your bank details. When leaving the country, present the receipt for the purchase together with the completed form to a French customs official. If you're at an airport, look for the window labeled *douane de détaxe*, and budget at least an hour for the intricacies of French bureaucracy. On a train, find an official or get off at a station close to the border. Once home, you must send a copy back to the vendor within six months; eventually the refunds will work their way into your account. Some shops

ESSENTIAL INFORMATION

THE EURO

The official currency of the 12 members of the European Union—Austria, Belgium, Finland, France, Germany, Greece, Ireland, Italy, Luxembourg, the Netherlands, Portugal, and Spain—is now the euro.

The currency has some important—and positive—consequences for travelers hitting more than one euro-zone country. For one thing, money-changers across the euro-zone are obliged to exchange money at the official, fixed rate (see below), and at no commission (though they may still charge a small service fee). Second, euro-denominated traveler's checks allow you to pay for goods and services across the euro-zone, again commission-free and at the official rate.

The following numbers are based on established August 2003 conversion rates:

US$1 = €0.88

€1 = US$1.13

CDN$1 = €0.64

€1 = CDN$1.56

UK£1 = €1.14

€1 = UK£0.71

AUS$1 = €0.58

€1 = AUS$1.72

NZ$1 = €0.52

€1 = NZ$1.92

ZAR1 = €0.12

€1 = ZAR8.32

exempt you from paying the tax at the time of purchase; you must still complete the above process. Food products, tobacco, medicine, firearms, unmounted precious stones, cars, means of transportation (e.g., bicycles and surfboards), and "cultural goods" do not qualify for a TVA refund. For more information, contact the Europe Tax-Free Shopping office in France, 4, pl. de l'Opéra, Paris 75002 (☎01 42 66 24 14).

MONEY

COSTS

"Budget travel in Paris" is somewhat of an oxymoron, but the cost of your trip will vary considerably depending on how you travel and where you stay.Before you go, spend some time calculating a reasonable per-day **budget** that will meet your needs. A modest daily budget (sleeping in hostels or budget hotels, eating one meal a day at a restaurant, going out at night) will probably fall between €40 and €45. If you stay in hostels and prepare your own food, you may be able to live on €20-25 per person per day.

Some simple ways to save money include searching out opportunities for free entertainment, splitting accommodation and food costs with fellow travelers, and buying food in supermarkets rather than eating out. With that said, don't go overboard with your budget obsession. Though staying within your budget is important, don't do so at the expense of your health or a rewarding travel experience.

CURRENCY & EXCHANGE

In 2002, the *franc français*, or **French franc**, was superseded by the **euro** (symbol €). The euro is divided into 100 cents. One euro is approximately equal to one US dollar. For current exchange rates, see **The Euro**, p. 307, or visit **www.xe.com**, **www.finance.yahoo.com**, or **www.letsgo.com.**

As a general rule, it's cheaper to convert money in France than at home. While currency exchange will probably be available in your arrival airport, it's smart to bring enough foreign currency to last for the first 24-72 hours. Watch out for commission rates and check newspapers for the standard rate of exchange (the margin between the buy and sell prices should be no more than 5%). Since you lose money with each transaction, convert in large sums. Using an ATM card or a credit card (see p. 308) will usually get you better rates. If you use traveler's checks or bills, carry some in small denominations (US$50 or less), especially for times when you are forced to exchange money at disadvantageous rates.

Banks generally have the best exchange rates; beware *bureaux de change* at airports, train stations, and touristy areas like the Champs-Elysées, which generally have less favorable rates. Many banks will exchange money from 9am-noon and 2-4:30pm. Banks near the Opéra (see **Sights,** p. 105) exchange money from 9am-5pm during the week and have 24hr. exchange machines. For more information, see **Service Directory** (p. 342).

CREDIT, DEBIT, & ATM CARDS

Credit cards are widely accepted in Paris, though usually only for purchases of over €15. Major credit cards can be used to extract cash advances in euros from associated banks and cash machines throughout France. Credit card companies get the wholesale exchange rate, which is generally 5% better than the retail rate used by banks and other currency exchange establishments. The most commonly accepted cards, in both businesses and cash machines, are **Visa** (also known as **Carte Bleue**; US ☎800-336-8472), and **MasterCard** (also called **Eurocard;** US ☎800-307-7309). **American Express** (US ☎800-843-2273) cards work in some ATMs, as well as at AmEx offices and major airports. Credit cards may also offer services such as insurance or emergency help, and are sometimes required to reserve hotel rooms or rental cars.

French-issued credit cards are fitted with a micro-chip (such cards are known as *cartes à puces*) rather than a magnetic strip *(cartes à piste magnétiques)*. Cashiers may attempt (and fail) to scan the card with a microchip reader. In such circumstances you should explain; say *"Ceci n'est pas une carte à puce, mais une carte à piste magnétique"* (This card doesn't have a chip, but a magnetic strip).

Twenty-four hour **cash machines** are widespread in France. Depending on the system that your home bank uses, you can probably access your own personal bank account. ATMs get the same wholesale exchange rate as credit cards. There is often a limit on the amount of money you can withdraw per day (usually about US$500, depending on the type of card and account). Your home bank may also charge a fee for using ATM facilities abroad.

The two major international money networks are **Cirrus** (US ☎800-424-7787; www.mastercard.com) and **Visa/PLUS** (US ☎800-843-7587; www.visa.com). Institutions supporting PLUS are: Crédit Commercial de France, Banque Populaire, Union de Banque à Paris, Point Argent, Banque Nationale de Paris, Crédit du Nord, Gie Osiris, and ATMs in many post offices. To locate ATMs around the world, call the above numbers, or consult www.visa.com/globalgateway. Most ATMs charge a transaction fee that is paid to the bank that owns the ATM.

ESSENTIAL INFORMATION

PINS & ATMS

To use a cash or credit card to withdraw money from a cash machine (ATM) in Europe, you must have a four-digit **Personal Identification Number (PIN).** If your PIN is longer than four digits, ask your bank whether you can just use the first four, or whether you'll need a new one. **Credit cards** don't usually come with PINs, so if you intend to hit up ATMs in Europe with a credit card to get cash advances, call your credit card company before leaving to request one.

People with alphabetic, rather than numerical, PINs may also be thrown off by the lack of letters on European cash machines. The following handy chart gives the corresponding numbers to use: 1=QZ; 2=ABC; 3=DEF; 4=GHI; 5=JKL; 6=MNO; 7=PRS; 8=TUV; and 9=WXY. Note that if you mistakenly punch the wrong code into the machine three times, it will swallow your card for good.

Debit cards are as convenient as credit cards but have a more immediate impact on your funds. A debit card can be used wherever its associated credit card company (usually Mastercard or Visa) is accepted, yet the money is withdrawn directly from the holder's checking account. Debit cards often also function as ATM cards and can be used to withdraw cash from associated banks and ATMs throughout Paris. Ask your bank about obtaining one.

TRAVELER'S CHECKS

Traveler's checks are one of the safest and least troublesome means of carrying funds, since they can be refunded if lost or stolen. In Paris, however, you may find that they are not widely accepted outside of tourist-oriented businesses, and many establishments only accept traveler's checks in euros. **American Express** and **Visa** are the most widely recognized brands. Check issuers provide refunds if the checks are lost or stolen, and many provide additional services, such as toll-free refund hotlines abroad, emergency message services, and stolen credit card assistance.

American Express: Checks available with commission at select banks and all American Express offices. US residents can also purchase checks by phone (☎888-269-6669) or order them online (www.aexp.com). AAA offers commission-free checks to its members. Checks available in US, Australian, British, Canadian, Japanese, and Euro currencies. *Cheques for Two* can be signed by either of 2 people traveling together. For more information on these checks, contact AmEx's service centers: in the US and Canada ☎800-221-7282; in the UK ☎0800 521 313; in Australia ☎800 25 19 02; in New Zealand ☎0800 441 068; elsewhere US collect ☎801-964-6665.

Visa: Commissioned checks available at banks worldwide. For the nearest office location, call the service centers: in the US ☎800-227-6811; in the UK ☎0800 89 50 78; elsewhere in UK collect ☎020 7937 8091. Available in US, British, Canadian, Japanese, and Euro currencies.

Travelex/Thomas Cook: In the US and Canada call ☎800-287-7362; in the UK call 0800 62 21 01; elsewhere call UK collect ☎1733 31 89 50.

Visa TravelMoney is a system allowing you to access money from any ATM that accepts Visa cards. (For local customer assistance in France, call ☎0800 90 1235.) You deposit an amount before you travel (plus a small administration fee), and you can withdraw up to that sum. The cards, which give you the same favorable exchange rate for withdrawals as a regular Visa, are especially useful if you plan to travel through many countries. Obtain a card by either visiting a nearby Thomas Cook or Citicorp office, by calling toll-free in the US ☎877-394-2247, or checking with your local bank or to see if it issues TravelMoney cards.

HEALTH

Common sense is the simplest prescription for good health while you travel. Drink lots of fluids to prevent dehydration and constipation, and wear sturdy, broken-in shoes and clean socks.

BEFORE YOU GO

People with **asthma** or **allergies** should be aware that Paris has visibly high levels of air pollution, particularly during the summer, and that non-smoking areas are almost nonexistent. Call ☎01 44 59 47 64 for information on air quality in Paris. (Open M-F 9am-2:30pm and 3:30-5:45pm, in French.) Consider bringing an over-the-counter antihistamine, decongestant, inhaler, etc., since there may not be a French equivalent with the correct dosage. Allergy sufferers might also want to obtain a full supply of necessary medication before the trip. Matching a prescription to a foreign equivalent is not always easy, safe, or possible.

In your **passport,** write the names of any people you wish to have contacted in case of a medical emergency, and also list any **allergies** or medical conditions you want doctors to be aware of. Carry up-to-date, legible prescriptions or a statement from your doctor stating the medication's trade name, manufacturer, chemical name, and dosage. Be sure to keep all medication with you in your carry-on luggage.

MEDICAL ASSISTANCE

Medical care is not hard to find in Paris (see **Once in Paris,** p. 33), but if you are concerned about being able to access medical support while traveling, you may want to look into support services. The *MedPass* from **GlobalCare, Inc.,** 2001 Westside Pkwy., #120, Alpharetta, GA 30004 (☎800-860-1111; fax 770-677-0455; www.globalems.com), provides 24hr. international medical assistance, support, and medical evacuation resources. The **International Association for Medical Assistance to Travelers (IAMAT)** has free membership, lists English-speaking doctors worldwide, and offers detailed info on immunization requirements and sanitation. (US ☎716-754-4883, Canada 716-754-4883, New Zealand 64 03 352-4630; http://www.cybermall.co.nz/NZ/IAMAT). **The American Hospital of Paris,** 63, bd. Victor Hugo (☎01 46 41 25 25), has English-speaking doctors. If your regular **insurance** policy does not cover travel abroad, you may wish to purchase additional coverage. If you go to a state hospital while in Paris, you will most likely have to pay in full and send in for reimbursement later on.

Those with medical conditions (e.g., diabetes, allergies to antibiotics, epilepsy, heart conditions) may want to obtain a **Medic Alert** identification tag ($35 the first year, $20 annually thereafter), which identifies the condition and gives a 24hr. collect-call info number. Contact the Medic Alert Foundation, 2323 Colorado Ave. Turlock, CA, 95382 (☎888-633-4298, outside US ☎888-633-4298; www.medicalert.org). For more on medical and emergency assistance, see the **Service Directory** (p. 342).

AIDS, HIV, & STDS

Acquired Immune Deficiency Syndrome (**AIDS; SIDA** in French) is a major problem in France. Paris has the largest HIV-positive community in Europe. France only recently lifted immigration bans on HIV-positive individuals. There are as many heterosexuals infected as homosexuals in France, and among heterosexuals, more women than men. The easiest mode of HIV transmission is direct blood-to-blood contact; *never* share intravenous drug, tattooing, or other needles. The most common mode of transmission is sexual intercourse. You can greatly reduce the risk of infection by using latex condoms.

For detailed info on **AIDS** in France, call the **US Centers for Disease Control's** 24hr. hotline at ☎800-342-2437, or contact the **Joint United Nations Programme on HIV/AIDS (UNAIDS),** 20 av. Appia 20, CH-1211 Geneva 27, Switzerland (☎+41 22 791 36 66; fax 22 791 41 87). France's AIDS hotline can be reached at ☎01 44 93 16 16. The Council on International Educational Exchange's pamphlet, *Travel Safe: AIDS and International Travel*, is posted on their web site (http://www.ciee.org/travelsafe.cfm), along with links to other online and phone resources.

If you think you may have contracted HIV or another sexually transmitted disease (STD; such as gonorrhea, chlamydia, genital warts, syphilis, herpes, or hepatitis B or C), see a doctor immediately.

BIRTH CONTROL

Contraception is readily available in most pharmacies (see **Service Directory,** p. 345). To buy **condoms** *(préservatifs)* in France, tell the pharmacy clerk, *"Je voudrais une boîte des préservatifs."* The French branch of the International Planned Parenthood Federation, the **Mouvement Français pour le Planning Familial (MFPF),** 10, r. Vivienne, *2ème* (☎01 42 60 93 20; www.planning-familial.org), can provide more information. Women on the pill should bring enough to allow for possible loss or extended stays. Bring a prescription, since forms of the pill vary a good deal.

GETTING THERE

BY PLANE

When it comes to airfare, a little effort can save you a bundle. If your plans are flexible enough to deal with the restrictions, courier fares are the cheapest. Tickets bought from consolidators and standby seating are also good deals, but last-minute specials, airfare wars, and charter flights often beat these fares. The key is to hunt around, to be flexible, and to persistently ask about discounts. Students, seniors, those under 26, and those who plan ahead should never pay full price for a ticket.

TIMING. Airfares to France peak between June and Sept.; Easter and Christmas are also expensive periods. Most cheap fares require a Saturday night stay. Traveling with an "open return" ticket can be pricier than fixing a return date when buying the ticket and paying later to change it. Most budget tickets allow no date or route changes made; student tickets sometimes allow date changes for a price.

FARES. Round-trip fares to Paris from the US range from US$250 to US$600 (during low season) to around US$400-800 (during the summer). From Australia, count on paying between AUS$1600 and $4500, depending on the season. From New Zealand, fares start at about NZ$5000 and climb all the way up to NZ$9000. Flights from the

UK to France are a comparative bargain, at UK£60-140 for a budget airline flight from London to Paris (one-way). A return (round-trip) flight from Dublin to Paris can cost as little as IR£140 during high season.

If Paris is only 1 stop on a more extensive globe-hop, consider a round-the-world (RTW) ticket. Tickets usually include at least 5 stops and are valid for about a year; prices range US$1200-5000. Try **Northwest Airlines/KLM** (US ☎800-447-4747; www.nwa.com) or **Star Alliance,** a consortium of 22 airlines including United Airlines (US ☎800-241-6522; www.staralliance.com).

BUDGET & STUDENT TRAVEL AGENCIES

Travelers holding **ISIC** and **IYTC cards** (see p. 306) qualify for big discounts from student travel agencies. Most flights from budget agencies are on major airlines, but in peak season some may sell seats on less reliable chartered aircraft.

CTS Travel, 30 Rathbone Pl., London W1T 1GQ, UK (☎020 7290 0630; www.ctstravel.co.uk). A British student travel agent with offices in 39 countries including the US. Empire State Building, 350 Fifth Ave., Suite 7813, New York, NY 10118 (☎877-287-6665; www.ctstravelusa.com).

STA Travel, 7890 S. Hardy Dr., Ste. 110, Tempe, AZ 85284 (24hr. reservations and info ☎800-781-4040; www.statravel.com). A student and youth travel organization with over 150 offices worldwide (check their web site for a listing of all their offices), including US offices in Boston, Chicago, L.A., New York, San Francisco, Seattle, and Washington, D.C. Ticket booking, travel insurance, railpasses, and more. In the UK, walk-in office 11 Goodge St., **London** W1T 2PF or call 0207 436 77 79. In New Zealand, Shop 2B 182 Queen St., **Auckland** (☎09 9349 4344). In Australia, 366 Lygon St., **Carlton** VIC 3053 (☎03 9349 4344).

Travel CUTS (Canadian Universities Travel Services Limited), 187 College St., Toronto, ON M5T 1P7 (☎416-979-2406 or 800-667-2887; www.travecuts.com). Canada's main student travel agent has offices throughout Canada and a few in the US, including Boston, Seattle, New York, and San Francisco. Books budget plane tickets for students and non-students. Also in the UK, 295A Regent St., London W1B 2H9.

USIT, 19-21 Aston Quay, Dublin 2 (☎01 602 1600; www.usitworld.com) Ireland's leading student/budget travel agency has 22 offices throughout Northern Ireland and the Republic of Ireland. Offers programs to work in North America.

Wasteels, Skoubogade 6, 1158 Copenhagen K. (☎3314 4633; fax 3314 0865; www.wasteels.dk/uk). A huge chain with 165 locations across Europe. Sells Wasteels BIJ tickets discounted 30-45% off regular fare, 2nd-class international point-to-point train tickets with unlimited stopovers for those under 26 (sold only in Europe).

COMMERCIAL AIRLINES

The commercial airlines' lowest regular offer is the **APEX (Advance Purchase Excursion)** fare, which provides confirmed reservations and allows "open-jaw" tickets. Generally, reservations must be made seven to 21 days in advance, with seven- to 14-day minimum-stay and up to 90-day maximum-stay restrictions. There are hefty cancellation and change penalties (fees rise in summer). Book peak-season APEX fares early. **Microsoft Expedia** (www.msn.expedia.com) and **Travelocity** (www.travelocity.com) can give you an idea of the lowest published fares. Low-season fares should be appreciably cheaper than high season (mid-June to Aug.).

FROM NORTH AMERICA

Basic round-trip fares to Paris average US$250-700. Commercial carriers like American (☎800-433-7300; www.aa.com) and United (☎800-241-6522; www.ual.com) will offer the most convenient flights, but they may not be the cheapest. You might find a better deal on one of the following.

Icelandair: ☎800-223-5500; www.icelandair.com. Flights to Paris with stopovers in Iceland at no extra cost. May-Sept. starting at US$650; Oct.-May starting at US$550. For last-minute offers, subscribe to their email Lucky Fares.

Finnair: ☎800-950-5000; www.us.finnair.com. Cheap round-trips from San Francisco, New York, and Toronto to Helsinki; connections throughout Europe.

FROM THE UK & IRELAND

Because of the many carriers flying from the British Isles to the continent, we only include discount airlines or those with cheap specials here. The **Air Travel Advisory Bureau** in London (☎020 7636 5000; www.atab.co.uk) provides referrals to travel agencies and consolidators that offer discounted airfares out of the UK.

Aer Lingus: Ireland ☎0818 365 000; www.aerlingus.ie. Return tickets from Dublin, Cork, Galway, Kerry, and Shannon to Paris (IR£102-244).

British Midland Airways: UK ☎0870 607 05 55; www.flybmi.com. Departures from throughout the UK. London to Paris (UK£71).

buzz: UK ☎0870 240 70 70; www.buzzaway.com. A subsidiary of KLM. From London to Paris (UK£50-80). Tickets can not be changed or refunded.

easyJet: UK ☎0870 600 00 00; www.easyjet.com. London to Paris (UK£47-136).

KLM: UK ☎0870 507 40 74; www.klmuk.com. Cheap return tickets from London and elsewhere in the UK to Paris.

Ryanair: Ireland ☎0818 303 030, UK 0870 156 95 69; www.ryanair.ie. From Dublin, London, and Glasgow to France. Deals from as low as UK£9 on limited weekend specials.

FROM AUSTRALIA & NEW ZEALAND

Qantas Air: Australia ☎13 13 13, New Zealand ☎0800 808 767; www.qantas.com.au. Flights from various cities in Australia and New Zealand to London for around AUS$2400.

Singapore Air: Australia ☎13 10 11, New Zealand ☎0800 808 909; www.singaporeair.com. Flies from Auckland, Sydney, Melbourne, and Perth to Paris.

Thai Airways: Australia ☎1300 65 19 60, New Zealand ☎09 377 02 68; www.thaiair.com. Auckland, Sydney, and Melbourne to Amsterdam, Frankfurt, and London.

FROM SOUTH AFRICA

Air France: ☎011 770 16 01; www.airfrance.com/za. Flies several times per week from Johannesburg to Paris.

British Airways: ☎0860 011 747; www.british-airways.com/regional/sa. Cape Town and Johannesburg to the UK and the rest of Europe from ZAR3400.

Lufthansa: ☎0861 842 538; www.lufthansa.co.za. From Cape Town, Durban, and Johannesburg to Germany and elsewhere.

Virgin Atlantic: ☎011 340 34 00; www.virgin-atlantic.co.za. Flies to London from both Cape Town and Johannesburg.

OTHER CHEAP ALTERNATIVES

STANDBY FLIGHTS

Traveling standby requires considerable flexibility in arrival and departure dates and cities. Companies dealing in standby flights sell vouchers rather than tickets, along with the promise to get to your destination (or near your destination) within a certain window of time (typically 1-5 days). Call in before your specific window of time to hear your flight options and the probability that you will be able to board each flight. Vouchers can usually be bought for both one-way and round-trip travel. You may receive a monetary refund if every available flight within your date range is full; if you opt not to take an available (but perhaps less convenient) flight, you can only get credit toward future travel.

Carefully read agreements with any company offering standby flights as tricky fine print can leave you in a lurch. To check on a company's service record in the US, call the Better Business Bureau (☎212-533-6200). It is difficult to receive refunds, and clients' vouchers will not be honored when an airline fails to receive payment in time. One established standby company in the US is Whole Earth Travel, 325 W. 38th St., New York, NY 10018 (☎800-326-2009; fax 212-864-5489; www.4standby.com) and Los Angeles, CA (☎888-247-4482), which offers one-way flights to Europe from the Northeast (US$169), West Coast and Northwest (US$249), Midwest (US$219), and Southeast (US$199). Connecting flights within the US or Europe cost US$79-139.

AIR COURIER FLIGHTS

Couriers help transport cargo on international flights by using their checked luggage space for freight. Generally, couriers must be over 21 (in some cases 18) and travel with carry-ons only. Most flights are round-trip only, with short fixed-length stays (usually one week) and a limit of a one ticket per issue. Most of these flights also operate only out of major gateway cities, mostly in North America. In summer, the most popular destinations usually require an advance reservation of about two weeks (you can usually book up to two months ahead). Super-discounted fares are common for "last-minute" flights (three to 14 days ahead).

FROM NORTH AMERICA

Round-trip courier fares from the US to Paris run about US$200-500. Most flights leave from New York, Los Angeles, San Francisco, or Miami in the US; and from Montreal, Toronto, or Vancouver in Canada. The organizations below provide members with lists of opportunities and courier brokers for an annual fee. Prices quoted below are round-trip.

Air Courier Association, 350 Indiana St. #300, Golden, CO 80401 (☎800-282-1202; www.aircourier.org). 10 departure cities throughout the US and Canada to Paris (high-season US$150-360). 1-year membership US$49.

International Association of Air Travel Couriers (IAATC), PO Box 980, Keystone Heights, FL 32656 (☎352-475-1584; fax 475-5326; www.courier.org). From 9 North American cities to Western European cities, including Paris. 1-year membership US$45.

Global Courier Travel, PO Box 3051, Nederland, CO 80466 (www.globalcouriertravel.com). Searchable online database. 6 departure points in the US and Canada to Paris. Lifetime membership US$40, 2 people US$55.

NOW Voyager, 315 W 49th St., New York, NY 10019 (☎212-459-1616; fax 262-7407). To Paris (US$499-699). Usually 1-week max. stay. 1-year membership US$50. Non-courier discount fares also available.

FROM THE UK, IRELAND, AUSTRALIA, & NEW ZEALAND

The minimum age for couriers from the **UK** is usually 18. **Brave New World Enterprises,** P.O. Box 22212, London SE5 8WB (www.courierflights.com) publishes a directory of all the companies offering courier flights in the UK (UK£10, in electronic form UK£8). **Global Courier Travel** (see above) also offers flights from London and Dublin to continental Europe. **British Airways Travel Shop** (☎0870 240 0747; www.batravelshops.com) arranges some flights from London to destinations in continental Europe (specials may be as low as UK£60; no registration fee). From Australia and New Zealand, Global Courier Travel (see above) often has listings from Sydney and Auckland to London and occasionally Frankfurt.

TICKET CONSOLIDATORS

Ticket consolidators, or **"bucket shops,"** buy unsold tickets in bulk from commercial airlines and sell them at discounted rates. The best place to look is in the Sunday travel section of any major newspaper, where many bucket shops place ads. Call early, as availability is typically extremely limited. Not all bucket shops are reliable, so get a receipt that gives full details of restrictions, refunds, and tickets, and pay by credit card (2-5% fee) so you can stop payment if you never receive tickets. For more, go to www.travel-library.com/air-travel/consolidators.html.

FROM THE US & CANADA

Travel Avenue (☎800-333-3335; www.travelavenue.com) searches for best available published fares and then uses several consolidators to attempt to beat that fare. **NOW Voyager,** 74 Varick St., Ste. 307, New York, NY 10013 (☎212-431-1616; fax 219-1793; www.nowvoyagertravel.com) arranges discounted flights to Paris and other European cities, mostly from New York. Other consolidators worth trying are **Interworld** (☎305-443-4929; fax 443-0351); **Rebel** (☎800-227-3235; www.rebeltours.com); **Travac** (☎800-872-8800; fax 212-714-9063; www.travac.com); **TravelHUB** (www.travelhub.com). Keep in mind that these are just suggestions to get you started in your research; *Let's Go* does not endorse any of these agencies. As always, be cautious and research companies before you hand over your credit card number.

FROM THE UK, AUSTRALIA, & NEW ZEALAND

In London, the **Air Travel Advisory Bureau** (☎0207 636 5000; www.atab.co.uk) can provide names of reliable consolidators and discount flight specialists. From Australia and New Zealand, look for consolidator ads in the travel section of the *Sydney Morning Herald* and other papers.

CHARTER FLIGHTS

Charters are flights a tour operator contracts with an airline to fly extra loads of passengers during peak season. Charter flights fly less frequently than major airlines, make refunds particularly difficult, and are almost always fully booked. Schedules and itineraries may also change or be cancelled at the last moment (as late as 48hr. before the trip, and without a full refund), and check-in, boarding, and baggage claim are often much slower. However, charter flights can be cheaper.

Discount clubs and **fare brokers** offer members savings on last-minute charter and tour deals. Study contracts closely; you don't want to end up with an unwanted overnight layover. **Travelers Advantage** (☎203-365-2000; www.travelersadvantage.com; US$60 annual fee includes discounts and cheap flight directories) specializes in European travel and tour packages.

BY TRAIN

SNCF (☎08 92 35 35 35, €0.34 per min; www.sncf.fr) offers a wide range of discounted roundtrip tickets for travelers in France called **tarifs découvertes**—you should rarely have to pay full price. Further discounts are available with the purchase of special cards, for those under 25, children, and adults traveling together. Get a calendar from a train station detailing *période bleue* (blue period), *période blanche* (white period), and *période rouge* (red period) times and days; blue gets the most discounts, while red gets none. Even without the cards, all of the above groups are automatically entitled to lesser reductions (usually 25% rather than 50%).

Reserve and purchase tickets at least one week **in advance.** Trains are especially full in the summer and on weekends. Buyer beware: unexpected strikes *(grèves)* are quite normal for the SNCF lines, so call ahead to confirm your departure time.

DESTINATIONS & RATES

The prices below are the **undiscounted fares** for one-way, second-class tickets unless otherwise noted. Summer schedules are listed. In general, prices and number of trips per day vary according to the day of the week, season, and other criteria. A word on **safety:** each terminal shelters its share of thieves. Gare du Nord and Gare d'Austerlitz are rough at night, when drugs and prostitution emerge. Official counters are the only safe (financially and otherwise) places to buy tickets. For the most current timetables and prices, consult the SNCF website at **www.sncf.fr.**

Gare du Nord: Trains to northern France, Britain, Belgium, the Netherlands, Scandinavia, the Commonwealth of Independent States, and northern Germany (Cologne, Hamburg) all depart

from this station. To: Brussels (1½hr., 28 per day, €66); Amsterdam (4-5hr., 6 per day, €87); Cologne (4hr., 7 per day, €78); London (by the Eurostar Chunnel; 3hr. approx. 12-28 per day, up to €299).

Gare de l'Est: To eastern France (Champagne, Alsace, Lorraine, Strasbourg), Luxembourg, parts of Switzerland (Basel, Zürich, Lucerne), southern Germany (Frankfurt, Munich), Austria, Hungary, and Prague. To: Luxembourg (4hr., 10 per day, €50); Strasbourg (4hr., 13 per day, €39); Zürich (6-7hr., 10 per day, €110); Munich (9hr., 14 per day, €130); Vienna (13hr., 5 per day, €180); Prague (16hr., 1 per day, €180).

Gare de Lyon: To southern and southeastern France (Lyon, Provence, Riviera), parts of Switzerland (Geneva, Lausanne, Berne), Italy, and Greece. To: Geneva (4hr., 7 per day, €69); Florence (13hr., 4 per day, €145); Rome (15hr., 4-5 per day, €160); Lyon (2hr., 23 per day, €35); Nice (6hr., 8 per day, €60); Marseille (4-5hr., 18 per day, €84).

Gare d'Austerlitz: To the Loire Valley, southwestern France (Bordeaux, Pyrénées), Spain, and Portugal. (TGV to southwestern France leaves from Gare Montparnasse.) To Barcelona (9hr., 1 per day, €97) and Madrid (12-13hr., 4 per day, €102).

Gare St-Lazare: To Normandy. To Caen (2hr., 9 per day, €26.20) and Rouen (1-2hr., 13 per day, €17.40).

Gare Montparnasse: To Brittany and southwestern France on the TGV. To Rennes (2hr., 30 per day, €46).

RAILPASSES

Those planning on leaving Paris for a time and train-hopping from city to city in Europe will profit from a railpass. Ideally, a railpass would allow you to spontaneously jump on any train, head to any destination, and alter your plans at whim. In practice, things are not that simple. You still wait in line to pay for supplements and seat and *couchette* reservations. Worse, railpasses aren't necessarily cost-effective. There are always discounts on rail travel in France and good deals (especially for those under 25) are usually waiting to be found. To evaluate your options more precisely, get the prices of relevant point-to-point tickets from the SNCF web site, add them, and compare with railpass prices. Both Europass and Eurailpass are harder to get in European cities, so you should consider buying one before you go.

Eurailpass (www.raileurope.com) is valid in most of Western Europe: Austria, Belgium, Denmark, Finland, France, Germany, Greece, Hungary, Italy, Luxembourg, the Netherlands, Norway, Portugal, the Republic of Ireland, Spain, Sweden, and Switzerland. It is not valid in the UK. **Standard Eurailpasses** are valid for a predetermined number of consecutive days; they work best if you spend a lot of time on trains every few days. **Flexipasses,** valid for any 10 or 15 days within a two-month period, are more cost-effective for those traveling long distances but less frequently. **Saverpasses** provide first-class travel for travelers in groups of two to five. **Youthpasses** and **Youth Flexipasses** provide parallel perks for those under 26. All the prices quoted below are for second-class travel, per person.

EURAILPASSES	15 DAYS	21 DAYS	1 MONTH	2 MONTHS	3 MONTHS
1st class Eurailpass	US$588	US$762	US$946	US$1338	US$1654
Eurail Saverpass	US$498	US$648	US$804	US$1138	US$1408
Eurail Youthpass	US$414	US$534	US$664	US$938	US$1160

EURAIL FLEXIPASSES	10 DAYS IN 2 MONTHS	15 DAYS IN 2 MONTHS
1st class Eurail Flexipass	US$694	US$914
Eurail Saver Flexipass	US$592	US$778
Eurail Youth Flexipass	US$488	US$642

BY BUS

British travelers may find buses the cheapest (though slowest) way of getting to Paris, with return fares starting around UK£50. Obviously, the bus trip will also entail a ferry trip or occasionally a descent into the Channel Tunnel; these extra trips are typically included in the price of a ticket. **Eurolines** is Europe's largest operator of international coach services; their return fares between London and Paris start at €30. They have offices in **London,** 4 Cardiff Rd., Luton, Bedfordshirt L41 IPP (UK ☎0990 143 219; fax 01582 400 694; www.eurolines.co.uk), and in **Paris,** 22, r. Malmaison, 93177 Banolet Cédex (☎01 49 72 57 80; fax 01 49 72 57 99; www.eurolines.fr).

BY CHUNNEL FROM THE UK

Traversing 27 mi. under the sea, the Chunnel is undoubtedly the fastest, most convenient, and least scenic route from England to France.

Eurostar, Eurostar House, Waterloo Station, London SE1 8SE (UK ☎0990 186 186; US ☎800-387-6782; elsewhere call UK +44 (0)20 7928 5163; www.eurostar.com; www.raileurope.com) runs frequent trains between London and the continent. Ten to twenty-eight trains per day run to Paris (3hr., US$75-159, 2nd class), Brussels (4hr., US$75-159, 2nd class), and Eurodisney. Routes include stops at Ashford in England, and Calais and Lille in France. Book at major rail stations in the UK, at the office above, by phone, or on the web.

Eurotunnel (UK ☎Customer relations, P.O. Box 2000, Folkestone, Kent CT18 8XY; www.eurotunnel.co.uk) shuttles cars and passengers between Kent and Nord-Pas-de-Calais. Return fares for vehicle and all passengers range from UK£219-317 with car, UK£259-636 with campervan. Same-day return costs UK£110-150, 5-day return UK£139-195. Book online or via phone. Travelers with cars can also look into sea crossings by ferry (see below).

BY BOAT FROM THE UK & IRELAND

The fares below are **one-way** for **adult foot passengers** unless otherwise noted. Though standard return fares are usually just twice the one-way fare, **fixed-period returns** (usually within five days) are almost invariably cheaper. Ferries run **year-round** unless otherwise noted. **Bikes** are usually free, although you may have to pay up to UK£10 in high season. For a **camper/trailer** supplement, you will have to add UK£20-140 to the "with car" fare. If more than one price is quoted, the quote in UK£ is valid for departures from the UK, etc. A directory of ferries in this region can be found at www.seaview.co.uk/ferries.html.

P&O Stena Line: UK ☎087 0600 0611; from Europe 44 13 04 86 40 03; www.posl.com. Dover to Calais (1¼hr.; every 30min.-1hr., 30 per day; UK£24).

Hoverspeed: UK ☎08705 240 24; France ☎008 00 1211 1211; www.hoverspeed.co.uk. Dover to Calais (35-55min., every hr., UK£24). Newhaven to Dieppe, France (2¼-4¼hr., 1-3 per day, UK£28).

SeaFrance: UK ☎08705 711 711; France ☎08 03 04 40 45; www.seafrance.co.uk. Dover to Calais (1½hr., 15 per day, UK£15).

Brittany Ferries: UK ☎08703 665 333; France ☎08 25 82 88 28; www.brittany-ferries.com. Plymouth to Roscoff, France (6hr.; summer 1-3 per day, low-season 1 per week; UK£20-58 or €21-46). Portsmouth to St-Malo (8¾hr., 1-2 per day, €23-49) and Caen (6hr, 1-3 per day, €21-44), France. Poole to Cherbourg (4¼hr., 1-2 per day, €21-44). Cork to Roscoff (13½hr., Apr.-Sept. 1 per week, €52-99), France.

Irish Ferries: France ☎01 44 88 54 50; Ireland ☎1890 31 31 31; UK ☎08705 17 17 17; www.irishferries.ie. Rosslare to Cherbourg and Roscoff (17-18hr.; Apr.-Sept. 1-9 per week; €60-120, students €48).

Stena Line: UK ☎44 1233 64 68 26; www.stenaline.co.uk. Harwich to Hook of Holland (5hr., UK£26). Fishguard to Rosslare (1-3½hr.; UK£18-21, students £14-17).

SPECIFIC CONCERNS

WOMEN TRAVELERS

Women traveling alone or with other women should expect to be hassled by men, even in busy areas, especially at night (see **Non Means No!,** p. 74). Women should exercise caution, maintain a confident gait, and avoid direct eye contact with intimidating men. Sunglasses will serve you well. Parisian women often respond to verbal harassment with an icy stare, but you should do your best to avoid conflict. Speaking to *dragueurs* (as the French call them), even to say "NO!", is only to invite a reply, but if you feel threatened don't hesitate to call out to others or to draw attention to yourself. A loud *"laissez-moi tranquille!"* ("leave me alone!") or *"au secours!"* ("help!") will hopefully send them on their way. Harassment can be minimized by making yourself as inconspicuous as possible, though in some cases you may be harassed no matter how you're dressed. Wearing a conspicuous wedding ring may dissuade unwanted overtures. *Let's Go: Paris* lists crisis numbers in **Once In Paris,** p. 25. **In an emergency, dial ☎17 for police assistance.**

TRAVELING ALONE

There are many benefits to traveling alone, among them greater independence and challenge. On the other hand, any solo traveler is a more vulnerable target of harassment and street theft. Lone travelers need to be well-organized and look confident at all times. Try not to stand out as a tourist, and be especially careful in deserted or very crowded areas. If questioned, never admit that you are traveling alone. Maintain regular contact with someone at home who knows your itinerary.

For more tips, pick up *Traveling Solo* by Eleanor Berman (Globe Pequot Press; US$17) or subscribe to **Connecting: Solo Travel Network,** 689 Park Road, Unit 6, Gibsons, BC V0N 1V7 (☎604-886-9099; www.cstn.org; membership US$35).

Alternatively, several services link solo travelers with companions who have similar travel habits and interests; contact the **Travel Companion Exchange,** P.O. Box 833, Amityville, NY 11701 (☎631-454-0880; www.whytravelalone.com; US$48).

OLDER TRAVELERS

In Paris, most museums, concerts, and sights offer reduced prices for visitors over 60. Tour buses and Seine River boat tours, such as the **Bateaux Mouches** (see **Tours** in the **Service Directory,** p. 346) enable you to see a large number of sights without walking great distances. *Let's Go: Paris* tries to list at least one hotel in every *arrondissement* that is accessible to those with limited mobility (see **Travelers with Disabilities,** p. 324). When booking your hotel, ask for a room on the first floor or inquire about access to the elevator. We've also tried to list at least one mid-priced quality hotel in each *arrondissement* so you can avoid the sometimes noisy young crowd at the hostels. Senior citizens are eligible for a wide range of discounts on transportation, museums, movies, theaters, concerts, restaurants, and accommodations. If you don't see a senior citizen price listed, ask, and you may be delightfully surprised. The books *No Problem! Worldwise Tips for Mature Adventurers,* by Janice Kenyon (Orca Book Publishers; US$16) and *Unbelievably Good Deals and Great Adventures That You Absolutely Can't Get Unless You're Over 50,* by Joan Rattner Heilman (NTC/Contemporary Publishing; US$13) are both excellent resources. For more information, contact one of the following organizations:

Elderhostel, 11 Ave. de Lafayette, Boston, MA 02111 (☎877-426-8056 M-F 9am-9pm; www.elderhostel.org). Organizes 1- to 4-week programs at colleges, universities, and other learning centers all over the world, including Paris. Must be 55 or over. For volunteer opportunities with Elderhostel, see p. 332.

The Mature Traveler, P.O. Box 15791, Sacramento, CA 95852 (☎800-460-6676; www.thematuretraveler.com). Deals, discounts, and packages for the 50+ traveler. Subscription $30.

Walking the World, P.O. Box 1186, Fort Collins, CO 80522 (☎800-340-9255; www.walkingtheworld.com), organizes trips to various destinations in France for travelers over 50.

BGLT TRAVELERS

Next to Berlin, London, and Amsterdam, Paris has one of the largest gay populations in Europe. Paris's queer communities are vibrant, politically active, and full of opportunities for fun (see **Festivals,** p. 18; **Nightlife,** p. 205; and **The Media,** p. 36). Listed below are contact organizations, mail-order bookstores, and publishers that offer materials addressing some specific concerns. **Out and About** (www.outandabout.com) offers a bi-weekly newsletter addressing travel concerns. See **Service Directory** (p. 343) for resources in Paris.

Gay's the Word, 66 Marchmont St., London WC1N 1AB (☎44 20 7278 7654; www.gaystheword.co.uk). The largest gay and lesbian bookshop in the UK, with both fiction and non-fiction titles. Mail-order service available.

Giovanni's Room, 1145 Pine St., Philadelphia, PA 19107 (☎215-923-2960; www.queerbooks.com). An international lesbian/feminist and gay bookstore with mail-order service (carries many of the publications listed below).

International Gay and Lesbian Travel Association, 4331 N. Federal Hwy. #304, Ft. Lauderdale, FL 33308 (☎954-776-2626; www.iglta.com). An organization of over 1350 companies serving gay and lesbian travelers worldwide.

International Lesbian and Gay Association (ILGA), 81, r. Marché-au-Charbon, B-1000 Brussels, Belgium (☎32 2 502 2471; www.ilga.org). Provides political information pertinent to traveling queers, such as homosexuality laws of individual countries.

ESSENTIAL INFORMATION

PACKING FOR PARIS

Pack lightly! Take half the clothes that you think you'll need, and twice the money.

CURRENT & ADAPTERS

In France, electric current is 220 volts AC, enough to fry any 110V North American appliance. A French electrical plug has two prongs and a round pin. Americans and Canadians should buy both an adapter (which changes the shape of the plug) and a converter (which changes the voltage; US$25). Don't make the mistake of using only an adapter, unless an appliance's instructions explicitly states otherwise. New Zealanders and South Africans (who both use 220V at home) as well as Australians (who use 240/250V) won't need a converter, but will need a set of adapters to use anything electrical.

FILM

Airport carry-on X-ray machines should not affect or in any way alter film of speeds 400 and under. Be sure to always pack film in your carry-on luggage, as higher-intensity X-rays are used on checked luggage.

FURTHER READING

There are several gay- and lesbian-oriented specialty travel guides, including *Spartacus International Gay Guide*, by Bruno Gmunder Verlag (US$33), and Damron Travel Guides' series of guides, including *Damron Men's Guide*, *Damron's Accommodations*, and *The Women's Traveller* (US$14-19). For further information on Damron titles, call ☎800-462-6654 or visit them online at www.damron.com. *Ferrari Guides' Gay Travel A to Z*, *Ferrari Guides' Men's Travel in Your Pocket*, and *Ferrari Guides' Inn Places* (US$16-20) are all available from Ferrari Publications; purchase the guides online at www.ferrariguides.com. *The Gay Vacation Guide: The Best Trips and How to Plan Them*, by Mark Chesnut, is available from Citadel Press (US$15).

TRAVELERS WITH DISABILITIES

Many of Paris' museums and sights are fully accessible to wheelchairs and some provide guided tours in sign language. Unfortunately, budget hotels and restaurants are generally ill-equipped to handle the needs of disabled visitors. Handicapped-accessible bathrooms are virtually non-existent among hotels in the one- to two-star range, and many elevators could double as shoeboxes. *Let's Go: Paris* tries to list at least one wheelchair-accessible hotel in each *arrondissement;* see "wheelchair-accessible" in the index for a full list of **wheelchair-accessible hotels.** Note that the hotels described as such are those with reasonably wide elevators or with ground-floor rooms wide enough for wheelchair entry. To ask restaurants, hotels, railways, and airlines if they are accessible, say: *"Etes-vous accessible aux fauteuils roulants?"* Many establishments can provide a ramp if you ask for one. If transporting a **seeing-eye dog** to France, you will need a rabies vaccination certificate issued from home.

The RATP and its personnel are generally well-equipped to assist blind or deaf passengers. Very few métro stations are wheelchair accessible, but RER lines A and B are. For a guide to métro accessibility, pick up a free copy of the RATP's brochure, *Lignes et stations équipées pour Personnes à Besoins Spécifiques* (☎01 45 83 67 77 for information regarding wheelchair-accessible stations; ☎08 36 68 41 14 for help in English), which provide a list of stations equipped with escalators, elevators, and moving walkways. Public buses are not yet wheelchair accessible except for line 20, which runs from Gare de Lyon to Gare St-Lazare. Taxis are required by law to take passengers in wheelchairs. **Airhop** (☎01 41 29 01 29; reserve 48hr. in advance) and **GIHP** (☎01 41 83 15 15) offer transport to and from the airport for the motion impaired (see **Once in Paris,** p. 23).

USEFUL ORGANIZATIONS

Mobility International USA (MIUSA), P.O. Box 10767, Eugene, OR 97440 (☎541-343-1284, voice and TDD; www.miusa.org). Sells *A World of Options: A Guide to International Educational Exchange, Community Service, and Travel for Persons with Disabilities* (US$35).

Society for Accessible Travel and Hospitality (SATH), 347 Fifth Ave., #610, New York, NY 10016 (☎212-447-7284; www.sath.org). An advocacy group that publishes free online travel information and the travel magazine *Open World* (US$18, free for members). Annual membership US$45, students and seniors US$30.

Directions Unlimited, 123 Green Ln., Bedford Hills, NY 10507 (☎800-533-5343). Books individual and group vacations for the physically disabled; not an info service.

The Guided Tour Inc., 7900 Old York Rd., #114B, Elkins Park, PA 19027 (☎800-783-5841; www.guidedtour.com). Organizes travel programs for persons with developmental and physical challenges in the US, Canada, Ireland, Cancún, and Paris.

AGENCIES IN PARIS

L'Association des Paralysés de France, Délégation de Paris, 17, bd. Auguste-Blanqui, 13*ème* (☎01 40 78 69 00; www.apf.asso.fr). M: Place d'Italie. Consult the web site for publications regarding wheelchair-accessible hotels in Paris. Open M-F 9am-noon and 2-5:30pm.

Audio-Vision Guides. Spoken service for the blind or vision-impaired, which describes the costumes, sets, and theater design. At Parisian theaters such as the Théâtre National de Chaillot, 1, pl. Trocadéro, 11 Novembre, 16*ème* (☎01 53 65 31 00), the Comédie Française, 2, r. de Richelieu, 1*er* (☎01 44 58 14 00), and the Théâtre National de la Colline, 15, r. Malte-Brun, 20*ème* (☎01 44 62 52 00).

FURTHER READING

Global Access (www.geocities.com/Paris/1502/disabilitylinks.html) has links for disabled travelers. Also try: *Access in Paris*, Gordon Couch (Quiller Press; US$12); *Resource Directory for the Disabled*, Richard Neil Shrout (Facts on File; US$14); and *Wheelchair Through Europe*, Annie Mackin (Graphic Language Press; US$13).

MINORITY TRAVELERS

Despite Paris's extraordinary diversity and its wealth of multi-ethnic restaurants and cultural events, racism is a serious problem here; France's postcolonial legacy is not, predictably, a happy one. Travelers of Arab, North African, or West African descent are more likely than Caucasians to be stopped by the police and may be met with suspicious or derogatory glances from passersby. In addition, incidents of anti-Semitism have become both more frequent and more violent in the last few years. While anti-Semitic sentiment is by no means the norm in Paris, which is home to half of France's nearly 600,000 Jews, Jewish visitors should be aware that religious tension is a current issue in Paris and throughout France. See **Life & Times** (p. 52) and **Alternatives to Tourism** (p. 331) for more information on these issues.

Should you confront race-based exclusion or violence, you should make a formal complaint to the police. It is also a good idea to work through either SOS Racisme or MRAP in order to facilitate your progress through a confusing foreign bureaucracy. (For additional listings consult **Minority Resources** in the **Service Directory,** p. 344.)

SOS Racisme, 28, r. des Petites Ecuries, 10*ème* (☎01 40 35 36 55; www.sos-racisme.org). Primarily helps illegal immigrants and people whose documentation is irregular. They provide legal services and are used to negotiating with police. Open M-F 9:30am-6pm.

MRAP (Mouvement contre le racisme et pour l'amitié entre les peuples), 43, bd. Magenta, 10*ème* (☎01 53 38 99 99; www.mrap.asso.fr). Handles immigration issues and monitors racist publications and propaganda. Open M-Sa 9am-noon and 2-6pm.

TRAVELERS WITH CHILDREN

Regardless of the fact that Paris offers a dizzying array of sights, sounds, and, above all, smells, those traveling with children will need to plan their days ahead. Given that their legs and attention span are generally shorter than those of adults, kids will soon tire and cease to care who painted the Mona Lisa, or who once drank thirty martinis at the Café de Flore.

Thankfully, there are a plethora of sights and attractions that are just for kids in Paris. For a *Let's Go* thumb in the right direction, see **Sights,** p. 94. A good way to plan the day with children is in bite-sized segments, allowing for an afternoon nap (especially in the August heat), and frequent, strategic breaks for the other great pacifier: Parisian sweets (see **Food & Drink,** p. 200). The other good news is that while the French might love to hate you, the attitude barrier does not apply to little ones, who will most often be accommodated in restaurants, cafés, and (heaven forbid) bars. Cheaper restaurants and chains often have children's menus. Hotels generally have a minimal charge for an extra bed or cot, called a *lit supplementaire.* Travelers with babies should have no problem finding the necessary supplies in supermarkets and pharmacies.

The Paris magazine *L'Officiel des Spectacles* (€0.35), available at any newsstand, has a section, entitled *Pour Les Jeunes,* that lists exhibits, programs, and movies appropriate for children. **Be sure that your child carries some sort of ID** in case of an emergency or in case he or she gets lost.

FURTHER READING

Helpful sources include: *Gutsy Mamas: Travel Tips and Wisdom for Mothers on the Road,* Marybeth Bond (Travelers' Tales, Inc.; US$8); *How to take Great Trips with Your Kids,* Sanford and Jane Portnoy (Harvard Common Press; US $10); *Trouble Free Travel with Children,* Vicki Lansky (Book Peddlers; US$9); *On the Go With Baby: A Stress Free Guide to Getting Across Town or Around the World,* Ericka Lutz (Sourcebooks Trade; $US15); and *The Penny Whistle Traveling-with-Kids Book,* Meredith Brokaw (Fireside; US$14).

DIETARY CONCERNS

Those with special dietary requirements may not find Paris to be the most accommodating of cities; **vegetarians** will find dining out difficult, **vegans** even more so. But there's hope: Paris has many ethnic restaurants and a growing number of strictly vegetarian ones. *Let's Go* has tried to list as many vegetarian- and vegan-friendly restaurants as possible (see **Food**, p. 167). For more info on vegetarian travel, contact the **North American Vegetarian Society** (P.O. Box 72, Dolgeville, NY 13329; US ☎518-568-7970; www.navs-online.org) for a copy of *Transformative Adventures, Vacations, and Retreats* (US$15). Another good resource is www.vegdining.com, which gives web sites and contact info for vegetarian and vegan restaurants worldwide.

Kosher delis, restaurants, and bakeries abound in the *3ème* and *4ème arrondissements*, particularly on r. des Rosiers and r. des Ecouffes. Contact the **Union Libéral Israélite de France Synagogue** (see **Religious Services** in the **Service Directory,** p. 345) for more information on kosher restaurants. **The Jewish Travel Guide,** edited by Michael Zaidner (Vallentine Mitchell; US$17), lists synagogues, kosher restaurants, and Jewish institutions in over 100 countries. In addition, www.shamash.org/kosher has a comprehensive kosher restaurant database.

FURTHER READING

The Vegetarian Traveler: Where to Stay if You're Vegetarian, Vegan, or Environmentally Sensitive, by Jed and Susan Civic (US$16), and *The Jewish Travel Guide*, by Betsy Sheldon (Hunter; US$17), are excellent sources.

OTHER RESOURCES

BOOKS

Cultural Misunderstandings: The French-American Experience, Raymonde Carroll, trans. Carol Volk. University of Chicago Press, 1990 (US$13). An interesting academic examination of cross-cultural communication; useful for Americans baffled by the French outlook on life.

Fragile Glory: A Portrait of France & the French, Richard Bernstein. Plume, 1991 (US$15). A witty, nuanced look at France by the former Paris bureau chief of *The New York Times*.

Wicked French: For the Traveler, Howard Tomb. Workman, 1989 (US$5). A hilarious guide to everything you really didn't need to know how to say in French.

A Traveller's Wine Guide to France, Christopher Fielden. Traveller's Wine Guides, 1999. (US$18). Exactly what it says it is, by a well-known oenophile.

The Food Lover's Guide to Paris, Patricia Wells. Workman, 1999 (US$18). A fabulous guide to all things culinary by the food critic for the *International Herald Tribune.*

Michelin Green Guides, Michelin. Around US$20. The authoritative guide to France, this series covers the country in 24 regional books with unbeatable information on towns and sights. You'll still need your trusty *Let's Go* for all your practical information, accommodations, and food needs.

WORLD WIDE WEB

Maison de la France (www.maison-de-la-france.com) is the main government tourist site. Up-to-date information on tourism in France, including a calendar of festivals and major events, regional info with links to local servers, and a host of tips on everything from accommodation to smoking laws. English version available.

France Diplomatie (www.france.diplomatie.fr) is the French Department of Foreign Affairs site, with information on visas and other official matters, as well as comprehensive info on French history, culture, geography, politics, and current affairs. English version available.

WWW.LETSGO.COM Our website, www.letsgo.com, now includes introductory chapters from all our guides and a wealth of information on a monthly featured destination. As always, our website also has info about our books, a travel forum buzzing with stories and tips, and additional links that will help you make the most of a trip to Paris. In addition, all nine Let's Go City Guides are available for download on Palm OS PDAs.

Secretariat for Tourism (www.tourisme.gouv.fr) has a number of government documents and press releases relating to the state of tourism in France, plus links to all the national, regional and departmental tourist authorities. In French.

Tourism in France (www.tourisme.fr) has information on all types of tourism in France and an extensive directory of links to local resources. In French and English.

Paris Tourist Office (www.paris-touristoffice.com) has information on everything from babysitting agencies to hotel reservations in Paris. In French and English.

Nomade (www.nomade.fr) and **French Excite** (www.excite.fr) are popular French search engines—though they're not very useful if you can't read French.

Pariscope (www.pariscope.fr) has the popular French publication's events listings. In French.

TF1 (www.tf1.com) is the home page of France's most popular TV station, with news, popular culture, and weather and traffic reports. In French.

Météo-France (www.meteo.fr) has 2-day weather forecasts and maps for France. In French.

PATISSERIES MAISON
Tarte aux fruits 28F
Crème brûlée 34F
Tarte aux Pommes 24F

INSIDE

Alternatives to Tourism

When we started out in 1961, about 1.7 million people were traveling internationally each year; in 2002, nearly 700 million trips were made, projected to be up to a billion by 2010. The dramatic rise in tourism has created an interdependence between the economy, environment, and culture of many destinations and the tourists they host. Every year, Paris alone welcomes millions of tourists.

Most of those tourists will see a Paris that is a capital of art, fashion, food, and culture; a Paris that ranks as one of the world's wealthiest cities, where the majority of people enjoy an extraordinarily high quality of life. But travelers driven to understand another side of Paris will find a city plagued by issues of social and economic injustice—and a number of organizations that work tirelessly to address those issues.

Unemployment remains at high rates (around 9%) in and around Paris; the poverty in the *cités* (housing projects) of the suburbs is especially grim, and the largely immigrant populations there also face racism and discrimination (as evidenced by the shocking success of the virulently anti-immigrant Front National in the 2002 election), as well as rising religious fundamentalism. Recently the traumas—from oppression and shame to gang rape and murder—endured by the women of *cités* have been the subject of protest and activism (for more on this, see **Modern Mariannes,** p. 109). Other issues of current concern in Paris include gay rights, AIDS research and support, anti-Semitism, and the rights of mentally and physically handicapped individuals. No traveler, obviously, can solve these problems, and "getting involved" is not as easy as we might wish. Nonetheless, opportunities for making a difference, however small, are available to those who seek them—and awareness is a powerful first step.

A NEW PHILOSOPHY OF TRAVEL

We at *Let's Go* have watched the growth of the "ignorant tourist" stereotype with dismay, knowing that the majority of travelers care passionately about the state of the communities and environments they explore—but also knowing that even conscientious tourists can inadvertently damage natural wonders, rich cultures, and impoverished communities. We believe the philosophy of **sustainable travel** is among the most important travel tips we could impart to our readers, to help guide fellow backpackers and on-the-road philanthropists. By staying aware of the needs and troubles of local communities, today's travelers can be a powerful force in preserving and restoring this fragile world.

Working against the negative consequences of irresponsible tourism is much simpler than it might seem; it is often self-awareness, rather than self-sacrifice, that makes the biggest difference. Simply by trying to spend responsibly and conserve local resources, all travelers can positively impact the places they visit. *Let's Go* has partnered with **BEST** (**Business Enterprises for Sustainable Travel,** an affiliate of the Conference Board; see **www.sustainabletravel.org**), which recognizes businesses that operate based on the principles of sustainable travel. Below, they provide advice on how ordinary visitors can practice this philosophy in their daily travels, no matter where they are.

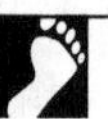

TIPS FOR CIVIC TRAVEL: HOW TO MAKE A DIFFERENCE

Travel by train when feasible. Rail travel requires only half the energy per passenger mile that planes do. On average, each of the 40,000 daily domestic air flights releases more than 1700 pounds of greenhouse gas emissions.

Use public mass transportation whenever possible; outside of cities, take advantage of group taxis or vans. Bicycles are an attractive way of seeing a community first-hand. And enjoy walking–purchase good maps of your destination and ask about on-foot touring opportunities.

When renting a car, ask whether fuel-efficient vehicles are available. Honda and Toyota produce cars that use hybrid engines powered by electricity and gasoline, thus reducing emissions of carbon dioxide. Ford Motor Company plans to introduce a hybrid fuel model by the end of 2004.

Reduce, reuse, recycle–use electronic tickets, recycle papers and bottles wherever possible, and avoid using containers made of styrofoam. Refillable water bottles and rechargable batteries both efficiently conserve expendable resources.

Be thoughtful in your purchases. Take care not to buy souvenir objects made from trees in old-growth or endangered forests, such as teak, or items made from endangered species, like ivory or tortoise jewelry. Ask whether products are made from renewable resources.

Buy from local enterprises, such as casual street vendors. In developing countries and low-income neighborhoods, many people depend on the "informal economy" to make a living.

Be on-the-road-philanthropists. If you are inspired by the natural environment of a destination or enriched by its culture, join in preserving their integrity by making a charitable contribution to a local organization.

Spread the word. Upon your return home, tell friends and colleagues about places to visit that will benefit greatly from their tourist dollars, and reward sustainable enterprises by recommending their services. Travelers can not only introduce friends to particular vendors but also to local causes and charities that they might choose to support when they travel.

VOLUNTEERING

Those looking to volunteer in the efforts to resolve the issues faced by the regions and communities they visit have many options. In this section, we recommend organizations that can help you find the opportunities that best suit your interests, whether you're looking to pitch in for a day or a year.

Most people who volunteer in Paris do so on a short-term basis, at organizations that make use of drop-in or once-a-week volunteers. The best way to find opportunities that match up with your interests and schedule may be to check with **www.volunteerabroad.com,** a resource which offers listings and descriptions of volunteer positions available all over the world, including Paris. Another option is to contact Care France (see below) for information on community service opportunities.

More intensive volunteer services may charge you a fee to participate. These costs can be surprisingly hefty (although they frequently cover airfare and most, if not all, living expenses). Most people choose to go through a parent organization that takes care of logistical details and frequently provides a group environment and support system. There are two main types of organizations—religious and non-sectarian—although there are rarely restrictions on participation for either.

Before handing your money over to any volunteer or study abroad program, make sure you know exactly what you're getting into. It's a good idea to get the name of **previous participants** and ask them about their experience, as some programs sound much better on paper than in reality. The **questions** below are a good place to start:

–What are the other participants like? How old are they? How much will you be expected to interact with them?

–Is room and board included? If so, what is the arrangement? Will you be expected to share a room? A bathroom? What are the meals like? Do they fit any dietary restrictions?

–Is transportation included? Are there any additional expenses?

–How much free time will you have? Will you be able to travel around?

–What kind of safety network is set up? Will you still be covered by your home insurance? Does the program have an emergency plan?

ORGANIZATIONS IN PARIS

Secours Populaire Françes, 9-11, r. Foissart, 75140 (☎01 44 78 21 00; www.secourspopulaire.asso.fr). A non-profit organization that provides aid and support to poor children and families into society through food and clothing provisions, as well as sports activities, social interaction, and a commitment to human rights. The organization's wide range of activities and assistance programs are made possible by its thousands of volunteers.

Secours Catholique–Delegation de Paris, 13, r. de Ambroisec, 74011 (☎01 48 07 58 21; www.secourscatholique.asso.fr). The Secours Catholique works to support those in need including the poor, the unemployed, children with social problems, foreigners, and other marginalized groups. Its operations throughout France and internationally rely heavily upon its thousands of volunteers.

Action Contra la Faim, 4, r. Niepce, 75014 (☎01 43 35 88 88; www.acf-fr.org). As an international organization combatting hunger, Action Contra la Faim can always use the help of volunteers. Among other things, volunteers play an integral role in organizing and carrying out the Race Against Hunger, a running competition to raise money for the cause.

Federation Familles de France, 28, pl. Saint Georges, 75009 (☎01 44 53 45 90; www.familles-de-france.org). Supports families in need by offering grants, help with resumes, educational assistance, and social organizations.

Twice as WICE

If you need a break from practicing your French and want to help foster a community at the same time, consider lending a hand at **WICE,** an organization dedicated to helping English-speakers transition into life in France. Founded in 1978 as part of the American College of Paris, the organization is run almost entirely by volunteers. It offers support and resources of various kinds, including courses on topics from art history to business strategies, opportunities for artists to show their work, social gatherings, a library, and information on health care. As a volunteer you can either help with day-to-day operations or plan and lead your own course. WICE offers volunteer opportunities of all length, whether you're in town just for a few months or permanently.

20, bd. du Montparnasse, 15ème (☎01 45 66 75 50; www.wice-paris.org). M: Duroc or Falgüiere. Closed July-Aug.

Care France, CAP 19, 13, r. de Georfes Auric, 75019 (☎01 53 19 89 89; www.care.org). This international humanitarian group fights worldwide problems like poverty, AIDS, and environmental destruction.

Les Papillons Blancs de Paris—APEI, 44, r. Blanche, 75009 (☎01 42 80 44 43; www.apei75.org). A non-governmental organization that aids the mentally handicapped and their families by providing transportation assistance, homecare, and friendship.

GENEPI, 4-14, r. Ferrus, 75014 (☎01 45 88 37 00; www.genepi.asso.fr). Promotes the social rehabilitation of those in prison by creating relationships between students and prisoners. All student volunteers. Offices throughout France, including in Paris.

Fondation Claude Pompidou, 42, r. du Louvre, 75001 (☎01 40 13 75 00; www.fondationclaude-pompidou.asso.fr). A charitable organization that aids the sick, elderly, or disabled by providing support, homecare, and companionship. Volunteers are welcome, but are expected to commit to a full year.

Arcat-Sida, 94-102, r. de Buszenval, 75020 (☎01 43 72 44 51; fax 01 44 93 29 30; www.arcat-sida.org). Association of doctors, journalists, sociologists, and volunteers offering information and support on HIV/AIDS as well as promoting AIDS research.

MRAP (Movement Against Racism and for Friendship Between Peoples), 43, bd. Magenta, 75010 (☎01 53 38 99 99; mrap@wanadoo.fr). Counseling and support for victims of racism and discrimination, including assistance for people experiencing difficulty with obtaining proper immigration documents.

REMPART, 1, r. des Guillemites, 75004 (☎01 42 71 96 55; fax 01 42 71 73 00; www.rempart.com). Offers summer and year-long programs geared toward protecting French heritage, including the restoration of monuments. Anyone 13 or over is eligible. Membership fee €35; most projects charge €6-8 per day.

Jeunesse et Reconstruction, 8, 10 r. de Travise, 75009 (☎01 47 70 15 88; www.volontariat.org). This international program offers work camps, building sites, agricultural camps, cultural stays in Paris, as well as long-term placements. For detailed program information see website or contact the organization via email or phone.

ORGANIZATIONS ABROAD

Elderhostel, Inc., 11 Ave. de Lafayette, Boston, MA 92111 (☎877-426-8056 www.elderhostel.org). Sends volunteers aged 55 and over around the world to work in research, teaching, and other projects. Costs average $100 per day plus airfare.

International Volunteer Program, 678 13th St., Oakland, CA, 94612, USA (☎510-433-0414; www.ivpsf.org). This organization places volunteers aged 18 and older in a 6-week summer position at a Paris non-profit organization. Room and board provided. Costs $1800.

STUDYING

Studying at a college or language program is another way to integrate yourself into the communities you visit, and Paris, with its centuries-long tradition of intellectual pursuit, is a destination for thousands of foreign students each year. Study abroad programs range from basic language and culture courses to college-level classes, often for credit. In order to choose a program that best fits your needs, you will want to research thoroughly before making your decision—determine costs and duration, as well as what kind of students participate in the program and what sort of accommodations are provided.

There are trade-offs to programs in which you will be surrounded by English speakers; you may feel more comfortable, but you will not have the same opportunity to practice French or to befriend other international students. As for accommodations, dorm life may provide a better opportunity to mingle with fellow students, whereas living with a family may give you a better chance to experience day-to-day life in depth.

Most university-level study-abroad programs are meant as language and culture enrichment opportunities, and therefore are conducted in French. Still, many programs do offer classes in English and beginner- and lower-level language courses. Those relatively fluent in French, on the other hand, may find it cheaper to enroll directly in a French university, although getting college credit may be more difficult. A good resource for finding programs that cater to your particular interests is **www.studyabroad.com.** The following is a list of organizations that can help place students in university programs abroad, or have their own branch in Paris.

AMERICAN PROGRAMS

Alliances Abroad, 702 West Ave., Austin, TX 78701, USA (toll-free in the US ☎888-6-ABROAD, elsewhere 512-457-8062; www.alliancesabroad.com). Opportunities for language study in Paris. Prices range from $1125-$7465 depending on program.

Central College Abroad, Office of International Education, 812 University, Pella, IA 50219, USA (☎800-831-3629 or 641-628-5284; www.central.edu/abroad). Offers internships, as well as summer-, semester-, and year-long programs in Paris. US$25 application fee.

GIVING BACK

Getting the FACTS

FACTS is a volunteer organization that provides HIV/AIDS counseling, treatment, information, support and education to English-speaking people of all nationalities in Paris. Unlike many volunteer organizations in Paris, FACTS eagerly welcomes English speakers (even those who don't speak French). Volunteers are asked to commit to a project rather than to a certain numbers of hours each week. Depending on the type of work, volunteers may be required to complete a training session (F evening and all day Sa-Su). All volunteers are asked to make monthly contributions of €20. Opportunities include:

FACTS-line: An anonymous HIV/AIDS helpline open M-F 11am-2pm. Trained "listeners" provide support and info to people living with HIV/AIDS (PLWA) and HIV-negative individuals. This is the only English-speaking helpline for PLWA in France.

Buddying: Volunteers pair up with PLWA to provide emotional and/or practical support, such as helping navigate the French social security system, assisting with immigration papers, or simply providing company.

190, bd. de Charonne (☎01 44 93 16 32; fax 01 44 93 16 60; assoc@yahoo.fr). FACTS-line (☎01 44 93 16 69) open M-F 11am-2pm.

Council on International Educational Exchange (CIEE), 633 3rd Ave., 20th floor, New York, NY 10017-6706, USA (☎800-407-8839; www.ciee.org/study). Sponsors work, volunteer, academic, and internship programs in Paris.

International Association for the Exchange of Students for Technical Experience (IAESTE), 10400 Little Patuxent Pkwy. Ste. 250, Columbia, MD 21044-3519, USA (☎410-997-2200; www.aipt.org). 8- to 12-week programs in Paris for college students who have completed 2 years of technical study. US$25 application fee.

Institute for the International Education of Students (IES), 33 N. LaSalle St., 15th fl., Chicago, IL 60602, USA (☎800-995-2300; www.IESabroad.org). Offers year-long, semester, and summer programs in Paris for college students. Internships offered. US$50 application fee. Scholarships available.

School for International Training, College Semester Abroad, Admissions, Kipling Rd., P.O. Box 676, Brattleboro, VT 05302, USA (☎800-336-1616 or 802-257-7751; www.sit.edu). Semester- and year-long programs in Paris run US$10,600-13,700. Also runs the **Experiment in International Living** (☎800-345-2929; www.usexperiment.org), 3- to 5-week summer programs that offer high school students cross-cultural homestays, community service, ecological adventure, and language training in Paris and cost US$1900-5000.

PROGRAMS IN PARIS

Agence EduFrance, 173, bd. St-Germain, 75006 Paris (☎01 53 63 35 00; www.edufrance.fr). A one-stop resource for North Americans thinking about studying for a degree in France. Information on courses, costs, grant opportunities, and student life in Paris and major student cities in France.

American University of Paris, 31, av. Bosquet, 75343 Paris Cedex 07 (☎01 40 62 06 00; www.aup.fr). Offers US-accredited degrees and summer programs taught in English at its Paris campus. Intensive French language courses offered. Tuition $9000 per quarter, not including living expenses.

Université de Paris-Sorbonne, 1, r. Victor Cousin, 75230 Paris Cedex 05 (☎01 40 46 25 42; fax 01 40 46 25 88; www.paris4.sorbonne.fr). The granddaddy of French universities was founded in 1253 and is still going strong. Inscription into degree courses costs about €400 per year. Also offers 3- to 9-month-long programs for American students.

LANGUAGE SCHOOLS

Language schools are frequently independently run international or local organizations or divisions of foreign universities; they rarely offer college credit. Language schools are a good alternative to university study for those seeking a deeper focus on language or a less rigorous courseload. Many French universities, as well as the **American University of Paris** (see above), offer language courses during the summer. Your national **Institut Français,** official representatives of French culture attached to French embassies around the world, can provide more information on language courses in Paris (contact your nearest French embassy or consulate). Some good programs include:

Eurocentres, 101 N. Union St. Suite 300, Alexandria, VA 22314, USA (☎703-684-1494; www.eurocentres.com) or in Europe, Head Office, Seestr. 247, CH-8038 Zurich, Switzerland (☎41 1 485 50 40; fax 481 61 24). Language programs for beginning to advanced students with homestays in Paris.

Alliance Française, 101, bd. Raspail, 75270 Paris Cedex 06 (☎01 42 84 90 00; www.alliancefr.org). Instruction at all levels, including specialized courses in legal and business French. Courses 1-4 months in length. Prices vary; written courses €267 for 16 2hr. sessions and €534 for 16 4hr. sessions.

AmeriSpan, PO Box 58129, Philadelphia, PA 19102-8129, USA (In US and Canada ☎1-800-879-6640, elsewhere ☎215-751-1986; www.amerispan.com). Offers French courses in Paris with the option of a homestay. See website for extensive list of program dates. Prices range from US$800-$2115 depending on length of stay.

Cours de Civilisation Française de la Sorbonne, 47, r. des Ecoles, 75005 Paris (☎01 40 46 22 11; www.fle.fr/sorbonne). French language courses at all levels; also a comprehensive lecture program on French cultural studies taught by Sorbonne professors. Must be at least 18 and at *baccalauréat* level to enroll in the school. Semester- and year-long courses are offered during the academic year (starting at €587) and 4-, 6-, 8-, and 11-week programs run in the summertime.

French Language Learning Vacations, French-American Exchange, 3213 Duke Street, #620, Alexandria, VA 22314, USA (☎1-800-995-5087; www.frenchamericanexchange.com). French language programs in Paris. Two-week sessions US$1015-$1340.

Institut de Langue Française, 3, av. Bertie-Albrecht, 75008 Paris (☎01 45 63 24 00; fax 01 45 63 07 09; www.inst-langue-fr.com). Language, civilization, and literature courses. Offers 4wk. up to year-long programs, 6-20 hr. per week, starting at €185.

Institut Parisien de Langue et de Civilisation Française, 87, bd. de Grenelle, 75015 Paris (☎01 40 56 09 53; fax 01 43 06 46 30; www.institut-parisien.com). French language, fashion, culinary arts, and cinema courses. Intensive language courses 10 (€95-117 per week), 15 (€143-177 per week), or 25 (€238-294 per week) hr. per week.

Langue Onze Paris, 15, r. Gamby, Paris, 70511 (☎01 43 38 22 87; www.langueonzeparis.com). Langue Onze is part of the Tandem International association of language schools (see www.tandem-schools.com/index.html). Langue Onze offers French language courses and homestays in Paris. Costs for the program average €160-€535 depending on course intensity and length of stay.

FRENCH UNIVERSITIES

For those who are fluent in French, direct enrollment in a French university can be more rewarding than a class filled with Americans, as well as up to four times cheaper, although academic credit at home is not a guarantee. French universities (except for the Grandes Ecoles; see below) must admit anyone holding a **baccalauréat** (French high school diploma) or a recognized equivalent to their first year of courses (British A-levels or 2 years of college in the US). Non-native French speakers must also pass a written and oral language test. At the end of the first year, exams separate the wheat from the chaff. The best of the best go on to the elite **Grandes Ecoles** after passing notoriously difficult entrance exams that require a year of preparatory schooling in themselves.

Students who apply directly to French universities should be prepared for earlier application dates (fall or early spring) and a required French language exam. Higher education in France is divided into three categories: *premier* cycle (first 2 years of undergraduate study), *deuxième* cycle (second 2 years of undergraduate study culminating in a *maîtrise*, or masters), and *troisième* cycle (graduate studies). For information on programs of study, requirements and grants or scholarships, visit **www.egide.asso.fr.**

EU citizens studying in France can take advantage of the **SOCRATES** program (www.socrates-france.org), which offers grants to support inter-European educational exchanges. Most UK and Irish universities will have details on the grants and the application procedure.

UNIVERSITÉ DE PARIS

In 1968, the Université de Paris split into 10 independent universities, each at a different site and offering a different program. The **Sorbonne,** now the Université de Paris IV, devotes itself to the humanities. The cultural services office at your nearest French consulate can provide more information. As a student at a French university, you will receive a student card *(carte d'étudiant)* upon presentation of a residency permit and a receipt for your university fees. In addition to standard student benefits, many additional benefits are administered by the **Centre Régional des Oeuvres Universitaires et Scolaires (CROUS).** Founded in 1955 to improve the living and working conditions of students, CROUS welcomes foreign students. The brochure *Le CROUS et Moi* lists addresses and info on student life. Pick up their guidebook *Je Vais en France* (free), in French or English, from any French embassy.

WORKING

Anyone hoping to come to France and slip easily into a job will be faced with a tough reality on arrival: French unemployment remains stubbornly at 9%, and unqualified foreigners are unlikely to meet with much sympathy from French employers. In general, the French are more conservative about their job choices, and there is a much slower turnover in terms of job openings. Those who find work can take comfort in government regulations that limit the work week to a rocking 35-39 hours, a measure intended to encourage hiring. **Non-EU citizens** will find it nearly impossible to get a work permit without a firm job offer. To hire a non-EU foreigner legally in France, the employer must prove that the hiree can perform a task which cannot be performed by a French person. For a frequently updated international internship and job database, try **www.jobsabroad.com**.

Those looking for work can also check **help-wanted columns** in French newspapers and the English-language *International Herald Tribune*, as well as **France-USA Contacts (FUSAC),** a free weekly circular filled with classified ads, available at Yankee hangouts. Many of these jobs are "unofficial" and therefore illegal (the penalty is deportation), but many people find them convenient because they often don't ask for presentation of a work permit. Youth hostels frequently provide room and board to travelers in exchange for work. Those seeking more permanent employment should have a **résumé** in both English and French. Type up your résumé for a prospective employer, but write the cover letter by hand. Handwriting is considered an important indicator of your character to French employers. The best tips on jobs for foreigners come from other travelers. Be aware of your rights as an employee, and always get written confirmation of your agreements, including official job offers.

VISA INFORMATION

EU citizens have the right to work and study in France without a visa. Others wishing to study in France for more than three months must apply for a student visa (US$47) and will need proof of admission to a French university, proof of financial independence, proof of residence (a gas or electric bill or a letter from your landlord), a medical certificate issued by a doctor approved by the French consulate, and proof of medical insurance. Foreigners studying in France must apply for a residence permit within two months of their arrival. Non-EU citizens wishing to work in France must have a firm offer of employment before applying for a long-stay visa (US$93); your employer should send you an official work contract, which must be presented upon arrival in France. Non-EU citizens must also apply to the prefecture of police for a residence permit within eight days of arrival. International students looking for part-time work (up to 20 hours per week) can apply for provisional work authorization upon completing their first academic year in a French university. For **au pairs, scientific researchers,** and **teaching assistants,** special rules apply; check with your local consulate.

EU CITIZENS

EU citizens can work in France without a visa or work permit, though they will need a **residency permit** (see p. 305). Those without an offer of employment have a grace period of three months in which to seek work and are eligible for social security benefits during this time. In order to receive benefits, you must make arrangements with your local social security office before leaving for France. Be aware that French bureaucracy often takes three months just to process the paperwork. If you do not succeed in finding work in that time, you must return home unless you can prove your financial independence. By law, all EU citizens must be given equality of opportunity when applying to jobs not directly related to national security, so theoretically, if you speak French you have as much chance of finding a job as an equally qualified French person.

FINDING A JOB

The organizations listed below all help foreigners to navigate the often difficult task of finding a job in Paris:

American Church, 65 quai d'Orsay, 75007 (☎01 40 62 05 00; fax 01 40 62 05 11; www.americanchurchparis.org). Posts a bulletin board full of job and housing opportunities targeting Americans and Anglophones. Open M-Sa 9am-10pm. Also hosts **The Information Center,** at the garden level (☎01 45 56 09 50), a clearinghouse of information and referrals providing immediate service to the English-speaking people of Paris. Maintains a comprehensive database of resources available to those in need of information regarding legal matters, medical resources, housing, language courses, and more. Open Tu-Th 1:15-4pm.

Agence Nationale Pour l'Emploi (ANPE), 4, impasse d'Antin, 75008 (☎01 43 59 62 63; www.anpe.fr). Has specific info on employment opportunities. Interested parties should bring a work permit and *carte de séjour.* Open M-W and F 9am-5pm, Th 9am-noon.

Centre d'Information et de Documentation Jeunesse (CIDJ), 101, quai Branly, 75740 (☎01 44 49 12 00; fax 01 40 65 02 61; www.cidj.asso.fr). An invaluable state-run youth center provides info on education, résumés, employment, and careers. English spoken. Jobs are posted on the bulletin boards outside. Open M, W, F 10am-6pm; Tu and Th 10am-7pm; Sa 9:30am-1pm.

European Employment Services (EURES), (☎33 0800 90 9700). Facilitates employment between EU countries. For EU citizens only.

Chamber of Commerce in France, 156, bd. Haussmann, 75008 Paris (☎01 56 43 45 67; fax 01 56 43 45 60; www.amchamfrance.org). An association of American businesses in France. Keeps résumés on file for 2 months and places then at the disposal of French and American companies. Open M-Th 9:30am-1pm and 2-5pm.

LONG-TERM WORK

If you're planning on spending more than three months working in Paris, job search in advance. International placement agencies are often the

in recent news

Métro Musicians

You can now take home a piece of the music that charms you during your endless hours of underground travel in Paris; **Correspondances** is the first ever compilation album by the musicians of the métro. Completed in 2003, the album was produced by **L'Espace Métro Accords (EMA)** and the company Mediabonus. The 14 artists represented on the album were selected from among 360 entries to showcase original talent and musical diversity. The album mixes French *chansons* with the sounds of Africa, South American, and Eastern Europe, a *mélange* not unlike what you'll hear while transferring from train to train on any given day. A number of today's best-selling musicians started out in train stations and on street corners, so you might want to check out the album to discover tomorrow's stars.

Most métro artists are accredited by the EMA, an organization created in 1997 to entertain commuters while representing and providing for artists. The EMA holds auditions twice a year, and listens to over 1000 artists before giving out about 350 licenses. Other major cities, including London and Tokyo, are following suit with similar governing bodies. *Correspondances* is available at record stores across France. For more information see **www.ratp.fr.**

easiest way to find employment, especially for teaching English. Internships, usually for college students, are a good way to segue into working abroad, although they are often unpaid or poorly paid. Be wary of companies that claim the ability to get you a job abroad for a fee—often the same listings are available online or in newspapers. Some good organizations include:

Council Exchanges, 52 Poland St., London W1F 7AB, UK (☎44 020 7478 2000; US☎ 888-268-6245; www.councilexchanges.org) charges a US$300-475 fee for arranging short-term working authorizations (generally valid for 3-6 months) and provides extensive information on different job opportunities in Paris.

French-American Chamber of Commerce (FACC), International Career Development Programs, 1350 Avenue of the Americas, 6th fl., New York, NY 10019, USA (☎212-765-4598; fax 765-4650). Has *Work In France* programs, internships, teaching, and public works.

TEACHING ENGLISH

Teaching jobs abroad are rarely well-paid, although some elite private American schools can pay somewhat competitive salaries. In almost all cases, you must have at least a bachelors degree to be a full-fledged teacher, although college undergraduates can often get summer positions teaching or tutoring. The Fulbright Teaching Assistantship and French Teaching Assistantship program through the French Ministry of Education are the best options for students and recent grads with little experience teaching. Another alternative is to make contacts directly with schools; the best time of the year is several weeks before the start of the school year.

Many schools require teachers to have a **Teaching English as a Foreign Language (TEFL)** certificate, or at least offer higher pay to certified teachers. Native English speakers working in private schools are most often hired for English-immersion classrooms where no French is spoken. Those volunteering or teaching in public, poorer schools, are more likely to be working in both English and French. The following organizations are extremely helpful in placing teachers in Paris.

International Schools Services (ISS), 15 Roszel Rd., Box 5910, Princeton, NJ 08543-5910, USA (☎609-452-0990; fax 609-452-2690; www.iss.edu). Hires teachers for more than 200 overseas schools; candidates should have experience teaching or with international affairs. 2-year commitment expected.

Fulbright English Teaching Assistantship, US Student Programs Division, Institute of International Education, 809 United Nations Plaza, New York, NY 10017 USA (☎212-984-5330; www.iie.org). Competitive program sends college graduates to teach in France.

French Ministry of Education Teaching Assistantship in France, Cultural Service of the French Embassy, 972 Fifth Ave., New York, NY 10021 USA (☎212-439-1400; fax 439-1455; www.frenchculture.org/education). Program for US citizens sends 1500 college students and recent grads to teach English part-time in France.

Office of Overseas Schools, US Dept. of State, Room H328, SA-1, Washington, DC 20522 USA (☎202-261-8200; fax 261-8224; www.state.gov/m/a/os). Keeps a list of schools abroad and agencies that arrange placement for Americans to teach abroad.

AU PAIR WORK

Au pairs are typically women, aged 18-27, who work as live-in nannies, caring for children and doing light housework in foreign countries in exchange for room, board, and a small spending allowance or stipend. Most former au pairs speak favorably of their experience—it can allow you to get to know the country well without the high expenses of traveling. Drawbacks, however, often include long hours of constantly being on-duty and mediocre pay. Much of the au pair experience really does depend on the family you're placed with. Check with the French embassy (see p. 304) for more information. The agencies below are a good starting point for looking for employment as an au pair.

Accord Cultural Exchange, 750 La Playa, San Francisco, CA 94121, USA (☎415-386-6203; www.cognitext.com/accord).

Au Pair Homestay, World Learning, Inc., 1015 15th St. NW, Suite 750, Washington, DC 20005, USA (☎800-287-2477; fax 202-408-5397).

Au Pair in Europe, P.O. Box 68056, Blakely Postal Outlet, Hamilton, Ontario, Canada L8M 3M7 (☎905-545-6305; fax 905-544-4121; www.princeent.com).

Childcare International, Ltd., Trafalgar House, Grenville Pl., London NW7 3SA, UK (☎44 020 8906 3116; fax 8906-3461; www.childint.co.uk).

InterExchange, 161 Sixth Ave., New York, NY 10013, USA (☎212-924-0446; fax 924-0575; www.interexchange.org).

L'Accueil Familial des Jeunes Etrangers, 23, r. du Cherche-Midi, 75006 Paris (☎01 42 22 50 34; fax 01 45 44 60 48; accueil@afje-paris.org). Arranges summer and 18-month *au pair* jobs (placement fee €108). Also arranges similar jobs for non-students which require 30hr. of work per week in exchange for room, board, employment benefits, as well as a métro pass.

FURTHER INFORMATION

For further information on alternatives to tourism, consult the following:

Alternatives to the Peace Corps: A Directory of Third World and U.S. Volunteer Opportunities, by Joan Powell. Food First Books, 2000 (US$10).

How to Get a Job in Europe, by Sanborn and Matherly. Surrey Books, 1999 ($US22).

How to Live Your Dream of Volunteering Oversees, by Collins, DeZerega, and Heckscher. Penguin Books, 2002 (US$17).

International Directory of Voluntary Work, by Whetter and Pybus. Peterson's Guides and Vacation Work, 2000 (US$16).

International Jobs, by Kocher and Segal. Perseus Books, 1999 (US$18).

Overseas Summer Jobs, by Collier and Woodworth. Peterson's Guides and Vacation Work, updated annually (US$18).

Work Abroad: The Complete Guide to Finding a Job Overseas, by Hubbs, Griffith, and Nolting. Transitions Abroad Publishing, 2000 ($16).

Work Your Way Around the World, by Susan Griffith. Worldview Publishing Services, 2001 (US$18).

Invest Yourself: The Catalogue of Volunteer Opportunities, published by the Commission on Voluntary Service and Action (☎718-638-8487).

Service Directory

ACCOMMODATION AGENCIES

Allô Logement Temporaire, 64, r. du Temple, 3*ème* (☎01 42 72 00 06; fax 01 42 72 03 11; alt@claranet.fr). M: Hôtel-de-Ville. Open M-F noon-8pm.

La Centrale de Réservations (FUAJ-HI), 4, bd. Jules Ferry, 11*ème* (☎01 43 57 02 60; fax 01 40 21 79 92). Affiliated with Hostelling International (HI). M: République. Open daily 8am-10pm.

Centre Régional des Oeuvres Universitaires (CROUS), 39, av. Georges Bernanos, 5*ème* (☎01 40 51 36 00; lodging ☎01 40 51 55 55; www.crous-paris.fr). RER: Port-Royal.

OTU-Voyage (Office du Tourisme Universitaire), 119, r. St-Martin, 4*ème* (☎08 20 81 78 17 or 01 49 72 57 19 for groups). Levies a €1.53 service charge. Open M-F 9:30am-7pm, Sa 10am-noon and 1:30-5pm. Another branch at 2, r. Malus, 5*ème* (☎01 44 41 74 74). M: Place Monge. Open M-Sa 9-6pm.

BIKE & SCOOTER RENTAL

Roulez Champions, 5, r. Humblot, 15*ème* (☎01 40 58 12 22; www.roulezchampions.com). Bike rentals from €15 per day. Also rents in-line skates. Open Apr.-Oct. daily 10am-8pm; Nov.-Mar. Su and Tu-Sa 11am-8pm.

Paris à velo, c'est sympa!, 37, bd. Bourdon, 4*ème* (☎01 48 87 60 01; www.parisvelosympa.com). M: Bastille. Rentals available with a €200 (or credit card) deposit. 24hr. rental €16; 9am-7pm €12.50; half day (9am-2pm or 2-7pm) €9.50. Open daily 9am-1pm and 2-6pm.

Paris-Vélo, 2, r. de Fer-à-Moulin, 5*ème* (☎01 43 37 59 22). M: Censier-Daubenton. Bike rental €14 per day. Open M-Sa 10am-12:30pm and 2-7pm.

SEjEM, 144, bd. Voltaire, 11*ème* (☎01 44 93 04 03; www.sejem.com). Rents bikes and scooters.Open M-F 9:15am-1pm and 2-7pm, Sa 10am-1pm and 2-6pm.

CAR RENTAL

Hertz, Carrousel de Louvre (☎01 47 03 49 12). M: Louvre. Open M-Th 8am-7pm, Sa 9am-1pm and 2-6pm, Su 9am-1pm. AmEx/MC/V.

Rent-a-Car, 79, r. de Bercy, 12*ème* (☎01 43 45 98 99; fax 01 43 45 65 00; www.rentacar.fr). Open M-Sa 8:30am-6pm. AmEx/MC/V.

Autorent, 98, r. de la Convention, 15*ème* (☎01 45 54 22 45; fax 01 45 54 39 69; autorent@wanadoo.fr). M: Boucicaut. Also at 36, r. Fabert, 7*ème* (☎01 45 55 12 54; fax 01 45 55 14 00). M: Invalides. Open M-F 8am-7pm, Sa 8:30am-noon. AmEx/MC/V.

CELL PHONE RENTAL

Call'Phone, 2, av. de la Porte de Saint-Cloud, (☎01 46 51 25 20; www.call-phone.com). Free cell phone rental. 5min. minimum charge daily (outgoing calls €0.70 per min). Incoming calls free. MC/V.

CHUNNEL RESERVATIONS

Eurostar, reservation ☎01 49 70 01 75; www.eurostar.co.uk.

Eurotunnel, ☎03 21 00 61 00; www.eurotunnel.com.

CURRENCY EXCHANGE

American Express, 11, r. Scribe, 9*ème* (☎01 47 14 50 00). M: Opéra or Auber. Open M-Sa 9am-6:30pm; exchange counters also open Su 10am-5pm.

Thomas Cook, 73, av. des Champs-Elysées, 8*ème* (☎01 45 62 89 55; fax 01 45 62 89 55). M: Georges V. Open M-Sa 9am-10:55pm, Su 8am-6pm.

DENTISTS & DOCTORS

Centre Médicale Europe, 44 r. d'Amsterdam, 9*ème* (☎01 42 81 93 33). M: St-Lazare. Open M-F 8am-7pm, Sa 8am-6pm.

SOS Dentaire, 87 bd. Port-Royal (☎01 43 37 51 00). RER: Port-Royal. Open daily 9am-6pm and 8:30-11:45pm. No walk-ins.

SOS Médecins, ☎01 48 07 77 77. Makes house calls.

SOS Oeil, ☎01 40 92 93 94. Open daily 6am-11pm.

SOS Optique Lunettes, ☎01 48 07 22 00. Open 24hr.

Urgences Médicales de Paris, ☎01 53 94 94 94. Makes house calls.

DISABILITY RESOURCES

L'Association des Paralysées de France, Délégation de Paris, 17, bd. Auguste Blanqui, 13*ème* (☎01 40 78 69 00; www.apf.asso.fr). M: Place d'Italie. Open M-F 9am-12:30pm and 2-5:30pm.

Audio-Vision Guides, at Parisian theaters such as the Théâtre National de Chaillot, 1, pl. Trocadéro, 11 Novembre, 16*ème* (☎01 53 65 30 00); the Comédie Française, 2, r. de Richelieu, 1*er* (☎01 44 58 15 15); and the Théâtre National de la Colline, 15, r. Malte-Brun, 20*ème* (☎01 44 62 52 00).

Comité National Français de Liaison pour la Réadaption des Handicapés (CNFLRH), 236bis, r. de Tolbiac, 13*ème* (☎01 53 80 66 66; fax 01 53 80 66 67; www.handitel.org). Open M-Su 9am-1pm and 2-5:30pm.

DRY CLEANING

Arc en Ciel, 62, r. Arbre Sec, 1*er* (☎01 42 41 39 39). M: Louvre. Open M-F 8am-1:15pm and 2:30-7pm, Sa 8:30am-1:15pm.

Belnet Pressing, 140, r. Belleville, 20*ème* (☎01 46 36 65 51). M: Jourdain. Open M-Sa 8am-1pm and 2-7:30pm. MC/V.

Buci Pressing, 7, r. Ancienne Comédie, 6*ème* (☎01 43 29 49 92). M: Odéon. Open M-Sa 8am-7pm. MC (for over €13).

Home Pressing, 140, r. Lamartine, 14*ème* (☎01 48 83 05 05; www.homepressing.com). Pick-up and delivery services provided. Open M-F 7:30am-5:30pm. AmEx/V.

Pressing de Seine, 67, r. de Seine, 6*ème* (☎01 43 25 74 94). M: Odéon. Open M-Sa 8am-7pm. Hours vary in Aug. MC/V

Pressing Villiers, 93, r. de Rocher, 8*ème* (☎01 45 22 75 48). M: Villiers. Open M-F 8am-7:30pm. MC/V.

EMERGENCY

Ambulance (SAMU), ☎15.

Fire, ☎18.

Poison, ☎01 40 05 48 48. In French, but some English assistance is available.

Police, ☎17. **For emergencies only.**

Rape: SOS Viol (☎08 00 05 95 95). Open M-F 10am-7pm.

SOS Help!, ☎01 46 21 46 46. An anonymous, confidential hotline for English speakers in crisis. Open daily (including holidays) 3-11pm.

ENTERTAINMENT INFO

Info-Loisirs, ☎08 92 68 31 12; €0.34 per min.

FITNESS CLUBS

The following listings of fitness clubs are by *arrondissement*.

Club Med Gym, 10, pl. de la République, 3*ème* (☎01 47 00 69 98; www.clubmedgym.com). Membership €140 per month. 36 locations throughout Paris.

Centre Sivananda de Yoga Vedanta, 123, bd. de Sébastopol, 2*ème* (☎01 40 26 77 49). M: Réamur-Sébastopol.

Espace Vit'Halles, 48, r. Rambuteau, 3*ème* (☎01 42 77 21 71). Membership €149 per month, students €119.20.

Centre de Danse du Marais, 41, r. du Temple, 4*ème* (☎01 42 72 15 42). M: Hôtel-de-Ville.

Squash Club Quartier Latin, 19, r. de Pontoise, 5*ème* (☎01 55 42 77 88). M: Maubert-Mutualité or Jussieu. Gym, weight room, pool, martial arts, squash, sauna, and jacuzzi. Open M-F 8am-midnight, Sa-Su 9:30am-7pm.

Gymnase Club Montparnasse, 149 r. de Rennes, 6*ème* (☎01 45 44 24 35). Membership €140 per month.

Gymnase Club Champs Elysées, 26, r. Berri, 8*ème* (☎01 43 59 04 58). Membership €140 per month.

Les Cercles de la Forme, 11, r. de Malte, 11*ème* (☎01 47 00 80 95). Membership €307 for 3 months (min).

Anthony's Studio Gym Club, 16, r. Louis Braille, 12*ème* (☎01 43 43 67 67). Annual membership €610, students €460.

Club Energym, 6, r. Lalande, 14*ème* (☎01 43 22 12 02). Membership €99 per month.

Jeu de Paume de Paris, 74ter, r. Lauriston, 16*ème* (☎01 47 27 46 86). M: Charles de Gaulle-Etoile. Squash and handball courts. Yearly membership required. Open daily 9am-10pm.

GAY & LESBIAN RESOURCES

ACT-UP Paris, 45, r. de Sedene, 11*ème* (☎01 48 06 13 89). M: Bréguet-Sabin.

Boobs Bourg, 26, r. de Montmorency, 3*ème* (☎01 42 72 80 86). Sign up at this bar to join a Paris-wide lesbian e-mail list with information on lectures and social events.

Centre du Christ Libérateur (Metropolitan Community Church), 5, r. Crussol, 11*ème* (☎01 48 05 24 48 or 01 39 83 13 44). M: Oberkampf.

Centre Gai et Lesbien, 3, r. Keller, 11*ème* (☎01 43 57 21 47; fax 01 43 57 27 93). M: Ledru-Rollin or Bastille. Open M-F 4-8pm.

Ecoute Gaie: ☎01 44 93 01 02. Crisis hotline. Open M-Tu and F evenings; if no one answers, a message will give the hours for the next 2 weeks.

SOS Homophobie: ☎01 48 06 42 41. Takes calls M-F 8-10pm.

GROOMING SERVICES

Space Hair, 10, r. Rambuteau, 3*ème* (☎01 48 87 28 51). M: Rambuteau. Cut and style women €37-46, men €24; about 15% discount for students. Open M noon-10pm, Tu-Sa noon-8pm.

Planet Hair, 26, r. Beaubourg, 4*ème* (☎01 48 87 38 86). M: Rambuteau. Women cut and style €42, men €26; student discount 20% Open Tu-W and F-Sa 10am-8pm, Th noon-9pm.

HOSPITALS

Hôpital Américain de Paris, 63, bd. Hugo, Neuilly (☎01 46 41 25 25). M: Port Maillot, then bus #82 to the end of the line.

Hôpital Franco-Britannique de Paris, 3, r. Barbès, in the Parisian suburb of Levallois-Perret (☎01 46 39 22 22). M: Anatole France. Has some English speakers, but don't count on it.

Hôpital Bichat, 46, r. Henri Buchard, 18*ème* (☎01 40 25 80 80). M: Port St-Ouen. Emergency services.

HOTLINES & SUPPORT CENTERS

AIDES, ☎0 800 84 08 00. Open 24hr.

Alcoholics Anonymous (AA), ☎01 46 34 59 65; www.aaparis.org. Holds both English and French meetings.

Free Anglo-American Counseling Treatment and Support (FACTS), HIV/AIDS information line ☎01 44 93 16 69. Open M and W 7-10pm.

HIV, 43 r. de Valois, 1*er* (☎01 42 61 30 04). M: Palais-Royal or Bourse. Open M-W 9am-5pm. HIV testing at 218, r. de Belleville, 20*ème* (☎01 40 33 52 00), M: Télégraphe. Open M-F 1-6pm. 3-5, r. de Ridder, 14*ème* (☎01 58 14 30 30), M: Plai-

sance. Testing M-F noon-6:30pm, Sa 9:30am-noon.

International Counseling Service (ICS), ☎01 45 50 26 49. Open M-F 8am-8pm, Sa 8am-2pm.

SOS Crisis Help Line Friendship, ☎01 46 21 46 46. English spoken. Open daily 3-11pm.

INTERNET ACCESS

Listings are by *arrondissement.*

Cybercafé de Paris, 15, r. des Halles. 1*er* (☎01 42 21 13 13). M: Châtelet. €8 per hr. Open 11am-11pm.

Artefak, 42 r. Volta, 3*ème* (☎01 44 59 39 58). M: Arts et Metiers or Temple. Early-bird specials (before 1pm), €2 per hr.; regular €3 per hr. Open daily 10pm-2am.

Internet Café, 30, Grenier St-Lazare, 3*ème* (☎01 42 77 12 21). M: Rambuteau. €3 per hour. Open M-Sa 10am-11pm.

Akyrion Net Center, 19, r. Charlemagne, 4*ème* (☎01 40 27 92 07). €2.40 per hr. Open M-Th 11am-10:30pm, F-Sa 11am-11pm, Su 2-9:30pm.

Le Jardin de l'Internet, 79, bd. St-Michel, 5*ème* (☎01 44 07 22 20). RER: Luxembourg. €2.50 per hr. Open daily 9am-11pm.

Luxembourg Micro, 83, bd. St-Michel, 5*ème* (☎01 46 33 27 98). M: St-Michel. RER: Luxembourg. €1.52-3 per hr. Open M-Su 10am-11pm.

Cyber Cube, 5, r. Mignon, 6*ème* (☎01 53 10 30 50). M: St-Michel or Odéon. €0.15 per min., €30 for 5hr., €40 for 10hr. Open M-Sa 10am-10pm.

Le Sputnik, 14-16, r. de la Butte-aux-Cailles, 13*ème* (☎01 45 65 19 82). M: Place d'Italie. €1 for 15min., €4 for 1hr.

XLnet, 103, r. de Tolbiac, 13*ème* (☎01 45 86 08 77). €5.34 per hr.

I Care Photo, 5, r. Liard, 14*ème* (☎01 45 80 52 24). M: Cité Universitaire. €5 per hr. Open M-Sa 9am-12:30pm and 2-7pm.

Taxiphone, 343, r. des Pyrénées, 20*ème* (☎01 43 15 68 25). M: Pyrénées or Jourdain. €3 per hr. Open daily noon-10pm.

LIBRARIES

The American Library, 10, r. Général Camou, 7*ème* (www.americanlibraryinparis.org; ☎01 53 59 12 60). M: Ecole Militaire. Short-term and annual memberships available, check website for details. Open Tu-Sa 10am-7pm.

Bibliothèque Marguerite Durand, 79, r. Nationale, 13*ème* (☎01 45 70 80 30). M: Nationale. Open Tu-Su 10am-7pm.

Bibliothèque National de France includes **Mitterrand** branch at 11, quai François Mauriac, 13*ème* (☎01 53 79 59 59). M: Quai de la Gare or Bibliothèque. Reading rooms open Tu-Sa 10am-8pm, Su noon-7pm. Branches at 66-68, r. de Richelieu, 2*ème* (☎01 47 03 81 26), M: Bourse; Bibliothèque de l'Opéra, 8, r. Scribe, 9*ème* (☎01 47 42 07 02), M: Opéra. Reader's card €3 per day; €30.50 per year, students €15.25.

Bibliothèque Publique, in the Centre Pompidou, 4*ème* (☎01 44 78 12 33). M: Rambuteau. Open M and W-F 11am-9pm, Sa-Su 11am-10pm.

MAIL

Federal Express, ☎0 800 12 38 00. Call M-F before 5pm for pick up. Or, drop off at 2, r. du 29 Juillet, between Concorde and r. du Rivoli, 1*er*. Open M-Sa 9am-7pm; drop off by 4:45pm. **Also** at 63, bd. Haussmann, 8*ème*.

Poste du Louvre, 52, r. du Louvre, 1*er* (postal info ☎01 40 28 20 40). M: Louvre. Open daily 24hr.

MINORITY RESOURCES

Agence Pour le Développement des Relations Interculturelles, 4, r. Réne-Villermé, 11*ème* (☎01 40 09 69 19). M: Père Lachaise. Open M-Th 9:30am-1pm and 2-6pm, F 9:30am-1pm and 2-5pm.

Association des Trois Mondes, 63bis, r. du Cardinal Lemoine, 5*ème* (www.cine3mondes.fr; ☎01 42 34 99 09). M: Cardinal Lemoine.

Centre Culturel Algérien, 171, r. de la Croix-Nivert, 15*ème* (☎01 45 54 95 31). M: Boucicault. Open M-F 9am-5:30pm.

Centre Culturel Coréen, 2, av. d'Iéna, 16*ème* (☎01 47 20 84 15). M: Iéna. Open M-F 9:30am-12:30pm and 2:30-6pm.

Centre Culturel Egyptien, 111, bd. St Michel, 5*ème* (☎01 46 33 75 67). M: Luxembourg. Open M-F 10am-7pm.

Maison de l'Asie, 22, av. du Président Wilson, 16*ème* (☎01 53 70 18 46). M: Iéna or Trocadéro. Open M-F 9am-6pm.

MRAP (Mouvement contre le racisme et pour l'amitié entre les peuples), 43, bd. Magenta, 10*ème* (☎01 53 38 99 99). Open M-F 9am-12:30pm.

SOS Racisme, 28, r. des Petites Ecuries, 10*ème* (☎01 40 35 36 55). Open M-F 10:30am-6pm.

PHARMACIES

Listings by *arrondissement.*

Pharmacie des Halles, 10, bd. de Sébastopol, 1*er* (☎01 42 72 03 23). M: Châtelet-Les Halles. Open M-Sa 9am-midnight, Su 9am-10pm.

Pharmacie Beaubourg, 50, r. Rambuteau, 3*ème* (☎01 48 87 86 37). M: Rambuteau. Open M-Sa 8am-8pm, Su 10am-8pm. MC/V

Pharmacie de l'Hôtel de Ville, 9, r. des Archives, 4*ème* (☎01 42 78 53 58). M: Hôtel de Ville. Open daily 10am-8pm. AmEx/MC/V.

Pharmacie Dhéry, in the Galerie des Champs, 84, av. des Champs-Elysées, 8*ème* (☎ 01 45 62 02 41). M: George V. Open 24hr.

British & American Pharmacy, 1, r. Auber, 9*ème* (☎01 42 65 88 29 or 01 47 42 49 40). M: Auber or Opéra. Open M-Su 8am-8:30pm.

Pharmacie Gacha, 361, r. des Pyrénées, 20*ème* (☎01 46 36 59 10). M: Pyrénées or Jourdain. Open M-Sa 10am-7pm.

RELIGIOUS SERVICES

American Cathedral (Anglican and Episcopalian), 23, av. George V, 8*ème* (☎01 53 23 84 00). M: George V. English services winter Su 9am, summer 9 and 11am. Open M-F 9am-5pm.

American Church in Paris, 65, quai d'Orsay, 7*ème* (☎01 40 62 05 00). M: Invalides or Alma-Marceau. Service in English Su 9 and 11am. Open M-Sa 9am-10:30pm.

Buddhist Temple, Centre de Kazyn Dzong, route de la ceinture du Lac Daumesnil, 12*éme* (☎01 40 04 98 06). M: Porte Dorée. Buddhist temple and meditation center. Meditations Tu-F 9:30-10:30am, 6 and 7:30pm; Sa-Su 10am-noon and 2:30-5:30pm.

Eglise Russe (Russian Eastern Orthodox), also known as **Cathédrale Alexandre-Nevski,** 12, r. Daru, 8*ème* (☎01 42 27 37 34). M: Ternes. Open Tu, F, Su 3-5pm. Services (in French and Russian) Su 10:30am.

Mosquée de Paris, Institut Musulman, pl. de l'Ermite, 5*ème* (☎01 45 35 97 33). M: Place Monge. Open Sa-Th 9am-noon and 2-6pm.

St. Joseph's Church (Catholic), 50, av. Hoche, 8*ème* (☎01 42 27 28 56). M: Charles de Gaulle-Etoile. English mass Su 11am and 6:30pm. Phone for other service times following renovations.

St. Michael's Church (Anglican and Episcopalian), 5, r. d'Aguesseau, 8*ème* (☎01 47 42 70 88). M: Concorde. Services in English Su 9:30, 11:15am, 6:30pm. Open M-Tu and Th-F 10am-1pm and 2-5:30pm.

Union Libéral Israélite de France (Jewish), 24, r. Copernic, 16*ème* (☎01 47 04 37 27). M: Victor Hugo. Services F 6pm and Sa 10:30am, mostly in Hebrew with a little French. Services in the evenings and mornings of High Holy Days; call for info. Open M-Th 9am-noon and 2-6pm, F-Sa 9am-5:30pm.

TAXIS

Alpha Taxis, ☎01 45 85 85 85.

Taxis 7000, ☎01 42 70 00 42.

Taxis G7, ☎01 47 39 47 39.

TICKET SERVICES

Kiosque Info Jeune, 25, bd. Bourdon, 4*ème* (☎01 42 76 22 60). M: Bastille. Open M-F 10am-7pm.

FNAC, 74, av. des Champs- Elysées, 8*ème* (☎01 53 53 64 64; www.fnac.fr). M: F.D. Roosevelt.

Virgin Megastore, 52, av. des Champs-Elysées, 8*ème* (☎01 49 53 50 00; www.virginmega.fr). M: F. D. Roosevelt. Open M-Sa 10am-midnight, Su noon-midnight.

TOURIST OFFICES

Bureau d'Accueil Central, 127, av. des Champs-Elysées, 8*ème* (☎08 92 68 31 12; www.paris-touristoffice.com). M: Georges V. Open high-season daily 9am-8pm; low-season Su 11am-7pm.

Bureau Gare de Lyon, 12*ème* (☎01 43 43 33 24). M: Gare de Lyon. Open M-Sa 8am-8pm.

Bureau Gare d'Austerlitz, 13*ème (*☎01 45 84 91 70). M: Gare d'Austerlitz. Open M-Sa 8am-8pm.

Bureau Tour Eiffel, Champs de Mars, *7ème* (☎08 92 68 31 12). M: Champs de Mars. Open May-Sept. daily 11am-6pm.

TOURS

Bateaux-Mouches (☎01 42 25 96 10; info ☎01 40 76 99 99; www.bateaux-mouches.fr). M: Alma-Marceau. 70min. tours in English. Departures every 30min. 10:15am-10:40pm (no boats 1-2pm) from the Right Bank pier near Pont d'Alma.

Mike's Bullfrog Bike Tours (☎01 56 58 10 54; www.mikesbiketours.com). New Segway tours! Tours meet by the south leg (Pilier Sud) of the Eiffel Tower. Daily Mar.-Nov., by appointment from Dec.-Feb. Check website for schedule and meeting point. Tickets €24, students €22; night tour €28, students €26.

Canauxrama, 13, quai de la Loire, *19ème* (☎01 42 39 15 00; fax 01 42 39 11 24). Reservations required. Departures either from Port de l'Arsenal (M: Gaures) or La Villette (M: Bastille) at 9:45am and 2:45pm. €13, students €11 except on weekends and holidays. Call ahead for departure point.

Paris à velo, c'est sympa!, 37, bd. Bourdon, *4ème* (☎01 48 87 60 01). M: Bastille. 3hr. tours 10am and 3pm. €30, under 26 €26. See **Bike & Scooter Rental.**

Paristoric, 11bis, r. Scribe, *9ème* (☎01 42 66 62 06; www.paris-story.com), M: Opéra. Shows daily on the hr. Nov.-Mar. 9am-6pm; Apr.-Oct. 10am-8pm. €8, students and children under 18 €5, under 6 and second child in a family free.

Paris-Vélo, 2, r. de Fer-à-Moulin, *5ème* (☎01 43 37 59 22). M: Censier-Daubenton. Call for group tours (6-8 people).

Vedette Pont Neuf Boats (☎01 46 33 98 38). M: Pont Neuf or Louvre. Departures daily 10:30, 11:15am, noon, every 30min. from 1:30-6:30pm, 7, 8pm, and every 30min. 9-10:30pm. 1hr. Leave from the Pont Neuf landing near the Eiffel Tower. €9, under 12 €4.50, under 4 free.

TRANSPORTATION

Aéroport d'Orly, (English info ☎01 49 75 15 15). Open 6am-11:45pm.

Aeroports de Paris (☎01 48 62 22 80; www.adp.fr). One stop for all info related to Charles de Gaulle and Orly Airports—ground transportation, flight times, delays, etc. 24hr. English hotline.

Air France Buses (☎08 92 35 08 20). Between Orly and Charles de Gualle and major Metro stops in Paris. Daily 6am-11pm. €11

Airport Shuttle (to both airports), (☎01 30 11 11 90). Door-to-door service. €29, smaller additional fee for each person going to same destination.

Eurolines, (☎08 92 69 52 52). Intercity and international buses.

Paris Airports Service (to both airports), (☎01 55 98 10 80 or 01 55 98 10 89).

Paris Shuttle (☎01 43 90 91 91). Serves both airports. Door-to-door service. €25 for one person. €15 person for groups of two people or more.

Régie Autonome des Transports Parisiens (RATP), (☎08 92 68 77 14, €0.34 per min.).

WOMEN'S RESOURCES

Bibliothèque Marguerite Duras, 79, r. Nationale, *13ème* (☎01 45 70 80 30). M: Nationale. Open Tu-Sa 2-6pm.

Centre de Planification et d'Education Familiale, 27, r. Curnonsky, *17ème* (☎01 48 88 07 28). M: Porte de Champerret. Open M-F 9am-5pm.

Mouvement Français pour le Planning Familial (MFPF), 10, r. Vivienne, *2ème* (☎01 42 60 93 20). M: Bourse. Open for calls M-F 9:30am-5:30pm. On F, the clinic is held at 94, bd. Massanna, on the 1st floor of the Tour Mantoue, door code 38145, *13ème* (☎01 45 84 28 25); F 10am-4pm call ahead. M: Porte d'Ivry.

Phrasebook

PRONUNCIATION & GRAMMAR

French pronunciation can be tricky, as many of the letters in a word are often silent. Do not pronounce any final consonants except L, F, or C; an E on the end of the word, however, means that you should pronounce the final consonant sound, e.g., *muet* is mew-AY but *muette* is mew-ET. This rule also applies to plural nouns—don't pronounce the final S. J is like the S in "pleasure." R is rolled in the front of the mouth. C sounds like *K* before A, O, and U; like *S* before E and I. A ç always sounds like *S*. Vowels are short and precise: A as the *O* in "mom"; E as in "help" (é becomes the a in "hay"); I as the *ee* in "creep"; *O* as in "oh." UI sounds like the word "whee." U is a short, clipped *oo* sound; hold your lips as if you were about to say "ooh," but say *ee* instead. OU is a straight *oo* sound. With few exceptions, all syllables in French words receive equal emphasis.

Le is the masculine singular definite article (the); *la* the feminine; both are abbreviated to *l'* before a vowel, while *les* is the plural definite article for both genders. Where a noun or adjective can take masculine and feminine forms, the masculine is listed first and the feminine in parentheses; often the feminine form consists of adding an "e" to the end, which is indicated by an "e" in parentheses: étudiant(e). In general, the plural is formed by adding an "s" to the singular form. *Tu* is the familiar form of second-person address, and *vous* serves as both the plural and the formal singular form. *Vous* should always be used to address strangers, authority figures, and older people; *tu* is traditionally used only for close friends and family, although it is now more frequently used among young people.

USEFUL WORDS & PHRASES

ENGLISH	FRENCH	PRONUNCIATION
GENERAL		
Hello/Good day.	Bonjour.	bonh-ZHOORRH
Good evening.	Bonsoir.	bonh-SWAHRRH
Hi!	Salut!	sah-LU
Goodbye.	Au revoir.	oh rhVWAHRH
Good night.	Bonne nuit.	bonn NWEE
yes/no/maybe	oui/non/peut-être	wee/nonh/p'TEHT-rh
Please.	S'il vous plaît.	seel voo PLAY
Thank you.	Merci.	mehrrh-SEE
You're welcome.	De rien.	de rrhee-ANH
Pardon me!	Excusez-moi!	ex-KU-zeh-MWAH
Go away!	Allez-vous en!	Ah-LAY vooz on!
Where is...?	Où se trouve...?	oo s'TRRHOOV..?
What time do you open/ close?	Vous ouvrez/fermez à quelle heure?	vooz ooVRHEH/ ferhMEH ah kel'URH?
Help!	Au secours!	oh-SKOORRH.
I'm lost.	Je suis perdu(e).	zh'SWEE pehrh-DU
I'm sorry.	Je suis désolé(e).	zh'SWEE deh-zoh-LEH

ENGLISH	FRENCH	ENGLISH	FRENCH
PHRASES			
Who?	Qui?	**No, thank you.**	Non, merci.
What?	Quoi?	**What is it?**	Qu'est-ce que c'est?
I don't understand.	Je ne comprends pas.	**Why?**	Pourquoi?
Leave me alone.	Laissez-moi tranquille.	**this one/that one**	ceci/cela
How much does this cost?	Ça coûte combien?	**Stop/Stop that!**	Arrête! (familiar) Arrêtez! (pl.)
Please speak slowly.	S'il vous plaît, parlez moins vite.	**Please repeat.**	Répétez, s'il vous plaît.
I am ill/I am hurt.	J'ai mal./Je suis blessé(e).	**Help!/Please help me.**	Aidez-moi, s'il vous plaît.
I am (20) years old.	J'ai (vingt) ans.	**Do you speak English?**	Parlez-vous anglais?
I am a student (m)/a student (f)	Je suis étudiant/étudiante.	**What's this called in French?**	Comment-dit on...en français?
What is your name?	Comment vous appelez-vous?	**The check, please.**	L'addition, s'il vous plaît.
Please, where is (are)...?	S'il vous plaît où se trouve(nt)...?	**I would like...**	Je voudrais...
a doctor	un médecin	**the cash machine**	le guichet automatique
the toilet	les toilettes	**the restaurant**	le restaurant
the hospital	l'hôpital	**the police**	la police
a bedroom	une chambre	**the train station**	la gare
with	avec	**single room**	une chambre simple
a double bed	un grand lit	**double room**	une chambre pour deux
a sink	un lavabo	**two single beds**	deux lits
a shower	une douche	**a bath**	bain
lunch	le déjeuner	**breakfast**	le petit déjeuner
dinner	le dîner	**without**	sans
included	compris	**hot**	chaud
cold	froid	**How's the weather?**	Quel temps fait-il?
DIRECTIONS			
(to the) right	à droite	**(to the) left**	à gauche
straight	tout droit	**near to**	près de
north	nord	**far from**	loin de
south	sud	**east**	est
follow	suivre	**west**	ouest
NUMBERS			
one	un	**two**	deux
three	trois	**four**	quatre
five	cinq	**six**	six
seven	sept	**eight**	huit
nine	neuf	**ten**	dix
eleven	onze	**twelve**	douze
fifteen	quinze	**twenty**	vingt
twenty-five	vingt-cinq	**thirty**	trente
forty	quarante	**fifty**	cinquante
hundred	cent	**thousand**	mille
TIMES & HOURS			
open	ouvert	**closed**	fermé
What time is it?	Quelle heure est-il?	**It's 11am.**	Il est onze heures.
afternoon	l'après-midi	**morning**	le matin

night	la nuit	**evening**	le soir
today	aujourd'hui	**yesterday**	hier
until	jusqu'à	**tomorrow**	demain
Monday	lundi	**public holidays**	jours fériés (j.f.)
Tuesday	mardi	**Friday**	vendredi
Wednesday	mercredi	**Saturday**	samedi
Thursday	jeudi	**Sunday**	dimanche
January	janvier	**July**	juillet
February	février	**August**	août
March	mars	**September**	septembre
April	avril	**October**	octobre
May	mai	**November**	novembre
June	juin	**December**	décembre

MENU READER

agneau (m)	lamb	**gâteau (m)**	cake
ail (m)	garlic	**gésier (m)**	gizzard
asperges (f pl.)	asparagus	**glace (f)**	ice cream
assiette (f)	plate	**cuisse de grenouille (f)**	frog's leg
aubergine (f)	eggplant	**haricot vert (m)**	green bean
bavette (f)	flank	**huîtres (f pl.)**	oysters
beurre (m)	butter	**jambon (m)**	ham
bien cuit (adj.)	well done	**lait (m)**	milk
bière (f)	beer	**lapin (m)**	rabbit
bifteck (m)	steak	**légume (m)**	vegetable
blanc de volaille (m)	chicken breast	**magret de canard (m)**	duck breast
boeuf (m)	beef	**maison (adj)**	homemade
boisson (f)	drink	**marron (m)**	chestnut
brochette (f)	kebab	**fraise (f)**	strawberry
canard (m)	duck	**miel (m)**	honey
carafe d'eau (f)	pitcher of tap water	**moules (f pl.)**	mussels
cervelle (f)	brain	**moutarde (f)**	mustard
champignon (m)	mushroom	**nature (adj.)**	plain
chaud (adj)	hot	**noix (f pl.)**	nuts
chèvre (f)	goat cheese	**œuf (m)**	egg
choix (f)	choice	**oie (f)**	goose
choucroute (f)	sauerkraut	**oignon (m)**	onion
chou-fleur (m)	cauliflower	**pain (m)**	bread
ciboulette (f)	chive	**pâtes (f pl.)**	pasta
citron (m)	lemon	**plat (m)**	course
citron vert (m)	lime	**poêlé (adj.)**	pan-fried
crème fraîche (f)	thick cream	**rillettes (f pl.)**	pork hash
crêpe (f)	thin pancake	**riz (m)**	rice
eau de robinet (f)	tap water	**salade verte (f)**	green salad
échalote (f)	shallot	**sanglier (m)**	wild boar
entrecôte (m)	chop (cut of meat)	**saucisson (m)**	sausage
escalope (f)	thin slice of meat	**saumon (m)**	salmon
escargot (m)	snail	**sel (m)**	salt
foie gras d'oie	fattened goose liver	**tournedos (m)**	beef filet
foie gras de canard (m)	fattened duck liver	**truffle (f)**	truffle
frais (fraîche) (adj)	fresh	**viande (f)**	meat

farci(e) (f)	stuffed	steak tartare (m)	raw steak
faux-filet (m)	sirloin steak	sucre (m)	sugar
feuilleté (m)	puff pastry	tête (f)	head
figue (f)	fig	thé (m)	tea

FRENCH-ENGLISH GLOSSARY

accueil (m): reception
abbaye (f): abbey
allée (f): lane, avenue
alimentation (f): food
aller-retour (m): round-trip ticket
appareil (m): machine (often telephone)
appareil photo : camera
arènes (f pl.): arena
arrivée (f): arrival
auberge (f): hostel, inn.
auberge de jeunesse (f): youth hostel
autobus (m): city bus
autocar (m): long-distance bus
autoroute (f): highway
banlieue (f): suburb
bibliothèque (f): library
billet (m): ticket
billeterie (f): ticket office
bois (m): forest, wood
bureau (m): office
carte (f): card; menu; map
cave (f): cellar, normally for wine
centre ville (m): center of town
chambre (f): room
chambre d'hôte (f): bed and breakfast room
chapelle (f): chapel
charcuterie (f): shop selling cooked meats
château (m): castle or mansion
cimetière (m): cemetery
cité (f): walled city
cloître (m): cloister
colline (f): hill
comptoir (m): counter (in a bar or café)
côte (f): coast; side (e.g. of hill)
côté (m): side (e.g. of building)
couvent (f): convent
cour (f): courtyard
cours (m): wide street
cru (m): vintage
dégustation (f): tasting
départ (m): departure
donjon (m): keep (of a castle)
douane (f): customs
école (f): school
église (f): church
entrée (f): appetizer or entrance
épicerie (f): grocery store
étudiant(e): student
faubourg (abbr. fbg; m): suburb (archaic)
fête (f): celebration, festival; party
ferme (f): farm
fleuve (m): river
foire (f): fair
fontaine (f): fountain
forêt (f): forest
galerie (f): gallery
gare or gare SNCF (f): train station
gare routière (f): bus station
grève (f): strike
guichet (m): ticket counter, cash register
horloge (f): clock
hors-saison: off-season
hôpital (m): hospital
hôtel (particulier) (m): townhouse, mansion
Hôtel-de-Ville (m): city hall
hôtel-Dieu (m): hospital (archaic)
île (f): island
jour (m): day
jour férié (m): public holiday
location (f): rental store
lycée (m): high school
magasin (m): shop
mairie (f): town hall
maison (f): house
marché (m): market
mer (f): sea
monastère (m): monastery
montagne (f): mountain
mur (m): wall
muraille (f): city wall, rampart
nuit (f): night
palais (m): palace
parc (m): park
place (f): town square
plan (m): plan, map
plat (m): main course (on menu)
pont (m): bridge
poste (PTT; f): post office
quartier (m): section (of town)
randonnée (f): hike
rue (f): street
salle (f): room; indoor seating in a café
sentier (m): path, lane
soir (m): evening
source (m): spring
supermarché (m): supermarket
tabac (m): cigarette and newsstand
table (f): table
terrasse (f): terrace, patio
TGV (m): high speed train
tour (f): tower
tour (m): tour
université (f): university
val (m)/vallée (f): valley
vélo (m): bicycle
vieille ville (f): old (part of) town
ville (f): town, city
visite guidée (f): guided tour
vitraux (m pl.): stained glass
voie (f): road
voiture (f): car

Index

B

D

E

F

I

J

K

L

M

Q

R

S

Y

Z

OPENING PHOTOS

Musée du Louvre
Champs-Elysées
Versailles
L'Arc de Triomphe
Musée d'Histoire Naturelle
Marché Montorgueil
Le Dépôt
Opéra Garnier
Christian Dior, av. Montagne
Versailles Gardens
Versailles Palace
Musée d'Orsay
Marais Café
Centre Pompidou

Map Appendix

INSIDE

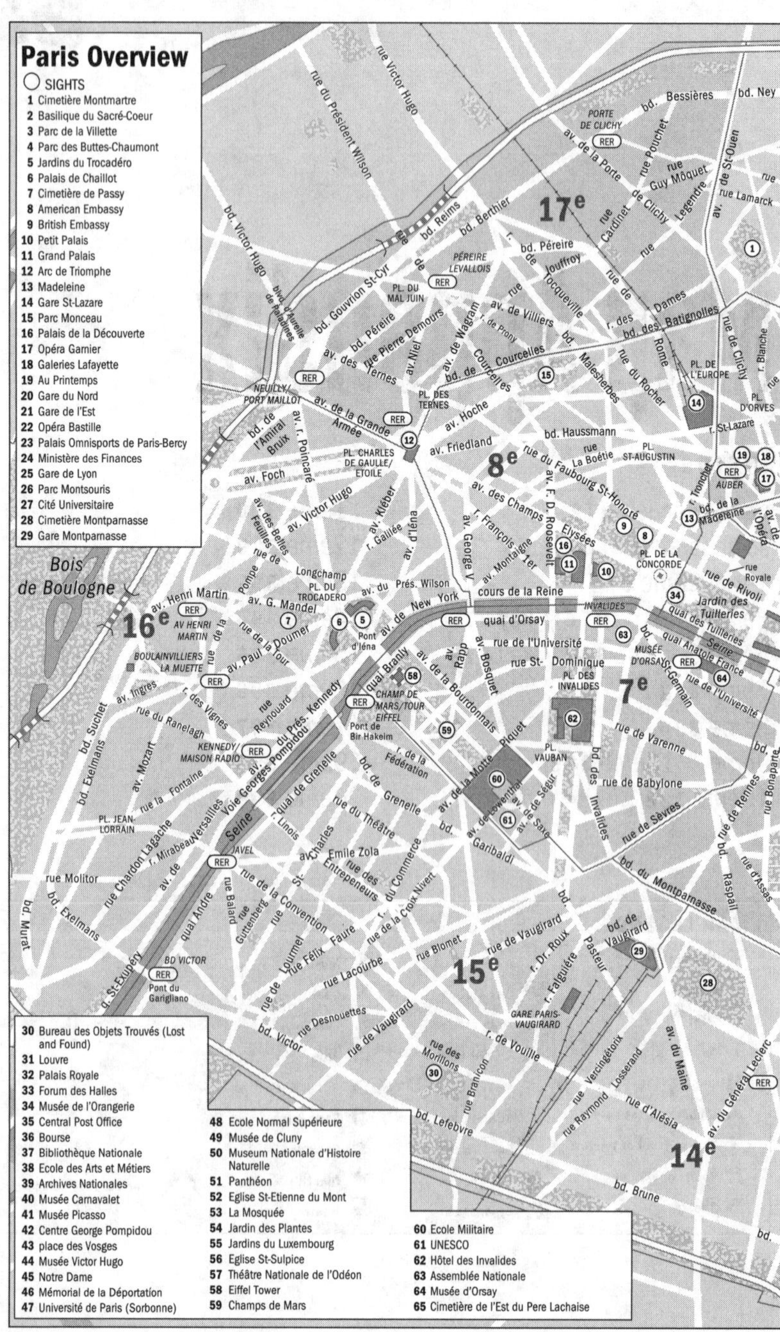
Paris Overview
SIGHTS
1 Cimetière Montmartre
2 Basilique du Sacré-Coeur
3 Parc de la Villette
4 Parc des Buttes-Chaumont
5 Jardins du Trocadéro
6 Palais de Chaillot
7 Cimetière de Passy
8 American Embassy
9 British Embassy
10 Petit Palais
11 Grand Palais
12 Arc de Triomphe
13 Madeleine
14 Gare St-Lazare
15 Parc Monceau
16 Palais de la Découverte
17 Opéra Garnier
18 Galeries Lafayette
19 Au Printemps
20 Gare du Nord
21 Gare de l'Est
22 Opéra Bastille
23 Palais Omnisports de Paris-Bercy
24 Ministère des Finances
25 Gare de Lyon
26 Parc Montsouris
27 Cité Universitaire
28 Cimetière Montparnasse
29 Gare Montparnasse
30 Bureau des Objets Trouvés (Lost and Found)
31 Louvre
32 Palais Royale
33 Forum des Halles
34 Musée de l'Orangerie
35 Central Post Office
36 Bourse
37 Bibliothèque Nationale
38 Ecole des Arts et Métiers
39 Archives Nationales
40 Musée Carnavalet
41 Musée Picasso
42 Centre George Pompidou
43 place des Vosges
44 Musée Victor Hugo
45 Notre Dame
46 Mémorial de la Déportation
47 Université de Paris (Sorbonne)
48 Ecole Normal Supérieure
49 Musée de Cluny
50 Museum Nationale d'Histoire Naturelle
51 Panthéon
52 Eglise St-Etienne du Mont
53 La Mosquée
54 Jardin des Plantes
55 Jardins du Luxembourg
56 Eglise St-Sulpice
57 Théâtre Nationale de l'Odéon
58 Eiffel Tower
59 Champs de Mars
60 Ecole Militaire
61 UNESCO
62 Hôtel des Invalides
63 Assemblée Nationale
64 Musée d'Orsay
65 Cimetière de l'Est du Pere Lachaise
17e
8e
16e
7e
15e
14e
Bois de Boulogne
Seine
PORTE DE CLICHY
PÉREIRE LEVALLOIS
PL. DU MAL JUIN
NEUILLY/PORT MAILLOT
PL. DES TERNES
PL. CHARLES DE GAULLE/ETOILE
PL. DE L'EUROPE
PL. D'ORVES
PL. ST-AUGUSTIN
AUBER
PL. DE LA CONCORDE
PL. DU TROCADERO
AV HENRI MARTIN
BOULAINVILLIERS LA MUETTE
KENNEDY/MAISON RADIO
CHAMP DE MARS/TOUR EIFFEL
INVALIDES
MUSÉE D'ORSAY
PL. DES INVALIDES
PL. VAUBAN
PL. JEAN-LORRAIN
JAVEL
BD VICTOR
GARE PARIS-VAUGIRARD
Pont d'Iéna
Pont de Bir Hakeim
Pont du Garigliano
bd. Bessières
bd. Ney
av. de la Porte de Clichy
rue Pouchet
rue Guy Môquet
rue Lamarck
av. de St-Ouen
rue Legendre
rue Cardinet
bd. Berthier
bd. Reims
bd. Péreire
r. Jouffroy
rue de Tocqueville
rue de Dames
bd. des Batignolles
rue de Rome
rue de Clichy
r. Blanche
rue du Rocher
bd. Malesherbes
av. de Villiers
r. de Prony
bd. de Courcelles
rue Pierre Demours
av. de Wagram
av. Niel
av. des Ternes
bd. Gouvrion St-Cyr
bd. Péreire
bvd. d'Aurelle de Paladines
bd. Victor Hugo
rue du Président Wilson
rue Victor Hugo
av. de la Grande Armée
av. Hoche
av. Friedland
bd. Haussmann
rue La Boétie
r. St-Lazare
r. Tronchet
bd. de la Madeleine
av. de l'Opéra
rue du Faubourg St-Honoré
av. des Champs Elysées
av. F. D. Roosevelt
r. François 1er
av. Montaigne
av. George V
av. d'Iéna
r. Galilée
av. Kléber
av. Victor Hugo
av. Foch
av. r. Poincaré
bd. de l'Amiral Bruix
av. des Belles Feuilles
rue de la Pompe
rue de Longchamp
av. du Prés. Wilson
av. de New York
cours de la Reine
rue Royale
rue de Rivoli
Jardin des Tuilleries
quai des Tuilleries
quai Anatole France
av. G. Mandel
av. Henri Martin
rue de la Tour
rue Doumer
av. Paul Doumer
quai d'Orsay
rue de l'Université
rue St- Dominique
bd. St-Germain
av. Rapp
av. Bosquet
av. de la Bourdonnais
quai Branly
rue de Varenne
rue de Babylone
rue de Sèvres
bd. des Invalides
av. de la Motte Piquet
av. de Lowenthal
av. de Ségur
av. de Saxe
bd. Raspail
rue de Rennes
rue Bonaparte
rue d'Assas
bd. du Montparnasse
av. Ingres
r. des Vignes
rue du Ranelagh
rue Reynouard
av. du Prés. Kennedy
Voie Georges Pompidou
quai de Grenelle
bd. de Grenelle
r. de la Fédération
bd. Suchet
bd. Exelmans
av. Mozart
rue la Fontaine
av. de Versailles
r. Mirabeau
rue Chardon Lagache
rue Molitor
bd. Murat
bd. Exelmans
d. St-Exupéry
quai André Citroën
rue Balard
r. Linois
av. Emile Zola
rue St. Charles
rue du Théâtre
rue des Entrepeneurs
av. du Commerce
r. de la Croix Nivert
bd. Garibaldi
rue de la Convention
rue Guttenberg
rue Félix Faure
rue Lacourbe
rue de Lourmel
rue Blomet
rue de Vaugirard
r. Dr. Roux
r. Falguière
bd. Pasteur
bd. de Vaugirard
rue Desnouettes
bd. Victor
rue de Vaugirard
rue des Morillons
r. de Vouille
rue Vercingétoix
rue Raymond Losserand
rue Branicon
av. du Maine
rue d'Alésia
av. du Général Leclerc
bd. Lefebvre
bd. Brune
RER

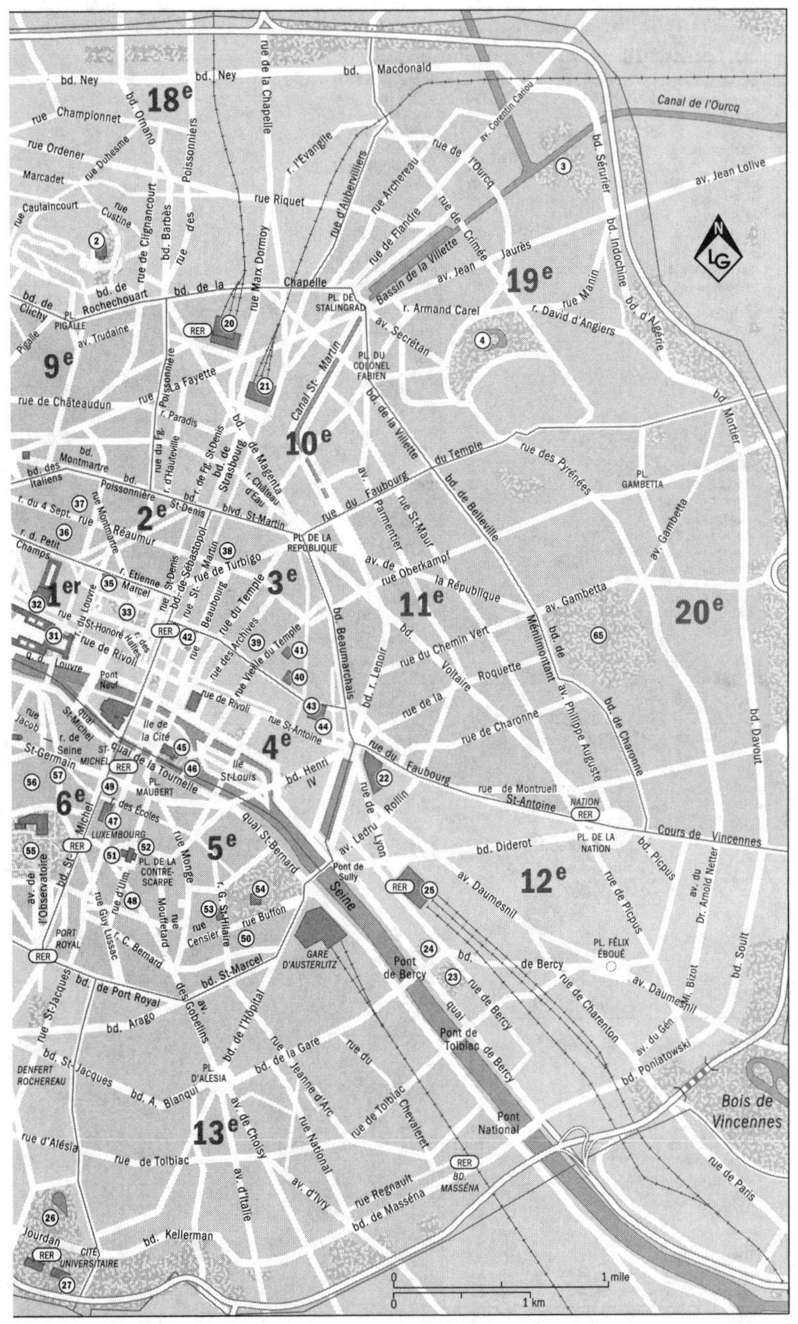

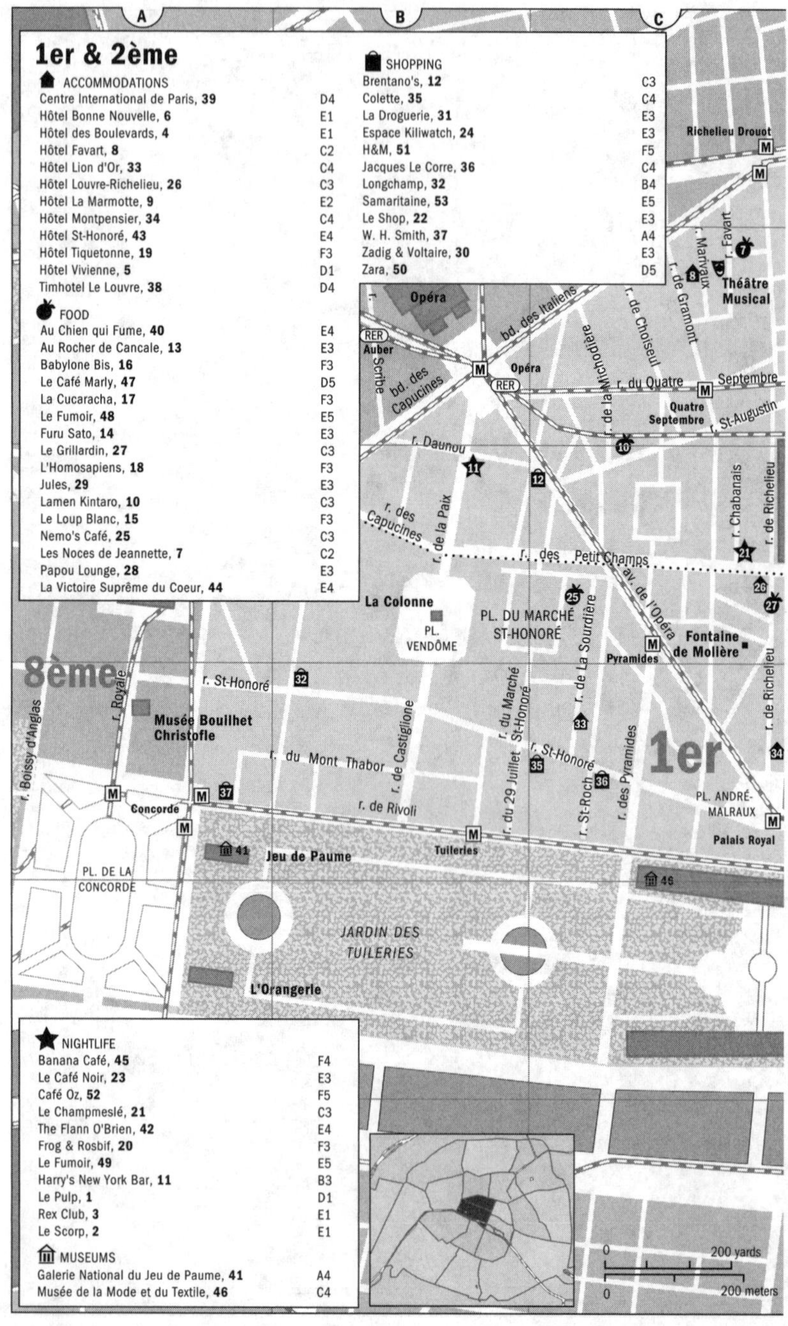
A
B
C
1er & 2ème
ACCOMMODATIONS
Centre International de Paris, 39 D4
Hôtel Bonne Nouvelle, 6 E1
Hôtel des Boulevards, 4 E1
Hôtel Favart, 8 C2
Hôtel Lion d'Or, 33 C4
Hôtel Louvre-Richelieu, 26 C3
Hôtel La Marmotte, 9 E2
Hôtel Montpensier, 34 C4
Hôtel St-Honoré, 43 E4
Hôtel Tiquetonne, 19 F3
Hôtel Vivienne, 5 D1
Timhotel Le Louvre, 38 D4
FOOD
Au Chien qui Fume, 40 E4
Au Rocher de Cancale, 13 E3
Babylone Bis, 16 F3
Le Café Marly, 47 D5
La Cucaracha, 17 F3
Le Fumoir, 48 E5
Furu Sato, 14 E3
Le Grillardin, 27 C3
L'Homosapiens, 18 F3
Jules, 29 E3
Lamen Kintaro, 10 C3
Le Loup Blanc, 15 F3
Nemo's Café, 25 C3
Les Noces de Jeannette, 7 C2
Papou Lounge, 28 E3
La Victoire Suprême du Coeur, 44 E4
SHOPPING
Brentano's, 12 C3
Colette, 35 C4
La Droguerie, 31 E3
Espace Kiliwatch, 24 E3
H&M, 51 F5
Jacques Le Corre, 36 C4
Longchamp, 32 B4
Samaritaine, 53 E5
Le Shop, 22 E3
W. H. Smith, 37 A4
Zadig & Voltaire, 30 E3
Zara, 50 D5
NIGHTLIFE
Banana Café, 45 F4
Le Café Noir, 23 E3
Café Oz, 52 F5
Le Champmeslé, 21 C3
The Flann O'Brien, 42 E4
Frog & Rosbif, 20 F3
Le Fumoir, 49 E5
Harry's New York Bar, 11 B3
Le Pulp, 1 D1
Rex Club, 3 E1
Le Scorp, 2 E1
MUSEUMS
Galerie National du Jeu de Paume, 41 A4
Musée de la Mode et du Textile, 46 C4
Richelieu Drouot
Opéra
Théâtre Musical
bd. des Italiens
r. de Choiseul
r. de Gramont
r. Marivaux
r. Favart
RER
Auber
r. Scribe
bd. des Capucines
r. de la Michodière
r. du Quatre Septembre
Quatre Septembre
r. St-Augustin
r. Daunou
r. des Capucines
r. de la Paix
r. Chabanais
r. de Richelieu
r. des Petit Champs
av. de l'Opéra
La Colonne
PL. VENDÔME
PL. DU MARCHÉ ST-HONORÉ
r. de La Sourdière
Pyramides
Fontaine de Molière
8ème
r. Boissy d'Anglas
r. Royale
r. St-Honoré
Musée Bouilhet Christofle
r. du Mont Thabor
r. de Castiglione
r. du Marché St-Honoré
r. du 29 Juillet
r. St-Roch
r. des Pyramides
1er
PL. ANDRÉ-MALRAUX
Palais Royal
Concorde
r. de Rivoli
Tuileries
Jeu de Paume
PL. DE LA CONCORDE
JARDIN DES TUILERIES
L'Orangerie
0 200 yards
0 200 meters

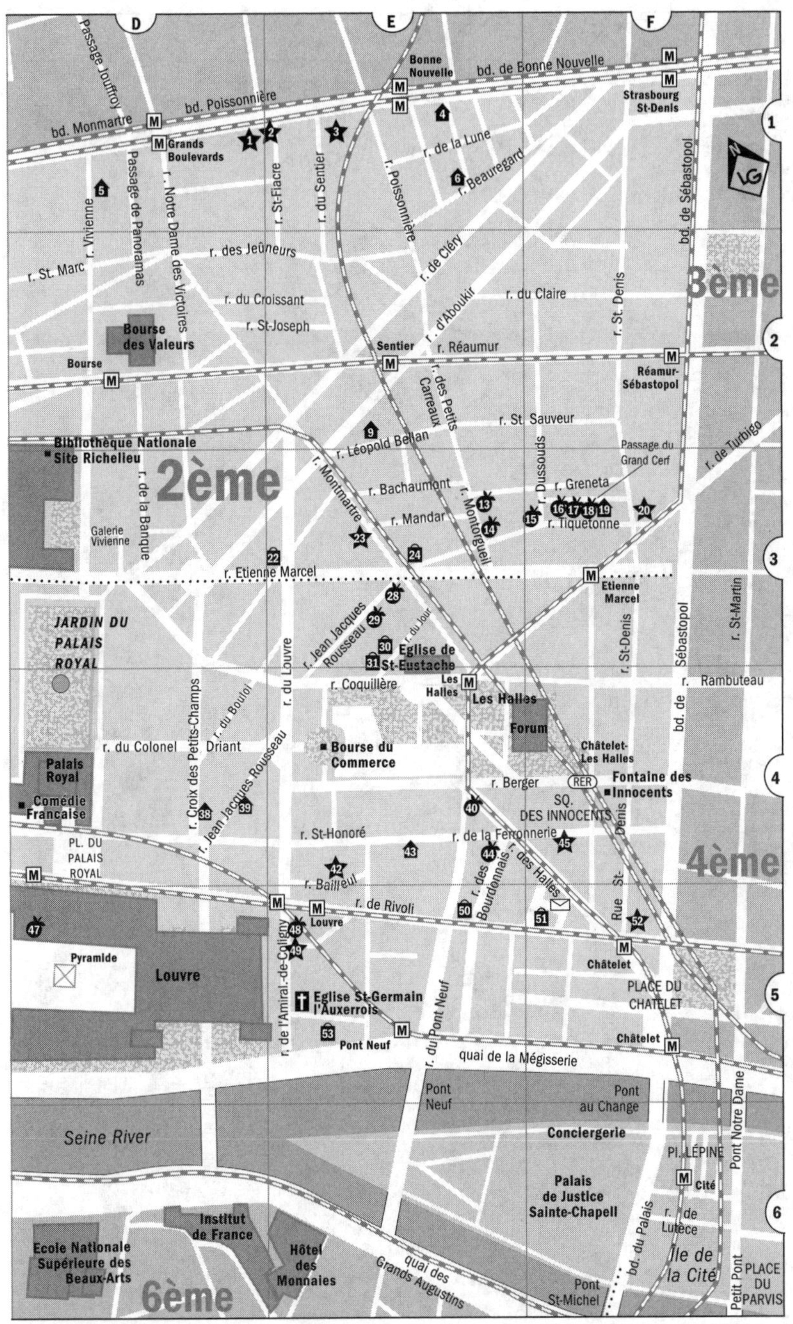

2ème
3ème
4ème
6ème
bd. de Bonne Nouvelle
bd. Poissonnière
bd. Monmartre
Bonne Nouvelle
Strasbourg St-Denis
Grands Boulevards
Passage Jouffroy
Passage de Panoramas
r. Notre Dame des Victoires
r. Vivienne
r. St-Fiacre
r. du Sentier
r. Poissonnière
r. de la Lune
r. Beauregard
bd. de Sébastopol
r. des Jeûneurs
r. St. Marc
r. de Cléry
r. du Croissant
r. St-Joseph
r. d'Aboukir
r. du Claire
r. St. Denis
Bourse des Valeurs
Bourse
Sentier
r. Réaumur
Réamur-Sébastopol
r. des Petits Carreaux
r. St. Sauveur
Bibliothèque Nationale Site Richelieu
r. Léopold Bellan
r. Montmartre
r. Dussouds
Passage du Grand Cerf
r. de Turbigo
r. de la Banque
r. Bachaumont
r. Greneta
r. Montorgueil
r. Mandar
r. Tiquetonne
Galerie Vivienne
r. Etienne Marcel
Etienne Marcel
JARDIN DU PALAIS ROYAL
r. Jean Jacques Rousseau
r. du Jour
Eglise de St-Eustache
r. du Louvre
r. St-Denis
r. St-Martin
r. Coquillère
Les Halles
r. Rambuteau
r. Croix des Petits-Champs
r. du Bouloi
Forum
r. du Colonel Driant
Bourse du Commerce
Châtelet-Les Halles
Palais Royal
Comédie Francaise
r. Berger
RER
Fontaine des Innocents
SQ. DES INNOCENTS
r. St-Honoré
r. de la Ferronnerie
PL. DU PALAIS ROYAL
r. Bailleul
r. des Bourdonnais
r. des Halles
r. de Rivoli
Louvre
Rue St-Denis
r. de l'Amiral-de-Coligny
Pyramide
Châtelet
PLACE DU CHATELET
Eglise St-Germain l'Auxerrois
r. du Pont Neuf
Pont Neuf
quai de la Mégisserie
Pont Neuf
Pont au Change
Seine River
Conciergerie
PL. LÉPINE
Pont Notre Dame
Cité
Palais de Justice Sainte-Chapell
r. de Lutèce
bd. du Palais
Institut de France
Ecole Nationale Supérieure des Beaux-Arts
Hôtel des Monnaies
quai des Grands Augustins
Pont St-Michel
Île de la Cité
Petit Pont
PLACE DU PARVIS
D
E
F
1
2
3
4
5
6

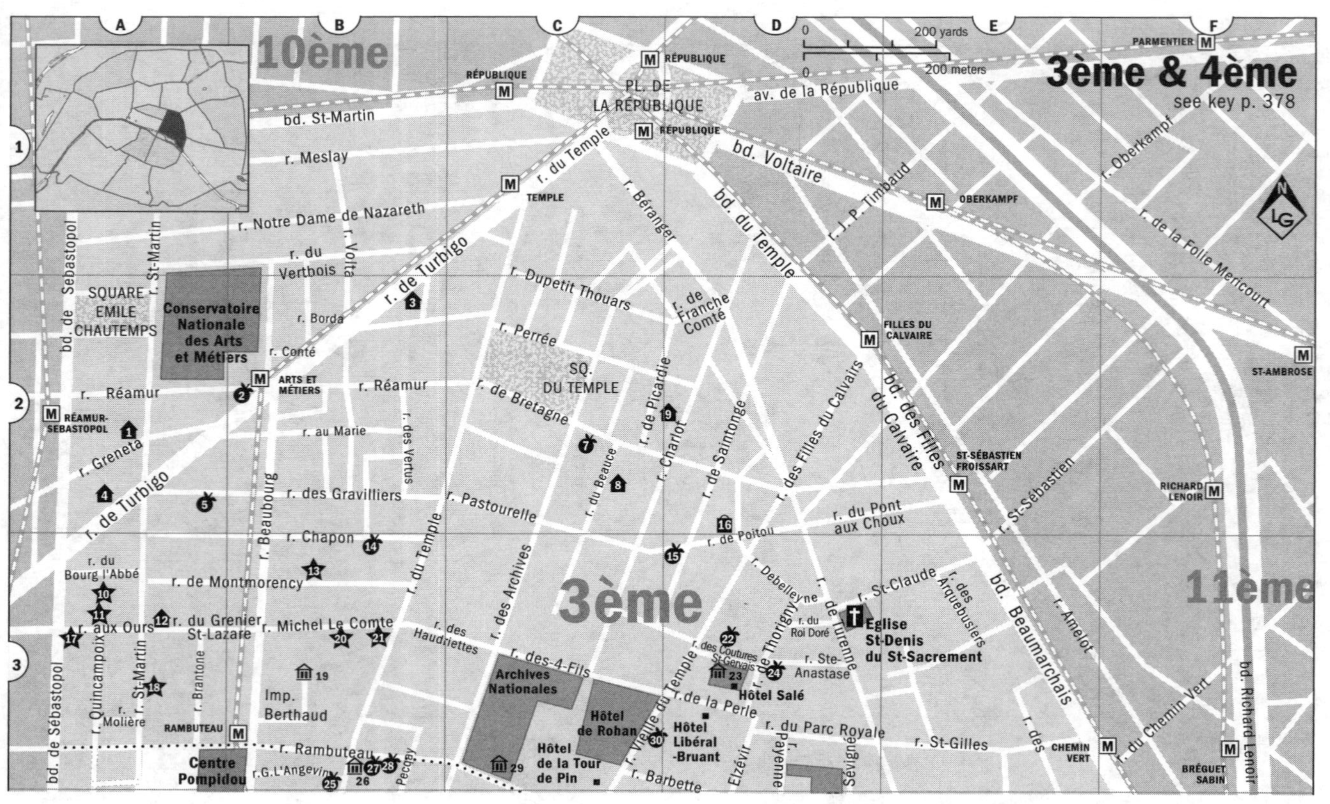

3ème & 4ème
see key p. 378
0
200 yards
0
200 meters
10ème
11ème
3ème
PL. DE LA RÉPUBLIQUE
RÉPUBLIQUE
PARMENTIER
av. de la République
bd. St-Martin
r. Meslay
r. du Temple
TEMPLE
bd. Voltaire
r. Oberkampf
OBERKAMPF
r. J. P. Timbaud
r. de la Folie Mericourt
r. Notre Dame de Nazareth
r. Volta
r. du Vertbois
r. de Turbigo
r. Béranger
bd. du Temple
r. Dupetit Thouars
r. de Franche Comté
SQUARE EMILE CHAUTEMPS
Conservatoire Nationale des Arts et Métiers
r. Borda
r. Conté
r. Perrée
SQ. DU TEMPLE
FILLES DU CALVAIRE
ST-AMBROSE
ARTS ET MÉTIERS
r. Réaumur
r. de Bretagne
r. de Picardie
r. des Filles du Calvairs
bd. des Filles du Calvaire
r. de Saintonge
RÉAUMUR-SEBASTOPOL
r. au Marie
r. des Vertus
r. Charlot
r. Greneta
r. du Beauce
ST-SÉBASTIEN FROISSART
r. St-Sébastien
RICHARD LENOIR
r. des Gravilliers
r. Pastourelle
r. du Pont aux Choux
r. Chapon
r. Beaubourg
r. de Poitou
r. des Archives
r. du Bourg l'Abbé
r. de Montmorency
r. Debelleyne
r. St-Claude
r. des Arquebusiers
bd. Beaumarchais
r. Amelot
r. aux Ours
r. du Grenier St-Lazare
r. Michel Le Comte
r. des Haudriettes
r. du Roi Doré
r. de Turenne
r. de Thorigny
Eglise St-Denis du St-Sacrement
r. des Coutures St-Gervais
r. Ste-Anastase
bd. de Sébastopol
r. Quincampoix
r. St-Martin
r. Brantone
Imp. Berthaud
r. des-4-Fils
Archives Nationales
r. Vieille du Temple
Hôtel Salé
r. de la Perle
r. du Chemin Vert
bd. Richard Lenoir
r. Molière
RAMBUTEAU
Hôtel de Rohan
Hôtel Libéral -Bruant
r. du Parc Royale
r. St-Gilles
r. des
CHEMIN VERT
BRÉGUET SABIN
r. Rambuteau
Centre Pompidou
r. G.L'Angevin
Pecquay
Hôtel de la Tour de Pin
r. Barbette
Elzévir
r. Payenne
Sévigné

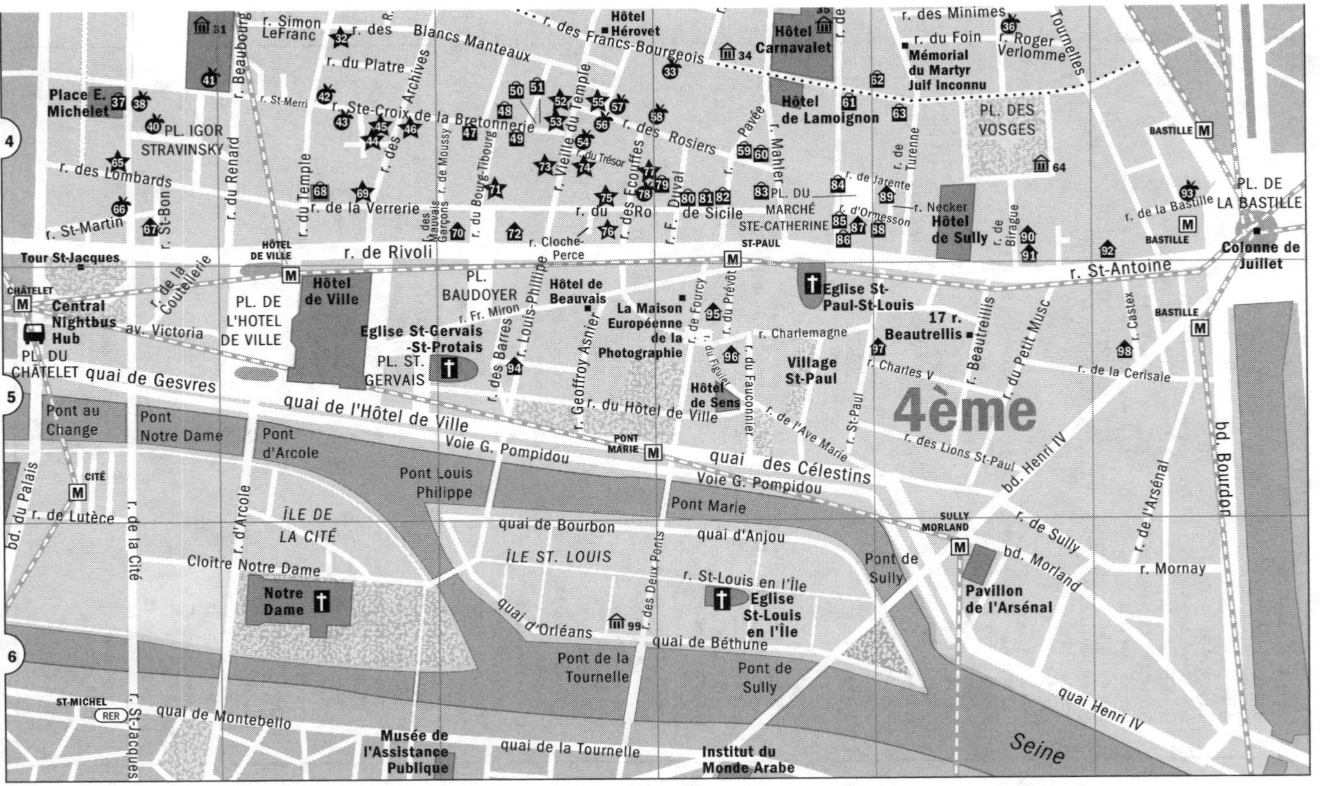
4ème
Seine
PL. DE LA BASTILLE
Colonne de Juillet
bd. Bourdon
BASTILLE
r. de la Bastille
r. St-Antoine
r. Castex
r. de la Cerisaie
r. de l'Arsénal
r. Mornay
quai Henri IV
bd. Henri IV
r. de Sully
bd. Morland
Pavillon de l'Arsénal
SULLY MORLAND
Pont de Sully
r. du Petit Musc
r. Beautreillis
17 r. Beautreillis
r. des Lions St-Paul
r. Charles V
r. St-Paul
r. de l'Ave Marie
quai des Célestins
Voie G. Pompidou
Eglise St-Paul-St-Louis
Village St-Paul
r. Charlemagne
r. du Fauconnier
r. du Prévôt
r. du Figuier
r. de Fourcy
Hôtel de Sens
r. du Hôtel de Ville
La Maison Européenne de la Photographie
Hôtel de Beauvais
r. Geoffroy Asnier
r. Louis-Philippe
r. des Barres
PL. BAUDOYER
r. Fr. Miron
Eglise St-Gervais -St-Protais
PL. ST. GERVAIS
PONT MARIE
Pont Marie
quai d'Anjou
Eglise St-Louis en l'Île
r. St-Louis en l'Île
quai de Béthune
Institut du Monde Arabe
r. des Deux Ponts
quai de Bourbon
ÎLE ST. LOUIS
quai d'Orléans
Pont de la Tournelle
quai de la Tournelle
Musée de l'Assistance Publique
Pont Louis Philippe
ÎLE DE LA CITÉ
Notre Dame
Cloître Notre Dame
r. d'Arcole
Pont d'Arcole
quai de Montebello
r. St-Jacques
RER
ST-MICHEL
r. de la Cité
Pont Notre Dame
Pont au Change
CITÉ
r. de Lutèce
bd. du Palais
quai de l'Hôtel de Ville
Hôtel de Ville
PL. DE L'HOTEL DE VILLE
HÔTEL DE VILLE
quai de Gesvres
av. Victoria
r. de la Coutellerie
PL. DU CHÂTELET
CHÂTELET
Central Nightbus Hub
Tour St-Jacques
r. St-Martin
r. des Lombards
r. St-Bon
PL. IGOR STRAVINSKY
Place E. Michelet
r. du Renard
r. Beaubourg
r. St-Merri
r. Simon LeFranc
r. du Temple
r. de la Verrerie
r. de Rivoli
r. du Platre
r. Ste-Croix de la Bretonnerie
r. des Archives
r. des Blancs Manteaux
r. des Mauvais Garçons
r. de Moussy
r. du Bourg-Tibourg
r. Vieille du Temple
r. du Trésor
r. Cloche-Perce
r. des Écouffes
r. des Rosiers
r. des Francs-Bourgeois
Hôtel Hérovet
r. du Roi de Sicile
r. F. Duval
r. Pavée
r. Mahler
PL. DU MARCHÉ STE-CATHERINE
ST-PAUL
Hôtel Carnavalet
Hôtel de Lamoignon
r. d'Ormesson
r. de Jarente
r. Necker
r. de Turenne
Hôtel de Sully
r. de Birague
PL. DES VOSGES
Mémorial du Martyr Juif Inconnu
r. du Foin
r. des Minimes
r. Roger Verlomme
Tournelles

3ème & 4ème

see map p. 376-377

ACCOMMODATIONS

Castex Hôtel, **98**	F5
Le Fauconnier, **96**	D5
Le Fourcy, **95**	D5
Grand Hôtel Jeannne d'Arc, **89**	E4
Hôtel du 7ème Art, **97**	E5
Hôtel Andrea, **67**	A4
Hôtel Bellevue et du Chariot d'Or, **4**	A2
Hôtel de la Herse d'Or, **92**	F4
Hôtel du Marais, **8**	C2
Hôtel de Nice, **72**	C4
Hôtel de la Place des Vosges, **90**	E4
Hôtel de Roubaix, **1**	A2
Hôtel de Sejour, **12**	A3
Hôtel Paris France, **3**	B2
Hôtel Picard, **9**	C/D2
Hôtel Practic, **87**	D4
Hôtel Rivoli, **70**	C4
Maubuisson, **94**	C5
Sully Hôtel, **91**	E4

FOOD

404, **5**	A2
L'Apparemment Café, **22**	D3
Aquarius, **42**	B4
Les Arts et Métiers, **2**	B2
L'As du Falafel, **58**	C/D4
Au Petit Fer à Cheval, **54**	C4
Bofinger, **93**	F4
Café Beaubourg, **40**	A4
Chez Janou, **36**	E4
Chez Marianne, **57**	C4
Chez Omar, **7**	C2
La Cure Gourmande, **38**	A4
Le Divin, **43**	B4
En Attendant Pablo, **30**	C3
Les Enfants Gâtés, **33**	D4
Fromages...ou Desserts, **27**	B3
Georges, **41**	A4
Le Grizzli, **66**	A4
Little Italy Trattoria, **28**	B3
Pain, Vin, Fromage, **25**	B3
Piccolo Teatro, **78**	C4
Le Réconfort, **15**	D3
Sacha Finkelsztajn, **56**	C4
Taxi Jaune, **14**	B3
La Verte Tige, **24**	D3

NIGHTLIFE

Amnésia Café, **55**	C4
Les Bains, **10**	A3
Le Bar du Palmier, **65**	A4
La Belle Hortense, **73**	C4
Boobs Bourg, **13**	B3
Café Klein Holland, **75**	C4
Le Café du Trésor, **74**	C4
Chez Richard, **52**	C4
Cox, **44**	A4
Le Dépôt, **11**	A3
Le Duplex, **20**	B3
Les Etages, **53**	C4
Lizard Lounge, **71**	C4
Le Masque Rouge, **32**	B4
Mixer Bar, **46**	B4
Open Café, **45**	B4
Le Quetzal, **69**	B4
Les Scandaleuses, **77**	C4
Stolly's, **76**	C4
L'Unity, **18**	A3
Utopia, **21**	B3
Villa Keops, **17**	A3

SHOPPING

Abou d'abi Bazar, **62**	E4
Alternatives, **80**	D4
Les Antiquaires de la Mode, **88**	E4
Bel ' Air, **60**	D4
Bernie X, **86**	D4
BHV, **68**	B4
Boy'z Bazaar, **49**	C4
Brontibay, **85**	D4
Culotte, **83**	D4
Fabien Nobile, **79**	D4
Free 'P' Star, **50**	C4
IEM, **48**	C4
Karine Dupont Boutique, **16**	D2
Loft Design by Paris, **84**	D4
Lollipops, **59**	D4
Monic, **63**	E4
Les Mots à la Bouche, **51**	C4
Plein Sud, **61**	D4
Pylones, **47**	C4
Sentimental, **81**	D4
Tokyoite, **82**	D4
Vertiges, **37**	A4

MUSEUMS

Maison de Victor Hugo, **64**	E4
Musée Adam Mickiewicz, **99**	C6
Musée d'Art et d'Histoire du Judaïsme, **26**	B3
Musée Carnavalet, **35**	D4
Musée Cognacq-Jay, **34**	D4
Musée de l'Histoire de France, **29**	C3
Musée National d'Art Moderne, **31**	A4
Musée Picasso, **23**	D3
Musée de la Poupée, **19**	B3

5ème & 6ème (see map p. 380-381)

ACCOMMODATIONS

Centre International de Paris, **50**	D3
Delhy's Hôtel, **24**	C2
Foyer International des Etudiantes, **95**	C5
Hôtel des Argonauts, **26**	C2
Hôtel le Central, **78**	D3
Hôtel de Chevreuse, **102**	B6
Hôtel d'Esmerelda, **27**	C2
Hôtel Gay-Lussac, **93**	C5
Hôtel du Lys, **35**	C2
Hôtel Marignan, **47**	C3
Hôtel des Médicis, **91**	C4
Hôtel de Nesle, **21**	B2
Hôtel St-André des Arts, **34**	B2
Hôtel Stella, **74**	C3
Hôtel St-Jacques, **61**	D3
Young and Happy Hostel, **97**	D5

FOOD

Au Port Salut, **87**	C4
Le Bistro Ernest, **20**	A2
Le Bistro d'Henri, **58**	A3
Café Delmas, **85**	D4
Café de Flore, **39**	A3
Café de la Mosquée, **94**	E4
Café Vavin, **98**	A6
Chez Henri, **49**	D3
Coffee Parisien, **53**	A3
Le Comptoir du Relais, **43**	B3
Comptoir Méditerranée, **64**	D3
Cosi, **32**	A2
La Crêpe Rit du Clown, **57**	A3
Crêperie St-Germain, **23**	B2
Les Deux Magots, **40**	A3
Les Editeurs, **42**	B3
Le Grenier de Notre-Dame, **29**	D2
Guen-Maï, **31**	A2
Le Jardin des Pâtés, **86**	E4
Le Machon d'Henri, **69**	A3
Octave, **96**	D/E4
Le Perraudin, **83**	C4
Le Petit Vatel, **60**	B3
Le Procope, **33**	B2
Savannah Café, **84**	D4
Le Sélect, **101**	A6

SHOPPING

Abbey Bookshop, **36**	C2
agnès b., **76**	A4
Bill Tornade, **54**	A3
Cacharel, **66**	A3
esprit, **67**	A3
Free Lance, **52**	A3
Gibert Jeune, **25**	C2
Gilbert Joseph, **45**	C3
L'Harmattan, **63**	D3
Muji, **70**	B3
No Name, **55**	A3
Om Kashi, **48**	D3
Petit Bateau, **99**	A6
Presence Africain, **61**	D3
San Francisco Book Co., **44**	B3
Shakespeare and Co., **28**	C2
Tara Jarmon, **51**	A3
Vanessa Bruno, **71**	B3
Village Voice, **56**	A3

NIGHTLIFE

L'Assignat, **19**	B2
Le Bar Dix, **73**	B3
Bob Cool, **22**	B2
Café Mabillon, **41**	A3
Le Caveau des Oubliettes, **38**	C2
Chez Georges, **68**	A3
Le Crocodile, **92**	C4
Finnegan's Wake, **79**	E3/4
Fu Bar, **72**	B3
Le Piano Vache, **77**	D3
Le Reflet, **75**	C3
Moosehead, **59**	B3
Who's Bar, **37**	C2

MUSEUMS

Grande Gallerie d'Évolution, **88**	E4
Institut du Monde Arabe, **65**	E2
Musée d'Anatomie Comparée et de Paléontologie, **80**	F3
Musée de Cluny, **46**	C3
Musée Delacroix, **30**	A2
Musée d'Histoire Naturelle, **89**	F4
Musée du Luxembourg, **81**	B4
Musée de Minéralogie, **90**	F4
Musée de la Monnaie, **18**	B2
Musée Zadkine, **100**	B5

Islands

ACCOMMODATIONS

Hôtel Henri IV, **1**	B1

FOOD

Amorino, **14**	D/E2
Au Vieux Paris d'Arcole, **4**	D1
Berthillon, **17**	E2
Brasserie de l'Ile St-Louis, **6**	D1
Cafê Med, **12**	D2
Le Caveau du Palais, **7**	B1
La Crêpe en l'Île, **16**	E2
Les Fous de l'Île, **10**	E1
Au Rendez-Vous des Camionneurs, **5**	B1
Le Rouge et Blanc, **2**	B1
Le Soleil d'Or, **3**	C1

SHOPPING

78, **9**	D1
Blasphème, **15**	E2
La Boutique Suèdoise, **8**	D1
Le Grain de Sable, **11**	D2
Pylônes, **13**	D2

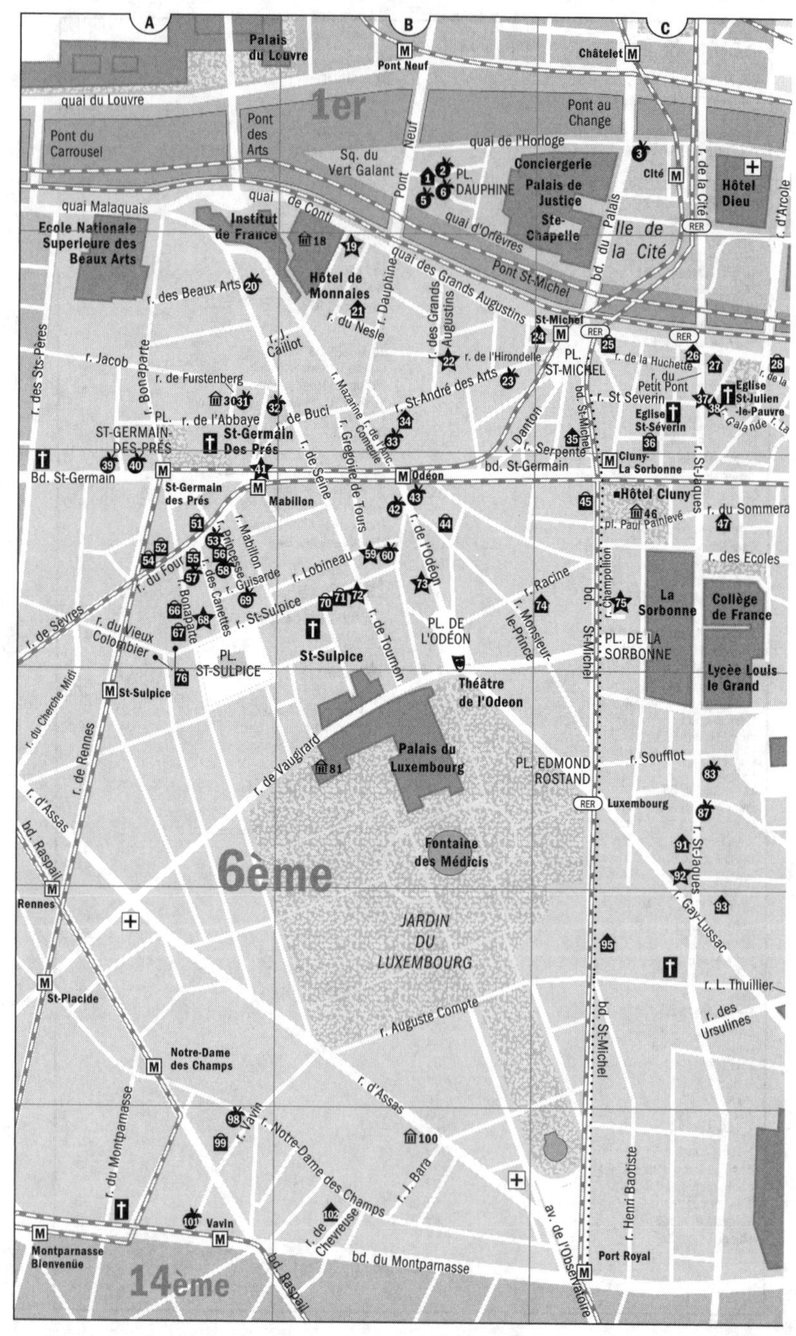

Palais du Louvre
Pont Neuf
Châtelet
1er
quai du Louvre
Pont au Change
Pont du Carrousel
Pont des Arts
Sq. du Vert Galant
PL. DAUPHINE
Conciergerie
Palais de Justice
Ste-Chapelle
Cité
Hôtel Dieu
quai Malaquais
quai de Conti
Institut de France
Ecole Nationale Superieure des Beaux Arts
Hôtel de Monnaies
quai d'Orfèvres
Ile de la Cité
quai des Grands Augustins
Pont St-Michel
quai de l'Horloge
r. des Beaux Arts
r. du Nesle
r. Dauphine
r. des Grands Augustins
St-Michel
PL. ST-MICHEL
r. de l'Hirondelle
r. de la Huchette
r. du Petit Pont
Eglise St-Julien -le-Pauvre
r. St Severin
Eglise St-Séverin
r. Galande
r. J. Caillot
r. Jacob
r. de Furstenberg
r. des Sts-Pères
r. Bonaparte
PL. ST-GERMAIN-DES-PRÉS
r. de l'Abbaye
St-Germain Des Prés
r. de Buci
r. Mazarine
r. St-André des Arts
r. Danton
r. Serpente
Cluny-La Sorbonne
Bd. St-Germain
bd. St-Germain
St-Germain des Prés
Mabillon
Odéon
r. de l'Anc. Comedie
r. Gregoire de Tours
r. de Seine
Hôtel Cluny
pl. Paul Painlevé
r. St-Jaques
r. du Sommerard
r. des Ecoles
r. Mabillon
r. Princesse
r. du Four
r. des Canettes
r. Guisarde
r. Lobineau
r. de l'Odéon
r. Racine
r. Monsieur-le-Prince
r. Champollion
La Sorbonne
Collège de France
r. de Sèvres
r. du Vieux Colombier
r. St-Sulpice
PL. ST-SULPICE
St-Sulpice
r. de Tournon
PL. DE L'ODÉON
Théatre de l'Odeon
PL. DE LA SORBONNE
bd. St-Michel
Lycée Louis le Grand
r. du Cherche Midi
r. de Rennes
r. de Vaugirard
Palais du Luxembourg
PL. EDMOND ROSTAND
r. Soufflot
r. d'Assas
bd. Raspail
Luxembourg
RER
Fontaine des Médicis
6ème
Rennes
JARDIN DU LUXEMBOURG
r. Gay-Lussac
r. L. Thuillier
r. des Ursulines
St-Placide
r. Auguste Compte
Notre-Dame des Champs
r. du Montparnasse
r. Vavin
r. Notre-Dame des Champs
r. J. Bara
r. Henri Baotiste
av. de l'Observatoire
Vavin
r. de Chevreuse
Montparnasse Bienvenüe
bd. du Montparnasse
Port Royal
14ème
A
B
C

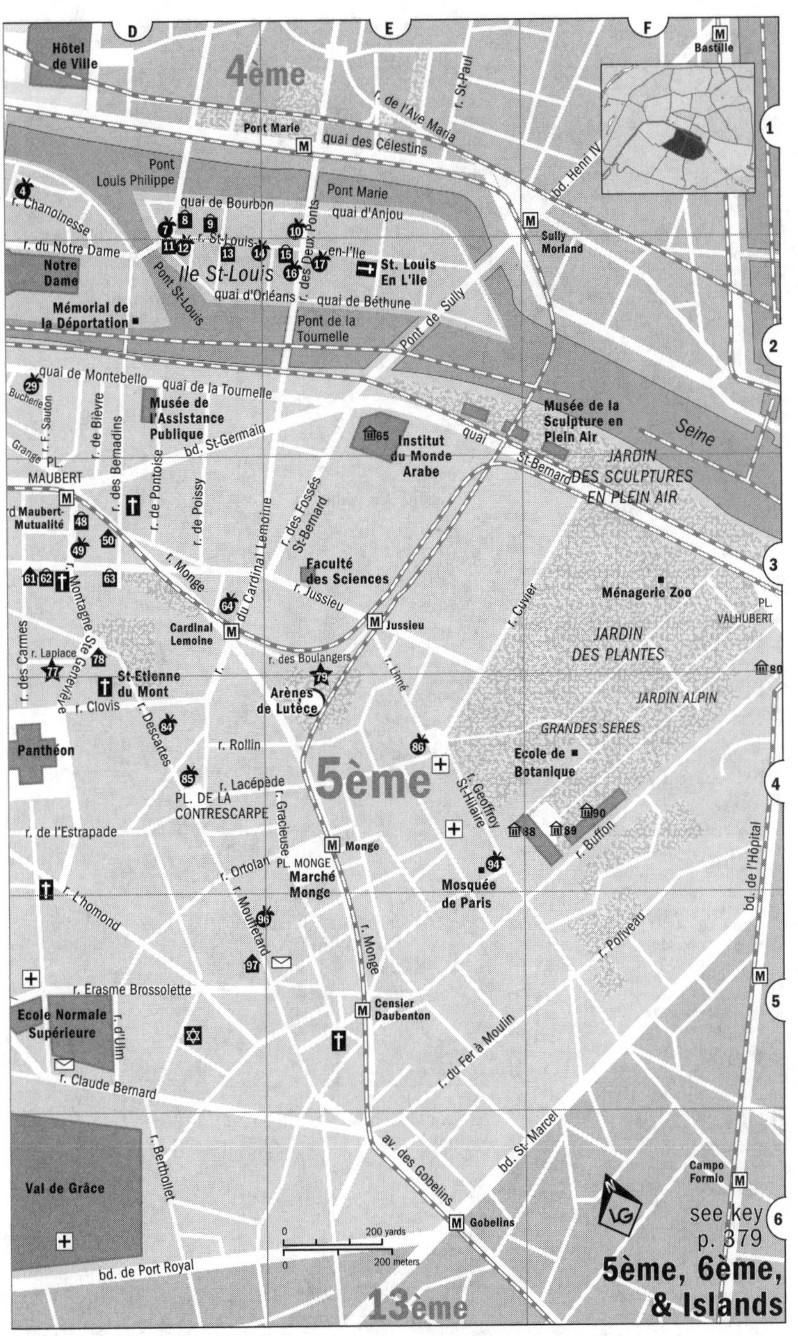

see key p. 379

5ème, 6ème, & Islands

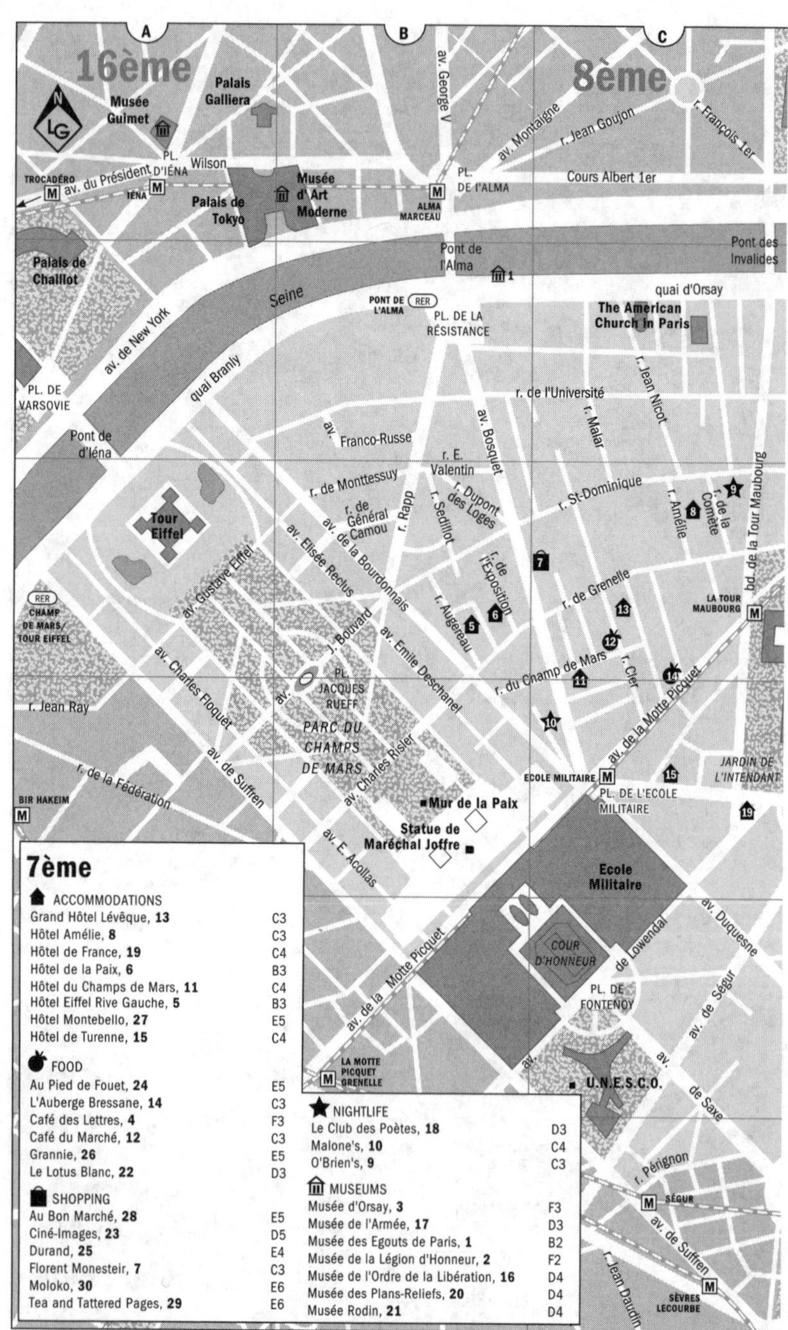
7ème
ACCOMMODATIONS
Grand Hôtel Lévêque, 13 C3
Hôtel Amélie, 8 C3
Hôtel de France, 19 C4
Hôtel de la Paix, 6 B3
Hôtel du Champs de Mars, 11 C4
Hôtel Eiffel Rive Gauche, 5 B3
Hôtel Montebello, 27 E5
Hôtel de Turenne, 15 C4
FOOD
Au Pied de Fouet, 24 E5
L'Auberge Bressane, 14 C3
Café des Lettres, 4 F3
Café du Marché, 12 C3
Grannie, 26 E5
Le Lotus Blanc, 22 D3
SHOPPING
Au Bon Marché, 28 E5
Ciné-Images, 23 D5
Durand, 25 E4
Florent Monesteir, 7 C3
Moloko, 30 E6
Tea and Tattered Pages, 29 E6
NIGHTLIFE
Le Club des Poètes, 18 D3
Malone's, 10 C4
O'Brien's, 9 C3
MUSEUMS
Musée d'Orsay, 3 F3
Musée de l'Armée, 17 D3
Musée des Egouts de Paris, 1 B2
Musée de la Légion d'Honneur, 2 F2
Musée de l'Ordre de la Libération, 16 D4
Musée des Plans-Reliefs, 20 D4
Musée Rodin, 21 D4
A
B
C
16ème
8ème
Palais Galliera
Musée Guimet
PL. D'IÉNA
Wilson
TROCADÉRO
av. du Président
IÉNA
Palais de Tokyo
Musée d'Art Moderne
av. George V
av. Montaigne
r. Jean Goujon
r. François 1er
PL. DE L'ALMA
ALMA MARCEAU
Cours Albert 1er
Palais de Chaillot
Pont de l'Alma
Pont des Invalides
Seine
quai d'Orsay
PONT DE L'ALMA
RER
PL. DE LA RÉSISTANCE
The American Church in Paris
av. de New York
quai Branly
PL. DE VARSOVIE
Pont de d'Iéna
r. Jean Nicot
r. de l'Université
r. Malar
av. Bosquet
av. Franco-Russe
r. E. Valentin
r. de Monttessuy
r. Dupont des Loges
r. St-Dominique
r. Amélie
r. de la Comète
bd. de la Tour Maubourg
r. de Général Camou
r. Rapp
r. Sedillot
Tour Eiffel
av. Elisée Reclus
av. de la Bourdonnais
r. de l'Exposition
av. Gustave Eiffel
r. Augereau
r. de Grenelle
LA TOUR MAUBOURG
CHAMP DE MARS/ TOUR EIFFEL
J. Bouvard
av. Emile Deschanel
r. Cler
r. du Champ de Mars
av. Charles Floquet
PL. JACQUES RUEFF
r. Jean Ray
PARC DU CHAMPS DE MARS
av. de la Motte Picquet
av. de Suffren
av. Charles Risler
JARDIN DE L'INTENDANT
ECOLE MILITAIRE
r. de la Fédération
PL. DE L'ECOLE MILITAIRE
BIR HAKEIM
Mur de la Paix
Statue de Maréchal Joffre
av. E. Acollas
Ecole Militaire
av. Duquesne
av. de la Motte Picquet
COUR D'HONNEUR
de Lowendal
PL. DE FONTENOY
av. de Ségur
LA MOTTE PICQUET GRENELLE
U.N.E.S.C.O.
av. de Saxe
r. Pérignon
SÉGUR
av. de Suffren
r. Jean Daudin
SÈVRES LECOURBE

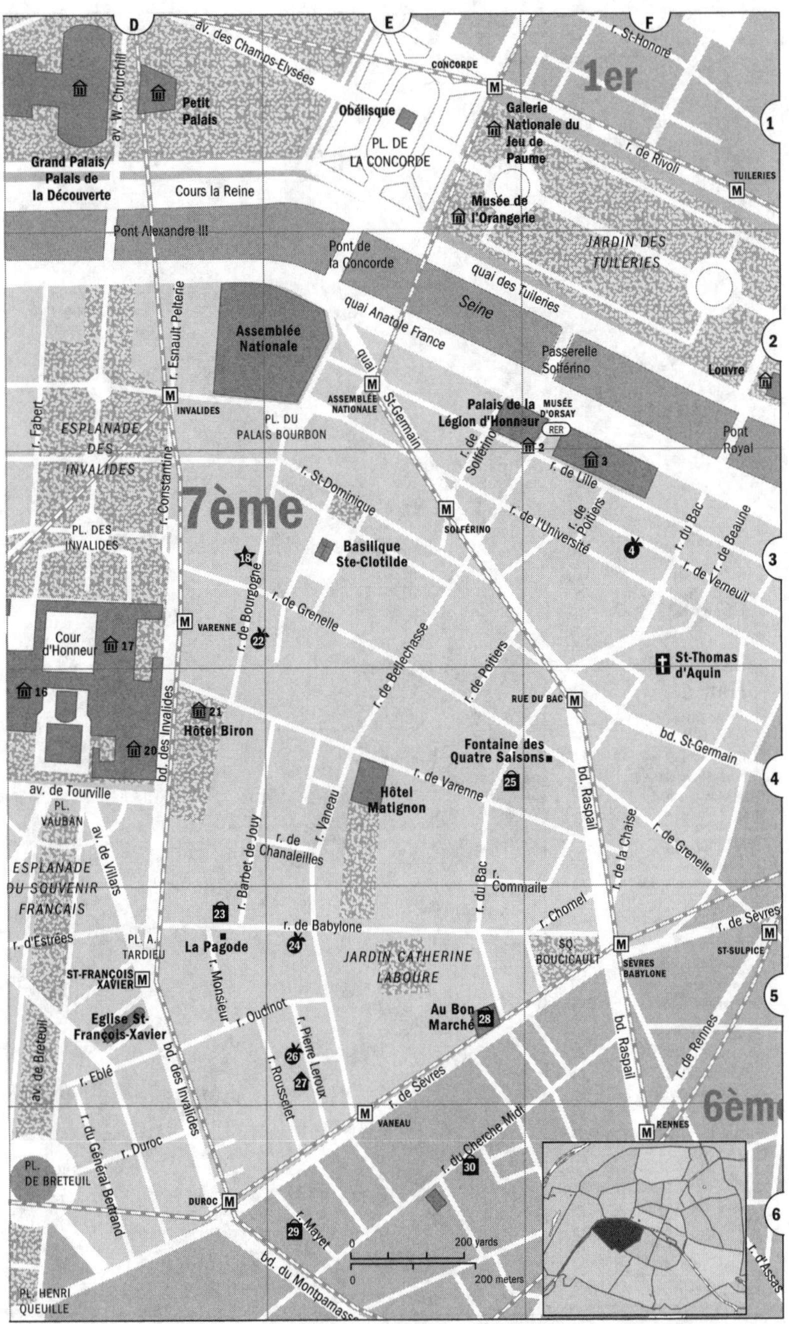

D
E
F
1
2
3
4
5
6
av. des Champs-Elysées
r. St-Honoré
CONCORDE
1er
Petit Palais
Obélisque
Galerie Nationale du Jeu de Paume
av. W. Churchill
PL. DE LA CONCORDE
r. de Rivoli
TUILERIES
Grand Palais/ Palais de la Découverte
Cours la Reine
Musée de l'Orangerie
Pont Alexandre III
Pont de la Concorde
JARDIN DES TUILERIES
quai des Tuileries
r. Esnault Pelterie
Seine
quai Anatole France
Assemblée Nationale
Passerelle Solférino
Louvre
quai St-Germain
ASSEMBLÉE NATIONALE
INVALIDES
PL. DU PALAIS BOURBON
Palais de la Légion d'Honneur
MUSÉE D'ORSAY
RER
r. Fabert
ESPLANADE DES INVALIDES
r. de Solférino
2
3
Pont Royal
r. Constantine
r. St-Dominique
r. de Lille
7ème
SOLFÉRINO
r. de l'Université
r. de Poitiers
r. du Bac
r. de Beaune
PL. DES INVALIDES
18
Basilique Ste-Clotilde
4
r. de Verneuil
r. de Grenelle
Cour d'Honneur
17
VARENNE
r. de Bourgogne
22
r. de Bellechasse
St-Thomas d'Aquin
16
r. de Poitiers
RUE DU BAC
bd. des Invalides
21
Hôtel Biron
bd. St-Germain
20
Fontaine des Quatre Saisons
25
av. de Tourville
r. de Varenne
Hôtel Matignon
PL. VAUBAN
bd. Raspail
r. Vaneau
r. Barbet de Jouy
av. de Villars
r. de Chanaleilles
r. de la Chaise
r. de Grenelle
ESPLANADE DU SOUVENIR FRANCAIS
r. du Bac
r. Commaille
23
r. Chomel
r. de Sèvres
r. de Babylone
r. d'Estrées
PL. A. TARDIEU
24
SQ. BOUCICAULT
ST-SULPICE
La Pagode
JARDIN CATHERINE LABOURE
SÈVRES BABYLONE
ST-FRANÇOIS XAVIER
r. Monsieur
Au Bon Marché
28
r. Oudinot
Eglise St-François-Xavier
r. Pierre Leroux
av. de Breteuil
26
bd. Raspail
r. de Rennes
r. Eblé
r. Rousselet
27
r. de Sèvres
VANEAU
6ème
RENNES
r. du Général Bertrand
r. Duroc
r. du Cherche Midi
30
PL. DE BRETEUIL
DUROC
r. Mayet
29
0
200 yards
0
200 meters
bd. du Montparnasse
r. d'Assas
PL. HENRI QUEUILLE

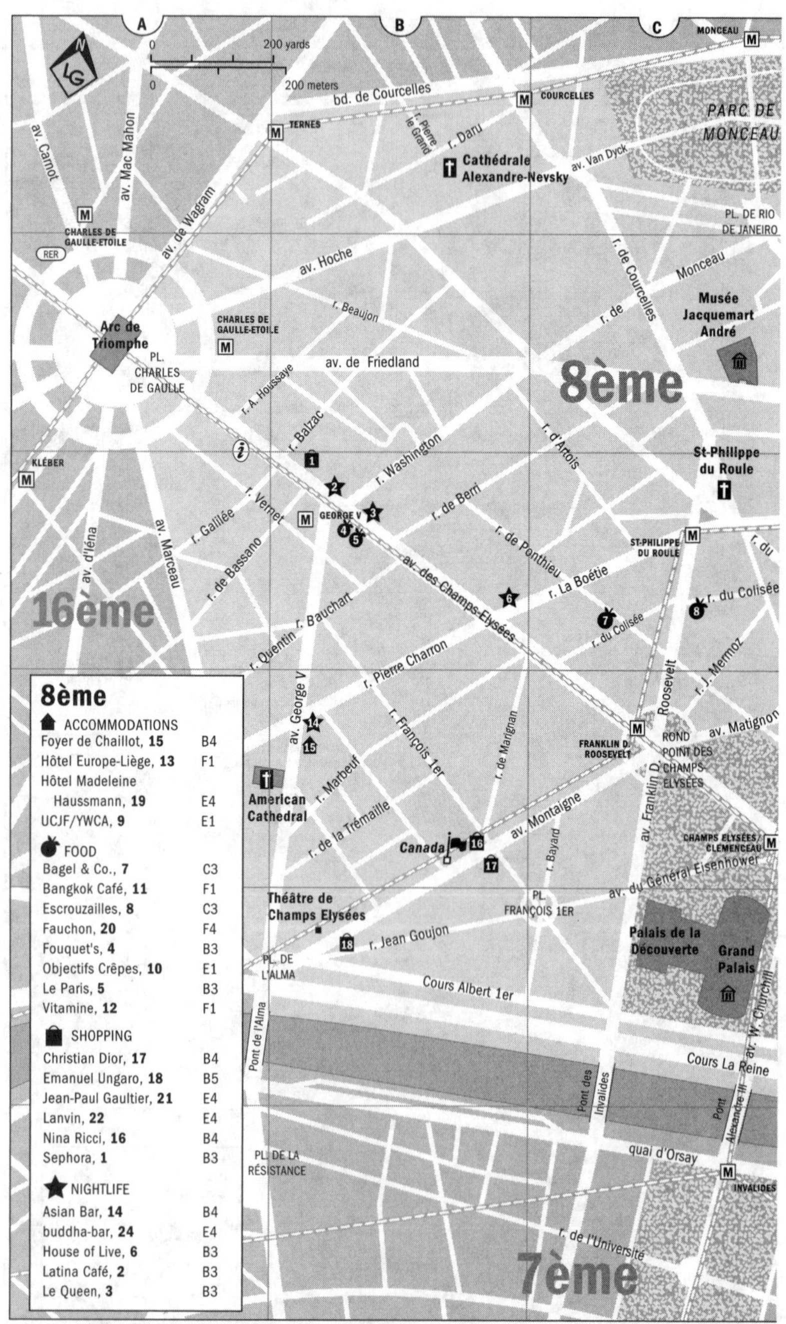

8ème

ACCOMMODATIONS

Foyer de Chaillot, **15**	B4
Hôtel Europe-Liège, **13**	F1
Hôtel Madeleine Haussmann, **19**	E4
UCJF/YWCA, **9**	E1

FOOD

Bagel & Co., **7**	C3
Bangkok Café, **11**	F1
Escrouzailles, **8**	C3
Fauchon, **20**	F4
Fouquet's, **4**	B3
Objectifs Crêpes, **10**	E1
Le Paris, **5**	B3
Vitamine, **12**	F1

SHOPPING

Christian Dior, **17**	B4
Emanuel Ungaro, **18**	B5
Jean-Paul Gaultier, **21**	E4
Lanvin, **22**	E4
Nina Ricci, **16**	B4
Sephora, **1**	B3

NIGHTLIFE

Asian Bar, **14**	B4
buddha-bar, **24**	E4
House of Live, **6**	B3
Latina Café, **2**	B3
Le Queen, **3**	B3

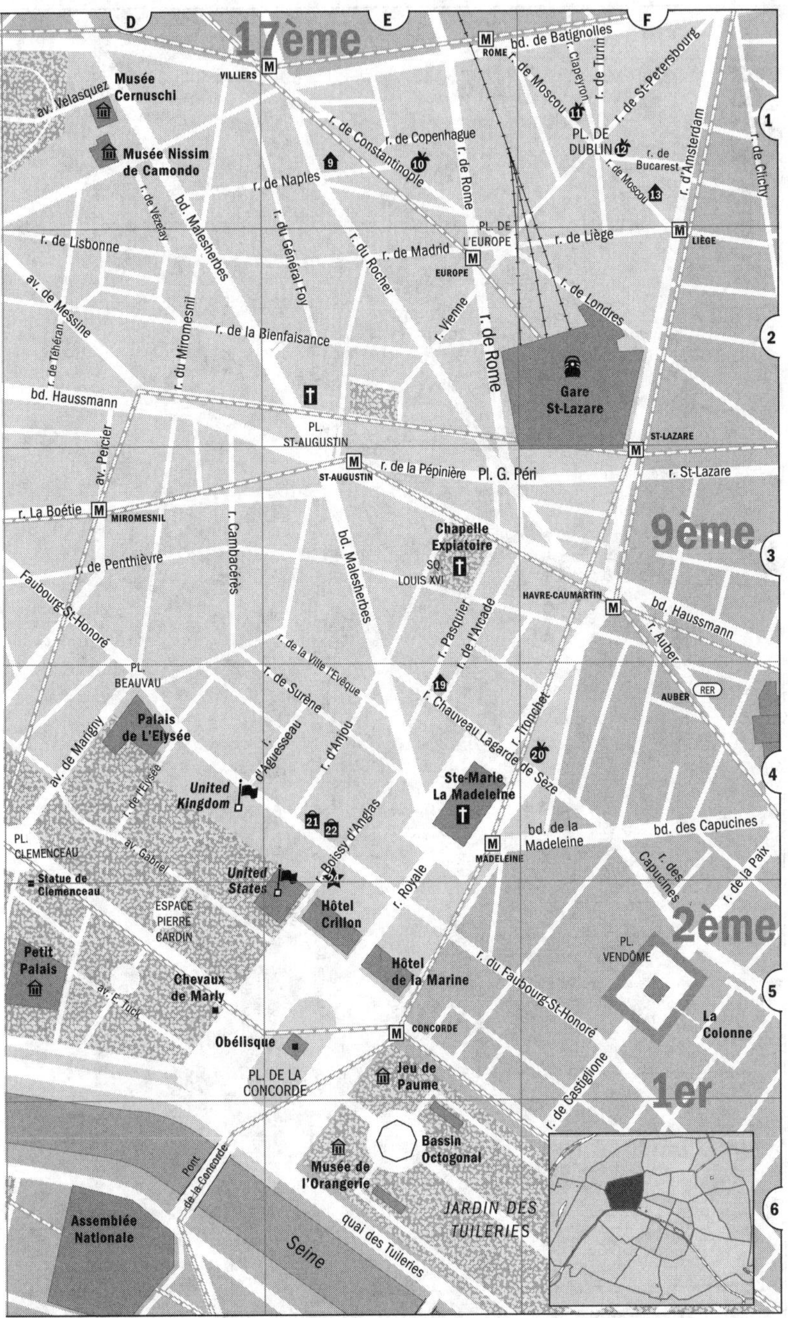

17ème
9ème
2ème
1er
Musée Cernuschi
Musée Nissim de Camondo
Gare St-Lazare
Chapelle Expiatoire
SQ. LOUIS XVI
Palais de L'Elysée
United Kingdom
United States
Ste-Marie La Madeleine
Hôtel Crillon
Hôtel de la Marine
Statue de Clemenceau
ESPACE PIERRE CARDIN
Petit Palais
Chevaux de Marly
Obélisque
PL. DE LA CONCORDE
Jeu de Paume
Bassin Octogonal
Musée de l'Orangerie
JARDIN DES TUILERIES
Assemblée Nationale
Seine
PL. VENDÔME
La Colonne
VILLIERS
ROME
EUROPE
LIÈGE
ST-LAZARE
ST-AUGUSTIN
MIROMESNIL
HAVRE-CAUMARTIN
AUBER
RER
MADELEINE
CONCORDE
PL. DE L'EUROPE
PL. DE DUBLIN
PL. ST-AUGUSTIN
Pl. G. Péri
PL. BEAUVAU
PL. CLEMENCEAU
bd. de Batignolles
r. de Moscou
r. Clapeyron
r. de Turin
r. de St-Petersbourg
r. d'Amsterdam
r. de Clichy
r. de Bucarest
r. de Constantinople
r. de Copenhague
r. de Rome
r. de Naples
av. Velasquez
r. de Vézelay
bd. Malesherbes
r. du Général Foy
r. du Rocher
r. de Lisbonne
r. de Madrid
r. de Liège
r. de Londres
av. de Messine
r. de Téhéran
r. du Miromesnil
r. de la Bienfaisance
r. Vienne
bd. Haussmann
av. Percier
r. de la Pépinière
r. St-Lazare
r. La Boétie
r. Cambacérès
r. de Penthièvre
Faubourg-St-Honoré
r. Pasquier
r. de l'Arcade
r. Auber
r. de la Ville l'Evêque
r. de Surène
r. Chauveau Lagarde
r. de Sèze
r. Tronchet
av. de Marigny
r. d'Aguesseau
r. d'Anjou
r. de l'Elysée
r. Boissy d'Anglas
bd. de la Madeleine
bd. des Capucines
r. des Capucines
r. de la Paix
av. Gabriel
r. Royale
r. du Faubourg-St-Honoré
av. E. Tuck
r. de Castiglione
Pont de la Concorde
quai des Tuileries
D
E
F
1
2
3
4
5
6
9
10
11
12
13
19
20
21
22
24

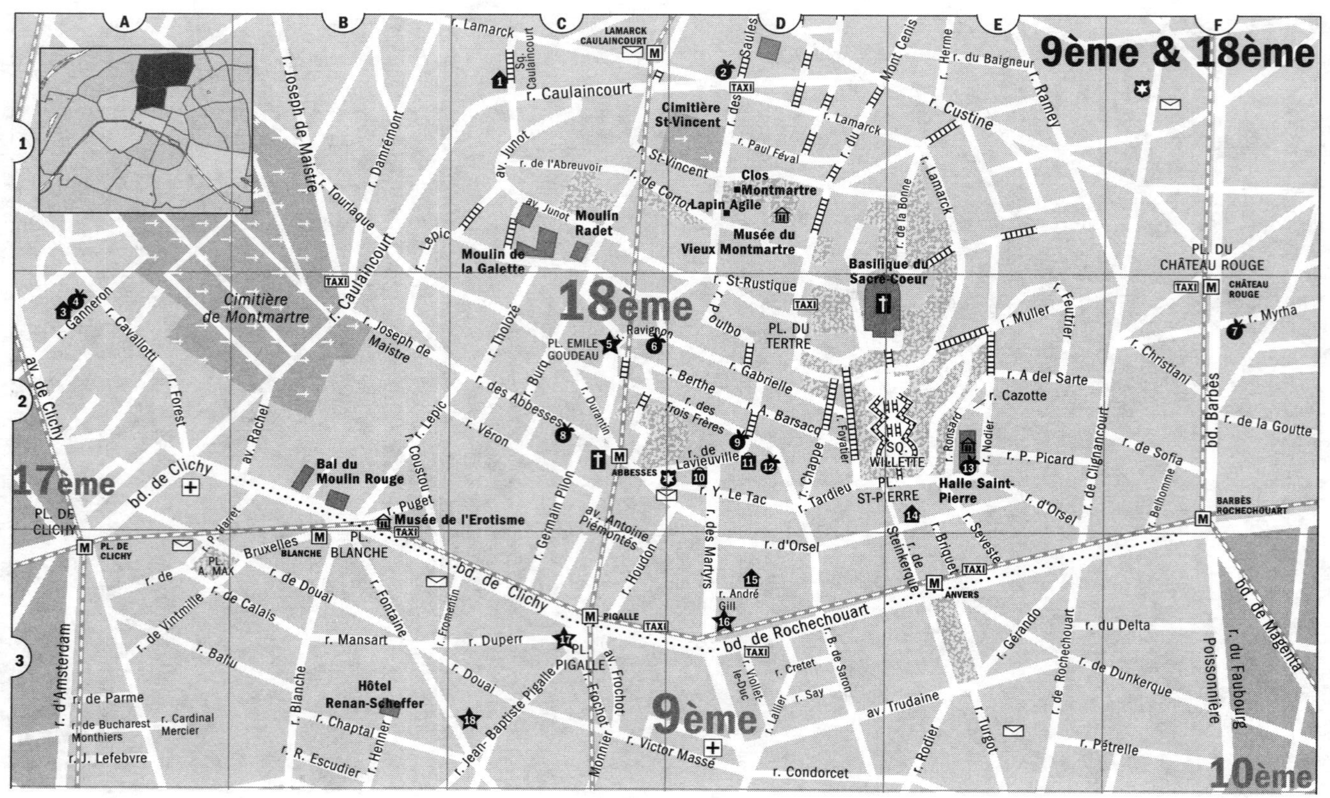

9ème & 18ème
18ème
9ème
10ème
17ème
Basilique du Sacré-Coeur
Cimitière St-Vincent
Clos Montmartre
Lapin Agile
Musée du Vieux Montmartre
Moulin Radet
Moulin de la Galette
Cimitière de Montmartre
Bal du Moulin Rouge
Musée de l'Erotisme
Halle Saint-Pierre
Hôtel Renan-Scheffer
PL. DU TERTRE
PL. EMILE GOUDEAU
PL. DU CHÂTEAU ROUGE
SQ. WILLETTE
PL. ST-PIERRE
PL. BLANCHE
PL. PIGALLE
PL. DE CLICHY
PL. A. MAX
Sq. Caulaincourt
LAMARCK CAULAINCOURT
ABBESSES
PIGALLE
BLANCHE
ANVERS
BARBÈS ROCHECHOUART
CHÂTEAU ROUGE
PL. DE CLICHY
bd. de Clichy
bd. de Rochechouart
bd. Barbès
bd. de Magenta
av. de Clichy
av. Junot
av. Trudaine
av. Rachel
av. Frochot
av. Antoine Piémontés
r. du Faubourg Poissonnière
r. Caulaincourt
r. Lamarck
r. Custine
r. Ramey
r. Joseph de Maistre
r. Lepic
r. des Abbesses
r. des Martyrs
r. Tholozé
r. Véron
r. Germain Pilon
r. Houdon
r. de Douai
r. Douai
r. Fontaine
r. Blanche
r. de Clignancourt
r. de Steinkerque
r. d'Orsel
r. Ronsard
r. Muller
r. Feutrier
r. Gabrielle
r. Berthe
r. St-Rustique
r. Poulbo
Ravignon
r. Durantin
r. Burq
r. Foyatier
r. Chappe
r. Tardieu
r. Y. Le Tac
r. de Lavieuville
r. des Trois Frères
r. A. Barsacq
r. Duperr
r. Jean- Baptiste Pigalle
r. Victor Massé
r. Condorcet
r. de Rochechouart
r. Turgot
r. Rodier
r. de Dunkerque
r. Pétrelle
r. du Delta
r. Christiani
r. de Sofia
r. Myrha
r. de la Goutte
r. Cavallotti
r. Forest
r. Ganneron
r. Damrémont
r. Tourlaque
r. Coustou
r. Puget
r. Fromentin
r. Mansart
r. Chaptal
r. Henner
r. R. Escudier
r. Ballu
r. de Vintimille
r. de Calais
Bruxelles
r. d'Amsterdam
r. de Parme
r. de Bucharest
r. Cardinal Mercier
Monthiers
r. J. Lefebvre
r. St-Vincent
r. de l'Abreuvoir
r. Paul Féval
r. des Saules
r. Mont Cenis
r. de la Bonne
r. Seveste
r. Briquet
r. Gérando
r. B. de Saron
r. Cretet
r. Say
r. Lallier
r. Viollet-le-Duc
r. André Gill
r. Frochot
r. Monnier
r. du Baigneur
r. Herme
r. Belhomme
r. P. Picard
r. Cazotte
r. A del Sarte
r. Nodier
TAXI
A B C D E F
1 2 3

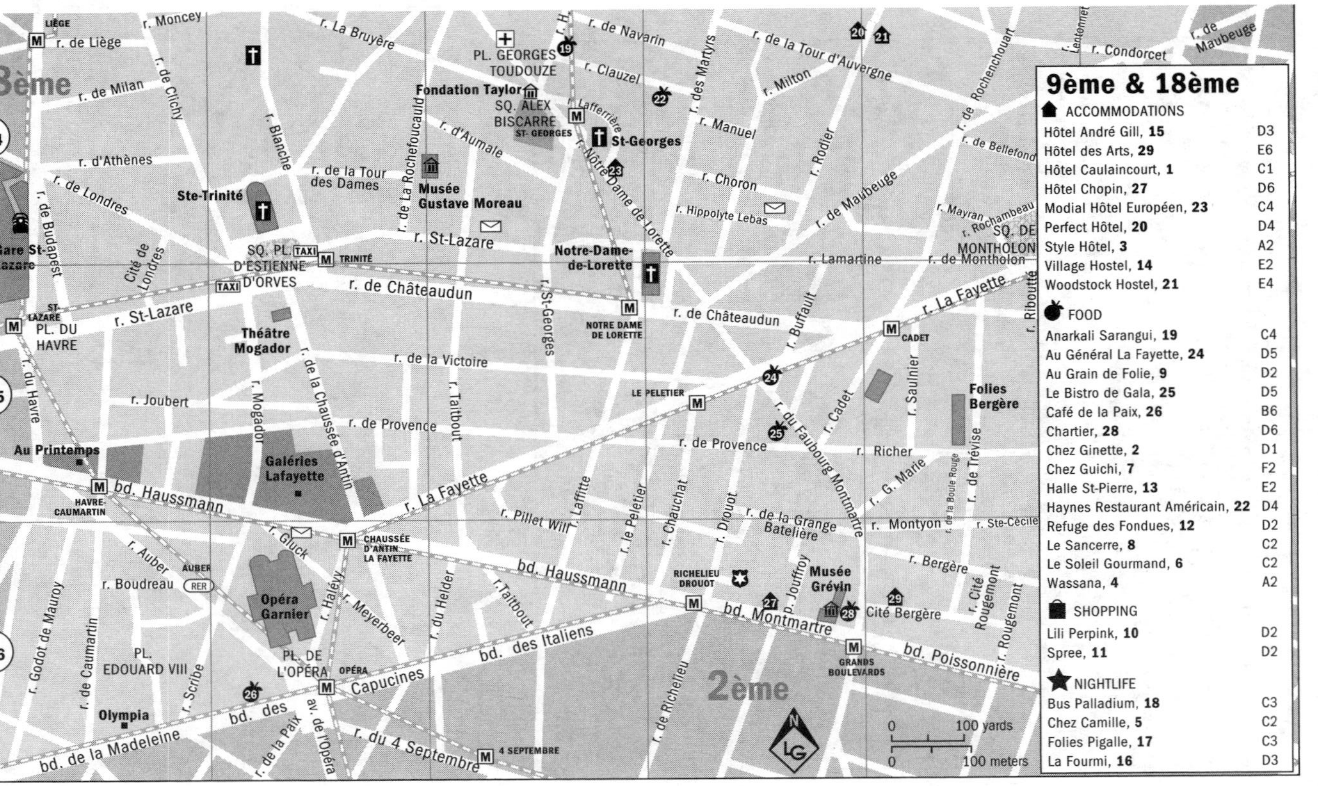
9ème & 18ème
ACCOMMODATIONS
Hôtel André Gill, 15 D3
Hôtel des Arts, 29 E6
Hôtel Caulaincourt, 1 C1
Hôtel Chopin, 27 D6
Modial Hôtel Européen, 23 C4
Perfect Hôtel, 20 D4
Style Hôtel, 3 A2
Village Hostel, 14 E2
Woodstock Hostel, 21 E4
FOOD
Anarkali Sarangui, 19 C4
Au Général La Fayette, 24 D5
Au Grain de Folie, 9 D2
Le Bistro de Gala, 25 D5
Café de la Paix, 26 B6
Chartier, 28 D6
Chez Ginette, 2 D1
Chez Guichi, 7 F2
Halle St-Pierre, 13 E2
Haynes Restaurant Américain, 22 D4
Refuge des Fondues, 12 D2
Le Sancerre, 8 C2
Le Soleil Gourmand, 6 C2
Wassana, 4 A2
SHOPPING
Lili Perpink, 10 D2
Spree, 11 D2
NIGHTLIFE
Bus Palladium, 18 C3
Chez Camille, 5 C2
Folies Pigalle, 17 C3
La Fourmi, 16 D3

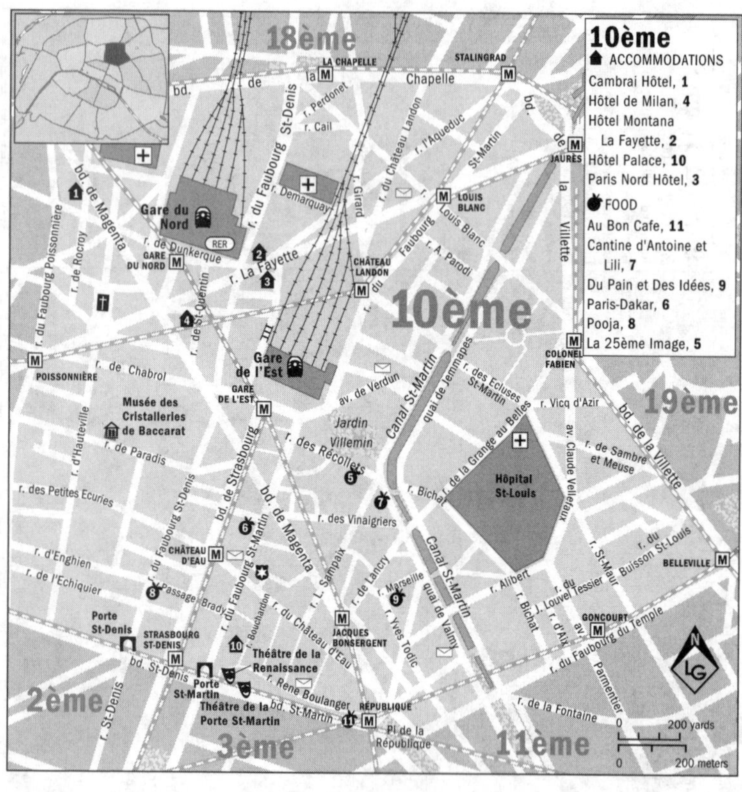
10ème
ACCOMMODATIONS
Cambrai Hôtel, 1
Hôtel de Milan, 4
Hôtel Montana La Fayette, 2
Hôtel Palace, 10
Paris Nord Hôtel, 3
FOOD
Au Bon Cafe, 11
Cantine d'Antoine et Lili, 7
Du Pain et Des Idées, 9
Paris-Dakar, 6
Pooja, 8
La 25ème Image, 5
18ème
19ème
2ème
3ème
11ème
10ème
Gare du Nord
Gare de l'Est
Musée des Cristalleries de Baccarat
Jardin Villemin
Hôpital St-Louis
Porte St-Denis
Porte St-Martin
Théâtre de la Renaissance
Théâtre de la Porte St-Martin
Pl de la République
Canal St-Martin
LA CHAPELLE
STALINGRAD
JAURÈS
LOUIS BLANC
CHÂTEAU LANDON
COLONEL FABIEN
GARE DU NORD
POISSONNIÈRE
GARE DE L'EST
CHÂTEAU D'EAU
STRASBOURG ST-DENIS
JACQUES BONSERGENT
RÉPUBLIQUE
GONCOURT
BELLEVILLE
bd. de la Chapelle
bd. de la Villette
bd. de Magenta
bd. de Strasbourg
bd. St-Denis
bd. St-Martin
r. du Faubourg St-Denis
r. du Faubourg St-Martin
r. du Faubourg Poissonnière
r. La Fayette
r. de Dunkerque
r. de Chabrol
r. de Paradis
r. des Petites Ecuries
r. d'Enghien
r. de l'Echiquier
r. d'Hauteville
r. de Rocroy
r. de St-Quentin
r. Perdonet
r. Cail
r. Demarquay
r. Girard
r. du Château Landon
r. l'Aqueduc
r. Louis Blanc
r. A. Parodi
av. de Verdun
r. des Récollets
r. des Vinaigriers
r. de Lancry
r. de Marseille
r. Yves Todic
r. L. Sampaix
r. Bouchardon
r. du Château d'Eau
r. Rene Boulanger
Passage Brady
quai de Jemmapes
quai de Valmy
r. des Ecluses St-Martin
r. Vicq d'Azir
r. de la Grange aux Belles
r. Bichat
r. Alibert
av. Claude Vellefaux
r. de Sambre et Meuse
r. St-Maur
r. du Buisson St-Louis
r. J. Louvel Tessier
r. d'Aix
av. Parmentier
r. du Faubourg du Temple
r. de la Fontaine
r. St-Denis
RER
0 200 yards
0 200 meters

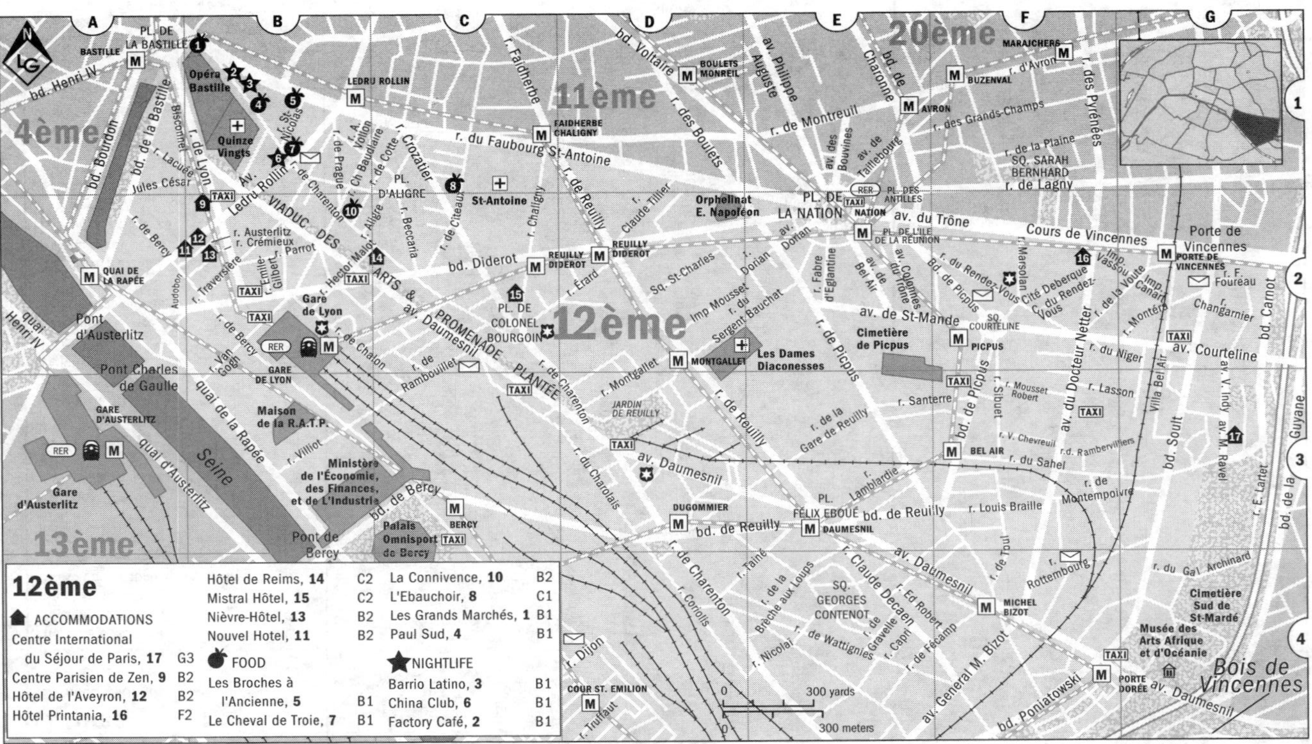
12ème
ACCOMMODATIONS
Centre International du Séjour de Paris, 17 G3
Centre Parisien de Zen, 9 B2
Hôtel de l'Aveyron, 12 B2
Hôtel Printania, 16 F2
Hôtel de Reims, 14 C2
Mistral Hôtel, 15 C2
Nièvre-Hôtel, 13 B2
Nouvel Hotel, 11 B2
FOOD
Les Broches à l'Ancienne, 5 B1
Le Cheval de Troie, 7 B1
La Connivence, 10 B2
L'Ebauchoir, 8 C1
Les Grands Marchés, 1 B1
Paul Sud, 4 B1
NIGHTLIFE
Barrio Latino, 3 B1
China Club, 6 B1
Factory Café, 2 B1
300 yards
300 meters

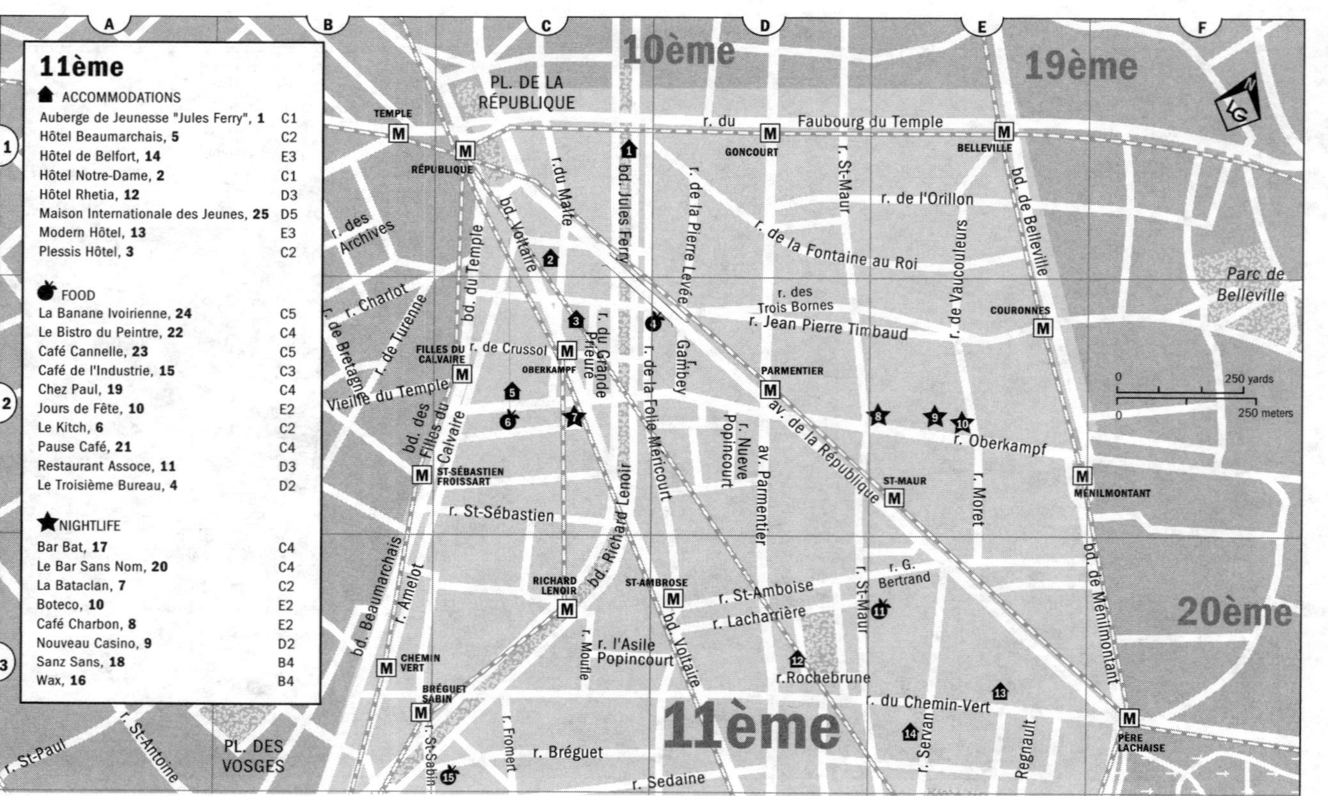
11ème
ACCOMMODATIONS
Auberge de Jeunesse "Jules Ferry", 1 C1
Hôtel Beaumarchais, 5 C2
Hôtel de Belfort, 14 E3
Hôtel Notre-Dame, 2 C1
Hôtel Rhetia, 12 D3
Maison Internationale des Jeunes, 25 D5
Modern Hôtel, 13 E3
Plessis Hôtel, 3 C2
FOOD
La Banane Ivoirienne, 24 C5
Le Bistro du Peintre, 22 C4
Café Cannelle, 23 C5
Café de l'Industrie, 15 C3
Chez Paul, 19 C4
Jours de Fête, 10 E2
Le Kitch, 6 C2
Pause Café, 21 C4
Restaurant Assoce, 11 D3
Le Troisième Bureau, 4 D2
NIGHTLIFE
Bar Bat, 17 C4
Le Bar Sans Nom, 20 C4
La Bataclan, 7 C2
Boteco, 10 E2
Café Charbon, 8 E2
Nouveau Casino, 9 D2
Sanz Sans, 18 B4
Wax, 16 B4
A
B
C
D
E
F
1
2
3
10ème
19ème
20ème
11ème
PL. DE LA RÉPUBLIQUE
PL. DES VOSGES
Parc de Belleville
TEMPLE
RÉPUBLIQUE
GONCOURT
BELLEVILLE
COURONNES
PARMENTIER
OBERKAMPF
FILLES DU CALVAIRE
ST-SÉBASTIEN FROISSART
ST-MAUR
MÉNILMONTANT
RICHARD LENOIR
ST-AMBROSE
CHEMIN VERT
BRÉGUET SABIN
PÈRE LACHAISE
r. du Faubourg du Temple
r. St-Maur
r. de l'Orillon
r. des Archives
r.du Malte
bd. Jules Ferry
r. de la Pierre Levée
r. de la Fontaine au Roi
bd. de Belleville
bd. Voltaire
r. des Trois Bornes
r. Jean Pierre Timbaud
r. de Vaucouleurs
r. Charlot
bd. du Temple
r. de Turenne
r. de Bretagne
r. de Crussol
r. du Grande Prieure
r. de la Folie Mericourt
r. Gambey
Vieille du Temple
bd. des Filles du Calvaire
r. Nueve Popincourt
av. Parmentier
av. de la République
r. Oberkampf
r. Moret
r. St-Sébastien
bd. Richard Lenoir
bd. Beaumarchais
r. Amelot
r. St-Amboise
r. G. Bertrand
r. Lacharrière
r. l'Asile Popincourt
r. Moufle
r.Rochebrune
r. du Chemin-Vert
bd. de Ménilmontant
r. Servan
Regnault
r. St-Paul
r. St-Antoine
r. St-Sabin
r. Fromert
r. Bréguet
r. Sedaine
0 250 yards
0 250 meters

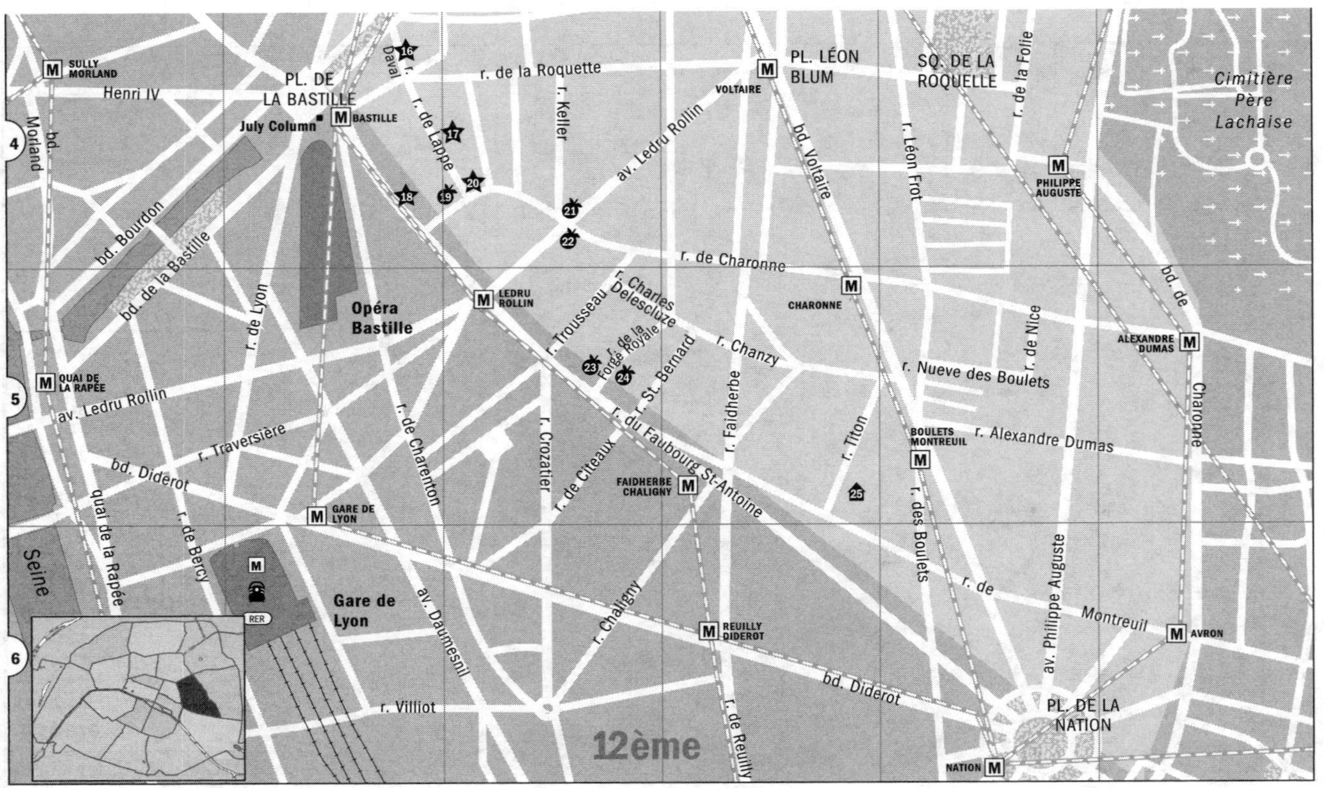

SULLY MORLAND
Henri IV
PL. DE LA BASTILLE
July Column
BASTILLE
Daval
r. de Lappe
r. de la Roquette
r. Keller
PL. LÉON BLUM
VOLTAIRE
SQ. DE LA ROQUELLE
r. de la Folie
Cimitière Père Lachaise
bd. Morland
bd. Bourdon
bd. de la Bastille
av. Ledru Rollin
bd. Voltaire
r. Léon Frot
PHILIPPE AUGUSTE
r. de Charonne
LEDRU ROLLIN
Opéra Bastille
CHARONNE
bd. de Charonne
ALEXANDRE DUMAS
r. de Lyon
r. Trousseau
r. Charles Delescluze
r. de la Forge Royale
r. Chanzy
r. de Nice
r. Nueve des Boulets
QUAI DE LA RAPÉE
av. Ledru Rollin
r. Traversière
r. de Charenton
r. Crozatier
r. de Citeaux
r. St. Bernard
r. du Faubourg St-Antoine
r. Faidherbe
r. Titon
BOULETS MONTREUIL
r. Alexandre Dumas
bd. Diderot
FAIDHERBE CHALIGNY
GARE DE LYON
quai de la Rapée
r. de Bercy
Seine
RER
Gare de Lyon
av. Daumesnil
r. Chaligny
REUILLY DIDEROT
r. des Boulets
av. Philippe Auguste
r. de Montreuil
AVRON
bd. Diderot
r. Villiot
12ème
r. de Reuilly
PL. DE LA NATION
NATION
4
5
6

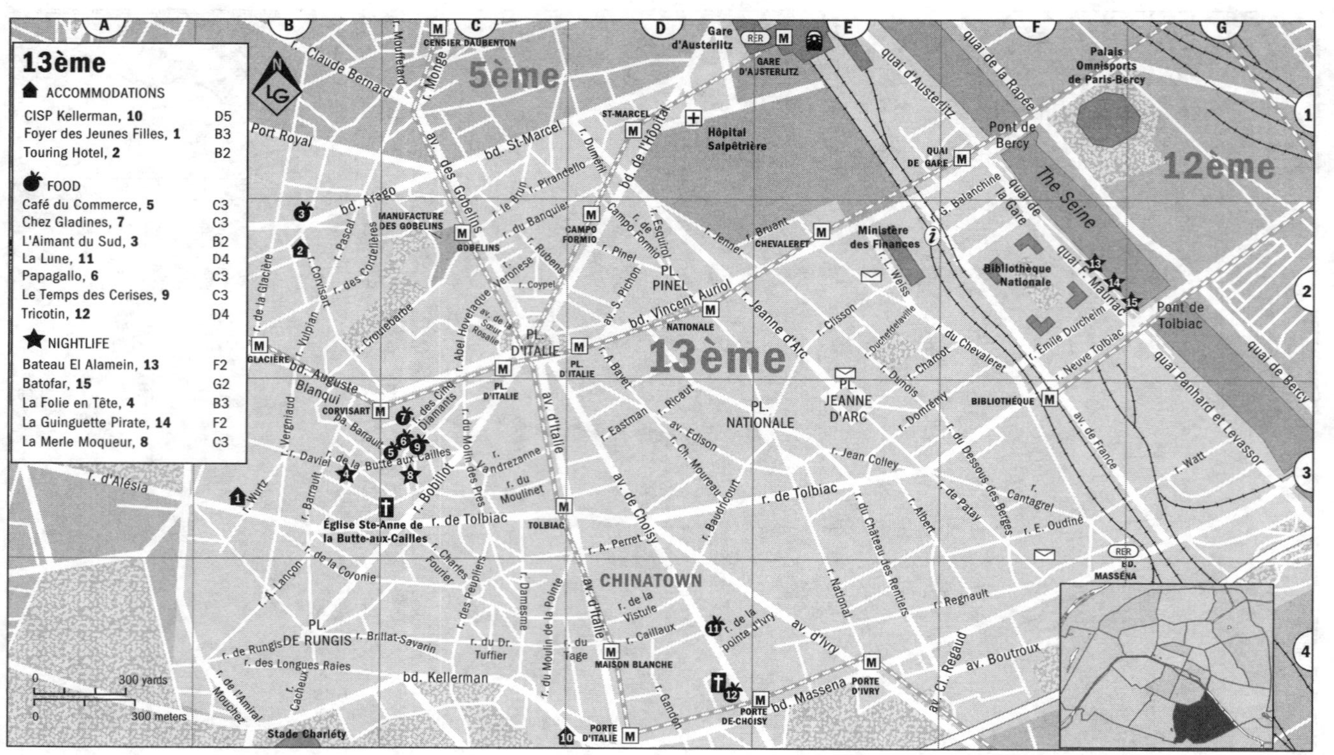
13ème
ACCOMMODATIONS
CISP Kellerman, 10 D5
Foyer des Jeunes Filles, 1 B3
Touring Hotel, 2 B2
FOOD
Café du Commerce, 5 C3
Chez Gladines, 7 C3
L'Aimant du Sud, 3 B2
La Lune, 11 D4
Papagallo, 6 C3
Le Temps des Cerises, 9 C3
Tricotin, 12 D4
NIGHTLIFE
Bateau El Alamein, 13 F2
Batofar, 15 G2
La Folie en Tête, 4 B3
La Guinguette Pirate, 14 F2
La Merle Moqueur, 8 C3
5ème
12ème
13ème
The Seine
CHINATOWN
Gare d'Austerlitz
Hôpital Salpêtrière
Palais Omnisports de Paris-Bercy
Ministère des Finances
Bibliothèque Nationale
Manufacture des Gobelins
Église Ste-Anne de la Butte-aux-Cailles
PL. D'ITALIE
PL. NATIONALE
PL. JEANNE D'ARC
PL. PINEL
PL. DE RUNGIS
Pont de Bercy
Pont de Tolbiac
Stade Charléty
300 yards
300 meters

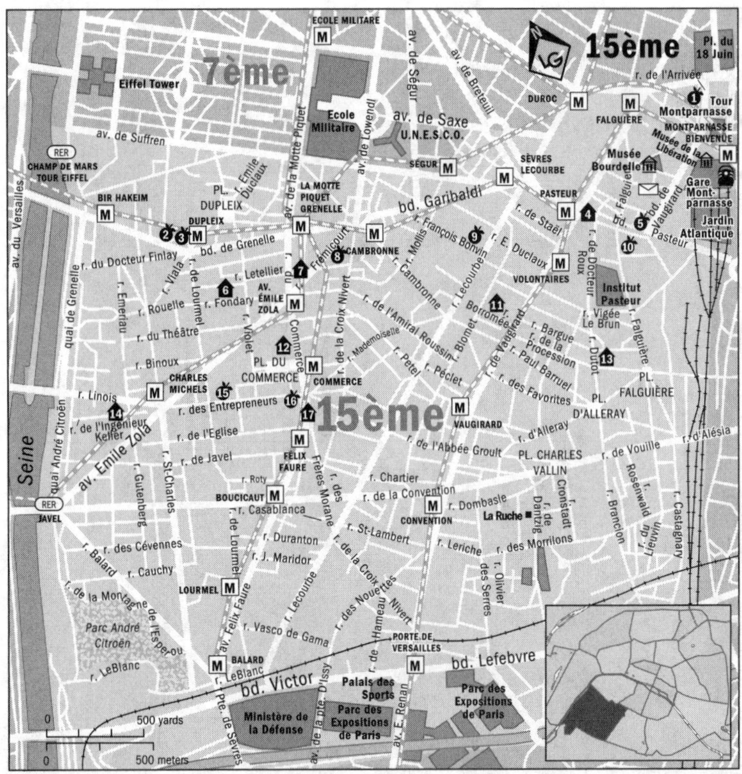

15ème

ACCOMMODATIONS

Aloha Hostel, **11**
Hôtel Camélia, **4**
Hôtel du Square, **12**
Hôtel Printemps, **7**
La Maison Hostel, **13**
Pacific Hôtel, **6**
Practic Hôtel, **14**
Three Ducks Hostel, **17**

FOOD

Au Coin du Pétrin, **16**
Aux Artistes, **10**
Chez Foong, **8**
Mozlef, **1**
Samaya, **2**
Thai Phetburi, **3**
Le Tire Bouchon, **15**
Le Troquet, **9**
Ty Breiz, **5**

14ème

see map p. 394-395

ACCOMMODATIONS

FIAP Jean-Monnet, **8**	F3
Hôtel de Blois, **11**	C3
Hôtel du Midi, **7**	E2
Hôtel du Parc, **4**	B1
Ouest Hôtel, **13**	A4

FOOD

L'Amuse Bouche, **9**	C3
Aquarius Café, **14**	B4
Au Rendez-Vous Des Camionneurs, **15**	C4
Chez Papa, **6**	C2
La Coupole, **1**	C1
Phinéas, **10**	B3

NIGHTLIFE

Café Tournesol, **5**	B1
L'Entrepôt, **12**	B3
Mustang Café, **2**	B1
Smoke Bar, **3**	B1

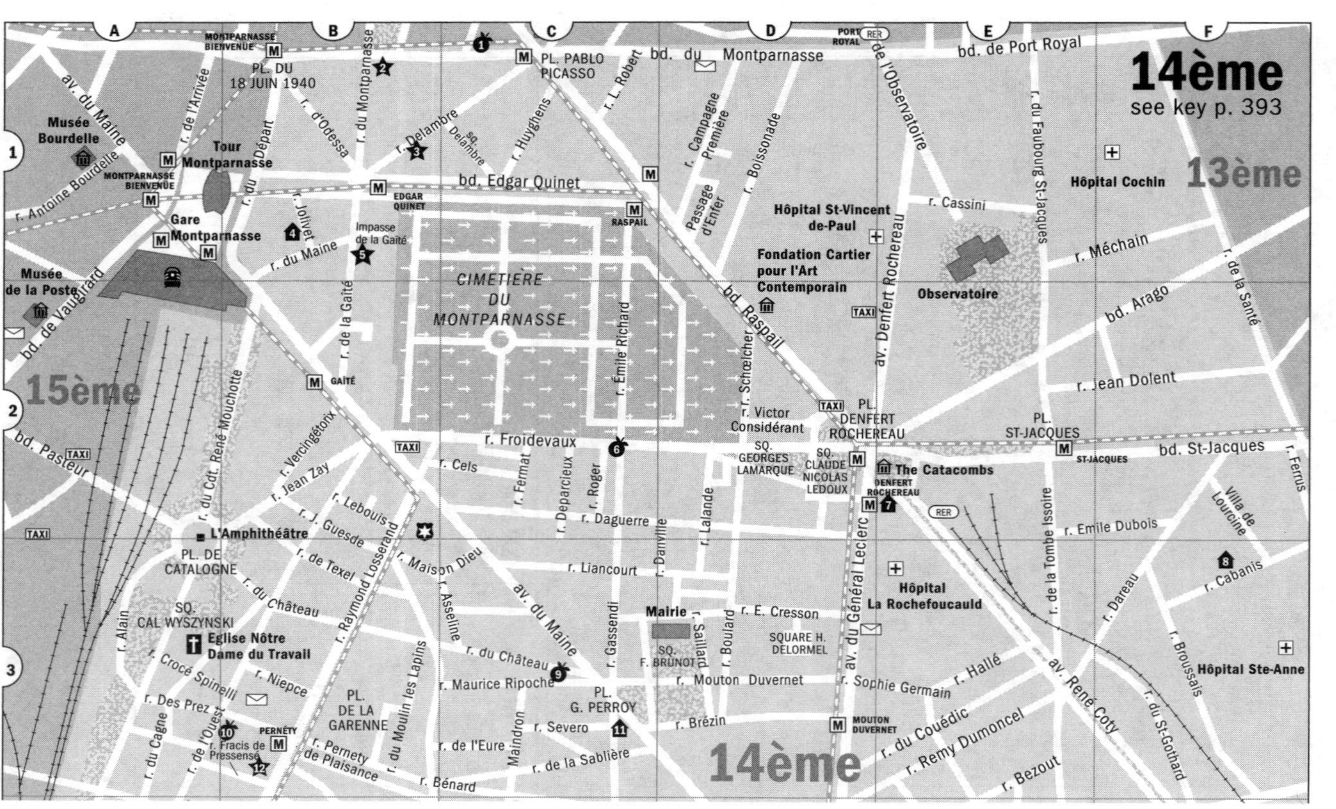

14ème
see key p. 393
13ème
14ème
15ème
Hôpital Cochin
Hôpital St-Vincent de-Paul
Fondation Cartier pour l'Art Contemporain
Observatoire
The Catacombs
Hôpital La Rochefoucauld
Hôpital Ste-Anne
CIMETIÈRE DU MONTPARNASSE
Tour Montparnasse
Gare Montparnasse
Musée Bourdelle
Musée de la Poste
Mairie
L'Amphithéâtre
Eglise Nôtre Dame du Travail
bd. de Port Royal
bd. du Montparnasse
bd. Raspail
bd. Edgar Quinet
bd. St-Jacques
bd. Arago
bd. Pasteur
bd. de Vaugirard
av. Denfert Rochereau
av. du Général Leclerc
av. du Maine
av. René Coty
r. de l'Observatoire
r. de la Santé
r. du Faubourg St-Jacques
r. Méchain
r. Jean Dolent
r. Cassini
r. Boissonade
r. Campagne Première
Passage d'Enfer
r. Schœlcher
r. Victor Considérant
r. L. Robert
r. Huyghens
r. Delambre
sq. Delambre
r. du Montparnasse
r. d'Odessa
r. Jolivet
r. du Départ
r. de l'Arrivée
r. Antoine Bourdelle
r. du Maine
r. de la Gaîté
Impasse de la Gaîté
r. Émile Richard
r. Froidevaux
r. Fermat
r. Cels
r. Deparcieux
r. Roger
r. Daguerre
r. Liancourt
r. Gassendi
r. Lalande
r. Danville
r. Boulard
r. E. Cresson
r. Mouton Duvernet
r. Brézin
r. Saillard
r. Sophie Germain
r. Hallé
r. du Couëdic
r. Remy Dumoncel
r. Bezout
r. de la Tombe Issoire
r. Emile Dubois
r. Dareau
r. Broussais
r. du St-Gothard
r. Cabanis
Villa de Lourcine
r. Ferrus
r. Asseline
r. Maison Dieu
r. du Château
r. Maurice Ripoche
r. Severo
r. Maindron
r. de la Sablière
r. de l'Eure
r. Bénard
r. du Moulin les Lapins
r. Raymond Losserand
r. Lebouis
r. J. Guesde
r. de Texel
r. Vercingétorix
r. Jean Zay
r. du Cdt. René Mouchotte
r. Niepce
r. Pernety de Plaisance
r. de l'Ouest
r. Fracis de Pressensé
r. Crocé Spinelli
r. Des Prez
r. du Cange
r. Alain
PL. PABLO PICASSO
PL. DU 18 JUIN 1940
PL. DENFERT ROCHEREAU
PL. ST-JACQUES
PL. G. PERROY
PL. DE LA GARENNE
PL. DE CATALOGNE
SQ. CAL WYSZYNSKI
SQ. GEORGES LAMARQUE
SQ. CLAUDE NICOLAS LEDOUX
SQUARE H. DELORMEL
SQ. F. BRUNOT
MONTPARNASSE BIENVENÜE
EDGAR QUINET
RASPAIL
GAÎTÉ
PERNÉTY
MOUTON DUVERNET
DENFERT ROCHEREAU
ST-JACQUES
PORT ROYAL
RER
TAXI

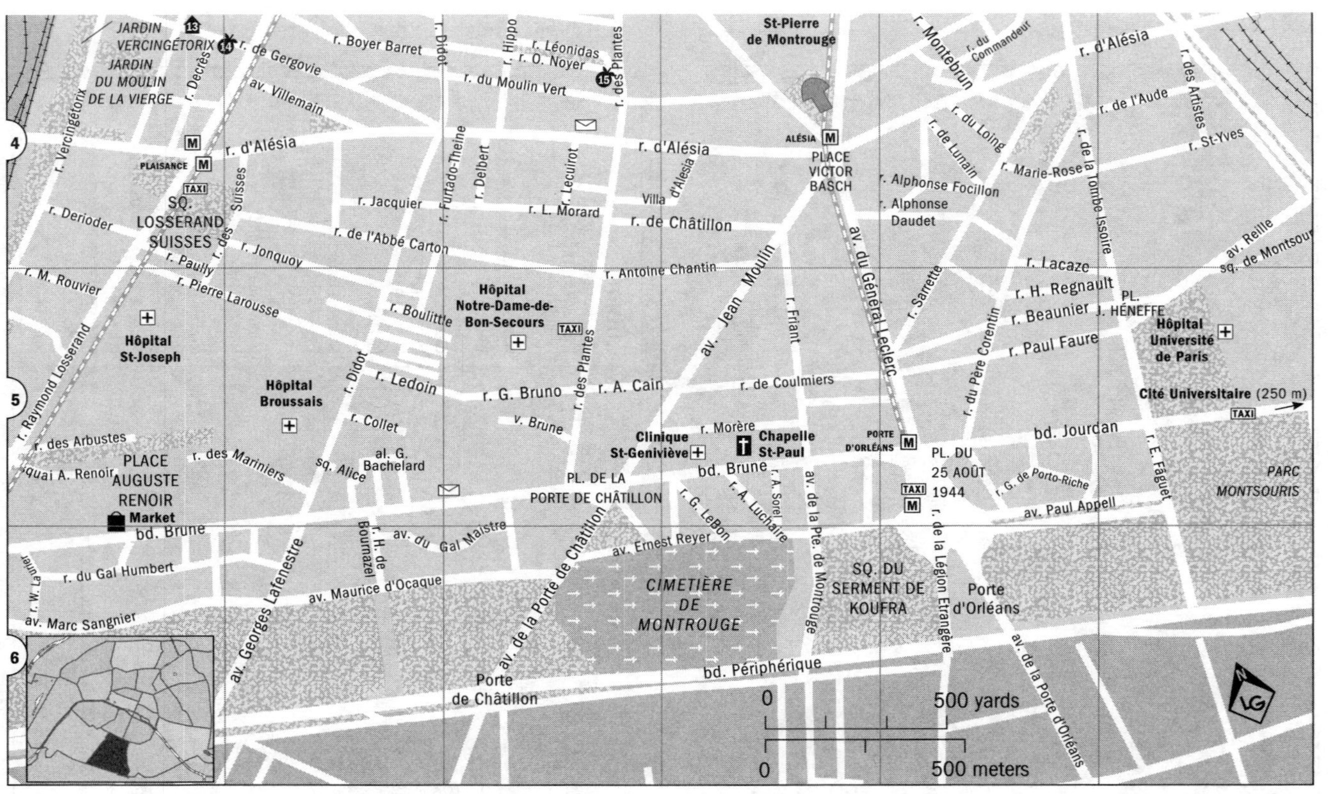

JARDIN VERCINGÉTORIX
JARDIN DU MOULIN DE LA VIERGE
r. Decrès
r. de Gergovie
r. Boyer Barret
r. Didot
r. Hippo
r. Léonidas
r. O. Noyer
r. des Plantes
r. du Moulin Vert
av. Villemain
St-Pierre de Montrouge
r. Montebrun
r. du Commandeur
r. d'Alésia
r. des Artistes
r. de l'Aude
r. St-Yves
r. du Loing
r. de Lunain
r. Marie-Rose
r. de la Tombe Issoire
r. Vercingétorix
PLAISANCE
r. d'Alésia
r. Furtado-Theine
r. Delbert
r. Lecuirot
Villa d'Alésia
ALÉSIA
PLACE VICTOR BASCH
r. Alphonse Focillon
r. Alphonse Daudet
SQ. LOSSERAND SUISSES
r. des Suisses
r. Derioder
r. Jacquier
r. L. Morard
r. de Châtillon
r. de l'Abbé Carton
r. Jonquoy
r. Pauly
av. Reille
sq. de Montsouris
r. M. Rouvier
r. Pierre Larousse
r. Antoine Chantin
av. Jean Moulin
av. du Général Leclerc
r. Sarrette
r. Lacaze
r. H. Regnault
r. Beaunier
PL. J. HÉNEFFE
Hôpital Université de Paris
Hôpital Notre-Dame-de-Bon-Secours
r. Boulitte
r. Friant
r. Paul Faure
Hôpital St-Joseph
r. Raymond Losserand
Hôpital Broussais
r. Didot
r. Ledoin
r. G. Bruno
r. A. Cain
r. de Coulmiers
r. du Père Corentin
Cité Universitaire (250 m)
r. Collet
v. Brune
r. Morère
Clinique St-Geniviève
Chapelle St-Paul
PORTE D'ORLÉANS
bd. Jourdan
r. des Arbustes
quai A. Renoir
PLACE AUGUSTE RENOIR
r. des Mariniers
sq. Alice
al. G. Bachelard
PL. DE LA PORTE DE CHÂTILLON
bd. Brune
r. A. Sorel
r. G. LeBon
r. A. Luchaire
PL. DU 25 AOÛT 1944
r. G. de Porto-Riche
r. E. Fâguet
PARC MONTSOURIS
Market
av. du Gal Maistre
r. H. de Bournazel
av. Paul Appell
av. Ernest Reyer
r. du Gal Humbert
av. Maurice d'Ocaque
CIMETIÈRE DE MONTROUGE
av. de la Pte. de Montrouge
SQ. DU SERMENT DE KOUFRA
r. de la Légion Etrangère
Porte d'Orléans
av. Marc Sangnier
av. Georges Lafenestre
av. de la Porte de Châtillon
Porte de Châtillon
bd. Périphérique
av. de la Porte d'Orléans
0
500 yards
0
500 meters
TAXI
4
5
6
13
14
15

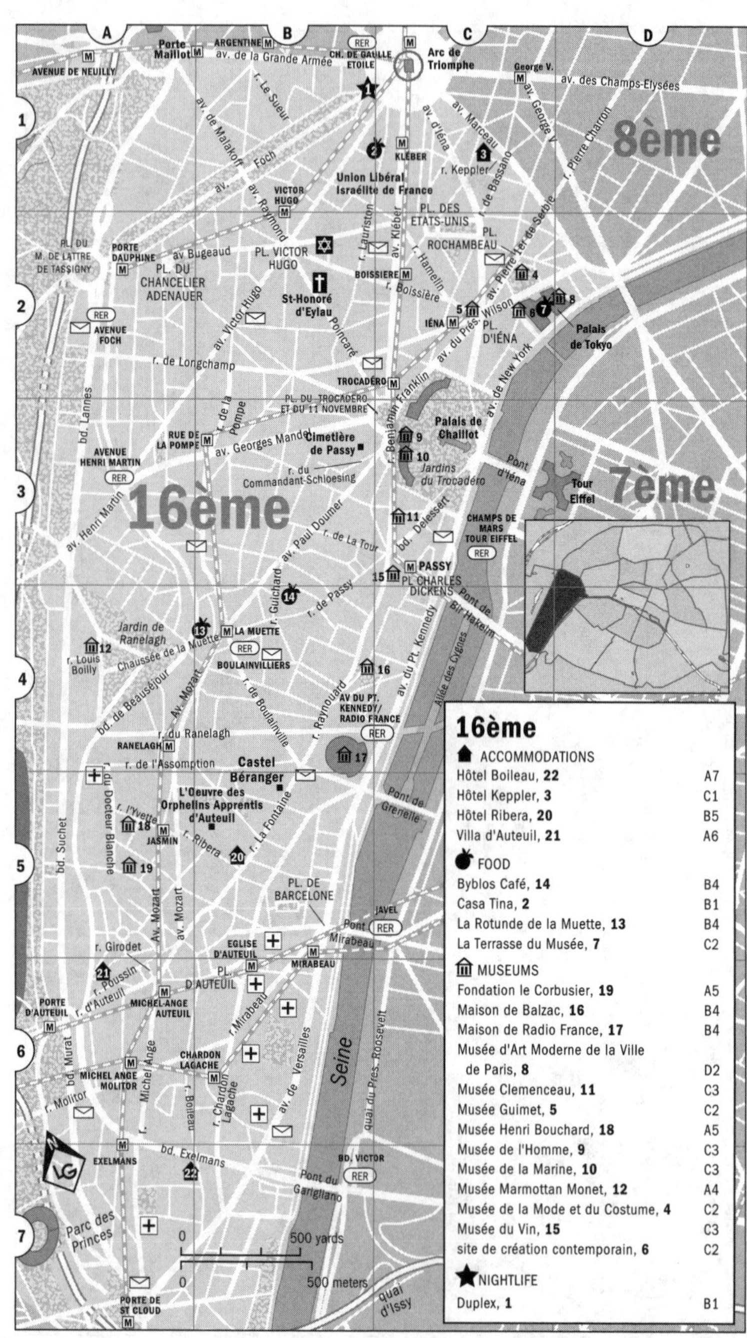
16ème
ACCOMMODATIONS
Hôtel Boileau, 22 A7
Hôtel Keppler, 3 C1
Hôtel Ribera, 20 B5
Villa d'Auteuil, 21 A6
FOOD
Byblos Café, 14 B4
Casa Tina, 2 B1
La Rotunde de la Muette, 13 B4
La Terrasse du Musée, 7 C2
MUSEUMS
Fondation le Corbusier, 19 A5
Maison de Balzac, 16 B4
Maison de Radio France, 17 B4
Musée d'Art Moderne de la Ville de Paris, 8 D2
Musée Clemenceau, 11 C3
Musée Guimet, 5 C2
Musée Henri Bouchard, 18 A5
Musée de l'Homme, 9 C3
Musée de la Marine, 10 C3
Musée Marmottan Monet, 12 A4
Musée de la Mode et du Costume, 4 C2
Musée du Vin, 15 C3
site de création contemporain, 6 C2
NIGHTLIFE
Duplex, 1 B1
8ème
7ème
16ème
Arc de Triomphe
Union Libéral Israélite de France
St-Honoré d'Eylau
Palais de Tokyo
Palais de Chaillot
Jardins du Trocadéro
Cimetière de Passy
Tour Eiffel
Castel Béranger
L'Oeuvre des Orphelins Apprentis d'Auteuil
Jardin de Ranelagh
Parc des Princes
Seine
0 500 yards
0 500 meters

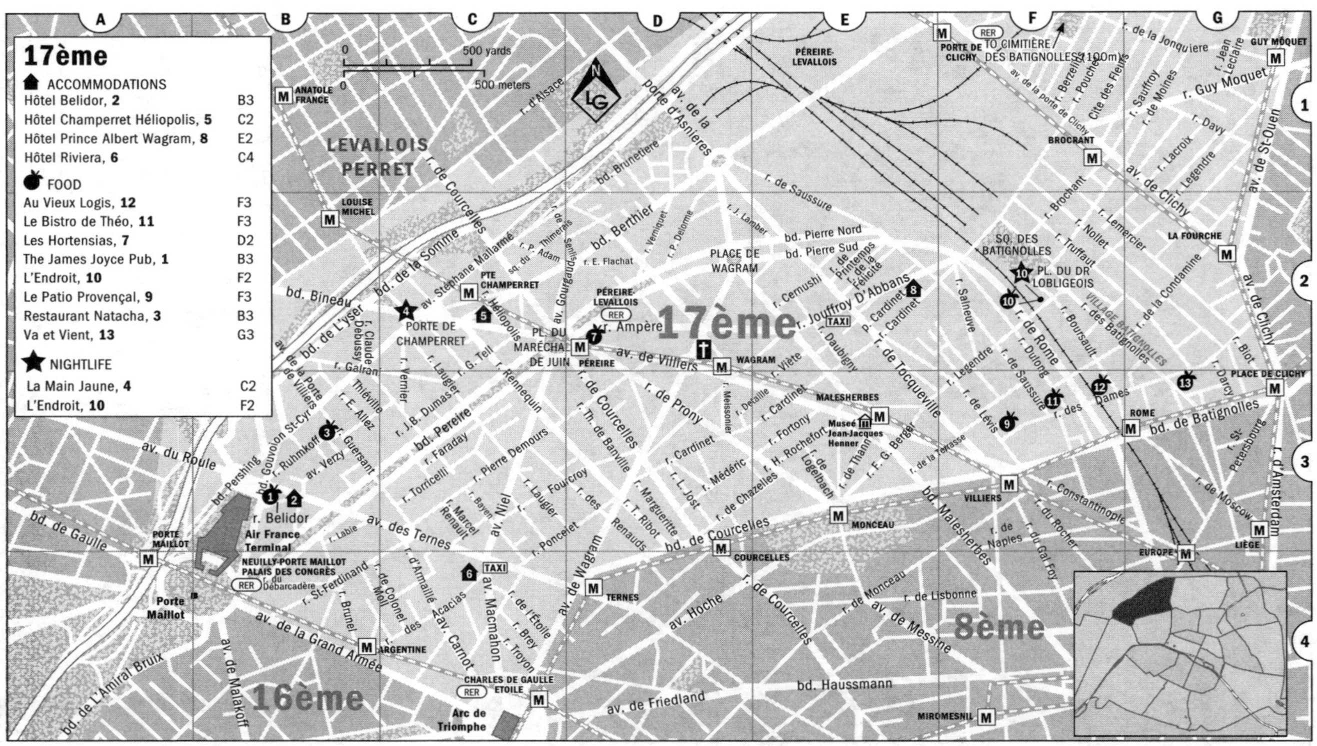
17ème
ACCOMMODATIONS
Hôtel Belidor, 2 B3
Hôtel Champerret Héliopolis, 5 C2
Hôtel Prince Albert Wagram, 8 E2
Hôtel Riviera, 6 C4
FOOD
Au Vieux Logis, 12 F3
Le Bistro de Théo, 11 F3
Les Hortensias, 7 D2
The James Joyce Pub, 1 B3
L'Endroit, 10 F2
Le Patio Provençal, 9 F3
Restaurant Natacha, 3 B3
Va et Vient, 13 G3
NIGHTLIFE
La Main Jaune, 4 C2
L'Endroit, 10 F2
0 500 yards
0 500 meters
LEVALLOIS PERRET
17ème
8ème
16ème
PLACE DE WAGRAM
SQ. DES BATIGNOLLES
PL. DU DR LOBLIGEOIS
PORTE DE CHAMPERRET
PL. DU MARÉCHAL DE JUIN
TO CIMITIÈRE DES BATIGNOLLES (100m)
Air France Terminal
NEUILLY-PORTE MAILLOT PALAIS DES CONGRÈS
Porte Maillot
Arc de Triomphe
Musée Jean-Jacques Henner
VILLAGE BATIGNOLLES

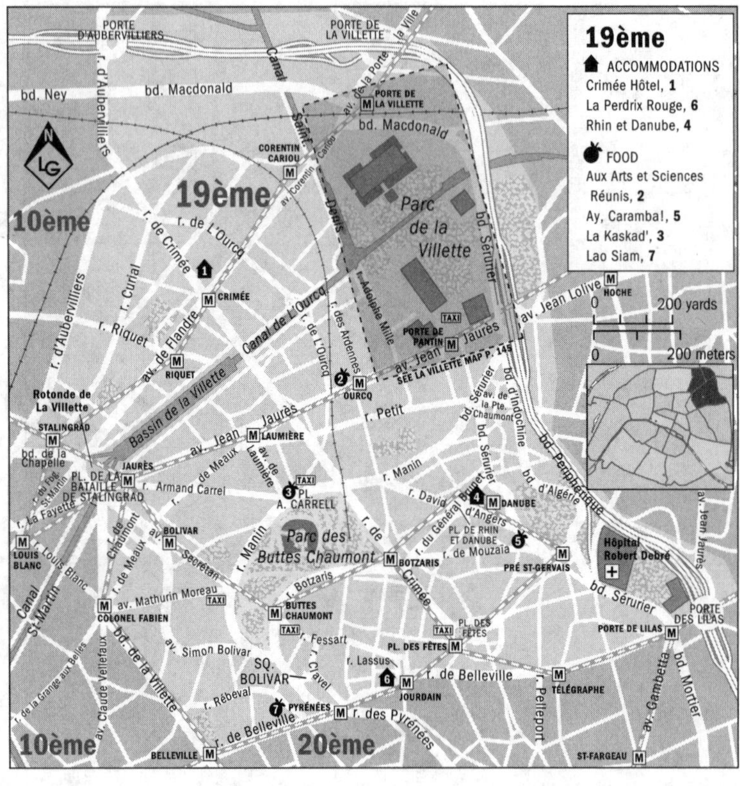
19ème
ACCOMMODATIONS
Crimée Hôtel, 1
La Perdrix Rouge, 6
Rhin et Danube, 4
FOOD
Aux Arts et Sciences Réunis, 2
Ay, Caramba!, 5
La Kaskad', 3
Lao Siam, 7
0 200 yards
0 200 meters
PORTE D'AUBERVILLIERS
PORTE DE LA VILLETTE
bd. Ney
bd. Macdonald
r. d'Aubervilliers
Canal Saint-Denis
PORTE DE LA VILLETTE
CORENTIN CARIOU
av. Corentin Cariou
Parc de la Villette
bd. Sérurier
10ème
19ème
r. de Crimée
r. de L'Ourcq
CRIMÉE
r. Curial
r. Riquet
av. de Flandre
RIQUET
Canal de L'Ourcq
r. Adolphe Mille
r. des Ardennes
PORTE DE PANTIN
av. Jean Jaurès
av. Jean Lolive
HOCHE
SEE LA VILLETTE MAP P. 145
OURCQ
Rotonde de La Villette
Bassin de la Villette
STALINGRAD
bd. de la Chapelle
LAUMIÈRE
r. Petit
JAURÈS
PL. DE LA BATAILLE DE STALINGRAD
r. Armand Carrel
r. de Meaux
av. de Laumière
PL. A. CARRELL
r. Manin
r. David d'Angers
DANUBE
r. du Général Brunet
bd. d'Indochine
bd. d'Algérie
bd. Périphérique
av. de la Pte. Chaumont
r. La Fayette
LOUIS BLANC
r. Louis Blanc
BOLIVAR
av. Secrétan
Parc des Buttes Chaumont
BOTZARIS
PL. DE RHIN ET DANUBE
r. de Mouzaïa
PRÉ ST-GERVAIS
Hôpital Robert Debré
av. Jean Jaurès
Canal St-Martin
av. Mathurin Moreau
COLONEL FABIEN
r. Botzaris
BUTTES CHAUMONT
r. de Crimée
PL. DES FÊTES
bd. Sérurier
PORTE DES LILAS
PORTE DE LILAS
av. Simon Bolivar
r. Fessart
SQ. BOLIVAR
r. Clavel
r. Lassus
PL. DES FÊTES
JOURDAIN
r. de Belleville
TÉLÉGRAPHE
r. Pelleport
av. Gambetta
bd. Mortier
r. de la Grange aux Belles
av. Claude Vellefaux
bd. de la Villette
r. Rébeval
PYRÉNÉES
r. des Pyrénées
r. de Belleville
10ème
20ème
BELLEVILLE
ST-FARGEAU
TAXI

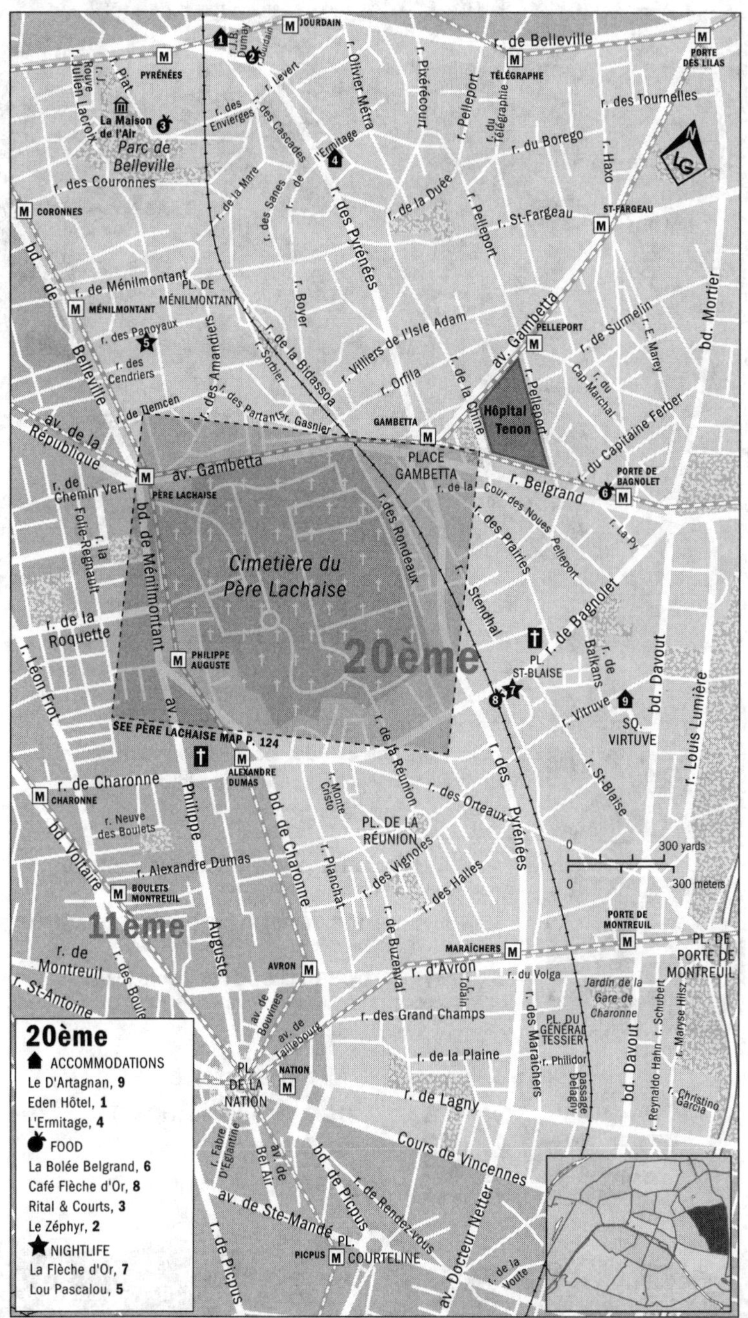
20ème
ACCOMMODATIONS
Le D'Artagnan, 9
Eden Hôtel, 1
L'Ermitage, 4
FOOD
La Bolée Belgrand, 6
Café Flèche d'Or, 8
Rital & Courts, 3
Le Zéphyr, 2
NIGHTLIFE
La Flèche d'Or, 7
Lou Pascalou, 5
Cimetière du Père Lachaise
SEE PÈRE LACHAISE MAP P. 124
Parc de Belleville
La Maison de l'Air
Hôpital Tenon
PLACE GAMBETTA
PL. DE MÉNILMONTANT
PL. ST-BLAISE
SQ. VIRTUVE
PL. DE LA RÉUNION
PL. DE LA NATION
PL. DE PORTE DE MONTREUIL
PL. COURTELINE
PL. DU GÉNÉRAL TESSIER
Jardin de la Gare de Charonne
11ème
JOURDAIN
PYRÉNÉES
TÉLÉGRAPHE
PORTE DES LILAS
CORONNES
ST-FARGEAU
MÉNILMONTANT
PELLEPORT
GAMBETTA
PÈRE LACHAISE
PORTE DE BAGNOLET
PHILIPPE AUGUSTE
ALEXANDRE DUMAS
CHARONNE
BOULETS MONTREUIL
PORTE DE MONTREUIL
MARAÎCHERS
AVRON
NATION
PICPUS
r. de Belleville
r. des Tournelles
r. du Borego
r. St-Fargeau
r. Pixérécourt
r. Pelleport
r. Olivier Métra
r. des Pyrénées
r. de Ménilmontant
r. des Couronnes
bd. de Belleville
av. de la République
av. Gambetta
r. Belgrand
r. de Bagnolet
bd. de Ménilmontant
r. de la Roquette
r. de Charonne
r. Alexandre Dumas
bd. de Charonne
bd. Voltaire
r. de Montreuil
r. d'Avron
r. des Grand Champs
r. de la Plaine
r. de Lagny
Cours de Vincennes
av. Docteur Netter
bd. de Picpus
r. de Picpus
av. de Ste-Mandé
bd. Davout
bd. Mortier
r. Louis Lumière
r. Haxo
r. de Surmelin
r. du Capitaine Ferber
r. Villiers de l'Isle Adam
r. de la Bidassoa
r. Orfila
r. de la Chine
r. des Rondeaux
r. Stendhal
r. des Prairies
r. Vitruve
r. St-Blaise
r. des Orteaux
r. des Vignoles
r. des Halles
r. de Buzenval
r. Planchat
r. de la Réunion
r. des Maraichers
r. de Rendez-vous
0 300 yards
0 300 meters